AF600094

Selected Correspondence of Bernard Shaw

Bernard Shaw and William Archer

Selected Correspondence of Bernard Shaw

Bernard Shaw and William Archer

Edited by Thomas Postlewait

UNIVERSITY OF TORONTO PRESS
Toronto Buffalo London

Published by University of Toronto Press
Toronto Buffalo London
www.utppublishing.com

ISBN 978-0-8020-4122-7 (cloth)

(Selected Correspondence of Bernard Shaw)

Library and Archives Canada Cataloguing in Publication

Shaw, Bernard, 1856–1950
[Correspondence. Selections]
Selected correspondence of Bernard Shaw.

Includes bibliographical references and indexes.
Contents: [v. 9] Bernard Shaw and William Archer / edited by Thomas Postlewait.

ISBN 978-0-8020-4122-7 (v. 9 : bound)

1. Shaw, Bernard, 1856–1950 – Correspondence. 2. Dramatists, Irish – 20th century – Correspondence. I. Title.

PR5366.A4 1995   822'.912   C959-301518

University of Toronto Press acknowledges the financial assistance to its publishing program of the Canada Council for the Arts and the Ontario Arts Council, an agency of the Government of Ontario.

Canada Council for the Arts | Conseil des Arts du Canada

Funded by the Government of Canada | Financé par le gouvernement du Canada

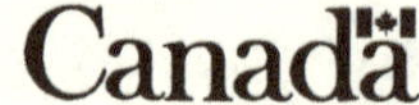

In Memory of Dan H. Laurence and J. Percy Smith
In Honour of L.W. Conolly
In Abiding Gratitude to Marilyn Brownstein

Contents

General Editor's Note

This volume is the ninth in the series entitled *Selected Correspondence of Bernard Shaw.* The first two volumes – *Bernard Shaw and H.G. Wells,* edited by J. Percy Smith, and *Theatrics,* edited by Dan H. Laurence – appeared in 1995. The third – *Bernard Shaw and Gabriel Pascal,* edited by Bernard Dukore – was published in 1996, and the fourth and fifth volumes – *Bernard Shaw and Barry Jackson,* edited by L.W. Conolly, and *Bernard Shaw and the Webbs,* edited by Alex C. Michalos and Deborah C. Poff – appeared in 2002. The sixth volume – *Bernard Shaw and Nancy Astor,* edited by J.P. Wearing – was published in 2005, the seventh – *Bernard Shaw and His Publishers,* edited by Michel W. Pharand – in 2009, and the eighth – *Bernard Shaw and Gilbert Murray,* edited by Charles A. Carpenter, in 2014.

The volumes in this series are of two kinds. Percy Smith's inaugural volume represents an example of the first kind: correspondence between Shaw and another individual of distinction in his or her own right. Bernard Dukore's, my own, J.P. Wearing's, Charles A. Carpenter's, and the present volume are further examples of this kind. *Bernard Shaw and the Webbs* is a minor variation of this model in that it deals with Shaw's relationship with *two* (in this case related) individuals.

This approach replicates other editions of Shaw correspondence published prior to this series: Christopher St John's *Ellen Terry and Bernard Shaw: A Correspondence* (1931) and Alan Dent's *Bernard Shaw and Mrs Patrick Campbell: Their Correspondence* (1952), among others. The advantage of this approach, of course, is that it gives the reader two (or more) voices rather than one, with all the stimulation that can arise from complementary or adversarial views on issues, events, or people. Such an approach also allows for insights into the nature of close personal and professional relationships, with all the emotional and intellectual drama that usually accompanies such Shavian associations. While matching the epistolary Shaw in full flow is a tough challenge, people such as Wells, Pascal, Jackson, the Webbs, Nancy Astor, and Gilbert Murray – hardened professionals all – were not easily intimidated by Shaw's sharp wit, searing logic, or intellectual aggression. Thus, the sparks sometimes fly, from which light as well as heat is generated.

The attempt to capture Shaw's *dialogue* with friends and colleagues differs, of course, from collections solely of Shaw's letters to individuals, be they single individuals, as in C.B. Purdom's *Bernard Shaw's Letters to Granville Barker* (1957) or Samuel Weiss's *Bernard Shaw's Letters to Siegfried Trebitsch* (1986), or hundreds of individuals as in Dan H. Laurence's monumental edition, *Bernard Shaw's Collected Letters* (4 volumes, 1965–88). And both of these approaches differ again from the second kind of volume in this *Selected Correspondence* series, Shaw's letters to a variety of individuals *on a particular subject*. Thus, Dan Laurence's *Theatrics* provides the opportunity to explore Shaw's ideas on theatre and theatricality, and *Bernard Shaw and His Publishers* deals comprehensively with Shaw's views on publishers and publishing.

And so, through a variety of approaches, the magnificent edifice of Shaw's correspondence is gradually constructed, drawing, in this series, largely on previously unpublished letters, and in all instances opening up new insights into Shaw's life and achievements, as well as the life and achievements of his correspondents. The correspondence between Shaw and theatre critic William Archer – the subject of this new volume in the *Correspondence* series – was spread over some forty years. The epistolary discussions of the hottest theatrical issues of their time, including Ibsen, the 'new drama,' 'new theatre,' Shaw's plays, Shakespeare's plays, censorship, and much more, were based on mutual respect, but that did not prevent frank and sometimes barbed exchanges. As editor Tom Postlewait points out, 'Even though they were united as colleagues, they had no qualms about pointing out the flaws and gaffs in one another's assumptions, reasoning, and intentions.' Shaw wondered if Archer had any brains at all. Archer told Shaw that he wanted to be Pope: 'Better order your triple crown at once.' Here, then, is the most comprehensive and detailed documentation yet gathered of what Postlewait argues is one of the most consequential partnerships ever between an artist and a critic.

Introduction

An Irishman and a Scotchman Transform the British Theatre

The historical development of modern British theatre depends in great measure upon the special partnership between Bernard Shaw (1856–1950) and William Archer (1856–1924). Indeed, their collective accomplishments proved to be without parallel in the history of the London stage. Together the two friends fought for the 'New Drama' and 'New Theatre,' and in the process offered a sustained critique of the Victorian theatre, which they perceived as staid and misguided. The unique quality of their critical voices established each of them as an intellectual force in the theatre. But equally relevant, their critical reviews and essays set new standards for the 'duties of dramatic critics.'[1] By means of these essays they developed models of dedicated criticism for the arts. Most importantly, they created the modern drama and theatre that they called for in their criticism. Shaw's plays as well as Archer's translations, publications, and productions of Ibsen's drama introduced the modernist drama and theatre to the British public. And in the process of mounting these campaigns for a new type of drama, theatre, and criticism, the two comrades provided selective support for other playwrights, such as A.W. Pinero, Henry Archer Jones, and Harley Granville Barker, whose works sometimes showed promising signs of modernist development.

Moreover, because they had little respect for Victorian Shakespeare, Archer and Shaw served as advocates for new staging methods of Shakespeare's plays. Opposed to Henry Irving's productions, which cut the plays in drastic ways, the two comrades carried out a sustained critique of scenic Shakespeare. In addition, they supported efforts to found and fund a national theatre that would feature Shakespeare as well as modern drama. Also, with Archer leading the way initially in the 1880s and early 1890s, they campaigned against stage censorship, which was imposed upon the theatres by the Lord Chamberlain's Office. Plays such as Ibsen's *Ghosts* and Shaw's *Mrs Warren's Profession* became touchstones in the anti-censorship battles. Thus, on six major fronts Archer and Shaw battled for the birth, development, and fulfilment of the modern theatre: the new drama, the new theatre, the new criticism, the establishment of a national theatre, the revitalization of Shakespearean theatre, and the opposition to stage censorship. Each of these commitments was a significant achievement; collectively, these six distinct yet interrelated projects transformed the modern theatre – in England and beyond.

Although both men moved to London in the late 1870s, they did not meet until 1884.[2] Yet already in 1881 Archer had begun the early stages of the campaign with articles on 'Henrik Ibsen,' 'Meiningen Realism,' and 'Will the Drama Revive?' Then in 1882 he published *English Dramatists of Today*, an attempt to identify promising playwrights. When Archer and Shaw met two years later, they quickly became colleagues with a shared mission. Their new partnership, as St John Ervine later observed, 'was the most momentous meeting of G.B.S.'s life.' From Ervine's perspective, 'No one could see G.B.S. and Archer together without perceiving their deep affection for each other.'[3] Together they launched Shaw's career, first as a critic of books, music, and theatre in the 1880s and 1890s, and then as a playwright, beginning with the co-authored *Rheingold*, which was an early draft of Shaw's *Widowers' Houses*, staged in 1892. During the 1890s, besides serving as the music critic at *The World* and then the theatre critic at the *Saturday Review*, Shaw wrote and published the seven dramatic works that constituted the two volumes of *Plays Pleasant and Unpleasant*, published in 1898 (the year he resigned as a theatre critic).

In this same decade Archer continued to distinguish himself with his theatre reviews, essays, and books, including the publication of the annual volumes of *The Theatrical 'World' of 1893, 1894, 1895, 1896,* and *1897.* And after translating and publishing *Pillars of Society, Ghosts, An Enemy of the People,* and *A Doll's House* in the late 1880s, he followed with five more of Ibsen's plays as they appeared in the 1890s. These translations and publications, even more than the arrival of Shaw's seven plays in 1898, stirred up the early controversies over the New Drama and New Theatre.

As their letters illustrate, their partnership set in motion a half-dozen distinct theatrical developments in London. For four decades the two friends engaged in their campaigns. The earliest surviving letter – a mentoring message from Archer – dates from January 1885. Their correspondence continued, with some notable gaps,[4] until Archer's death in December 1924 at the age of sixty-eight. Shaw lived another quarter-century until 1950, when he died at the age of ninety-four.[5]

These efforts featured productions of a few of Shaw's plays, including *Widowers' Houses* and *Arms and the Man*, but also the London premieres of a dozen of Ibsen's plays which Archer had translated and published. Behind the scenes he also helped to rehearse and stage several of the productions, especially those featuring the actress Elizabeth Robins in the 1890s. These productions achieved a new realism that defined and distinguished the presentation of the New Drama. Then, of course, with the staging of Shaw's own plays, especially the major productions at the Court Theatre (1904–7), the London stage entered the modern era. In the first decade of the twentieth century, he wrote and staged some of his most innovative plays, including *Man and Superman* and *Major Barbara.*

Shaw's development as a critic and playwright in the 1890s signalled the growth of a creative genius, and his arrival as a playwright in the Edwardian era was a full triumph. But little about his early life, including the first decade in London, suggested that these major achievements were likely to happen. In the main, his early decades showed little promise of the major figure he became. His years in Dublin, as he later described his childhood, were defined by 'shabby-genteel poverty.' He compared his education to prison life.[6] Apparently his home had few books, though he proudly recalled the reading of plays by Shakespeare and novels by Dickens. And he discovered John Bunyan's *The Pilgrim's Progress.* He also enjoyed visits to the National Gallery.[7] And occasionally, when he had a few extra coins, he could afford a visit to the theatre. Most notably, music, especially opera, was a major feature of the Shaw household because George John ('Vandeleur') Lee, the conductor and music teacher, lived with the family. Lee trained Shaw's mother, Lucinda Elizabeth ('Bessie'), as a singer. When Lee conducted opera productions in Dublin, he sometimes featured her in mezzo-soprano roles.

Consequently, during those early years Shaw was exposed to operas by Verdi, Donizetti, Gounod, and Bellini.

Upon finishing his formal education in 1871, Shaw became at the age of fifteen an office boy in a land agent office. Then in 1873 he was promoted to a position of clerk and cashier. Such was the development of his unpromising career in Dublin. He seemed resigned to his less than appealing future that provided more clerking jobs and limited opportunities. Not even the break-up of family life in June 1873 delivered a release for Shaw. Suddenly, his mother and his sister Agnes moved to London, abandoning the constraints of provincial Dublin. Bessie decided to change her life. Seeking a professional career in music, she decided to follow Lee to England. The other sister, Lucinda ('Lucy'), soon followed after them.[8] Yet Shaw remained behind. He continued to live with his father and to work in a boring job. Finally in 1876 he too bolted for England, leaving his father alone in Dublin.[9]

Shaw arrived in London at the age of nineteen. He was uncertain about the direction for his life, but he knew that escape from Ireland was imperative. In London he lived with his mother, who taught singing lessons. Over the next few years, before he met Archer, Shaw struggled to discover and create his adult selfhood – a striking identify which eventually became the articulate and impervious G.B.S. In 1879 he wrote *Immaturity*, the first of his five novels. But he had no success in finding a publisher. For a short period in 1879–80 he worked as a clerk for the Edison Telephone Company. He also published a few ghost-written music reviews for Lee's music column in *The Hornet*. In 1880 he joined the Zetetical Society, and began his activities as a public speaker on social and political issues. With each engagement his public persona was beginning to emerge. In 1881 he made his first attempt at maintaining a vegetarian diet. A year later he became involved with Alice Lockett in an unconsummated love affair. He also took up boxing with Pakenham Beatty, perhaps as compensation for the unsuccessful affair. Three more years would pass before he commenced his sexual affair with the Irish widow Jenny Patterson. In 1882, after hearing a lecture by Henry George on the nationalization of land and a single tax, he read George's *Progress and Poverty*, which proved to be a catalyst for his economic and political ideas. Then in 1883 he began to read Karl Marx's *Das Kapital* in the French translation. During this same period he made an effort to learn

French, with limited success. In 1884 he participated in the first meetings of the Fabian Society, and published 'A Manifesto,' the first of many Fabian essays. In this same year he met Archer.

Basically, Shaw's first decade in London, between 1876 and 1885, had been defined by his stumbling searches for direction. As his diary revealed, he was living primarily off of the donations of his mother and occasional cheques his father sent. His major accomplishment, since writing his first novel in 1879, was to write four more novels (*The Irrational Knot, Love among the Artists, Cashel Byron's Profession,* and *An Unsocial Socialist*). Although publishers rejected each novel, the last one appeared serially between March and December 1884 in *To-Day,* a new socialist magazine. Three years later this novel was finally published in book form. From all outward appearances Shaw was yet another inglorious novelist to be displayed in George Gissing's *New Grub Street.*[10] But with the arrival of Archer in his life everything changed, beginning with writing assignments for the journals. Finally, after almost three decades of misguided developments, Shaw's career as a writer was launched.

In contrast to Shaw, Archer was already a quite successful young man by 1884. There was nothing provincial about him. He had already converted his prospects into an impressive set of accomplishments. Born in Perth, Scotland, in 1856, he lived mainly there as a young man with his parents, six brothers, and one sister. The family's economic conditions were lean, but each summer, beginning when Archer was one year old, he travelled to Larvik, Norway, to stay with the extended paternal family. By the time he attended Edinburgh University in the early 1870s, he was a fluent speaker of Norwegian, Danish, German, and French. He graduated with an M.A. degree in 1876. While still in school he held a job in Edinburgh as a theatre critic. He also wrote plays and novels. In 1876 his play *Mesmerism; or Quits* was performed in Edinburgh by the local Library Association. In 1877, with his friend Robert Lowe, he published a controversial pamphlet, *The Fashionable Tragedian,* which criticized the acting methods of Henry Irving. Facing possible libel threats, Archer and Lowe had to withdraw the pamphlet. In March 1878 his two-act play *Rosalind* was performed in Edinburgh; Lowe played one of the roles. With his friend E.V.R. Dibdin he collaborated on a one-act farce called *Our Special Correspondent.* This was the first of several farces or burlesques that they wrote under the pseudonym of E.V. Ward. The name was derived from the first letters of their names. They also wrote two comic operas, *The Khan of Kashgar*, based loosely on Aristophanes' *Lysistrata*, and *Blue and Buff, or The Great Muddlesborough Election*, a satire of Gilbert and Sullivan. (For descriptions of these works see Whitebrook: 23–33.) Archer's early creative efforts had also been directed toward fiction writing. Between 28 September 1875 and 15 January 1876, his novel *The Doomed of the Damned*, which was a parody of Sir Walter Scott, had been serialized in *North Briton*, a weekly journal.

Upon graduating at the age of twenty-one, Archer travelled to Australia, where family members had moved (see Stanley). After spending a few months on the family homestead and then journeying by horse and hunting in the bush in Queensland, he left Australia and sailed to America. He then travelled from San Francisco to New York City on the newly completed railroad. He then completed his first of several world trips with a voyage from New York to Glasgow. International travel had settled in his blood.

When Archer arrived in London in the autumn of 1878, he was already a sophisticated young man and an accomplished writer for several journals. He spent his first year in London preparing for and attaining a law degree (to satisfy the wishes of his parents), but he had already committed himself to a career in journalism. After completing the law degree, he became a theatre critic for *The London Figaro* and *Progress*. In 1879 he travelled to Paris to prepare twenty articles on the forty-one plays that the Comédie Française planned to stage on a visit to London in May. He also adapted and staged Ibsen's *The Pillars of Society* as *Quicksands* for a matinee in London in 1880. In 1881 he travelled to Rome, walking across France and northern Italy. In Rome he held several meetings with Ibsen, who informed him that *Ghosts* had just been published. Upon reading the play Archer committed himself to the mission of translating Ibsen's drama. In 1882, back in London, he published *English Dramatists of Today*, and in 1883 he published *Henry Irving, Actor and Manager: A Critical Study*, which went through three editions by 1884. He became the theatre critic for *The World* in 1884, and with this steady, if hardly grand, income flowing into his banking account, he married Frances Trickett, whom he had met in Rome in 1881.

Given their quite different experiences and achievements, Shaw and Archer were unlikely candidates to become friends and comrades. And yet the friendship between provincial Shaw and cosmopolitan Archer was immediate and lasting. Soon after they met Archer took up Shaw and provided the missing direction for his life. Why? Because, as Archer observed soon after they had met, Shaw was 'a remarkable man, one of the most interesting studies in character, I ever came across.'[11] From Shaw's perspective, Archer was equally remarkable. His energy, experiences, intelligence, and commitments were just the spark that Shaw needed. Archer opened the doors into the world of journalism at exactly the right time for Shaw, who was ready to deliver his intellectual talents to the world, receptive or not. That determination and brilliance excited Archer, as if he had discovered a lost comrade, a brother in arms. They bonded, and then argued like family members who understood that the bonds were permanent. For the next forty years they were comrades in a series of campaigns to transform and modernize the London stage. Their partnership, despite the striking differences in not only their backgrounds and experiences but also their temperaments, became invaluable for both of them.

There can be no doubt that meeting Archer was a life-changing event for Shaw. Even though his genius was already maturing, especially as he developed into a political spokesman for social causes, Shaw's artistic career was at a stalemate because of his failed attempts to become a novelist. After almost a decade in London he seemed to have reached a dead end. Apparently he was without any alternative direction. Of course his career may well have taken off in the 1880s without the intervention of Archer, but such speculation is unnecessary. Archer did show up. He took control of Shaw, with Shaw's blessings and gratitude. In the process, a powerful jolt of energy finally launched Shaw into the critical and artistic directions that made all the difference for his eventual success as an essayist and playwright.

Archer transformed the unsuccessful novelist into a playwright. No doubt Shaw had refined his writing talent by drafting the novels, but he had not yet found the proper release and direction for his smouldering talent. The irony, of course, is that the transformation of Shaw into a playwright developed out of the belaboured attempts of the new friends to co-author the play *Rheingold* between 1884 and 1887 (see Shaw's letter of 4 October 1887). Finally in 1892, after Shaw had jettisoned Archer's plot and reconceived the play's social topics, he composed *Widowers'*

Houses. Although Archer had failed as a playwriting partner, he quite successfully launched Shaw into the field of journalism during the first decade of their friendship. Consequently, by the mid-1890s the two aspects of Shaw's writing genius became joined as he poured forth his ideas as both a playwright and a journalist. These two strains of his masterful genius culminated in his determination to write plays with long prefaces. These plays and prefaces defined the full voice of G.B.S., that powerful and unique persona that had emerged during the early years of Archer's mentoring. The journalism of the 1880s and early 1890s, including the brilliant music criticism, provided a vital and enduring quality of his playwriting.

As for Archer's career, it too received valuable support and purpose from this new friendship. But in the main Archer would have followed the same direction that he had already set in motion since the 1870s. Even if he had never met Shaw, he would have translated Ibsen's plays and participated in the Ibsen campaign at the end of the Victorian era. And he would have met Elizabeth Robins and become involved with her in the productions of Ibsen's plays during the 1890s. In brief, Archer was already on the path to become the translator of Ibsen's plays. And of course he would have continued to develop his career as a theatre critic, which had already become his daily livelihood. Moreover, by the mid-1880s he had established himself as the major critical voice in opposition to Henry Irving's approach to Shakespearean theatre. He had also begun his campaign for an endowed national theatre. And he would have remained the major foe of stage censorship, for by 1884 he had written several strong essays against the institution of the Lord Chamberlain's Office. Without question, he benefitted substantially from having Shaw as his new partner in these several battles – for a new drama, a new theatre, a new criticism, a new Shakespeare, a national theatre, and a stage free of debilitating and hypocrical censorship – but Shaw was not the instigator. Instead, he proved to be the genie who, once released from the magical bottle, provided the amazing critical voice that joined Archer's in these battles, and expanded the reach and power of the opposition to the old systems, attitudes, and values. More importantly, and this was the greatest payoff for Archer, Shaw became the playwright who delivered the revolution that Archer sought in the lesser figures of the English stage, such as A.W. Pinero and H.A. Jones. From the 1890s forward

Shaw's plays, along with the great voice of G.B.S. in his theatre reviews and prefaces, became responsible for the outpouring of Archer's dozens upon dozens of reviews and articles on Shaw that completed the circle of energy between these two leaders of the revolution of the British stage.

Despite the striking differences in their experiences and termperaments, Acher and Shaw quickly became comrades, dedicated to the modernization of the London theatre. Of course, they were not alone in this undertaking. They were joined by other dedicated individuals, many of whom were also outsiders. Indeed, the transformation of London theatre in the late nineteenth and early twentieth centuries depended in great measure on an invasion of aliens. Besides Archer and Shaw the outsiders included Elizabeth Robins (American), J.T. Grein (Dutch), J.M. Barrie (Scottish), Gilbert Murray (Australian), Hans Lien Brækstad (Norwegian), Charles Frohman (American), Oscar Wilde (Irish), and George Moore (Irish). And additional Irish contributors included J.M. Synge, W.B. Yeats, and Lady Augusta Gregory, who were central figures in the modern transformation of drama and theatre in London, not just in Dublin.[12]

Crossing Swords: The Pleasures of Debate

During the first decade of their friendship Archer took on the role of mentor, steering Shaw into positions at several London journals as a music critic, book reviewer, art critic, and then music critic at *The World.* These efforts culminated in 1895 when Shaw became a theatre critic for the *Saturday Review.* (See letter of 28 December 1894.) Throughout this period Archer continued to serve as the theatre critic for *The World.* Their weekly reviews provided a platform for their critiques of the staid Victorian theatre, as Max Beerbohm recalled in 1907: 'The goal in Mr Archer's eyes was practically the same as the goal in G. B. S.'s. It was only as to the means of reaching it that the two men differed. G. B. S. was violent, Mr Archer was all for diplomacy. G. B. S. was for burning the rubbish-heaps that cumbered the path. Mr Archer was for making them stepping-stones to higher things.'[13]

Even when Archer and Shaw were in basic agreement on a specific campaign, they often differed in their tactics and judgments. In their theatre reviews, for example, Archer supported the new plays by A.W. Pinero and Oscar Wilde, but was often critical of those by H.A. Jones and

St John Hankin. Shaw rallied for Jones and Hankin, but found fault regularly with Pinero and Wilde. As for Shakespearean productions, they concurred in their criticism of the spectacles that Henry Irving presented at the Lyceum Theatre, but they divided company in their commentary on William Poel's productions for the Elizabethan Stage Society, with Shaw supporting and Archer attacking them.

> Shaw: 'I welcome the advent of The Elizabethan Stage Society ... I do seriously suggest that our leading actors might occasionally come down and take a turn on the stage of the E.S.S., at Gray's Inn Hall or elsewhere.' (SR, 20 July 1895; Dukore 2: 399)

> Archer: 'Can nothing be done to make the Elizabethan Stage Society a useful, instead of a ridiculous, institution?' (*Study and Stage*, 10 February 1898: 231)

Most significantly, they engaged in a series of debates about Shaw's plays, beginning with *Widowers' Houses* and continuing across the decades. Indeed, their public – as well as private – debates about his plays became the sixth major topic in their multifaceted campaigns. At times these exchanges were more pronounced than those about the new theatre, censorship, Shakespeaean theatre, or a national theatre. Although Archer admired, and often praised, most of Shaw's plays, he still felt compelled to identify any of Shaw's lapses in plot development, characterization, and subject matter. He complained repeatedly that the plays, though brilliant in their comic effects, were hindered by the Shavian politics and philosophical theories. His primary complaint was that the G.B.S. persona dominated not only the prefaces but also the plays. Although Archer usually praised the prefaces as brilliant expressions of Shaw's genius, he felt that several of the characters in the plays, such as Tanner in *Man and Superman*, were ineffective because they served as spokesmen for Shaw's ideas. Shaw the orator compromised Shaw the dramatist. Responding to these critiques – and even anticipating them in some of his letters, articles, and prefaces – Shaw accused Archer of being wilfully blind to his creative innovations.

Quite often, when confronted by Archer's latest review, article, or letter, Shaw would deliver one of his droll dismissals. He was masterful in his quips, wisecracks, ribbings, and putdowns:

> 'Oh William Archer, William Archer: where are your brains?' (26 October 1891).
>
> 'You have a perfect rag shop of old ideas in your head which prevent you getting a step ahead' (23 April 1894).
>
> 'As I said before, *you* don't matter: your dunderheadedness will only give rise to your national sport of argument' (24 January 1900).
>
> 'Your review [of *Man and Superman*], apparently colossally stupid, is really blind and careless' (2 September 1903).
>
> 'Confound you for a romancing idiot' (12 May 1904).
>
> 'You are the laziest man in London. The way you calmly leave me to do all your thinking for you is beyond words' (15 November 1905).
>
> 'Father William, you are no longer fit to be at large' (c. 26–7 May 1907).
>
> 'Oblige me with a hammer, a saw, a beetle and a couple of wedges that I may operate on your all but impervious knowledge box' (19 June 1923).

Having announced his jesting discontent in the opening sentence of a letter, Shaw would then launch into an argument on their latest disagreement.

Archer was no match for Shaw in the art of the jest, but on occasion he offered his own ribbing, usually in response to the latest assault by Shaw:

> 'I have always said you wd end by being Pope, & now I'm sure of it. Better order your triple crown at once' (26 October 1891).
>
> 'Ever since I read that Nietzschean motorcar [*Man and Superman*], I have had vials of remonstrance simmering within me which the possession of your address causes to boil over' (1 September 1903).
>
> 'I never in my life read a document more utterly beside the mark than your letter' (18 November 1905).
>
> 'It won't do. In your determination to defend your later manner of play-writing against all the rest of the world, your earlier self included, you have undertaken to re-make the English language' (20 June 1923).

These disputes spread through their conversations, letters, reviews, articles, and books. Often the private disputes expanded into public exchanges in the newspapers and journals. And in some cases the debates would spread over several days or weeks. (See, for example, the letters bunched around 25 October 1891, 31 July 1897, or July and August 1906.)

In one case, their disagreements over cutting Shakespeare's plays for production went back and forth in the letters and journals for several months. (See letters of 17 May and 6 September 1919.)

Even though they were the closest of friends and united as colleagues, they had no qualms about pointing out the flaws and gaffs in one another's assumptions and ideas. And yet, after pages of assault, the letters would regularly conclude as if there had been no disagreement. Shaw, for example, after assaulting Archer, Elizabeth Robins, and the New Century Theatre Company for several paragraphs on 27 January 1900, closed with 'We shall expect you [for lunch] on Friday, as arranged.' Archer, in turn, after defending himself in his letter of 26 October 1891, concluded with 'Look out for me after the Flying Dutchman tonight – shall be in the pit. Yours incorrigibly, W.A.'

Both men were completely self-confident in their opinions and judgments. And both were equally certain that the other one should change his ways. Their scraps and tiffs, accordingly, demonstrated a principle that Archer articulated in 1891: 'Two men of letters crossing swords, on equal terms, can adjust their differences without ill-feeling, and take nothing but pleasure in the bout of fence.'[14] For four decades they engaged in these rhetorical bouts with the greatest of pleasure. The exchanges were part of the fun, for they both enjoyed and expected the raillery.

Although they were quite serious in their arguments, the purpose was never personal invective. There was no malice in their arguments with one another. To strive for total defeat or to impose an argument would have run counter to the very spirit and purpose of their raillery, as Shaw recognized in a marvelous statement he made toward the end of one extended debate:

> Do not suppose that when I insist on my view of a question that I am reproaching you for not being a Shaw. The notion of two Shaws corresponding with one another is one which staggers even me. Your pugnacity, wit, knowledge &c are undoubtedly mixed in different proportions to mine, and the result is both quantitatively and chemically different. I sometimes, when a good side of you comes out by chance against a bad side of me, feel apologetic for the difference; but as we clearly could not stand one another if the difference were abolished, whether by the Archerization of Shaw (with Mrs Archer in the background wondering which was the real Antipholus) or the Shawation of Archer, let us rejoice that it exists.[15]

Shaw rejected the idea of the two of them being twins, like the brothers in *The Comedy of Errors.*

Shaw also articulated another principle of their mutual regard when he praised Archer for his 'exceptional ability,' and for putting his brain to as good a use as he was capable of. They expected the highest standards of one another, and when one of them failed to maintain the rigorous dedication to honesty and truth, the other one would call him on it. In a series of letters in early November 1891, for example, Shaw insisted that Archer had misrepresented certain facts in his argument with Shaw over the issue of Archer's integrity as a critic. Neither of them, Shaw insisted, could avoid making some accommodations with the 'environment' in which they worked. But in making his argument Shaw was not urging Archer to abandon his own distinct traits and judgments. Just the opposite. In making their arguments they did not expect or want the other person to abandon his own distinct traits, abilities, and judgments. What they expected – because they admired and respected one another – was the fulfillment of their highest abilities. When either of them, in the judgment of the other, fell short of his exceptional character and intelligence, then the arguments and indictments emerged.

In these debates, Archer and Shaw saw themselves as realists, committed to the facts. In turn, they often accused one another of being an idealist or 'apriorist,' that is, a self-deluding person who occupies an a priori world of his own intellectual construction. The problem with Shaw, from Archer's perspective, was that he too readily embraced one cause after another, such as taking up Jaeger suits. Archer was especially annoyed, for instance, by Shaw's indulgent embrace of the philosophical ideas of Schopenhauer in *The Quintessence of Ibsenism.* This was a case of apriorism or 'Shawpenhauerism.' (See Archer's open letter of 25 October 1891 and his regular letter of 26 October.) 'The trouble with you ... is that you are incurably credulous. Someone comes along & tells you that wool is the only wear; & instantly you go in for woolen boots, which lead, in due time, to a course of crutches. Then Wagner comes along, & you are a Wagnerite. Ibsen, & you are an Ibsenite (I never was); Nietzsche, & you are a Nietzschean; Bergson, & you are a Bergsonian.'[16]

Yet from Shaw's perspective Archer was the idealist and apriorist. For Shaw, Archer's many attempts to place the plays of A.W. Pinero in the camp of Ibsen were based upon false and self-deceiving comparisons. (See Shaw's letter of 21 August 1893.) As for Archer's abiding faith in liberalism, Shaw insisted that he should join the Fabian Society and get a little truth knocked into him. In both of these matters Archer was locked into 'apriorist' assumptions that blinded him to the factual truths of Shaw's judgment and world view.[17]

By means of these argumentative dichotomies, they usually equated a realistic perspective to inductive thinking and an idealist perspective to deductive thinking, as Shaw stated in the letter of 25 October 1891. Archer accused Shaw of being an idealist because of his dependence upon social and philosophical theories. And Shaw accused Archer of being a self-deceived idealist because of his 'romantic portrait' of himself as an incorruptible critic. In making these dichotomies, Shaw, who read Continental philosophy, may have had in mind the epistemological distinctions between *a priori* and *a posteriori* thinking. But Archer primarily used the terms of *a priori* and *idealist* interchangeably as handy synonyms, without reference to the heritage of philosophical distinctions.

Decade after decade, as Charles Archer noted, Shaw's arguments and exhortations were expressed in 'the usual affectionately abusive terms' of teasing banter (C. Archer: 363). The two friends chided and assaulted one another relentlessly. Candour was the norm; honesty was a requirement. To someone who did not understand the special nature of their friendship, their statements might seem mean-spirited, and perhaps motivated by malice. Yet beneath the banter, a deep and abiding respect for one another guided the friendship and mutual love. It is possible to misunderstand the tone and purpose of their traded comments, but Michael Holroyd, to his credit, correctly described some of the basic features of the relationship when he noted that Shaw and Archer 'teased, goaded, celebrated and admonished each other, and under the device of open disagreement made a secret code of their affection' (Holroyd 1: 135).

Shaw never tired of ribbing Archer. Yet when he mistakenly mailed a letter intended for Archer to Frank Harris, he was quite embarrassed: 'Horror on horror's head: I have put your letter into Harris's envelope – and such a letter! Description would be futile: you must read the letter when he sends it on in order to realize the awful situation. I am really very sorry' (9 November 1891). Shaw understood, of course, that people were quite capable of misinterpreting his rhetorical assaults.[18] (See letters of 7, 9, 10, and 13 November 1891 for the case of the misguided letter.)

Beginning a Friendship: The 1880s

For most years of their friendship, Shaw was the confident – and often over-confident – G.B.S. This persona was ever present and often dominant. By the time he had written *The Quintessence of Ibsenism* in 1891 and *Widowers' Houses* in 1892, the theatrical Shaw had arrived. And with the success of *Plays Pleasant and Unpleasant* in 1898 Shaw had completed his transformation into G.B.S. Although he still had to wait a few years for the Court Theatre productions to declare to the world his greatness, he announced to Archer in 1900 that he was 'the best English-language playwright since Shakespear' (letter of 27 January 1900). In this same letter he also proclaimed that Archer had become 'the worst critic now alive.' But this familiar Shaw – the man who apparently was incapable of doubting himself – had not fully emerged in the 1880s. During those early years in London he was still dependent, at least under certain conditions, on Archer's judgment and guidance for the development of his career.

Although the earliest surviving letters are from 1885, Archer and Shaw probably met in the spring or early summer of 1884. The exact date, location, and occasion remain buried in the shadowy past.[19] Yet even before they were introduced, Archer had observed Shaw in the British Museum (perhaps even in 1883). Archer described his sighting of Shaw in a now famous anecdote from his 1892 review of the performance of *Widowers' Houses*:

> Partly to facilitate the labours of Mr. George Bernard Shaw's biographers, and partly by way of relieving my own conscience, I think I ought to give a short history of the genesis of *Widowers' Houses*. Far away back in the olden days, while as yet the Independent Theatre slumbered in the womb of Time, together with the New Drama, the New Criticism, and the New Humour, and all the other glories of our renovated world, I used to be a daily frequenter of the British Museum Reading Room. Even more assiduous in his attendance was a young man of tawny complexion and attire, beside whom I used frequently to find myself seated. My curiosity was piqued by the odd conjunction of his subjects of research. Day after day for weeks he had before him two books, which he studied alternately, if not simultaneously – Karl Marx's *Das Kapital* (in French), and an orchestral score of *Tristan und*

> *Isolde.* I did not know then how exactly this quaint juxtaposition symbolized the main interests of his life. Presently I met him at the house of a common acquaintance, and we conversed for the first time.[20]

This description, besides reminding us that Shaw carried on his self-education in the Reading Room, provided a singular portrait of his dedication to the economic and artistic revolutions of his time.

As for *Widowers' Houses*, Archer explained that its genesis could be traced back eight years to 1884 when the two of them agreed to write a play together.[21] 'I learned from himself that he was the author of several unpublished masterpieces of fiction. Construction, he owned with engaging modesty, was not his strong point, but his dialogue was incomparable.' Because Archer considered himself a 'born constructor,' he 'proposed, and Mr. Shaw agreed to, a collaboration' that would produce a popular love story, based upon mistaken identity. Archer outlined, 'scene by scene, the scheme of a twaddling cup-and-saucer comedy.' With Archer's plot guiding him, Shaw began the task. After several attempts in 1884, 1885, and 1887 at composing scenes, Shaw completed two acts of the play (first called *The Way to a Woman's Heart*, then *Rhinegold*, and then *Rheingold*). On 4 October 1887 he left a transcript of the incomplete play at Archer's flat. (See letter of this date.) On 6 October, he 'went up to Archer's and read the unfinished drama. A long argument ensued, Archer having received it with great contempt' (Diaries 1: 304).

Archer's rejection, though probably not an expression of contempt, was a major disappointment for Shaw, who still needed and depended upon his friend's support in the 1880s.[22] During the early years of their friendship Archer was the authority on London drama. He had introduced Shaw to the contemporary theatre, especially the plays of Ibsen – even before Archer's translations were published. Already in the 1880s, as Shaw appreciated, Archer had established himself as a progressive theatre critic. Archer understood how the contemporary theatre was developing (and failing to develop).

Of course, despite his admiration for Archer and his accomplishments, Shaw seldom missed an opportunity during these early years to argue with him on theatrical matters. (See, for example, the letters of 16 April 1886 and 4 September 1888.) But playwriting was uncharted territory for Shaw, as he admitted on 24 February 1888 in a letter to the actress Alma

Murray: 'I wish I could write you a play myself, but unfortunately I have not the faculty. I once wrote two acts of a splendid play, and read them to an eminent drama critic. He laughed the first to scorn, and went asleep in the middle of the second; so I made him a present of the MS (to his intense indignation) and set to work to destroy the society that makes bad plays possible' (CL 1: 188). Typically of Shaw at this point of his literary struggles, the letter conceals any self-doubts behind a protective mask of self-assertion. Five years later, when he completed and staged *Widowers' Houses,* he could ignore, dismiss, or deny those earlier doubts. In 1887, however, he lacked the full Shavian confidence that would define the G.B.S. persona by the end of the decade.[23]

Also, in the 1880s Archer was more sophisticated than Shaw, a provincial young man who was still confined to a room in his mother's flat until he married in 1898. He made his first trip to Continental Europe in 1889. His world in the 1880s had been defined by conditions of poverty, and limited to Dublin and London. His life as a writer was primarily a record of repeated rejections by the publishers. By constrast, Archer, after attaining his M.A. degree, had travelled to Australia and United States in the 1870s. Fluent in several languages, he travelled regularly in the 1880s to major European cities to see theatre and opera productions and to write about them. He had married in 1884, and was father of a son, Tom, who was born on 2 August 1885. In London the Archers had rooms at 16 John Street, which is where Shaw delivered the incomplete *Rheingold* in 1887. In 1890 they had acquired a second place in the small village of Cobham in Surrey, which is where Shaw read the first draft of *The Quintessence of Ibsenism* to Archer and A.B. Walkley (see Archer's open letter of 25 October 1891).

Moreover, as Shaw knew, Archer had written a few plays in the days before the two of them met. These satires and melodramas, rapidly turned out between 1876 and 1881 in collaboration with Edinburgh friends, were not serious works. Indeed, though these youthful efforts had been staged in Edinburgh and London, they were minor achievements that Archer made no attempt to publish.[24] Nonetheless, these early plays, along with Archer's critical publications on English theatre and his emerging translations of Ibsen, established a basis fact: Archer had the theatrical experience that Shaw lacked.[25] Thus, his rejection of Shaw's incomplete manuscript served as a temporary judgment that

Shaw could not ignore. If Shaw wished to pursue a career in theatre, Archer, his closest and trusted friend, was the most reliable – but also the most demanding – guide.[26] Of course, this initial deference to Archer's judgment, though important in 1887, was set aside by 1892. Even though he may have masked his confidence with a certain amount of bluster and hyperbole in those early years, Shaw's self-regard and defiance rapidly asserted itself in the 1890s. From that point forward he never relented. Shaw's self-regard rapidly asserted itself in the 1890s. And his self-doubt basically disappeared.

Archer and the First Stage of the Campaign: 1880s and 1890s

Archer's self-confidence was already in place in the 1880s. After an imposed lull in 1880–1, which included the weeks in Rome, the discussions with Ibsen, and the dedication to a career in journalism, he quickly established himself as a theatre critic. Besides serving as the weekly theatre critic for *The World*, he also wrote essays in the 1880s for various other journals and newspapers, including *Theatre*, *National Review*, *Nineteenth Century*, *Longman's Magazine*, *New Review*, and *Fortnightly Review*. British drama and theatre were his primary topics, but he also wrote on French, German, and Danish theatre. In addition, he turned out essays on Shakespeare's sonnets, Elizabethan theatre architecture, John Webster, Charles Lamb, Eleonora Duse, Maeterlinck, and music halls. And he published essays on Robert L. Stevenson, with whom he had established a friendship in the 1880s. As for Ibsen, in 1878 Archer translated *The Pillars of Society* and published an essay entitled 'Henrik Ibsen's New Drama.'[27] *Pillars* was the first of Ibsen's twelve major prose plays. Archer's recognition of the Norwegian playwright thus occurred even before Ibsen had written *A Doll's House*. More essays on Ibsen followed on a regular basis in the 1880s and 1890s (see Prophet: 139–59). During this period he communicated with Ibsen regularly whenever a new play appeared. Also, after his initial set of meetings in Rome with Ibsen in 1881, Archer continued to seek him out in Munich, the village of Saeby in Denmark, and Christiania (Oslo) in the 1880s and 1890s.[28] (See, for example, the letter of 21 August 1890.)

Moreover, Archer became a small factory in book publishing. Even before he met Shaw in 1884, he had published *English Dramatists of Today*

(1882) and a critical study of *Henry Irving, Actor and Manager* (1883).[29] In 1886 he published *About the Theatre* (see letters of 26 March and 16 April 1886). Then in 1888, after interviewing dozens of European actors, he published *Masks or Faces? A Study in the Psychology of Acting* (see letter of 4 September 1888). In 1890 he published a book on the actor William Macready; then in 1891 he commissioned and edited books on the actors Thomas Betterton and Charles Macklin. Then between 1894 and 1896, he co-edited with Robert W. Lowe three volumes of *Dramatic Essays* by (1) Leigh Hunt, (2) William Hazlitt, and (3) John Forster and George Henry Lewis. Also, after a trip to America in 1899, he published a series of articles on contemporary America, which a year later became *America Today: Observations and Reflections.*

Archer also translated several works, including A.L. Kjelland's *Tales of Two Countries* (1891), Fritjiof Nansen's *Eskimos Life* (1893) and *Farthest North* (2 vols, 1897), and two books by Georg Brandes, *William Shakespeare: A Critical Study* (1899) and *Henrik Ibsen, Björnsterne Björnson: Critical Studies* (1899). And because he was fluent in French and German as well as the Scandinavian languages, he translated and published Gerhart Hauptmann's *Hannele: A Dream Poem* (1894) and Maurice Maeterlinck's *Interior* (1899).

And yet all these books and translations, though a marvellous series of accomplishments by the time he was forty years old, were secondary to Archer's major undertaking in the 1880s and 1890s: the translation of Ibsen's plays. Committed to the development of an alternative theatre movement, he decided that Ibsen plays and productions should be the catalyst for change in the London theatre. They would define and determine the direction of the campaign for a new drama. Shaw concurred, as he stated in 1898: 'The New Theater would never have come into existence but for the plays of Ibsen.'[30] Archer's articles and reviews were part of his campaign, but his translations and publications of Ibsen's plays were even more important. By 1892, Archer had translated and published fifteen of Ibsen's plays. The major achievement was *Ibsen's Prose Drama*, published in five volumes (1890–1), which contained all of the realistic plays up to 1892 and the history plays such as *Vikings at Helgeland, The Pretenders*, and *Emperor and Galilean.* Also, with his brother Charles, he published a lyrical translation of *Peer Gynt* in 1892 (and then a revised version in 1896). *Ibsen's Prose Drama* sold quite well, and these volumes were supplemented by inexpensive 'shilling' editions of several of the single plays. He published each of these separate editions in conjunction with a production, including *A Doll's House* (1889), *Hedda Gabler* (1891), *The Master Builder* (1893), *Little Eyolf* (1896), and *John Gabriel Borkman* (1897). Over 40,000 copies of the Ibsen translations were sold in the 1890s. The final single volume was Ibsen's last play, *When We Dead Awaken*, translated and published in 1900.[31]

Besides these publications, which made the Ibsen campaign possible, the movement gained full momentum and high visibility with the productions of the plays. The staging of *A Doll's House* in June 1889, with Janet Achurch, launched the Ibsen movement in the London theatres. (See letter of 11 June 1889.) A trim production of *Rosmersholm* followed in 1891, with Shaw working closely with Florence Farr on the rehearsals. The movement turned into a major controversy in March 1891 because the government imposed censorship on the production of *Ghosts* by the Independent Theatre Company. And then a month later *Hedda Gabler*, with Elizabeth Robins, advanced the cause, and demonstrated the greatness of Ibsen for the modern actress. (See letter of 23 April 1891.) In turn, Robins and Archer were responsible for the productions of *The Master Builder* (1893), *Little Eyolf* (1896), and *John Gabriel Borkman* (1897). Also, the Independent Theatre Company presented *The Wild Duck* in 1894, with a revival of it in 1897, and a revival of *A Doll's House* with Janet Achurch, also in 1897. There was even a West End production of Ibsen when Herbert Beerbohm Tree displayed a heroic Dr Stockmann in *An Enemy of the People* at the Haymarket in 1893 for seven performances.

Ibsen's plays, their translations, and their London productions anchored the alternative theatre movement at the end of the Victorian era. Beginning with the production of *Hedda Gabler* in 1891, Archer and Robins became partners in the movement. And selectively he turned out articles about the plays and some reviews about the productions. Likewise, Shaw wrote about several of the productions, beginning with *A Doll's House*; but it is quite misleading to claim, as Holroyd did, that 'Shaw assumed the generalship of the British campaign' for Ibsen with the publication of the *Quintessence* (Holroyd 1: 200).[32] Several other people, including Robins, Grein, Achurch, and Charrington, were significant contributors to the Ibsen campaign. But without question Archer was the leader (see Prophet).

It is no surprise, of course, that the topic of Ibsen's drama weaves its way into the correspondence between Archer and Shaw. In some letters there is little more than a brief mention of Ibsen or a play, but quite often the commentary is substantial. For example, *A Doll's House* is the topic in twenty-two of the letters; *The Pillars of Society* is mentioned six times; *Ghosts* appeared in twenty letters; *Rosmersholm* in ten; *Hedda Gabler* in thirteen; *An Enemy of the People* in five; *The Wild Duck* in ten; and *Little Eyolf* in eleven. Even *Peer Gynt* was the topic in a dozen letters, despite there being no London production to generate discussion. There was, however, a French production of this great play in 1896, and Shaw travelled to Paris for it.[33] Also of note, the Independent Theatre Company, which staged three of Ibsen's plays in the 1890s, was the topic in nineteen letters, and Elizabeth Robins, who produced and performed in a half-dozen productions, received attention in at least twenty letters.[34] And two of the major playwrights who contributed to the 'New Drama,' Arthur Wing Pinero and Henry Arthur Jones, received plenty of attention from Shaw and Archer in their letters. Pinero was discussed in thirty-one letters and Jones was mentioned on twenty-three occasions.

Shaw and the First Stage of the Campaign: 1880s and 1890s

For both Archer and Shaw, Ibsen's plays made possible the first of two progressions in their campaign to transform the London stage. The translations, publications, and productions anchored Archer's efforts. And Shaw also found in Ibsen a commitment that gave definitive purpose to his own efforts to move the British theatre in a new direction. Ibsen became the paramount catalyst in the arrival of modern drama on the British stage. And while those plays dominated the campaign and controversies in the 1890s, Shaw began to emerge himself as a playwright, and in time became the major catalyst for the second stage of the revolution. But what happened before the new century?

Although the collaborative project on *Rheingold* in 1887 had been a notable failure for the two comrades, Shaw had several other options for developing his career. But how should he proceed? Fiction was one possibility, for he had recently published two novels, *Cashel Byron's Profession* (1886) and *An Unsocial Socialist* (1887). Also, besides maintaining a busy schedule of political lectures throughout the country, he worked closely with Sidney Webb in the administration of the new Fabian Society. Even if he had failed to develop a literary career in the 1880s, he was demonstrating his substantial talents in the social, economic, and political causes that defined his Fabian activities. These commitments became even more evident by 1889 when he edited and wrote two essays for *Fabian Essays in Socialism.*

In addition, Shaw's work in journalism opened up two possible directions for his talents. He could dedicate himself to political journalism and advocacy, for he was becoming an accomplished political commentator. Or he could develop a career in the criticism of literature, art, music, and theatre. In 1885, thanks to Archer's guidance, he began to write book reviews on fiction and biography in the *Pall Mall Gazette.* Then in 1886 he became the art critic for *The World.* Most notably, he was already becoming a brilliant music critic. By 1889, under the pseudonym of Corno di Bassetto, he was publishing brilliant musical reviews in *The Star.* Then with the shift to *The World* in 1890, he became G.B.S., a masterful writer on the musical scene (see letter of 22 October 1889). Most likely, a whole career could have been developed in musical criticism.

If anything, Shaw had too many options, for by the late 1880s he had already developed several possible writing careers. Except for playwriting, which he had apparently failed to develop, Shaw was emerging as an accomplished writer on various cultural and political topics. Yet despite the setback over *Rheingold,* he remained tempted by the possibility of writing plays. In late 1890, after a three-year lull, he wrote a 'scene of the third act' for *Rheingold,* as he noted in his diary for 28 December. Then finally during the summer of 1892 he returned to the manuscript, which he renamed *Widowers' Houses.* He revised the old cup and saucer play, completing and renaming it by November. Five years after the collapse of the collaboration, Shaw had circled back into the theatre. The original love story of *Rheingold* was now forcefully joined to an indictment of respectable middle-class people who profited as slum-landlords. Shaw's political and theatrical identities were joined. In December 1892 *Widowers' Houses,* produced by the Independent Theatre Society, had two matinee performances.

At the age of thirty-six, Shaw had finally launched his playwriting career.[35] But in what direction? In 1893 he wrote two plays, *The Philanderer* and *Mrs Warren's Profession,* but no one wished to produce them. The

Independent Theatre, under the leadership of J.T. Grein, had staged Shaw's first play. Grein had also produced a private performance of Ibsen's *Ghosts* in 1891 when the play was denied a licence by Edward F. Smyth Pigott, the Examiner of Plays. (For Shaw's judgments on Pigott, see letters of 10 October 1892 and 30 April 1895.) So Grein was not opposed to controversy. Up to a point he was prepared to stage challenging and disturbing plays. But he did not take up Shaw's second and third plays, which were much too unpleasant for his taste. He felt, for example, that *Mrs Warren's Profession* was unfit for a female audience. (See headnote for Shaw's letter of 2 January 1902.)

Archer agreed with Grein that these two plays represented women in disturbing ways, but he had a more complex response than Grein to these plays. He disliked the 'baseness' of *The Philanderer*, which had failed to honour the moral vision and seriousness of Ibsen's drama, especially the representation of the Ibsen Club. In the case of *Mrs Warren's Profession*, however, Archer had none of Grein's uneasiness about the topic of prostitution. Like Ibsen's *Ghosts*, this play offered a profound study of hypocritical social and ethical values. And in its generational divisions and struggles, it captured the kinds of complex intellectual disturbances that Ibsen brilliantly represented in *Ghosts*. From Archer's perspective, Shaw had created a 'masterpiece' with *Mrs Warren's Profession*. Its profound qualities justified its profane topics. He admired 'Vivie's thorough intellectual competence.' 'There are speeches whose irony takes you by the throat.' Except for a few lapses in dialogue, Shaw had done justice to Ibsen's dramatic influence, whereas he had failed to do so in *The Philanderer*, which lacked the artistic and thematic power of the new play. Archer thus distinguished between the crass liabilities of the second play and the subtle qualities of the third. When the play was published in 1898, Archer proclaimed that '*Mrs Warren's Profession* is not only intellectually but dramatically one of the very ablest plays of our time.'[36] (See also letter of 21 April 1898.)

And yet, without production opportunities, Shaw's career as a playwright in 1893, when he wrote *Mrs Warren's Profession*, seemed even less successful than his career as a novelist. Getting his plays produced was proving to be more difficult than finding publishers for his novels. Indeed, the odds tilted slightly toward fiction writing because at least two novels had been published (belatedly in 1887),[37] whereas only *Widowers'*

Houses had been published, and the sales were dismal. But so were the sales for the two novels. From all apparent signs Shaw's literary career was in the doldrums. The novels had failed to find readers, and both *The Philanderer* and *Mrs Warren's Profession* raised major doubts about his ability or his willingness to write for the commercial theatre.[38]

But then, just when hope, if not self-confidence, might have been forsaken, the doors of the Avenue Theatre swung open. In April 1894 Shaw's fourth play, *Arms and the Man*, was produced, and it ran for over two months. This turn of events was made possible because an anonymous person, Miss Annie E.F. Horniman, a wealthy patron of the theatre who lived in Manchester, provided financial backing to the actress Florence Farr (with whom Shaw had been involved in a relationship since 1890).

In the spirit of the occasion, Archer opened his review with a comic complaint that Shaw, of all people, has written a popular play:

> No one with even a rudimentary knowledge of human nature will expect me to deal impartially with a play by Mr. George Bernard Shaw ... He is not only my esteemed and religiously-studied colleague, but old and intimate and valued friend. We have tried our best to quarrel many a time. We have said and done such things that would have sufficed to set up a dozen lifelong vendettas between normal and rightly constituted people, but all without the slightest success, without engendering so much as a temporary coolness. Even now, when he has had the deplorable ill-taste to falsify my frequently and freely-expressed prediction by writing a successful play, which kept an audience hugely entertained from the rise to the fall of the curtain, I vow I cannot work up a healthy hatred for him. Of course I shall criticize it with prejudice, malice, and acerbity; but I have not the faintest hope of ruffling his temper or disturbing his self-complacency. The situation is really exasperating. If only I could induce him to cut me and scowl at me, like an ordinary human dramatist, there would be some chance of his writing better plays – or none at all. But one might as well attempt 'to bully the Monument.'[39]

Archer obviously took great pleasure in crafting this ironic lament. Pleased by Shaw's good fortune, he praised the comic success of the play:

'There is not the least doubt that *Arms and the Man* is one of the most amusing entertainments at present before the public.'[40]

Yet true to form Archer also lodged some complaints, as he was to do with many of Shaw's plays over the following decades. Countering Shaw's claim that the play is a realistic comedy, he insisted that it is a farce in the manner of W.S. Gilbert – an observation that was bound to irritate Shaw. Archer also dismissed the realism of the Bulgarian subject matter, and he complained about the unrealistic love affairs. Rather oddly, Archer found Shaw's vision of human life too cynical: 'To look at nothing but the seamy side may be to see life steadily, but is not to see it whole.' Shaw immediately responded with two letters – both written on 23 April 1894 – that challenged Archer's assessment, including his complaint about the 'seamy side' of life. Continuing the debate, Archer replied two days later. Then in July Shaw advanced his argument for the realistic integrity of the play with an article in the *New Review* entitled 'A Dramatic Realist to His Critics.' Proclaiming his moral superiority to theatre critics, he announced that unlike a theatre critic, who 'derives all his knowledge of life from witnessing plays,' he draws upon 'objective life' for the reality of the dramatic action. 'I simply discovered drama in real life.'[41]

With the success of *Arms and the Man* in 1894, Shaw had apparently opened the door to the London stage. Although it had taken nearly forty years, his self-confidence was finally justified. But then the theatre doors quickly closed. The production opportunities failed to develop throughout the rest of the decade. By 1900 he had written ten plays, including *Candida, You Never Can Tell, The Devil's Disciple,* and *Caesar and Cleopatra,* but the London theatres remained closed to him.[42] Except for the productions of *Widowers' Houses* and *Arms and the Man,* he remained exiled from the London theatres.[43] In 1897 there was the possibility of a West End production, but negotiations to stage *You Never Can Tell* at the Haymarket Theatre unravelled. (For Shaw's versions of these negotiations, see letters of 12 January 1903, 7 September 1903, and 14 December 1924.) Not until he was almost fifty years old did he receive his due with the series of productions at the Court Theatre (1904–7). Finally, he attained his rightful place in the London theatres.

This belated arrival must have tested Shaw's patience. Although he had diligently committed himself in the 1890s to becoming a playwright who could change the modern theatre, he had not yet delivered the revolution he believed in. He was fully committed to the campaign to revolutionize the London stage, but in comparison to his colleague he remained a secondary figure in the theatres. Most of Shaw's contributions for a new theatre until June 1898, when he married and retreated from London because of medical disabilities, had depended primarily on journalism. It is true, of course, that in 1893 he published *Widowers' Houses*, with an appendix addressed to theatre critics. And of course his three and one-half years as the critic for the *Saturday Review* was a major contribution to the campaigns. But we need to remember that until 1895 his journalism was dedicated to music criticism, art criticism, book reviews, and Fabian politics, not theatre reviews. Most notably, he published several hundred music reviews which established him as a masterful authority in the field. But until January 1895, when he became theatre critic at the *Saturday Review*, his efforts for the New Drama were limited to a letter to an editor and an article on American stage rights in 1885, three short articles in 1889 on the production of *A Doll's House*, two articles in 1891 on *Rosmersholm* and *Brand*, a letter to an editor in 1891, two letters to editors on *Widowers' Houses* in 1892, a defence of *Arms and the Man* in 1894, and a preface to Archer's *The Theatrical World of 1894*, which appeared in 1895.[44]

The one important exception to his absence from the theatrical cause was the publication in 1891 of *The Quintessence of Ibsenism*, which appeared a year before *Widowers' Houses*. The book generated a fair amount of interest, selling approximately 2000 copies over a six-year period.[45] Archer took advantage of the occasion to review *The Quintessence* in an open letter in the *New Review*, offering his mixture of praise and criticism. Because he hoped to generate more controversy over Ibsen (as had occurred earlier in 1891 with the productions of *Ghosts* and *Hedda Gabler*), Archer urged Shaw to respond in the *New Review*. The editor Archibald Grove extended an invitation. But untypically of Shaw, he avoided a public response to Archer's challenging review. (See the open letter, which Archer shared with Shaw on 25 October, and their exchange of letters on 25 and 26 October 1891.) *The Quintessence* caused a bit of a stir among the true believers in the Ibsen revolution. But the book did not yet attain the importance that it subsequently achieved in the twentieth century when Shaw published the expanded and revised edition in 1912–13.[46]

The *Saturday Review* position finally gave Shaw a critical platform for judging, and often indicting, the London theatre. Although the West End theatres were still not interested in his plays, he had partial revenge by becoming a theatre critic. Frank Harris had first offered the position to Archer in December 1894, but he turned it down after receiving a raise at *The World*. Harris then offered the position to Shaw. (See letter of 28 December 1894.) Between January 1895 and April 1898 Shaw proceeded to write some of the most impressive – and aggressive – theatre criticism in the English language, comparable in quality and lasting significance to his valuable music criticism. These theatre reviews provided an ideal forum for his descriptive and analytical talents. His rhetorical voice, perfected in the music criticism, proclaimed his authoritative identity as G.B.S. By shifting from music to theatre criticism, he was now able to join Archer in the journalistic campaign. Finally in 1895 they became full-time comrades in the theatrical campaign. They became Max Beerbohm's violent and diplomatic critics (the bad and good cops) who interrogated the actor-managers and theatrical conditions of London.

Shaw's other important book publication during the 1890s – and by far his most important achievement that decade – was *Plays Pleasant and Unpleasant*, which was published in two volumes on 19 April 1898. Although he had initially expressed doubts to the young publisher Grant Richards about putting out a collection of his plays, he soon saw the advantage. Archer reminded him of Ibsen's success in publishing his own plays.[47] *Plays Pleasant and Unpleasant* did not generate the volume of sales that Archer's translations of Ibsen's plays had achieved. But with these two volumes, along with his argumentative prefaces, Shaw demonstrated that he was becoming a major playwright, despite the limited number of productions in London. To his credit he remained confident that things would change. His time would arrive.

In celebration of the appearance of these volumes, Archer wrote a long, two-part essay for the *Daily Chronicle* on the 19 and 21 April.[48] The appearance of *Plays Pleasant and Unpleasant* was 'an event, literary and theatrical, of the first magnitude.' He celebrated both *Candida* and *Mrs Warren's Profession* as 'works of genius.' He knew, of course, that *Mrs Warren's Profession* could not be performed because of stage censorship, so he made a point of extolling it. As for *Candida*, he loved and lauded the play. This brilliant reworking of Ibsen's *A Doll's House*, with Marchbanks instead of Nora walking out the door, revealed for Archer that Shaw was capable of carrying forward the modernist movement that Ibsen had initiated. If Shaw would write more plays like *Candida*, Shaw could be 'a pillar of fire to our dramatic movement.' With such plays he 'might have the future of the English theatre in his hands.'

Archer admired 'the ingenuity and beauty, the humour and tenderness' that Shaw had achieved with *Candida*. Like Marchbanks, Archer fell in love with the character of Candida, whose 'radiant beauty and sanity' represented for him an ideal image of womanhood.[49] By contrast, the women and love affairs in *Widowers' Houses* and *The Philanderer* were, from his perspective, unappealing, even vulgar. The scenes between the women and their lovers offer a 'bloodless erotics.' This topic of proper and improper womanhood became a key issue in the review as Archer struggled, rather unsuccessfully, to come to terms with Shaw's representations of women and their love affairs. Although he had accepted the sexual dynamics in Ibsen's *A Doll's House*, *Ghosts*, *Hedda Gabler*, and *Rosmersholm*, he was bothered by the sexual coarseness of Shaw's dialogue.

In 1892 Shaw had been bemused by Archer's uneasiness over the character of Blanche. Responding to Archer's review of *Widowers' Houses*, he dismissed Archer as a 'sentimental Sweet Lavendery recluse' and celebrated himself as someone who had 'philandered with women of all sorts & sizes.' (See letter of 14 December 1892.) But by 1898 Shaw showed less patience over Archer's criticisms of the sexual matters in the first two plays. Ignoring Archer's mostly positive commentary in the long review, Shaw unloaded on his friend in his letter of 2 May 1898:

> Well I am DAMNED! Your *analysis* of my limitations! Why, you stupendous ass, you draw a line through my plays which represents your own limitations in your most fatuously lazy mood; and you then proceed to explain that everything outside that line is mere Shawism (which doesn't in the least account for it), and everything inside it is heavenborn genius. You are getting a great deal worse than Clement Scott: everything that is not a stagily sentimental *coup de théâtre* makes you simply petulant.

Shaw's comparison of Archer to Scott was a well-aimed dagger, reminding Archer that Scott had been unable to understand and appreciate Ibsen's *Ghosts* just a year earlier.

In his comments on *Arms and the Man,* Archer granted its comic appeal, as he had done in 1894, but he continued to insist that the action is farcical, not realistic. He also expressed disappointment with *You Never Can Tell.* But eight years later, after seeing a production of the play at the Court Theatre, he would call it a 'classic.' This critical reversal amused Shaw, who teased Archer about his shifting judgment. (See the letter of 10 July 1906, another well-aimed dagger.) Archer had little to say about *The Man of Destiny,* in part because he had already reviewed the play in 1897 when it had received a terrible production in Croydon, outside of London proper. Shaw had nothing to do with that blundering staging. (See the open letter of 31 July 1897 for Archer's assessment.)

Archer's review of *Plays Pleasant and Unpleasant* established a pattern that he would follow, with rare exceptions, for the next twenty-five years. He repeatedly praised Shaw as an artistic genius, yet lamented that didactic messages and philosophical reflections hampered many of the plays. Unlike Ibsen and Shakespeare, Shaw imposed his personal views and identity onto specific characters in each of the plays. The fact that Archer was already comparing Shaw to Ibsen and Shakespeare did not matter. His negative comments – not the critical praise – provided ammunition for Shaw's counter-attacks. (See, for example, their letters of 21 April, 26 April, 30 April, and 2 May 1898.) Shaw's responses also established a pattern that he would follow, with a few exceptions, for the next twenty-five years. He thus dismissed Archer's complaints about the presence of G.B.S. in the plays because, as he told his German translator in January 1903, 'Archer knows me so well personally that he cannot understand how anybody can read my books without seeing that it is 'only Shaw talking,' and not literature' (Trebitsch: 37).

The Second Stage of the Campaign: 1900 to 1914

During the expansive Edwardian era Archer continued to serve as the weekly theatre critic at *The World* until January 1906. (See letters of 1 and 3 January 1906.) He then shifted to the *Tribune* for two years, followed by two more years at the *Nation* (November 1908 to December 1910). In addition, he continued to write regularly for the *Daily Chronicle* until 1910 (various articles, some unsigned). And he wrote a column for the *Morning Leader* from 1900 to 1916 (except for an interlude in 1912 when he took a world tour to the Far East and India). Until 1908 the column was called 'Study and Stage,' then 'Things in General' to 1916. In 1913 he became the theatre critic for *The Star*, an assignment that he continued through the war until 1920. During this period he also maintained a column called 'On Things in General' in the *Daily News* until 1918. Throughout these years he wrote occasionally for other London journals, including the *Fortnightly Review* and *Pall Mall Magazine*, and in New York City for both *The Critic* and *McClure's Magazine*. In a typical week he published two to four articles, and sometimes more. Theatre remained a major commitment. Besides the *Collected Works of Henrik Ibsen* in 1906 (12 vols in both London and New York), he published *Playmaking: A Manual of Craftsmanship* (1912), which sold quite well. And he and H.G. Barker published *A National Theatre: Scheme and Estimate* in 1907. But he also published an impressive range of books beyond the topic of theatre, including *America Today* (1900), *Poets of the Younger Generation* (1902), *Real Conversations* (1904), *Let Youth But Know: A Plea for Reason in Education* (1905), *Thro'Afro-America: An English Reading of the Race-Problem* (1910), and *The Life, Trial, and Death of Francisco Ferrer* (1910).

As this outpouring of books illustrates, Archer's career had expanded substantially beyond the campaign for a 'New Drama' and 'New Theatre.' For example, he was commissioned in 1908 by *McClure's Magazine* to write about the 'colour problem' in the United States. In preparation for this investigation, he read widely on the issues, and spent two months in the United States, interviewing a number of people, from President Roosevelt in the White House to the 'man in the street.' He also met with both Booker T. Washington (1856–1915) and W.E.B. Du Bois (1868–1963) – both of whom impressed him in their distinctive ways. He travelled for several weeks in the southern states, observing communities and living conditions. He met with black people and white authorities, and even attended a black church service. His investigation resulted in a series of featured articles in *McClure's Magazine* in 1909, followed by his book *Thro' Afro-America: An English Reading of the Race Problem* (London, 1910). The book is a valuable record of attitudes and conditions during the first decade of the twentieth century. Yet despite Archer's sympathies for the sufferings of blacks and his firm judgment that slavery had been a crime, he still believed in innate biological and intellectual differences between whites and blacks. He was still a prisoner – like almost all whites of the era as well as the scientific community – of racial prejudices, including the belief in 'the innate inferiority of the negro race' (221). His book is thus an important but flawed document of its time, written from a liberal yet still racist perspective (see Whitebrook: 272–6).

By contrast, Shaw dedicated himself to drama during this period, with a major increase in productions. Although he continued to write on social, political, and economic issues for the Fabian Society, his major publications featured an outpouring of brilliant plays, with the notable appearance of *Man and Superman* (1903), *John Bull's Other Island* (1904), and *Major Barbara* (1905). The German translations began to appear in 1903, as did productions in Austria and Germany. Likewise, the American stage expanded its offerings. For a few years in London Shaw had to depend upon matinee productions by the Stage Society: *Candida* in 1900, *Mrs Warren's Profession* in a private performance in 1902, *The Admirable Bashville* in 1903. Then everything changed with the Court Theatre productions (1904–7). Even though the location of the Royal Court in Sloane Square was some distance from the West End theatre district, the series of productions by the Vedrenne-Barker management propelled Shaw into the front ranks of London theatre.

Archer concurred in this assessment. In an article on the three seasons at the Court, he pointed out that thirty-two plays by seventeen dramatists were featured. Eight of the plays were one-acts. Three were Greek tragedies by Euripides, translated by Gilbert Murray. Eleven of the plays were by Shaw. Out of a total of 988 performances during the three years, 701 were of Shaw's plays.[50] Besides featuring many of the plays that appeared in *Plays Pleasant and Unpleasant*, the Court Theatre produced *Captain Brassbound's Conversion*, *Man and Superman*, *John Bull's Other Island*, *Major Barbara*, and *The Doctor's Dilemma*. These plays and productions established Shaw's works as the modernist voice in English drama. The confident voice that guided the criticism at the *Saturday Review* (1895–8) found full justification in the genius who wrote the plays.

These productions, which were followed by stagings of *Getting Married* (1908), *Misalliance* (1910), *Fanny's First Play* (1911), *Androcles and the Lion* (1913), and *Pygmalion* (1914), solidified Shaw's reputation as the most innovative dramatist in the English language. With the publications and productions of his plays he easily displaced Ibsen as the primary focus of the campaign for a new theatre. And he also displaced the two British playwrights, A.W. Pinero and Henry Arthur Jones, who had appeared for a few years as possible leaders in the revival of English drama. Shaw even found his way into the inner sanctum of the West End theatres, with *Getting Married* at the Haymarket, *Misalliance* at the Duke of York's, *Androcles and the Lion* at the St James's, and *Pygmalion*, featuring Herbert Beerbohm Tree and Mrs Patrick Campbell, at His Majesty's. With charm and bluster, Shaw had captured the London theatrical world – until the turmoil of the First World War.

In the years before the war there continued to be Ibsen productions, but the shock of the new had worn off for many people. There were no new plays, of course, so a retrospective spirit began to emerge. For example, the Stage Society, continuing its subscription program of one or two performances per play, presented four plays that had not yet appeared in London: *The League of Youth* (1900), *The Lady from the Sea* (1902), *When We Dead Awaken* (1903), and *Lady Inger of Östrät* (1906). Eleonora Duse visited in 1903 and 1905 with *Hedda Gabler*. The Court Theatre, under Vedrenne-Barker management, staged *The Wild Duck* in 1905 and *Hedda Gabler*, starring Mrs Patrick Campbell, in 1907. In 1911 Lillah McCarthy and Norman McKinnel appeared in *The Master Builder* with H.G. Barker as director (28 performances). Herbert Beerbohm Tree revived *An Enemy of the People* for a few performances in 1905 and 1909. Florence Kahn (Lady Max Beerbohm) staged *Rosmersholm* in 1908 (8 perfs.). And in 1911 Lydia Yavorska was featured in productions of *A Doll's House* (52 perfs.) and *Hedda Gabler* (25 perfs.). Except for the Stage Society presentations, all these plays had premiered in the Victorian era.[51]

Not surprisingly, few people were interested in performing Ibsen's history plays, but besides the Stage Society's *Lady Inger of Östrät*, London saw Gordon Craig's *The Vikings* [*at Hegleland*] in 1903, with a revised translation by Archer. The staging at the Imperial Theatre (30 perfs.) was controversial not only because of the scenic effects but also because of the decision to feature Ellen Terry in a major role. (For Archer's review, see the headnote for the letter of 15 April 1903.) Another history play, *The Pretenders*, was staged in 1913 by Laurence Irving at the Haymarket (35 perfs.). Otherwise, between 1900 and 1914 the Ibsen productions were minor revivals for a few performances of the most popular of the realistic plays.

By contrast, the major Shaw productions during this period were of new plays. Shaw thus became for Archer the primary focus of the campaign for a new drama. Keeping up with Shaw was Archer's new mandate. Until 1898 he had written only a half-dozen or so reviews and essays on Shaw's works, though on several occasions he created ways to mention Shaw in articles on other topics. But from 1898 on, when he published his long two-part essay on *Plays Pleasant and Unpleasant,* until 1914, the pace quickened. Whenever Shaw published a new play, Archer reviewed it. Whenever any play was staged, he reviewed it. And after reviewing the opening performance, he would often write another essay on a specific aspect of the play. He regularly published two or three articles on each production. In the case of *The Doctor's Dilemma,* he wrote four articles during the run. And quite often these reviews generated debates with Shaw, who sometimes replied in the newspaper or journal. Just as often he unloaded on Archer with a private letter or two, as this collected correspondence illustrates.

Month after month, year after year, Shaw's plays called forth a steady flow of articles from Archer. Between May 1904, when he reviewed the production of *Candida,* to the end of December 1907, when he reviewed a revival of *Arms and the Man,* Archer wrote 66 reviews and essays about Shaw and his works – both the book publications and the productions. Then, for the years between May 1900, when he reviewed a production of *You Never Can Tell,* and May 1914, when he discussed Shaw's *The Dark Lady of the Sonnets,* Archer published, by my count, 126 articles and essays in which Shaw's plays, prefaces, productions, and ideas were discussed. Even when there was no new publication or production, Archer found ingenious ways to introduce the topic of Shaw into articles on quite separate topics. He did so not only in discussions of other plays and playwrights (such as Arthur Conan Doyle's *A Story of Waterloo,* a German production of Lessing's *Nathan Die Weise,* or Gilbert Murray's *Andromache*), but also in articles on copyright law, censorship, endowed theatres, religion, science, spelling reform, book printing, amateur acting, Mark Twain, Eleonora Duse, Shakespeare, tenement dwellers, Aristotle, the Sir Walter Scott club in Edinburgh, and in a comparison of Shaw to Thomas Huxley and Matthew Arnold as intellectuals. By means of these dozens upon dozens of reviews and articles, Archer established Shaw as the most important playwright in the English drama. Even when he lamented that Shaw was not fulfilling his genius, Archer insisted that Shaw had the potential to not only transform the modern theatre but also provide leadership in the modern world (if, that is, he would stop being a clown).

In celebration of the Court's first season, Archer published a fancy booklet of fifteen pages, *The Vedrenne-Barker Season. 1904–05: A Record and a Commentary*. Besides offering photographs of Vedrenne, Barker, Shaw, and the performers, the booklet featured the cast lists and length of runs for each production. Archer described each production. He insisted that the Vedrenne-Barker enterprise was approaching the model of a repertory company, a topic dear to his campaign for an endowed theatre (which he and Harley Granville Barker were developing at this time). When the Court Theatre decided to devote the end of the first season (1904–5) to a nine-week evening season of *Candida, You Never Can Tell*, and *John Bull's Other Island*, Archer identified Shaw as 'the Chelsea Shakespeare' (*The World*, 9 May 1905). Shaw had conquered Sloane Square in Chelsea as Shakespeare had prevailed in Southwark.[52]

Unfortunately, except for a few comments by Shaw, the extant letters failed to take up the topic of the Court Theatre plays and productions. Dozens of reviews by Archer exist, but only three of Archer's letters from these years have survived, and none of them discussed the Court Theatre productions. Shaw wrote most of the surviving letters for 1904 through 1907, but even when the Court theatre plays and productions emerged as the topic, he was usually responding to an article by Archer, not a letter.[53] (See, for example, 1 January 1906 on *Major Barbara* and 10 July 1906 on *You Never Can Tell.*) Before and after the period of the Court Theatre productions, the letters offered at least a partial record of how Archer and Shaw communicated. Although it was still the case that Shaw was often responding to a published article rather than to a previous letter, a few letters discussed a production. (See, for instance, his letter of 17 June 1908 on *Getting Married.*)

Yet despite the missing letters and gaps in the correspondence, it is still possible to track the spirited arguments between the two men by attending to Archer's articles. For example, on 22 August 1903 Archer published an article in the *Morning Leader* on 'Mr Shaw and Mr Pinero.' Then two days later, on 24 August, he published a review in the *Daily Chronicle* of *Man and Superman.* Then on 2 September he published an essay entitled 'Das moderne Drama in England' in the German newspaper *Die Zeit.* Shaw, who was in Scotland, still received the articles. On 27 August he wrote a letter in response to Archer's *ML* article, and on 28 August he also published a letter to the editor of *ML* on the same topic. In reply Archer wrote a long, nine-page letter on 1 September that countered Shaw's private letter and the letter to the editor. This was a defence of his *ML* article on Pinero-Shaw and his *DC* review of *Man and Superman*. A day later, on 2 September, Shaw expanded his assault on Archer. Then on 7 September he wrote a letter in response to Archer's essay in *Die Zeit*. These three articles, the letter to the editor, and the private letters captured the spirit of the heated debates between Archer and Shaw on Pinero's plays, *Man and Superman*, and the overall campaign for modern drama in England. Archer also wrote a letter on 2 September, which responded to Shaw's attacks; he continued his defence of his articles and review, but this letter has not survived. Nonetheless, it is possible to reconstruct some of the topics of the missing letter on the basis of an additional letter from Shaw on 8 September. Given this typical combination of articles and letters (and missing letters), I have made a point in my headnotes of offering sufficient summaries of Archer's articles so that the letters have their full context.

Shaw's plays are the most prevalent topic in the extant letters, exceeding references to Ibsen or Shakespeare. For example, the topic of *Mrs Warren's Profession* occurred in no less than twenty-five of the letters. *Widowers' Houses* was mentioned twenty-one times (and *Rheingold* an additional eleven); *Arms and the Man* was commented upon nineteen times; *Candida* twenty six; *The Man of Destiny* fourteen; *Captain Brassbound's Conversion* fourteen; *Plays Pleasant and Unpleasant* ten; *The Devil's Disciple* fifteen: *Caesar and Cleopatra* nine; *Man and Superman* twenty; *John Bull's Other Island* three; *The Admirable Bashville* six; *Major Barbara* nine; *The Doctor's Dilemma* seven; *Getting Married* six; *Misalliance* three; *Androcles and the Lion* six; *Pygmalion* seven; *Heartbreak House* seven; *Back to Methuselah* six; and *Saint Joan* six. These numbers would be even higher if the missing letters by Archer had survived.

The War and After

Shaw and Archer held opposing views during the First World War on the British government and its leadership. Whereas Shaw mounted a series of sharp attacks on the government, Archer not only defended the policies but also served in the government in several capacities. Despite their differences, the friendship held. (See letters of 11 November 1914 and

23 February 1916.) But they saw one another only occasionally during the war years. Only a few letters were exchanged, and Archer wrote far fewer reviews than he had poured out during the Edwardian era.

At the beginning of the war Shaw published *Common Sense about the War*, a blistering critique of both the German and British governments. His statements angered many people, including a number of his colleagues in the theatre community and the Fabian Society. Henry Arthur Jones denounced Shaw as an enemy of the country. Some people called him a traitor. In his opposition to British authority, Shaw once again took on his preferred role as a political outsider. The war turned him into a polemicist. As H.G. Wells stated during the turmoil, Shaw 'flings himself upon his typewriter and rattles out his broadsides.'[54] He seemed to thrive and gain purpose in opposition.

Because of his political views, Shaw was highly visible during the war. But in the London theatre world he became almost invisible – a notable reversal of his status in the years before the war. He had continued to receive solid, if not spectacular, support in 1913 and 1914. *Androcles and the Lion*, which was directed by Barker and starred Lillah McCarthy, had been staged on 1 September 1913 (St James's, 63 perfs.). *Great Catherine*, a sketch that featured Gertrude Kingston and Norman McKinnel, opened on 18 November 1913 (Vaudeville, 44 perfs.). *The Music Cure*, 'a piece of utter nonsense' which served as a curtain raiser for Gilbert Chesterton's *Magic*, opened on 28 January 1914 (Little Theatre, 68 perfs.). And then *Pygmalion* appeared at His Majesty's Theatre on 11 April 1914 and ran until 24 July (118 perfs.) – just a few days before the guns of August shattered the tenuous peace. Starring Mrs Patrick Campbell and Herbert Beerbohm Tree, the production, which Shaw directed, was a major achievement, even though the two stars were inappropriate for their roles.

For the next five years, however, there was only one London production of a full-length play by Shaw.[55] On 13 Februrary 1915 Lena Ashwell braved the political controversies that Shaw had generated by opening a revival of *Fanny's First Play* at her Kingsway Theatre (49 perfs.).[56] Except for this production there were few sightings of Shaw's plays for the next four years. Two performances of *Augustus Does His Bit* were presented privately by the Stage Society on 21 and 22 January 1917. This minor piece was staged jointly with J.M. Synge's *The Tinker's Wedding* (which was even more controversial than Shaw's work because of the scene of a priest tied up in a bag). At the end of the year, on 16 December 1917, Shaw directed a single performance of *The Inca of Perusalem* for Edith Craig's Pioneer Players at the Criterion Theatre. The final glimse of a Shaw play occurred when *Annajanska, the Bolshevik Empress* had a single performance as one of the offerings in a variety show at Oswald Stoll's London Coliseum Theatre on 21 January 1918. Not surprisingly, Shaw had stated to Lillah McCarthy in August 1917 that 'the war is playing the deuce with my income.' He was completing *Heartbreak House,* yet he admitted that he was 'not very keen on having the play produced at all just now ... What with the war, and the fact that it will be some time before we can be quite our old selves again, my heart is not on the stage at present' (CL 3: 498). Shaw had to wait more than four years for a London production of the play.

He did not begin to regain his place in the London theatre until December 1919, when *Arms and the Man* was revived (Duke of York's, 72 perfs.). This production featured Robert Loraine and Mrs Campbell. Then in May 1920 *Pygmalion* was revived, with C. Aubrey Smith and Mrs Campbell, and Shaw directing. In the main, between the two productions of *Pygmalion* in 1914 and 1920 Shaw had lost his place in the London theatres.[57] Without the support of the women – Lena Ashwell, Edith Craig, and Mrs Campbell – Shaw might well have been completely abandoned during these years. As had been the case in the 1890s, but for quite different reasons, his plays lacked support. But whatever his frustration and possible gloom, he had continued to create new work: *Heartbreak House* was written in 1916 and 1917. And *Back to Methuselah* – all five parts – was written between March 1918 and May 1920.

It is true, of course, that during the war only a few worthy plays and productions were staged, including a cut version of Thomas Hardy's *The Dynasts,* which opened on 25 November at Ashwell's Kingsway Theatre (71 perfs.). This play about the Napoleonic war was staged by H.G. Barker. Few candidates for 'new drama' emerged during the war, though Harold Brighouse's *Hobson's Choice* found a supporting audience at the Apollo in 1916 (228 perfs.). Among the established playwrights, Pinero had revivals of *His House in Order* in 1914 and *Trelawney of the 'Wells'* in both 1915 and 1917. His one new play that garnered some praise was *The Big Drum* in December 1915 (St James's, 111 perfs.). Less impressive were *The Amazons* in 1917 (36 perfs.) and *The Freaks, an Idyll of Suburbia* in 1918 (51 perfs.). J.M. Barrie was quite popular throughout the war with revivals of *Peter Pan, The Professor's Love Story,* and *Dear Brutus.* And of course the pantomimes held their vital place in the Christmas season. Likewise, Shakespeare's plays were featured regularly in the West End theatres, especially *Henry V* and some of the comedies. Perhaps the most laudable and tenacious accomplishment during the war years belonged to Lillian Baylis, who maintained her rigorous schedule of theatre and opera at the Royal Victoria Hall [Old Vic]. Without fail each year her players staged a dozen or more of Shakespeare plays, a few comedies by Sheridan and Goldsmith, and at least a half-dozen operas (e.g., Mozart, Donizetti, Verdi, Bizet, Puccini).[58] Year after year, the war was incapable of diminishing her ambition and dedication.

Many offerings in the West End theatres during these troubled years were patriotic reviews, pageants, musicals, melodramas, and comedies – exactly the kinds of entertainment that angered Shaw (though he avoided all of them). The titles often revealed the war themes: *For England, Home, and Beauty; Or, Comrades in Arms* in 1915, *Home on Leave* in 1916, and *Seven Day's Leave* in 1917 which ran for 718 performances at the Lyceum. By far the most popular production during and after the war was *Chu Chin Chow,* the 'musical tale of the East' by Oscar Asche, with music by Frederic Norton. A costume extravaganza based loosely on *Ali Baba, and the Forty Thieves,* it ran for an amazing 2238 performances, from 31 August 1916 until 22 July 1921.

Perhaps wisely, Archer and Shaw avoided discussions about the war – both privately and publicly. In contrast to Shaw, Archer had aligned himself with the governmental policy as soon as the war began.[59] Although he was too old to enlist as a soldier, he sought employment in the government. For one of his first assignments, he accepted a position in the postal censorship office in Edinburgh for a few months. The irony did not escape him. He soon moved to the War Intelligence Bureau in London, where he wrote several pamphlets and books in opposition to German militarism (Whitebrook: 316). In response to the German invasion of Belgium, he published *The Thirteen Days: July 23–August 4 1914: A Chronicle and Interpretation.* He held Germany fully responsible for beginning the war. Shaw, by contrast, had rejected this explanation, and instead held the British government equally responsible. Despite – or perhaps because of – Archer's dedicated service to the government, the daily reports on the war gave him 'a sense of black oppression.' By 1916 he felt that the war was a nightmare, 'a pain unspeakable.'[60]

Throughout the war, in addition to his full-time governmental work, Archer continued to turn out theatre reviews for *The Star*, though the stortage of paper reduced most reviews to little more than short notices. He provided a supportive review of *Fanny's First Play*, which he described as 'a humorous creation of extraordinary brilliancy. We all enjoyed it immensely on Saturday evening. For myself, I laughed with a heartiness that almost recalled the Golden Age before the war' (16 February 1915). Besides *The Star*, Archer wrote for the *Daily News*, which featured his political and social commentary. But this newspaper ceased publication in 1917. Archer's most significant commentary on London theatre during this period was a series of reports he sent to *The Nation* in New York (C. Archer: 348). In April 1917, for example, he noted that the Stage Society had presented Shaw's *Augustus Does His Bit*, a 'one-act trifle' which was a satire 'upon aristocratic incompetence in military and other matters.' The piece was amusing, but 'there are some things for which war destroys one's palate, and Mr. Shaw's persiflage is one of them.' Archer then expanded upon his concerns:

> After the war, those of us who are still above ground will no doubt relish our Shaw again; but in the thick of its storm and stress he somehow seems an incongruity. His whole habit of mind is out of place in such a crisis; and I cannot but think that an uneasy consciousness of this fact leads him to exaggerate his foibles, and to assume an aloofness, not to say a callousness, which he does not really feel. He gives one the impression of caring for nothing so long as he can crack his joke and exhibit his *Besserwissen* on every conceivable topic. I am sure that in this he does his real nature injustice. He is simply the victim of an ineradicable habit of mind which happens to be sadly out of place in war-time. In days like these, it is surely a maxim of plain common-sense that he who cannot say anything helpful had better hold his tongue; and anything less helpful than *Augustus Does His Bit* it would be hard to imagine. (*The Nation*, 26 April 1917)

Archer, like most people in those years, had lost his taste for Shaw's disturbing, irreverent voice. Although Archer had not joined those who opposed Shaw, he felt that Shaw's tactics were misguided.

Unlike Shaw, Archer had been engaged personally in the war ever since his son joined one of the Scottish regiments in 1914. (See Shaw's letter of 11 November 1914.) Tom survived until the spring of 1918, but then Archer, Mrs Archer, and Tom's young wife Alys received official word that Tom was wounded and missing in action. During the following weeks and months of uncertainty, when rumours circulated that Tom might have suffered a head injury and lost his memory, Archer, the dedicated rationalist, consulted spiritualist mediums in the hope of making contact with his lost son. Even though he had doubts about clairvoyants – and kept these activities secret from his wife and Alys (and Shaw) – he tried to believe that the exercises might allow him to communicate with Tom. But after two years of these futile searches in the spirit worlds, he forsook them. He finally concluded that Tom was dead, not just missing. Three long years passed before confirmation finally arrived in July 1921 of his death. The report stated that Tom had actually died in 1918 in a German hospital and was buried in West Flanders. (See letters of 19 April 1919 and 22 June 1921.) When Archer, Mrs Archer, and Alys visited the grave in the late summer of 1921, he informed a close friend that 'it makes one feel that one has no right to be alive.'[61]

Despite the many trials and hardships of the war, both Archer and Shaw made occasional attempts to reconnect in a familiar way. In 1916, when Shaw sent a copy of the newly published *Androcles and the Lion, Overruled,* and *Pygmalion,* Archer responded and even made a half-hearted attempt to resume the swordplay. He argued against Shaw's version of Jesus Christ in the long preface to *Androcles.* Shaw replied a few months later. (See Archer's letters of 4 January and 18 July 1916, and Shaw's delayed response on 30 December 1916.)

The war had taken its toll on Archer, as Shaw recognized. In 1919, when Archer published *War Is War* – a laboured play in which he attempted to represent the German atrocities – Shaw made a point of reviewing it. And he made an even more important point of writing to Archer about his insistence upon reviewing it. In the lengthy, heartfelt, and exhaustive letter of 19 April 1919, Shaw reached out to his dear friend in a time of uncertainty over the fate of Tom. Although sentimentality was forbidden, Shaw used the occasion to praise Archer's determination to write a play, and he urged Archer to commit himself to writing more plays, for the war had given him something to argue about. Praising

Archer was not, however, Shaw's primary aim in this letter. Instead, he felt that the best strategy for dealing with a melancholy Archer was to engage him in argument once again. By evoking their early friendship and their debates during the three decades before the war, including the initial disagreements over *Rheingold* and *Widowers' Houses*, Shaw renewed and revitalized their relationship by purposefully challenging Archer. In his adversarial manner, he attempted to renew their old debates. The best way to do this was to re-establish the 'running fight' that had yoked them together 'for forty years.' In the process of stirring up old debates, Shaw seemed to grab Archer's old umbrella in order to whack him over the head. It was the right tactic, for the contentious juices began to flow again for both of them.

Having stirred up the old and familiar topics, Shaw then shifted to current matters. He challenged Archer on the issues that most concerned them, from political debates over how to achieve peace to theatrical debates about staging Shakespeare. By covering several large topics, he quite earnestly sought to reconnect with Archer, and in the process to reconstitute their friendship. Even when he proclaimed the end of his 'thousand and somethingth lesson' he was just warming up, for he then criticized Archer on the matter of cutting Shakespeare's plays for production. If there is any doubt about the depths of the friendship, Shaw's complex letter should be required reading. From Shaw's perspective, the best physic for reconnecting with his comrade-in-arms was a full-scale debate, not sentiment and sympathy. Shaw offered what he did best – the fine art of fencing.

War Is War, though an ineffectual play, had allowed Archer to describe the horrors of war, and in the process to achieve a moral assessment (and at least a partial emotional release over the probable death of Tom). Then his next play, *The Green Goddess*, which came to him in a dream, allowed him to create a spirited melodramatic triumph of good over evil. In 1919 Archer had appealed to Shaw, Pinero, and then Barker to help with the writing of the play, but each of them turned him down and told him to trust in himself. Despite his adamant 'no,' Shaw did discuss some ideas with Archer. And Barker helped with some rewriting during rehearsals. But the play was Archer's. (See letters of 6 September 1919, 17 September 1919, 9 October 1919, 18 October 1919, 8 November 1920, and 16 March 1921.)

The Green Goddess opened in New York City on 18 January 1921, after a December tryout in Philadelphia. It ran for 440 performances, and then toured in the northeastern states for over a year, racking up a total of over 800 performances. (See letter of 16 March 1921.) The play then opened in London on 6 September 1923 at the St James's Theatre, and had 419 performances.[62] The play, which had no pretensions of being the 'new drama,' was nonetheless an accomplished melodrama that pitted British moral character against the unscrupulous and hypocritical values of a dictator, the Raja of Rukh, who oversees a frontier kingdom near India. No doubt the play's opposition between East and West offered an adventurous tale in the manner of Dion Boucicault's *Jessie Brown or the Relief of Lucknow*, which was set in India. In this manner the basic plot delivered a predictable struggle between civilization and barbarism. Yet Archer was able to weave into *The Green Goddess* several of the ironies, contradictions, and ambiguities of the colonial conditions of his era, including some of the complexities of the Indian continent under British rule. He had travelled there for five months in 1912, and visited with his brother Charles, an agent of the government, who was located in Balochistan in the north. Subsequently Archer had written about the country and British colonialism in *India and the Future* (1917). The play also evoked some of the horrors of the war he had represented in *War Is War*. And on a deeply emotional level, Archer's melodrama delivered some quite personal motifs, including a secret version of the love between Archer and Elizabeth Robins: two people who love one another but cannot announce their love because one of them is married. In this version of true love, the woman is the married one. She has maintained a loveless marriage because of her children. In the last act, when the hero and heroine, Traherne and Lucilla, must face death by the evil Raja, they are able to declare their love because Lucilla's husband, in an act of heroism, sacrifices himself in opposition to the Raja. Finally they can acknowledge their love and the price they have paid because of the secrecy.

> Traherne: I wonder if you guess what it has meant to me, ever since we met ..., to see you as another man's wife, bound to him by ties I could not ask you to break. It has been hell, hell!
>
> Lucilla: Yes, Basil, I know. I have known from the beginning.

> Traherne: Oh, Lucilla, have we not been fools, fools? We have sacrified to an idol as senseless as that – [with a gesture towards the Green Goddess image] all the glory and beauty of life! ...
>
> Lucilla: Oh, Basil – you are going back on your own wisdom.
>
> Traherne: Wisdom! What has wisdom to say to love, thwarted and unfulfilled? You were right when you said that it is a mockery to speak of love without hands to clasp, without lips to kiss. We may be going to some pale parody of life: but in our cowardice we have killed love forever and ever.
>
> Lucilla: No, Basil, don't call it cowardice. I, too, regret – perhaps as much as you – that things were – as they were. But not even your love could have made up to me for my children.[63]

For Traherne and Lucilla, as for Archer and Robins, a great sacrifice has been paid, yet a special honour has also been achieved. This scene carried a private message just for Archer and Robins. And for Archer alone there was also another expression of private emotion, for he presented a scene about communication between the living and dead that paralleled his own spiritual attempts to communicate with his son Tom who died in the war.[64]

For the first time in his life Archer achieved financial stability, even riches (despite the taxes imposed by both countries). In 1920 he concluded his weekly theatre reviewing. After four decades he was exhausted. And some aspects of modernism were moving beyond him, including the plays of Chekhov and O'Neill, Expressionist scene design, and American jazz). To a certain extent he withdrew into his familiar self during the last four years of his life. Yet he did not abandon theatre. He wrote three history plays, including one on Martha Washington.[65] He also accepted the invitation to present a series of lectures of the history of British theatre. In 1923 these lectures became *The Old Drama and the New.*

As is clear from this book, Archer had recovered sufficiently from the war years to argue with Shaw again. This renewed spirit of friendship is also strikingly evident in the series of disputes between them in June 1923 when he delivered a copy of his new book to Shaw. It led to a stirring debate about the construction of Shaw's plays. (See the six long letters written between 8 and 23 June.) The two friends, to their delight, were once again fully engaged in argumentative swordplay, each quite convinced that he was right and the other hopelessly wrong. The friendship concluded as it had begun four decades earlier. It had only deepened.

The Other Campaigns

Besides their major campaigns for the 'New Drama,' the 'New Theatre,' and new standards for criticism, the two colleagues were actively involved in three additional projects: the battle against stage censorship, the founding of an endowed national theatre, and the transformation of the acting and production methods for Shakespeare's plays. The topic of censorship was discussed in seventeen letters, the issue of an endowed national theatre arose in thirteen letters, and the concerns over Shakespearean theatre, including debates over production methods and the cutting of the texts, showed up in no less than forty-four letters – almost one-quarter of the extant letters.

On the issue of censorship, for example, both of them were opposed to the Examiner of Plays, who worked out of the Lord Chamberlain's Office. Shaw was appalled by the hypocrisy of E.F. Smyth Pigott and George Alexander Redford, who denied performance licences for *Ghosts* and *Mrs Warren's Profession*, but had no problem sanctioning obscene sex farces. (See the letter of 10 October 1892.) For Archer the campaign against censorship was maintained throughout his full professional career. From the early 1880s forward he wrote critiques of the system of stage censorship. In 1892 he was the lone person who testified against censorship when the government held a national hearing on the theatre industry. Then in 1909, when the Joint Select Committee of Parliament again held public hearings on stage censorship, Archer was joined by Shaw and several other people, including H. Granville Barker and J.M. Barrie. They all testified against the continuation of the policy. (See letter of 10 August 1909.) When the Select Committee refused to accept and read Shaw's lengthy *Statement of the Evidence*, he published it later as the preface to *The Shewing-up of Blanco Posnet*, which had been refused a licence for performance in England.

The campaign for the founding of an endowed national theatre was a major undertaking for Archer and Shaw. Here too Archer had first begun to advance arguments for a national theatre early in his career during the 1880s. By 1902 Shaw had joined the discussions in earnest. (See the letters of 24 February, 1 March, and 4 March 1902.) In 1904 Archer and Granville Barker wrote a 'blue book' for a national theatre and circulated it privately to various influential people in the theatre community and the government. Then in 1907 they published the revised plan as *A National Theatre: Scheme and Estimates.* Shaw supported the project, though of course he argued with Archer and Barker over some details in the proposal. (See the letter of 3 July 1908.) This project subsequently became part of a national campaign when the Shakespeare Memorial National Theatre Committee was established. (See letters of 3 November 1908 and 4 March 1909.) Shaw and Archer were members of the committee. (On the politics of the SMNTC see letters of 8 June 1922, 10 June 1922, and 13 June 1922.)

As for their campaigns for a revitalized Shakespearean theatre, Archer and Shaw were leading advocates not only in their journalism but also in their support for performers, directors, producers, and financial backers who were committed to a modern transformation of staging practices. The matter of Shakespeare engaged them on several fronts, not limited to the campaign for a national theatre. It shows up in the letters for the first time on 16 March 1885, when Shaw complained about a production of *As You Like It.* After seeing the performances by the Kendals and John Hare, he wrote: 'My opinion of Shakespeare has gone up prodigiously: my opinion of Victorian stage culture is below zero.' Shaw and Archer continued their campaign in their debates over the production of *Cymbeline* with Ellen Terry and Henry Irving. (See the letter of 6 October 1896.) Both of them, on several occasions, voiced their opposition to Irving's productions, which featured elaborate sets, long intermissions, and truncated playtexts. Besides the Lyceum productions, they also argued over the efforts of William Poel and his Elizabethan Stage Society. On several occasions Shaw defended Poel's idiosyncratic efforts, but Archer maintained a steady flow of criticism. They were not divided, however, over the efforts of Harley Granville Barker.

They were strong supporters of his three productions of Shakespeare in 1912 and 1914, but unfortunately the extant letters do not offer descriptions and evaluations. And because of his world tour in 1912, Archer missed the first two productions.

During the First World War there was limited opportunity and inclination to mount battles for the arts. But in 1919 Shaw and Archer returned to the Shakespeare campaign. They carried out a series of debates over the birth of the Shakespeare Memorial Theatre at Stratford-upon-Avon that William Bridges-Adams had established and was directing. (See the letter of 19 April 1919, and the subsequent debate articulated in the letter of 8 June 1922.) They also had several heated arguments over the cutting of the plays, with Archer attempting to justify selective cuts and Shaw opposing any. (See, for example, the letters for 22 April 1919, 17 May 1919, and 6 September 1919.) And in 1923, eighteen years after the death of Henry Irving, they still complained about productions of Shakespeare's plays that had 'elaborately built sets' and 'interminable entr'actes.' (See the letter of 19 June 1923.)

Obviously, these three campaigns sometimes overlapped with one another, and with the other three campaigns for the new drama and new theatre. For Archer and Shaw the various campaigns were all part of their collective endeavours to bring about a modern transformation of the British stage.

Conclusion

There is much to admire about the missions and achievements of Shaw and Archer. Given their individual and collective accomplishments over four decades, it is sometimes difficult to determine what was more important at key moments – their partnerships on the various projects or their separate endeavours and talents. Whatever their specific methods of working together and individually, they transformed the modern British theatre. And yet, there remains one troubling feature of their relationship. Year after year, decade after decade, Archer continued to insist upon the supposed faults in a number of Shaw's plays. In some cases his judgments were misguided, and some of his statements remain inexplicable. How could he be so dense? We may smile at – or perhaps shake our heads over – Archer's struggles to accept and appreciate several of Shaw's plays. Yet we need to keep in mind that often he was purposefully setting up a debate with Shaw in order to maintain or continue a public campaign. Crossing swords was an imperative of the friendship for both men. Also, as many letters and reviews illustrate, Archer regularly delivered a negative evaluation upon first reading a play; yet his assessment often improved when he saw a production. Reversals in his judgments were not uncommon. Because he often wrote three or four separate articles and letters on a specific play, we need to measure his assessments as collective pronouncements (sometimes stretching over the years). For example, in 1903, when *Man and Superman* was published, he wrote an extended review that rejected the philosophical commentary on the superman, by way of Schopenhauer and Nietzsche. Although he granted that the 'Epistle to A. B. Walkley,' 'The Revolutionist's Handbook by Jack Tanner,' and the play itself 'crackle with wit and tingle with cerebral activity,' he despaired that Shaw would ever write well-crafted plays like *Candida, Mrs Warren's Profession,* and *The Devil's Disciple.* Instead of these gems, Shaw delivered in *Man and Superman* a 'symbolic extravaganza,' a 'morality in four acts and a dream,' and an 'allegorical farce.'[66] But he failed to write a self-contained drama. (For Shaw's dismissive response to this review see his long letter of 2 September 1903.)

In 1905, however, Archer's judgments modified when he reviewed the Court Theatre production of *Man and Superman.* He still lamented, as he had done in 1903, that Shaw had overloaded the play with philosophical and political statements. But in 1905 Archer had come to a more complex understanding: 'Every play of Mr. Bernard Shaw's is the result of a collaboration of three distinct personages: the dramatist, the philosopher, and the wit.' Shaw had limitations as a dramatist, but 'he is something rarer, if not better – a philosophical humorist, with the art of expressing himself in dramatic form.' Archer concluded that Shaw may not be a great modern dramatist, but *Man and Superman,* which Archer described as 'a fantastic allegory,' is something special because Shaw's 'wit is unique, personal, priceless.' The wit, in fact, is the man, and we are unreasonable 'to wish that he were not himself, but someone else.'[67]

In this assessment Archer had a moment of recognition (and a partial reversal in his own understanding of Shaw's drama):

> It has taken me some time to arrive at this perception. Hitherto I have wrestled earnestly with Mr. Shaw to try to make a serious playwright of him. *Candida* and some scenes in *Mrs. Warren's Profession* awakened false hopes in

> me, and I strove, by a judicious blending of flattery and insult, to foster the artist in him at the expense of the humorist. It was a mistake, and I hereby renounce it. The artist, at his best was essentially inferior to the humorist. I was labouring for the survival of the unfittest. Had I succeeded (a preposterous assumption) we should have been the richer by an inferior Ibsen, the poorer by an individual, inimitable, irritating, tantalizing, incalculable, delightful Shaw. It would have been an unhappy exchange.[68]

A few months later, when the Court production moved into the evening slot, Archer attended the revival. He praised the play's 'abounding, irresistible humour' and the admirable performances.[69] His comments were mostly positive. Then in 1907 the Court finally presented the dream play, which had been removed from the 1905 productions. Archer was enthralled by *Don Juan in Hell*: 'I enjoyed intensely the piece which is ... a brilliant freak.' Summing up the flow of ideas, Archer announced that the separate experience of act 3 was profound. 'Fundamentally the pleasure one received was simply that of listening to a continuous stream of thought, expressed in an amazingly vivid, supple, stimulating, irritating, fascinating, rhetorical form. "Don Juan in Hell" is nothing more nor less than the exposition of a philosophy, coloured, and deeply coloured, by a temperament. One might almost go further and call it a philosophical autobiography.' Enthralled by the 'mature Shaw,' Archer proclaimed: 'Don Juan's gospel of the contemplative intellect is a quite genuine *gospel*, and will one day be recognized, I verily believe, as a forecast of the religion of the future.' Archer praised the staging, which 'was quite delightful.' As for the acting, 'the four performers, Lillah McCarthy (Dona Ana), Robert Loraine (Don Juan), Michael Holbrooke (Statue), and Norman McKinnel (Devil), were excellent.'[70]

Archer's several reviews of *Man and Superman* suggest that from 1905 forward he was ready to accept Shaw's drama on its own terms. To a certain extent this was the case. For example, at the end of 1907 he wrote: 'We have long ago come to recognize in Mr. Shaw a playwright who is a law unto himself and on whom technical criticisms are almost entirely wasted. It is not his methods that matter, but his message, and the wit with which it is delivered.'[71] And yet, over the following years Archer continued to express doubts about certain aspects of Shaw's plays, from

Widowers' Houses to *Heartbreak House.* Even in 1923 he was still finding fault with Shaw's plays because they combined philosophical ideas with clowning. In turn, Shaw continued to complain that Archer was wedded to the well-made play as his model for dramatic plotting. In some sessions of their debates the two friends kept repeating versions of their well-crafted identities. Accordingly, it is easy to string together several of Archer's negative statements about Shaw's plays, and thus conclude, as Archibald Henderson did, that Archer was a terrible theatre critic:

> He protested against Shaw's introducing the most advanced ideas in the theater, crassly laughed at him for being ahead of his age, spoke in solemnly regretful tones of his most brilliant qualities, tacked deprecatory characterizations upon some of his best and most effective plays, took him to task for not writing plays as he, Archer (the author of *The Green Goddess* – shades of the Adelphi!), thought they should be written ... Could misinterpretation of fact go further?[72]

Ever since Henderson published his biographies (1911, 1932, 1956), some observers have perceived Archer as a flawed and limited critic. From Henderson's perspective, Archer failed to understand Shaw and his works: 'Archer meant well; but his perspective was execrable' (Hend 3: 605–6). This condescending attack in 1956 is so absolute that we must wonder why Shaw took the trouble to have anything to do with Archer. We may not join Henderson in such a negative and misleading judgment on Archer, but when Shaw aimed his barbs at Archer (e.g., accusing him of having 'a perfect rag shop of old ideas' in his head), it is easy – perhaps too easy – to concur.[73] But in our rush to judgment against Archer we should keep in mind G.K. Chesterton's own judgment: 'The fame of having first offered Shaw to the public upon a platform worthy of him belongs, like many other public services, to Mr. William Archer' (Chesterton: 65).

As is now apparent, Archer's deep admiration for the realism of Ibsen's well-crafted plots and methods of characterization made it difficult for him to accept some of Shaw's unconventional dramatic methods. Shaw recognized, of course, that Archer was a prisoner of his ideas on dramatic form – ideas that established Ibsen's realistic plays as the required model for the development of modern drama. Shaw saw quite correctly that Archer's perspective was limited by some of his reigning ideas that he advocated in *Play-making* (1912) and *The Old Drama and the New* (1923). If, though, we dismiss Archer because of these limitations, we fail the historical challenge of understanding how and why he was the most outstanding theatre critic on Shaw during their shared time together. We fail to contend with the ambiguities and contradictions that define Archer and his judgments. The many articles, reviews, and books he wrote about Shaw are the most extensive contemporary record of Shaw's drama, from *Widowers' Houses* to *Saint Joan.* The outpouring of reviews and essays, even the negative ones, provided important and vital commentary on the plays and the productions.

Like the surviving letters, the reviews and essays offer us a valuable documentary record of not just the fascinating friendship but also the development of Shaw's drama from the perspective of the most important theatre critic in London between the 1880s and the First World War. The reviews and essays often provide the missing cause, context, and condition for the exchange of ideas in their correspondence. We may indeed question Archer's judgments on some matters, as seems most appropriate in a number of cases. Yet despite his critiques and repeated complaints about Shaw's plays, he understood and appreciated Shaw's subject matter and rhetorical style, and he recognized and admired many traits of Shaw's genius and accomplishments. If we doubt this, we might keep in mind that in 1924 he argued that Shaw was the leading candidate in English literature for the Nobel Prize.[74] In this case his judgment was right on target, even though he did not live to witness the moment when the prize was awarded in 1926.

As for the friendship, it cannot and should not be separated from their engaged debates. Archer and Shaw expected great achievements from one another, and they expected and required the highest standards of judgment. Because the friendship was tied directly to the critical judgments and challenges that they generated over the years, the two comrades, each in his own way, benefited from the debates. Given the temperaments and sensibilities of the witty Irish playwright and the dour Scottish critic, they seldom removed their well-crafted personas, even in their personal letters. Indeed, these articulate personas defined much about their relationship with one another, and protected them from expressions of personal emotion and sentiment (which they dismissed usually as sentimentality).[75] Both men avoided these kinds of displays in their writings. But occasionally the deep regard and love was expressed.

In Archer's last letter to Shaw, which announced his impending surgery for a tumor on his liver, he declared his steadfast friendship: 'This episode gives me an excuse for saying, what I hope you don't doubt – namely, that though I may sometimes have played the part of the all-too candid mentor, I have never wavered in my admiration & affection for you, or ceased to feel that the Fates had treated me kindly in making me your contemporary & friend. I thank you from my heart for forty years of good comradeship' (letter of 17 December 1924). A week later Archer died, unable to recover from the surgery.

Shaw and Mrs Shaw had left London for a trip to Madeira right after the surgery, assuming that Archer would recover (which seemed possible for a day or two). But he died on 27 December. When the Shaws arrived in the lobby of their hotel in Madeira, they were greeted by a news bulletin: 'Death of Mr. William Archer.' The news threw Shaw 'into a transport of fury,' as he wrote a year and one-half later in 'How William Archer Impressed Bernard Shaw.' In that long obituary essay Shaw allowed his private emotions to be expressed in the public statement about his friend:

> The operation had killed him ... My rage may have been unjust to the surgeons; but it carried me over my first sense of bereavement. When I returned to an Archerless London it seemed to me that the place had entered on a new age in which I was lagging superfluous. I still feel that when he went he took a piece of me with him.[76]

The loss of Archer was not as consequential for Shaw as the meeting in 1894, but it was still a significant moment, the closing event for the four decades of friendship. Recalling those four decades, Shaw announced: 'I have not a single unpleasant recollection.'[77]

Archer and Shaw, Shaw and Archer – they were, in their very special ways, joined together in one of the most consequential partnerships in the history of any relationship between an artist and a critic.

NOTES

1 This was the title of an essay Archer published in February 1885 in the journal *Nineteenth Century*.

2 The evidence on their first meeting is sketchy, but most likely it occurred in 1884, perhaps in the rooms of a young poet named Ernest Radford. See the third section of this Introduction – 'Beginning a Friendship: The 1880s' – for Archer's anecdote on observing Shaw in the Reading Room of the British Museum. The most famous version of this event appeared in 1892 when Archer reviewed the production of *Widowers' Houses,* but the more reliable version was first described by Archer in his letter to R.L. Stevenson in 1886.

3 Ervine, 329, 173. For the identification of bibliographical sources see the section entitled 'Abbreviations and Works Cited,' which is located directly after the Editor's Note.

4 See my Editor's Note for a description of the gaps in the correspondence.

5 In 1927 Shaw published 'How William Archer Impressed Bernard Shaw,' his tribute to Archer. It is a heartfelt statement that serves as the foreword to *Three Plays by William Archer*, vii–xxxvii. Shaw closed the essay with Archer's last letter to Shaw on 17 December 1924.

6 Holroyd 1, 13, 33–6. On Shaw's early life in Dublin, see Holroyd 1, Gibbs 2, and Embryo.

7 On the relationship of Shaw and his wife Charlotte Shaw to the National Gallery of Ireland, as spelled out in their wills, which have been administered by the National Trust, see Holroyd 4. The events have made for a grim, often grotesque comedy.

8 Lucinda Shaw (1853–1920) was also a singer, and had a successful career in the 1880s and 1890s, often touring with musical and light opera companies. When in London she stayed with her mother and Shaw. After contracting tuberculosis in the late 1890s, she was forced to discontinue her career (Gibbs 1, 14–15).

9 Shaw's decision to leave for England in 1876 was also in response to the death of his sister Agnes at the age of twenty-one. She died of tuberculosis in a hospital on the Isle of Wight. A few days later Shaw joined his mother and Lucy at her burial site (Gibbs 1, 34).

10 *An Unsocial Socialist* was the fifth and last of Shaw's attempts at novel writing. As he noted with wry wit in 1896: 'I had given up humiliating editors and publishers by exposing them to the stupidity of failing to see any merit in me. Archer, regarding this as mere inertia on my part (not without some

reason), took my affairs in hand.' Bernard Shaw, 'Nine Answers,' *Chap-Book* (Chicago, 1 November 1896); reprinted in I&R, 25.

11 This comment was made in 1886, in a letter to R.L. Stevenson (BL 45295 f 96).

12 In 1894 both Yeats and Shaw had plays performed in London when the actress Florence Farr, who received anonymous support from Annie E.F. Horniman, presented a spring season of new drama. A decade later Yeats participated in the Court Theatre productions in 1904 and 1905. Most impressively, the Irish National Theatre Society, which featured plays by Yeats, Synge, Lady Gregory, and several other Irish writers, was able to present a series of productions in London in 1904, 1907, 1910, 1911, 1912, 1913, and 1914. Even during the war, in 1915, the Irish Players from the Abbey Theatre, led by Synge, Yeats, and Gregory, returned to London for a spring season at the Little Theatre. Twenty plays by seven playwrights ran across four weeks. *Playboy of the Western World* had 13 performances, *The Gaol Gate* had 7, *Kathleen ni Houlihan* had 6, and most of the other plays had 2 to 4 performances. The outsiders triumphed against great odds.

13 Max Beerbohm. 'G. B. S. Republished,' in *Last Theatres 1904–1910*, ed. Rupert Hart-Davis. (New York: Taplinger Publishing Co, 1970), 292–5. This article, published on 27 April 1907, offered an assessment of Shaw's theatre criticism for the *Saturday Review* between January 1895 and May 1898. We should note that Archer could sometimes be quite brash, disrespectful, and even savage, as he was in his attacks on the institution of stage censorship. And Shaw could be civil, tactful, and generous, as he often was when describing the acting of Mrs Patrick Campbell and Ellen Terry.

14 William Archer, 'The Free Stage and the New Drama,' FR, November 1891, 670.

15 See letter of 13 November 1891.

16 Letter of 12 June 1923.

17 In this context, a comment by G.K. Chesterton in 1910 deserves mention: 'Shaw is so much of an idealist about his ideals that he can be a ruthless realist in his methods' (Chesterton, 24).

18 Some Shaw scholars have mistakenly interpreted Shaw's voice in these letters as primarily one of annoyance and irritation with Archer. No doubt both men could be peevish and prickly on occasion, but Charles Archer was surely correct in seeing that deep affection and mutual respect were the predominant emotions that guided the friendship and correspondence over the years.

19 The lack of letters for 1884 is one of several mysteries of the correspondence. Surely some letters were written in 1884, for this is the period when they

decided to write a play together. Yet for whatever reason the extant letters begin in 1885.

20 W. Archer, 'Widowers' Houses,' World, 14 December 1892, 14–15. When Shaw published the play in 1893, he reprinted Archer's review in his 'Author's Preface.' He justified this decision in a letter to Archer on 24 March 1893. As for the description of Shaw in the British Museum, Archer wrote a much earlier version on 10 March 1886 in a letter to R.L. Stevenson: 'Before I even knew his name, I used to sit beside him at the British Museum where he excited my curiosity by studying simultaneously Karl Marx's "Das Capital" and an eight-part score of Wagner's "Tristan und Isolde." The combination struck me as highly poignant. Then I heard vaguely of him from common acquaintances as a Socialist lecturer and a man who had written about a half-dozen novels which all publishers praised but no publisher would print. Then I met him and found him without exception the most entertaining man I had ever come across, and a man of very varied knowledge' (British Library, Add MS 45295, ff 94–6). In a much later retelling by Archer in 1921 (see Stanley, xxii), Shaw was wearing a Jaeger outfit; but this is incorrect, for he did not purchase his first Jaeger suit until 1885, following the receipt of a small payment from his father's insurance policy upon his death (Diaries 1: 191).

21 Although Archer judged *Widowers' Houses* a 'failure,' his judgment was mild compared to the anonymous statement by A.B. Walkley who, despite being Shaw's friend, called him 'a detestable dramatist' when he reviewed the production. *The Star*, 10 December 1892.

22 It is most unlikely that Archer ever felt anything close to 'contempt' or 'scorn' for his friend, but of course hyperbole is one of the familiar signatures of Shaw's style.

23 In the late 1880s, as his diaries record for 1888, he struggled at times with colds, 'bellyaches,' and nausea. On these occasions he would become 'exceedingly depressed and out of sorts' (Diaries 1: 334). The physical ailments, including dental problems, sometimes contributed to minor cases of psychological uncertainties. But he remained very busy with his many activities, as his diaries also show. His spirits improved, and his engagement with the theatre soon became a commitment with the reading of Ibsen's plays, as Archer translated them. Also, the 1889 production of *A Doll's House*, which launched the Ibsen movement in London, contributed directly to Shaw's engagement with theatre. Then the writing and staging of *Widowers' Houses* became the key turning point in his playwriting commitments.

24 Besides the several farces and burlesques that he wrote with Edinburgh friends in the years after he graduated from Edinburgh University, Archer

co-wrote two works that appeared briefly in London in 1881. *Blue and Buff,* a curtain raiser with music by William Frost, was performed at the Bijou Opera House in an amateur production. It closed after five performances, a failure. But his melodrama *Australia, or The Bushrangers,* written under the pseudonym of A.G. Stanley with his friend Hector Mackenzie, was staged in Shoreditch at the Grecian Theatre in 1881. This production ran for a few weeks. Having spent several months in Australia in 1876, Archer had drawn upon some of his experiences of hunting and camping in the outback. The play also tapped the exploits of the infamous Kelly Gang for its dramatic action. Four decades later Archer had amazing success with another melodrama, *The Green Goddess.*

25 By contrast, Shaw's critical judgment on music outshone Archer's limited understanding. When Archer wrote a study of Richard Wagner in the 1880s, he asked Shaw to review the manuscript. Based upon Shaw's assessment, Archer decided not to publish the book, even though he had received the proofs from the publisher.

26 In his biography on Shaw Michael Holroyd offered an assessment of the failed collaboration: 'Archer's opinion was important to Shaw. Though he had trained himself to do without encouragement – even to interpret the lack of it as a compliment – he needed the support of this man who had given him so much of his theatrical education. Not receiving it, he was lost' (Holroyd 1, 277). Shaw was not 'lost,' but Holroyd recognized that Shaw's reliance on Archer for support and advice during these years was a key aspect of the friendship.

27 In 1880 Archer adapted his translation of *Pillars of Society* as *Quicksands, or The Pillars of Society.* It had one matinee performance. He soon regretted this misguided effort, and apologized to Ibsen at their meeting in Rome in 1881.

28 In 1906, when Ibsen died, Archer published 'Ibsen as I Knew Him.' The essay describes their meetings, and Archer's impressions and admiration. See Ibsen Essays, 107–24.

29 This study of Irving was a revision and expansion of a satiric pamphlet that Archer and Robert W. Lowe had written in 1877.

30 B. Shaw, 'Preface Mainly about Myself,' in CP 1, 16.

31 There was no production of *When We Dead Awaken,* but the review by the young James Joyce appeared in the *Fortnightly Review* in April 1900.

32 Of course he was not alone in this claim. For example, Josephine Johnson claimed that 'Bernard Shaw, at his own admittance, had assumed charge of the campaign for the so-called New Drama in England' (Farr, 46).

33 B. Shaw, 'Peer Gynt in Paris,' SatRev, 21 November 1896. Biblio 2, C1174; Dukore 2, 698–704.

34 These numbers are notable, and if more of Archer's letters had survived, the commentary on Ibsen in the correspondence would have been even more impressive. See the Editor's Note for a discussion of the missing letters in the correspondence.

35 As several of the letters reveal, Shaw and Archer argued for forty years over the reasons for this failed collaboration in playwriting. See, for example, the letters of 4 October 1887 and 19 June 1923. Their memories were often selective and faulty. After Archer died, Shaw had the last word when he described the collaboration yet again in 'How William Archer Impressed Bernard Shaw' (Three Plays, xxvi–xxix).

36 W. Archer, 'Mr. Shaw's Plays,' DC, 19 and 21 April 1898. The several quotations are from this long review of *Plays Pleasant and Unpleasant,* published on 19 April.

37 *Cashel Byron's Profession* was published in 1886 by The Modern Press, and *An Unsocial Socialist* was published in 1887 by Swan Sonnenschein in 1887. Both novels had previously been serialized in 1884 and 1885 in the journal *To-Day*. Also, in 1885 *The Irrational Knot* was serialized in *Our Corner*, another political journal.

38 The first public production of *The Philanderer* did not occur in London until 1907, and *Mrs Warren's Profession,* because of censorship, was not staged publicly until 1925 (though it did receive a private production by the Stage Society in 1902).

39 Archer, World 94, 109–10. The reference is to Christopher Wren's Monument in London built in memory of the London Fire of 1666. See Alexander Pope's *Moral Essays,* epistle 3, line 339, for a description of the column as a 'tall bully.' Archer suggested that Shaw, like the abiding Monument, was unalterable.

40 Ibid., 109–18.

41 CP 1, 485–511. Comparing himself to Cervantes, Shaw stated that he presents characters who, like Don Quixote, are imprisoned in a life of self-deception and fantasy – as are the theatre critics who cannot perceive reality. This dismissal of critics, which ignored the fact that Shaw was a music critic, was published six months before he became the theatre critic at the *Saturday Review.* The confident voice of G.B.S. was not to be hindered by present conditions and future developments.

42 Only a few minor productions occurred in the 1890s. *The Man of Destiny* was poorly staged at the Grand Theatre in Croydon in July 1897. *The Devil's Disciple* was produced at the Princess of Wales's Theatre in Kennington in September 1899. And the Stage Society offered *You Never Can Tell* for a single private performance at the Royalty Theatre in November 1899.

Between 1900 and 1903 few Stage Society's matinees kept Shaw alive in the alternative theatre movement, but there were no West End productions. Until 1904 Shaw continued to be a marginal playwright. Even the Court Theatre productions in 1904–7 were located beyond the central district of the West End theatres.

43 The one encouraging sign in the 1890s of Shaw's arrival as a playwright occurred in America. Richard Mansfield staged *Arms and the Man* in New York City in late 1894, and then Shaw had major success in 1897 with *The Devil's Disciple*, which had an extended run in New York City, and then toured. For the first time he was financially solvent.

44 See Dukore 1, 33–4, 105–10, 113–14, 203–10, 210–18, 218–21, 221–2, 224–32.

45 When Constable published a second edition in 1913, 'now completed to the Death of Ibsen,' a run of 5000 copies was printed. And in New York an additional run of 1000 copies was printed by Brentano's. For further details on the several editions of *Quintessence*, see Biblio 1, 16–19.

46 Of course, this book has gained greater significance in modern times because both Ibsen and Shaw are major figures in the modernist movement in the arts. For a valuable perspective on the historical significance of *Quintessence*, see J.L. Wisenthal, *Shaw and Ibsen: Bernard Shaw's The Quintessence of Ibsenism and Related Writings* (Toronto: University of Toronto Press, 1979).

47 In the era before copyright laws protected the rights and royalties for plays, Ibsen had demonstrated that by publishing his plays he could assert at least some financial and textual control over his works. In the Scandinavian countries he was able to create and expand a reading public that became the foundation for his theatre audiences. In turn, the translations of his plays expanded his income and his audiences. This was especially the case in Germany and Austria, but also in the English-speaking world thanks to Archer's translations, which were distributed and sold not only in Britain but also in Ireland, the United States, and the nations of the Empire. When Shaw decided to publish his plays, he urged Grant Richards, the publisher, to use Archer's translations of Ibsen, published by Walter Scott, as the model for the layout of *Plays Pleasant and Unpleasant*. See CL 1, 766–7, 808, 811, 816, 838.

48 When Archer published *Study and Stage*, 'a yearbook' of his major criticism for 1898, this review of twenty-two pages opened the book.

49 See Shaw's letter of 24 January 1900 for a critique of Archer's abiding love affair with *Candida*. Four years earlier, in a letter to Ellen Terry, Shaw called it 'a very sentimental play' that would appeal to women, if not men (CL 1, 632).

50 Archer, 'From the Court to the Savoy,' Tribune, 29 June 1907.

51 There was, though, one notable achievement. The censorship was lifted on Ibsen's *Ghosts* in 1914, twenty-three years after the private production by the Independent Theatre Company in 1891. Single performances occurred in April, May, and July 1914. Then somewhat surprisingly during the war, this production of *Ghosts* was revived; it had a run of 96 performances in 1917 at Kingsway Theatre, followed by 17 more at the St James's Theatre.
52 Fittingly, Shaw's *Shakespeare v. Shaw* was produced by Cyril Maude this same month of May 1905 at the Haymarket.
53 Because of the importance of Archer's public writings on Shaw, there needs to be a published volume of Archer on Shaw: The Major Essays. Such a collection would be a valuable supplement to the correspondence.
54 Holroyd 2, 355.
55 The one rather bizarre exception to the disappearance of Shaw did not please him. It was a revival of *The Chocolate Soldier* by Oscar Straus (music). The comic opera, which had premièred in London for 500 performances in 1910, was revived on 5 September 1914 at the Lyric Theatre and had 56 performances. Shaw had dismissed this adaptation of *Arms and the Man* as 'a dirty farce.'
56 For this revival, unlike the première in 1911, Shaw was identified as the playwright.
57 Beyond London, Shaw did not disappear during these war years. For example, Barker and McCarthy took *Androcles and the Lion* to New York City in January 1915. *Misalliance* had its first American production in 1917. And in Ireland, which opposed the British war effort and hoped that Germany would support the independence movement, Shaw was welcomed, with several productions of his plays by the Abbey Theatre, including *Widowers' Houses, Arms and the Man, Man and Superman,* and *John Bull's Other Island.* Also, the Abbey, which had premiered *The Shewing-Up of Blanco Posnet* in 1909, brought the play to Liverpool in April 1916. After the war, in 1920, the Theatre Guild presented the premiere of *Heartbreak House* in New York; the play also had productions in Stockholm and Vienna before it appeared in London in late 1921.
58 Although both Shaw and Archer tended to dismiss Baylis and the Old Vic productions, Baylis became more successful than them in creating a national theatre. And in the process she also provided the foundation for national opera and dance institutions.
59 Before the war Archer had been an advocate for international peace. His *The Great Analysis: A Plea for a Rational World-Order* (1912) was an ambitious plan for the creation of an international organization that would compile research on world problems and seek ways to share the information among

all nations of the world. But this idealistic proposal was ignored, and had no influence on the order of the world. He published *The Great Analysis* anonymously because he feared that an appeal from a theatre critic would not be taken seriously. He convinced Gilbert Murray, however, to write the preface.

60 C. Archer, 363.

61 See Peter Whitebrook's biography on Archer's involvement with mediums and clairvoyants (pp. 334–8).

62 For a detailed study of play, production, and film versions see Veronica Kelly, '*The Green Goddess*: William Archer's Great War Play,' *Nineteenth Century Theatre and Film* 40.2 (Winter 2013): 2–30. She also reprinted the play, with annotations: 31–124.

63 Goddess, 119–20. Despite attempts by H.G. Barker and the producer Winthrop Ames to revise this scene, and to eliminate the marriage of Lucilla, Archer insisted upon no revisions or deletions. He wanted the play to parallel aspects of his own loveless marriage and his true love for Elizabeth Robins (Whitebrook, 363).

64 The heroine Lucilla wonders if she will be able to communicate with her children after she dies.

Lucilla: Shall I see them again, Basil? Tell me that.

Traherne: Who knows? … But I do sincerely think you may.

Lucilla: You think there is a sporting chance?

Traherne: More than that. This life is such a miracle – could any other be more incredible?

… You may be with them this very night – with them, unseen, but perhaps not unfelt, all the days of their lives (Goddess, 116–17; see also Kelly, 118, note 129).

Sometimes, life is a melodrama, but ideal conclusions, such as those in *The Green Goddess*, are seldom realized. Mrs Archer outlived Archer; he and Robins remained apart. Consequently, when Archer was facing major surgery in 1924, he was desperate about the love letters that he and Robins had written to one another over the years. He wanted them destroyed. They both sought to protect the privacy of their affair, but Robins was unable to destroy all the letters, even though she removed his signature from some of the letters she kept. (See Prophet, 116–20; and Whitebrook, 314–16.)

65 The three plays, *Martha Washington, Beatriz Juana,* and *Lidia,* were published posthumously in 1927. Shaw wrote the foreword to be book, which delivered his invaluable essay on Archer entitled 'How William Archer Impressed Bernard Shaw.' See Three Plays, vii–xxxvii.

66 Archer, 'Mr. Shaw's Pom-Pom,' DC, 24 August 1903.
67 Archer, World, 30 May 1905.
68 Ibid.
69 Archer, World, 31 October 1905.
70 'Mr. Shaw in Hades,' Tribune, 5 June 1907.
71 Archer, Tribune, 31 December 1907.
72 Hend 3, 605–6.
73 As we reflect upon this dismissal, we might keep in mind that it was stated in 1894, early in their partnership to transform the London stage. If we perceive a tease as a serious judgment, we probably will misunderstand much about the relationship between Shaw and Archer.
74 W. Archer, 'The Psychology of G. B. S.,' *The Bookman*, no. 399, 67 (December 1924): 135–41. For Archer the other candidate in English literature was Thomas Hardy, whose poems and novels Archer greatly admired. See his interview with Hardy in *Real Conversations.*
75 Shaw made a special point about Archer's repressed emotions in his essay 'How William Archer Impressed Bernard Shaw.' When Archer read his newly translated text of Ibsen's *Little Eyolf* to Shaw and two others, his emotions overwhelmed him, despite his method of reading 'without a trace of emotion.' When Archer came to the last pages 'he suddenly handed me the book, and said, formally and with a marked access of woodenness, "Shaw: I must ask you to finish the reading for me. My feelings will not allow me to proceed"' (Three Plays, x).
76 Three Plays, xxxvii. The obituary essay was written in July 1926.
77 Ibid., xxxvi.
78 When Archer died in 1924, his papers were donated to the British Drama League, which was founded in 1919. The large archive (collection, holdings, or materials) contained Archer's private library, drafts and proofs of articles and books, translations, numerous files of correspondence, fifty years of theatre programs, many photographs, some of the records of both the New Century Theatre Company and the Memorial National Shakespeare Theatre committee, and several dozen scrapbooks that contain hundreds of his magazine articles and several thousand press clippings of his theatre and book reviews. All of these materials were stored in a back room. No catalogue was available. The Drama League, always short on funds, ceased to exist in 1972. Its holdings became the property of the British Theatre Association, which oversaw the building on Fitzroy Square. When the BTA became insolvent in the 1980s, the Archer collection was boxed up and stored at Regent's College. After the BTA went bankrupt in 1989, the collection was shifted to Cranbourn Mansions. Apparently some materials

were stored at Drury Lane Theatre. Then between 1990 and 1992, during two years of negotiations on the fate of the BTA collection, the Archer holdings were deposited with the new Theatre Museum in Covent Garden. But financial difficulties also plagued the Museum, which the V&A closed in 2006. Yet again the Archer holdings, still lacking a catalogue, were boxed up and moved. The new home became Blythe House near Olympia stadium. Finally, thanks to efforts by volunteers, the Archer materials have been catalogued. The V&A administers the theatre collection at Blythe House. Appointments can be made to carry out research there – when and if the room is open.

Editor's Note

The letters in this volume, which extend from 6 January 1885 to 17 December 1924, are printed without any cuts. Of the 181 letters collected here, 125 were written by Shaw to Archer. Several of Shaw's letters were dictated to Charlotte Shaw. These are part of the 125 letters credited to Shaw. In addition, Shaw wrote four letters to Frances E. Archer (Mrs Archer) and Charlotte Shaw wrote eight short letters to Archer. Shaw's letters to Mrs Archer and Charlotte Shaw's letters to Archer are also included in this edition. Mrs Shaw was not just G.B.S.'s amanuensis; her letters to Archer were part of the familiar relationship between the Shaws and Archer. Overall, a total of 137 letters came from the Shaws, but only 44 letters came from Archer. Although he wrote occasionally to Mrs Shaw, those letters are missing. Nor have any of Mrs Archer's letters to the Shaws survived.

Archer's letters make up slightly less than one-fourth of the letters in this edition. Why this large discrepancy? For example, between 7 November 1891 and 23 April 1894 there are fifteen letters from Shaw, but only one from Archer. This was the period in which Shaw wrote his first four plays: *Widowers' Houses, The Philanderer, Mrs Warren's Profession,* and *Arms and the Man.* During this period the two colleagues were engaged in a wide range of shared activities and discussions, including debates about these plays. Indeed, on the basis of the entries in Shaw's diaries, he met with Archer more often than with anyone else between 1885 and 1897 (the years of the diaries). Why, then, was the correspondence so one-sided? Unfortunately, this was not the only disappearing act by Archer. Between 1 February 1900 and 1 September 1903 there are sixteen letters to Archer from Shaw and an additional three from Charlotte Shaw, but not one letter from Archer.

Most troubling, there are no surviving letters from Archer between 8 June 1906 and 8 June 1912, even though we have twenty-two letters written by Shaw. This was the period in which Shaw wrote not only *The Doctor's Dilemma* – in response to a public challenge from Archer to compose a serious play that featured death – but also *Getting Married, The Shewing-Up of Blanco Posnet, Misalliance,* and *Fanny's First Play.* The two colleagues were closely involved with one another during these years. For example, between June 1906 and June 1912 Archer wrote no less than 59 reviews and essays about Shaw, his plays, and the productions. A number of these articles caused Shaw to write rebuttal letters to Archer. Debates and rhetorical sword play were the norm. Yet if we judge by the available letters, Archer was a disappearing act, year after year.

Most of the gaps in the surviving correspondence between Shaw and Archer result from the absence of Archer's letters, but on a few occasions Shaw appeared to have gone silent. For example, there are no extant letters from him between 15 May 1910 and 11 November 1914. Given Archer's apparent silence during part of this period, the gaps in letter writing seem to suggest that the two friends failed to communicate with one another between 15 May 1910 and 8 June 1912 (when Archer sent two letters from Japan at the beginning of his world tour). Likewise, except for a single letter from Charlotte Shaw, no letters were apparently exchanged between 30 December 1916 and 7 April 1919. Perhaps the letter writing by Archer and Shaw decreased in the years before and during the Great War. Perhaps the two friends had less need or desire to communicate. Yet these conjectures fail to provide a convincing explanation for the absence of letters. It is much more likely that the two friends did communicate during most, if not all, of the years between 1885 and 1924, but for some reason – or set of reasons – many of the letters have disappeared. Did Shaw destroy some of them? That seems most unlikely. Whatever the case, we are limited to vague surmises about the reasons for the gaps in the letters, especially the shortage of letters from Archer.

The easiest assumption about this shortage would be that Archer wrote only 44 letters to Shaw during the four decades – basically one letter per year. But we can dismiss this explanation. Quite often Shaw's letters were written as direct responses to missing letters from Archer. It is clear that

Archer wrote to Shaw on a number of occasions during these three periods of 1891 to 1894, 1900 to 1903, and 1906 to 1912. But where are these letters? Perhaps they are buried in some untapped collection or archive. Or perhaps they have not survived. Whatever the explanation, the mystery of the missing letters became a major difficulty for this edition of their correspondence. This difficulty has also contributed to my uncertainty over the proper identification for these letters. I have used several different descriptions when referring to them as 'missing,' 'lost,' 'unavailable,' 'no longer extant,' 'unaccounted for,' or 'destroyed.' Or I have noted that a letter 'has disappeared' or 'has not survived.' But because the status of these various letters has remained uncertain, these designations are inexact, even misleading. I therefore urge readers to keep in mind this problem of identification as they come across one of these ambiguous designations in the headnotes to the letters.

When I first became aware of the gaps in the correspondence, I assumed that a trove of Archer's letters must exist somewhere. I just needed to do more digging in the archives. Perhaps in one of the uncatalogued collections I would find the letters. For example, until most recently the large Archer collection has remained uncatalogued.[78] Over the recent years, as time and funds allowed, I made additional research trips to London and elsewhere in quest of missing letters. But these searches resulted in the discovery of only a few more letters – and those were from Shaw. Of course I was glad to find these letters, and up to a point I was even amused by the irony that my extra sleuthing had increased instead of decreased the ratio of Shaw's letters to those by Archer. But the mystery remained: at least a few dozen of Archer's letters had disappeared or were buried somewhere unknown. I was proving to be a very poor sleuth.

After several extra years of searching in the United Kingdom and the United States, I was becoming reconciled to the likelihood that I would not find any of the missing letters from Archer. Also, a few years ago I became aware of a significant pattern in Shaw's correspondence with key people. Upon examining his exchange of letters with H.G. Wells that J. Percy Smith had published (University of Toronto Press, 1995), I noted Shaw's letters greatly outnumbered those written by Wells. The edited volume has 152 letters. They cover the years from 1901 to 1946, but only 51 were written by Wells, including the two letters he sent to Charlotte Shaw.

Because the ratio of Shaw/Archer and Shaw/Wells letters is similar, I began to think that I should discontinue my search for missing letters from Archer. For whatever reasons, a number of the letters from both Archer and Wells had disappeared. I should accept the basic fact that far more of Shaw's letters have survived than those written by Archer or Wells. But when I examined another set of letters, the problem became more complicated and contradictory. In the correspondence between Shaw and the film director Gabriel Pascal, edited by Bernard F. Dukore (Toronto, 1996), there are 268 letters, extending from 1935 to 1950. Of these, 130 letters are from Pascal, 138 from Shaw. Basically a balanced correspondence existed in the extant letters, with no mysteries about missing letters. Did it matter that these letters were exchanged during the last years of Shaw's life? Most of Pascal's letters were sent to Ayot St Lawrence, where Shaw lived almost exclusively between 1939 and 1950. Did this fact account for the protection and saving of the letters from Pascal? Also, was it possible that the business nature of the Shaw/Pascal correspondence contributed to the survival of the letters? Did Shaw's secretary, Blanche Patch, who increasingly oversaw his business matters, organize and save the letters from Pascal? Other explanations are possible, but the immediate significance for me was that I should continue to search for Archer's letters to Shaw. If Pascal's letters did not disappear, perhaps Archer's letters were also still extant.

I went back to archives, and expanded the possible locations for Archer's letters. I was also aware of the ratio of letters in the correspondence between Shaw and Barry Jackson that L.W. Conolly had published (Toronto, 2002). Of the 183 letters in this edition, Shaw provided 120 letters, and in addition Charlotte Shaw sent 17 letters to Jackson, while Blanche Patch' sent 9 more letters. By contrast, Jackson had written only 37 letters. The correspondence extended from 1923 to 1950. The number of Shaw letters overwhelmed the number of Jackson letters: 146 to 37. Here again, as with the Shaw/Archer letters, the ratio of letters is four to one. On a number of occasions, as Conolly clarified in his notes, important letters from Jackson were absent. Also, some of Shaw's letters were written as replies to missing letters from Jackson.

Given the recurring problem of missing letters in Shaw's correspondence with Archer, Wells, and Jackson, the balance in letters between Shaw and Pascal was apparently an anomaly. But this conclusion became doubtful with the publication of the correspondence of Shaw and Gilbert Murray (Toronto, 2014), edited by Charles A. Carpenter. In this edition 85 letters were written by Shaw and 86 by Murray. Almost a perfect balance. Their letters stretched over several decades, as did Shaw's correspondence with Archer, Wells, and Jackson. The total number of letters in all four collections was roughly the same: 171 for Shaw/Murray, 181 for Shaw/Archer, 152 for Shaw/Wells, and 183 for Shaw/Jackson. Yet why was the Shaw/Murray correspondence balanced, when the distribution of letters in the other three cases was so out of balance? Why the discrepancy?

One thing – and perhaps only one thing – was obvious: the asymmetrical pattern of letters repeated itself in three out of four cases. Although the pattern has proved nothing, there can be no doubt that some letters are missing. Was it still possible that some, if not all, of these unaccounted for letters might turn up? Perhaps they still existed somewhere; but if so, where were they? If, however, they were lost or destroyed, the search for them was pointless. The only conclusion, then, would seem to be that Shaw's correspondents, including Archer, Wells, and Jackson, did a better job than Shaw at preserving letters across the years. But without definite evidence that the missing letters no longer existed, the whole situation remains a mystery. Uncertainty and frustration prevail.

Despite the reassuring balance of letters in the editions of Shaw/Pascal and Shaw/Murray, there might be two possible explanations for the disproportion of letters in Shaw/Archer, Shaw/Wells, and Shaw/Jackson. These two explanations are directly connected to the last decade of Shaw's life.

Many of the letters sent to Shaw by Archer, Wells, and Jackson may have been destroyed by the bombings of London during the Second World War. Yet because of the haphazard nature of destruction during the war, it was also possible that the letters from Murray and Pascal survived. Because of the bombs and fires, the Shaws had settled in Ayot St Lawrence early in the war. Only a very few trips were made to the Whitehall Court flat in London (CL 4: 583–5). Also, because of Charlotte's poor health Ayot was a better location. After she died on 12 September 1943, Shaw seldom went to London. The first major loss he experienced from German bombs was not letters but the printed pages of some of his recent works. The loss occurred on 18 September 1941 when a bomb destroyed close to

90,000 unbound sheets and dust jackets at the bindery of Constable & Co. on the London docks (CL 4: 578–9). Then in June 1944 German bombs hit Whitehall Court or near it. The London flat was badly damaged, and this was not the only explosion that wrecked the flat, as Shaw explained in a letter to Gilbert Murray on 4 July 1944: 'My Whitehall flat has been blasted again, this time by a Robot. A window in my study was shivered into smithereens, my front door blown in, the grandfather clock prostrate, one of Charlotte's Tang horses shattered, and – *comble de Malheur* – Strobl's bust of Lady Astor done in' (CL 4: 716). No doubt other things were also battered or destroyed. Ayot St Lawrence was a safer location, even though the bombs also threatened Shaw there. In one case a German V bomb took out a window at Ayot on 25 July 1944.

Yet the occasional bomb in the rural neighborhood turned out to be a minor problem for Shaw compared to the daily turmoil within the house. This domestic havoc, which increased throughout the last decade of Shaw's life, may well have contributed to the loss of many letters. Ever since Charlotte's death, life at Ayot had become chaotic. Shaw was suffering from 'blunders and forgetfulness,' as he had explained to Murray. He was surrounded by a disarray of housekeepers, nurses, Clara Higgs, Alice Laden, Stephen and Clare Winsten, and the impulsive John Wardrop. At the centre of the unrest and disorganization were Blance Patch, Lady Astor, and F.E. Loewenstein, whom Shaw had begrudgingly designated his literary executor, to the dismay and frustration of Patch and Lady Astor, who battled him in every way possible. Loewenstein, whom Shaw sanctioned and protected, yet called 'an unholy terror' (CL 4: 467), drove Shaw and everyone else crazy with his compulsive efforts to organize Shaw's life and papers. In a letter to him on 20 July 1944, Shaw exclaimed: 'Dont send me things I have to return ... Dont mention the Shaw Society to me. Dont forget that I am fully occupied with my present and future and have no time to attend to my past over again' (CL 4: 718). Adding to the confusion, Shaw had decided to turn over the Ayot estate, now called Shaw's Corner, to the National Trust. The Sturm und Drang of the Ayot menagerie increased after the war. (For a description of 'this unhappy scramble swirling round Shaw since Charlotte's death,' see Holroyd 3: 452–72.)

Under these conditions, the loss of various items, including letters, was probably inevitable at both Ayot and Whitehall Court. In the haphazard ways of Shaw's last years, as various people wilfully asserted partial controls over him and his estate, some of the letters from Archer, Wells, and Jackson likely disappeared, along with other papers and documents. Adding to the confusion, in 1949 Shaw, the absentee tenant of 116 Whitehall Court, had everything shifted out of this flat into a much smaller 'two-roomed furnished flat downstairs' (Holroyd 3: 506). In turn, many things had to be either redistributed from the small flat to Ayot or eliminated. Patch, who took over the small flat, oversaw much of the packing and allotment of possessions, though Lowenstein and others tried to assert themselves into the division of the kingdom as much as possible.

It thus seems quite possible that many items and papers disappeared in the 1940s, without proper supervision by Shaw, who had lost control of his affairs. Yet these conjectures, however convincing they may be, fail to prove that some of Archer's letters were destroyed by either bombing or the disarray that overwhelmed Shaw's life and households in those final years. I still remained uncertain about the possible survival or destruction of those letters. Even if I expanded my analysis to Shaw's correspondence with Ellen Terry, Mrs Patrick Campbell, and Lady Nancy Astor, the number of letters from each writer in each of those collections would not change the conditions that have shaped and determined the fate of the correspondence between Shaw and Archer. The missing letters were still missing.

Accordingly, whatever I might conclude about the possible reasons for the absence of letters from Archer, Wells, and Jackson, I also recognized that the gaps in their correspondence with Shaw had to be acknowledged and accepted. Many crucial letters are unavailable (lost, missing, etc.). I also recognized that the gaps in the correspondence are quite significant and troubling. Even though the surviving letters offer invaluable information about the relationship between Shaw and each man, each edition offers an incomplete portrait. Because far more of Shaw's letters have survived, these editions of his correspondence make for a misleading, even distorted, perspective on each relationship. The absence of so many letters from Archer, Wells, and Jackson serves to silence each of them in crucial ways. In reading these editions one needs to proceed with caution. Of course, the surviving letters between Shaw and each man are rich documents. But in order to get a fuller sense of the interactions in each case, additional evidence should be consulted.

Luckily, and most fortunately in the case of Shaw and Archer, there exists a unique and expansive supplement to the surviving letters, a supplement that complements the letters. During his career as a journalist Archer published thousands of reviews and essays in dozens of journals and newspapers. Over two hundred of these articles discussed Shaw and his works, often as the primary or exclusive topic. In those reviews and essays, and in sections of some of his books, such as *Play-making: A Manual of Craftsmanship* (1912) and *The Old Drama and the New* (1923), Archer wrote about Shaw, his plays and prefaces, his productions, and his essays and books. The reviews and essays, like the letters, contributed to the debates and arguments that engaged both men. Many of Archer's letters are missing, but we can still gain a considerable understanding and appreciation of the exchanges between Archer and Shaw by attending to what Archer wrote in the reviews and essays. These articles provide a vital compensation, and in some ways a balance to Shaw's voice in the letters. In at least a few cases they even replace some of the missing letters.

Much of the correspondence is about what they published. Throughout the forty years they read one another's publications, and they argued about those publications. Shaw responded, of course, to reviews and essays about his works, but he also responded quite often to Archer's articles on other topics. Accordingly, in the headnotes and endnotes, I have described the publications. From his article on Shaw's *The Quintessence of Ibsenism,* published in October 1891, to his final essay 'The Psychology of Shaw,' published in December 1924, Archer presented his challenging assessments of Shaw and his publications. Shaw read many of these articles, including those from 1891 and 1924. Of the two hundred reviews and essays on Shaw that Archer published, half of them appeared in one decade, from 1898 to 1908. On several occasions Shaw was responding to not only a recent article by Archer but also a recent letter. We may lack the letter, but we still have the article that provides much of the subject matter and context for Shaw's letter. Consequently, in my headnotes and endnotes, besides offering commentary on the letters, I have identified, described, and summarized many reviews and essays, and I have quoted selectively from them whenever Shaw had responded to one or more of them. To a certain extent this information compensates for the missing letters; but more importantly these articles provide an expanded perspective on the relationship between these two friends who never tired in demanding the best of one another. The letters and articles, when considered together, provide a full and complex perspective on the friendship and partnership between Bernard Shaw and William Archer.

As for the extant letters themselves, their distribution across four decades, from 1885 to 1924, reveals that most of the missing letters are from 1890 to 1910:

1885 through 1889: 17 letters have survived; 9 by Shaw, 8 by Archer.
1890 through 1899: 54 letters have survived; 43 by Shaw, 11 by Archer.
1900 through 1909: 61 letters have survived; 53 by Shaw, 8 by Archer.
1910 through 1919: 21 letters have survived; 11 by Shaw, 10 by Archer.
1920 through 1924: 16 letters have survived; 9 by Shaw, 7 by Archer.

In addition, the eight letters that Charlotte Shaw sent to Archer were written during the twentieth century, from 1902 to 1919. And the four letters that Shaw sent to Frances E. Archer were written on 18 March 1885, 12 January 1887, 27 October 1905, and 23 January 1915.

The breakdown of the letters by decades reveals that there was a balance of letters during three separate periods: the 1880s, the 1910s, and the 1920s. The letters from 1885 to 1889 capture the developing nature of the special friendship between Shaw and Archer. This was the period in which Archer guided Shaw into journalism. By contrast, the letters from the last fifteen years of the correspondence, from 1910 through 1924, provide a vital perspective on their relationship during the mature years in which they both had realized major accomplishments and achieved national and international reputations.

The majority of the letters in this volume were written between 1890 and 1909, the two decades in which Archer and Shaw were most active in their campaigns for the 'New Drama' and 'New Theatre.' During these decades the gaps in the letters were most severe, with 96 letters from Shaw but only 19 from Archer. Yet this was also the period in which Archer translated, edited, and published all of Ibsen's plays, and he wrote the introductions for each play in the *Works* (1906–12). Moreover, he was involved as co-director and literary adviser in a half-dozen productions of Ibsen's plays, and wrote most of his major essays about Ibsen. During the same twenty years Shaw wrote twenty-three plays, from *Widowers' Houses* to *Misalliance.* Two of these plays were staged in the 1890s; then in the 1900s most of the twenty-three plays were produced, sometimes on more than one occasion. For example, *You Never Can Tell* had five productions during the decade: 1900, 1905, 1906, and 1907 for two separate stagings.

Some of Shaw's letters to Archer have been published previously. Twelve letters by Shaw to Archer are included in Charles Archer's biography of his brother, *William Archer: Life, Work, and Friendships* (1931). Eight of these twelve letters, however, are incomplete. Charles Archer also printed seven of Archer's letters to Shaw. Three of these letters are also incomplete. More recently, and more significantly, Dan H. Lawrence, the editor of *Bernard Shaw: Collected Letters* (1965–85), published eighty of Shaw's letters to Archer. Five of these letters had appeared at least partially in Charles Archer's biography. Most of these eighty letters are reproduced in full, though Laurence made selective cuts of sentences and paragraphs in twelve letters. Also, in a few of his headnotes, and an occasionally endnote, Laurence printed excerpts from Archer's letters.

Lawrence's decision to publish so many of Shaw's letters to Archer was quite appropriate. He understood the central importance of Archer in Shaw's career. Some of these letters are among the most entertaining in Shaw's correspondence, and of course they are among the most feisty. The advantage of having these letters in the *Collected Letters* has been substantial. But caution is required, not only because some of these letters are incomplete. Laurence's notations are necessarily brief and selective in most cases, and they contain some errors which I have been able to correct in this volume. Nonetheless, Laurence was absolutely right to feature some of the most valuable letters that Shaw wrote to any of his colleagues. My advantage, obviously, has been to present both sides of the correspondence between Shaw and Archer, and also to draw upon dozens of Archer writings about Shaw, the plays, and the productions.

In editing this volume of letters, I am pleased to join the previous publications in the *Selected Correspondence of Bernard Shaw* by the University of Toronto Press. For each letter, I have provided four pieces of information: the number for the letter, the recipient of the letter (in boldface), the location from which the letter was mailed, and the date for the letter. Then in brackets I identify the primary source for the letter and its location (e.g., a holograph letter located at the British Library). Abbreviations are used for the types and sources of each letter. For example: the designation of ALS: BL 45296 ff 151–2 informs readers that the letter is an autographed letter that Shaw signed, and that it is located at the British Library in catalogue 45296, folios 151–2. If a letter has been previously published, I have added this information to the source information: ALS: BL 45296 ff 151–2: CL 2 – that is, *Collected Letters*, volume 2.

The various codes that I use in the headings for the letters are listed in the section entitled 'Abbreviations and Works Cited' that follows directly after this Editor's Note. In that section I have also identified the abbreviated codes for published works by Shaw and Archer. In addition, I have provided codes for a few of the newspapers and journals that Archer and Shaw wrote for regularly (e.g., PMG refers to *Pall Mall Gazette*, FR refers to *Fortnightly Review*). And in this section I have also listed the important biographical and scholarly publications on Shaw, Archer, and theatre history that I have relied upon as an editor.

The headnotes for each letter supply the immediate context and the connecting narrative for each letter, including biographical information. I also describe any relevant theatrical information about the people and events that Shaw and Archer name and discuss in their letters. J.P. Wearing's calendars on London productions during this whole era have proved to be invaluable. Also, whenever appropriate, I offer basic details on the relevant historical, political, literary, or cultural events that pertain to the letter. In the case of a missing letter, I have attempted to describe what the writer – usually Archer – had possibly communicated. Given the number of missing letters, this task is a common one in the headnotes.

For the endnotes I identify the people, references, allusions, and quotations that Shaw and Archer mentioned in their letters. For these annotations each subject is identified in boldface. A short identification is provided, including birth and death dates within parentheses. For example, Robert L. Stevenson is mentioned in nine letters. The preliminary information on him appears in the endnote for the first letter in which he is mentioned, and then when references to him were made in subsequent letters by Archer or Shaw, I provide a few more details that are relevant to the specific letter.

In transcribing the letters for this volume I have honoured and reproduced Shaw's idiosyncrasies of spelling ('Shakespear') and contractions (wont, youve, havent). And I have tried to follow the punctuation methods of each writer. I have thus avoided the editorial use of [*sic*] for minor spellings or typing errors. For example, Shaw writes *Love Labor Lost* and *Love's Labor Lost* instead of *Love's Labor's Lost.* I have left the title as he wrote it. Otherwise, if the typing or spelling errors were minor, I have silently corrected them (e.g., 'unskillfully' rather than 'unskilfully' in letter #13 by Shaw). If, however, any such error seemed to carry added significance, I have provided a comment in the endnote. Overall, though, I have reproduced the styles and grammatical traits of each writer. If Shaw or Archer underlined any words, phrases, or sentences, I have translated the underlining into italics. If they underlined titles of plays, newspapers, or journals, I have used italics. But if they did not underline such titles, I have left the titles as presented in the letters. Often they made partial identifications for these titles (e.g., *Chronicle* for *Daily Chronicle, Pall Mall* for *Pall Mall Gazette, Tanqueray* for *The Second Mrs Tanqueray*). I have attempted to provide clarity, not necessarily a complete title or a compulsive consistency in the designations. The majority of my identifications are in the endnotes, but in a few cases I have inserted identifying information within the text of a letter (e.g., a person's full name, a missing play title). This insertion is placed within brackets. Otherwise, all identifications and corrections appear in the endnotes. As for the signatures at the end of a letter or notecard, I have printed them as written. If, though, there was no signature I point this out by adding '[no signature]' before the endnote. The designation for the person who stages a theatre production is usually 'producer' in British parlance but 'director' in American sources. For consistency, I use 'producer' to identify the person who oversees financial arrangements and overall management, and the word 'director' for the person who stages the production, such as Harley Granville Barker and Shaw for most of the Court Theatre performances.

Acknowledgments

I undertook this edition because of the encouragement and guidance of Dan H. Laurence. His support and gentle nudging convinced me to join the Toronto series, despite my initial reservations because of other commitments. The arrival in the mail of Dan's notecards, letters, and packets became one of the special rewards and pleasures of agreeing to edit the correspondence. He was always making sure that I had not missed any letter or relevant document, including items from his own collection. I deeply regret that he did not live to see this edition. He was the initiator and justifier. I am one of many grateful people who have stood on his shoulders and benefited from his knowledge, good will, and standards of scholarship.

When I finally signed a contract and began to delve into the archives in search of missing letters, J. Percy Smith, as the general editor for the *Selected Correspondence of Bernard Shaw*, became my mentor. It was a pleasure to work with him, for he was always supportive and encouraging. I also benefited from his practical guidance. Sadly, he too did not live to see that I have finally carried through on this commitment. That knowledge belongs to L.W. Conolly, who became the general editor and guardian scholar for this project. He guided me down the slow, winding track toward the finish line. His evaluation of the manuscript was exactly what I needed. Conolly is a model of scholarly understanding and patience, especially when confronted by my turtle pacing. In carrying out my research and in editing these letters, I have benefited from the impressive critical and biographical scholarship on Shaw, beginning most notably during his lifetime with G.K. Chesterton's *Bernard Shaw* (1910) and Eric

Bentley's *Bernard Shaw* (1947), then continuing across the decades since Shaw's death. Likewise, I am beholden to the various scholars who have edited Shaw's correspondence, interviews, letters to editors, and collections of essays. (See, however, the General Editor's Note at the beginning of this volume for the list of eight previous editions of Shaw correspondence published by University of Toronto Press.) I won't – or wont – make any effort to catalogue the many scholarly works here, but consult the following section, 'Abbreviations and Works Cited,' for at least a partial list of my obligations, starting with the scholarship of both Dan H. Laurence and Stanley Weintraub, and extending to several dozen dedicated scholars listed in Charles A. Carpenter's *A Selective, Classified International Bibliography of Publications about Shaw* and Michel Pharand's *A Chronology of Works by and about Bernard Shaw* (listed on the Shaw Society website). In great measure Shaw has been well served by two generations of scholarly editors, biographers, critics, and bibliographers.

In the case of William Archer's works, I have had the great pleasure of immersing myself in the many reviews, articles, and books that he published. His own scrapbooks, which have bounced around during recent years, are now held by the Victoria and Albert Museum at Blythe House. They are a major repository of his journalism. In addition to these scrapbooks, there are two quite helpful biographies: Charles Archer's *William Archer: Life, Work, and Friendships* (1931) and Peter Whitebrook's *William Archer* (1993). I have benefited substantially from both of them. Likewise, I have drawn upon biographical studies of Elizabeth Robins, as noted in the section 'Abbreviations and Works Cited.'

Now that the volume is finally prepared, I am most grateful to Richard Ratzlaff, editor of humanities at the University of Toronto Press, for his support and guidance. I am also grateful for the two anonymous readers who offered most helpful reports on the rambling manuscript that I had delivered to the press. Their assessments as well as their nudges, questions, and challenges have guided my preparation of the manuscript. I offer special thanks to John St James, who navigated and solved the editorial challenges of the manuscript, including the texts of the 181 letters and my commentary in the headnotes, endnotes, Introduction, and these Editor's Notes. I also extend my gratitude to Barbara Porter.

I also wish to acknowledge the Society of Authors, acting for the Estate of Bernard Shaw, and the trustees of the will of Charlotte Shaw, for permission to publish the letters in this volume. I am also beholden, yet again, to the late Elinor Archer, who years ago granted access to William Archer's extant letters, manuscripts, articles, and books, and the rights to publish Archer's writings, published and unpublished. I also thank Dr David Sutton of the Library, University of Reading. He has served as the director of UK Watch Office, and supplied answers to my questions on copyright for William Archer since the death of Elinor Archer. I am grateful as well to the following archives and libraries for permission to publish the letters in their collections: the British Library, the De Coursey Fales Library of New York University, the Burgunder Collection of Cornell University Library, the Backsettown Trustees for the Elizabeth Robins Papers, the Harry Ransom Center at the University of Texas, and the Victoria and Albert Museum, which oversees the Theatre and Performance Collection at Blythe House. I extend my sincere gratitude to the resourceful librarians and staff members at these institutions.

I am also grateful to the libraries and archives in which I carried out research: the British Library, Edinburgh University Libraries, the National Library of Scotland, the Bodleian Library at Oxford University, the Enthoven Collection at the Victoria and Albert Museum, the library of the Garrick Club in London, the Brander Matthews collection at Columbia University, the New York City Library at Lincoln Center, the Theater Collection at Harvard University, the Library of Congress, the Ohio State University Libraries, and the University of Washington Libraries, including the Drama Library. I offer my gratitude to each of these institutions and their dedicated staff members.

I also offer my warm greetings and sincere regards to my ex-students who participated in my seminars on several aspects of British theatre history and historiography. Likewise, I thank my colleagues at Indiana University, Ohio State University, and University of Washington for their institutional support. I extend a special thank you to Michael Connolly, who wrote on Archer, and also to Eric Samuelsen and Jennifer Schlueter for their assistance in transcribing letters and preparing computer files when I initially began to undertake this project. To my scholarly colleagues who have contributed, in one way or another, to this project and the refinement of my own scholarship, I offer my appreciation: Tracy C. Davis, Joseph Donohue, J.P. Wearing, Charles A. Carpenter, Arthur Ganz, Bruce McConachie, David Mayer, Marvin Carlson, Charlotte Canning,

Bernard Dukore, Eric Bentley, Veronica Kelly, Michel Pharand, Jacky Bratton, Claire Cochrane, Stephen Johnson, Dennis Kennedy, Joanne E. Gates, Angela V. John, Cary Mazer, Gay Gibson Cima, Kirsten Shepherd-Barr, Stephen Johnson, Anna Sica, Brian Singleton, Kate Newey, Jim Davis, Victor Emeljanow, Heidi Holder, Peter Bailey, Joseph Roach, Ellen Gainor, Holly Carver, Matthew Yde, Laurence Senelick, Mark Shanda, Lesley Ferris, and Nena Couch at the Theatre Research Institute. I also offer my heartfelt regards to the members of the Theatre Historiography Working Group of the International Federation for Theatre Research. And I extend my deep regards to the several dozen scholars who published books in the theatre history series that I edited at the University of Iowa Press from 1990 to 2014. Working as an editor with these scholars has been a major commitment of time and energy, but more importantly a major lesson in scholarly endeavours. Although these scholars and colleagues did not contribute directly to this edition of the Shaw/Archer letters, they provided models of excellent scholarship that greatly expanded my understanding and judgment of the discipline of theatre history and its cultural conditions. My gratitude to each scholar.

Because this project stretched over too many years I may well have forgotten to mention other people to whom I owe credit. I apologize for any absences, and lift a glass of wine, a bottle of lager, and/or a cup of tea to each colleague.

I dedicate *The Correspondence of Bernard Shaw and William Archer* to Leonard Conolly and the memory of Dan H. Laurence and J. Percy Smith. Finally, and most importantly, I honour my wife Marilyn Brownstein, who knows, far better than anyone, what this project has required – of both of us.

Abbreviations and Works Cited

Type of correspondence

ACCS	Autograph 'compliments' card signed
ADS	Autograph draft signed
ADU	Autograph draft unsigned
ALS	Autograph letter or letter-card signed
ALU	Autograph letter or letter-card unsigned
AMCU	Autograph marginal commentary unsigned
ANS	Autograph note signed
APCS	Autograph postcard signed
APCU	Autograph postcard unsigned
ASU	Autograph shorthand unsigned
CALS	Copy of autograph letter signed
TDU	Typed draft unsigned
TEL	Telegraph or cable
TLS	Typed letter signed
TLU	Typed letter unsigned
TT/C	Typed transcription or copy

Sources of the correspondence

BL	British Library, Department of Manuscripts, London
BM	British Museum
BTA	British Theatre Association (Fitzroy Square)
BTM	British Theatre Museum (Covent Garden)

CUL	Cornell University Library, Department of Rare Books
DHL	Dan H. Laurence, private correspondence
FALES	De Coursey Fales Library, Special Collections, New York University
HRC	Harry Ransom Humanities Research Center, University of Texas at Austin
V&A	Victoria and Albert Museum, Theatre and Performance Collection, Blythe House

Publications, Newspapers, Journals, and Organizations

Afro-America	William Archer, *Through Afro-America: An English Reading of the Race Problem* (London: Chapman & Hall, 1910)
Agits	Bernard Shaw, *Agitations: Letters to the Press 1875–1950*, ed. Dan H. Laurence and James Rambeau (New York: Frederick Ungar, 1985)
Auto 1,2	Bernard Shaw, *Shaw: An Autobiography*, 2 vols, ed. Stanley Weintraub (New York: Weybright & Talley, 1969, 1970)
Barker	Bernard Shaw, *Bernard Shaw's Letters to Granville Barker*, ed. C.B. Purdom (New York: Theatre Arts Books, 1957)
Bentley	Eric Bentley, *Bernard Shaw: A Reconsideration* (New York: New Directions, 1947; reprint New York: W.W. Norton, 1976)
Biblio 1,2	Dan H. Laurence, *Bernard Shaw: A Bibliography*, 2 vols (Oxford: Clarendon Press, 1983)
Biblio 3	Dan H. Laurence, 'A Supplement to Bernard Shaw: A Bibliography,' *Shaw: An Annual* 20 (2000): 3–128.
Booth	Michael R. Booth, *Theatre in the Victorian Age* (Cambridge: Cambridge University Press, 1991)
C. Archer	C. [Charles] Archer, *William Archer: Life, Work, and Friendships* (New Haven: Yale University Press, 1931)
Carpenter	Charles A. Carpenter, *A Selective, Classified International Bibliography of Publications about Bernard Shaw* (web address: harvey.binghamton.edu/~ccarpen/ShawBibliography/)
Chesterton	G.K. Chesterton, *George Bernard Shaw* (New York, 1910; reprinted New York: Hill and Wang, 1956)

CL 1,2,3,4	Bernard Shaw, *Collected Letters*, 4 vols, ed. Dan H. Laurence (London: Reinhardt, 1965, 1972, 1985, 1988)
CP 1,2,3,4,5,6,7	Bernard Shaw, *Collected Plays with Their Prefaces*, 7 vols, ed. Dan H. Laurence (London: Bodley Head, 1970–4)
Davis 1	Tracy C. Davis, *The Economics of the British Stage 1800–1914* (Cambridge: Cambridge University Press, 2000)
Davis 2	Tracy C. Davis, *George Bernard Shaw and the Socialist Theatre* (Westport, CT: Praeger, 1994)
DC	*The Daily Chronicle*
Dent	*Bernard Shaw and Mrs Patrick Campbell: Their Correspondence*, ed. Alan Dent (New York: Alfred A. Knopf, 1952)
Diaries 1,2	Bernard Shaw, *Bernard Shaw: The Diaries*, 2 vols, ed. Stanley Weintraub (University Park: Pennsylvania State University Press, 1986)
Donohue	Joseph Donohue, *Fantasies of Empire: The Empire Theatre of Varieties and the Licensing Controversy of 1894* (Iowa City: University of Iowa Press, 2005)
Douglas	*Bernard Shaw and Alfred Douglas, A Correspondence*, ed. Mary Hyde (New Haven: Ticknor & Fields, 1982)
DraRev	*The Dramatic Review*
Dreams	William Archer, *On Dreams*, ed. Theodore Besterman, preface by Gilbert Murray (London: Methuen & Co., 1935)
Dukore 1,2,3,4	Bernard Shaw, *The Drama Observed*, 4 vols, ed. Bernard F. Dukore (University Park: Pennsylvania State University Press, 1993)
Dukore Director	Bernard Dukore, *Bernard Shaw, Director* (Seattle: University of Washington Press, 1971)
Dukore Screenplays	*The Collected Screenplays of Bernard Shaw*, ed. with intro. by Bernard Dukore (Athens: University of Georgia Press, 1980)

Dunbar Janet Dunbar, *Mrs G.B.S.: A Portrait* (New York: Harper & Row, 1963)

Edwardes Thomas Postlewait, 'George Edwardes and Musical Comedy: The Transformation of London Theatre and Society, 1878–1914,' in *The Performing Century*, ed. Tracy C. Davis and Peter Holland (Houndmills, Basingstoke, Hampshire: Palgrave Macmillan, 2007), 80–102

Embryo Stanley Weintraub, *Bernard Shaw* before His First Play, The Embryo Playwright (Greenboro, NC: ELT Press, 2015).

Ervine St John Ervine, *Bernard Shaw: His Life, Work and Friends* (London: Constable, 1956)

Evans T.F. Evans, ed., *Shaw: The Critical Heritage* (London: Routledge & Kegan Paul, 1976)

Farr Josephine Johnson, *Florence Farr: Bernard Shaw's 'New Woman'* (Gerrards Cross: Colin Smythe, 1975)

Ferrer William Archer, *The Life, Trial, and Death of Francisco Ferrer* (London: Chapman & Hall, 1911)

FR *The Fortnightly Review*

Franchi Francesca Franchi, *Directory of Performing Arts Resources*, 3rd ed. (London: Society for Theatre Research & Theatre Museum, 1998)

Gainer J. Ellen Gainer, *Shaw's Daughters: Dramatic and Narrative Constructions of Gender* (Ann Arbor: University of Michigan Press, 1991)

Gänzl 1,2 Kurt Gänzl, *The British Musical Theatre*, 2 vols (New York: Oxford University Press, 1986)

Gates Joanne E. Gates, *Elizabeth Robins, 1862–1952: Actress, Novelist, Feminist* (Tuscaloosa: University of Alabama Press, 1994)

Gibbs 1 A.M. Gibbs, *A Bernard Shaw Chronology* (Houndmills, Basingstoke: Palgrave, 2001)

Gibbs 2 A.M. Gibbs, *Bernard Shaw: A Life* (Gainesville: University of Florida Press, 2005)

Goddess William Archer, *The Green Goddess* (New York: Alfred A. Knopf, 1921)

Harris *The Playwright and the Pirate: Bernard Shaw and Frank Harris. A Correspondence*, ed. Stanley Weintraub (University Park: Pennsylvania State University Press, 1982)

Hend 1	Archibald Henderson, *George Bernard Shaw: His Life and Works* (London: Hurst & Blackett, 1911)
Hend 2	Archibald Henderson, *Bernard Shaw: Playboy and Prophet* (New York: D. Appleton & Co., 1932)
Hend 3	Archibald Henderson, *George Bernard Shaw: Man of the Century* (New York: Appleton-Century-Crofts, 1956)
Holroyd 1,2,3,4	Michael Holroyd, *Bernard Shaw*, 4 vols (New York: Random House, 1988, 1989, 1991, 1992)
Howard	Diana Howard, *London Theatres and Music Halls 1850–1950* (London: Library Association, 1970)
Ibsen Essays	William Archer, *William Archer on Ibsen: The Major Essays, 1889–1919*, ed. Thomas Postlewait (Westport, CT: Greenwood Press, 1984)
Ibsen Letters	*Ibsen Letters and Speeches*, ed. and primarily trans. Evert Sprinchorn (New York: Hill & Wang, 1964)
Ibsen Works	Henrik Ibsen, *Collected Works*, ed. and trans. William Archer, 12 vols (London: Heinemann, 1906–12)
India	William Archer, *India and the Future* (New York: Alfred A. Knopf, 1918)
I&R	Bernard Shaw, *Interviews and Recollections*, ed. A.M. Gibbs (London: Macmillan/Iowa City: University of Iowa Press, 1990)
IT	Independent Theatre Company
John	Angela V. John, *Elizabeth Robins: Staging a Life 1862–1952* (London: Routledge, 1995)
Journey	Stanley Weintraub, *Journey to Heartbreak: The Crucible Years of Bernard Shaw 1914–18* (New York: Weybright & Talley, 1971)
Kelly	Veronica Kelly: '*The Green Goddess*: William Archer's Great War Play,' *Nineteenth Century Theatre and Film* 40.2 (Winter 2013): 2–124
Kershaw	Baz Kershaw, ed. *The Cambridge History of British Theatre*, vol. 3 (Cambridge: Cambridge University Press, 2004)
LCC	London County Council
Masks/Faces	William Archer, *Masks or Faces? A Study in the Psychology of Acting* (London: Longmans, Green, 1888)

Meisel	Martin Meisel, *Shaw and the Nineteenth Century Theater* (Princeton, NJ: Princeton University Press, 1963)
Meyer	Michael Meyer, *Ibsen: A Biography* (Garden City, NY: Doubleday & Co., 1971)
ML	*Morning Leader*
Morgan	Margery Morgan, *File on Shaw* (London: Methuen, 1989)
Music 1,2,3	Bernard Shaw, *Shaw's Music: The Complete Musical Criticism of Bernard Shaw,* 3 vols, 2nd rev. ed., ed. Dan H. Laurence (London: Bodley Head, 1989)
NCT	New Century Theatre Company
Old Drama	William Archer, *The Old Drama and the New, An Essay in Re-Evaluation* (Boston: Small, Maynard and Co., 1923)
OTN 1,2,3	Bernard Shaw, *Our Theatres in the Nineties,* 3 vols (London: Constable, 1948)
Oxford	*The Oxford Companion to the Theatre,* ed. Phyllis Hartnoll, 1st and 2nd ed. (London: Oxford University Press, 1951, 1957)
Patch	Blanche Patch, *Thirty Years with G. B. S.* (New York: Dodd, Mead & Company, 1951)
Pearson Shaw	Hesketh Pearson, *Bernard Shaw: His Life and Personality* (London: Methuen, 1961)
Pearson Tree	Hesketh Pearson, *Beerbohm Tree: His Life and Laughter* (London: Columbus Books, 1988)
Pen Portraits	Bernard Shaw, *Pen Portraits and Reviews* (New York: Wm. H. Wise & Co, 1932)
Peters	Margot Peters, *Bernard Shaw and the Actresses* (Garden City, NY: Doubleday, 1980)
Pharand	Michel Pharand, *A Chronology of Works by and about Bernard Shaw,* http://www.shawsociety.org/ShawChron 2017.pdf
Platform	Bernard Shaw, *Platform and Pulpit,* ed. Dan H. Laurence (New York: Hill & Wang, 1961)
Play-Making	William Archer, *Play-Making: A Manual of Craftsmanship* (Boston: Small, Maynard & Co., 1912)
PMG	*Pall Mall Gazette*

Prefaces 1,2,3	Bernard Shaw, *The Complete Prefaces*, 3 vols, ed. Dan H. Laurence and Daniel J. Leary (London: Allen Lane / Penguin Press, 1993, 1995, 1997)
Prophet	Thomas Postlewait, *Prophet of the New Drama: William Archer and the Ibsen Campaign* (Westport, CT: Greenwood Press, 1986)
Real	William Archer, *Real Conversations* (London: William Heinemann, 1904)
Religion	*The Religious Speeches of Bernard Shaw*, ed. Warren Sylvester Smith (University Park: Pennsylvania State University Press, 1963)
Salt	S. Winsten, *Salt and His Circle*, preface by Bernard Shaw (London: Hutchinson, 1951)
SatRev	*Saturday Review*
Schmid	Hans Schmid, *The Dramatic Criticism of William Archer* (Bern: A. Francke AG Verlag, 1964)
Shaw/Jackson	*Bernard Shaw and Barry Jackson: Selected Correspondence of Bernard Shaw*, ed. L.W. Conolly (Toronto: University of Toronto Press, 2002)
Shaw/Wells	*Bernard Shaw and H.G. Wells* (Selected Correspondence of Bernard Shaw), edited by J. Percy Smith (Toronto: University of Toronto Press, 1995)
Smith	J. Percy Smith, *Unrepentant Pilgrim: Light on Bernard Shaw's Private Life & Formative Years* (London: Gollancz, 1966)
SMNTC	Shakespeare Memorial National Theatre Committee
SNT	Shakespeare National Theatre (Stratford-upon-Avon)
Speaight	Robert Speaight, *William Poel and the Elizabethan Revival* (London: Heinemann, 1954)
SS	Stage Society
SSS	Bernard Shaw, *Sixteen Self-Sketches* (New York: Dodd, Mead, 1949)
Stanley	Raymond Stanley, ed., *Tourist to the Antipodes: William Archer's 'Australian Journey: 1876–77'* (St Lucia, Queensland: University of Queensland Press, 1977)
Stevenson	*The Letters of Robert Louis Stevenson*, 9 vols, ed. Bradford A. Booth and Ernest Mehew (New Haven: Yale University Press, 1994–8)

Study-Stage	William Archer, *Study and Stage: A Yearbook of Criticism* (London: Grant Richards, 1899)
Terry/Shaw	*Ellen Terry and Bernard Shaw: A Correspondence*, ed. Christopher St John (New York: G.P. Putnam's Sons, 1932)
Theatrics	Bernard Shaw, *Theatrics* (Selected Correspondence of Bernard Shaw), ed. Dan H. Laurence (Toronto: University of Toronto Press, 1995)
Three Plays	William Archer, *Three Plays*, foreword by Bernard Shaw (New York: Henry Holt, 1927)
Trebitsch	Bernard Shaw, *Bernard Shaw's Letters to Siegfried Trebitsch*, ed. Samuel A. Weiss (Stanford, CA: Stanford University Press, 1986)
Tribune	*The Tribune*
Tyson 1,2	Bernard Shaw, *Bernard Shaw's Book Reviews*, 2 vols, ed. Brian Tyson (University Park: Pennsylvania State University Press, 1991)
Tyson Story	Brian Tyson, *The Story of Saint Joan* (Kingston and Montreal: McGill-Queen's University Press, 1982)
Wagner	George Bernard Shaw, *The Perfect Wagnerite. A Commentary on the Niblung's Ring* (London: Grant Richards,1898; 4th ed., London: Constable & Co., 1923; reprint New York: Dover Publications, 1967)
Wearing Biblio	J.P. Wearing et al., *G.B. Shaw: An Annotated Bilbiography of Writings about Him* (Dekalb: Northern Illinois University Press, 1986–7)
Wearing 1890	J.P. Wearing, *The London Stage 1890–1899: A Calendar of Plays and Players*, 2 vols (Metuchen, NJ: Scarecrow Press, 1976)
Wearing 1900	J.P. Wearing, *The London Stage 1900–1909: A Calendar of Plays and Players*, 2 vols (Metuchen, NJ: Scarecrow Press, 1981)
Wearing 1910	J.P. Wearing, *The London Stage 1910–1919: A Calendar of Plays and Players*, 2 vols (Metuchen, NJ: Scarecrow Press, 1982)
Webb 1,2,3,4	*The Diary of Beatrice Webb*, 4 vols, ed. Norman MacKenzie and Jeanne MacKenzie (London: Virago Press, 1982)

Weintraub — *Bernard Shaw on the London Art Scene 1885–1950*, ed. Stanley Weintraub (University Park: Pennsylvania State University Press, 1989)

WH — Bernard Shaw, *Widowers' Houses, Facsimiles of the Shorthand and Holograph Manuscripts and the 1893 Published Text*, intro. by Jerald E. Bringle (New York: Garland Publishing, 1981)

Whitebrook — Peter Whitebrook, *William Archer: A Biography* (London: Methuen, 1993)

Wilde — *The Complete Letters of Oscar Wilde*, ed. Merlin Holland and Rupert Hart-Davis (New York: Henry Holt and Co., 2000)

Wisenthal — Bernard Shaw, *Shaw and Ibsen: Bernard Shaw's The Quintessence of Ibsenism and Related Writings*, ed. J.L. Wisenthal (Toronto: University of Toronto Press, 1979)

World — *The World*

World 93 — William Archer, *The Theatrical 'World' for 1893* (London: Walter Scott, 1894)

World 94 — William Archer, *The Theatrical 'World' of 1894* (London: Walter Scott, 1895)

World 95 — William Archer, *The Theatrical 'World' of 1895* (London: Walter Scott, 1996)

World 96 — William Archer, *The Theatrical 'World' of 1896* (London: Walter Scott, 1997)

World 97 — William Archer, *The Theatrical 'World' of 1897* (London: Walter Scott, 1998)

Yde — Matthew Yde, *Bernard Shaw and Totalitarianism: Longing for Utopia* (New York: Palgrave Macmillan, 2013)

Figure 1 Bernard Shaw in July 1891, before he wrote *Widowers' Houses.* Courtesy of Cornell University Library, Department of Rare Books.

c

"The lyfe so short, the craft so long to lerne."

CHAUCER.

William Archer.

Figure 2 William Archer (circa 1890). Courtesy of Cornell University Library, Department of Rare Books.

Figure 3 Lord Howard de Walden, William Archer, J.M. Barrie, G.K. Chesterton, and Bernard Shaw, in the process of making the cowboy film *How Men Love*, by Barrie and Granville Barker. July 1914.

Letters

1 / To G. Bernard Shaw

2 Queen Sq. Place
6th January 1885

[APCS: BL 50528 f 29]

Archer and Shaw, born in 1856, migrated to London in the 1870s. Archer came from Edinburgh, Shaw from Dublin. The met in 1884, and soon became close friends. By 1885 Archer was an established theatre citric in London. He had already published two books on London theatre: English Drama of Today *(1882) and* Henry Irving, Actor and Manager: A Critical Study *(1883). By contrast, Shaw's career was yet to develop. Living with his mother, Lucinda Elizabeth ('Bessie') Shaw (1830–1913), he had resisted appeals from his father, George Carr Shaw (1814–85), to 'get something to do to earn some money' (Holroyd 1: 81). His most notable achievement during this period was the writing of five novels, all unpublished except for an unpaid serialization in 1884 of* An Unsocial Socialist, *which appeared in a new socialist journal called* To-Day. *Since arriving in London in 1876, his life was defined, as he later wrote, by 'nine years of shabby genteel destitution during which my attempts to gain a footing in literature were a complete and apparently hopeless failure. I was rescued from this condition by William Archer' (Music 1: 29). Eighteen eighty-five was 'a year of firsts in Shaw's writing and journalistic career' (Gibbs 1: 54). As Shaw recorded in his new diary, Archer 'procured me an appointment as musical critic to* The Dramatic Review, *a journal started in February by an Irishman named Edwin P. Palmer' (Diaries 1: 53).*

My dear Shaw

I looked into the B.M. this afternoon but you were not at home.

I told Mr E. Palmer, *Dramatic Review,* 13 or 14 Catherine Street Strand, that you would call upon him *re* musical notes & criticism, and will always find him in. He has got someone who *says* he will do the musical business for nothing; but I pointed out to him that gratis work was generally the dearest, & he seemed to agree. So dont be too moderate in your demands.

Look me up either before or after you go to see him.

Yours
W. Archer

During their first two decades in London, Shaw and Archer carried out much of their reading and some of their writing in the Reading Room at the **B.M.** (British Museum). Shaw's first article for the **Dramatic Review** was published appeared on 8 February (Music 1: 208–13). Entitled 'Herr Richter and His Blue Ribbon,' it offered a brief historical survey of the annual Wagner festivals at Albert Hall. Wagner himself had directed several concerts during the first festival in 1877. Hans Richter (1843–1916), who had conducted the first *Ring* cycle at Bayreuth in 1876, came to London in 1877 with Wagner. He also conducted some concerts, and in 1879 became the primary conductor of the annual 'Orchestra Festival Concerts.' Richer held this post until 1897.

2 / To G. Bernard Shaw

2 Queen Sq. Place
7th February 1885

[APCS: BL 50528 f 30]

Having taken Shaw's affairs in hand, Archer made sure that Palmer's door remained open. Shaw's second review, published on 15 February, was a full-scale blast at Franz Liszt's 'shallowly conceived and detestably expressed' Dante Symphony, *which Liszt had based upon* The Divine Comedy. *Shaw was unimpressed by Liszt's 'exceptionally loud' musical depiction of the Inferno (Music 1: 213–19). With this review Shaw settled into his new position, though he had to convince Palmer to publish his reviews on a regular basis (CL 1: 118–19). 'At first I contributed only signed articles, but later in the year I wrote a set of paragraphs every week for the musical column' (Diaries 1: 53). Palmer ran out of funds by midsummer, yet for six more months Shaw continued to publish notices on the musical scene. Despite no payments, Shaw derived substantial benefit from attending the weekly concerts: 'My practical interest in music was revived by my duties as critic of* The Dramatic Review*' (Diaries 1: 54).*

I see Bache's Liszt concert comes off on Thursday Dannreuther conducting – great occasion isn't it? Shall I tell Palmer you're going to it? I think you'd better if you can.

W.A.

Walter **Bache** (1842–88), a concert pianist and conductor, taught piano at the Royal Academy of Music. Dedicated to the performance of Franz Liszt's works, he staged a series of concerts in London. Shaw admired Bache's talents. Edward **Dannreuther** (1844–1905), a German pianist, conductor, and music scholar, was best known for championing Wagner's operas. In 1872 he founded the London Wagner Society. He also published an English translation of Wagner's *On Conducting*, which Shaw reviewed (PMG, 28 May 1887; Music 1: 496–9).

3 / To William Archer

36 Osnaburgh St NW
16th March 1885

[ALS: BL 45296 ff 3–4; CL 1]

As You Like It *was staged at the St James's Theatre. Managed by William Hunter Kendal and John Hare, the production starred Mrs Kendal as Rosalind and featured Kendal as Orlando and Hare as Touchstone. Also in the cast were Linda Dietz as Celia, Herbert Waring as Oliver, A.M. Denison as Duke Frederick, and Henry L. Vernon as Charles the Wrestler.*

In 1885 Shaw's familiarity with the staging methods for Shakespearean theatre was still limited. Before leaving Dublin he had seen a few productions, including the touring of Barry Sullivan (1821–91) in Hamlet. *But after the move to London he seldom had the funds to attend the theatre. No doubt he had read many of the plays before he left Dublin, and by the 1880s he was becoming well versed in the Shakespearean canon. In April 1880 he drafted but failed to publish his first theatre review, an overwritten analysis of the Lyceum production of* The Merchant of Venice *with Henry Irving and Ellen Terry. This was his first exposure to them. He complained of cuts in the text, yet lavished praise on Terry's 'gift of acting' and her 'genius.' This was the beginning of his fascination with her (Dukore 1: 3–10). The review remained unpublished until 1993.*

I have just been to 'As you Like it.' If you want matter for a Palmeresque paragraph you may describe poor Rosalind's bad cold. Exposure in the forest of Arden and an immutable resolution not to blow her nose before the audience did their deadly work. Then at her exit in the third act she made a mistressly stroke of business out of them. She fainted, slipping from the neck of Linda Dietz with a beautiful stage fall in the patent collapsible manner. Orlando, with unconcealed scepticism as to the cause of the tragedy, and brutally marital blindness to its timeliness and attractiveness, bundled her off promptly. Well might she ask in the next act whether she had not counterfeited excellently. It was the only good piece of acting I saw. Such allround abject, utter, abysmal, bottomless incompetence I hope I may never see again. The direct cause of the failure of the revival is the frightful badness of Oliver and Frederic. Had they been even presentable, Charles the Wrestler would have made a good start for the play in spite of Orlando, whose stupidity I never before fully realised. Mrs Kendal, without a cold, could be made a good Rosalind by a few hints from me. But the decadence of the stage is awful. We have our work cut out for us, I can tell you. My opinion of Shakespeare has gone up prodigiously: my opinion of Victorian stage culture is below zero.

I write by this post to Sonnenschein giving him a concise sketch of the history of publishing in England from 1885 to 1900, shewing the great increase in value of good copyrights that must take place, and declining a 15 years lease at 10%. Adroitly interwoven plagiarisms from Braekstad give an air of practical knowledge to the forecast.

Braekstad, by the bye, has sent me a copy of 'True Women.' I read some of it between 'As you Like it,' and think it good so far. It smells of Ibsen.

Kielland ought to be regarded with loathing by a boa constrictor like you. He does not even preserve the order of events in the scenes, much less the order of the scenes. The chapters that did me most impress are the description of Garman's garden (Trianon overgrown with rushes &c), the kissing of Sarah by Fennefos, and – from a partly comic point of view – that scene between Worse and Randulf which you translated for Foote. Fennefos & Sarah were particularly startling in their naturalness. I left the book for you this afternoon. When I keep books long, butter, porridge, jam, cocoa, and orange juice accumulate between the leaves and disgust the next reader.

GBS

A **Palmeresque paragraph** was a brief report on current events in the theatre; it sometimes featured an amusing, satiric, or even hostile statement that a critic might deliver in an unsigned notice. Both Shaw and Archer were capable of delivering well-aimed barbs in their reviews, signed or unsigned. In the **Victorian stage culture**, the Kendals and John Hare were major figures. **Mrs Kendal** (1849–1935, née Margaret 'Madge' Robertson) was the sister of the playwright Thomas William Robertson (1829–71). She married W.H. Kendal in 1869. After four successful decades in the London theatre, often appearing in adapted French plays, the Kendals retired in 1908. They were models of respectability in the Victorian theatre. In 1926 she was made Dame Commander of the British Empire, and in 1927 received the Order of the Grand Cross. The actor-manager **William Hunter Kendal** (1843–1917) performed at the Haymarket Theatre in the late 1860s and 1870s. He and Hare became business partners at the St James's Theatre in 1879. In 1886 Archer published an essay on the Kendals in volume 5 of *Actors and Actresses of Great Britain and the United States*, edited by Brander Matthews and Laurence Hutton. **John Hare** (1844–1921), also an actor-manager, performed at the Prince of Wales's with the Bancrofts in the plays of Tom Robertson, beginning in 1865 with *Society*. In 1889 Hare took over the Garrick Theatre, which William Schwenck (W.S.) Gilbert (1836–1911) built for him. There he staged *The Profligate* (1889) by A.W. Pinero (1855–1934), and starred in *A Pair of Spectacles* (1890, 1891, 1895) by Sydney Grundy (1848–1914). He later managed the Globe Theatre, where he featured *The Gay*

Lord Quex (1899) by Pinero and revivals of Robertson's plays. Hare was knighted in 1907. **Linda Dietz**, who played Cecil, and A.M. Denison, who played Duke **Frederic**, had limited careers in the West End theatres. **W.H. Vernon** (1834–1905), an actor and director, worked with Archer twice in the staging of Ibsen's plays. In 1880 they presented *Quicksands; or, The Pillars of Society* for a single matinee. This crude adaptation, which Archer quickly came to regret, was the first staging of Ibsen in England. In 1897 Vernon played the lead role in *John Gabriel Borkman* in a production by the New Century Theatre Company. The actor **Herbert Waring** (1857–1932) worked with Archer on several productions, including Ibsen's *A Doll's House* (1889) and *The Master Builder* (1893). He also appeared in Archer's melodrama *The Green Goddess* (1921).

William Swan **Sonnenschein** (1855–1931) guided the publishing company Swan Sonnenschein and Co. After several rounds of negotiation over copyright control and royalties, Shaw and Sonnenschein reached agreement on the publication of *An Unsocial Socialist.* Hans Lien **Brækstad** (1845–1915), a Norwegian, had settled in London as a journalist; he wrote on contemporary events and literature, including Norwegian and Swedish works, including the plays of Ibsen. He was the literary agent for Archer's *English Dramatists of Today* (1882). In several capacities, he served the Norwegian government in London, and in 1906 became the Norwegian vice-consul. In 1883 Brækstad translated the Swedish play ***True Women***, written by Anne Charlotte Edgren, Duchess di Cajanello (1849–92). He had apparently shared the manuscript with Shaw, for the translation was not published until 1890. Shaw's reference to Henrik **Ibsen** was the first mention of the playwright in any of his writings (Wisenthal: 5). Except for what he had learned from Archer, he knew little about Ibsen's drama in 1885, though he probably read Frances Lord's translation of *Ghosts*, which appeared in the Socialist magazine *To-Day* in early 1885. Also, it is quite likely that Shaw joined Archer at an amateur production of *Nora* by the Scribblers' Dramatic Society in late March. The play was an adaptation of Ibsen's *A Doll's House* that Lord had translated in 1882. Archer's review of the amateur production appeared in *The World* on 1 April, and his 'Ibsen in England' was published in DraRev on 4 April (Prophet: 142). Shaw mentioned Lord's *Nora* in a letter to the editor of DraRev on 27 June 1885 (Dukore: 34). Because Archer had already published several articles on Ibsen's plays, he surely shared them with Shaw. It is uncertain, however, that Archer showed him the unpublished *Quicksilver, or the Pillars of Society*, which he had translated in 1878. Mrs Archer lent Shaw a copy of the novel *Skipper Worse*, written by Alexander L. **Kielland** (1849–92), a Norwegian novelist and playwright (Diaries 1: 70). The translation, published in 1885, was by Henry John Moreton, 3rd Earl of Ducie. Under the pseudonym of 'Norman Britton,' Archer translated and published a short portion of the novel within his essay entitled 'Kielland Again' that appeared in *Progress* (Dec. 1883). In 1891 Archer translated and published Kielland's novel *Tales of Two Countries.*

4 / To Frances E. Archer

36 Osnaburgh St NW
18th March 1885

[ALS: BL 45296 f 5; CL 1]

Archer and Frances E. Trickett (1855–1929) met in Rome during the winter of 1881–2. She was touring Europe with her father; Archer was meeting with Ibsen, who lived in Rome between 1880 and 1885. During this period Ibsen wrote Ghosts, An Enemy of the People, *and* The Wild Duck. *Back in London, Frances and William were married on 23 October 1884 in a simple ceremony at the Kensington Register Office. She – and she alone – called him 'Willy.'*

Shaw's review of the performance of Johann Sebastian Bach's Mass in B Minor *appeared in the* DraRev *on 28 March 1885. In preparation, he attended a rehearsal on 19 March and the performance on 21 March, score in hand.*

Dear Mrs Archer

Your friend from the north shews an utter disregard of my convenience and indeed of human possibility in selecting Thursday for his visit. I have to go to the Albert Hall to the rehearsal of the Bach festival. This, which was yesterday a prospect of pleasure, is now one of sacrifice. Kismet!

Moonenschein not yet replied. I have paralysed him for a post or two.

yours faithfully
George Bernard Shaw
(I am forming the habit of signing the name by which posterity will revere me)

The visiting **friend** from Edinburgh, whom Shaw did meet four days later, was Edward Rimbault Vere Dibdin (1853–1941). He was the great grandson of Charles Dibdin (1745–1814), the famous songwriter of popular ballads. Edward Dibdin and Archer had become close friends during Archer's student days at Edinburgh University (1872–6). Under the pseudonym of E.V. Ward (based on the combined initials of their names), they wrote and published satiric poems and plays, including *The Khan of Kashgar,* based on Aristophanes' *Lysistrata* (1879), and *Blue and Buff, or The Great Muddlesbourgh Election* (1881), a satire of Gilbert and Sullivan. Dibdin later served as an art critic for the *Liverpool Courier* (1887–1904), and in 1904 became curator of the Walker Art Gallery, Liverpool. The **Bach festival** was part of the bicentennial celebration for the works of Johann Sebastian Bach (1685–1750). **Moonenschein** was Shaw's coinage for the publisher W.S. Sonnenschein, with whom he was negotiating a contract for *An Unsocial Socialist.* Despite Shaw's parenthetical statement on his signature, he disliked his first name. Yet for articles, books, and business correspondence in the 1880s and 1890s he used either 'George Bernard Shaw' or 'G. Bernard Shaw.' But by the late 1890s and beyond he preferred 'Bernard Shaw.' For letters to friends and colleagues he usually identified himself as 'GBS' or 'G.B.S.'

5 / To G. Bernard Shaw 2 Queen's Square Place, Bloomsbury, WC
Tuesday [c. late March 1885]

[ALS: BL 50528 f 31]

After several emendations to the contract for An Unsocial Socialist, *Shaw finally signed the agreement with the publisher Swan Sonneschein on 6 April 1885. The novel appeared in February 1887 with a projected run of 1000 copies, but 'only 244 copies seem to have been bound in cloth' (Biblio 1: 10). Because the novel sold poorly, a cheap, cut-down edition of the remaining copies was published in 1888. This edition featured an appendix letter from Sidney Trefusis, the protagonist, to the author.*

Shaw!

(I see you have given up conventional terms of endearment, but somehow I dont seem quite to know who I'm writing to unless there is a name at the top of the paper.) Sorry we were away when you called, as I wanted to tell you that I took the liberty of laying your little business with Moonenschein pretty fully before Braekstad, in whose practical knowledge of publishers & their ways I have much faith, and he agrees with me that Sonnenschein's proposition is by no means despicable (as the publishing trade goes) and that you would be a fool to quarrel with it. Certainly they have treated you absurdly in the matter of the *Time* story; but stinginess does not necessarily argue absolute dishonesty, and my own opinion is that a publisher in the hand is worth two in the bush – Sonnenschein *in praesenti* (the association of *ex/in praesenti* has probably led to this plunge into the classics) is worth Macmillan & Blackwood *in futuro.*

My wife sends her kind regards. Glad to see you whenever you like.

Yours sententiously
W.A.

At the bottom of the letter Archer wrote 'Comrade G. B. Shaw, 36 Osnaburgh St' for the mailing address. Besides his contractual hassles over **Sonnenschein's proposition** for his novel, Shaw bargained unsuccessfully with the publisher over payment for his mystery story 'The Miraculous Revenge,' published in the shilling magazine ***Time*** in March 1885 (CL 1: 122, 143). A year after Shaw's death, the story was retitled 'The Grave of Brimstone Billy' and published in the *Ellery Queen's Mystery Magazine* (October 1951, vol. 18: 16–31). Archer's laboured witticism of **in praesenti** and **in futuro** suggests the Latin phrase *Praesentem mulgeas, quid fugientem insequeris* (loosely, 'a bird in hand is worth two in the bush'). **Macmillan** & Co. and **Blackwood** & Sons were British publishers. As Archer likely knew from previous conversations with Shaw, the two birds in the bush, Macmillan and Blackwood, had rejected Shaw's first novel *Immaturity* in 1880.

6 / To G. Bernard Shaw

2 Queen Sq. Place
Sunday [3rd May 1885]

[ALS: BL 50528 f 32]

Besides serving as the weekly drama critic at The World, *Archer wrote occasional book reviews for the* Pall Mall Gazette, *an evening newspaper and review. Having set up Shaw as a music critic at* DraRev, *Archer now sought to place him at* PMG *as a book reviewer. To this purpose, Archer gave him a novel entitled* Trajan *to review.*

My dear Shaw

Will you dine with us tomorrow at one thirty? H. A. Jones, the playwright, wd like to meet you. We'll try not to poison you with the stench of the fleshpots.

Morley of the Pall Mall is clamoring for the review of 'Trajan' (very much to my surprise). I'm afraid I must ask you either to hurry up with it or to let me pitch into it myself tomorrow, in which case we will try our experiment with some other book.

Yours ever
W. Archer

Shaw accepted the invitation to dine with the playwright **Henry Arthur Jones** (1851–1929). Even before Jones and Henry Herman (1832–94) had written and staged the popular melodrama entitled *The Silver King* in 1882, Archer had praised Jones's playwriting talent, which he discussed in *English Dramatists of Today*. But in 1884, when Jones and Herman adapted Ibsen's *A Doll's House*, as *Breaking a Butterfly*, Archer complained that they had distorted Ibsen's play 'to fit the narrow prejudices and attenuated powers of thought of British Philistinism' (World, 12 March 1884). Set in England, the action shows how Flossie, the weak wife, is protected by her strong husband, Humphrey Goddard. Goddard saves the marriage; Flossie does not walk out the door. Archer wrote three reviews that criticized the radical changes in the text. Shaw, a vegetarian, attempted to avoid **the stench of the flesh-pots** whenever he dined. (See Exodus 16:3 for reference to flesh pots.) Charles Robert **Morley** (1853–1916), the nephew of John Morley (1838–1923), served as the literary editor of PMG. John Morley, who had edited *Fortnightly Review* from 1866 to 1882, was PMG editor from 1880 to 1883, then was replaced by W.T. Stead (1848–1912). In 1880, as editor of the PMG, Morley had rejected reviews submitted by Shaw and urged him 'to get out of journalism' (CL 1: 30–2). Five years later his nephew Charles Morley hired Shaw. Over the next four years Shaw became a regular reviewer for PMG, publishing a total of 111 reviews. All of the reviews, excepting one, were unsigned. Shaw's review of Henry F. Keenan's ***Trajan:*** *A Novel* appeared on 16 May (Tyson 1: 19–21). Morley thanked Archer for procuring the review, and wrote, 'Your man shall certainly have more books.' Archer's **experiment** had worked. On 18 May Morley then sent 'a small batch of books' to Shaw, and told him that *PMG* sought 'a certain flippant gaiety – *when* we can get it.' No doubt Shaw's closing line in his review satisfied this appeal. *Trajan*, he announced, will appeal to 'persons whose time is of comparatively small value.' A couple of months later Archer introduced Morley and Shaw to one another (Diaries 1: 100).

7 / To G. Bernard Shaw

[no address]
Friday night, 12th November 1885

[ALS: BL 50528 f 33]

Throughout 1885 Archer continued to find reviewing opportunities for Shaw. Besides the DraRev *and the* PMG, *he located Shaw with the* The Magazine of Music, *a monthly journal out of Edinburgh. Shaw's first music review – on the sound of period instruments – appeared in August (Music 1: 319–24). In June Shaw himself tapped another source of income when he began to write a monthly note on the arts for* Our Corner, *a socialist journal edited by Annie Besant (1847–1933). In addition, Shaw's mother, who offered singing lessons, was able to give him small payments during most months (e.g., 10 shillings on three occasions in November according to diary entries). And the monthly checks from* PMG *for book reviews provided a few pounds. But Shaw's financial situation remained precarious, even though he lived with his mother. The two of them no longer received the monthly 30 shillings from Shaw's father, who had died in April, though they were paid £100 in July from his life insurance policy (CL 1: 132–5). Shaw's portion was spent on a new Jaeger suit, coat, vest, and pants (Diaries 1: 91 and 103).*

Shaw's earnings had diminished by late 1885 because Palmer had not paid Shaw since the summer for the weekly reviews and occasional notes he continued to write for the Dramatic Review. *Archer thus conceived a credit and debit scheme to address Palmer's missing payments. The details of this plan are unclear, although Shaw recorded a single payment on 14 November from* DraRev *for 15 shillings, despite Palmer's lack of funds (Diaries 1: 125). This arrangement, whatever its method for transferring funds, did not continue to operate. If Shaw deemed Archer's plan an act of charity, he would have rejected the payment, as events a month later revealed with another of Archer's payment schemes. (See three letters of December 1885.) Likewise, he would not accept a loan.*

Shaw!

The enclosed will explain itself.

If you are damned fool enough not to accept the money, return it *to me* and destroy my note to Palmer. If you have the sense to stick to it, send on my note to Palmer and when you next write him state that you have received £11 through me, & that your account is accordingly reduced to £sd – whatever it is, in fact.

Seriously, I think you shd take the money – I certainly should in your place. I suppose Palmer has sent you too a guinea & your expenses. If I were you, I would stick to the guinea saying the same thing of it – namely that you apply it to the liquidation of your original account.

By the by[e], if Palmer's bankruptcy puts you for the moment in a tight place, I am making more money than I have any present need for, and shall always be glad to help you to keep going until one or other of your argosies comes home. I hope you will not hesitate to let me know if (or when) I can be of any service to you in that way. I shall charge you the same interest as I get at the bank – viz *nil.*

Tea at 6:30 tomorrow – but I shall probably see you at the B.M.

W.A.

Shaw's **argosies**, like those of Antonio in *The Merchant of Venice*, were long delayed in reaching port. He did not even have a bank account, so Archer served as his surrogate banker. When Shaw received payments from the journals, he and Archer would go to Archer's bank to make a deposit. Then Archer would withdraw the equivalent sum in cash or write an 'open cheque' for Shaw (e.g., Diaries 1: 139, 146, 219, 223, 244, 291, 297, 323). It is unclear how many years these financial arrangements operated, but Shaw did not open his first bank account until 5 November 1894 (Diaries 1: 1048, Weintraub's note). Thanks to the American and British royalties of £340 for *Arms and the Man*, Shaw finally became a participating member of the capitalist banking system in 1894 – eighteen years after his arrival in London.

8 / To William Archer 36 Osnaburgh St NW

12th December 1885

[ALS: BL 45296 ff 6–7; CL 1]

Archer began serving as The World*'s dramatic critic in March 1884. Then in November 1885, when the journal's art critic suddenly abandoned his position, the editor Edmund H. Yates (1831–94) urged Archer to take on this additional assignment. Reluctantly he agreed, but instead of signing the reviews 'W.A.', as* *he did for his theatre reviews, he credited the art criticism to 'F.B.' This was his private reference to Frederick Bayham, a character in* The Newcomes, *a satiric novel by William Makepeace Thackeray (1811–63) that represents the pretensions of British artists. From November 1885 through January 1886 Archer credited the reviews to 'F.B.' In the novel Bayham describes himself as a 'barrister ... but without business – a literary man, who can but seldom find an opportunity to sell the works of his brain' (chapter 12). Bayman's self-description apparently caught Archer's fancy because he too had studied the law, but did not practise it. And now he was making his living by selling the works of his brain as a suspect art critic. Feeling unqualified to write art reviews, he appealed to Shaw to join him on the visits to the galleries. They visited two galleries on 20 November, three galleries on 28 November, and two galleries on 5 December (Diaries 1: 125–9). Archer then wrote the weekly reviews by cribbing some of Shaw's comments. Given this dependence on Shaw, he decided to offer Shaw part of the payment received from Yates. These joint visits continued for two months. Then Yates gave Shaw the art criticism job (see letter of 12 February 1886).*

In 1945, when describing Yates to the biographer Hesketh Pearson (1887–1964), Shaw offered a misleading version of the Fred Bayham pseudonym. Shaw claimed, 'I had to write for him on fiction at fivepence a line, and I got very tired of it, and of having to sign myself F. B. – you know, Fred Bayham, a character in Thackeray's Newcomes' (Pearson Shaw: 442). Besides misappropriating Archer's pseudonym from 1885, Shaw confused his fiction reviewing for W.T. Stead at PMG *with his art reviewing at* The World. *His first art review on 4 February 1886 was signed Atlas, the pen-name for Yates (Diaries 1: 143). Most of his subsequent art reviews and notes for* The World *were unsigned, as were his music reviews for* DraRev *(February 1885–January 1886). Likewise, the miscellaneous music reviews in* PMG *(1886–8) and the regular book reviews in* PMG *(1885–8) were unsigned. Initially his music reviews for* The Star *appeared unsigned (April 1888–January 1889), but subsequent weekly music reviews for* The Star *were signed 'Corno di Bassetto' or 'C. di B.' (February 1889–May 1890). In turn, the weekly music reviews for* The World *were signed 'G.B.S.' (May 1890–August 1894). And his theatre reviews for the* SatRev *were also signed 'G.B.S.' (January 1895–May 1898).*

Your mind is in a thoroughly morbid condition with regard to the pictures. I return the cheque, and recommend more exercise and earlier hours. My 'moral ground' is this. If you are a competent critic, you do not need my assistance. If you are not competent, you are imposing on Yates, and I cannot share the proceeds of a fraud. This, I hope, is conclusive. If it is not, I can easily find a fresh position equally elevated and inexpugnable.

Robertson has sent me a ticket for his lecture. I shall look in there on my way to an appointment down Kensington way.

My lecture came off well enough; but I was sorry to miss you, as I laid down a formula for scientific criticism expressly on your account. It excited general loathing. Morris & Crane came, and spoke.

Furnivall has just revealed the Shelley Society to me. I thought it would be a tip; but have seen it in yesterday's P.M.

Damn this pen. I left my own at home (I am au Musée).

GBS

Edmund **Yates** (1831–94) served as editor of *The World* from 1874 until his death from a heart attack in May 1894. For Shaw, who prided himself on his pugilist skills, the best defence in an argument with Archer was a combative offence. He was **inexpugnable**, that is, unyielding and unconquerable, as he demonstrated with the clever punching and counterpunching in the exchange of letters on 12, 13, and 14 December. John Mackinnon **Robertson** (1856–1933), a close friend of Archer's from Edinburgh, was a dedicated rationalist and secularist who influenced Archer's own beliefs. After moving to London in 1885, he became an assistant editor for Annie Besant's *Our Corner*. He also wrote for the *National Reformer*, edited by the secularist and social reformer Charles Bradlaugh (1833–91). Robertson took over as editor in 1891 when Bradlaugh died. During the 1890s he continued to write for radical journals and was active in the South Place Ethical Society. Shaw lectured on 13 December 1885 at St George's Hall. On several occasions in 1885 Shaw and Archer discussed the possibility of writing a **scientific criticism** (e.g., Diaries 1: 110, 113). Both Shaw and Robertson were active in the New Shakspere Society, founded in 1873 by Dr Frederick James **Furnivall** (1825–1910), who also established societies on Shelley, Browning, Chaucer, Early English Texts, the English Ballad, and Philology. The **Shelley Society** was responsible for a private production on 5 May 1886 of *The Cenci* by Percy Bysshe Shelley (1792–1822). The Examiner of Plays, E.F. Smyth Pigott (1824–95), had refused a licence for the play because of its sexual subject matter. Both Archer and Shaw, though opposed to stage censorship, found fault with the play. They wrote negative reviews – Archer in *The World*, Shaw in *Our Corner*. Shaw's **appointment** in Kensington was with Vandeleur Lee (1831–86), who had taught singing to Shaw's mother and sister Lucy (1853–1920) in Dublin when he lived with the Shaw family (1866–73). After Lee moved to London, Mrs Shaw soon followed. Three years later in 1876, when Shaw moved to London, he acted as a ghostwriter for Lee's music column in *The Hornet*. Shaw later came to regret this duplicity. On 10 December Shaw gave a **lecture** on 'Art' at the Bedford Debating Society; he argued for a redistribution of wealth to break the capitalist model of buying and selling. Walter **Crane** (1845–1915) and William **Morris** (1834–96) were leaders of the British decorative art movement, and like Shaw embraced socialist ideas. Crane, a painter and illustrator, was also an art teacher and the director at the Royal College of Art. Besides his many illustrations in books (e.g., Spenser's *The Faerie Queen*), he contributed political cartoons to socialist journals. Morris, a designer, craftsman, poet, and novelist, was the proprietor of the Kelmscott Press. He wrote the novel *Sigurd the Volsung and the Fall of the Niblungs* (1876). Shaw attended several of Morris's socialist lectures during 1885, and dined some evenings at Kelmscott House, where he became charmed by Morris's daughter, May (1862–1938). Shaw wrote book reviews for the **P.M.** – that is, the *Pall Mall Gazette* – and on many days he bought a copy of the newspaper, as he recorded in his diary.

9 / To G. Bernard Shaw

[no address]
Sunday evg [13th December 1885]

[ALS: BL 50528 ff 34–9]

Unwilling to accept Shaw's reasons for rejecting the payment for the art articles, Archer rallied with this series of logical counter-punches. Perhaps unwisely, he declared that his argument was 'categorically' unanswerable. Such a claim, of course, was an open invitation to Shaw, who delivered his own counter-punches in the following letter.

My dear Shaw

I fled from Mrs. Besant this evening; & in any case I'd just as soon put in writing my opinion of your folly in the matter of this cheque.

I am *not* a competent critic of art, and I dont believe for a moment that you could appreciably help me to become one. Yates does not want a competent critic of art; what he wants is a man competent to write about art in a particular fashion, and that, with your help, I apparently am. Therefore I am not imposing upon Yates. I hope this is conclusive.

You may say that I do not require your aid to write about art as Yates wants; but surely I'm the best judge of that. If you took the trouble to read what I do write you would see that every second idea is yours, while I can assure you that even the ideas which are my own would not occur to me if you were not there. I dont mean to say that I should be absolutely incompetent to grub up anything to say if I went to a picture gallery alone, but my work would be heavy and labored, and would be produced at the cost of such exertion and ennui to myself that the waste of tissue involved would be most inadequately paid at £4 an article instead of £2. Besides your refusal of this cheque is an absolute breach of contract. On the day when Yates proposed the matter to me, I spoke to you about it, asked if you would agree in the meantime to come with me to the galleries, saying that we would 'share the spoils' (my *ipsissima verba*) & speculating upon the possibility of retiring from the thing altogether & getting you shoved in in my place. I assure you that if you had then rejected this proposal I should in all probability have written to Yates & declined the job. When I spoke of 'sharing the spoils' the idea in my mind was to halve them; but I now see that so long as I do the actual writing this would be an unfair division, & the proportion represented by the enclosed cheque seems to me to be the fair one. You must surely see that I cannot possibly occupy your time by dragging you round these galleries & sucking your brains at the same time without sharing with you the results of what is strictly a collaboration. As I have undertaken absolutely to give the thing its literary form I cant, without laying the matter before Yates, ask you to do the actual writing of the articles; but if I could and if you wanted me to go with you to the galleries & give you what ideas occurred to me, I assure you I should stick to a third of the proceeds with the utmost alacrity. I am sincerely anxious to shuffle out of the business altogether & hand it over to you; but I must have some reasonable excuse for making the proposal to Yates and of course the longer I hold on the more influence is my recommendation of you likely to have. If you continue to behave like a damned ass in this matter you will put me in a very unpleasant hole indeed. I utterly shrink from going alone to these confounded shows – besides making my writing about them poor & pointless it will make my life a burden to me; and I utterly decline to take you with me except on sharing terms. So be a good fellow & stow your logic (which is not logic but turns on an ambiguity in the word 'critic') and fulfil your engagement – else the next time we make an arrangement about anything I'm damned if I wont put in black & white & have it stamped at Lamerset House. The only excuse I could accept would be that you can occupy your time more profitably (pecuniarily) in other ways, in which case it would simply become a question of the market value of your time, & I should have to offer better terms.

I am going to Aveling's show on Tuesday but dont want my second ticket. Will you use it? or have you already a place?

I had the pleasure of making Mr Edmund Barnard's acquaintance yesterday. He is in want of work and prepared to write about anything from any point of view, but draws the line at attacking the infallibility of the Pope!

Yours cogently, unanswerably, irrefutably, categorically and above all sincerely

W. Archer

Annie **Besant's** *Our Corner* not only featured Shaw's monthly article on the arts but also the serialization of two of his novels: *The Irrational Knot* (1885–7) and *Love among the Artists* (1887–8). Mrs Besant supported various social and political causes, and became a colleague of Shaw's in the new Fabian Society. In 1887 she proposed a common-law marriage to Shaw; he refused. In 1889, turning away from secular causes, she embraced Theosophy, and in 1907 served as president of the Theosophical Society. She later moved to India. The meaning of the Latin phrase **ipsissima verba** is 'the very words.' **Lamerset House** certified various kinds of personal documents, from birth to death. Edward Bibbins **Aveling** (1851–98) was a journalist and an occasional playwright (under the pseudonym of Alec Nelson). Shaw and Archer attended the performance of Aveling's play *Beeton's* on 15 December. Like Shaw, Aveling wrote for DraRev in 1885, before Palmer ran out of funds. Divorced from his first wife, he lived with Karl Marx's daughter Eleanor (1855–88), who became his common-law wife. With Samuel Moore, he translated volume one of Karl Marx's *Das Capital*, which Shaw reviewed in the *National Reformer* (7, 14, and 21 August 1887). In 1906 Shaw used Aveling as a partial model for the character of Louis Dubedat in *The Doctor's Dilemma.* In his 1911 biography of Shaw, Archibald Henderson (1877–1963) claimed that Aubrey Beardsley was the model for Dubedat. In response to Henderson's biography, Shaw published a critical and corrective letter in the *Morning Post* on 2 May 1911 (Biblio 2: 644). Edmund **Barnard**, whoever he was, briefly entered and quickly disappeared from Archer's world.

10 / To William Archer

36 Osnaburgh St NW
14th December 1885

[ALS: BL 45296 ff 8–9; CL 1]

Shaw's diary for 14 December offered a condensed version of this letter: 'Archer's cheque back again. Again returned it. Took tea at Archer's' (Diaries 1: 131). Despite Shaw's refusal to accept any payments, he continued to join Archer at the gallery showings on 31 December, 7 January, 23 January, and 30 January. What Shaw failed to mention in this exchange of letters is that he used these gallery visits to produce monthly articles on the arts for Annie Besant's Our Corner *(Biblio 2: C174, C197). For example, he received £3/6/3 from Besant on 26 January (Diaries 1: 141). So, despite his claim here of seeing the galleries without the need of 'writing the articles,' he did in fact evaluate the paintings. Also, despite his refusal of a payment from Archer, he accepted two mysterious payments from Archer of £1 on 15 January and £2 on 22 March (Diaries 1: 139, 155). He offered no explanation for these two payments, but if they were not for art criticism in* The World, *they may have covered Archer's credit and debit scheme for the notices that Shaw had published in Palmer's* Dramatic Review *(see letter of 12 November 1885). (For a psychological interpretation of Shaw's refusal, see Holroyd 1: 139–40.)*

I rereturn the cheque, and if you rerereturn it, I will rererereturn it again ('again' being here, as you justly observe, tautological). The considerations which induce me to do so follow in no particular order.

1. The idea of one man sucking another's brains is a depraved individualist idea. No man has a right of property in the ideas of which he is the mouthpiece. The law does not permit a man to patent a discovery, but only an invention concreted as a machine. The ideas of your criticism are mere natural raw material which neither of us is entitled to monopolize. You have only to imagine Norman, Morley, Lowe, Robertson, Dibdin, and myself sending in our claims whenever we detect in your writings an idea to which our conversation with you led up (and which therefore would never have occurred to you without us), to perceive the frightful and anarchical impossibilism to which your proposition of private property in ideas – especially critical ideas – must lead in practice. If I am to be paid for what I suggested to you, for example, the painters must clearly be paid for what they suggested to me. This is the *reductio ad absurdum.* The devil has presented you with a depraved conception disguised as conscientiousness.

For what, then, are you to be paid by Yates? For the ideas in your article? Certainly not. Only for the skilled labour of producing with hand, ink, and pen, a certain instrument for the utilization and distribution of these ideas. The reading world must feed you whilst you write for it. *Must,* mind you, solely because you wouldnt write the article if they didnt, whereas you would think away all the same, pay or no pay. But they must also feed you whilst you are going through the galleries, because otherwise you would never darken their doors. Ergo, you say, they must also feed me whilst I walk through the galleries. But they do not; they pay only one man's time – yours. Yet I go. Observe: I am under no external compulsion to go, yet I do so. Obviously then, it pays me to go without direct remuneration; and for me under these circumstances to take the cheque would be to pocket a bonus to which I am not entitled, and to shorten your life by one half. The latter point is too obvious to need detailed explanation. You are, by the RicardoLassalle iron law, working at a bare subsistence wage. For the two hours (say) you spend in a gallery, you only get two hours subsistence. Of this you give me one hour, although I am already provided for (as shown by my willingness to come for nothing apparently). Consequently you can only support life for one hour instead of two for which you have been provisioned by society & Yates. Therefore the division shortens your life by one half, whereas I, having half as much again as I need, suffer from surrepletion.

As it is, I have the advantage of seeing the galleries for nothing without the drudgery of writing the articles. I do not like to lose the record of the art life, and yet going to a gallery by myself bores me so much that I let the Academy itself slip last year, and should have done so this year but for your bearing me thither one day. (I perceive your manly form stooping at the catalogue desk, and moving along as if your hat had blown off and were making three or four knots before a gentle breeze). If you decline to utilize your complimentary tickets in future for my benefit, you will be perpetrating an act – or series of acts – of wanton and fiendish malignity. Pray observe that I am not actuated by motives of generosity. You are much better off than I am, and any pecuniary consideration on my part for you would be senseless. I perceive the proposed arrangement to be unjust, and therefore I am proof against your special pleading that you are placed in 'an unpleasant hole' by my obduracy. Were you to be placed naked in a blast furnace, my decision would be the same. *Fiat justitia: ruat coelum.* (Latin!)

Here you approach in person, evidently resolved to confer – at least it is like your footstep and shadow. 'Hallo &c'

GBS

Sir Henry **Norman** (1858–1939) and Charles **Morley** served on the editorial staff of the PMG. Archer's close friendships with John Mackinnon **Robertson**, Edward Rimbault Vere **Dibdin**, and Robert William **Lowe** (1853–1902) began in Edinburgh, before he moved to London. In 1877 Lowe and Archer published a pamphlet, *The Fashionable Tragedian: A Criticism*, which derided the acting of Henry Irving (1838–1905). When threatened by a possible lawsuit, they destroyed the copies of the first edition and then published a toned-down second edition. By the 1890s Lowe had established himself as a distinguished historian of British theatre. David **Ricardo** (1772–1823), an English economist, developed 'Ricardo's Law' on wages, rent, and profit. Ferdinand **Lassalle** (1825–64), a German social theorist, derived his theory of the 'iron law of wages' from Ricardo. Unlike Karl Marx (1818–83), Lassalle supported a class-based society. At the same time that Shaw discovered Marx, he also read Ricardo and Lasselle on economics and social theory. But by the late 1880s Shaw modified or rejected key aspects of the theoretical ideas of Ricardo and Lasalle. (For a summary see Holroyd 1: 174–82.) The word **surrepletion** is Shaw's coinage for excessive repletion. The Royal **Academy of Art** held an annual show of contemporary painters. The phrase ***Fiat justitia ruat coelum*** means 'Let justice be done though the heavens should fall.' The several parenthetical inserts of words, phrases, clauses, and sentences are all by Shaw.

11 / To G. Bernard Shaw [no address]
Tuesday mg [12th February 1886]

[APCS: BL 50528 f 41]

In his diary entry for 2 February 1886, Shaw reports that 'Archer proposes that I shall take over The World *art criticism.' Archer urged Shaw to write 'a specimen article' that he could show to Yates. Two days later Shaw produced a review of the shows at the three galleries that he and Archer had visited on 30 January. The unsigned review, 'What the World Says,' was shown to Yates, who then published it on 10 February (Biblio 2: 533). (It is retitled 'Landscapes and Meissoniers' in Weintraub: 73.) Impressed by the review – and by Archer's advocacy for Shaw – Yates decided to offer the art criticism post to Shaw. On 11 February he wrote to Archer: 'Your friend – I have most idiotically forgotten his name – seems to understand his business, & I would be glad, as you wish it, to transfer the art criticism to him. Here is a crumb, to commence with.' Archer included Yates's note and the payment in this letter to Shaw on 'Tuesday mg.' Archer had achieved his aim, as he reported later to his brother: 'Shaw didn't know much more about painting than I, but he thought he did, and that was the main point' (C. Archer: 135).*

Shaw served as the art critic for The World *from February 1886 until December 1889. Six decades later, looking back on this moment, Shaw proudly wrote: 'When William Archer delegated to me a job as a critic of painting which had been pushed on him, and [for] which he was quite unqualified, I rose like a rocket. My weekly feuilletons on all the fine arts in succession are still readable after sixty years' (SSS: 116).*

Yates has apparently a stranger sense of humor than I credited him with – or else a more vivid appreciation of your critical genius. I am very glad, even at the cost of my reputation as a prophet; but don't, for heaven's sake, presume too much on this initial triumph.

By the by[e], what have Ferdinand & Isabella to do with *Measure for Measure*? Shade of Shakespeare! art thou confounded with Prescott.

WA

Ferdinand II (1452–1516) and **Isabella I** (1451–1504), who married in 1469, were king and queen of Spain, as well of Sicily and Naples. In 1492, besides supporting the voyage of Christopher Columbus to the new world, they instituted the Inquisition in Spain in order to create a unified Catholic country. This campaign led to the expelling of all Jews (1492) and Moors (1502) who would not convert. Archer's statement on ***Measure for Measure*** refers to a talk Shaw delivered on 12 February at the New Shakspere Society. Shaw mistakenly identified the character of Claudio as Ferdinand. Despite Archer's comment, he repeated the mistake six weeks later in an art review in which he described William Holman Hunt's 'Scene from *Measure for Measure*.' Shaw saw the Hunt exhibition on 16 March; the review was published in *The World* on 24 March. William Hickling **Prescott** (1796–1859), American historian, wrote *The History of the Reign of Ferdinand and Isabella* (1837), which was well received. He also wrote histories of Mexico (1843), Peru (1847), and Philip II of Spain (1855–8, 3 vols, unfinished).

12 / To G. Bernard Shaw

[no address]
26th March 1886; Friday

[APCS: BL 50528 f 42]

Beginning on 28 March and continuing for nine separate days in April between the 3rd and 25th, Shaw corrected proof pages for Archer's About the Theatre *(Diaries 1: 156–64). They met on several occasions in April to discuss Shaw's suggestions. In addition to these comments on the book, Shaw apparently looked over the proofs for Archer's study of Richard Wagner's operas. When travelling in Europe in 1882 Archer had attended Wagner productions in Munich and elsewhere. He drafted a Wagner manuscript in 1883 and 1884, and found a publisher by 1886. But he never published the book. Shaw, who had initially read the Wagner manuscript in February 1885 (Diaries 1: 61), may have discouraged Archer from publication. The manuscript and page proofs have disappeared.* About the Theatre; Essays and Studies *was published in late 1886 by T. Fisher Unwin; it included essays on the problem of censorship of the British stage, the ethics of theatrical criticism, and the 'advancing' qualities of British playwriting. None of the contemporary playwrights warranted strong praise, but Archer expressed measured support for W.S. Gilbert and two young writers, H.A. Jones and A.W. Pinero.*

As I have rolled your log will you help me to plane mine? I send you herewith a small installment of the proofs of my great work on wh I beg that you will make (in pencil) any remarks that occur to you as to orthography, etymology, syntax, prosody, matter, form, style, sentiments, opinions; in short anything that occurs to you. I wd specially call your attention to the marginalia (in red ink); any improvement you can suggest in the way of making them shorter, pithier or more to the point will be gratefully considered. Mrs A. is grateful for your note – she has not an accordion to dispose of at present, but if a tambourine wd suit you perhaps you and Master J.A. might do a 'swap.'

W.A.

Shaw's **note** to Mrs Archer is lost. Archer may have been referring to his younger brother James as **Master J.A.** Shaw first met James in September 1885.

13 / To William Archer 36 Osnaburgh St NW
16th April 1886

[ALS: BL 45296 ff 10–11; CL 1]

Shaw continued to proofread pages for Archer's About the Theatre.

All the points about the actor are wrong. As you recapitulate them on Slip 57 they conflict with the following facts.

1. Acting destroys morbid self consciousness by making the actor a master of the science of appearances. Just as the man is less *morbidly* self conscious than the youth, so is the actor than the man. 2. Amounts only to the fact that the actor must be particularly careful not to make an ass of himself. Expectation of applause is not constantly present to a good actor, because such a one puts a lot of work into his acting, and this work keeps his attention fully occupied. You cannot do two things at once. If you are thinking of the applause you are either not acting, or acting mechanically, like Diderot's couple who interpolated a private quarrel between their lines. An actor may of course be much mortified if, after he has done his work thoroughly, the audience do not seem to appreciate it – so may any other artist. The truth is that 'the somnambulism of genius' (which is bosh) does not leave room for eager expectation of applause which you suppose to leave no room for anything else. No 3 is not a bit more true of acting than of painting, poetry, composition, or anything else. The same remark applies to No 4. An unappreciated actor can persist in taking theatres and offering himself to the public just as I used to persist in writing novels and offering them to the publishers. It is true that unless he can educate the public to accept him within fifteen years, his chance will be gone for ever; but as a matter of fact every man of genius gains his verdict within that time unless his views are so exceptional as to make him hopelessly dependent on posterity in which case he is a monstrous premature birth. 5. The supply of first places on the stage is not less in proportion to the aspirancy than in other professions named by you at the top of slip 57. You mention sculptors: go and talk to any sculptor about the commission for the Gordon statue or the Wellington statue. There are a dozen opportunities of playing Hamlet for one PRA ship, or chance of a London statue or public building of the first magnitude, to say nothing of frescoes and all artistic work above

the level of cabinet pictures. And surely there are heaps of chances for cabinetpicture actor & actresses.

As to Shakespere, I suspend judgment until the argument is fully unrolled. But I contend that our feeling that blank verse is artificial and flat is based on blank verse that *is* artificial & flat, or that is unskilfully uttered so as to appear so. The ruinousness of Shakespere is only an excuse for bad performances. Given one of his tearing good plays acted and mounted as adequately as The Scrap of Paper and success is as certain in one case as in the other. But it is ten times as hard to get a decent performance of 'As You Like It' as of 'A Scrap of Paper': hence a London manager is ten times safer with a play of Sardou's than with a play of Shakespere's. This is the sort of thing that needs saying from time to time. You spar with the actors & Shakespere in a highly scientific manner; but it seems to me that you do not lead off enough, except in your bout with the Censor. The public needs to be roused by some destructive as well as evasive fighting.

In haste
GBS

PS Never mind my pencil nicks on the proof. There is only one to be attended to – that about 'resulting from' which I take to be a tortology.

Besides editing the famous *Encyclopédie*, Denis **Diderot** (1713–84) wrote philosophical dialogues and plays. His essay on acting, *Le pardoxe sur le comédien* (1773, published in 1830), was translated into English by Walter H. Pollock (1850–1926) in 1883 and published by Unwin. It presented the scene of private quarreling between two actors as they delivered lines in *Le dépit amoureux* by Molière (Jean-Baptiste Poquelin, 1622–73). (See letter of 4 September 1888 for an expanded debate between Archer and Shaw on Diderot's *Paradox*.) Counter to Shaw's statement here that the actor 'cannot do two things at once,' both Archer and Shaw concluded in 1888 that both the actor and the spectator are quite capable of dual or double consciousness during a performance. Statues of the Duke of **Wellington**, Arthur Wellesley (1769–1852), were commissioned after the defeat of Napoleon's army at Waterloo; statues of Charles George **Gordon** (1833–85) began to appear soon after his death at Khartoum in 1885. Artists sometimes received a commission or fellowship tendered by the **PRA** (President of the Royal Academy). Victorien **Sardou** (1831–1908), the skilful playwright of *Les pattes de mouche*, translated as ***A Scrap of Paper***, wrote often for Sarah Bernhardt (1845–1923), including the popular *La Tosca*, *Fédora*, *Thermidor*, and, with Émile Moreau (1852–1922), *Madame Sans-Gêne*. In the 1890s, when Bernhardt visited London regularly, both Archer and Shaw wrote reviews of her performances. In his *Saturday Review* criticism Shaw dismissed Sardou's plays as 'Sardoodledom.' Whenever possible in his publications, Archer launched a **bout with the Censor** – a campaign against stage censorship. Shaw's coinage of **tortology**, on the model of tautology, teased Archer for using the obfuscating discourse of lawyers.

14 / To Frances E. Archer 36 Osnaburgh St NW
12th January 1887

(ALS: CUL)

In 1886 Frances Archer wrote a romantic novel about a young woman and her suitors. She asked Shaw to read the manuscript. On 12 and 13 January he wrote this long evaluative letter to her (Diaries 1: 233). The immediate and primary significance of Shaw's long letter derives from what it expressed about his ideas – both basic and idiosyncratic – on literary diction, dialogue, descriptive detail, and the 'immense subject of punctuation.' Here in one letter Shaw offered a compact lecture on grammar, punctuation, and style. The letter is also significant in a less obvious way because it may have contributed to some changes in the relationships between Shaw and Mrs Archer, Shaw and Archer, and even Archer and Mrs Archer. These incidental developments emerged slowly over the years.

Because of his blunt and sometimes harsh criticism, Shaw may have unsettled Mrs Archer, and thus contributed to her decision to drop the project. The novel was never published; the manuscript has disappeared. Did she show this letter to Archer? Did they discuss it? Did he side with her or Shaw? There is no direct record of how the Archers responded, and apparently Shaw and the Archers remained on good terms. Over the days following Shaw's critique he remained a regular visitor at the Archers' flat on John St. On 15 January he showed up for tea, and on 16 January he returned for the reading by H.A. Jones of his new play Hard Hit. *He also came for tea on 25 January. Four weeks later, on 8 February, the three of them went to the theatre together to see Pinero's farce* Dandy Dick; *afterwards they returned to the flat for dinner. On such occasions Mrs Archer and Shaw sometimes played duets at the piano. However unsettling the letter may have been for Mrs Archer, her relationship with Shaw showed no noticeable changes – at least during the short term. If we were tempted to make conjectures about possible tension over the critique, we might consider an entry in Shaw's diary for 5 February: 'Went to Archer's and had tea there. He thinks* The Irrational Knot *[Shaw's second novel] is not good enough to republish' (Diaries 1: 239–40). Was this a delayed case of tit for tat? Probably not, for neither Archer nor Shaw settled scores in petty ways. Neither of them went roundabout. They were open and direct in their communications with one another. Besides, as Shaw wrote in his entry on 5 February: 'I agreed.'*

In sum, though Shaw's rejection of the romantic novel did not cause any immediate distancing between himself and Mrs Archer, the critique hardly enhanced their relationship. And over time this incident, when placed within the context of subsequent events and conditions (as described in the Introduction), may have been an early contributing factor in the distance between them. It may also have served as one of several disillusioning episodes that accumulated in an increasingly unromantic marriage.

Dear Mrs. Archer

I have at last made time to go carefully through your MS; and I advise you to do the same without loss of time. When you have put in a few stops, and made the diction as accurate and logical as you know how, then write another. Correct that; and write a third, and, if you have patience enough, a fourth. By that time you will have sufficient command of your ideas and the art of expressing them, to put your first story into artistic shape. You might get a success of indulgence even now by trading on your own naïveté; but I will assume that you are strong-souled enough to disdain this. Besides, the naïveté is not true naïveté: it is ineptitude. As some American critic put it. You are a knowledgeable person; but you cant yet write worth a cent. This, however, is a sign of originality. You will have to make your style to fit your ideas. People with readymade styles have their ideas also readymade – by somebody else. You have variety of construction already – more than you know how to punctuate.

Your weakest point at present is your inability to see all round your scenes. In a dialogue, there are two things to be dealt with simultaneously. 1. The personal feelings of the people towards one another. 2. The subject of their conversation. No. 2 determines what they are to say, No. 1 how they are to say it. You do not forget No. 2 – no one ever does; but it often puts No. 1 out of your head for a moment; and in that moment you become purely argumentative, and betray yourself by slipping into literary terms of expression. On p. 111, an agitated father says to an agitated daughter – 'as you justly observe,' which is quite unnatural. In real life he would most likely say 'Why, you minx, you said yourself just now, &c.' In going through the dialogue, you will find other bits of the same sort, and each of them will mark a place where the human interest has slipped away from you. Grip will only come with practice and wisdom. It is the quality of qualities in a writer; and you will be astonished at how awful and earnest you will become when you begin to feel it securely.

Your attention also wanders to insignificant external details. Never describe anything that an intelligent reader would infer. When you want to convey that a man lets himself into his house, dont say that he mounted the steps; paused on the platform between them and the threshold; put his hand in his pocket; drew out a key; inserted it in the keyhole; turned it firmly from right to left; and pressed against the ponderous door, which swung back on its hinges at his touch. This would hardly be worse than your description of how Rivington, before he began his sketch of Edith, got out of handshaking distance. There are other instances, particularly concerning smiles, lifted eyebrows, and the like. *Rule.* Never describe a normal action. Only describe such as are peculiar to the speaker, or which one would not infer as a matter of course from the situation. For instance, '"You dont say so!" she exclaimed, opening her eyes in surprise' is bad; but '"You dont say so," she cried, turning several somersaults in her astonishment,' is necessary, because no one could infer the somersault from the speech, as they could the eye-opening. And above all, be careful not to make your people go through gestures and grimaces which are not observed, but only evolved by the amateur-actor process. Staggering, sobbing, swooning, turning deadly pale, raising the head nobly – beware of these.

There are certain comparisons that occur to us when we want to describe ideals or dream figures, but are never suggested by people whom we really know. You write on p. 13 of a woman with 'a smile like sunshine on the sea.' That strikes her unreal at once: no human face is like the sea. A sunshine smile is admissible, but not sunshine on the sea. You would never describe Braekstad or any real person in such terms. *Rule* – dont introduce people as ornaments only.

On p. 229 there is a most desperately shallow account of the rector. The few accidental circumstances you throw together do give easily satisfied people a notion of a sort of country parson; but there are fifty different men whom they would fit equally. Only walking gentlemen and lay figures should be treated in this way. You must describe the souls of the real people. You, in this instance, have already made a fair first attempt at a bit of his soul; and to descend from this to a mere Mellish pastiche is almost worse than if the rector were pastiche all through.

Edith in one or two places is too frank. I doubt whether it is possible for a young woman speaking to an almost strange man to free herself as completely as she does from all influences except that of her intellectual aspirations. However, you know as much about this as I do.

On p. 155 and thereabouts, it seems to me that the visitors go too straight to the point. The men declare their designs on Edith's hand before the rector has time to ask them how they do. It is in places like this that bits of comedy are indispensable. Mere padding to break the news will not do.

Misters Diapason & Reed, the organ builders, of course destroy all the illusion, and reduce the affair to the level of farce. I am astonished at you. What would you say if I were to rechristen a celebrated work of mine 'The Adventures of Hammer Hardfist and Miss Moneybags'? Diapason & Reed is franker than Peddle and Sticker or Pipes Clef but it is all the more insufferable.

You will find some terribly tangled and clumsy sentences here and there. On p. 96 there is, in the first paragraph, a labyrinth of imagining and mistaking and supposing and desiring and approving, to which the 'I coulds' and 'you coulds' and 'you could that I coulds' are hardly sufficient here. And you really must not make people say 'You can imagine therefore that the matter of your share in this conversation has been a heavy blow to me.' Revising this at yearly intervals, you will see it evolve in this way: 'You can imagine therefore that your share in this conversation has been a heavy blow to me.' 'You can imagine therefore that the conversation has been a heavy blow to me.' 'What you have just said has been a heavy blow to me.' 'What you have said has been a heavy blow to me.' 'You have hit me hard, Edith.' 'I cant help feeling disappointed, Edith, after building so much on your companionship.' Observe how the process is one of merely husking down the unsatisfactory sentence, until the right word – 'disappointment' – comes instead of the hackneyed metaphor of the 'heavy blow,' when the utterance expands freely. From the 'completely stunned' at the beginning of the speech to the heavy blow at the end, the metaphor weighs on the expression in a dull and brutal manner which adds a little to the idea of Roger's character as you unsympathetically wish to paint him, but which makes the reader feel like Clarence at the bottom of the sea. The mixed metaphors about refreshment, asphyxiation, marrow, and the skeleton on p. 104 are overbold. You must contrive to explain about the innocent Edith's guilty-looking blush on p. 108 without discoursing on foreign motives and inadequate minds. It is impossible for a reader to maintain cordial relations with an author who comes [at] it in this manner: 'I have not an amount of regard for him which would warrant &c.' is a very bad version of 'I have not enough regard for him to &c.' Beware of this word 'amount.' It implies a mass heaped up by successive increments and not merely quantity or degree, for which it is so often misused. Why do you put 'energy of intelligence' for 'intelligence' [which of course implies energy] on p. 146, and 'full extent of difficulty' for 'full difficulty' on p. 192? And dont you think 'If you dont wish your friends at Bucknall to know where you are' just a little more human than 'if you are still desiring to preserve your location unknown to your friends at Bucknall'? p. 215. Just read p. 217, and see how absurdly the young woman goes on about 'no intention of instituting a search' instead of saying 'I thought they had given me up by this time' or the like. On p. 128 'hearty human laugh' is a second-hand phrase. It should be 'hearty laugh,' or else you must find the right word for 'human,' which is nonsense. You must never adopt a readymade *fancy* in expression: it is plagiarism. And be careful of the word 'singularly' (230). It is a worn-out literary affectation, except of course when it is literally exact. 'A clammy dread gathering about the heart' is one of your strokes of genius; but it a risky mixture of the abstract & the concrete (129). 'Dividing his peregrinations into districts' (225) is bad. A walk in London is no more a peregrination than five minutes is an epoch. Calling a man 'a plague of vacillation in their triangular intercourse of friendship' (123) is very extreme.

Always select the most differentiated expression you can find. For instance, you can call cheese subsistence, or, better still, food, or fare, or wherewithal for the inner man (a vile phrase, but better than subsistence); but the shortest word that leaves nothing uncertain as to the nature of the food is 'cheese.' Windbags on the platform always talk of houses as dwellings, of Macbeth as 'the works of Shakespere,' the French as 'Europeans,' and so on. You also sometimes seek refuge in the remoter categories, and become cumbrous instead of crisp in consequence. If you revise with an eye to getting closer to your exact meaning, you will find plenty of words to alter.

On page 205 you say that second hand goods do not come under the same conditions as new ones. This is sophistry on the part of Mr Reeves. Was it so intended? On 207 you mention Stevenson's 'Child's Garden of

Verses.' I respectfully suggest that logrolling should be confined to periodical literature. I am not clear that the alliteration of Reeves, Rogers, & Rivington is, on the whole, advisable. The delegation [?] ought to be beyond the three Rs. However, I am doubtful on the point. Perhaps you are right.

I now come to the immense subject of punctuation. Your style, unlike W A's, requires all the stops. On p. 102 you have this sentence. 'Forgive me, and make all allowance – I see you do – for my sorrow.' Here the comma should be a semi-colon, thus. 'Forgive me; and &c. A comma would be proper in such a sentence as 'Forgive me, and Jack, and Bill, and all poor sinners this night.' You will see the vital distinction by comparing. In the one you ask a person to do two separate things: in the other you ask him to do the same thing to several objects. On p. 151 you have 'I am not sure, it depends on a good many things,' which should be 'I am not sure: it depends &c.' On p. 115 you have 'You are one individual, I am another. You cannot compress me into your mould, I must be free. I must go, I can stay no longer.' All three commas should be colons. They are six distinct sentences; but they are grouped in twos. A colon stands between the members of a group of sentences. But when the sentences are less independent – where one turns on the other or is modified by it, the second one begins always with a but, an and, or a for. In that case, put a semi-colon. For instance – 'Her hair was red; she looked like a beacon in the summer night.' 'Her hair was red; but she was evidently in the habit of dipping it in cochineal.' 'Her hair was red; and I believe its color was natural.' 'Her hair was red, and naturally so.' Another use of the semicolon may be illustrated by a passage from p. 77. 'He supervised his children's education himself, directed his wife in all matters, great and small, and left no stone unturned to secure &c.' Now the comma before 'great' is right; but evidently then the other two must be wrong. They should be semi-colons. If you omit 'great and small', the commas will pass well enough; and you will find plenty of precedents for the misuse of them; but they are wrong, for all that. For instance, 'He took a dagger, twisted like a corkscrew, and stabbed himself' means that he stabbed himself with a corkscrew-shaped dagger. But 'He took a dagger; twisted like a corkscrew; and stabbed himself' means that he twisted himself about like a corkscrew before stabbing himself with an ordinary dagger. On p. 108, Edith says 'You are mistaken Papa.' This means that the rector is known as 'mistaken Papa' just as Dryden was known as 'glorious John.' On page 111 'Nor ever will he by me father' is only an Irish way of saying 'Nor ever will he by my father.' You should write, 'You are mistaken, Papa', and 'Nor ever will he by me, father.' But there are other forms of the same difficulty. Here are illustrations.

Mama: may I eat this volume of Goethe?

No, Tommy, you may not.

Would it make me as wise as Goethe, mamma?

Perhaps so, Tom; but it would also give you indigestion.

I don't care: I mean to have a try, anyhow.

Tommy: put down that book this instant. Do you hear?

I hear you, mamma; but I cannot forget that knowledge is power &c &c &c &c

Here you have the three stops used with the name.

If the last of a group of sentences is linked by an and, use semi-colons instead of colons, in order to forewarn the reader as to the management of his voice. Thus,

'The rose is red: the violet's blue: white is the lily.

'The rose is red; the violet's blue; the lily's white; and so are you.

You will soon pick up all this; but I dwell on it in detail because I know you will have to struggle against most baleful domestic influences in the matter of punctuation.

This is all I can tell you – all I know about our trade that is communicable. Dont waste time bothering about publication; but start another book as soon as you can; and keep hammering away until you have learned the business in the only possible way – by practice. After all, it is easier than pianoforte playing. It will aid in ten thousand pound copyrights, rescue of the eminent critic from the imminent abyss of journalism, and endowment of my biographer on a scale sufficient to enable him to donate his life to the literary monument which he is destined to raise.

Excuse prolixity & illegibility,
GBS

A **walking gentleman** was a character type or 'line of business' in a theatre company. In stock companies, such as the travelling companies of the eighteenth and nineteenth centuries, supporting actors specialized in lines of business and had the appropriate costumes for these stereotypical roles (e.g., low comedian, courtesan). The term **Mellish pastiche** may be a reference to the character Bob Mellish who is in Shaw's novel *Cashel Byron's*

Profession. Both of the Archers had recently read the boxing novel. This **celebrated work** was serialized in a magazine called *To-Day* from April 1885 to March 1886; it was then published by the Modern Press in March 1886. Robert Louis [originally Lewis] Stevenson (1850–94) published ***A Child's Garden of Verses*** in 1885. Upon reading Archer's anonymous review in the PMG, he wrote a one-sentence letter to the journal on 26 March 1885: 'Now *who* are you?' (BL 45295 f 59). Archer replied the following day, and thus began a friendship in correspondence between the two men during the last decade of Stevenson's life. John Dryden (1631–1700), who excelled in drama, satiric verse, and prose, was admired as '**glorious John**' by writers of the eighteenth century, including Joseph Addison (1672–1719) and Alexander Pope (1688–1744). Shaw's advice to Mrs Archer to **start another book** as soon as possible reflected his own experience with his five novels. This prompting became his standard advice for writers. In 1895, when Gilbert Murray (1866–1957) showed Shaw his play *Carlyon Sabib,* Shaw told him to not worry about revising it. Instead, he should 'write another and another; when you have written a dozen, you'll know ever so much more about it' (G. Murray, 'A Few Memories,' *Drama,* Spring 1951).

15 / To William Archer

29 Fitzroy Square W
4th October 1887

[ALS: BL 45296 ff 12–13; CL 1]

In 1884 Archer proposed that the two friends should write a play together that would be successful in the commercial theatre. He would provide the scenario, Shaw the dialogue. Archer derived the plot loosely from Émile Augiers's La Ceinture Dorée. *Over a period of eight years, from 1884 to 1892, this developing play – first called* The Way to a Woman's Heart, *then* Rhinegold, *and then the German* Rheingold *– would eventually become* Widowers' Houses, *Shaw's first play. He drafted two acts and the beginning of the third act in shorthand between August and November 1884 (Diaries 1: 33). On 25 August 1885 he copied 'out some of the drama I began last year' (Diaries 1: 106–7). Then on 3 September 1887, 'at Archer's suggestion,' Shaw began to transcribe and revise 'the play I began in 1884' (Diaries 1: 296). During September he fleshed out the early notes, producing in longhand two acts of the dialogue for five characters. At this point he asked Archer for more plot details because he had used up those that Archer had previously given him. On 1 October he appealed to Mrs Archer to convince Archer to try 'his luck with the drama in collaboration with me' (Diaries 1: 302). On 4 October 1887, the same day as this letter, Shaw 'finished copying the play and left the MS. at Archer's' (Diaries 1: 303).*

Two days later Shaw brought a newly copied draft of the two acts to a meeting with Archer. According to Shaw, they 'read the unfinished drama. A long argument ensued, Archer having received it with great contempt' (Diaries 1: 304). At the beginning of 1888, when Shaw wrote out the summary 'Notes' in his diary on his activities during 1887, he described the play and meeting of 6 October in this way: 'When it was finished (that is, the transcript, not the drama) Archer ridiculed it. I then dropped it, and left it with him, subsequently suggesting that he should give it to H. A. Jones, who might borrow a notion from it for a drama touching socialism' (Diaries 1: 228). On the failed collaboration, also see Shaw's letter to the actress Alma Murray (1854–1945) on 24 February 1888 (CL 1: 187–8). The description of the meeting had been modified somewhat, for he complained to her that Archer 'laughed the first [act] to scorn, and went to sleep in the middle of the second.'

I have left the first two acts of the Rheingold at John St, in longhand. They are not supposed to be complete; but they present a series of consecutive dialogues in which your idea is prepared and developed. The central notion is quite perfect; but the hallucinations with which you surrounded it are absent: you will have to put them in yourself. The bathing place is impossible; and I dont see how the long lost old woman is to be introduced without destroying the realism and freshness of the play: she would simply turn the thing into a plot, and ruin it. I think the story would bear four acts; but I have no idea of how it is to proceed. The peculiarity so far is that there is only one female character; and her social isolation is essential to the situation. Will you proceed either to chuck in the remaining acts, or provide me with a skeleton for them? You will perceive that my genius has brought the romantic notion which possessed you, into vivid contact with real life.

I should prefer the St. Jas's Theatre, with Mrs. Kendal as Blanche, Hare as Sartorius, Mackintosh as Lickcheese, Arthur Cecil as Cokane, and Kendal as Trench. Or Ellen Terry as Blanche, Wilson Barrett as Sartorius, George Barrett as Lickcheese, Irving as Cokane, and Gardiner as Trench. Harry Nicholls or Edward Terry might understudy Cokane; and Alma Murray might in extremity be allowed to play Blanche.

What is your opinion? I think, by the bye, that the title Rheingold ought to be saved for a romantic play. This is realism.

GBS

PS Never mind clerical errors: I have not read it over. And the details as to the hotel garden, the time &c, are all at sixes and sevens.

In this letter Shaw, who knew his Wagner, used the German **Rheingold** for the play's title, not the anglicized *Rhinegold.* But when Archer reviewed *Widowers' Houses* in 1992, he identified the early version as *Rhinegold.* This uncertainty over the correct title has continued in scholarship ever since. Shaw and his mother moved to **29 Fitzroy Square** on 21 March 1887, after having lived at 36 Osnaburgh St for five years. **St. Jas's Theatre** – that is, St James's Theatre – was managed by the Kendals and John Hare between 1879 and 1888. George Alexander took it over in 1891. Although *Rheingold* was supposed to be a popular play, especially as Archer conceived it, there was little possibility that it would appeal to Henry **Irving** and **Ellen Terry** (1847–1928). Ever since 1878, when Irving had established a partnership with Terry, the productions at the Lyceum Theatre usually featured historical melodramas and the works of Shakespeare – not contemporary plays such as *Rheingold.* Shaw's idea of Irving for the character of Cokane may have been a joke for Archer's benefit, for Shaw knew that Archer had criticized Henry Irving's acting in two earlier publications: a pamphlet written with Robert W. Lowe entitled *The Fashionable Tragedian: A Criticism* (1877) and a book entitled *Henry Irving: Actor and Manager* (1883). Also, given the disdain that Shaw expressed for the Kendals and John Hare in his letter of 11 March 1885, it is difficult to believe that he intended this realistic play for them. Even though the list was fanciful, it revealed that despite having written only a partial draft of the play, Shaw had already conceived the major characters that would appear five years later in *Widowers' Houses.* William **Mackintosh** (1855–1929) was an accomplished character actor. Arthur **Cecil** (1843–96) was a comic actor. **George Barrett** (1849–94) performed in the company of his brother **Wilson Barrett** (1846–1904). In February 1886 Shaw saw him play Tribulation Tizack in Henry Arthur Jones's *The Lord Harry.* **Harry Nicholls** (1852–1926) appeared regularly in Drury Lane productions. **Edward O'Connor Terry** (1844–1912) was a popular comic actor (but not part of the famous Terry family). Shaw may have seen him at the Gaiety Theatre, where the manager John Hollingshead (1827–1904) featured burlesque. Terry later managed his own theatre, which he called Terry's. There he staged Pinero's *Sweet Lavender* and other comedies. Edward W. **Gardiner** (1862–99) starred at Drury Lane; he was the husband of Kate Rorke (1866–1945), who would star in *Candida* in the 1904 production at the Court Theatre.

16 / To William Archer

[no address]
4th September 1888

[AMCU: BL 45296 ff 14–17]

No letters from October 1887 to September 1888 have survived. Perhaps, after the disagreements over Rheingold *in October 1887, the letter writing diminished for a while. Yet as the entries in Shaw's diaries verify, they continued to meet together regularly in the days, weeks, and months after Archer rejected the draft. Although they were no longer meeting several times a week, as had been the case in 1885 and 1886, they still met for tea, dinner, and the theatre on a regular basis. They also continued to read and edit the drafts of one another's articles. And on occasion Shaw played piano with Mrs Archer, and even took her to the theatre. The friendship was as solid as it had always been. Increasingly, however, Shaw's time was dedicated to making political lectures around the country. His social and political communities had enlarged rapidly. And he continued to meet with Jane (Jenny) Patterson (c.1840–1924), the Irish widow with whom he had been carrying on a sexual affair since 1885.*

During five days in September Shaw spent many hours 'reading proofs of Archer's book on Diderot's paradox and annotating it with my own theory of the matter' (Diaries 1: 408; also 412, 413, 414, 415). Masks or Faces? A Study in the Psychology of Acting *was published in late 1888. It was Archer's response to Denis Diderot's* Paradoxe sur le Comédien, *written in 1770; published in 1830. The English translation by Walter Herries Pollock had appeared in 1883. A year later Archer published 'Diderot's* Paradox of Acting*' in* The Theatre *(March 1884). Shaw and Archer had initially engaged in discussions on Diderot when Archer published* About the Theatre *(1886). See letter of 16 April 1886. Over a year later (18 and 20 October, 22 November 1887), they met to 'discuss Archer's series of questions on the Diderot Paradox about acting' (Diaries 1: 307, 317). In late 1887, after sending a series of questions about acting methods to actors in England and France, Archer collated their responses and wrote three articles entitled 'Anatomy of Acting,' which appeared in* Longman's Magazine *(January, February, and March 1888). He then expanded the articles into the book* Masks or Faces? *at the end of the year. Shaw offered marginal commentary on the page proofs, and then on the reverse side of the proofs he wrote out this separate message to Archer on emotions, acting, and audiences.*

Shaw challenged Archer's assertion in chapter 3 that 'Diderot's psychology of the audience is surely as false as his psychology of the actor.' In his critique of Diderot, Archer used the terms 'emotionalist' and 'anti-emotionalist' to describe how actors related to the characters they played, but he admitted that these 'clumsy' terms are inadequate. He insisted, though, that effective portrayals can be delivered by both types of actors – those who immersed themselves in the emotions of their characters and those who maintained or established distancing techniques. Both Shaw and Archer granted that emotions contribute to acting, but they rejected the idea that effective acting requires a psychological process of identification by the actor. They also rejected the idea that spectators maintained an illusionist belief in the representation. As Archer stated, 'the real paradox of acting … resolves itself into the paradox of dual consciousness' for the actor and the spectator (chapter 10).

Despite Shaw's reservations about Archer's ideas on acting and spectators, he cribbed some statements from Masks or Faces? *for a talk he delivered on 5 February 1889, 'Acting, By One Who Does Not Believe In It: Or the Place of the Stage in the Fool's Paradise of Art' (Dukore 1: 92–104).*

It seems to me that there is a confusion in your statement of the issue: You speak of emotionalist & anti-emotionalist & then imply that they are the same as illusionist and anti-illusionist. Now the truth of the matter is as plain as a pike staff. Emotions are not simple but compound. There is a nervous condition into which a man may be thrown, which I will call abstract (non-specific) emotion. It is generally set up by a specific cause – such as the death of a friend or relative – in which case it takes a specific object, and is called not emotion in the abstract but grief. The ordinary person, being no psychologist, instead of considering emotion as one thing which assumes various objects according to the various specific causes which produce it, believes that there are as many emotions as there are provocations of emotion, & speaks of 'the emotions,' separating grief, love, mirth, &c from one another abstractly as well as specifically. Just so did the savage, instead of recognizing the singleness of pain, and its independence of its accidental locality, speak of leg-woe, headwoe, toothache, bellyache, instead of correctly observing that he had pain (not *a* pain) in his head, or his belly, or elsewhere. Abstract emotion can be produced without external stimulus by the imagination, by whiskey (an external stimulant) and by other causes, including infection, probably. The emotion of the actor is abstract emotion. It is however by itself, senseless and uninteresting. It must become apparently specific, and play a part in a story, before it can interest an audience or elude them. Now this can only be contrived by deliberate simulation. Let us take a vulgar instance – bellyache. The actor's abstract emotion is to be made interesting to the audience by seeming to be produced in Napoleon by the consciousness that he is losing the battle of Waterloo because his stomach is out of order (the instance is historical: that was actually the case). The scene painter paints a tent: in it a camp bed is placed: men in uniform come and go: the roar of battle is initiated by suitable noises outside: bricks, supposed to be heated, are applied to the stomach of the actor, who groans and belches in a heartrending manner. Of all this nothing is genuine except the actor's emotion. That which seems to give it a specific character is all a sham; and the actor knows that it is a sham just as a child imitating a railway train, though it pleases itself with pretending, knows perfectly well that it is not an engine. Diderot, Dr. Johnson, & the rest were quite right in insisting that all this simulation could not produce an illusion in the actor, or that, if it did, he would instantly become ridiculous. Salvini is quite right in insisting that no illusion can be produced upon a keen audience, nor any effect upon their sympathies, except by an actor in a state of emotion. But if you miss the distinction, if you slip from emotion to illusion, from nervous condition to imitation of the effects of sensation, from experience to make-believe, from abstract to specific categories, then you will have confusion worse confounded. I entirely protest, by the bye, against your slighting the subject as unimportant. It is evidently a psychological investigation of the very primest moment. We are all actors. Act well your part, then all the world's a stage, &c &c &c.

Finally, since it is proven by experiment that abstract emotion does not destroy the power of simulation, the question is whether it heightens it or diminishes it. The rising of the curtain does not necessarily throw the actor into an emotional state. Nevertheless he must and does go through the whole simulative process, probably omitting no mechanical detail of his performance on the previous night, when he was, let us suppose, deeply affected. What will the effect be: Coquelin & Diderot say 'all the better': Salvini says 'all the more.' The weight of testimony seems to me to support Salvini. But it is conceivable that Coquelin's normal condition may be one of sufficient nervous sensibility to need no intensification for stage purposes. In that case he would obviously declare against 'emotion,' which implies *abnormal emotion.*

[no signature]

Dr Samuel **Johnson** (1709–84), poet, essayist, biographer, novelist, and travel writer, edited an edition of Shakespeare, wrote biographical and critical essays on the major English poets, and, perhaps most famously, published *A Dictionary of the English Language* (1755). He is also admired for his moral and critical essays. He rejected the idea of illusionism for actors and spectators because both of them know that 'the stage is only a stage' (*Preface to Shakespeare,* 1765). Constant-Benoît **Coquelin** (1841–1900), a French actor, was admired for his tragic performances. He performed with the Comédie-Française for years, then after 1886 toured in Europe and America. In the 1890s he directed the Théâtre de la Porte-Saint-Martin, where he starred in *Cyrano de Bergerac* by Edmond Rostand (1868–1918). He supported Diderot's position. Tommaso **Salvini** (1829–1916), an Italian tragedian, became an international star in the 1870s and 1880s, most famous for the role of Othello. He performed in England and the United States on several occasions. In 1893 he published his memoirs. He rejected Diderot's position.

17 / To William Archer

Hotel de Vienne,
24 Rue de la Tourche, Brussels
18th April 1889

[ALS: BL 45296 f 18; CL 1]

Travelling with Sidney Webb (1859–1947), Shaw made his first trip to the Continent (17–24 April). Ever since they met in 1880 at the Zetetical Society, Shaw and Webb were colleagues who supported political, economic, and social reforms in British society. Webb, who was a lawyer, joined Shaw in the Fabian Society in 1885. They became leaders in the Society, and wrote many of its essays, pamphlets, and books. Webb and his wife Beatrice (née Potter; 1858–1943) were married in 1892; they founded the London School of Economics and Political Science in 1895. In 1913 they established the New Statesman. *They were major contributors to political policy in the Labour governments of Ramsay MacDonald (1866–1937).*

If Shaw's complaint about sightseeing in Belgium is to be believed, the trip proved to be a great disappointment. But after only one day in Belgium, Shaw travelled to the Netherlands. He thought better of The Hague, Rotterdam, Utrecht, and Amsterdam, where he saw a Dutch production of Ibsen's A Doll's House *(two months before the first London production).*

My worst forebodings have been realized. I have seen nothing that I was not already tired of except the Musée Plantin at Antwerp, which nobody seems to care about, and which is worth a dozen such whitened dog-holes as the Cathedral. These cathedrals are all rot: none of them are finished; the building of a certain sort of tracery at a prodigious height to get a lace work effect is a mere trick; and the insides are ugly and full of vile modern stained glass. I thought the San Carlo Borromeo church at Antwerp the most horrible experience of my life until I went into the picture gallery, which is a pretty nightmare to cross the ocean to see. Antwerp is exactly like Limerick, only duller. I spent an hour in Mechlin; saw the cathedral and another barrack of the same army; and fled howling to Brussels, where I went to the Theatre de la Monnaie and was driven out after one act by Mounet Sully declaiming Oedipus with a lot of the Français people. The weather has been magnificent; but Nature conspires with you in vain to palm off the Continent on me as a success. My only piece of luck was not seeing the descent from the cross, because of Easter. Off to the Hague on Sat^{y} and back Wed^{y} morn^{g}.

GBS

Jean Sully Mounet (1841–1916), known as **Mounet-Sully**, was a star of the Comédie-Française; he often performed in tragic roles. Shaw had little patience for French classical acting styles.

18 / To William Archer 29 Fitzroy Square W
11th June 1889

[ALS: BL 45296 ff 19–20; CL 1]

The London production of A Doll's House, *which ran from 7 to 28 June, was staged at the Novelty Theatre by Charles Charrington (c. 1860–1928), who played Dr Rank. His wife Janet Achurch (1864–1916) portrayed Nora, and Herbert Waring played Torvald Helmer. Gertrude Warden (1862–?) appeared as Mrs Linden and Royce Carleton (1858–95) as Krogstad. Archer provided the translation. The production received several quite positive reviews, and many reviews were divided between positive and negative assessments. Even some of the negative notices, while dismissive of the play, praised the acting (Prophet: 40–8).*

For Archer and Shaw this production offered their first major opportunity as collaborators to mount a substantial campaign to modernize the London stage. Their efforts on several fronts became a model for their activities during the 1890s. In Archer's case, the mission for A Doll's House *began in late March when he published 'Ibsen and the English Stage.' He made the case for staging* A Doll's House *instead of* Ghosts. *He feared that* Ghosts, *more controversial and more difficult to stage, would create a nasty backlash against Ibsen among English critics. Charrington and Achurch took up Archer's challenge. Yet despite his advocacy, he did not review the production because of his public identity as translator (and also because of his behind-the-scenes role as literary adviser and co-director). But in* The World *on 12 and 19 June, he wrote about Ibsen and the play, and in the process he commented on Achurch's performance. He also published a limited edition of* A Doll's House *in June that featured several illustrations from the production. Then in July he published in the* Fortnightly Review *a long essay, 'Ibsen and English Criticism,' which celebrated Ibsen as a great playwright and poet (Ibsen Essays: 13–22). Over the following months he dedicated himself to translating or retranslating Ibsen's plays, which were published in five volumes under the title of* Ibsen's Prose Drama *in 1890–1. This set included thirteen of the prose plays, extending chronologically from* Lady Inger of Östrät *to* Hedda Gabler *(Prophet: 143–4).*

Shaw also contributed to their campaign on several fronts. Seven days before A Doll's House *opened, he published a note, signed 'No Gentleman,' in the* Penny Illustrated Paper *about the forthcoming production (Biblio 2: 558, C581). He then attended the opening on 7 June and returned four days later. As arranged by Archer, Shaw reviewed the production on 8 June for the* Manchester Guardian *(Biblio 2: 559, C588). Then on 13 June in the* PMG, *he responded to a negative article by Robert Buchanan (1841–1901) entitled 'Is Ibsen a Zola with a Wooden Leg?' Shaw's reply, 'Is Mr Buchanan a Critic with a Wooden Head?,' offered a spirited defence of Ibsen as well as a dismissal of Buchanan's plays as 'idle twaddling' (Biblio 2: 559, C 591; Dukore 1: 108–10). (Buchanan was notorious for his attack years earlier on Dante Gabriel Rossetti's poetry. His title was* The Fleshy School of Poetry.*) On 21 June, writing under the name of Corno di Bassetto in a music review in* The Star, *Shaw described the dinner which took place at the Novelty Theatre on 16 June to honour the production (Biblio 2: 559, C597). He sat next to Janet Achurch, thus beginning his infatuation with her. On 20 June he returned to an evening performance of* A Doll's House, *sitting with Mrs Archer. His excessive praise of Janet Achurch, a married woman, offended Mrs Archer, who found some of his remarks improper. On 23 June he and Archer 'talked about Ibsen and some unlucky offense I had given Mrs Archer by going on about Miss Achurch' (Diaries 1: 514). Months later Shaw was still worrying over how Mrs Archer judged his infatuation with Janet Achurch (CL 1: 238–9).*

Six months later Walter Besant (1836–1901), the popular novelist, published a satiric sequel to Ibsen's play in which Nora is portrayed as a successful novelist, but Torvald is a drunkard, a son is a forger, and a daughter commits suicide. In response to Besant in February 1890 Shaw published 'Still after The Doll's House,*' which appeared in* Time *(and was reprinted in* The Transatlantic *in Boston) (Biblio 2: 565, C 680). Shaw blamed respectable society and its conformist codes for making Nora an outcast. As he wrote to Charrington and Achurch – who were touring in Australia after concluding the run of* A Doll's House *– his aim was to stir up more controversies about Ibsen and to counter Archer's 'inveterate pessimism' (CL 1: 237–41) about the public and critical resistance to Ibsen's drama.*

I noticed a good many shortcomings tonight that escaped me before, & that ought to be remedied somehow. The cardinal one is that the situation in the second act is not made clear. The audience does not understand her [Nora's] idea that Helmer will take the forgery on himself. When she exclaims 'He *will* do it' they dont know what it means. I asked my neighbor – who was intensely interested – at the end of the act whether he understood this; and he was quite in the dark. His companion (Lleyewellyn Smith of Toynbee, who did a lot of the work for that book of Booth's on East London) knew; but he had read the play; and he agreed with me that the point did not come out in the acting. In several places, the piece wants playing up. In spite of Julius Floemmochser I am alive to the necessity of perfect diction when an attempt is made at realism in the pitch of the conversation. I was in the fourth row of the pit, which is not unreasonably far back; but I lost several lines, and was conscious of a great relief when they spoke out or made their words tell. One unfortunate pittite at last cried out respectfully but imploringly 'speak up'; and my sympathies were entirely with him. One of the scenes which needs to be brought out is that between Nora & the nurse. Mrs. Linden is fading into nothing; and I have come to the conclusion that Krogstad is bad, an opinion which I found shared by Stepniak. They are all relapsing into their ordinary stage tricks now that they are at their ease & the strain of the first night off. Miss A actually bowed to the applause on her entrance, a proceeding which so ruined the illusion – she was the only one who did it – that I have resorted to the 'last device of a coward,' an anonymous letter, begging her not to do it again. If she shews it to you – mum!

Charrington is better: the exit is greatly improved.

GBS

Sir Hubert **Lleyewellyn Smith** (1864–1945) was an economist; he later served as permanent secretary to the Board of Trade. Charles **Booth** (1840–1916) and his team of assistants published *Life and Labour of the People in London* (1889–1903) in 17 volumes, a major sociological study of urban life, trade, and working conditions. The first volume, to which Shaw refers here, described conditions in East London. Under the pseudonym of **Julius Floemmochser**, Shaw had written a letter to 'Spectator' – A.B. Walkley (1855–1926) – at *The Star* on 1 February 1889, attacking French actors for their formal elocution. He was responding to Walkley's review of a production by a French company at the Royalty Theatre. Shaw's coinage of **pittite** refers to someone who sits in the pit. Sergius **Stepniak** was the pseudonym for Sergei Mikhailovich Kravchinski (1852–95), a Russian writer who fled St Petersburg in 1884 following a failed attempt to assassinate the head of the secret police. After he settled in London, he was active in the socialist movement, and wrote *Russia under the Czars* (1885) and *The Career of a Nihilist* (1889).

19 / To William Archer

29 Fitzroy Square W
22nd October 1889

[ALS: BL 45296 ff 21–2; CL 1]

Despite Shaw's hyperbole, the negotiations with Edmund Yates, editor of The World, *were performed on respectful terms. On 18 October Shaw sent to Yates his resignation (Diaries 1: 550). Yates genuinely regretted the need to cut or drop some of Shaw's art reviews. In his reply to Shaw he apologized, and announced his desire to keep Shaw as a contributor. But Shaw turned down the generous offer and resigned in November, though he delivered a few more signed reviews until 8 January. Yates finally sent a termination letter on 10 March 1890 (Diaries 1: 597), yet Shaw provided several more unsigned pieces until May 1890. Then suddenly the music position at* The World *became available with the departure of the music critic Louis Engel, who had to leave the country because of trouble over 'an affair of gallantry,' as Shaw later recalled the situation. Archer 'assured Yates that I was the only possible successor to the fugitive' (SSS: 68; CL 3: 453). On 16 May 1890 Yates wrote to Archer: 'I am grateful for your suggestion, on which I at once acted: with the result that G.B.S. begins work next week as my musical critic' (BL 45297). Accepting the offer, Shaw discontinued his Corno di Bassetto column for* The Star. *He served as the music critic for* The World *until August 1894.*

You may be interested and amused by the fact that I went for Yates at last on Friday in four glorious pages beginning 'Your treatment of me as art critic is monstrous, scandalous &c &c &c' *crescendo molto alla fine.* My proposal was that he should hand over the job to Lady Colin Campbell, who could include the exhibitions in her 'Woman's Walks' and so save the £29 odd per an. which I absorb, & which doesnt pay me. Edmund, in reply, is gracefully magnanimous, munificent, pleasantrative, proud of the connection, remorseful for inevitable editorial stinginess as to space. He offers to put all the minor exhibitions on to Lady C. C; to take eight articles a year on the big exhibitions at the usual rate; and to pay me besides £52 a year as retainer. After this I cannot complain as to money; but I am hanged if I know what to say. Taking £52 a year for refusing to write about pictures more than 8 times a year is out of the question; and if I offer, as I probably shall, to undertake the 8 articles alone, leaving myself free to do what I please in other directions, I shall lose the run of the minor shows, which are really necessary to keep one *au courant* with the art world. And yet I cannot afford to go to them on the old paragraph system.

Can you suggest anything? I am tolerably clear about my reply – i.e. refuse the £52; offer to do the eight articles for him; warn him that if some other paper offers me a free run for its money I will transfer my services; and make it clear that the only way to 'retain' me is to give me a column a week as well as a pound. All this of course to be put with the tact for which I am famous. But I am not so clear about it as to be indisposed to consider any other view of the case that may occur to you; for I have been so up to the neck in the final throes (mixed; but never mind) of 'Fabian Essays' that I have not had time to lay my mind to the thing fairly.

If you can spare the time so soon let me have a line by return, as Y[ates]'s letter languishes unanswered.

GBS

PS Advice to accept the offer as it stands will be rejected as a base dictate of Caledonian prudence.

In a sensational court trial in 1886 **Lady Colin Campbell** (née Gertrude Elizabeth Blood, 1858–1911) separated from her husband, Lord Colin Campbell (1853–95), the youngest son of the 8th Duke of Argyll, on the grounds of cruelty and infidelity. They had married in 1881. Lord Campbell held a seat in the House of Commons from 1878 to 1885; he died of syphilis in 1895. After the trial, Lady Campbell supported herself as a journalist and dramatist. In May 1890 she became the art critic for *The World*, replacing Shaw, who became the music critic. In October 1889 Shaw was in the **final throes** of editing the *Fabian Essays in Socialism*. The collection, published in December, included two of his essays. It sold well. Archer's reply, however **Caledonian** it might have been, is lost.

20 / To William Archer

29 Fitzroy Square W
27th April 1890

[TLS: BL 45296 f 23; CL 1]

On 14 March Shaw purchased a used Bar-Lock typewriter (CL 1: 376) from H.W. Massingham (1860–1924), the editor of The Star. *Of the typed letters to Archer, this is the first to survive.*

I was prevented from coming to tea by the plight of my drunkard, who, still in a state of horror, was surrounded by his whispering relatives who were assembled as if for a funeral. I dispersed them with roars of laughter and inquiries after pink snakes &c, an exhibition of bad taste which at last converted the poor devil's wandering apprehensive look into a settled grin. I then took him out for a walk, and endeavored to relieve his mind of the strong illusion that nothing can ever tempt him to taste liquor more. Tomorrow he goes to a retreat at Rickmansworth, to be reformed. When we got back to the house it was too late for the train before the 7, which does not reach Paddington until 7–20. In the train I wrote an article; but I jumped out before the train stopped; and the damned thing fell under the wheels and was *coupé, haché*, like the two men in 'La Bête Humaine.' So I had to hurry home and write it over again.

I am to send all Ibsen's works to Rickmansworth to help in restoring the lowered moral tone of the patient. They forced him to make his will in the crisis of his agony; and he cannot get rid of the notion that the next thing must be his funeral.

GBS

The **drunkard** was Shaw's Irish friend Pakenham Beatty (1855–1930), with whom Shaw sometimes boxed. Beatty's drinking, which he blamed on his troubled marriage, led to a case of 'delirium tremens,' as Shaw identified the problem (Diaries 1: 611). The treatment centre for Beatty was located in the town of **Richmansworth,** northwest of London beyond Harrow. Despite this crisis and the writing of his will, Beatty lived for forty more years. The lost **article**, later rewritten and published anonymously in *The Hawk*, was a review of Sir Frederic Cowen's opera *Thorgrim* (Music 2: 41–4). The novel ***La Bête Humaine*** (1890) was by Émile Zola (1840–1902). Few **Ibsen works** were available in translation by April 1890. Besides Archer's limited edition of *A Doll's House* (1889), Havelock Ellis (1859–1939) had edited and published three of the plays in 1888: *Pillars of Society*, and *Ghosts* (translated by Archer), and *An Enemy of the People* (translated by Eleanor Marx-Aveling). With diligence, Shaw might have been able to find a copy of Catherine Ray's 1876 translation of *Emperor and Galilean*. Not until November did Archer publish four of the five volumes of *Ibsen's Prose Drama*. (See note to letter of 21 August 1890.)

21 / To William Archer

29 Fitzroy Square W
17th August 1890

[TLS, with ALS postscript: BL 45296 ff 24–5; CL 1]

Between 29 July and 10 August Shaw and Sidney Webb made a Continental trip that featured short visits to Brussels, Cologne, Mainz, Frankfurt, Munich, Augsburg, Stuttgart, and Strasbourg. The highlight of their trip was a stay in Oberammergau to see a performance of the Passion Play. After his return to London Shaw published 'Opera and Oberammergau' on 13 August in The World. *On the same day his article 'Ibsen and Socialism' appeared in the* Daily Chronicle. *On 12 August the DC's Berlin correspondent travelled to Munich to interview Ibsen. He told Ibsen that English Socialists had declared that Ibsen was a member of their party. This interview, which was published in* DC *on 13 August, suggested that Ibsen angrily rejected such a claim. The published interview became the source for Shaw's request to Archer in this letter to explain to Ibsen what had and had not been said in his lecture on Ibsen which he delivered to the Fabian Society a month earlier on 18 July. On 18 August, when Ibsen became aware of the* DC *article by the Berlin correspondent, he wrote to H.L. Brækstad and asked him to translate and publish a corrective statement that countered the 'misconstruction' of his position on socialism. This statement was published in* DC *on 28 August. (For Ibsen's letter to Brækstad, see Ibsen Letters: 291–3.) See also Archer's letter to Shaw, 21 August 1890, about visit with Ibsen in Munich.*

Archer travelled to Bavaria, leaving London on 17 August, the day of this letter from Shaw. Archer also saw the Passion Play, but his primary mission was to meet with Henrik Ibsen, his wife, and son in Munich. Ibsen was angry with the Berlin interviewer, not with Shaw, as Archer explained in a letter to Shaw on 21 August. He also wrote to his brother Charles (1861–1941) about the controversy. This letter to Charles was subsequently reproduced in Archer's 'Ibsen as I Knew Him,' published in 1906 after Ibsen's death that year. (Archer's article is also available in Ibsen Essays*: 107–23, 300–1.) Archer returned home on 26 August. Two days later Ibsen's corrective statement of his views on socialism appeared in the* DC, *as arranged by Brækstad.*

I have written nothing about the Passion Play except a paragraph in my World article, which has been borrowed from me by somebody. However, I can give you the gist of it without waiting to get another copy and send it on. I first said that though you had come fast enough to Bayreuth, where you had no business, you had refused to come to the Passion Play, and had recommended me to spend the cost of the trip on a bicycle instead. This was my apology for trespassing on your province. I denounced Meyer as a stick, grumbled at his perpetual pose as the Man of Sorrows, objected to his not letting himself go, and being such an insufferably superior person that the wonder was, not that they crucified him, but that they stood him so long. I admitted his skill and endurance as a poseur, but pointed out that all the Oberammergauers were experts in that department (they teach it in school there) and based my dissatisfaction on the want of feeling in his dialogue, of humor in his repartee, on his quoting texts instead of holding human intercourse, and so on. I called him the Christ, not of the elder Holbein, nor of Von Unde (modern realist), but of Ary Scheffer and Sir Noel Paton. I swept away John and the B.V.M. in the same condemnation.

Their notion of being divine was simply not being human nor anything else, for fear of being irreverent. I praised the acting of the secular people, especially of Pilate, Nathanael, Caiaphas, Judas, and several of the minor characters. My criticism of the play was that the excision of the devil for the sake of gentility had spoiled it by weakening the motive of Judas's treachery. I also opined that the fatalistic apathy of Christ before Pilate and Herod was inadequately motivirt. This, with a detailed criticism of the music, was all I said, at no greater length than I have said it above.

Oberammergau seems to be run by two women who speak all known languages, and run the Burgomaster's office and the post office alternately. We were much disheartened when we arrived and found ourselves in the middle of [a] lamenting, seatless, lodgingless horde of English and American trippers; but when we at last got up the stairs of the Rathaus and into the office, Webb had no sooner got out the words 'Bitte, Vebb –' than our billet was handed to a boy guide and off we went in triumph. Webb had written to the Burgomaster; and we had arrived on the day we named. This apparently settled the affair for us, though we had had no reply. Webb's letter was couched in terms which are only used in Germany in addressing the Emperor. We were unlucky in applying too late to have covered seats reserved for us: we could only get five shilling ones, much superior to the ten shilling places for seeing and hearing, but roofless. However, as it was a most beautiful Saturday afternoon, we rejoiced in having saved five shillings apiece. Our rejoicing was shortlived. At about eight in the evening a horrible dust storm suddenly charged into the village, turning the balmy eve into a scene of darkness and confusion, in which men and women wildly held their hats on, bent their heads, shut their eyes nine tenths, and in that condition rushed about looking for their lodgings in the unaccustomed streets. By the time we were abed, the dust was succumbing to rain. In the morning it was raining as if it had no idea of leaving off; and what is more, it did not leave off. I was sustained from 8 a.m. to 5 p.m. only by the consciousness that Caiaphas (the Burgomaster) was getting as wet as I was, and that the sou'wester, unique in central Europe, was an unprecedented success.

If you leave Munich by the early (not the midday) train for Oberau, you will get to the village in time to have an afternoon there, and to see enough of it to make you content to return to Munich immediately after the performance. The best way to spend the afternoon on Saturday is to ascend the Alpine peak with the cross on the summit. The path is up through the trees beside the peak on the right. The last ten minutes of the ascent presents a mild feat of cragsmanship. If you slip, you break your neck; and the Matterhorn can do no more for you than that. There is edelweiss, and a view, and generally an American at the foot of the cross, which owes its flashing appearance to a plating of tin. Altogether it is a useful, lung opening, fifty minutes climb. I did it alone, Webb preferring to sit among the trees at the base, writing an article on municipal death duties for the Speaker.

At Munich the modern pictures in the Exhibition are worth seeing; and the Passion Play throws a light on the old German pictures in the Pinacothek. We left Munich by a very early train (seven or thereabouts); broke our journey at Augsburg; went on in the afternoon to Ulm (glorious cathedral, satisfactory restaurant called Goldener Löwe, and delightful feeling about the town in the evening light); and went on to Stuttgart, where we slept and put in a whole day, which it was not specially worth except for the rest. Then to Strassburg, where I paid two marks for an order to go to the tiptop of the cathedral spire. I outfaced agonies of terror that no typewriter can describe until the municipal steeplejack who accompanied me invited me to ascend by a naked flight of steps, each of the size and shape of a small slice of cheese, to a pinnacle, and there to stand like one of the statues and admire the view. And this, mind you, on the outside of the steeple, at a height that makes me sick to remember. How much higher I could have gone for the money I dont know; for we were still thirty of forty feet from the horrible apex of the thing; but I said 'Ist genug' with what dignity I could muster, and admired the view with an intelligentforeigner air from where I was. And yet when, after a fearful descent, I was safe in the streets, I had a craving to try again – a remorse at having given in, that would have ended in my going another two marks, and leaving my invaluable brains on the pavement of the Munsterplatz if we had stayed another week there. We got home after a night in Brussels, and a stay of a few hours at Lille. The sou'wester proved a sovereign preventive of sickness. I escaped without a qualm, both going and coming. The water was uncommonly smooth.

If you go to see Ibsen I wish you would explain a matter to him which concerns me. The Daily Chronicle published a half column or so of sensational extracts from my lecture; and its Munich correspondent thereupon went to Ibsen and told him that the London Social Democrats had been claiming him as one of themselves, and exploiting his reputation to bolster up their theories. Naturally Henrik was infuriated, and declared that he had nothing to do with the dogmas of the Social Democrats. Will you tell him if you get the chance that the true state of the case is that an eminent socialist critic made his plays the text for a fierce attack on the idealist section of the English Social Democrats, comparing them and their red flag to Hilmar Tonnesen and his 'banner of the ideal.' Also that the effect was to bring down on the critic the fiercest denunciation from the organ of the Social Democratic Federation, which calls me a pig incapable of understanding Beethoven's sonatas, and repudiates my socialism as 'socialism of the sty.' I did not read to you this section of the paper, as its interest was too purely Fabian; but the following scraps from it will shew you how it ran.

> I now come to the bearing of Ibsen's thesis on ourselves as Socialists. Ibsen himself has made no such application; for he is not a socialist: he was born in the year 1828, and therefore formed his political opinions whilst socialism was still the most outrageously idealist of all the new 'isms.' —— The only ideal that is specially obnoxious to us as practical socialists, and that Ibsen has directly attacked, is the ideal of Law and Order. Property and Thrift he lets alone; and Laissezfaire he would probably endorse, not as an ideal, but as a tolerably safe rule to adopt when Tom, Dick, and Harry begin to call themselves Society and The State, and start meddling with the moral deportment of individuals. His attitude towards Democracy I have dealt with in describing 'An Enemy of the People.' His opinion of the Fabian Society is not known – probably it has not yet been formed, since he does not read English &c. &c. —— Ibsen and Morris both hold mainly to the point that as long as people deliberately let themselves be idealized into doing what they dont like, thereby not only making themselves unhappy, but creating a social pressure on other folk to do the same, no mere turning of the wheels of public machinery will set them free. —— With Ibsen's

> thesis in one's mind, it is impossible to think without concern of the appalling adaptability of Socialism to idealist purposes. —— We (the socialists) are perhaps little troubled with the pet ideals of middleclass England, such as the honor of a gentleman, the glory of the nation, or patriotism, which Dr. Johnson, prophetically inspired for the moment with Ibsenism, described as the 'last refuge of a scoundrel.' Still less are we tainted with those ideals of duty and discipline which are used to cloak the abject slavery of the soldier. Above all, we are fairly free from that archideal called God, which concentrates into a single concept all the essential evil and incidental good of idealism. But socialism itself as an 'ism' or ideal is as capable of mischief as any of these. —— My socialism may thus lead me to compromise my principles, to trample on the red flag, and to be proved a traitor by Mr Herbert Burrows; but I cannot help that, anymore than I can help the other series of crimes which I am accused of under the laws of conduct laid down by the genteel idealists, who have satisfactorily proved over and over again that I have committed every conceivable atrocity, from breaking my mother's heart to damning my own soul. For the life of me I cannot see that the chains of socialistic idealism are less burdenless than those of genteel idealism, or that they lead to less obstructive and hurtful conduct.

[Shaw inserted the long dashes or ellipses throughout this self-quoted text in order to indicate his own cuts.]

I set great store by the settingright of Ibsen about this matter; and even if you don't see him I wish you would drop him a line to say that his interviewer got hold of the wrong end of the stick, and that any hasty strictures of his on Social Democracy, based on the assumption that it is as dogmatic and unpractical in England as in Germany, will be represented here as repudiations of the very section which is trying, and so far with remarkable success, to rid socialism of the dogmatism, sectarianism, and absolutism of which he complains!

You may add, if you please, that I am extremely sorry that my total ignorance of Norwegian prevented my calling on him during my stay in Munich to explain his plays to him.

The Fabian, by the bye, is getting known in Germany. A recent work by a German author mentions the Fabian as the really important motor in English Social Democracy.

GBS

PS In the interview with the Daily Chronicle man, Ibsen again declared that 'The Doll's House' was founded on fact – that Nora was a real person who had actually walked out & slammed the door.

When will you be back in England?

Walkley writes his column now from Boulogne, which he calls 'Oberammergau sur mer.' I got a card from him from Somme, in which he says that the Star obituary portrait of Cardinal Newman [on 12 August] was really a portrait of Lafontaine as 'L'Abbe Constantin' which once adorned a Spectator column.

Joseph Mayr, not **Meyer**, portrayed Jesus in the Oberammergau Passion Play. Hans **Holbein** the elder (c.1465–1524), a painter and draftsman, excelled in his altarpieces and portraits. Fritz von **Uhde** (1848–1911) was a German painter; he often featured religious subjects. In the 1890s he joined the Munich and later the Berlin Secession movements. **Ary Scheffer** (1795–1858) was a portrait painter. Sir Joseph **Nöel Paton** (1821–1901) was a Scottish painter of religious and allegorical topics. **B.V.M.** is the Blessed Virgin Mary. Although **motivirt** was probably Shaw's version of the German 'motiviert' (*motivieren*, to motivate), it also has the teasing quality of a Shaw coinage that joined 'motive' to 'virtue' to suggest sacred motivation. The **Pinacothek** museum in Munich, now divided into the Alte, Neue, and Moderna, featured an exhibition of modern portrait paintings in August 1890. Shaw's reference to **my lecture** was to his two-hour talk on Ibsen which he delivered to the Fabian Society at St James's Restaurant on 18 July 1890. Shaw developed the lecture into *The Quintessence of Ibsenism* (1891). For the text of the lecture, its historical context, and the controversy over linking Ibsen to socialism, see Wisenthal: 8–15, 81–96. **Hilmar Tönnesen** is a character in Ibsen's *The Pillars of Society*. The Fabians were opposed to the doctrinaire Marxism of the **Social Democratic Federation**, led by Henry Mayers Hydman (1842–1921). The socialist **William Morris**, like Shaw, separated himself from Hydman and the SDF in the mid-1880s. Dr Samuel **Johnson's** statement about patriotism appears in James Boswell's *Life of Johnson*. In 'Socialism of the Sty,' published in *Justice* on 26 July, **Herbert Barrows** (1845–1922), a member of the Social Democratic Federation, attacked Shaw's lecture of 18 July on Ibsen. The false **portrait of Cardinal Newman** appeared in *The Star* on 12 August. John Henry Newman (1801–90) was an English theologian and writer of the Church of England who converted to the Catholic Church. His writings include his autobiography *Apologia Pro Vita Sua* (1865–6). He became a cardinal in 1879. The poet Jean de **La Fontaine** (1621–95) wrote fables; many were derived from Aesop.

22 / To G. Bernard Shaw

[Munich]
21st August 1890

[APCS: BL 50660]

Archer spent two days in Munich with Ibsen. This was their third meeting. The first occurred in Rome (1881–2) and the second in Jutland (July 1887). In the 1890s they met on several occasions when Archer visited Christiania (Oslo). Ibsen had remained in exile for twenty-seven years, except for a few brief visits to Norway. When he resettled in Christiania in 1891, he was welcomed as a literary giant. The Norwegian people embraced and honoured him.

While in Munich, Archer joined Ibsen on a visit to the Pinacothek museum. Among the modern portraits was one of Ibsen, which he refused to observe. Although they discussed the controversy created by the Daily Chronicle *article (see letter of 17 August), they talked primarily about productions and translations of Ibsen's plays. Ibsen was pleased by his growing fame in the English-speaking world. And Archer was equally pleased that Ibsen was 'profuse in his acknowledgement of my share in bringing it about' (C. Archer: 170). In order to control the copyright for his plays in England, Ibsen had designated Archer as his preferred English translator. By means of staged readings and publications, Archer protected his translations. Ten plays, with separate introductions by Archer, were issued by the publisher Walter Scott (1826–1910). Four volumes of* Ibsen's Prose Drama *appeared in November 1890. Vol. 1:* The League of Youth, The Pillars of Society, *and* A Doll's House*; vol. 2:* Ghosts, An Enemy of the People, *and* The Wild Duck*; vol. 3:* Lady Inger of Östrät, The Vikings at Helgeland, *and* The Pretenders*; and vol. 4:* Emperor and Galilean. *These volumes feature revised translations. A fifth volume was issued in 1891 (*Rosmersholm, The Lady from the Sea, *and* Hedda Gabler*). Archer published all of the plays in 1906–8.*

Have been all day with Ibsen who is infuriated against the *Chronicle* man & no one else. What he said to him was that he had never belonged to any party & in all probability never would, but that he was (pleasantly) surprised to learn that English socialism, working on scientific lines, had arrived at something like the same results at which he had arrived on the dichterisch line. This interviewer seems to have twisted into an expression of (unpleasant) surprise at the audacity of anyone calling him a socialist. He says that on the contrary he expressed a sympathetic interest in socialism as one of the forces of the future. Meanwhile all Europe is aflame over the business. It is in the German, Danish and Norwegian papers, & Herr Vollmar, a leading German socialist & friend of the old min's, has written to him asking what the devil he means. Ibsen has himself written to Braekstad a letter designed for the English papers, wh[ich] you have no doubt seen by this time. Am thinking of cutting Oberammergau & stopping to see *En Folkefiende* here – not that I love J.C. less but that I love H.I. more.

W.A.

Archer's playful reference to Ibsen's **dichterisch line** depends on the German word for poet, Der Dichter. Ever since the 1870s, Archer and his brother Charles referred to Ibsen respectfully as the '**old min**,' the old man. He was twenty-eight years older than Archer. Ibsen's letter, sent to H.L. **Brækstad**, was not published in the DC until 28 August, so Shaw had not yet seen it. Archer attended the Passion Play at Oberammergau for only a half-day, then returned to Munich for the production of ***En Folkefiende*** (*An Enemy of the People*) at the Residenz Theater. 'It was vilely staged – if they'd have let me direct a couple of rehearsals, I'd have made a different play of it' (C. Archer: 171).

23 / To William Archer

29 Fitzroy Square W
14th March 1891

[ALS: BL 45296 f 26; CL 1]

No extant letters have survived from 21 August 1890 to this date. The production of Ibsen's Ghosts, *which Archer had translated in 1888, was by the new Independent Theatre Company, founded by Jacob Thomas Grein (1852–1935), a London dramatic critic who was born in the Netherlands. It was staged on 12 and 13 March 1891. The performances were designated private, thereby circumventing the censorship of the Lord Chamberlain's Office. Nonetheless, several dozen critics attended, and published their reviews. Most reviewers expressed outrage over the supposed immorality of the play. Four weeks later in the* PMG, *Archer compiled the abusive statements from the press for a satiric article, a British Schimplexikon, called '*Ghosts *and Gibberings' (Ibsen Essays: 23–7). Shaw later incorporated part of this article into* The Quintessence of Ibsenism, *published in October 1891.*

Massingham turned up for the M. G. I forgot to post my answer to your letter, and had to telegraph; but I infer that the telegram was not delivered before you left.

The performance was simply a tremendous success; and I fully expect that today the gloves will be off & the fighting agog in earnest.

GBS

Because Archer was involved as translator and adviser for the production of *Ghosts*, he asked the journalist Henry William **Massingham** to substitute for him as the reviewer for the **M.G.,** *Manchester Guardian*. Massingham wrote on politics and theatre. In 1888, as assistant editor at *The Star*, he hired Shaw to write on political topics. In 1890 Massingham replaced Thomas Power O'Connor (1848–1929) as editor of *The Star*. This was the first of four publications he edited between 1890 and 1923, including the *Daily Chronicle* (1895–9), *Daily News* (1901–6), and *The Nation* (1907–23), for which Archer served as theatre critic from November 1908 to December 1910.

24 / To William Archer

29 Fitzroy Square W
23rd April 1891

[ALS: BL 45296 ff 27–8; CL 1]

Ibsen published Hedda Gabler *in 1890; the first London production opened at the Vaudeville Theatre on 20 April 1891. After ten matinee performances, the production moved into the evening slot for the full month of May. Hedda was portrayed by Elizabeth Robins (1862–1952), Thea Elvsted by Marion Lea (1861–1944), Tesman by W. Scott Buist (1860–?), Judge Brack by Charles Sugden (1850–1921), and Lövborg by Arthur Elwood (1850–1903). Robins and Lea were the co-producers; Robins and Archer served as co-directors. Although Archer had assumed that he would publish the copyrighted translation, the young publisher William Heinemann (1863–1928) outfoxed him by buying the rights directly from Ibsen even before the Norwegian text was published in Copenhagen. After publishing a copy of the Norwegian text in December, Heinemann hired Edmund Gosse (1849–1928) to do a quick English translation in January. This text thus had to be identified as the official one for the April production. But Archer, who launched a major public assault on Gosse's poor translation when it was published, substantially revised it for the production (Whitebrook: 115–29). Robins convinced Heinemann to provide a shilling edition of* Hedda Gabler, *'to be sold at the theatre doors.' This edition, she insisted, had to be based on Archer's revised text. She wanted spectators to know, as she wrote to Archer, 'how entirely we are indebted to you for what is best in our stage version' (BL 45295 ff 32–3). Later in the year, with Ibsen's support, Archer circumvented Heinemann's copyright control of the play by publishing his own translation in volume 5 of* Ibsen's Prose Drama.

Despite productions in London of Rosmersholm *and* Ghosts, *as well as a revival of* A Doll's House, *during the first three months of 1891, Archer had not written any production reviews because of his direct involvement as translator and behind-the-scenes director. But he had written articles about the plays, and had published '*Ghosts *and Gibberings.' He broke his silence as a reviewer with the* Hedda Gabler *production, fully supported by his editor Edmund Yates. As soon as he finished a draft, he asked Shaw to apply his critical eye. The revised article appeared in* The World *on 29 April, nine days after the opening performance.*

Besides writing this letter to Archer about the draft of the review, Shaw also sent a letter to Robins after the opening performance. He praised the closing scene of Hedda's suicide: 'I never had a more tremendous sensation in the theatre.' But he catalogued several failings of the actors, and was 'violently disappointed' that Robins altered 'do it beautifully' to 'do it gracefully' when Hedda urges Løvborg to self-destruction. He also claimed that she failed to make clear in act 1 that Hedda was disturbed by her possible pregnancy (CL 1: 291–2). Although Robins willingly accepted notes from Archer after each performance, she complained to Archer about receiving any criticism from Shaw.

On page 2 of the MS, four lines from the bottom, you had better strike out 'under the joint management &c' which gives the sentence the air of an advertisement. There is a certain elaborate House-of-Lords unnaturalness about the whole article which can be remedied by striking a word out here & there. For instance, why do you Desire to record Emphatically the deep impression made by the Production &c &c, instead of saying 'I want, then, to record the deep impression made upon me by *Hedda Gabler* last Monday afternoon at the Vaudeville'? And again, 'that fact, I say [my lords & gentlemen] [Shaw's brackets] is not without its interest as a human document.' Cant you say 'that fact, I hope, has its interest as a h.d.'? It is this unlucky half page that flavors all the rest: if you alter it as I suggest, the spell will be broken completely.

Common decency demands that you should modify the claim to normal impartiality in your first sentence, which should end '– any approach, not to impartiality, which I hope I know better than to pretend to in any case, but to freedom from flagrant & immediate personal and even pecuniary bias.'

You have, in your remark (p. 5, two lines from foot) about the respectable British householder, gloriously missed the real point of the conventional objection. Why, man alive, it is Thea, whom you so naively praise, and not Hedda, the modern Lucretia, who preferred death to dishonor, at whom the householder holds up his hands (*vide* daily papers).

With these reservations I approve immensely of the article. There is no reason why Yates should not print it. I could quite understand his objecting to your *not* noticing Ibsen plays & thereby cutting his paper clean out of the theatrical movement; but he cannot, without wantonly picking a quarrel with you, suppress this article. Why the deuce should you anticipate such a vagary on his part?

My 'feminine' point in the letter to Miss R. was à propos of her cutting out the cause of her agitation in the first act and yet leaving the agitation in. My contention is that the women who are mad to play Rebecca, Hedwig, Hedda, Nora &c, recoil from the jar of the peculiarly Ibsenite passages. Ibsen says, in effect, 'Here is a beautiful part for you to play, on condition that you face a laugh or two, a jar or two, a misunderstanding or two, in giving it to the unprepared public in all its completeness & reality.' And immediately they set to work to see how they can get the beautiful part & yet escape the condition by cutting out all the bits that raise the laughs & the jars & misunderstandings. This I call the great feminine problem because all the beautiful parts are women's parts. Perhaps it was unfair as seeming to infer that the men were any less cowardly than the women; but I did not mean it so. The truth is that all the performances lately have been very poor specimens of the moral courage of the stage hero & heroine: they have shirked pretty nearly everything that could be shirked. Mrs Theodore Wright is by far the pluckiest of the lot.

I am off to Wolverhampton this afternoon to lecture. Hanley on Friday, and back again on Saturday morning.

GBS

The American actresses Elizabeth Robins (1862–1952), **Miss R.**, and Marion Lea (1861–1944), provided the **joint management** for the production. Lea acted in London between 1890 and 1892, then returned to the United States and married the American playwright Langdon Mitchell (1862–1935). Working closely with Archer, Robins became the leading Ibsen producer and performer in London during the 1890s. She was also a novelist, writing under the pseudonym of C.E. Raimond. As a supporter of the women's suffrage movement, she wrote the play *Votes for Women!*, staged at the Court Theatre by the Vedrenne-Barker management in 1907. The femme fatale **Lucretia** Borgia (1480–1519), daughter of Pope Alexander VI (1480–1519), was infamous for her ruthless sexual and political escapades. She had several affairs, three marriages, and eight children in her thirty-nine years of life. She was featured in Machiavelli's *The Prince* (1513) and was the heroine of the stage play *Lucrèce Borgia* (1833) by Victor Hugo (1802–85) and the opera *Lucrezia Borgia* (1834) by Gaetano Donizetti (1797–1848). It is a stretch to compare Hedda Gabler to her. **Mrs Theodore Wright** (d. 1922) played the role of Mrs Alving in the production of *Ghosts* in March 1891. A Fabian, Mrs Wright became an active support of socialist causes and the new theatre. Shaw lectured in **Wolverhamton** and **Hanley** on capitalist profits and the distribution of wealth.

25 / To G. Bernard Shaw

[no address]
25th October 1891

[*New Review*, November 1891]

Archer wrote this 'open letter' in response to Shaw's The Quintessence of Ibsenism, *which had been published in September. A copy of this letter was delivered to Shaw on 25 October. He replied on the same day. By publishing this open letter, Archer sought to continue the public campaign for Ibsen. He felt that a public debate in the* New Review *would be timely because it would complement the Ibsen productions, the publication of the plays, the critical articles, and the debates with the London critics. From Archer's perspective, Shaw's* Quintessence, *whatever its flaws, was yet another important event in 1891 that had already featured the premieres of* Ghosts, Rosmersholm, *and* Hedda Gabler. *Archer thought that a controversy over Shaw's book would keep the subject of Ibsen before the public. It would help to rally the supporters of Ibsen, just as his* 'Ghosts *and Gibberings'* *had heightened the critical controversy over Ibsen. Also, a public debate between the two friends might help to attract buyers for* Quintessence, *which apparently sold two thousand copies during its first six years on the market. It was not reprinted, however, until 1912–13, when Shaw revised the text and expanded a new edition to accommodate Ibsen's last four plays.*

My Dear G. B. S.,

On that summer afternoon of last year when you read your Fabian Essay on Ibsen (it was not yet quintessentiated) to A.B.W., my wife, and myself, under the elm-trees by Walden Pond, I fear you found us the very worst audience you ever addressed. A.B.W. confesses that after a brief but desperate effort to adjust his mind to your novel terminology, he gave it up in despair, and fell to considering the prospects of the root-crops. For my part, I was seasoned beforehand to your freakish irrationalism, your perverse Schopenhauerism – may I say your Shawpenhauerism? I was thus in a position, while recognizing the acuteness and ingenuity of your analyses of individual plays, to scoff at the jargon in which you had chosen to expose the ground-work of your theory – a darkening counsel (so it seemed to me) by sheer metaphysical verbalism. My criticisms, like the remarks of Bret Harte's Californian controversialist, were so 'frequent and painful and free,' that I have ever since regarded your self-restraint in not pitching me into the alluringly viscous horse-pond as a sufficient refutation of your doctrine of human motives. You maintain that we do not 'do things for reasons,' but simply 'find reasons for what we want to do.' Now you will scarcely deny that you *wanted* to plunge me into the duckweed – that your Will, with a big W, made for my immersion; and no one who knows your powers of casuistry will doubt that you could have found a score of excellent reasons for so doing. (I will not insult so eminent a light-weight [boxer] as the author of *Cashel Byron's*

Profession by suggesting that any physical difficulty could act as a deterrent.) The fact remains, however, that the depths of the tarn (as Ibsen is our theme, let us be Ibsenesque) are as yet unplumbed by me; whence it ensues that your action was not governed by your Will with a big W, but was the resultant of a plexus of perfectly comprehensible motives acting upon your (lower-case) will; or, in other words, that you behaved, in spite of yourself, not like a high-and-mighty Realist (to adopt your terminology), but like a groveling, logic-chopping, 'canny' Rationalist. And this, although your opening chapters are devoted to proclaiming that you 'don't believe there's no sich person!'

Indeed, I cannot but suspect you of having taken my criticisms more rationally than I had ventured to hope. It seems to me that there is less jargon in the completed book than there was in the initial essay. You may point to this as proof that I am gradually becoming a convert to Shawpenhauerism, alleging that the difference lies, not in your text, but in the eyes with which I read it. Perhaps so; but a very little labour of the file may do a great deal in the way of dejargonisation. But this as it may, the *Quintessence* as it now stands is in every way a great improvement on the first draft. The analyses of the plays are little masterpieces of dialectical and literary dexterity. Your treatment of *Brand* and *Peer Gynt* fills me with envious awe. I have read and re-read these poems until I know them as intimately as Mr. Ruskin knows Giotto's Campanile; you, on the other hand, have never read them at all, but merely picked up a vague, second-hand knowledge of their outlines; yet you have penetrated their mystery (I speak in all seriousness) much more thoroughly than I have – more thoroughly even than Mr. P. H. Wicksteed, whose marvelous familiarity with their texts far surpasses mine. The reason is plain enough: Mr. Wicksteed and I (philosophical bias apart) are bewildered by the multitudinous details, fantastic, mystical, often, to all appearance, mutually destructive, the touches of local and temporary satire, the outbursts of tumultuous creative rapture, by which you remain blissfully undisturbed. You study the great twin-towered cathedral, so to speak, on paper, taking in at a glance the ground-plan and elevations; we see it in all its amazing lavishness of form and colour, light and shade, fretwork and tracery, an elaborately-orchestrated piece of 'frozen music.' I do not believe and you do not pretend, that the architect himself, while rearing the pile, had the ground-plan and elevations as clearly in his mind's eye as you have them in yours; but they may be substantially correct for all that. In your accounts of the later plays, and especially *Rosmersholm* and *Hedda Gabler*, there are several details of interpretation with which I cannot agree; and you have throughout reduced the poet's intentions and motives of his characters to diagrammatic definiteness which will tend to strengthen the predisposition, already inveterate in some quarters, to regard Ibsen, not as a poet, but as the showman of a moral wax-work. That cannot be helped; it is a drawback inseparable from expository criticism. I do not for a moment doubt that, on the whole, your analyses will help the candid reader not only to understand Ibsen as a thinker, but to appreciate him as a poet; as for the uncandid reader, he must be left to time and his own conscience. Not that I accuse all those who 'see nothing in Ibsen' of disingenuousness. Most of them suffer from sheer obtuseness to the higher order of dramatic effects – a malady which may co-exist with more than average sensitiveness to other forms of literary excellence.

Granting, however, that you have succeeded in the main in following up the line of thought which runs through Ibsen's plays, from *Brand* onwards – granting, too, that your peculiar use of the terms 'Idealist' and 'Realist' is justified by convenience – I return to the consideration of what I still regard, even in its modified form, as your perverse Shawpenhauerism. Why give your doctrine a wantonly obscurantist air by vapouring about 'the will to live,' as though that were a substantive discovery of Schopenhauer's, and not merely a convenient and luminous name for a phenomenon or group of phenomena which had been more or less clearly recognized from time immemorial? That the name, and the philosophic synthesis it implies, marked a great advance towards lucidity of thought, I, for the most part, most potently believe. I profess myself a convinced Schopenhauerist. I have not read Schopenhauer any more than you have; but I had thought my way to many of his conclusions (and Hamlet's) before I had so much as heard his name. This I say to show that my objection to your Shawpenhauerism arises from no mere sectarian prejudice, unless it be a prejudice to shrink from attributing Mesopotamian blessedness to any formula whatsoever. My point is that by juggling with the words 'will' and 'reason,' you not only make a simple matter needlessly obscure, but give countenance to other word-jugglers who use their sleight-of-hand to reactionary ends. Because the eye is an imperfect organ – because it cannot see what is not in sight and is subject to illusion in what it *does* see – are we therefore to renounce its aid altogether and elect to walk blindfolded? I assure you that is a perfectly natural – I will not infuriate you by saying 'logical' – deduction from your babble about 'the age of reason going its way after the age of faith.'

The quintessence of Ibsen's doctrine, according to you, is simply that circumstances alter cases. 'He protests,' you say, 'against the ordinary assumption that there are certain supreme ends which justify all means used to attain them; and insists that every end shall be challenged to show that it justifies the means. Our ideals, like the gods of old, are constantly demanding human sacrifices. Let none of them, says Ibsen, be placed above the obligation to prove that they are worth the sacrifices they demand.' Well and good; but what is this but the old utilitarian, rationalist morality? I am firmly convinced that you originally wrote 'to prove that they are consistent with the greatest good of the greatest number,' and then suddenly remembered that that phrase smacked of the Age of Reason, now happily transcended. But, having expunged it, you promptly restated it in a vaguer form; small blame to you, say I, for your beloved 'will to live' is implicit in the Benthamite formula. Of course that formula, like all the rest, must be challenged and put on trial –and that, mark you, in the Court of Reason. As it stands, the phrase is what you call an Ideal, what Ibsen calls a 'Genganer' – for who denies that rationalism as well as theology has its 'Ghosts'? Strictly considered, indeed, it is meaningless; for there is nothing to show whether it implies 'the greatest number consistent with the highest good' or 'the highest good consistent with the greatest possible number.' But whatever its verbal defects, it points in the right, because in the only possible, direction, and you, my ingenuous sophist, in the very act of scoffing at it, are throwing the search-light of reason along the path it indicates. Whither that path will lead us I do not pretend to foresee. You, with charming inconsistency, appear to look forward to a time when there shall be no general rules of conduct, but every act shall be regulated by a special judgment, a deliberate ratiocination, as to its utility. My faith in human reason is not so robust. I am rather inclined to speculate upon a scientific morality, a set of formulas or ideals, if you choose to put it so, based upon a thorough knowledge of what we are as yet but groping after – the laws of physical and mental hygiene; a morality to which the human will (psychological, not metaphysical), tamed, and, as Ibsen would say, acclimatized, in the course of generations, shall submit without a struggle and with no conscious sacrifice of freedom. You may object that this implies an unthinkable state of stable equilibrium; but the approach to perfect civilization may be asymptotic, not absolute; and furthermore, how do you know that the 'constant growth of the will,' which you so confidently postulate, may not prove to be a 'Genganger'? I admit that my stable moral world will not be at all amusing; but perhaps by the time our sense of humour will have been tamed, along with so many other inconvenient spiritual promptings.

Mr. Birrell has remarked somewhere or other that if Macaulay were to come to life again, a good many of us would be more careful than we are in how we write about him. This saying came to my mind, with Voltaire's name in place of Macaulay's, as I read your curt dismissal of his immortal *Je n'en vois pas la nécessité.* What fun he would have made of your 'universal postulate,' your solemn quibbling with the word 'necessity,' and your ingenuous belief that you had proved Reason to be nowhere in the race when you had only shown, what no one dreamed of denying, that Instinct, or if you prefer it, 'will to live,' has always had a certain start of her! Why, man alive, where do you find any necessity – natural, logical, or moral – for the individual life? Nature, it is clear, 'does not see the necessity' any more than Voltaire or 'the late lamented guillotine,' as Ibsen calls it. By a convenient metaphor, we call her 'careful of the type,' but she is notoriously 'careless of the single life.' You, I suppose, will scarcely maintain the theological position that –

We, like sentries, are obliged to stand
In starless nights, and wait the appointed hour.

There remains only the logical necessity, deduced from your 'universal postulate' of the will to live; and hourly experience proves to us that it is not universal at all. We are all of us answering the question 'To be, or not to be?' every moment of our lives, and our answer at any given moment is the resultant of a complex set of forces of which instinct or habit is only one, though doubtless in most cases the most potent. We can all conceive circumstances which would turn the scale against the primal instinct; every day of the year, every hour of the day, some of us – a certain percentage – find ourselves placed in such circumstances. And remember that the suicides who come within the ken of the coroner are but a vanishing minority of those who deliberately die because the will to live is not their strongest motive. Is it not clear, indeed, that the man who first 'did not see the necessity' was the founder of civilization? (By the way, he was probably a woman.) We are what we are in virtue of the impulse which causes some more or less human ancestor of ours to tag an adverb to his will to live. The instinct is no longer crude and absolute, even among the higher animals. Among men, it has developed into the will to live nobly, or respectably, or ostentatiously, or (in nine cases out of ten) comfortably. Our dear Hedda Gabler was full of the will to live beautifully, and when she found that she had mistaken the way, when she no longer believed in vine-leaves in the hair, her will was to die beautifully – and she fulfilled it. Poor little Hedvig, too – did *she* 'see the necessity'? No, it was her father who acknowledged himself 'face to face with the universal postulate.'

Hjalmar, having seen her body
  Borne before him on a shutter,
True to Shawpenhauerism,
  Went on eating bread-and-butter,

And no doubt making phrases about the will to live.

I know, my dear G.B.S., that this is a wrangle about words; that we do not differ as to the facts; and you will be prepared with ingenious vindication of the set of terms you choose to employ. My point is that in using them you play into the hands of superstition and reaction. And you do yourself injustice; for let me end this diatribe by saying that the affection I have long felt for you – no pitiful false shame shall make me fall back on a more conventional word – is founded on the belief that less, perhaps, than any other man I have ever known, do you 'see the necessity.'

William Archer

Shaw had delivered his **Fabian essay on Ibsen** at a meeting of the Fabian Society on 18 July 1890. A week later he read the essay to Archer, Mrs Archer, and **A.B.W.**, that is, Arthur Bingham Walkley, the theatre critic. This reading occurred at **Walden Pond**, the name for the Archer family cottage in the village of Cobham in Surrey. As a gift, E.R.V. Dibdin had carved the title of 'Walden' onto a board. Archer, his wife Frances, and their son Tom moved to the country place in May 1890. Archer also maintained a London flat at 40 Queen Square. In his own review of the *Quintessence* when it was published in 1891, Walkley reported that Shaw's talk at Walden Pond the previous year had bewildered him:

'In sheer desperation I fell to speculating on the prospect of the **root crops**' (*The Star*; quoted in Diaries 1: 638). The philosopher Arthur **Schopenhauer** (1788–1860), often identified as a pessimist, wrote *The World as Will and Idea* (1818; English trans. 1883). **Bret Harte** (1836–1902), the American short-story writer, wrote for the weekly *Californian* in the 1860s, and was famous for his stories of the Wild West. For **California controversialist** also see the character of Clarence in Harte's *A Waif of the Plains and Other Tales* (1890). ***Cashel Byron's Profession*** is Shaw's novel about boxing. The line 'don't believe there's no sich person!' derives apparently from a Bret Harte story.

From Shaw's perspective **Voltaire** (François-Marie Arouet, 1694–1778) was a Rationalist who had been limited by his 'blind faith in the intellect' or Reason. This faith was a form of Idealism in Shaw's formulation. Schopenhauer and Ibsen, identified as Realists, stripped away illusion and reason; they supposedly rejected Rationalism by recognizing the necessity of individual will in human thought and action. In this philosophical formation, Shaw saw himself as a Realist, but Archer accused him of propagating rationalistic confusion. Although Shaw was familiar with *Peer Gynt*, neither it nor *Brand* was yet translated into English when Shaw wrote the *Quintessence*. In *The Stones of Venice* (1851–3), John **Ruskin** (1819–1900) wrote about the Campanile, the bell tower of the Florence Cathedral that the painter **Giotto** (c.1266–1337) worked on towards the end of his life when he served as supervisor of the cathedral. Philip H. **Wicksteed** (1844–1927), a classical scholar and translator of Dante, was one of the early supporters of Ibsen in England. He lectured on Ibsen in 1888 at the Chelsea Town Hall (after being denied space at London University). Two of these lectures were published in *The Contemporary Review* (1889, 1891), then in 1892 he published *Four Lectures on Henrik Ibsen*. Like Archer, he argued for Ibsen the poet over Ibsen the social philosopher. The phrase **'frozen music'** was used by John Ruskin (1819–1900) in *Seven Lamps of Architecture*. Preceding him, however, Johann Wolfgang von Goethe used the phrase in *Conversations with Goethe* by J.P. Eckermann (1792–1854) on 29 March 1829: 'Music is liquid architecture; architecture is frozen music.' Goethe, in turn, credited the *Philosophy of Art* (1807) by Friedrich von Schelling (1775–1854) as his source: 'Architecture is music in space, as if it were a frozen music.' Archer himself had previously used the phrase in a letter to Dibdin on 31 March 1885 (BL MS 65373 f35).

In the *Quintessence* Shaw defined an **Idealist** as a deluded and self-deceiving thinker. By contrast, a **Realist**, such as Ibsen, was able to see life and conditions as they are. Shaw divided human beings into three groups: Philistines, Idealists, and Realists, and in a parallel analogy he distributed them into three progressive ages: **age of faith**, **age of reason**, and age of individual will. Complicating matters, Shaw identified a thinker of the Age of Reason, such as Voltaire, as an idealist instead of a realist because of his commitment to rationalism and reason. In the compressed opening sections to the *Quintessence*, 'The Two Pioneers' and 'Ideals and Idealists,' Shaw attempted to set up these various historical and philosophical distinctions. (On Shaw's terminology, including definitions of idealist and realist, see Wisenthal, esp. 26–40.) Jeremy **Bentham** (1748–1832), the English philosopher, was the founder of the English utilitarian school of philosophy, which argued for a social ethic based on the idea that an action should be dedicated to and serve a principle of the greatest good, which could be understood as the greatest happiness for the greatest number of people. **Genganger** in Norwegian means ghost, spirit. Augustine **Birrell** (1850–1933), who wrote prolifically on literary topics, produced a study of Thomas Babington **Macaulay** (1800–59), the essayist and historian who became famous for his opinionated writings and his 'Whig view of history' that celebrated modern Britain as the 'best of all possible worlds.' The phrase ***Je n'en vois pas la nécessité*** ('I do not see the necessity') appears in the 'Discours préliminaire,' a preface to Voltaire's play *Alzire*. But the phrase originated with Comte d'Argental, censor of the press for Louis XV, who made this statement when a political writer excused his own political squibs by saying, 'I must live.' Alfred Tennyson's *In Memoriam*, LV, is the source for '**careless of the single life**.' The quoted lines '**We, like sentries ... appointed hour**,' are derived from John Dryden's *Don Sebastian, The King of Portugal: A Tragedy* (II, i). Ibsen's ***Hedda Gabler***, in which the heroine commits suicide, premiered in London on 20 April 1891. **Hedvig** is the daughter of Hjalmar in Ibsen's *The Wild Duck*. The translation was published in 1890 in Archer's edition of *Ibsen's Prose Drama*, vol. 2.

26 / To William Archer

29 Fitzroy Square W
25th October 1891

[TLS: BL 45296 ff 29-30; CL 1]

Although Shaw refused to publish a public response to Archer's open letter, this private letter allowed him to defend and explain his philosophical argument in the Quintessence. *This letter is the first – but hardly the last – of Shaw's laments that Archer failed critically in his assessment of Shaw's works because he evaluated the author instead of the book. Shaw continued to make this complaint during the following decades.*

Grove has just sent me your open letter with a suggestion that I should write a reply to it. On reading it over I have formed a strong opinion that you ought without further ado to burn it. Everybody will expect something specially good from you on the subject; and this is quite exceptionally bad. Its badness is twofold. In the first place it entirely omits the really serious question of the review – that is to say, whether my interpretation of Ibsen is right or wrong, or how much right and how much wrong, and if wholly wrong what Ibsen's meaning actually is. As to this there is nothing in the letter, absolutely nothing. You must have something at the bottom of Walden Pond, if you ask the public to dive into it. Either the language of The Wild Duck means something or nothing. If something, is it something particular, or is it the ordinary meaning – is Relling simply Clement Scott or Buchanan? If the latter, why has it puzzled and revolted Clemmy? If the former, am I right or wrong; and if wrong, put your finger on the error. And if you do put your finger on it, shew whether it is common to myself and Ibsen (in which case I should be right in my interpretation, though we should be both wrong in our philosophy) or whether it has led me to miss Ibsen's meaning. That is the job which the book presents to the illustrious W.A. from the public point of view. Instead of doing it, you have written a criticism of *me*, leaving it to be inferred that you do not demur to the identity between Ibsen's philosophy and what you call mine, and that you dismiss them both as worthless.

The worst of it is that your criticism of me is nothing but a mere crudity. It is like a country parson's criticism of Socialism. Socialism is an attack on property: that is enough for him: how could we get on without property: we should have universal theft and anarchy: in a week things would be as they were &c, &c, &c. Now there is no poorer sort of dialectical game than that which proceeds by each party assuming that the other means what he cannot possibly mean – that he is an idiot, in short. This is what the parson does and this is what you do. You see an attack on Reason; and you immediately go ahead to shew how impossible it is to do without reason. That is what everybody does in the first five minutes, and what nobody has any excuse for doing in the second five. When you have once thought out the position that the real and of course eternally indispensable function of Reason is to devise the means for the satisfaction of the will, whereas the essence of Rationalism is to set it up as being the prime motor of human action – the steam instead of the engine – you will then find not only that the book is precise on the point, but that it contains the most emphatic and explicit warning against the error you have fallen into. In the place where you call me an ingenuous sophist, you blunder in an amazing manner into the reductioadabsurdum of your own assumption about the extinction of reason. My book is closely reasoned from cover to cover. Precisely, says you: therefore you have not got rid of reason after all. Exactly, I reply; and now, in the name of Reason, itself, may I ask you which of us you suppose that stone has brained?

The phrase about the age of reason going its way after the age of faith, by the bye, is not a rhetorical flourish, but an allusion to Tom Paine's proclamation of the Age of Reason as the successor to the Age of Faith. And he meant that Reason was to ascertain the Divine Will instead of taking the Church's word for it.

What you say of the Voltaire point is hopelessly fudged by your overlooking my careful limitation of the meaning of his 'necessity' to logical necessity. The whole gist of my criticism of him is that he did regard lack of logical necessity as lack of real necessity. If you can shew from other writings and sayings of his that he was not really under any such confusion, and that he saw eye to eye with Schopenhauer on the point, then you will throw a new and startling light on his character. And, observe, you will then have changed the complexion of his 'Je n'en vois pas &c.,' from a fundamentally honest though mistaken home truth to a brutal quibble. You accuse me of quibbling, by the bye. You will always find that when one man has a tight grip of the meaning of a word, and another man has a loose and perpetually shifting one, the latter always accuses the former of quibbling. I defy you to pick out one passage in which I have used the Voltairean 'necessity' in any other sense than the one expressly claimed for it at the outset. So there!

As to Schopenhauer, you have seized only the vaguest generalization of his synthesis – so vague that it seems identical with your equally vague generalization of mine. In vain have I warned you in the book itself against confusing his metaphysics with his philosophy. I have taken his distinction between the intellect and the will, a natural fact which has always been preached (as I have pointed out) in one form or another, but which he undoubtedly brought clearly into the light of modern thought. That does not make me a Schopenhaurist, or Ibsen one. His pessimism, and his conviction that the will was the devil and the intellect the divine saviour, marks him off from me and from Ibsen in the clearest and most fundamental way. You might just as well call me a Herbert Spencerist because I accept the doctrine of evolution. My whole book is a protest against that Genganger, the dread of the will and the blind faith in the intellect. And as to pessimism, not only ought the last page of my first Fabian Essay to publicly absolve me from all suspicion of it, but the Quintessence first disposes of it by implication on the simple ground that it *is* an ISM, and then deals with it explicitly in the pages dealing with the survivals in Ibsen's mind of the old middle class pessimism as shewn in Emperor & Galilean &c. The fact is, you have done just what you think I did: you have fished one notion out of Schopenhauer, or rather out of his reputation, and you call that Schopenhauerism. In any case, the second and third sentences of your third paragraph simply mean that I have given 'my' doctrine a wantonly obscurantist air by using the terms of a philosophic synthesis which marked a great advance towards lucidity of thought. Of course you dont mean this; but just conceive the confusion of mind you must have attained in order unsuspectingly to leave such holes in your article.

Your objection that the distinction between the Will and the Reason is not new (after which you go on, as usual in such cases, to deny that it exists) brings the letter down to the level of the Noodle's oration. I do not say this merely because I have not only pointed out the antiquity of the distinction myself, but mentioned the most familiar and convincing forms of its recognition before Schopenhauer's grandfather was born. It is because Ibsen has put forward as novel certain consequences of it which have been so completely overlooked that our moral standards have become seriously corrupted. That is where the novelty is; and that is where it is claimed. Now if you mean to say that the novelty is no novelty – that the criticism of life in Ghosts or the Wild Duck is stale and trite, then you are an ass; and matters are so far irremediable. But if you have only missed the point, then you have merely made an ass of yourself, which is remediable by suppressing your oversight.

Another Noodle's Oration phrase, and a quite inexcusable one, is 'showman of a moral waxwork.' It is a base desertion of Ibsen – a deliberate going over to the haters of light who cant about art for art's sake. And it is a most unworthy and inadequate treatment of my very careful demonstration of the point at which Ibsen's delight in the exercise of his artistic faculty came at last under complete subjection of his impulse as a moralist. (And observe, the artistic faculty may work harder under the compulsion of the moral impulse than in freedom, just as the reason is far keener as the servant of the will than when it is merely taking exercise in the academy.)

It is impossible for me to go on any further. I have already cursed you up hill and down dale for forcing me on a very busy day to say all this over again which I have so laboriously said before merely because you will go fooling over a serious bit of thinking. Out of the depths of a pessimism induced by your actual observation of the fact (for statistics see 'Facts for Socialists,' one penny) that out of every five men in the country four live uncomfortably, one dishonorably, and most of them miserably both one and the other, you find yourself under such a necessity to whittle down and disparage any clear statement whatever, that you proceed to inform the world that the will to live now means the will to live nobly, or at least comfortably. Now if there were any sort of satisfaction to you in this, I would not attempt to baulk you in it. But since it is only your way of swearing you will ne'er consent; since it will do you no credit and me no good; since it includes Ibsen in the depreciation of what has been said as not worth saying; and since the occasion is one on which you will be expected to put forward your sharpest and closest dialectical power – since finally it is all the blastedest evasion, misunderstanding, and nonsense, I most vehemently recommend you to either cancel it or do it over again.

In hottest haste
GBS

Archibald **Grove** (1855–1920) was the editor of the *New Review*, which William Heinemann published. **Relling**, the doctor in Ibsen's *The Wild Duck*, is the realistic critic of Greger Werle's self-deceptive idealism. Eric **Clement Scott** (1841–1904), who served as theatre critic for the *Daily Telegraph*, was opposed to Ibsen's drama. In *Quintessence* Shaw analysed Scott's rejection of *Ghosts*. When Robert W. **Buchanan** was not attacking Ibsen and the new drama, he wrote popular comedies and melodramas. The philosopher **Herbert Spencer** (1820–1903), who prided himself on his scientific reasoning, adapted and promulgated reductive versions of Darwinian evolution for a social theory of human evolution, progress, and individualism. Shaw used the Norwegian **Genganger** ('ghost,"spirit') to identify what he described here as 'the dread of the will and the blind faith in the intellect.' The title of Ibsen's play is *Gengangere*, Ghosts. ***Emperor and Galilean*** (1873) is Ibsen's 'world history play' about the dialectical struggle between Paganism and Christianity during the reign of Julian the Apostate in the fourth century CE. Archer translated and published the play in November 1890; Shaw read it that December (Diaries 1: 675). Sydney Smith (1771–1845), co-founder and editor of the *Edinburgh Review*, created the phrase **Noodle's Oration** in a review of Jeremy Bentham's *Book of Fallacies* (1824). Smith criticized 'a vast number of absurd and mischievous fallacies, which get accepted readily in the world for sense and virtue. The whole of these fallacies may be gathered together in a little oration, which we will denominate the "Noodle's Oration."' Shaw appropriated the phrase, using it here and twice in book reviews (29 April 1892, 30 May 1902) to identify anti-rationalist, anti-socialist, and anti-progressive fallacies in politics. '**Facts for Socialists**' was Fabian Tract no. 5, written by Sidney Webb, revised by Shaw, and published in June 1887 in *The Commonweal* (see Biblio 2: C321 and Biblio 1: BB3; Diaries 1: 223, 231).

27 / To William Archer

29 Fitzroy Square W
26th October 1891

[ALS: BL 45296 ff 31–2; CL 1]

Archer's reply to Shaw's previous letter is missing. He apparently again challenged Shaw's ideas on Rationalism and appealed to Shaw to accept Grove's request for a reply to the open letter. Besides the frustration of contending with Archer over the Quintessence, *Shaw had to face the dentist on 26 October 'for the whole day' (Diaries 2: 762).*

This crackbrained proposal really finishes me. You must have your way as to publishing your letter; but no public reply from me is possible. Quem Deus vult asinare, prius dementit. An awful silence will fall on your little world when the New Review appears: your friends will breathe only by stealth. I write to Grove to say, No answer.

Evidently your underlining means that I am a Rationalist because I deal in rational ideas. Doubtless I am also a Positivist because I deal with positive facts, and you a Chiropodist because you have corns.

If you like, you may put my reply at the foot of your letter in these terms – 'Oh William Archer, William Archer: where are your brains? G.B.S.'

GBS

Shaw's loose Latin clause of **Quem Deus vult asinare, prius dementit** offers a modification of the Latin proverb *Quem Deus vult perdere, prius demantat* ('Whom God wishes to destroy he first drives mad'). The Latin phrase, in turn, has been credited to a Greek tragic couplet by Sophocles.

28 / To G. Bernard Shaw [no address]
[26th October 1891]

[ALS: BL 45296 ff 31–2; CL 1]

In the margins and empty spaces of Shaw's short letter, Archer wrote this reply, which he immediately returned to Shaw.

Undisturbed by Shaw's negative response, Archer maintained his resolve to publish his open letter in the November issue of the New Review. *Because Archer appreciated the ways that the G.B.S. persona and voice could attract an audience and stir up a controversy, he continued to push back at Shaw. He was still hoping to entice, goad, or badger Shaw into an 'ingenious vindication of the set of terms you choose to employ,' as he had stated in the open letter. Although Archer admired Shaw's interpretations of the plays – 'The analyses of the plays are little masterpieces of dialectical and literary dexterity' – he felt that the philosophical sections in the* Quintessence, *though clever, misrepresented Ibsen views. The opening section offered a Shavian manifesto on will power and metaphysical philosophy that Shaw had imposed on Ibsen's drama. The two friends were thus at odds with one another, despite their shared advocacy for Ibsen's drama. Whereas Archer mostly admired the drama for its poetry, its symbolic significance, and its dramatic form,*

Shaw sought to celebrate its representation of human morality and individual action. Shaw chose the title of 'Ibsenism' for his interpretation, but Archer preferred the dismissive title of 'Shawpenhauerism.' Consequently, in 1891 they were bound to argue, though Shaw would modify and drop some of his ideas by the time he prepared the revised edition of Quintessence *in 1912–13. (On Shaw's ideas and how they modified over time see Wisenthal: 23–73.)*

I have always said you wd end by being Pope, & now I'm sure of it. Better order your triple crown at once. Only not content with being infallible yourself you insist on everyone else being infallible, & want to have all bad reasoning burnt by the common hangman. Very likely my reasoning *is* bad; but I insist on my inalienable right to reason badly if I please. And let me add that if all your unborable revolutionists are going to be infallible logic machines, I think they'll have a mighty dull time of it. But that's a contingency I face with equanimity. The probability is that neither of us is anywhere near right, but it's very likely that you have the right end of the stick & I the wrong. All I want you to do is to pull.

Of course I think you're doing precisely what you think I'm doing. If there ever have been rationalists idiotic enough to make reason the prime motor in human conduct, why worry about them at this time of day? I say you are setting up an idiotic rationalism (which may or may not have some sort of historic foundation) & thinking you've done a mighty fine thing when you've knocked it down again. I dont think I'm quite as bad as that, for the position I attribute to you (whether it's yours or not) is not idiotic, only injudicious. In a word, I accuse you of deifying the mainspring of the watch & reviling the regulator; you accuse me of deifying the regulator & ignoring the mainspring; of course the latter blunder would be the more imbecile of the two; but 'who deniges of it Betsy Prig'?

As to answering or not answering, the difference between us is this: I want you to accept the Socratic method of working towards truth, you howl because I haven't put all Ibsen & all myself into a newspaper article (for you know it wasn't intended even for a Review) with Herbert Spencerian precision. And remember, I'm not casting myself for Socrates – Socrates, I take it, is the fellow who comes best out of the skirmish, & as you're a practised debater & I'm not, it would be more shame to you if that wasn't you. As a matter of fact your position is not Socratic but

Clement Scottish – you say 'Yah, here comes a beastly pessimist – the only thing I can do is to 'eave 'arf a brick at him, & as I dont care to do that I'll do nothing.'

Look out for me after the Flying Dutchman tonight – shall be in the pit.

Yours incorrigibly
W.A.

The question **'who deniges of it Betsy Prig'?** is from *Martin Chuzzlewit* by Charles Dickens (1812–70). Because Shaw referred to Clement Scott in his letter of 25 October, Archer retaliated by dismissing Shaw's position as **Clement Scottish.** On several occasions in their debates both Shaw and Archer employed the rhetorical tactic of comparing the other to Scott, the dramatic critic (see Wisenthal: 18). The comparison was not, however, a demeaning insult, but instead an easy – and rather pointless – taunt in their fencing matches. The phrase **'eave 'arf a brick at 'im** appeared in a *Punch* cartoon which showed two miners observing a well-dressed man in the street. First native: 'Who's 'im, Bill?' Second native: 'A stranger.' First native: ''Eave 'arf a brick at 'im.' The *Punch* cartoon appeared in 1854; the phrase was repeated often in other contexts during and after the Victorian era to express a closed-minded attitude. For example, Annie Besant used the phrase to illustrate prejudice against others in her essay 'Wake Up, India' (1913). In his review of Signor Antonio Lago's production of Wagner's ***The Flying Dutchman***, Shaw dismissed the performance as a 'miserable travesty' (Music 2: 443–50). No doubt after the performance the two friends continued their argument over the *Quintessence.*

29 / To William Archer

29 Fitzroy Square W
7th November 1891

[TLS, with ANS postscript: BL 45296 f 33; CL 1]

In the PMG *on 9 September, the novelist George Moore (1852–1933) stirred up controversy by proclaiming that English theatre reviewers, except for Archer, were incompetent and often took gifts from theatrical people. Recognizing a hot topic, Frank Harris (1856–1931), editor of the* Fortnightly Review, *invited Archer, Shaw, and others to submit essays on the issue of theatre reviewing in London. Archer used the occasion to submit 'The Free Stage and the New Drama,' which described recent developments in the alternative theatre movement, especially the Ibsen productions in London and the arrival of J.T. Grein's Independent Theatre. He also praised André Antoine (1858–1943) and the Théâtre Libre in Paris. Only towards the end of the essay did he take up Moore's accusation. Contrasting the 'jaded, theatrical journalists' in London with the 'men of letters' in Paris, Archer concurred with Moore that theatre reviewing in London was incompetent. He observed that some theatre critics were controlled by the actor-managers and dramatists. Then, in a feckless endeavour to separate himself from other London critics, he offered a self-deprecating statement: 'No one has as yet thought it worth while to make the slightest attempt to buy my goodwill' (FR, November 1891: 671). This statement served as an open invitation to Shaw, who ridiculed 'William the Anchorite' in this letter.*

But instead of mailing this teasing letter to Archer, Shaw mistakenly sent it to Frank Harris. At this time Shaw and Harris barely knew one another; they did not meet until 1893. Four days later, on 11 November, Harris returned Shaw's misguided letter. In his attached letter Harris wrote: 'I will confess to a sense of mystification upon reading the enclosed letter of yours, which none the less afforded me much amusement. I tried to look upon it as the eccentricity of a clever writer, but failed to comprehend its drift. I felt as Alice may have felt in Wonderland' (BL 45296 f 39).

With the letter for 'William the Anchorite' back in his hands, Shaw wrote out the handwritten note at the bottom of this letter and then belatedly mailed it to Archer.

I have just had a letter from Frank Harris asking me to put my oar into the discussion on criticism. I have refused on the ground that I have said all that need be said in the appendix to the Quintessence. The magnanimity of this resolution consists in my abstaining from exposing the monstrous hypocrisies of your own article. When I see you posing as the incorruptible Archer, assuring the public with an air of primeval simplicity that you would not know how to set about getting half a crown for a notice if you wanted to, and that no monk knows less of teas with pretty actresses than William the Anchorite, I really feel a moral revulsion. How if I were to tell the world that I have hardly once dropped in on you unexpectedly at Queen Square without disturbing a teteatete between you and some pretty actress or another; so that your stock excuse became that I did it on purpose, having got wind of the appointment? Marion la bionda today: Elizabeth la bruna tomorrow. Have you forgotten Hampstead Heath and Mary Anderson? do the photographs of the fascinating Janet no longer plaster your walls? is your table already cleared of the gift books of the irresistible Rehan, the reward of your shameless recantation? If Leporello, with his catalogue in his pocket, had ever come upon an article by Don Juan expressing an artless surprise that no pretty woman ever tried to 'get at' him, he would have felt much as I feel over the Fortnightly. I can see all those beauteous eyes winking as they read your audacities, and their owners making private notes not to believe men who wear incorruptible collars. The amazing, staggering, breath bereaving part of it all is that I actually believe that you thought you were perfectly sincere in what you wrote. Why, man alive, there is not an ambitious actress in London whose first move is not to get at William Archer. And they do it with perfect security under cover of your theory that the thing is impossible and consequently never happens. Your theory that your name has never been publicly connected with Ibsen's, and that you have in fact hardly ever alluded to that obscure foreigner, is nothing to your pretty actress theory.

I have just received the New Review article. The oftener I read it, the more flagrantly does it proclaim itself pure Clement Scott. Its hideous superficiality has destroyed my faith in your intellectual solidity as completely as the Fortnightly has destroyed my belief – what was left of it – in your moral integrity. A man who can assert that the only safe way to work the L & M Railway is to draw up an absolute and unalterable time table, and start the trains at the appointed speed and hour without regard to earthquake, landslip, accident, snowfall, fog or certain death (since the human mind is incapable of any other guidance except blind idealistic adherence to the letter of the timetable) is a man who ought not to be at large. Now either you mean this, or you are incapable of seeing that an ordinary timetable is no violation at all of the principle that 'circumstances alter cases,' in which case you are a manifest idiot. Altogether the article is one which you will have to live down.

If you would like to print the first part of this letter in the next Fortnightly as a reply to your article, I have no objection whatever. In fact, I think it ought to be done in the public interest.

Walkley says he is bringing out a book. Why did you let him throw away his copyright permanently?

GBS

11th Nov. 1891
Has anything more unspeakably awful ever happened than my sending this to Harris & his letter to you?

Frank Harris edited the *Fortnightly Review* from 1886 to 1894; he then became editor of the *Saturday Review*. In the 1891 **appendix** to the *Quintessence*, Shaw described the new modern actors in the London productions of Ibsen, and castigated the critics for their inability to recognize and appreciate realistic, rather than idealistic, acting. He noted that the 'resistance of the old playgoers to the new plays' was supported by 'the elder managers, the elder actors, and the elder critics' (Wisenthal: 229). In the last several pages of the appendix Shaw expressed his disdain for the London critics such as Clement Scott, though he praised Archer and Walkley as independent critics (Wisenthal: 233–7). Archer had moved into a London flat on **Queen Square** Place in late 1889 or early 1890. This was his city address in 1891; on the weekends he joined his wife and son Tom at the 'Walden' cottage in the village of Cobham in Surrey. **Marion la bionda** (Marion Lea) and **Elizabeth la bruna** (Elizabth Robins) produced and acted in *Hedda Gabler* in 1891; **Janet** Achurch was in *A Doll's House* in 1889. **Mary Anderson** (1859–1940) was an American actress with whom Archer had taken a walk on Hampstead Heath. Acclaimed for her classical beauty and rich voice, she appeared in London regularly in the 1880s before she retired from the stage in 1889. Archer admired her Shakespearean roles, including the doubling of Perdita and Hermione in *The Winter's Tale.* **Ada Rehan** (1860–1916) was the leading actress in the American company of Augustin Daly (1839–99). During the 1880s and 1890s she performed regularly in New York and London, starring in productions of Shakespeare's comedies (e.g., the roles of Katherina, Rosalind, Viola, Miranda, and Portia). Archer's open letter on *The Quintessence of Ibsenism* appeared in the **New Review**. By proclaiming that Archer could '**print the first part of this letter**' in the *Forthnightly Review,* Shaw offered a jesting counter-proposal to his refusal to write a response to the open letter. In 1891 A.B. **Walkley** published *Playhouse Impressions,* a collection of his reviews for *The Star* (1888–90). He wrote under the name of 'Spectator.' Shaw reviewed the book in *The Star* on 9 January 1892.

30 / To William Archer

29 Fitzroy Square W
9th November 1891

[ALS: BL 45296 f 34; CL 1]

Archer received this letter two or three days before the misguided letter of 7 November finally reached him, probably on 12 November. In both letters Shaw accused Archer of being a self-deceiving idealist or 'apriorist' who needed 'a little realism knocked' into him. Shaw also continued his assault on Archer's essay 'The Free Stage and the New Drama' in Harris's Fortnightly Review. *To this end, Shaw expanded his critique of Archer's pose of critical integrity by sending a letter to Elizabeth Robins on this same day. He asked her opinion of Archer's claim of incorruptibility. 'What do you think of that, you, who put him in your pocket with one flash of your dark?!! eyes so ridiculously easily that I blushed for him? Do write an article entitled "How to get at William Archer; by one who has done it"' (FALES, box 23: 9 November 1891). Shaw's letter, which offended her, was 'an outrageousness too outrageous even to be shown to WA' (as she wrote on a note that she attached to Shaw's letter). She ordered Shaw to stop making insinuations. He replied: 'I did not mean that you deliberately took his scalp. But I assure you the scalp went all the same – walked spontaneously off his head and hung itself to your belt without the least help from you or conscience on his part' (FALES, 10 November;*

Whitebrook: 137). Despite Shaw's gesture toward an apology to Robins and his suggestion that his comment was innocent, he failed to calm her anger. She was not amused by his suggestion that she would use her sexual wiles to charm Archer. Ever since the production of Hedda Gabler *in April 1891, Robins had felt indignant over his unmannered familiarity with her and his prankish remarks. Archer could be amused by Shaw's 'affectation of omniscience,' but not Robins (Prophet: 77–9; 81–2).*

Horror on horror's head: I have put your letter into Harris's envelope – and such a letter! Description would be futile: you must read the letter when he sends it on in order to realize the awful situation. I am really very sorry. Fortunately, he will probably take it to be pure chaff.

Your point about antiIbsen criticism needing no hypothesis of corruption to explain it is one which I quite catch. I ought to, considering that you have stolen it from my appendix (see page 160, lines 6 – 16). In your letter, you say, waking up suddenly to a sense of real life, that people have often tried, and do continually try, to chicken and champagne you. In the article you solemnly declare that no one has yet thought it worth while to make the slightest attempt to buy your good will. Which of these two positions is the apriorist and which the realist one? You also say in your letter that corruption, *as regards Ibsen*, does not come into play. What, then, is your view of, for instance, the terrific row made by Yates when Lady C[olin] C[ampbell]'s article on Ghosts got into the paper during his absence at Bath? Was it his conscientious Puritanism or his country house circulation that was imperilled then? Or do you suppose that this was a solitary and accidental incident? Or have you forgotten it? Further, there is in your article no limitation of your denial of corruption to criticism of Ibsen, any more than there is in my appendix.

The fact is, you have not yet realized that what you have read about and talked about as 'getting at' critics, is just what is happening to you and me and Lady C. & Austin & Davenport Adams & Knight & Massingham & all the rest that you know. You are like Agatha in 'An Unsocial Socialist,' regarding yourself as an exceptional person whose experiences do not belong to the common categories. You have, in short, talked prose all your life without knowing it. The other evening, at the Shaftesbury, Thompson of the Star came up to me with tears in his eyes (positively) and showed me 'her last gift.' It was a handsome cigar box which Giulia

Ravogli had given him on her departure. Poor Thompson was as void of all guile in the matter as you were when you were taking tea with Miss Robins. To him it only meant that he liked Giulia and that she had been kind to him. To the public it meant that 'Piccolo' had been got at. In Thomson's place I, being an older man, should have returned the cigar case. In your place I should have taken tea with Miss Robins – possibly have gone to greater extremities; but my article in the Fortnightly should have been a graceful explanation of how the corruption actually worked – how different it was from the fancy picture of gross bribery & blackmail painted by apriorists. And I should not have flatly contradicted either George Moore or the author of a document so very carefully drawn up and so scrupulously based on observation of facts as the appendix to the Quintessence.

Seriously, I think that page 671 of the Fortnightly is a most outrageous piece of trifling – not to say petulance. You should join the Fabian & get a little realism knocked into you.

GBS

In the **appendix** for *The Quintessence of Ibsenism* Shaw argued that the anti-Ibsenite theatre critics are not necessarily corrupt; instead, they were motivated by several factors, including the demands placed upon them by their editors and by legal concerns over possible libel suits. Only a few theatre critics, such as A.B. Walkley and William Archer, have been capable of independent thinking (Wisenthal: 233–7). Both Archer and Shaw enjoyed labelling one another an **apriorist** – that is, a person who resides in an idealistic or *a priori* world of his own intellectual construction. This dismissive tag recurred often in their exchanges. (See, for example, letters of 22 August 1893, 25 and 27 January 1900, 1 September 1903, 22 April 1919, and 14 December 1924.) The earliest extant evidence of this labelling appeared in a letter Archer wrote to R.L. Stevenson on 10 March 1886; he praised Shaw, but also described him as 'an *a priori* novelist' – an Irishman who was guided by his fads, such as Jaeger suits, and his idealism, such as socialist politics (BL: MS 45295 f 94). Decades later Archer repeated the apriorist idea in his last essay on Shaw, 'The Psychology of G. B. S.,' published in December 1924. Louis Frederick **Austin** (1852–1905) was the theatre critic for the *New Review*, and he served as a paid secretary for Henry Irving. William **Davenport Adams** (1851–1904) wrote reviews for several newspapers; in 1891 he edited *A Book of Burlesques* and published *With Poet and Player: Essays on Literature and the Stage*. Joseph **Knight** (1829–1907), the drama critic for *The Atheneum*, published *Theatrical Notes* (1893), a collection of his reviews since 1874; he also wrote a biography of David Garrick (1894). After editing *The Star* (1890–1), H.W. **Massingham** edited the *Daily Chronicle* (1895–9), the *Daily News* (1901–6), and *The Nation* (1907–23). Both Shaw and Archer wrote for these publications on various occasions. Massingham was a member of the Fabians in the early 1890s. ***An Unsocial Socialist*** (1883) was Shaw's fifth novel. In 1890, when Shaw became music critic at *The World*, Sidney R. **Thompson** replaced him as the music critic for *The Star*. He wrote under the pen name of 'Piccolo.' **Giulia Ravogli** (1850–1910) was a highly respected and accomplished Italian soprano. In 1891, for example, at Covent Garden she sang the roles of Carmen, Ortrud in *Lohengrin*, Venus in *Tannhäuser*, and Euridice in Gluck's *Orfeo ed Euridice*. Shaw's first introduction to Elizabeth Robins occurred on 21 January 1891 when she and Marion Lea were **taking tea** at Archer's flat on Queen Square (*Diaries* 2: 689). The Irish novelist **George Moore** was best known for *A Modern Lover* (1883), *A Mummer's Wife* (1885), and *A Mere Accident* (1887). The latter novel, which features a rape and a suicide of young women, was reviewed by Shaw in PMG (19 July 1887): 'The objection, in fact, to Mr. Moore, is not that he is realistic, but that he is a romancer who, in order that he may take liberties, persuades himself that he is a pathologist' (Tyson 1: 303). In 1893 Shaw continued his criticism of Moore when he reviewed the publication of his play *The Strike at Arlingford*. (See Dukore 1: 218–21; also Shaw's letter to Archer, 23 February 1893.)

31 / To William Archer

29 Fitzroy Square W
10th November 1891

[ALS: BL 45296 ff 35–8; CL 1]

In this and the following letter Shaw offered his most serious argument against Archer's rather thoughtless claim that as a critic he was free of any influence by theatre people. At this date Archer had not yet seen the letter of 7 November that Shaw had mailed by mistake to Frank Harris. He had responded to Shaw's letter of 9 November, but that response has not survived. In addition to that lost letter, Archer apparently enclosed a draft of a letter he was preparing for the editor of PMG. *It was an attempt to clarify or justify what he had said in his article 'The Free Stage and the New Drama,' which he had published in the* Fortnightly Review. *Archer felt that he should respond to comments that George Moore had written to the editor of* PMG *about the critical debate. But after receiving this letter of 10 November from Shaw, Archer decided against sending a defensive letter to* PMG.

Yes, but look here. You havent said that chicken and champagne dont matter; what you have told the public is that they dont exist. And that is precisely why I have made so much of this occasion. Hitherto the difference between us has always been, not as to facts, but as to how much the facts mattered. But now, for the first time, you have misstated the facts themselves. It is one thing to say to George Moore, 'My good sir, you are quite mistaken if you suppose that we critics spare Harris or Wyndham one jot because they have chicken and champagned us,' and quite another to say, 'You are an ignorant liar: critics are never chickened and champagned; and if I wanted a liver wing or a glass of dry Monopole tomorrow, I should not, after all these 12 years, know where to turn for it.' Now that I have had the trouble of sticking to you like a bulldog for about a week, I have forced you to come down to reality and, as you say, to agree with me as to the facts. But is it possible that you do not see that if you published this last letter of yours in the Pall Mall [Gazette] tomorrow, it would be received with amazement as a complete confession of the utter falsehood of your description of your personal experience in the Fortnightly?

I insist on the point because I have been watching your writing, and find that whilst it has lately gained considerably in eloquence, freedom, and wilfulness in the better sense, it is also getting unscrupulous & careless. Letting yourself go on the generous side, you also let yourself go on the ungenerous side without making up and verifying your case with your old caution. A few years ago it would have been impossible for you to have conducted a controversy with Moore in such a fashion as to enable him to put you in the wrong at every step of the argument, whatever the merits of your conclusion might be.

Take the case as to me, too. Formerly you stuck to your facts and though I sometimes thought you saw too few of them at a time, or weighted them unjudgmatically, or grouped them badly, yet I never felt that you were misleading people, and never felt the smallest impulse to contradict you, knowing pretty well that you would finally come unconsciously round to my view in the course of time, when the kaleidoscope had shifted a bit, just as I have sometimes come round to yours. But now you have said the thing that is not – you have drawn a romantic portrait of yourself which is not true, exactly as [Clement] Scott draws maudlin groups of himself, Tomlins & Co. which are not true. And you have also offered me the indignity – of which I mildly complain, on principle – of dismissing me contemptuously with a blow beneath the belt by denying the facts on which my induction was based, and thereby pretending to convict me of pure deduction.

As to the Ghosts incident, let me first call attention to the extraordinary jump you have made from the position that undue influence was nil in the special case of Ibsen, to the position that Ibsen is so specially obnoxious to editorial influence that it is unfair to argue from it to ordinary plays. This by the way, as a revelation of how your grip slips. But the main point to be grasped is that if you mean, by your 'negligable [*sic*] quantity' that in the vast majority of cases the play raises no question of morals or politics, and that neither critic, editor nor proprietor has an axe to grind in the matter one way or another, then I grant you the first part, and admit, as to the second, that it is rather the abstract sense of danger in speaking out than any definite bias for or against the play in question that operates. And even in this I am making the shallowest of concessions; for a moment's reflection will convince you that though a drama by [Robert] Buchanan or Ohnet apparently raises no moral question – and really as well as apparently does not do so in the mind of the conventionally moralled critic – yet you and Walkley and all the abler men have a fundamental quarrel with the Ohnetesque morality which you never dream of raising seriously, simply because, in your case, of Mrs. Archer and Tom. Under the circumstances it is not worth doing. But if you were in as independent a position as Samuel Butler, you would think it worth doing, and would do it, if not thoroughly, at least far more than you do now. Suppose you were a critic of commonplace ability – one who could be dismissed and replaced without loss to your paper, as is necessarily the case with most critics. Suppose the only berth that offered itself was one on the Sunday Times, or a private secretaryship to Irving. Would you ever think of telling the whole truth about a Drury Lane or Lyceum performance? Suppose by chance you had not translated Ghosts, and you had had Lady Colin's job, and Yates had been in town. Would you have ventured to say, Either my criticism goes in or I go out? You know that I lost about £100 a year for refusing to criticise in the private interests of Mrs Labouchere. Do you doubt that Mrs Labouchere interferes in the dramatic criticism as well, considering her past? Most men lose their sense of the omnipresent corruption just as they lose their sense of the taste of water, which is always in their mouths; but I think, if you quite seriously examine your career as a writer from the days when you signed Norman Britton to the Fortnightly Review period you will see that you have had to trim your work to suit your paper, Pall Mall [Gazette], Pioneer, World, [Manchester] Guardian or what not. You now do it instinctively, without feeling it, as I do myself. But compare my Fabian Essays and my Quintessence with my World articles, bold as the last affect to be; and you will find the butter on my mother's bread and my own sticking to my fingers. What would my writing be if I had a wife and family, and had no more ability than any of the men who are craving for my berth today? This is not Stupidity: it is Poverty and Servitude. I prostitute myself as honestly as I can; but I am bought and sold for all that. I do not take a £10 note for a notice; nor does Judge Hawkins take a £50 note for a favorable summing up; nor would [Joseph] Chamberlain take £1000 for backing a private Bill. And so, by putting your standard at our level, you may say that criticism, the Bench, and Parliament are pure, just as you can express your satisfaction with Helmer because he is so far superior to Uriah Heep. You know two journalists who may fairly be called uncompromisingly honest in their utterances. One is Robertson, the other is Foote. Both of them are a good deal honester than I am, because, although they do not publish more extreme opinions, yet they have to serve them up without Shaw sauce; and it was a strong sense of this that provoked Robertson to say, in the N.R. [*National Reformer*], that I never said anything that was not palatable to my audiences. Think of all the compliances you have made that they have refused to make; and say is it fair to hold yourself and the rest of the critics, from Wedmore down to Scott, up as uncorrupted and incorruptible? The pretension is valid at Ohnet's standard. Is it so at Ibsen's standard? Or at any standard worth setting up?

However, I have run away from my point that, granting that only a narrow upper margin of dramatic literature raises any controversy at the ordinary standard, no ordinary critic dare, for his livelihood's sake, strike a blow for the antiidealist side.

By the bye, you have got Voltaire on the brain (vide recent World par.). The saying 'that which is too silly to say, one sings it' is in the first act (I think) of Beaumarchais' Mariage de Figaro. Just think of what you have come to when I have to set you right on points of French dramatic literature.

GBS

Augustus **Harris** (1851–96), nicknamed 'Druriolanus,' owned and managed Drury Lane Theatre, where he staged melodramatic spectacles and Christmas pantomimes. He was knighted in 1891 for serving as London mayor, not for his theatrical activities. Charles **Wyndham** (1837–1919) was one of the most popular actor-managers of his era. In the Criterion Theatre, which he renovated in 1879, he and his second wife Mary Moore (1862–1931) produced and performed in several of H.A. Jones's plays in the 1890s. At the height of his success, he built two new playhouses, Wyndham's (1899) and the New Theatre (1903). He was knighted in 1902. The **maudlin groups** of theatre critics were, from Shaw's perspective, foolishly sentimental is their self-serving comments on their integrity. Shaw warned Archer that he was in danger of joining these critics in his self-regarding and self-celebrating article. Frederick G. **Tomlins** (1804–67) served as the drama and art critic for the *Morning Advertiser*. Georges **Ohnet** (1848–1918), a French novelist and dramatist, wrote the novel *Le maître de forges*, which A.W. Pinero adapted for the stage as *The Ironmaster*

(1884). In his series of novels, *Les batailles de la vie,* he portrayed idealistic characters and actions. The **Ghosts incident** was the controversial London production of Ibsen's play in 1891. Archer's son **Tom** (1885–1918), also called Tomarcher, was the Archers' only child. **Samuel Butler** (1835–1902), a satirist and novelist, was best known for *Erewhon: or Over the Range* (1872) and *The Way of All Flesh,* published a year after he died. His *Luck or Cunning* (1887), which Shaw reviewed in the PMG on 31 May 1887, made the case for the role of will power rather than chance in evolutionary events (Tyson 1: 277–81). Butler's theory influenced Shaw's idea of Creative Evolution. Clement **Scott** began his career writing for the **Sunday Times**; Louis Frederick Austin, besides serving as the drama critic for the *New Review,* held the **secretaryship to** [Henry] **Irving. Mrs Labouchere,** also known as the actress Henrietta Hodson (1831–1912), was married to Rt Hon. Henry Labouchere (1831–1910), owner of the journal *Truth.* She apparently attempted to induce Shaw – when he wrote occasional art reviews for *Truth* – to puff the art of Frederick Goodall. He refused (Weintraub: 303). **G.W. Foote** (1850–1915), an atheist and socialist, edited *Progress.* When he was imprisoned in 1883 for blasphemy, Archer kept the journal going, writing under the pen name of **Norman Britton**. Foote became president of the National Secular Society in 1890. Archer's admiration for Foote began in October 1881: 'I heard Foote lecture for the first time last Sunday night: what a first-rate speaker he is!' (C. Archer: 95). In 1885 Archer introduced Foote to Shaw. **Judge Hawkins** was Sir Henry Hawkins, Baron Brampton (1817–1907); he acquired the name 'Hanging Hawkins' because of the number of murder cases he decided as a trial judge. Joseph A. **Chamberlain** (1836–1914) began his political career as the 'reforming' mayor of Birmingham. In Parliament he served the Liberal Party, but in 1891 he joined the Liberal Unionists, who opposed home rule for Ireland. A strong supporter of colonial policy, he shifted to the Conservative Party in 1895. He supported the South African War of 1899–1901. John Mackinnon **Robertson** was a brilliant and argumentative writer, always ready for a dispute. Besides his early work as a journalist, editor, and leader of rationalist and secular movements, he wrote a number of critical books on social, economic, and religious topics. Later in his career he became a Liberal member of Parliament (1906–18) and a major Shakespearean scholar of his era. Archer and Shaw greatly admired him. **Helmer** Torvald is the husband in Ibsen's *A Doll's House.* **Uriah Heep** is the devious 'umble clerk in Dickens's *David Copperfield.* Sir Frederick **Wedmore** (1844–1921) served as art critic at *The Standard.* Although Archer credits **Voltaire** with stating that 'Anything that is too stupid to be spoken is sung,' this is a misattribution. **Beaumarchais** is the source, as Shaw corrects Archer. But the phrase '*Aujourd'hui ce qui ne vaut pas la peine d'etre dit, on le chante*' ('Today one sings what isn't worth saying') appears in *The Barber of Seville* (1, ii), not *The Marriage of Figaro.* A decade later Shaw retrieved this error and transferred it into *Man and Superman* (CP 2: 610):

Tanner: Let me remind you that Voltaire said that what was too silly to be said could be sung.

Straker: It wasnt Voltaire, it was Bow Mar Shay.

Tanner: I stand corrected. Beaumarchais of course.

Shaw gave Archer's mistake to Tanner, but if he came to recognize his own mistake over which play is the source, he did not assign the mistake to Starker. Just as well, for Straker should be flawless at this moment. In 1907 Archer acknowledged the topic and correction when he argued in a review that Shaw's *The Man of Destiny* should be an operetta. It 'demands a musical setting for the reason laid down (as Mr. 'Enery Starker reminds us) by 'Bowmarshay' (28 December 1907, *The Tribune*).

32 / To William Archer

29 Fitzroy Square W
13th November 1891

[TLS, with APCU postscript: BL 45296 f 40; CL1]

Archer wrote at least two and probably three letters to Shaw between 7 and 14 November. And Shaw wrote letters on 7, 9, 10, and 13 November. All of Shaw's letters have survived, but none of Archer's has shown up. These exchanges on the topic of critical integrity extended for over a week. And the discussion likely continued when they met together on 13 and 14 November (Diaries 2: 767). Unfortunately, because Archer's letters have disappeared, it is not always clear what Shaw is responding to in this letter. But we can still identify some features of Archer's missing correspondence. Upon receiving Shaw's previous letter of 10 November, Archer asked Shaw to clarify several of his statements, including his assertion that Archer had let himself 'go on the ungenerous side' in his recent critical writings. This judgment concerned, and perhaps even worried, him. Also, based upon what Shaw stated in his reply, Archer must have defended the editorial decisions of Edmund Yates at The World.

When Shaw first read Archer's 'Free Stage' essay on 7 November, he surely noted this statement: 'Two men of letters crossing swords, on equal terms, can adjust their differences without ill-feeling, and take nothing but pleasure in the bout of fence' (FR, November 1891: 670). In the spirit of this statement (which I quoted in the Introduction), Shaw countered Archer with his own 'style of sword-play.' In these four letters of 7, 9, 10, and 13 November he delivered his own aggressive thrusts that taught Archer some fundamental fencing principles.

We need to keep in mind, however, that we lack Archer's thrusts and parries. Without his letters, we have only a partial portrait of this bout. Basically, Shaw's letters demonstrate not only his impressive argumentative skills, but also his ability to craft a captious portrait of Archer. From our historical perspective Shaw dominated the exchanges; he shaped our perception of Archer and his ability – or lack thereof – to define and defend his positions. Apparently Archer was specifically overmatched in this fencing match. Shaw was masterful, of course, in his ability to present his side of an analysis and argument, yet we need to be careful not to rush into easy judgments. We might note that in his letter Shaw toned down and modified some of his assertions in the previous letters. What Archer wrote in his letters remains unavailable.

Much obliged for fancy portrait of yourself on the old lines. Artistically drawn, but not in the least like the original. Have invariably proceeded with satisfactory results – on the assumption that it was a fancy sketch.

Meaning of the phrase about generous and ungenerous simply that you have lately praised more effusively and blamed more abusively than you used to – that you write to express your feeling without the old preoccupation as to the abstract merits of the case. Meaning re Ohnet, that his plays are vitiated by 'idealist' morals, and that this is the real objection to them.

You must observe that in my remarks on compromise, or corruption, or what you choose to call it provided you consistently mean the operation of external causes in inducing a man to suppress, modify, or veil his opinions, I was not delivering a series of moral judgments. The question at issue is not for a moment whether there are some rascally editors and critics. There are black sheep in every flock. The question is, assuming a man to be normally upright, independent and clean handed, will he under existing circumstances criticize without fear or favor. I say no. In such concessions as he makes he may feel quite justified – may feel that he would demand them if he were in the editor's (or other concessionaire's) place. But it is one thing to say that the critic is not to blame for making certain concessions: it is quite another to assert that the concessions are not made, or to infer that because they dont matter individually they dont matter socially. In saying that you are not to blame and that Yates is not to blame and that you sympathise with Yates and that he would have let you go further than another writer whom he could have more easily done without, you do not for a moment prove that the World is incorrupt. All you shew is that the corruption is not the fault of the editor and critic.

Again, take the comparison of your case and that of G. W. F[oote]. It shews at once that you are muzzled, because F., though himself muzzled in other directions, bluntly says things which you are glad to have said, and which you would probably say yourself sometimes if there was no reason to the contrary. But it does not at all shew that G.W.F. is a nobler character than you. He occupies the most eminent position that his ability and opportunity brought within his reach. In spite of what I said about Shaw sauce I should laugh at Robertson if he claimed to be a braver man than I because my style of swordplay, which he cannot manage, is a safer one than his. We all go as far as our styles will carry us. All four of us get further than the rank and file of our competitors by dint of our exceptional ability. If we cannot get beyond a certain point, it is obvious that the rank and file of the critics get turned back far sooner. The man who gets as far as he wants to go – to say all that he wants to say – must be so completely of the color of his environment that his being a critic as distinct from a mere reporter is hardly conceivable.

Do not suppose that when I insist on my view of a question that I am reproaching you for not being a Shaw. The notion of two Shaws corresponding with one another is one which staggers even me. Your pugnacity, wit, knowledge &c are undoubtedly mixed in different proportions to mine, and the result is both quantitatively and chemically different. I sometimes, when a good side of you comes out by chance against a bad side of me, feel apologetic for the difference; but as we clearly could not stand one another if the difference were abolished, whether by the Archerization of Shaw (with Mrs Archer in the background wondering which was the real Antipholus) or the Shawation of Archer, let us rejoice that it exists. But as to our putting our brains to as good a use as they are capable of, it is as plain as a pikestaff to me that our environment is too many for us in several ways, including some that are pernicious both to ourselves and our neighbors. But I grant you that what we come in conflict with is not opposing faiths in art or religion. It is simply proprietary interests, all powerful, and vested in the darkness of mind of the people.

I do not think that there is anything in the notion that your 'layin low and sayin nuffin' may have been more baneful to you than if you had upset the apple cart. But I wonder whether you defrauded your parents of a necessary part of their education? For instance, if the same thing should happen with Tom, would you not rather he spoke out than shut you out of his life that way?

GBS

PS I shall be at the Wheatsheaf tomorrow at two. I have a fearful cold, and paid my sixth visit to the dentist yesterday. I have taken annoyingly to getting my teeth drilled.

Antipholus is one of the twin brothers in Shakespeare's *The Comedy of Errors.* Uncle Remis, the narrator of the African American folktales published in 1881 by Joel Chandler Harris (1848–1908), advocates '**layin low and sayin nuffin.**' The Uncle Remis stories, widely read in England, influenced Rudyard Kipling (1865–1936), Beatrix Potter (1866–1943), and A.A. Milne (1882–1956). Shaw regularly ate at the vegetarian restaurant **Wheatsheaf**. Of note, during this same period, from late 1888 to 1892, another regular diner at Wheatsheaf and other cheap vegetarian restaurants was a law student named Mohandas Karamchand (Mahatma) Gandhi (1869–1948). Influenced by the writings of Henry Salt (1851–1939),

Gandhi became a member of the Vegetarian Society. Years later Shaw and Gandhi met in 1931 and proclaimed their mutual respect. Shaw praised Gandhi as a saint and superman for opposing the British Raj. Gandhi called Shaw 'a Puck-like spirit' and the 'Arch Jester of Europe' (Holroyd 3: 286). This assessment coincided with Archer's lament in 1923 that despite Shaw's international fame, his influence in the world was greatly hindered by his 'clowning' (Old Drama: 355). Archer came to believe, in the twentieth century, that Shaw had the ability to make progressive changes in the modern world – if only he would restrain his jesting persona.

33 / To William Archer 29 Fitzroy Square W
10th October 1892

[CALS; BTA; original lost]

There is no extant correspondence between November 1891 and October 1892. I discovered this letter when I carried out research at the now-defunct British Theatre Association in Fitzroy Square. It was folded within the pages of a scrapbook of Archer's articles on censorship. I made a copy, and left the original with the BTA *librarian, Enid Foster. But the letter disappeared at some point during the shifts of the Archer archive from the* BTA *to the Theatre Museum, and then to Blythe House. See note 78 in the Introduction on the migrations of Archer's archive.*

With a view to further combat with the Censor you ought to see *Incognita* at the Lyric. The second act is so gross that Grein would be prosecuted if he put it on at the I. T. The two main incidents are – 1. The hero, on the wedding night, indecently assaults an old woman in order to get turned out of the house, because he does not want to consummate the marriage. Instead of resisting, however, she is delighted, and at last, to get rid of her, he throws her on the floor, where she lies placidly with the remark 'See where you've left me, Ducky.' [2.] After this the bride's father enters in his nightgown & listens at the door of the nuptial chamber, chuckling as he hears kisses, and finally declaring that he really must get married again. I have written to the Chronicle in the character of an outraged Paterfamilias, declaring that Pigott has evidently been bribed by the Lowenfeld syndicate, but I don't know whether Fletcher will put my letter in. If not we must seize the opportunity in some other way.

GBS

Alfred Ewen **Fletcher** (1841–1915), editor at the *Daily **Chronicle**,* did not publish Shaw's letter, but Shaw 'seized the opportunity' to write a review on 12 October 1892 in *The World* about ***Incognita***, a comic opera by Francis C. Burnand (1836–1917), Charles Lecocq (1832–1918), and Harry Greenbank (1866–99). The production, an anglicized rendering of Lecocq's *Le coeur et la main*, had some success, running for 103 performances. In his review Shaw described the father, in nightcap and bedgown, 'chuckling as he listened at the door of his daughter's bridal chamber.' Shaw congratulated London audiences who, a year after shuddering 'with horror at the wickedness' of Ibsen's *Ghosts*, now accepted the gross sexual jokes of this comic opera (Music 2: 706). In 1892 Edward F. Smyth **Pigott**, the Examiner of Plays for the Lord Chamberlain's Office, testified before the Parliamentary Select Committee on the regulation of the theatres. Pigott announced that the characters in Ibsen's plays were 'morally deranged,' but he allowed the productions of *A Doll's House*, *Rosmersholm*, and *Hedda Gabler* because he assumed that audiences would laugh the plays off the stage. He dismissed Archer, the lone person who testified against censorship, as a person with 'very limited' experience of the stage. When Pigott died in 1895, after twenty years as the governmental censor, Shaw crafted an assault on him (SatRev, 2 March 1895; Dukore 1: 272–8). He described Pigott as 'a walking compendium of vulgar insular prejudice,' and accused him of 'wallowing all his life in the cheapest theatrical sentiment.' Then, as an example of how Pigott encouraged 'lewd farce at the expense of fine drama,' Shaw again described the sexual scenes in *Incognita*. The **Lowenfeld** syndicate was run by Henry Lowenfeld, the tycoon for 'Kops Ale.' This syndicate was one of several limited liability companies, such as the famous Moss Empires, Ltd., that took over ownership of theatres and music halls between 1880 and 1920. By the 1920s these business cartels displaced the actor-manager system (Davis 1: 159–200, 267–72).

34 / To William Archer

29 Fitzroy Square W
14th December 1892

[APCS: BL 45296 f 41; CL 1]

Widowers' Houses, *a 'Didactic Realistic Play' in three acts, was staged by the Independent Theatre Company at the Royalty Theatre for two matinee performances on 9 and 13 December. J.T. Grein was listed as director, but Shaw ran the rehearsals, including special sessions with Florence Farr (1860–1917), who took the role of Blanche. His diary during this period has descriptions of rehearsals and performances (Diaries 2: 871–94). Given the brief run of the play, the Royalty was available a week later for the opening of* Charley's Aunt *by Brandon Thomas (1856–1914). It had 1469 performances, beginning at the Royalty and continuing until 19 December 1896 at the Globe.* Widowers' Houses *versus* Charley's Aunt *– the two extremes of London theatre.*

Archer shared his review with Shaw before publication. Shaw made some corrections. Apparently neither of them felt that this practice raised any concerns about critical integrity. Then on 13 December Shaw amused himself 'during the [train] journey by writing a letter to Archer which I afterwards tore up' (Diaries 2: 881). He replaced that letter with this one. In his review (World, 14 December), Archer recounted his version of the play's development between 1884 and 1892 (which should be compared to Shaw's narrative in his letter of 4 October 1887). He praised the character of Lickcheese, played by James Welch (1866–1917), but dismissed the rest of the characters as unrealistic 'monsters.' The play is a 'failure,' primarily because the 'psychology and stagecraft' for the love story 'are alike found wanting.' 'If Mr. Shaw would or could divest his mind of theory, I think he would see that these lovers of his are not human beings at all … Truly, for a set of blood-suckers, Mr. Shaw's middle-classes are strangely bloodless.' For the next thirty years Archer offered versions of these complaints about Shaw's dependence on theory and his harsh representation of women and love affairs. (On Blanche see Gainor: 185–8.) Shaw responded calmly and even generously to the critics in a long letter to the editor of The Star *in 19 December (Dukore 1: 203–8). Then on 31 December he provided a defence of the play's realism in* The Speaker *(Dukore 1: 208–10).*

I have come to the conclusion that Moy Thomas (who sat it out again yesterday; every line) is the greatest critic of the age, and Massingham entirely right in his estimate of you and Walkley. A more amazing exposition of your Shaw theory even I have never encountered than that World article. Here am I, who have collected slum rents weekly with these hands, & for 4 1/2 years been behind the scenes of the middle class landowner – who have philandered with women of all sorts & sizes – and I am told gravely to go to nature & give up apriorizing about such matters by you, you sentimental Sweet Lavendery recluse. Get out!

GBS

William **Moy Thomas** (1828–1910), theatre critic for the *Daily News,* praised the play, which 'is, in spite of a tedious and almost superfluous first act, really a very remarkable production.' He insisted that the play is not 'a Fabian pamphlet' and the characters are not 'mere abstractions attired in human clothing.' Because each character 'speaks according to his kind,' the satire is 'as diverting as it is clever.' Shaw 'exhibits many of the qualities which go to the making of a dramatist of the first rank' (Evans: 44–6). A.W. Pinero's ***Sweet Lavender*** premiered in 1888, and was revived in 1890 and 1899. Long on stereotypical characters and sentiment, it featured the comedian Edward Terry as a drunken but good-hearted old lawyer. In his review of Archer's *The Theatrical World of 1894* Shaw proclaimed that among Archer's half-dozen identities, one is that of a 'sentimentalist' who 'gushes over *Sweet Lavender*' (SatRev, 13 April 1895; Dukore 1: 307–12).

35 / To William Archer

29 Fitzroy Square W
23rd February 1893

[ALS: BL 45296 f 43; CL 1]

The Irish novelist George Moore served as a manager for J.T. Grein's IT, *which produced his play* The Strike at Arlingford *on 21 February (Opera Comique, 1 perf.). In his review in* The World *on 1 March Archer concluded that neither Moore's play nor Shaw's* Widowers' Houses *was suited 'to the ordinary commercial stage,' but each was 'a very remarkable dramatic experiment.' The acting for* Strike, *however, was poorer than that for* Widowers' Houses. *Clearly influenced by this letter from Shaw, Archer wrote: 'I am credibly assured that Mr Moore's sociology is all wrong, that he has confounded socialism with trades-unionism, muddled up two different classes of capitalists, and thereby earned the pronounced disesteem of the Fabian Society.' Yet Archer insisted, despite this flaw, that Moore's play had 'ten times more flesh and blood' than Shaw's play, which demonstrated 'unimpeachable Fabianism but doubtful humanity' (World 93: 70–5). When Moore's play was published in June, Shaw reviewed it in* The Star. *He criticized the representations of socialism and labour leadership in the play, but he found the basic plot 'technically sound' (27 June; Dukore 1: 218–21).*

I do not know whether it is altogether fair for me, as a rival dramatist, to blow the gaff on Moore; but dont let yourself in for endorsing his strikology. He has confused the master collier class (ironmasters, manufacturers &c) with the financial class, & has taken Lionel Rothschild as his model when he should have taken Livesey. Steinbach's speech, 'if only we were as well organised as they' is too ludicrously opposed to the facts to be fully appreciated by anyone who does not know how the masters out-organise the men in every colliery district. The confusion of Trade Unionism with Socialism and with Louise Michellism is utter and inextricable. The notion of sending for the military under circumstances which would have ensured their presence in considerable strength weeks beforehand is another blunder. In fact, from the realistic point of view, the whole play is utter nonsense: it was so unreal to me that it bored me to distraction. The first act only needed some practical knowledge to be made very amusing, especially the deputation. Moore's counterpoint is weak; he runs too much into duets. A master of polyphony like myself would have made a fine concerted piece out of that quartet & chorus. John Reid was simply Ingarfield over again. *Do* blow up the I.T. about the acting: even my lot, though they had not had half the rehearsal, did better than poor Moore's. I have written to him to warn him that his sociology is not what it might be, & to put him on his guard against leaving in that brutal speech about the public house in Manchester, where they are starving just now.

GBS

Baron **Lionel Nathan de Rothschild** (1808–79) inherited the leadership of the House of Rothschild in England from his father, Nathan (1777–1836). Both father and son were astute financiers, especially in their international loans. In 1847 Lionel Rothschild was elected to the House of Commons as a Liberal MP, but he did not assume his seat until 1858 when he could take the oath in accordance with his Jewish faith. He was the first Jewish Member of Parliament. Sir George **Livesey** (1834–1908), who headed an engineering firm, was director of the South Metropolitan Gas Co. and a promoter of partnership between business and labour. Louise **Michel** (1830–1905), a French anarchist, lived in London from 1886 to 1895. **John Reid** is a character in Moore's *Strike*; Philos **Ingarfield** is a character in Henry Arthur Jones's *The Crusaders* (1891).

36 / To William Archer

[40 Queen Square WC]
Friday afternoon [24th March 1893]

[TLS: BL 45296 f 42; CL 1]

Shaw's diary entry for this day reads: 'After dinner called on Archer; and as he was not in, wrote a letter on his typewriter and left it for him with his article and proofs of Widowers' Houses*' (Diaries 2: 917). Because Shaw wrote this letter in Archer's flat, I have followed the lead of Dan H. Laurence, who provided in the* Collected Letters *the above address of Archer's flat, not Shaw's own address at Fitzroy Square (CL 1: 386). (Of note, this was not the only occasion on which Shaw was able to enter Archer's flat when no one was there. Either the flat was often left unlocked or, more likely, Shaw had a key.)*

Archer's article 'The Mausoleum of Ibsen' (reprinted in Ibsen Essays: 32–52) – which Shaw proofread and commented upon in this letter – appeared in FR *(July 1893). As he had done with '*Ghosts *and Gibberings' in 1891, Archer prepared another* Schimpflexikon *– A Dictionary of Abuse – that illustrated the vituperative opposition by London critics to the Ibsen plays and productions, including* The Master Builder, *which Robins and Archer had staged for thirty-one performances (20 February–25 March 1893). He quoted dozens of invectives from the critics, including Clement Scott. He also noted that since 1889 the publishing of Ibsen translations had been quite successful, despite the fact that the English* *public had 'lost the habit of reading plays' (p. 49). Leading the way were the thirteen plays in his* Ibsen's Prose Drama *(5 vols, 1890–1) and also the 'schilling' editions of individual plays. Archer estimated that 'one hundred thousand prose dramas by Ibsen had been bought by the English-speaking public in the course of four years' (48). As for the London productions, he pointed out that several of them had paid their way, despite the fact that Ibsen's plays 'represent society in a small and little-known country' and were performed 'at second-rate theatres' (51) such as the Novelty, the Vaudeville, and the Trafalgar Square Theatre.*

Archer proofread Widowers' Houses *and the 'Author's Preface.' The play was published in May 1893 in the new book series that J.T. Grein had conceived for the Independent Theatre. Perhaps 400 to 500 copies were printed by Henry and Co., but not all of these were bound. About 200 copies sold over the next couple of years. Shaw probably ended up with a pile of unbound copies, though in the late 1890s he had another publisher bind some copies of the play (Biblio 1: 22–4). In his preface Shaw quoted part of Archer's production review that had been published in* The World *on 14 December 1892. In that review Archer had offered a history of the joint venture to write* Rhinegold *in 1884 and 1887. Based upon Archer's comments on the proofs – as well as his own experiences with the rehearsals and two performances – Shaw made some revisions in the play, including a few cuts in Blanche's harshness toward her maid. He also tightened the reconciliation scene between Blanche and Trench (WH: xxvii).*

I leave the article, which seems to me good enough in spite of its inhumanity, except on one point. The explanation of the success of the translations on the stage is that in middle class social and political life Norway is the microcosm and England is the macrocosm. As I have often told you, if you would only join the local caucus, you would see at once that An Enemy of the People comes home to Holborn as closely as A Doll's House comes home to Brixton and Holloway, which are just as narrow and provincial as Norway. Ninetyfive per cent of an Ibsen play is as true of any English town as it is of Christiania; and the odd five per cent is not sufficient to make the performance in the least puzzling. Probably this is less true of France; but modern commercialism levels all nations down to the same bourgeois life, and raises the same problems for realist playwrights, though not for romantic ones. This is what destroys the whole parallel between Molière and Co. (as far as translation is concerned) and Ibsen; and I think you owe it to your reputation to shew that the difference is within the sphere of your consciousness in the article. Even apart from realist plays the drama is more international than you represent it; for most of the adaptations – especially the most successful ones – are very close translations. It is the ultraadapted ones that fail.

The note about the theatres on page 76 of the MS had better come out, because the description of the Novelty is, I think distinctly libellous, and the other two instances are more of the nature of apologies.

The tone of the article generally is one of devilish malignity towards the unfortunate Scott and the rest. They may deserve it; but when Widowers' Houses celebrates its six hundredth night, Scott will have his revenge.

I leave you the two sheets of W. H. which were missing from the set of proofs I sent you before. There are two points to admire: first, the ingenuity with which I have secured a preface by William Archer without running any of the risks which destroyed poor Jones; and second, the sublime preface by Grein, with its adroit allusion to the play 'setting the machinery of public opinion in motion and SUPPLYING BRICKS' &c. The proof of the final sheet is unique, and will be readily saleable for ten guineas in view of the champion misprint which has produced the sentence beginning on the last line of page 121.

I make no apology for lifting your copy out of the World, as I confined myself strictly to that part which is clearly made out of my own flesh and blood.

Please let me know whether you are going to publish *A Visit* in the series (or anything else) as I see I shall have to do the whole volume, advertisements and all, myself.

GBS

Archer did not remove the phrase about 'second-rate theatres,' but in response to Shaw's concern about a possible libellous statement, he added a footnote that softened the description of the **Novelty** Theatre, which was 'hidden away in a by-street.' In turn, he identified the Vaudeville Theatre, where *Hedda Gabler* was staged in 1891, as a 'popular' venue. And he described the Trafalgar Square, which featured *The Master Builder* in 1893, as 'the pleasantest and best-appointed' theatre in London (295). Shaw's reference to **Molière and Co.** is a response to Archer's claim that Ibsen's plays have been more successful on the English stage than any of the plays by major French, Spanish, and German playwrights. Even though these plays were occasionally performed, they were poorly adapted. In a footnote he stated that the adaptations of Goethe's *Faust* and two plays by Victor Hugo were deplorable. In his 'Editor's Preface' to *Widowers' Houses,* J.T. Grein praised Shaw's 'most remarkable play,' which '**supplied bricks** and mortar' that consolidated the IT. Archer translated ***A Visit*** (*De Besuch*) from the Danish in 1891. Written by Edvard Brandes (1847–1931), brother of Georg Brandes (1842–1927), *A Visit* was staged by the IT at the Royalty Theatre with two short plays: *The Kiss*, a Pierrot idyll by Theodore de Banville (1823–81) and *The Minister's Call* by Arthur Symons (1866–1945). The production had only one performance, on 4 March 1892. In a missing letter or a conversation, Archer informed Shaw of his decision about publishing *A Visit*. See the following letter for explanation.

37 / To William Archer

29 Fitzroy Square W
27th March 1893

[ALS: BL 45296 f 44; CL 1]

Although J.T. Grein had planned to publish separate editions of the plays by Shaw, George Moore, and Edvard Brandes, only Widowers' Houses *appeared in the new* IT *book series. Moore decided to place* The Strike at Arlingford *with Walter Scott, publisher of Archer's translations of Ibsen. He believed that Scott was a more reliable publisher than Henry and Co. As for Brandes's play* A Visit, *the publishing decision belonged to Archer, who had translated the play. One of his concerns was that he did not want the play published with the two curtain-raisers –* The Kiss *and* The Minister's Call *– that had been performed with Brandes's play a year earlier. The key factor, however, in his decision against publication was a matter of censorship. When* A Visit *was in rehearsal in March 1892, Archer discovered that someone had amended the rehearsal script. He initially held Grein responsible for making the cuts. Archer assumed that Pigott, the Examiner of Plays, had insisted upon the cuts. He was irate that Grein would bow to Pigott. Opposed to censorship and frustrated by Grein's silence, he printed a leaflet of four pages that contained the excised passages. On the day of the performance he placed copies of the leaflet on the seats at the Royalty Theatre.*

But a few days later Archer discovered that George Moore, not Grein or Pigott, was the culprit. It is a mystery why Moore, who had repeatedly fought against censorship of his novels and campaigned for the translation of Zola's novels, would have anything to do with trimming Brandes's play, but apparently in his role as Grein's stage manager he made the cuts. He did so without informing Archer. The whole matter angered Archer, who voiced his disapproval in PMG *(12 March 1892). He criticized not only Moore but the whole system of censorship that operated in the London theatre. Then a month later, in May 1892, he testified against censorship during the hearings of the Parliamentary Select Committee on the topic of the regulation of the theatres – the only person to do so. All other critics and theatre managers who appeared before the committee supported the current system, overseen by Pigott, who, when he testified, attacked Archer (Whitebook: 138–9). (See also letter of 10 October 1892.)*

In his 1892 review of the production of Widowers' Houses, *Archer admitted that the first act was 'ten times better' than the 1884 scenario he had offered to Shaw. Even so, 'the first act, in which some faint traces of my conception remain, is the one thoroughly dull and ineffectual portion of the play.' But in the second act, 'where Mr. Shaw gets upon his own ground of economic theory and fact, he at once becomes competent and entertaining' (World, 14 December 1892). Archer was appalled, however, by the characterization of Blanche Sartorius. Instead of being the well-mannered Victorian woman he had imagined, she is a 'vixen.' Archer judged the play a failure in both characterization and plot construction because Shaw lacked the ability to create realistic characters, a critique Shaw dismissed. In his preface for the 1893 publication of the play, he proclaimed it was 'a propagandist play – a didactic play – a play with a purpose' (CP 1: 44). 'It is saturated with the vulgarity of the life it represents: the people do not speak nobly, live gracefully, or sincerely face their own position' (45).*

I am writing to Grein to alter the advertisement of the 2nd vol. of the I.T. series on the ground that you are resolved not to have any other play in the same book with 'A Visit.' I suppose that is all right. I am also writing to Moore asking him whether he is still bent on taking 'The Strike' to Scott.

About that first act, I am prepared to admit that it is no great shakes, except that Cokane is a creation, and my one French critic was right when he said that 'la composition de cette lettre à laquelle Sartorius est appelé à collaborer pendant que les deux amoureux s'en vont reflirter dans le fond du jardin, constitue une scène de réelle et bonne comédie, au dialogue piquant et serré.' Your objection to both is bad taste pure and simple; but as for the rest I do not press its excellence, provided you allow for the inevitable postponement of the glimpse of the under world to the second act caused by your own insistence on my beginning on the Rhine. 'Tu l'as voulu, George Dandin.'

GBS

The unidentified **French critic** praised Shaw for delivering good, realistic comedy, 'with dialogue both piquant and compact.' The scene he described was at the end of act 1: Sartorius is collaborating with Cokane in the composition of the letter to Trench's family about the social status of Sartorius; Trench and Blanche are flirting in the garden. The character **George Dandin** appears in Molière's play of this name. Shaw modified Dandin's repeated statement about his humiliated dignity, 'Vous l'avez voulu, George Dandin.' The phrase translates as 'You asked for it,' or 'It's your own fault.'

38 / To William Archer

29 Fitzroy Square W
28th April 1893

[APCS: FALES; CL 1]

The anonymous play Alan's Wife, *starring Elizabeth Robins, was produced by the Independent Theatre at Terry's Theatre on 28 April and 2 May. Shaw saw the first performance. Despite the speculations about the identity of the author – with Archer, Elizabeth Robins, and Lucy Clifford being prime candidates in the gossip – the secret held for several years. Florence Bell (1851–1930) wrote the play, with some contributions offered by Robins. Bell and Robins became close friends during this period. They insisted that the identity of the authors should remain anonymous.*

Because Archer shared with Robins some of the correspondence to him from Shaw, especially in the 1890s, some of the Shaw letters ended up in the Robins archive, now housed at the Fales Library at New York University. In volume 1 of the Collected Letters *of Shaw, Dan H. Laurence misidentified Robins instead of Archer as the recipient of this letter. The lack of a heading misled him. But Laurence subsequently corrected this mistake.*

Whoever wrote that play, it is of the Kingdom of Clifford from beginning to end – superstitious atheism – sensational anti-Goddity all over. Wallas has made a bet that it is Mrs. C.

GBS

The surprising answer to **Whoever wrote the play** was Florence Bell, who became Lady Bell in 1876 when she married Sir Hugh Bell, 2nd Baronet, Middlesbrough. She was the stepmother of her husband's children, including Gertrude Bell (1868–1926), who became the famous explorer, archeologist, spy, governmental mediator for the breakup of Ottoman Empire, and founding administrator for Iraq after WW1. She also worked with T.E. Lawrence (1888–1935) in Palestine. Florence Bell also had three children during the first decade of the couple's marriage. In 1918 she was created a Dame Commander of the Order of the British Empire. After the death of Gertrude Bell in 1926, Dame Bell edited the letters of her celebrated stepdaughter. Graham **Wallas** (1858–1932), a member of the executive committee of the Fabian Society (1888–95), became director of the London School of Economics, which was founded in 1894 by Sidney and Beatrice Webb. He later served as professor of political science at London University (1914–23). Beatrice Webb (1858–1943) called Wallas, Shaw, and her husband Sidney the 'troika' of the Fabian society. **Mrs C.** was Lucy Clifford (Mrs William Kingdon Clifford, 1846–1929). She became a novelist after the death of her husband (1879), who was a mathematician. By 1893 she had written *Anyhow Stories* (1882), *Very Short Stories* (1886), and *Love Letters of a Worldly Woman* (1891). She also wrote the play *A Woman Alone* (1898).

39 / To William Archer

29 Fitzroy Square W
11th May 1893

[TLS: BL 45296 ff 45–6; CL 1]

Alan's Wife *was based upon the short story* Befraid *by the Swedish writer Elin Ameen (1852–1913; see John: 88–90). In 1891 Archer read the story and developed a scenario for a play of three scenes, which he described to Elizabeth Robins. A year later she informed him that his 'scheme had been entirely thrown overboard' (World 93: 115) because she and Florence Bell had developed their own version. She swore him to secrecy about the identity of the joint authors. The play opens with the death of the husband Alan, crushed by machinery in the mines. Alan's wife, Jean Creyke, is devastated. When she later gives birth to a deformed son, she decides to kill him. Imprisoned and condemned to death, she refuses the appeals of her mother and a minister to admit that she committed a crime. In her performance Robins presented a defiant young woman.*

Although there were only two matinee performances of Alan's Wife, *the controversial topic of the play stirred up debate for several months. Because of his behind-the-scenes involvement in the play and production, Archer did not write a review. But he still published an article about its origin and subject matter (Westminster Gazette on 6 May; reprinted in World 93: 114–22). He rejected the arguments of some theatre critics, including A.B. Walkley, that the topic of infanticide is inappropriate for the stage. Archer praised the production, and defended the play's 'rare simplicity and directness of style' (World 93: 119). Shaw avoided the temptation to write about the production because of his close ties to the* IT, *which produced the play.*

You shew a deplorable want of grasp of the business talents of your compatriots. Miss Elsie has cultivated me with the greatest care ever since Hector introduced me to the household some years ago. She called, consulted me, and bound me over to attend the concert weeks ago. I abstain from returning the ticket so as not to deprive you of your excuse for not going.

You are perfectly right in your sketch of the right treatment of *Alan's Wife.* A woman capable of thinking for herself on questions of life and death would, obviously, quarrel with such a softheaded old mother and would have gusty times with her husband.

I believe the real difference between us is caused by the play being real to me in a way that it is not to you, or to the author. To you the incident is imaginary. Now to me it is comparatively common. Women do, as a matter of fact, polish off invalids and children on the ground that it is the most sensible and humane thing to do. Infanticide on that and other grounds is not a thing that women confess to; but every coroner knows how frequent it is. As to women who, if they dont exactly give Oswald the morphia, nevertheless deliberately and affectionately read the doctor's instructions backwards, you would not doubt their existence if you wore a sympathetic looking collar instead of giving your head the appearance of being stuck in a jam pot, and so repelling the confidence of clever women. Such women are not in the least like Jean, and never do it in Jean's way. They dont get hung; and they dont repent: on the contrary, they are invariably proud of having done the right thing. The tragedy, if there is tragedy, lies in the fact, and not in the fuss that is made about it. To represent a woman killing her child in such a way as to convince nine tenths of the audience that she is suffering from puerperal mania, and then getting hung for it, is to my mind shirking the problem as completely as it can be shirked without ignoring it altogether.

If I were to treat the subject, I should represent Jean as a rational being in society as it exists at present; and I should shew her killing the child with cool and successful precautions against being found out. I should then represent her mother and the parson and all the neighbors as being morally certain that she had done it, and herself as keeping up no greater pretence to the contrary than might be needed to save her neck. And I should represent their theories as to their own horror and her remorse as breaking down signally in practice, leaving her, when she had recovered from the natural grief produced by the sawing episode and so forth, the happiest and most sincerely respected woman in the parish. I should, by the bye, have married her to the parson, and, out of the struggle between the poor little chap's piety and his common sense (enlightened by his love), made a roaring good part for Welch. When I think of that wasted opportunity, I feel more than ever contemptuous of this skulking author who writes like a female apprentice of Buchanan.

The reason I cannot rush publicly into the controversy is that I should be unable to dissociate the problematical aspect of the play from its artistic aspect. You admire the execution, its large simplicity and so on. I dont. You may call *East Lynne* largely handled if you like, or the end of *Froufrou*, or *La Joie fait peur*, or anything else that uncorks the eye of the emotional actress, with almost as much chance of gaining my full assent. But I quite admit that the picture is painted with a full brush, and is a remarkable example of the fact that the sort of work that has hitherto been supposed proper to the novel only will do on the stage as well as and a good [deal] better than the shoppy stage style. But I still think that the pathos and the ideas are most horribly common; and as to the character creation, what bungler could not fake up that dreadful old woman and her gossip, not to mention the minister who, thanks to Welch, looked like a character until he opened his mouth and twaddled. These opinions I must, as a comrade Independent, keep to myself.

As to what you say about greenness, freshness, youth, susceptibility to enjoyment and so on, I can only say, with Rossetti, that

The thumb as it goes
To the end of the nose

conveys my opinion of this quintessence of the Clement Scott illusion. Why the devil dont you write a play instead of perpetually talking about it? You can do it well enough if you will only face making an ass of yourself in the preliminary trials, as you had to when you learnt to cycle. I've all but finished another play [*The Philanderer*] myself, quite as promising a failure as Widowers' Houses, but a step nearer to something more than talk about what plays ought to be. Just think of all the horrors you could revel in for the mere sake of telling Nature that you knew her real character and were not afraid to look her in the face.

What a chap you are!

GBS

The singer **Miss Elsie** Mackenzie was the sister of Archer's friend Sir Hector Mackenzie (1856–1929). Shaw attended her concert on 11 May. In Ibsen's *Ghosts* **Oswald** is the son who appeals to his mother, Mrs Alving, to give him morphine tablets because of his debilitating illness. In *Alan's Wife* James A. **Welch**, who played the role of Lickcheese in *Widowers' Houses*, took the role of Jamie Warren, a pious minister. The playwright Robert **Buchanan**, who led the attacks on Ibsen's plays, wrote sentimental dramas. ***East Lynne*** (1861), the popular novel by Mrs Henry (Ellen) Wood (1814–87), was adapted on several occasions for the English stage. Likewise, adaptations of the French play ***Frou-frou*** (1869), written by Henri Meilhac (1831–97) and Ludovic Halévy (1834–1908), were produced in London almost yearly in the 1880s and 1890s. ***La Joie fait peur*** was written by Delphine de Girardin (1804–55). Adapted by Dion Boucicault (1820–90), who titled it *Kerry*, it appeared at Terry's Theatre in January 1893, featuring Edward Terry. The poem, 'Hop-o'-my-thumb and little Jack Horner,' which appeared in *Sing-Song: A Nursery Rhyme Book* (1893), was written by Christina Georgina **Rossetti** (1830–94). Her brother was the painter and poet Dante Gabriel Rossetti (1828–82), who was a leader of the Pre-Raphaelite Brotherhood.

40 / To William Archer

29 Fitzroy Square W
21st August 1893

[ALS: FALES; TLS copy at HRC Texas; CL 1]

Although Shaw and Archer occasionally attended the music halls, such as the Empire Theatre of Varieties that George Edwardes (1852–1915) controlled, they were hardly enthusiastic supporters. Whatever the value of the variety acts, both men were bothered by the smoke, drink, and noise of the halls. In principle Shaw supported the plebian ambiance of the halls, and Archer appreciated Augustus Harris's practice of featuring leading music hall performers, such as Marie Lloyd (1870–1922) and Dan Leno (1860–1904), in the Drury Lane pantomimes (World 93: 7–8). But neither of them was attracted to the halls, even though Shaw's attitude had modified somewhat since 1887 when he dismissed the 'stupid and depressing Music Hall entertainment' (Diaries 1: 327). He even wrote a review on 27 August 1890 of the ballet and singing at the Alhambra Theatre of Varieties (Music 2: 157–64), though he admitted that in August there was little else for a music critic to feature.

Shaw criticized Archer for throwing himself into all manner of controversy, such as the debates with A.B. Walkley in the Daily Chronicle *over infanticide and suicide. He failed to mention, however, that on this same day he himself 'wrote a letter to* The Chronicle *on the suicide question,' though this letter apparently did not get published (see S. Weintraub's note in Diaries 2: 963). On 16 August Archer lent Shaw a private-circulating copy of A.W. Pinero's* The Second Mrs Tanqueray*; then on 17 August, after reading the play under a tree in Richmond Park, Shaw wrote a letter to Archer about the play (Diaries 2: 962). That letter is lost.*

I somehow dont feel that the Music Halls need a report sufficiently to justify an editor in rising to the occasion. Of course if we were to follow it up and eventually publish a conspectus of the art of the day – music halls, concerts, opera, & theatres – there might be some interest in it for the bookmakers of posterity. But I dont feel that we should have any real grip of the subject, because we have no experience of it. If we had been constant music hall goers for the last 20 years, then we could really apply the historical method & produce something valuable; but as we have probably not made twenty visits between us in our lives, we should have to fall back on apriorism and bare description of what is not worth describing. However, if you have a call, I am willing to go round and help.

The restless energy with which you are throwing yourself into all manner of controversies suggests to me that you are going mad. Or rather, you have at last thrown off the restraints that used to keep up your character for sanity, and are recklessly exhibiting yourself to the public in your true character of a Nihilist. The cynical lunacy of your fundamental propositions used to be veiled partly by your own reserve, and partly by the air of sobriety given to your logical superstructure by the contrast with my superficial extravaganza on a hidden bed rock foundation of reality and common sense. But your letter to the Chronicle and other recent exploits of yours are blowing the gaff. Further, by throwing all your energy & excitability into trifles, you are forcing yourself to find adequate material in them to work on, and as they dont in themselves provide this you magnify them imaginatively until they are big enough to exercise all your powers; and then you wrestle with them to the great astonishment of the public, which sees you struggling with grasshoppers as if they were giants. All these terrible combats with Walkley & others on behalf of Wilde, Pinero, Harris &c. &c. &c. belong to Piona and not to the wakeaday world. Le Gallienne, otherwise twaddly enough, is right in complaining that you shew no sense of proportion, the reason being that you are wreaking all your powers on small jobs with a magnifying glass in your eye. I therefore return to my old position as to your business in the world. All this trouncing of Walkley out of positions which he does not really hold, and which you manufacture out of his obvious carelessness of expression, is [a] waste of time – mere cat'scradle work, which will soon bore even the few who now care to watch it. When the Westminster Gazette started, Cook said to me, as an objection to my suggestion of a dramatic feuilleton, that nobody really wanted the 'My dear A.B.W. business'; and I am inclined to think that he was right in hesitating to dedicate a column of the paper to – possibly – an interminable controversy about nothing. When that confounded preface to Alan's Wife appears, it will land you at the extreme limit of human patience. Sooner or later – unless you wait until it is too late – you will have to turn your dramatic instinct into its legitimate channel, and write plays yourself. If you spend the next six months in writing a play, it will no doubt not be a *very* first rate one; but at all events it will be more respectable than the product of all the hours you have spent over the question of whether Walkley saw a streak of red paint or not. It is already quite evident that unless you take your part in the production of 'the new drama,' you will be driven by the inner necessity of justifying yourself to yourself, to abuse it frantically, and to champion the reactionary drama against it. The one fact that is clear about Alan's Wife is that you should have written it yourself. You would then have had the right to put a preface to it. Instead of that you leave it to another, and then, with a monstrous want of sense of the position, come forward to explain and defend and justify your own undone work in front of the unhappy person who did it. If Walkley has only the gumption to see this opening he can send you to the bottom with a single shot; and for my part I hope he will. Defend yourself and your own work and your own plays by all means; but do have the good sense to drop the pretence that Pinero & the author of Alan's Wife & the rest of them are all William Archers, and that therefore you are the proper person to answer for their notions. No matter how cleverly you do it, the fictitiousness of the whole position makes it tedious.

You could very easily provide Grein with a horrible drama for next season on purely mechanical lines, and from that you could go on to improve the quality of your horrors until you did something in the tragic line. You will have to become as a little child again and consent to make an ass of yourself publicly by making your debut as dramatic author; but surely that will be better than 'My dear A.B.W.' ad. lib., with the proceeds invested in Australian banks.

You will admit – as far as you are at present capable of admitting anything – that I am an extremely patient man; but the years are flying. I told you about eight years ago that you had 'a good education, instead of which you went about stealing turnips.' Your answer was to go and get married – checkmate for years to come. In about four years, I mentioned the subject again, only to find Tom Archer and the Australian banks in complete command of the situation. Now, after four years more, I again suggest that it is time to begin. As journalists we have had our turn; and if there is nothing higher before us – if the future, as Mrs Tank says, is only to be the past entered through another gate – why, then, the lethal chamber is the proper place for us.

GBS

The phrase **blowing the gaff** was British criminal slang for revealing a secret or hidden information. A gaff was a barbed stick used for fishing and other tasks. Searching in the wilderness, Moses and his people report that 'we saw the **giants**, the sons of Anak, which come of the giants: and we were in our own sight as **grasshoppers**' (Numbers 13:33, King James Bible). **Piona**, a fantastical realm free of the restraints of reality, was the imaginary kingdom of Archer's son, Tom. Richard **Le Gallienne** (1866–1947), a poet and essayist, reviewed books at *The Star* under the pseudonym 'Logroller.' Active in the decadent arts movement, he contributed to *The Yellow Book.* He also joined the debates about the topic of life and death in *Alan's Wife.* Shaw, who dismissed him as a 'sensitive plant,' wrote two dismissive reviews in 1892 of his poetry books, *Narcissus* and *English Poems* (Tyson 2: 84–6, 151–9). In 1893 Archer mounted '**combats**' for the new productions of *A Woman of No Importance* by (World 93: 105–13) by Oscar **Wilde** (1856–1900) and *The Second Mrs Tanqueray* by A.W. **Pinero**. He also noted that Augustus **Harris** had increased the use of music hall performers in the Christmas pantomimes. The game of **cat's cradle** is played by one or more people by weaving a tied string into figures. Sir Edward Tyas **Cook** (1857–1919) became editor of PMG in 1890; when a Tory purchaser bought the paper in 1893, Cook became editor of the new *Westminster Gazette.* Then in 1895 he shifted to the *Daily News* until 1901. He subsequently wrote for the *Daily Chronicle* and edited the works of John Ruskin. He was knighted in 1912, and was created knight commander in 1917. When reviewing *Alan's Wife,* A.B. Walkley complained about the bloody body of the husband being carried onto the stage. In rebuttal, Archer pointed out that there was no stage blood – or **red paint** – on the body.This vivid image occurred only in Walkley's imagination. Shaw believed that Archer's career became constricted when he decided to **go and get married.** In 1889 Shaw began a play, *The Cassone,* about the restraints imposed on Archer by his marriage (Diaries 2: 517; Holroyd 1: 278). Shaw also felt that the birth of the son Tom and the loss of money in **Australian banks** kept Archer tied to journalism. On the advice of family members, Archer had deposited most of his savings in three Australian banks, two of which went bankrupt during the economic crash of 1893. Abel Magwitch in *Great Expectations* recalled an early life of **stealing turnips.** Pip, by contrast, gains an education from money provided by Magwitch. **Mrs Tank** is a reference to A.W. Pinero's *The Second Mrs Tanqueray,* which starred George Alexander and Mrs Patrick Campbell (1865–1940). It opened at the St James's Theatre on 27 May, and ran for 223 performances. Archer wrote three supportive reviews: one in *The World* on 31 May, a second in *St. James's Gazette* on 3 June, and a third in *The World* on 27 December (World 93: 125–36, 137–44, 292–7).

41 / To G. Bernard Shaw

40 Queen Square, WC
1:15 a.m., just back from Southwold [22nd August 1893]

[TLS: HRC; copy at FALES]

Archer had become overly involved with Alan's Wife *– not only in his advocacy for the play but in his need to justify his campaigns for its critical status and its publication. Besides writing an essay about the play in the* Westminster Gazette, *he produced a long introduction for the published book. By writing the introduction, he had assumed a misleading – and perhaps inappropriate – role in the presentation of the anonymous play. His excessive investment in the play was at odds with his normal critical responsibilities. Florence Bell became frustrated because he had become the public voice for the play.*

Initially, the play involved Archer in only one act of secrecy. But besides honouring Bell's demand that her role as author should not be revealed, he had to maintain a protective shield for Elizabeth Robins – in part because of her own secret role as a co-author but also because of his secret affair with her. These promises of secrecy added another 'principle' to his argument with Shaw, but not one that he could name or defend adequately. Further complicating matters, Archer showed his and Shaw's recent letters to Robins – yet another secret withheld from Shaw.

Besides this exchange of letters, Shaw and Archer had even more to say in their debate over the play and Archer's activities. In his diary for 22 August Shaw reported that he wrote 'to Archer in reply to his reply to my letter of yesterday' (Diaries 2: 963). Unfortunately, Shaw's reply is missing. In turn, Archer's response to this letter has also disappeared.

My dear G.B.S.

Goodness knows what you're maundering about. I think it's you that is controversy-mad if (as I almost gather) you want to controvert my letter to the Chronicle, which is not controversial at all, but a plain statement of my own feeling on a particular question. I fancy it's shared by a good many people, and I believe by you among the rest, in your saner moments. But that's neither here nor there – I cannot see how you fit a statement of even a reprehensible and detrimental feeling on a question of life and death into your indictment of my tendency to controversy on trifles. It does not deal with a trifle, and it does not controvert anybody –except the coroner's juries with their tedious 'Temporary Insanity.' I haven't read Le Gallienne's letter, and don't propose to, simply because I *don't* want to be drawn into a controversy on this matter – least of all with a man who discusses religion with Buchanan, which seems to be about the lowest depth to which a human being can sink.

Of course you're right, in a sense, about ALAN'S WIFE – if I could afford it, I'd cancel the introduction to-morrow. I've had the fun of writing it, but it seems rather foolish that I should mortally offend the author of the play, on the one hand, and Walkley on the other, by publishing it. And of course it *is* quite disproportionately long – I deliberately wrote out everything to its greatest length because I knew the publishers wanted to make up the book to a decent size. However, as aforesaid, I admit that it is a case in which my innate love of stating a case and marshalling arguments got the better of me. And yet I don't know either – I don't think I would cancel it altogether. If I had the time, and could reasonably make the publishers reset it, I'd go over it and cut it down by about one half, so as to reduce the mere disproportion of bulk (which is, after all, a mechanical and secondary matter) but I don't believe I'd cancel the thing altogether even if I were paid to do so. After all there *is* a principle at stake, and the importance of the principle is not to be measured by the importance of the work – the play – exemplifying it.

As for the old formula of wanting me to write plays, you might just as well insist that I should compose a grand opera. I wonder when you'll recover from this mania far enough to realize that the paltriest criticism you or I ever wrote was better worth doing, yes, and a better work of art, than WIDOWERS' HOUSES.

What an odd thing is author's vanity. Here are 4 plays: Widowers' Houses, The Strike at Arlingford, The 2nd Mrs T[anqueray], and Alan's Wife. You are full of leniency for the faults and enthusiasm for the merits of W's H. and of scorn for the other three. Moore (I have it under his own hand and seal) supposes from its reception that The Strike is not a masterpiece, but can't for the life of him see in what respect it falls short of perfection, while for your play, Pinero's and A's W. [*Alan's Wife*] he has a hearty contempt. Pinero, I have no doubt, thinks the 2nd Mrs T., in spite of its success, a much underrated performance, and can see nothing whatever in The Strike – the only one of the other plays that he has seen so far as I know. I, again, have probably a certain amount of author's vanity with regard to A's W., though the actual author thinks me a contemptuous beast; but at least I so far retain my sanity as to be able to recognize and to assert that with all its faults and limitations the 2nd Mrs T. is a piece of competent dramatic literature, such as we haven't had in England in *our* time, and that the man who speaks of it in the same breath as the PROFLIGATE simply doesn't know what he is talking about.

As for Cook and his 'My dear A.B.W. business,' perhaps if he'd had a little more of the dear A.B.W. business his paper might have been not only better but more successful. The public wants whatever is well done. I don't know any form of criticism to which more *a priori* objections might be alleged than your own in the World, but Yates, having some glimmerings of sense, knows that the form is nothing, the man and the matter is everything. (This is very badly put.)

The term Nihilist has no terrors for me, any more than the term parallelogram (fewer in fact, for I can spell Nihilist and I can't the other word). Very likely I *am* a Nihilist – it all depends on definition – only I haven't the nerve to worry around with nitro-glycerine.

Our ignorance of the music-hall is precisely what seems to me to qualify us to render a useful report of its state and prospects. But perhaps we fall between 2 stools – it is neither quite unfamiliar nor quite familiar to us. Anyhow, as your mania for controversy leads you to controvert my theory that the world is hungering for our report on Music-Hall Land, we'd better let it drop.

I have received a tremendous communication from Bolas – he has really taken a whacking lot of trouble. Yours impenitently W.A.

Archer's **letter to the Chronicle** – that is, the *Daily Chronicle* – was part of his debate with A.B. Walkley over *Alan's Wife*. On Richard **Le Gallienne**, see previous letter. Archer's disdain for Robert **Buchanan** matched that of Shaw's. A.W. Pinero's ***The Profligate***, a farce, appeared in 1887. Despite Archer's dismissive comments on the *Westminster Gazette* and its editor, Edward Tyas **Cook**, he wrote for it on several occasions between 1893 and 1910. His article on *Alan's Wife* appeared in it. Likewise, despite Edmund **Yates**'s conservative ideas on some topics, both Archer and Shaw continued to write for *The World*, with Yates's full approval. A few anarchists, if not **nihilists**, were setting off bombs in London in the 1880s and 1890s, memorably represented in *The Secret Agent* (1907) by Joseph Conrad (1857–1924). It's unclear what trouble Thomas **Bolas** (1848–1932) had taken on, but it probably had something to do with *The Practical Socialist*, a journal he edited, and for which Shaw and others wrote. Bolas was an advocate for 'evolutionary socialism.'

42 / To William Archer c/o Sidney Webb. The Argoed. Monmouth.
30th August 1893

[APCS: BL 45296 ff 47–8; CL 1]

On 26 August Shaw journeyed to Monmouth in Wales to visit the Webbs. He stayed until 18 September. In the mornings he worked on Mrs Warren's Profession *and in the afternoons he took walks. He also proofread and edited the Webbs's* The History of Trade Unionism *(Biblio 1: 494–5), published in 1894. By November he finished the draft of the play (though he would later revise the ending of act 3). Although the play was published in 1898 in* Plays Pleasant and Unpleasant, *it was not licensed for performance in London until 1924. But the Stage Society presented a 'private' staging on 5 January 1902 (CP 1: 230). The New York City production of 1905 was closed down by the police. (On the New York controversy, see letters of 8, 15, and 18 November 1905.)*

My address is as above for the moment. I dont know how long I shall stay – perhaps into next week, perhaps only 'til the end of this.

Your reasons for not doing your duty by your own daemon are so conclusive that they would have shut up Shakespere if they had occurred to him.

I have finished the first act of my new play, in which I have skilfully blended the plot of The Second Mrs. Tanqueray with that of [Shelley's] The Cenci. It will be just the thing for the I. T.

GBS

Archer's **duty** to his **daemon** – his resistance to writing plays – was apparently explained in a missing letter, written between 23 and 25 August when he and Shaw exchanged another round of letters. Those letters have not survived. Shaw continued his campaign, nonetheless, as is evident at the close of letter 44, written seven months later.

43 / To William Archer 29 Fitzroy Square W

23rd April 1894

[ALS: BL 45296 ff 51–2; CL 1]

The correspondence between September 1893 and April 1894 is missing. During this period, besides finishing Mrs Warren's Profession, *Shaw wrote* Arms and the Man, *which was staged at the Avenue Theatre in 1894, thanks to funding provided anonymously to Florence Farr by Annie E.F. Horniman (1860–1937), an independent woman financially, socially, and intellectually. This was the first of Horniman's theatre projects, which in time expanded to the Abbey Theatre in Dublin and the Gaiety Theatre in Manchester. Farr launched a spring season at the Avenue Theatre. She received plays from John Todhunter (1839–1916), W.B. Yeats (1865–1939), and Shaw. The plays of Todhunter and Yeats were part of a double bill, opening on 29 March. Todhunter's* A Comedy of Sighs *was a disaster in late March and early April; it ran for 16 performances. Yeats's* The Land of Heart's Desire, *a verse play, was somewhat more successful, carrying forward for 33 performances. But audiences were slight. With only a week for rehearsals, Shaw's* Arms and the Man *replaced* Heart's Desire. *Farr took the role of Louka, Alma Murray played Raïna, Yorke Stephens (1862–1937) was Bluntschi, Bernard Gould (the stage name for the artist Bernard Partridge, 1861–1945) was Sergius Seranoff, and James Welch, who had played Lickcheese in* Widowers' Houses, *was a hit as Major Paul Petkoff. The production opened on 21 April 1894 and ran for either 50 performances (as per CP 1: 387–8) or 75 performances (as per Wearing*

1890: 388). The comedy was a success. When Shaw published his preface to Plays Pleasant *in 1898, he described these three productions as part of the history of the 'New Drama' and 'New Theatre' (Prefaces 1: 40).*

This letter is the first of two that Shaw dated 23 April. This one was started on late 22 April and finished on 23 April. In both letters he criticized aspects of Archer's review, which was published on 25 April. But by the evening of 22 April he had already shared the first draft of it with Shaw. In the final version Archer incorporated Shaw's taunt in this letter that Arms and the Man *'totally shatters your theory that I cannot write for the stage.' With Shaw's words in mind, Archer opened his review with this statement: 'I have long ago satisfied myself that Mr Shaw cannot write a play ... Even now, when he has had the deplorable ill-taste to falsify my frequently and freely-expressed prediction by writing a successful play, which kept an audience hugely entertained from the rise to the fall of the curtain, I vow I cannot work up a healthy hatred of him. Of course I shall criticise it with prejudice, malice, and acerbity; but I have not the faintest hope of ruffling his temper or disturbing his self-complacency.' Archer praised the comic effects of the play, which combines 'drama, farce, and Gilbertian irony.' The first act 'is genuine fantastic comedy, sparkling and delightful' (World 94: 109–18). But Archer dismissed the Bulgarian motifs as unrealistic. He also complained that the farcical methods of the second act descended into verbal games similar to those in W.S. Gilbert's* Palace of Truth *(1870). A.B. Walkley also compared Shaw to Gilbert in his review.*

Three months later Shaw countered his critics in The New Review *with 'A Dramatic Realist to His Critics' (CP 1: 485–511), which opened with this sentence: 'I think few people know how troublesome dramatic critics are.' A few months later on 1 November in the* Pall Mall Budget, *Archer again took up the Shaw-Gilbert comparison in a review of* His Excellency *by Gilbert and F. Osmond Carr (1858–1916). He repeated his claim that Shaw sometimes adopted 'Mr Gilbert's technical devices,' but he granted that Shaw 'triumphantly proved that whereas his criticism was leveled at traditional ideals, Mr Gilbert's banter implied an unquestioning acceptance of these ideals, and spent itself upon reductions-to-absurdity of the mere phrases and catchwords in which they are formulated.' In this sense, Gilbert's 'talent is almost exclusively verbal.' He 'has little more than the superficial observations of a journalist' (World 94: 296–7). This review probably made Shaw smile, for after six months his arguments against the Gilbert analogy were beginning to refine Archer's own arguments.*

I must really clear that Gilbert notion out of your head before you disgrace yourself over Arms & the Man. You have a perfect rag shop of old ideas in your head which prevent you getting a step ahead.

Gilbert is simply a paradoxically humorous cynic. He accepts the conventional ideals implicitly, but observes that people do not really live up to them. This he regards as a failure on their part at which he mocks bitterly. This position is precisely that of Sergius in the play, who, when disilluded, declares that life is a farce. It is a perfectly barren position: nothing comes of it but cynicism, pessimism, & irony.

I do not accept the conventional ideals. To them I oppose in the play the practical life & morals of the efficient, realistic man, unaffectedly ready to face what risks must be faced, considerate but not chivalrous, patient and practical; and I not only represent the woman as instinctively falling in love with all this even whilst all her notions of fine mannishness are being outraged; but I dot the i's by making him say in audible words – 'You mean, dont you, that I am the first man that has ever taken you *quite* seriously &c' – 'Now that you've found out that life isnt a farce, but something quite sensible & serious &c' and so on. You will not find a trace of this in Gilbert, and only some broken glimpses of it in Ibsen, who is by old habit a pessimist. My whole secret is that I have got clean through the old categories of good & evil, and no longer use them even for dramatic effect. Sergius is ridiculous through the breakdown of his ideals, not odious from his falling short of them. As Gilbert sees, they dont work; but what Gilbert does not see is that there is something else that does work, and that in that something else there is a completely satisfactory asylum for the affections. It is this positive element in my philosophy that makes Arms & The Man a perfectly genuine play about real people, with a happy ending and hope & life in it, instead of a thing like 'Engaged' which is nothing but a sneer at people for not being what Sergius & Raïna play at being before they find one another out. Every touch in Engaged is false: not one speech or action in it is possible. In the first act of Arms & The Man there is not one speech of Bluntschli's that is not faithful in fact & spirit to the realities of soldiering. All the effect is got out of facts stated in the simplest terms. The chocolate, the effect of a third day under fire, the dirt, the sleepiness, the cavalry charge are prosaically accurate. The effect is produced by an adroit contrast of this reality with the unreality of the woman's notions, which are, of course, largely the conventional stage notions. If you could only rid yourself of the intense unreality of your own preconceptions, and of your obsession by the ideals which you grow pessimistic over, you would not find that an effect due to the ridiculous obviousness and common sense of realism breaking through the mist & glamor of idealism, was a mere mechanical topsyturvyism.

But my chief object in writing this letter is to call your attention to the fact that last night, whether it leads to a commercial success or not, totally shatters your theory that I cannot write for the stage. Your notice of Widowers' Houses was one of the stupidest things you ever perpetrated, except perhaps your notice of Arms & The Man, which will no doubt explain matters virtually on the old ground that I am a supernatural being. Now the theory of *my* dramatic incompetence was part of a general theory involving *your* dramatic incompetence too. If you write a play, which you can do if you will sit down sincerely to amuse yourself, it will get produced as easily as Arms & the Man. And I still think that you ought to try. You dont intend to spend the rest of your life reviewing for the P.M.G., do you?

GBS

In 1877 W.S. Gilbert wrote ***Engaged***, a satire that featured young Victorians who grubbed for money and scorned the ideals of romantic love and marriage. From Michael Booth's perspective, 'Gilbert tore to shreds' the familiar character types of the loving female, obedient daughter, tender father, and noble male. The audience's 'cherished ideals of romantic love, marriage, the home, selflessness and filial relationships were under attack' (Booth: 187). Gilbert was, on occasion, quite capable of criticizing contemporary values, but Shaw rejected his cynical or pessimistic perspective. The condition of **topsyturveyism** – of being upside down or inverted – is one of reversal, confusion, and disorder. Gilbert and Alfred Cellier (1844–91) created the one-act operetta *Topsyturveydom* in 1874. Based on one of Gilbert's *Babs Ballads*, it opened on 21 March at the Criterion (25 perfs.). In 1884 a reviewer of *Princess Ida* identified Gilbert as the King of Topsy-Turveydom. More generally, the word *topsy-turvy* has been applied to the Gilbert and Sullivan operettas, and was used as the title for the 1999 film about the two men that Mike Leigh (1943–) directed. The word, however, has a long and various history that predates Gilbert. For example, Washington Irving (1783–1859) used it twice in 'The Legend of Sleepy Hollow' (1820). The *Oxford English Dictionary* traces the phrase to 1528, but it was 'probably in popular use from an earlier period.'

44 / To William Archer

29 Fitzroy Square W
23rd April 1894

[ALS: BL 45296 ff 49–50; CL 1]

This is the second of two letters that Shaw wrote in response to Archer's review of the production of Arms and the Man. *In the draft, which he shared with Shaw, Archer had praised the comic success of the play, but he had some reservations. He found the quick shift of Raïna's love from Sergius to Bluntschli 'in the course of six hours' quite unrealistic. Because she seemed 'bloodless' to him, Archer complained that Shaw has a 'peculiar habit of straining all the red corpuscles out of the blood of his personages.' In consequence, the play delivered a cynical representation of 'the seamy side' of human life (World 94: 113–16). Archer also applied this 'seamy' judgment to* Widowers' Houses, The Philanderer, *and* Mrs Warren's Profession.

Come, what did I tell you? Your first column, in which you describe things sanely and objectively, is capital. Then you strike on 'the seamy side,' the good old seamy side, and immediately the whole notice goes to pieces. It might have been written – from that point on – by a Bulgarian idealist. Do you think war is any the less terrible & heroic in its reality – on *its* seamy side, as you would say – than it is in the visions of Raïna & of the critics who know it from engravings of Elizabeth Thompson's pictures in the Regent St shop windows? And so on as regards the whole material of the play.

Your 'transfer of Raïna's affections' is a masterpiece of obtuseness. I offer to submit the point to your wife as arbitrator. The reference is to be 'Did Raïna love Sergius & then *transfer* that love to Bluntschli; or did she, after imaginatively living up to an ideal relation with Sergius, and conceiving a subconscious dislike for him under the strain, fall in love for the first time with Bluntschli?' Mrs. Archer will tell you straight off that the latter is the true solution, and that it is written large on the play, staring your amblyopia out of countenance. (I am convinced, by the way, that Mrs. Archer used to be just like Raïna). Poor Sergius struggling with your idiotic view of the seamy side, and heroically marrying Louka because he *will* not be a coward and a trifler (as per that idiotic view) is patent even to a man's understanding, if the man's eyes are open. You ought to be ashamed of yourself for applying such a word as 'bloodless' to a man who is bleeding from fifty wounds to his spirit – a perfect Banquo's ghost.

GBS

Shaw's statement about the '**first column**' referred to the layout of the page in *The World*, not to a separate essay by Archer. The journal published two columns of text per page, which measured 9 ½ inches wide by 14 inches long. In the first column Archer praises *Arms and the Man*, but the rest of the review offerred a critique of Shaw's 'unrealistic' characterization. **Elizabeth Thompson** (1844–1933) was born in Switzerland but settled in England, where she became a popular painter of military scenes. Shaw accused Archer of suffering from **amblyopia**, a lack of sharp clarity in one's vision. By contrast, in the preface 'Mainly about Myself' for *Plays Unpleasant* (1898), Shaw announced that he had 'normal eyesight' – that is, 'the power to see things accurately' which is 'enjoyed by only about ten per cent of the population' (CP 1: 12). Despite the hyperbole of comparing himself to **Banquo's ghost** in *Macbeth*, Shaw was not bloodied by Archer and the other critics. With the production of *Arms and the Man*, he achieved his first substantial success in the London theatres.

45 / To G. Bernard Shaw

[no address]
[c. 25th April 1894]

[TLU: FALES]

The original of this letter has disappeared; a partial copy survives in the papers of Elizabeth Robins. In defence of his review of Arms and the Man, *Archer attempted to justify his complaint that the characters, especially Bluntschli and Raïna, are 'bloodless' in their sexual identities. He had also dismissed the lovers in* Widowers' Houses *as 'strangely bloodless.' Although he was quite capable of admiring the poetic battle of the sexes in* Much Ado about Nothing, *the cynical (and often silly) confrontations in Gilbert's works, or the troubled sexual struggles in Ibsen's plays, he could not come to terms with Shaw's unsentimental and often harsh versions of sexual relations. By constrast, Oscar Wilde, upon the publication of* Widowers' Houses *in May 1893, informed Shaw: 'I admire the horrible flesh and blood of your creatures' (Wilde: 563–4). But Archer rejected any such sentiment about the creatures – or monsters.*

Archer was thus determined to reject the contemporary battles that Shaw represented. And because Shaw was still at the early stage of his career in 1894, Archer – the committed (if sometimes misguided) mentor – felt justified in delivering his own hyperbole, as he did in this letter. But Shaw, to his credit, ignored such warnings. Save for his creation of the alluring Candida, who seduced Archer as well as Marchbanks, Shaw rejected Archer's well-meaning guidance. He continued to serve his own daemon in the writing of sexual scenes.

In this case there is not the slightest symptom of sex in either of the parties concerned, except a pair of trousers & a petticoat. Now, there you have a fundamental fact quite apart from all theories of cynicism or idealism or anything else – you have totally failed to make me feel that there is an atom of sex-attraction between any of the lovers. That is why I call them bloodless, & Sergius' 'bleeding spirit' has nothing whatever to do with the matter. You might as well argue that Othello wasn't copper-coloured on the grounds that he was a 'white man' in the American sense of the words.

And mind you this same bloodlessness vitiates a great deal of *Mrs Warren* as well. You have made your love-scenes nauseous enough, heaven knows, but it is a sort of frigid nauseousness that is indescribably revolting.

[I reject] the absolute froggishness of your characters, especially where love is concerned. If you can't realize & correct that, you'll never be worth a cent as a writer for the stage.

[no signature]

46 / To William Archer

29 Fitzroy Square W
27th November 1894

[ALS: FALES]

In November 1894 Ibsen sent Little Eyolf, *his newest play, to Archer, who translated it within four weeks so that a copyright performance could be held. Once the play was read aloud in a theatre space, the British copyright would be secure; but until then Archer was trying to keep the play a secret. Upon receiving Shaw's letter, Archer wrote to Robins, enclosing Shaw's letter in the mailing. He informed her that he had telegraphed Shaw 'to hold his tongue, as I have no doubt he will.' Archer also sent a letter to Shaw, but it is no longer extant. In his letter to Robins, however, he describes what he had written to Shaw: 'I cannot think how the rumors he mentions have got about, and that at any rate I am determined they shall not get about through me.' He also told Shaw, as reported in the letter to Robins, that he had said nothing to Florence Farr except that 'the play had knocked me over' (ALS: Fales, 28 November).*

Both Archer and Robins were concerned that Shaw would spread word about Ibsen's play to the Charringtons and others. Their worries were justified; on this same day Shaw began the first of several attempts to get the play away from

Robins and Archer. In a letter to the publisher William Heinemann, who held the publishing rights for the translation, Shaw suggested that he should appeal to Robins to relinquish any priority for the staging of the play, which could then be transferred to the IT. *As Shaw conceived matters, he and Charles Charrington would then be able to feature Janet Achurch in an* IT *production. Throughout 1895 and much of 1896 Shaw's meddling caused many complications and struggles over the control of* Little Eyolf, *which was finally produced by Robins in November 1896. Throughout the disagreements and negotiations over the play Archer remained aligned with Robins (Prophet: 120–8; Whitebrook: 175–8, 182–7).*

Is the secret of the Ibsen play officially out – yet? I see it stated in the Chronicle with all possible firmness that the title is to be 'Little Whatshisname.' I saw Mrs. Emery the other day; and she declares boldly that various scraps of information are afloat, and have been imparted to her in dreadful secrecy, you being the only person who did not pledge her to silence. I sat tight & said nothing, except to correct an impression of hers that the 'untasted champagne' scene was in the present tense of the play instead of the past. What she knew did not, as far as I could make out without pursuing the subject, come to very much. As it is absurd for me to solemnly keep an open secret, I wish you would let me know how far you want anything to leak out. I write because I expect to see the Charringtons tomorrow; and they will probably ask me for news of the new play.

I have withdrawn the Philanderer from Wyndham's hands on seeing it announced that he is (very wisely, as I think) going to follow up the H.A.J. vein of gold.

GBS

Mrs Emery – the actress Florence Farr – had staged *Arms and the Man* in 1894, and was looking for a new project. In act 1 of *Little Eyolf,* Rita, the wife of Alfred Allmers, says to him: 'There stood the champagne, but you tasted it not.' This sexual allusion to herself as **untasted champagne** is an indictment of Allmers for not making love to her upon his return from his reclusive retreat into the mountains. Shaw offered ***The Philanderer*** to several actor-managers without success. In the 1890s the actor-manager Charles **Wyndham** staged several of the plays of **H.A.J.** – Henry Arthur Jones. He premiered Jones's *The Case of Rebellious Susan,* which opened on 3 October 1894 (164 perfs.). Although he did not produce any of Jones's plays in 1895 or 1896, he staged Jones's *The Physician* (78 perfs.) in March 1897. It was followed in October by a long run of *The Liars* (328 perfs.). Then in September 1900

Wyndham had another success with Jones's *Mrs Dane's Defence* (207 perfs.). Wyndham and his wife Mary Moore played the leads in these previous productions, but Lena Ashwell (1872–1957) replaced Moore in *Mrs Dane's Defence*.

47 / To William Archer

29 Fitzroy Square W
6th December 1894

[TLS: BL 45296 f 53; CL 1]

In The Theatrical 'World' for 1893 *Archer had written an 'Epistle Dedicatory to Mr Robert W. Lowe,' one of his closest friends. The epistle paid homage to 'our unfaltering friendship of twenty years' and 'our love of the theatre.' It recounted fondly their experiences of attending theatre together in Edinburgh and London, and celebrated 'our craze, our mania, for the stage of the past.' The epistle then justified their professional careers in theatrical criticism and scholarship (World 93: ix–xxxv). Although this personal epistle had been well received, Archer sought a Shavian voice to open* The Theatrical 'World' of 1894. *Relunctantly, Shaw agreed to write the preface, but instead of offering a personal piece, he took the opportunity to criticize the commercial basis of the actor-manager system in London and to praise the emergence of a few actress-managers, such as Elizabeth Robins and Florence Farr. When the book was published, Shaw then reviewed it (SatRev, 13 April 1895; Dukore 1: 307–12). This was one of many cases that Shaw and Archer rolled one another's logs.*

On 3 December Shaw and H.W. Massingham, who served as editor of DC, *attended a private reading of* Little Eyolf *at Archer's flat. Shaw quickly drafted a review, which he shared with Archer, who quoted from it in his letter of 8 December (see below). But it was never published. Archer's criticism in that letter probably did not deter Shaw, but Massingham, who had asked Shaw for an assessment, may have changed his mind about publishing the review. Or perhaps Archer – or even William Heinemann – asked Shaw to not write about the new play until it was published or performed. Whatever the case, Massingham decided to publish his own commentary about the play on 12 December 1894 (Diaries 2: 1051). Shaw did not publish anything about* Little Eyolf *until November 1896, when he reviewed the production staged by Elizabeth Robins.*

There is one serious objection to my doing the preface; and that is that I have hardly been half a dozen times to the theatre (including all that I saw of 'Arms and The Man') in the course of the year. I should have to make that fact the text of my discourse, I suppose. Further, I have always been of opinion, and am still, that the custom of getting Jones to write a preface for Smith's book is a very idiotic one. I remonstrated strongly with H.A.J. the other day for publishing *Judah* with a preface by Joe Knight. Not that I objected to Knight, but that I wanted to know what Henry Arthur had to say about his own work, and not what Joseph thought of it – as to which there was evidence already in the Athenaeum and elsewhere. Your last dedicatory preface to Lowe was interesting: I heard people talking about it with considerable feeling, though personally I thought it deficient in profundity of sentiment. But it did not at all explain your point of view as a critic. It seems to me that such a book is incomplete without a general review of the dramatic movement of the year; and this can only gain charm by being put in the form of the critic's confession as to how far he has been compelled to throw himself into one or other of the parties which are inevitably formed for progress or conservation whenever a movement takes place. I know your enormous reluctance to realise your own experience in this fashion; but it is assuredly a thing you must do, whether you write it down or not, if you are to progress in consciousness – which is the only sort of progress possible to a critic. Why not use such an excellent opportunity as the annual preface to the Theatrical World for this purpose? It is easier this year to get me to do something; and next year and the year after there may be a sparkler or two still left to fall back on. But think of the inevitable time when, if you keep up this silly shirking practice of getting an alien preface, you will have to fall back on the nobodies who will consider that they are laying you under a huge obligation by writing something of which you will be secretly ashamed. This appears to me to make out a heavy case against the preface. If in spite of it you persist in calling in outside aid, call in mine sooner than anyone else's by all means; but the right man for the work is clearly William Archer and nobody else.

I sympathise with you so entirely – in the sense of knowing how you feel about it – that on Monday, in spite of Massingham's appeal for my presence and support, I two or three times almost made up my mind to spare you the agony of my appearance on the scene. But I think you will admit that it was desirable to get as much horse power as possible into the discussion of the play on your reading it, and that this was no less important in view of my own review than of Massingham's. I have always been one of the most indulgent of fathers to you up to the point at which your petulances and protervities are clearly spoiling good business. At that point, I cannot be blamed for asserting that I, too, have my validity in the universal scheme.

By the way, so far from backing my proposal for a page of reviews [of *Little Eyolf*] you received it with pathetic dismay, and plainly impressed on Massingham that he would be doing the most cruel violence to your finest feelings if he thus exposed your darling naked in the slave market to be priced by a horde of filthy reviewers. If you doubt this, ask him.

Why don't you set yourself to find out what you mean when you say that I never saw or felt a play in my life? You are quite right insofar as you mean something, and something which I quite understand; but you know perfectly well that the something is not that I never saw or felt a play in my life. If you were to say that the Adelphi theatre was not in the Strand, I daresay I should find out what you really meant by that statement; but I should also suspect you of not having precisely cornered your own meaning, judging from your very loose expression of it. You must find a more plausible Shaw formula, if it were only to save you from open disaster in criticising my plays. It is true that what are to you the solid and permanent elements in 'Little Eyolf' are to me the illusory and transitory ones, and that the solution which you announced as conventional and disappointing is as real to me as the solution that breakfast brings to my morning's appetite – and by the solution, remember, I do not mean the mere material dress of the matter – the huts and the boys and so on – but the new feeling which these indicate. The transition from the passionate, idealistic world of love and hate (two names for the same thing), lust and murder, sacrifice and expiation, virtue and advice, and all the rest of it, to the real, creative, maternal world, comes just in that way. And the entry into the second costs the plunge into the first. Perhaps it may a little disappoint you, after the fantastic solution of Peer Gynt, and the no-solution of Rosmersholm, that a real solution is only found in something that brings the great Ibsen into line with Monsieur Toutlemonde; but that, in my view, is the final *pièce de conviction.*

I shall not need the book (at least not indispensably) for my review, which is already finished and sent to the printer. But I should like to study that point about the letters, as I can see at present no function for them except that of explaining Asta's objection to live with the Allmers before the play begins. This does not seem sufficient: besides, why should she not be his sister in reality? It would improve the case instead of damaging it.

I write by this post to Heinemann to ask him when I may let my review loose.

G.B.S.

Although Robert H. **Lowe** worked as an insurance broker, he was also an accomplished theatre scholar. In 1888 he published the *Bibliographical Account of English Theatrical Literature*, an indispensable reference work. He also edited a new edition of Colley Cibber's *Apology* (2 vols, 1889) and wrote a biography of the Restoration actor Thomas Betterton (1891). Together, Lowe and Archer edited the dramatic essays of Leigh Hunt (1894) and William Hazlitt (1895). Henry Arthur Jones's ***Judah***, which premiered on 21 May 1890 at the Shaftesbury Theatre (122 perfs.), was revived at the Avenue Theatre on 30 January 1892 (22 perfs.). Besides serving as theatre critic for *The Athenaeum*, **Joseph Knight** also edited *Notes and Queries*. William **Heinemann** held publishing rights to *Little Eyolf*, and thus controlled the performance as well as the publishing of the play.

48 / To G. Bernard Shaw

[no address]
8th December 1894

[ALU: Fales]

This unsigned and incomplete letter, which resides in the papers of Elizabeth Robins, is not in Archer's hand. But the letter is clearly a direct response to Shaw's letter of 6 December, and it represents Archer's voice and persona. Archer composed the letter, but someone else transcribed it. We cannot be certain, however, that the letter, either complete or incomplete, was delivered to Shaw. Adding to the puzzle, this letter quoted from Shaw's unpublished draft of a review of Little Eyolf. *As for Archer's statement that Shaw had 'never seen a play,' this may have been said during the reading of Ibsen's play at Archer's flat on 3 December. If, though, the statement was made in a letter to Shaw in early December, that letter has also disappeared. Another intrigue, less cryptic, arises with Archer's fantasy of human psychology in the distant future when people will be rational instead of emotional. He anticipated – almost three decades before the fact – Shaw's vision of human development, as represented by the contemplative Elders in* Back to Methuselah.

To G.B.S.

I must decline to construct a complete Shaw formula until I am bound to. Wait till I write a preface to a book of yours. For expressing the effect produced on me by a play, no formula is needed. What I meant by saying that 'you had never seen a play' was clumsy enough for all practical purposes. You have seen productions in the theatres in which fictitious personages express, or fail to express, certain ideas, approximate or fail to approximate to your philosophy. You have also had a certain intellectual insight into the playwright's technical skill or lack of skill. But you have never (mind, I am not speaking of opera) *felt with* an author's characters simply as hurt and suffering human beings. The analysis you apply to Little Eyolf is absolutely destructive of drama. 'Ibsen means,' you say, 'to show that these people are fussing extravagantly over nothing.' Very likely; but because people *do* fuss and suffer over these things, he means in the first place that we shall *feel with them*, as I do & as you don't. In other words, he is writing a drama, not a pamphlet to prove the absurdity of drama. Remember, I believe your analysis of the thing is in the main rational. I believe that the average man of about A. D. 2500 may think & feel as you do, and then the theatre will be given up to ironical farce like Arms and the Man. About A. D. 2700 they will probably have ceased even to ironise, and then there will be no theatre at all – and a good thing too. But in the meantime, I am a man of this age, and I propose to make the most of the qualities of its defects. Since laws and prejudices are still strong enough, since human nature is still blind enough, to afford matter for poignant drama, Ibsen & I are bent on getting what fun we can out of it. And I am not sure that in A. D. 2894, when the theatre is only a department of the museum of antiquities, people may not see Little Eyolf played, perhaps on Ibsen's birthday, & think to themselves, 'Oh, how I shld have liked to live in the days when men & women could feel & suffer like that! Of course all their drama was a mere insensate fuss, arising out of foolish habits of thought, some of which had crystalised into written & unwritten laws. But I think I would exchange our majestic calm for the possibility of plunging back again into that picturesque, ridiculous, heroic hurly burly.'

[no signature]

49 / To William Archer West Cliff Hotel, Folkestone
28th December 1894

[ALS: BL 45296 ff 54–5; CL 1]

In late December Shaw took a short vacation in Folkestone with Graham Wallas. He escaped London but not Archer, who kept Shaw busy by mailing page proofs for The Theatrical World of 1894. *During the second half of 1894 Archer was uncertain about the future of his position at* The World *because the publisher Edmund Yates had died suddenly in May. In August Shaw had resigned as music critic and Archer was unhappy over his meagre salary. In November Frank Harris, who had recently purchased the* Saturday Review, *asked Archer to become the drama critic at £5 per week. But Archer turned down the position, after securing a raise in salary from £3 to £5 per week from Major Arthur Griffiths (1838–1908), the new proprietor of* The World *(C. Archer: 208; Whitebrook: 169). In early December Harris then approached Shaw, who negotiated for* £6 per week *(SSS: 69). In* My Life and Loves *(1925), Harris claimed that he had only negotiated with Shaw for the position, offering £8 per week. But Harris was often unreliable in his statements.*

In December Shaw finished a draft of Candida, *written for Janet Achurch, but had no luck in enticing George Alexander to produce the play. Alexander was already rehearsing* Guy Domville *by Henry James (1843–1916). It opened on 5 January 1895 to weak reviews. The run was stretched out for 32 performances while Alexander rushed Oscar Wilde's* The Importance of Being Earnest *into rehearsal. It opened on 14 February and ran until the end of the season in May for 83 performances. The run may have been extended, but Wilde's trial and guilty verdict caused Alexander to close down the production. Shaw and Archer reviewed both plays and their productions.*

I return to town tomorrow afternoon to take up the duties, fairly forced on me by Harris, of dramatic critic to the Saturday Review; so do not send on any more proofs to Folkestone. It is questionable whether it is quite decent for a dramatic author to be also a dramatic critic; but my extreme reluctance to make myself dependent for my bread and butter on the acceptance of my plays by managers tempts me to hold to the position that my real profession is that by which I can earn my bread in security. Anyhow, I am prepared to do anything which will enable me to keep my plays for twenty years with perfect tranquillity if it takes that time to educate the public into wanting them.

I read 'Candida' to Alexander before I came down here. He instantly perceived that it was Marchbank's & Candida's (that is, Esmond's & Janet's) play and not his. He said he would produce it if he could get down to the poet's age; but he would not play Morell. He had acted that sort of part, he said, until people were declaring that he could not act. By so doing he has made money enough to make him independent of playing anything but parts which will give him, as he put it, a property in himself as well as in his theatre. This, being intelligent, delighted me, and I took off 'Candida' in high spirits. However, as he said he wanted to act a clever man, I suggested The Philanderer, who is an extremely clever man. He asked me to let him read it. I sent it to him & have not heard from him since. He said he wanted a play, because neither Jones nor Pinero was ready. He meant ready to step in on the failure of Henry James's play; but naturally he did not say so.

I am desperately floored by your confounded proofs. A year or two ago, when there was some question of republishing my World articles, I looked through a few of them, and found them, apart from the context of time and place for which they were originally designed, quite impossibly dull, stale and ineffective. I will not go so far as to say that your articles are so afflicting; but they are sufficiently damnable. Who now cares for a discussion of the probability of the plot of 'A Bunch of Violets'? What further use to Carte is your attempt to make yourself agreeable, kindly & tolerant over such a ghastly and foredoomed insanity as *Mirette*? Is it tolerable to have Ibsen and Duse, not to mention myself, cut into strips by twothousandword lengths of mere regurgitation of the year's refuse, which is sufficiently chronicled elsewhere in the Dramatic Year & the files of the Era? I am in utter despair: I dont know what to write by way of preface. If your laziness had led you to follow my example & leave the articles buried, I could not have complained; but I am now more than ever convinced that you should either let your year's work alone or else rearrange it all as an annual article having the same excellence as its parts originally had as weekly articles. You tell me that the experiment of last year was not a financial success. I tear my hair and desperately ask you, why should it? I declare before high Heaven that Scott is a fool, and you a shirk, to publish a book that is no book. If it paid you, you would have some excuse; but it doesnt.

I am also greatly hampered in even trying to think out a preface by the overwhelming obstacle which you make so light of – that I have not seen the plays you deal with. I must at least try to see the New Woman & Rebellious Susan when I come up.

I have read a Scott novel down here. On my trip to Italy last September I read 'Catriona.' And, making all due allowance for the inferiority of 'Catriona' as a specimen of R.L.S., and for the fact that 'Old Mortality' is not one of Scott's failures, I cannot see the sense of forcing the comparison between the two men as everyone is doing just now. I wonder what Stevenson's work would have come to if he had lived to bring it to its full realisation. His death seems to me a complete 'cutoff' of a man who had never got to close quarters with life & who was only beginning to peep carefully over his palisade of cleverness at it. Here ringeth the table d'hôte bell.

GBS

Shaw's statements in the first paragraph about Frank **Harris**, the ***Saturday Review***, and waiting **twenty years** for his plays to be accepted by the public repeated a quite similar set of observations he wrote in his diary on the same date (Diaries 2: 1054). Having completed the writing of *Candida* in December 1894, Shaw decided that the role of Marchbanks should be acted by Henry V. **Esmond** (1862–1922), who had appeared in A.W. Pinero's *The Magistrate* (1892) and *The Second Mrs Tanqueray* (1893), and H.A. Jones's *The Masqueraders* (1894). But Courtney Thorpe (1854–1927), not Esmond, played Marchbanks in the first production in 1897 in Aberdeen (CP 1: 514). And when the play was given a private performance by the Stage Society on 30 July 1900, the role of 'Eugene Marjoribanks' (Wearing 1900: 42) went to Harley Granville Barker (1877–1946), with Shaw's full approval. Then when two additional productions of *Candida* occurred in 1904 (see letter of 12 May 1904), Barker again played Marchbanks. With these productions in 1904 Shaw finally achieved his mission as a playwright. Thus, instead of having to wait twenty years to capture the public for his plays, he only had to be patient for a little less than ten years. Of course, he was almost fifty years old by 1904, and had been in London for close to thirty, not twenty, years. His patience was surely tested during those years. Alexander anticipated the **failure of Henry James's play**, but he correctly felt that a play by Oscar Wilde was a much safer choice than *The Philanderer* by Shaw.

Sydney Grundy wrote ***A Bunch of Violets***. The comic opera ***Mirette***, by Michel M. Carré (b. 1865) and André Messager (1853–1929), opened on 3 July 1894 at D'Oyly **Carte**'s Savoy Theatre, and ran for five weeks. Eleonora **Duse** (1858–1924) performed in London in 1893 and 1894; she appeared at Daly's Theatre in *La dame aux camélias* (Alexandre Dumas fils, 1824–95), *Fedora* (Victorien Sardou, 1831–1908), *La Locandiera* (Carlo Goldini, 1707–93), and *Cavalleria Rusticana* (Giovanni Verga, 1840–1922). She even performed Ibsen's *A Doll's House* and Shakespeare's *Antony and Cleopatra*. Each year Archer wrote several reviews of her performances: 'She is, without exception, the most absorbingly interesting actress I ever saw' (World 93: 126). ***The Dramatic Year Book***, intended by its editor C.S. Cheltman to be an annual like the **Era**, only appeared in 1892. The **experiment of last year** was *The Theatical 'World' of 1893. The* ***New Woman***, written by Sydney Grundy, starred Winifred Emery (1862–1924). It opened at the Comedy on 1 September 1894 (173 perfs.). H.A. Jones's *The Case of* ***Rebellious Susan***, starring Charles Wyndham and Mary Moore, opened at the Criterion on 3 October 1894 (164 perfs.). Archer reviewed both productions (World 94: 223–2, 266–75). The publisher Walter **Scott** issued five volumes of *The Theatrical 'World'* annuals, covering 1893–7. Scott Publishing, which had produced the five volumes of Archer's translations of Ibsen (1890–1), was also responsible for a revised edition of Shaw's *Cashel Byron's Profession* (1889) and *The Quintessence of Ibsenism* (1891). The novelist Sir Walter **Scott** (1771–1832) published *Old Mortality* in 1816. In 1893 **R.L.S.** (Robert Louis Stevenson) published *Catriona* (American title, *David Balfour*); he died on 3 December 1894.

50 / To William Archer

29 Fitzroy Square W
18th March 1895

[TLS: BL 45296 f 56; CL 1]

A. W. Pinero's The Notorious Mrs Ebbsmith, *which starred Mrs Patrick Campbell, premiered at the Garrick Theatre on 13 March (86 perfs.). Archer praised 'the design of the play' and aspects of Mrs Campbell's acting, but felt that the character of Agnes Ebbsmith 'can scarcely pass muster as a well-observed type.' Pinero failed to understand the traits and discourse of the new woman. Although Agnes Ebbsmith is supposed to be the daughter of 'a revolutionary Socialist, atheist,' she does not 'know the phraseology of her party.' She reduces her father's economic beliefs to a vague statement about the 'division of wealth, and the rest of it' (World 95: 75–85). Shaw disliked Pinero's play: 'To tell the truth, I disliked the play so much that nothing would induce me to say anything good of it.' He dismissed it as bad, artificial, unreal, feeble, degraded, hackneyed, gross, and insufferable; the characters were bloodless. 'Mr Pinero has not the faintest idea of what such a woman's career is in reality.' But Shaw was charmed by Mrs Campbell, 'a wonderful woman.' At a key moment in the play Mrs Ebbsmith tosses a Bible into a stove; then, as Shaw writes, 'with a wild scream, she plunges her hand into the glowing stove and pulls out the Bible again. The Church is saved; and the curtain descends' (SatRev, 16 March; Dukore 1: 283–7).*

On 16 March Janet Achurch departed for New York City to act in a production of Candida, *to be staged by the American actor Richard Mansfield (1857–1907). But in April, during rehearsals, Mansfield cancelled the production because he did not like the play (just 'talk, talk, talk') and could not abide Achurch, whose wild appearance and debilitating vices of drugs and drinking appalled him (Holroyd 1: 320–5).*

The 'division of wealth' passage is all right. If only he [Pinero] had used the word, 'distribution' he would have cleared the reef.

I am greatly dissatisfied with my article on the play. I was in the middle of the worry and overwork thrown on me by the necessity of getting *Candida* ready for the boat on Saturday, with the parts all corrected and the full score provided with a minutely detailed plan of the stage action and so on. The production of the play on Wednesday rushed me mercilessly, as the paper has to be ready to catch the foreign mails on Friday afternoon; so that I was quite unable to get into a sympathetic, humane mood, and could only express the – in short, what I did express. However, I should not at all mind seeing Pinero driven back into the comic line. It is in that line alone that he shews the smallest fertility. Mrs Ebbsmith, like the other two wouldbe serious plays, not only shews awkwardness, constraint, and impotence on its intellectual side, but apparent exhaustion and sterility on its inventive side. All the characters in it bundled together, and squeezed in a wine press would not produce blood enough to make Dick Phenyl. 'The Hobby Horse' is a masterpiece of humor and fancy in comparison. It seems to me that it is only by the frankest abandonment of himself to his own real tastes and capacities that he can do anything worth doing now on the stage. But he won't do that, because he is a Jew, with the Jew's passion for fame and effect and the Jew's indifference to the reality of the means by which they are produced. A man who, at Pinero's age and in his position and with his secure bank account, could bring himself to that Bible business, is hopelessly damned. You might as well try to fertilise a mule. We shall have to take these plays of his for exactly what they are, without trying to appeal for better to a will which he simply hasn't got in him. After all, I don't know that I could have done anything more for him than what I did; and that was to alter the words 'silly and cowardly' to 'less sensible and less courageous.'

I think you are wrong about the pioneering. He is, and always has been, a camp follower and not a leader. That sort of man, in his lust for effect, sometimes tries to catch the public imagination by *bizarrerie*, and since genuinely original and faithful work always strikes the mob at first as bizarre, the real bizarrerie may accidentally help to secure a hearing for the work that is mistaken as bizarrerie. You have of course the champion instance of Meyerbeer (a Jew) leading up in this way to Wagner, who abhorred him and all his works. But I believe myself that the gain is wiped off with a heavy balance to the bad by the loss. Pinero is only cutting the grooves deeper that I wish to lift the drama out of. To the man who is touched and fascinated by Pinero, Shaw will be the merest sand and saw-dust, all the more irritating because it would appear so very easy to give my subjects the Pinerotic effect. In the long run, of course, he can do me no harm; but in the meantime I am bound, not to be grateful to him as my John the Baptist, but to let him have his show goodhumoredly whilst it lasts. And in speaking of myself here, I do not mean myself individually, but my school, or rather the school to which I belong, which is the great classic school.

I am going to hear Olivier's play on the 27th at Miss Brooke's in Hampstead. Is there any other fixture – at Hartley's, for instance? But you needn't trouble to answer this, as I am sure to hear from Olivier himself.

I suggest that you should reconsider your position concerning Mansfield and Peer Gynt. I have put it into his head that if he succeeds as Eugene he should follow it up with Oswald, and that as nobody has ever made anything in England of Lovborg, he should try his hand at Hedda Gabler with Janet. I still fail to see any better man to back.

G.B.S.

Dick Phenyl is a character in Pinero's *Sweet Lavender* (1888), which, like ***The Hobby Horse*** (1886), is a comedy. In his statement about the **Jew's passion for fame and effect** Shaw voiced a pervasive Jewish stereotype of the era. Evoking Wagner's anti-Semitism did not help the matter. Wagner was a greater composer than Meyerbeer and Shaw was a greater playwright than Pinero, but Shaw's Jewish explanation for the limitations of Meyerbeer and Pinero was irrelevant and small-minded. Shaw's alignment of himself with Wagner under these terms was – and remains – a nasty comparison. Both Shaw and Archer, on occasion, settled too easily into anti-Semitic clichés and generalizations about all Jews that were prevalent in the era. Even Shaw's first theatre review in 1880 of *The Merchant of Venice*, which rejected Henry Irving's generous portrayal, referred to the 'habitual greed' of Shylock, who is a 'common Jewish type' who 'clings to the money' (Dukore 1: 5). On Shaw's disturbing commentary on the 'Jewish problem' under Hitler, see Yde: 15–16, 61, 152–3. Yet Shaw bent over backward to accommodate Dr Fritz Loewenstein, who fled Nazi Germany in 1933 and appealed to Shaw as 'a Jewish refugee.' For Shaw's struggles to accommodate Loewenstein, see Holroyd 3: 462–8, 470–2. It is important to note that Shaw's judgments on Jews could be more complex and ambiguous than was expressed in some of his clichés and statements. See the exchange of articles in 1925 with the French playwright Henry Bernstein (Biblio 2: 706, item C2575); reprinted as 'On the Jews' with invaluable commentary and notes by Michel W. Pharand in the *Shaw Annual* (2012; vol. 32: 16–30). Giacomo **Meyerbeer** (1791–1864) was a German composer of Jewish decent. He became a great success in French Grand Opera with *Robert le diable, Le prophète, Les Huguenots,* and *L'Africaine.* Wagner admired aspects of Meyerbeer's talent, but still unleashed anti-Semitic remarks against him. Sydney (later Baron) **Olivier** (1859–1943) was a Fabian who served on its executive committee (1887–99); he entered the colonial service, and held various posts, including assignments in Honduras, Jamaica, and India. The amateur reading of Olivier's play was a singular event; there's no record in the 1890s of a London production of a play by Olivier. Emma **Brooke** (d. 1926) served on the Fabian executive committee (1893–6), and wrote several anonymous novels, including *Transition,* which offers a portrait of Sidney Webb. Eustace D. **Hartley** (d. 1897) was also a Fabian. For years Archer had resisted the idea of Richard **Mansfield** (1857–1907) performing an abridged version of his translation of ***Peer Gynt.*** But in 1906 he relented. Mansfield cut eleven scenes from the text, and trimmed others. The production opened in Chicago in October, then moved to New York City in February 1907, the year of his death.

51 / To William Archer

29 Fitzroy Square W
29th April 1895

[TLS: FALES]

In 1894 and 1895 a series of national debates took place over the supposed immorality of the music halls and variety theatres. As this letter and the two following letters illustrate, Shaw and Archer resisted the efforts of the National Vigilance Association to close down the Empire Theatre of Varieties and the Palace Theatre. They were opposed to stage censorship, but they disagreed over methods and rhetorical tactics for defending the theatres. They also disagreed over the artistic value of music hall entertainment. Archer doubted, for example, that the principle that guided their defence of Ibsen's plays could be applied to the display of semi-nude women at the Palace.

*Shaw's initial involvement in the controversy had occurred six months earlier when Laura Ormiston Chant (1848–1923) and other social reformers campaigned to close down the Empire Theatre because prostitutes visited its balcony promenade. The battles between Mrs Chant and George Edwardes became a major public controversy over the licensing of the Empire Theatre (Donohue: 31ff.). In 'The Empire Promenade' (PMG, 16 October 1894; Agits: 30–4), Shaw criticized Mrs Chant for ignoring the social and economic conditions that caused prostitution. Then in early April 1895 he returned to the music hall controversies. In 'The Living Pictures' (SatRev, 6 April 1895; Dukore 1: 301–7), he denounced William Alexander Coote and his followers, who wanted the London County Council (*LCC*) to close down the Palace Theatre (Donohue: 90–6). In opposition to Coote, who denied that the exhibition of sixteen ostensibly nude women had any artistic quality, Shaw proclaimed that 'the living pictures are works of art.' By this means he announced his* *support for the aims and methods of Charles Morton, the manager of Augustus Harris's Palace Theatre.*

*Archer also opposed the moral reformers, but he was less adversarial than Shaw. In 'The County Council and the Music Halls' (*Contemporary Review, *March 1895: 317–27), he appealed to the LCC to apply 'calm reason' in its regulation of the halls. He urged the council members to resist 'the influence of Puritan bigotry and busy-bodyism' that guided the National Vigilance Association. Three weeks later in the* Pall Mall Budget, *Archer published 'Theatre and Music Hall' (28 March 1895; World 95: 96–103). Here too he called for reasonable judgment, but his concern in this case was not the reformers but instead the avid supporters of the halls. Though quite willing to praise the talent of a few of the performers, Archer rejected the 'cant about the art of the music halls.' He had little patience for enthusiasts such as George Moore who, in the process of celebrating the artistic qualities of the halls, declared the death of West End theatres. Archer's moderating essay displeased Shaw.*

Now the matter is settled with a vengeance. The Vigilance Committee is not alone in its opinion: the Gaiety Theatre is on its side. Men of such different ways of thinking as Mr Coote and Mr Seymour Hicks are found agreeing on this great public question. Why not interview Arthur Roberts on the subject?

What I want to fix in your mind is the fact that Coote is not going to proceed against Morton in court. He is going to try and induce the County Council to deal with Living Pictures exactly as they dealt with the Empire Promenade. Any theatre in London has really the same power to play 'Ghosts' as Morton has to exhibit the pictures: the penalty in both cases is the same in fact if not in law: namely, the withdrawal of the license.

Suppose [Augustus] Harris produces *Das Rheingold* with the three Rhinedaughters skirtless, will that be art or will it not? Is a *tableau vivant* art or is it not? Is the living picture of Gretchen at the spinning wheel exhibited by Mephistopheles to Faust, or the apotheosis of Gretchen, or the apparition of Guinevere in the prologue to *King Arthur* at the Lyceum, art or not? If not, why not? If so, the Palace picture of Marguerite clothed is clearly art. The sole difference between Marguerite and the Naiad is that M. is dressed and the Naiad is not? Kindly explain how the disappearance of the skirt involves the disappearance of the artistic character of the picture. Do you surrender the whole pictorial side of the art of the stage, since that is necessarily the art of presenting living pictures? Have you ever devoted two minutes serious thought to the question?

I think you are wrong to publish the letter and the article. I have not exercised my veto because that would be simply a resort to force majeure; and you are responsible for your own actions. The reason I think it will damage you is Lassalle's reason: History forgives all errors and failures, but want of conviction it never forgives. In the letter I reproach you with that unpardonable want; and I am afraid of the reproach sticking. In making copy for the [Pall Mall] Budget, you meddle in all sorts of controversies in a dilettante way, not caring much about them one way or another, and therefore not having the will-force to centre them. You amuse yourself with picking holes in the argument, detaching an illustration here and there and putting some contradictory illustration against it, and letting yourself be led finally into quite monstrous misstatements of your own attitude. For instance, if Morton, misled by the criticisms of Watson, were to produce *The Doll's House* under the impression that it was an immoral play, and would attract the public on that account, and an elaborate and successful revival of the play were the result, you would not say 'By all means let the performance be stopped.' You don't balance yourself on the fence: you loaf about the field throwing stones. That gets on the nerves of the public finally. You will not give your strength to anyone or any cause; and consequently you lose the air of force that an individual can only get when he heads a rush. Further, judging from my own experience, the two articles a week are too much for human strength. You cannot do your World article, and then turn to at once and undo my Saturday [Review] article, or undertake any other job that requires hard application. You should play light in that Budget, and play upon feather weights.

This letter is not for publication.

G.B.S.

***William Alexander* Coote** (1842–1919), a spokesman for the National Vigilance Association, opposed the *tableaux vivants* at the Palace Theatre. **Seymour Hicks** (1871–1949) began his career as a performer in the music halls, and soon became a star of musical comedy at the Gaiety Theatre in the 1890s. Often performing with his wife Ellaline Terriss (1871–1971), he developed into a successful actor-manager and dramatist (e.g., *Bluebell in Fairyland,* 1901). Though he supported George Edwardes (1852–1915), who managed both the Gaiety and the Empire Theatre of Varieties, he also tried to avoid a confrontation with the LCC. **Arthur**

Roberts (1852–1933) was a comedian who began in music halls, then appeared in pantomimes, burlesques, and musical comedies. In a review of *Gentleman Joe*, a musical farce at the Prince of Wales' Theatre, Shaw complained of the 'indecency' of Roberts's coarse ribaldry ('Mr Arthur Roberts as a Gentleman,' SatRev, 9 March 1895; Dukore 1: 279–82). Charles **Morton** (1819–1904), known as the 'father of the halls,' opened the Canterbury Hall in 1851 (Howard: 40). In 1895 he managed Augustus Harris's Palace Theatre, which featured the **'Living Pictures'** of semi-nude women in 'artistic' poses. The production of ***King Arthur***, starring Henry Irving as King Arthur and Ellen Terry as Guinevere, premiered at the Lyceum on 12 January 1895 (105 perfs.). The play was written by Joseph W. Comyns Carr (1849–1916), who usually adapted French plays or novels for the English stage. Both Shaw and Archer reviewed the production. The Living Pictures presented several 'classical' poses, such as a **Naiad**. The theorist Ferdinand **Lasalle**, a German social leader and legal scholar, was committed to social reform and a German socialist state, but he opposed the ideas of Marx and Engels. Responding to the Palace Theatre controversy, Archer sent an essay and a letter to the **Pall Mall Budget** in late April. Alfred Edward Thomas **Watson** (1849–1922) was the theatre critic for *The Standard*, a Tory newspaper. Like Clement Scott, he opposed the new drama.

52 / To G. Bernard Shaw

[no address]
30th April 1895

[TLS: FALES]

Archer was primarily responding to Shaw's overheated letter of 29 April, but he also had in mind Shaw's attack on W.A. Coote in the Saturday Review *on 6 April. In a nasty dismissal of Coote, Shaw had declared that he is 'a most intensely stupid man, and on sexual questions something of a monomaniac.' Archer disapproved of this personal assault. As Archer attempted to remind Shaw, the entertainments at the Gaiety and Empire Theatres were quite popular. Archer also had disapproved of Shaw's scathing personal attack on E.F. Smyth Pigott, the Examiner of Plays, following Pigott's death in February 1895 (SatRev, 2 March 1895; Dukore 1: 272–8). But Archer then joined Shaw in the assault on Pigott with a public dismissal of the man (DC, 9 March 1895). And two weeks later he began his critique of the new Examiner of Plays, George Alexander Redford (1846–1916) by making a joke that yet another 'ordinary middle-class Englishman' of no discernable competence would be selected for the position (World, 24 April 1895).*

My dear G.B.S. Make your mind easy – I wouldn't do you the injustice of publishing this letter. It shall be preserved for posterity, & will probably figure in elementary handbooks to logic with the superscription 'Point out & classify the fallacies in this stupendous production.'

In the first place, as you are not for the moment 'heading a rush' at me, is it really worth while to let on that you think I quoted that verse as giving the opinion of Mr. Seymour Hicks? Mr. Seymour Hicks very likely thinks the tableaux 'perfectly modest' – & it doesn't matter a straw what he thinks. That verse represents not the opinion of Mr. Seymour Hicks, but the mental attitude of the 100,000 people (at a very low estimate) to whom it is addressed & by whom it is applauded. These people see nothing in the tableaux, & care to see nothing, but a handful of posing prostitutes – & if that isn't a sufficient refutation of your assertion that only 'Coote & Co.' see anything indecent in the Living Pictures, then I don't know what is. Interview Arthur Roberts, forsooth! As if there were any necessity for that! As if he & his following – shall we put them down at half a million or so? – hadn't given *their* opinion on the matter clearly enough any time in the last twelve months!

GENERAL RULE: In any controversy, the man who assumes his opponent to be an imbecile has the weaker case. In this paragraph about 'Mr. Coote & Mr. Seymour Hicks' you assume me to be an imbecile. Perhaps I may not have made my meaning clear, though I don't see where the obscurity comes in. But even if you didn't at first sight see what I meant, it would surely have been better to try to cipher it out than to waste time in reducing to absurdity what I obviously did *not* mean. If I had meant to cite the opinion of Mr. Seymour Hicks *as* Mr. Seymour Hicks, the friendly course would have been to come round with a strait waistcoat & have me conveyed to Colney Hatch.

If you must have this part of the argument in syllogistic form, here it is: The songs & gags of Messrs Seymour Hicks & Arthur Roberts represent not the 'opinions' – that is too large a word – but the feelings of the great mass of the GaietycumEmpire public – in a word the varietyshow public. It is perfectly clear from these songs & gags, that the great mass of that public – in other words the great mass of those who support the Living Pictures – think of them as indecent & chuckle over them as such. That may not be a reason for suppressing them – I have never said that it was – but it's certainly a reason for not simply flouting Coote & Co, as a set of disgracefully prurient people who see evil where no one else does.

I never supposed for a moment that Coote was going to take the L.P. into court. I presume if he does anything at all, he will do again what he did before – lay the matter before the Licensing Committee of the

County Council. And if they say to Mr. Morton 'Unless you can run your show without exhibiting naked women, your license is in danger,' I don't think he will have anything to complain of. I don't in the least understand you in this matter – I thought you supported the County Council as the regulative authority for the musichalls, though, like myself, you rather sat on the fence with regard to their action on the particular question of the Empire Promenade. Even in your Saturday [Review] article, I didn't understand that you departed from that position – I took it that you were simply arguing against Coote at the bar, so to speak, of the County Council. But from this letter it appears as though you had chopped round & were wanting to reject & abolish County Council control. Anyway, you surely don't flatter yourself you are 'heading a rush' in this matter. Clement Scott headed the rush with 'Prudes on the Prowl' – you are heroically bringing up the rear.

In the paragraph about Art, & the Rhinemaidens & Gretchen & other fearful wildfowl, you are off again on the verbal juggle, & trying to come it over me as you came it over the defenceless Coote. The word 'Art' has roughly speaking about half a dozen meanings, all perfectly legitimate in themselves & so long as they are clearly understood. What is not legitimate is to use them all in turn, just as it suits your convenience, & pretend that you've been talking about the same thing all the time. I can't be bothered disentangling them for you here & now – indeed I admit it is not easy – the ambiguity is one of the oldest in the world & one of the most fruitful of bad reasoning. But the main threads are clear enough to any one who has ever thought about the matter, & so far as this particular question is concerned, you ought never to have tangled them.

I haven't time to deal with the flagrant sophistry that 'any theatre in London has the same power to play GHOSTS as Morton has to exhibit the Pictures.' It is precisely on a par with saying 'Smith has the same right to jump off the Monument that Jones has to walk over London Bridge.' You can very easily prove that it is so – but you know quite well that it isn't.

Finally, as to the general question of 'heading a rush' – we have all our *métier* in this world, & that doesn't happen to be mine. Mind, I'm not sneering at it or speaking of it with contempt – I often wish it *were* my métier. But there are other functions that come into the day's work & are not quite without their part in the economy of the universe. It is one of your pet manias to want to make your own particular & very peculiar talent & temperament a law for everyone else, – as if an engine should consist of nothing but pistonrods. The flywheel too has its uses, & even the harmless necessary safetyvalve. The use you would put it to is to sit on it.

You may publish this letter if you like. Also you may let me know when you're game for a day's cycling in Surrey, & I'm your man. Did you write the interview with Miss Achurch? If not, you have evidently a formidable rival in New York.

Yours W.A.

Colney Hatch 'Lunatic Asylum,' which opened in 1851, was located in north London; it later became known as Frien Hospital, and closed in 1993. Clement Scott, the theatre critic for the *Daily Telegraph,* may have been responsible for the dismissive phrase of **Prudes on the Prowl**, though it may have been created by a typesetter at the newspaper. In early October 1894 the phrase was used by the *Daily Telegraph* to feature various letters to the editor, pro and con, about the campaign of Mrs Chant and the liscensing of the Empire Theatre by the LCC (Donohue: 118). That controversy was the catalyst for Shaw's 'The Empire Promenade' (PMG, 16 October 1894). Having learned how to operate bicycles, which had become the new craze, Archer and Shaw became tempted by the adventure of **a day's cycling**. From the perspective of Gilbert K. Chesterton (1874–1936), Shaw's impulse to make his beliefs **a law for everyone else** was a defining Puritan trait: 'His instincts upon all social customs and questions are Puritan' (33). This impulse manifested itself as a 'strange pugnacity' (25). In New York City on 17 April an interview with Janet **Achurch** appeared in the *Evening Sun.* The piece was written by Acton Davies. Then in London on 28 April the *Weekly Sun* reprinted the interview, with a brief editorial insert by Shaw about Mrs Manfield having played Nora in *A Doll's House* in New York.

53 / To G. Bernard Shaw

[no address]
3rd May 1895

[TLS; FALES]

Archer was responding to a missing letter from Shaw (written on 1 or 2 May). In his letter Shaw had returned to the topic of the Living Pictures (see letter 51). He also justified his attack on W.A. Coote, secretary of the National Vigilance Association, who had delivered an address in March 1895 to the Church and Stage Guild. Published in the Church Reformer *(vol. 14, April 1895: 84–6), the talk rallied supporters for his campaign against the Palace Theatre. He proclaimed: 'What cant to talk about "Art" in connection with these living picture exhibitions!' Determined to answer Coote, Shaw 'hurried off to see the Living Pictures at once.' He wanted to discover 'whether Mr Coote's opinion is worth anything or not.' He then published his assessment in the* Saturday Review *on 6 April, declaring that the women, 'all practically undraped,' offered an impressive artistic display. 'I urge every father of a family who cannot afford to send his daughters the round of the picture galleries ... to take them all (with their brothers) to the Palace Theatre.'*

I have registered a vow not to exceed this sheet, so don't be surprised if this letter comes to an abrupt end.

It would have served no purpose for me to read Coote, so far as this discussion was concerned. It was not Coote that was in question, but your answer to Coote. A jury is perfectly justified in stopping a trial at the end of the case for the prosecution, if they are convinced that the prosecution, on its own showing, has no case. They are not bound to wait on the chance that the defence may be badly conducted. I only mentioned the fact that I hadn't read Coote's paper because a phrase in your letter seemed to extend the discussion to Coote's whole paper, & I wanted to make it clear that I was concerned only with what you had yourself quoted or condensed from it. Coote's general moral attitude is another story. He may be quite wrong about artists' models & quite right about the L.P.s – or he may be quite wrong about the L.P.s, & yet you may have answered him wrongly & in such a way as to obscure the issue.

You didn't *say* that Coote & Co were the only people who thought the L.P.s indecent (at least I take your word that you didn't) but you certainly did not admit that any others did, as I think you were bound to if you were going to make a fair statement of the case. Now you try to make out that they are held indecent only by two sections – the morbidly 'pure' at the one end of the line & the morbidly filthy at the other, the implication being that to the great mass in the middle they are beautiful & ennobling works of art. But no – I see you admit that even in this golden mean 'a great many vulgar Philistines think them indecent' but you don't take them into account because 'they don't propose to interfere with the people who want to see the pictures.' Certainly not – because they *are* the people who want to see the pictures. That is precisely my argument; you have admitted all I want; the only practical question between us is the numerical value to be attached to the phrase 'a great many.' You use it to indicate a negligible minority – I believe that it ought to indicate a large majority of the musichall public – & one of my strongest pieces of evidence is precisely the HicksRoberts evidence at which you jeer. Don't pretend that Hicks & Roberts represent only 'the young gentlemen in the Gaiety stalls' – it is the herringpacked pit & gallery that yell with frenzied delight at their jocosities over your perfectly modest works of art.

The fact is, (& just give this suggestion a little thought) neither you nor I dare state quite frankly & fundamentally the reasons why we don't think these pictures ought to be put down, because to do so, even if our editors would print the exposition, would be to frighten respectable hypocrisy over to the side of the Puritans. We go as near it as we think politic, & then you proceed to talk about Art.

As to the County Council, your position is now clear – they are to have control of the front of the house, but their jurisdiction is to cease at the footlights, & the only competent tribunal beyond that boundary is to be a court of law. Well, I don't think that is feasible, but it is conceivable & rational enough. Only if that is to be the way of it, why didn't you state this very clear & simple distinction at the time of the main discussion? Why wait until you had seen the Living Pictures? [Handwritten statement at bottom of first page: 'Vow broken, as usual.'] The competence of the tribunal is a totally distinct question from the merits of the particular case, & you ought to have stood by Morton when Coote first went for him, without waiting to enquire whether the Pictures were indecent or not. Coming along at this time of day, your apportionment of jurisdiction has an *ex post facto* air which isn't in its favour. But of course I don't deny your right to change your mind or systematize your ideas more thoroughly in the light of further observation & reflection. On the contrary, I would even encourage you to carry the process a little further.

Yours W.A.

54 / To William Archer c/o Sidney Webb, The Argoed. Monmouth
6th August 1895

[ALS: BL 45296 ff 57–8; CL 1]

This is the only extant letter between 3 May 1895 and 29 January 1896. Shaw was replying to a missing letter from Archer. For the birthday of Tom, his ten-year old son, Archer decided to purchase a bicycle. Providing 'up-to-date' wisdom on the quality of bicycles, Shaw consulted the London bicycle manufacture Charles Friswell & Company. During August and September Shaw stayed with the Webbs at their cottage, 'The Argoed,' in the Wye Valley in South Wales. While there, he finished The Man of Destiny *and undertook long bicycle rides, including a forty-mile cycling trip in Wales with Sidney and Beatrice Webb in September. But on occasion, when descending a hill 'at full speed,' he would crash. On 12 September, while bicycling with Bertrand Russell (1872–1970), he 'had a most awful bicycle smash – the quintessence of ten railway collisions' (Diaries 2: 1090–1).*

In the absence of any shadow of an argument in favor of the deliberate debasement of Tom's bicycle, I decline to do him that wanton injury. You might as well send him to bed with a tallow candle and snuffers on the ground that he is too young for the modern article. In five years he will want a new machine. He will then delight himself with whatever the latest thing will be; and he will partly defray the cost by selling the old one, which will only be saleable on condition of its having been quite uptodate when it was new. A solid tyred machine would not be worth fifteen shillings the day after it was purchased; it would disappoint Tom more than no bicycle at all, besides demoralising him by giving him the habit of putting up with obsolete and inferior things instead of being always abreast of his epoch; it would disgust the manufacturer, who would take no interest in supplying a universally despised article; it would be a bad machine even of its own kind, the art of building for solid tyres being a decaying one; it would rob its owner of the amusement of using the inflator (on which Tom lays great stress) and prevent him from acquiring the accomplishment of repairing punctures: in short, it would add to the disadvantage of its direct and obvious inferiority, every conceivable contingent disadvantage. Your peculiar modesty would on these grounds undoubtedly entitle you to a solid tyred bike for yourself (why not a hobby horse, to carry the principle through?); but I entirely object to that virtue being imposed on Tom. He conveyed to me, within the due limits of his instinctive delicacy, that the air tyre, blown on to the wheel like a bubble, as it were, was *the* thing; and I am resolved not to prove unworthy of his confidence. I have told Friswell that in every respect save the mere luxuries of superfluous nickel plating & the like, I expect him to come up to the mark; and he has undertaken that Tom shall toe the 1895 line. Tom's attitude on the question seems to me sound and intelligent: his father's, feeble & superstitious. I consider that I am giving him an excellent start in life; and I trust he may never learn that his unnatural parent attempted to put him back by five or six years out of mere wanton shrinking from the front seats. Impress on him the motto 'Always up to date,' and bid him take warning by you and me, who at forty are only where we ought to have been at 22 if only we had had the courage.

GBS

PS Ought I to come up to town any time during Aug & Sep for theatre openings & the like? This is a bad place for news. If anything important threatens, drop me a card. GBS

55 / To William Archer

29 Fitzroy Square W
29th January 1896

[ALS: BL 45296 ff 59–60; CL 1]

Wilson Barrett's The Sign of the Cross, *a spectacle of Christian martyrdom set in Nero's Rome, opened on 4 January at the Lyric Theatre (438 perfs.). In their reviews, Archer and Shaw offer contrasting critical strategies. Whereas Archer delivered a severe assault, Shaw offered ironic praise. From Archer's perspective, the production's 'tawdry tableaux' of Christian sacrifice and rapture provided 'a combination of the penny dreadful with the Sunday-school picture-book.' The play's 'hideous vulgarity' and 'pretentious puerility' appealed 'to the shallowest sentiments and lowest instincts of the mob' (World 96: 9–11). By contrast, Shaw announced his 'unbounded delight' with Barrett's courageous staging of the 'perverted voluptuousness of the Christians, with their shuddering exaltations of longing for the whip, the rack, the stake, and the lions.' Barrett delivered 'a tremendous moral lesson' that displays the misguided 'raptures of sacrifice' of the Christians (SatRev, 4 January 1896; Dukore 2: 495–6). Because of Archer's negative review, Charles Hudson, one of the actors in the production, wrote a letter to* The World *in defence of the play. Although the letter was published, Archer did not respond. But Shaw did in the* Saturday Review. *He praised Hudson's skill in writing a long letter, and urged other actors to 'shew the critics their ideas of dramatic criticism.' If Hudson 'perseveres for a few years' he may become an 'average critic' (SatRev, 1 February; Dukore 2: 512–13).*

In February 1896 Archer published 'George Henry Lewes and the Stage' in the Fortnightly Review. *Lewes (1817–78) had been its founding editor, taking up the position in 1865. Archer and R.W. Lowe edited and published the dramatic essays of Lewes and John Forster (1896). Lewes briefly acted in London, and in 1875 published* On Actors and the Art of Acting. *On 25 January 1896, in response to Shaw's 'On Going to Church' (*The Savoy, *1 January 1896: 13–28), Archer published in the* Daily Chronicle *an unsigned review entitled 'A Yellow*

Book Hinterland.' He had great fun teasing Shaw for purging Christianity of its doctrines and re-edifying it according to the ideas of John Ruskin: 'Every new virus with which Mr. Shaw is vaccinated "takes" violently, but, mingling or clashing with former inoculations, is apt to produce amazing complications. At present, Mr. Shaw is in the hot fit of Ruskinian cinquecentism, which he must perforce bring into harmony with Schopenhauerism (attenuated through Wagner), Fabianism, vegetarianism, Shelleyism, and a dozen other 'isms,' superimposed upon the fundamental and congenital Shawism. The result is the gratifying discovery that the Church, purged of Christianity and re-edified according to Ruskin, is the true public-house of the modern world, to which our vegetarian progeny will resort for that stimulation which, oddly enough, is not to be found in lentils alone.'

It may have seemed in 1896 that Shaw had abandoned all beliefs that pertained to Christianity, but he had not become an atheist, even though he made such proclamations in the 1880s when he aligned himself with Shelley. And by the time he wrote Androcles and the Lion *in 1912, he appeared to be a prodigal son who had returned to the Church and Christ, as the 'Preface on the Prospects of Christianity' could easily lead one to conclude. His spiritual ideas were always complex, and often contradictory. Temperamentally he was incapable of being a fundamentalist about any system of belief.*

Hudson has by no means risen to the level of being beneath notice, though you cannot very well notice him. I am not alluding in any way to the 'Sign of the Cross' question, or to you. I have simply flicked the insect off the window frame in passing, *pour encourager les autres.*

The article on Lewes is interesting. His failure on the stage was probably of the nature of the failures of musicians & composers as pianists. He had not the trained and hardened face and speech muscles of the actor who has been at it for years. It was not a question of *optique du theatre*: the evidence is that he looked all right, which he wouldn't have done if he had missed the scale of the picture even in his conception of the action. Barry Sullivan thought him a poor weak creature, I expect, just as Paderewski might think Arthur Sullivan a poor weak creature if he were challenged to play against him. If he could have beaten Barry at making faces and repeating the alphabet, he'd probably have beaten him as an actor.

The review in the Chronicle was most disgraceful. It should have been signed Norman Britton. Where do you expect to go when you die? You talk of the beauty of 13th (not 14th) century work as 'Ruskinism,' as if it had no objective reality – as if I criticised with my imagination, as you do, instead of with my laboriously sharpened eyes and ears. I have been for years trying to educate you out of the common rationalistic secularism of the N.S.S.; and here you relapse into the most benighted and splenetic phase of it at the mere mention of a beautiful church. You will presently lose your temper with somebody for declaring that Bunyan wrote better than Tom Paine, or for preferring 'Onward, Christian soldiers' to 'Ca ira.' I urge you to leave prayer and belief outside when you enter San Zeno: you evidently believe that the building would be wasted unless scientific lectures were given there by Foote. You are so inveterately imaginative that you cannot believe that any effect is due to a real cause, or that any cause produces a real effect. However, you must waken yourself: there is no use shouting at you. See you tomorrow, I presume.

GBS

Barry **Sullivan**, a Shakespearean actor, was a star of the provincial circuits in England, Wales, and Scotland. He also toured in Ireland, where the young Shaw saw him. Ignace Jan **Paderewski** (1860–1941), a Polish pianist and composer, appeared regularly in London. In the 1890s Shaw wrote often about his performances and compositions. He admired Paderewski's technical skill at the piano, but disliked his 'blinding passion' (Music 2: 250). **Norman Britton** was Archer's pseudonym in 1883–4 when writing for *Progress*, the journal of G.W. **Foote**. Foote's secularist lectures and essays influenced Archer, who supported the **N.S.S.** – the liberal National Secular Society. Shaw greatly admired the *Pilgrim's Progress* of John **Bunyan** (1628–88) and the political writings of Thomas **Paine** (1737–1809). In his mention of **San Zeno**, Shaw, who visited Pisa, Italy, in 1894 with the Art Workers' Guild, is likely referring to the site and church in Pisa that dates from 1029 when it was a monastery of the Camaldolese monks. But the Basilica of San Zeno Maggiore in Verona, also of eleventh-century origin, is more famous for its architectural features. If Shaw and Archer intended to identify the century for the origin of San Zeno, they both misdate it. When asked about the likelihood of an American republic, Benjamin Franklin answered Ça ira ('It will go'; 'It will succeed'); this popular phrase was often inserted in songs during the French Revolution.

56 / To William Archer

29 Fitzroy Square W
2nd February 1896

[APCS: BL 45296 f 61; CL 1]

The copyright reading of Archer's translation of Ibsen's Little Eyolf *had occurred in December 1894. (See letters of 27 November, 6 December, and 8 December 1894.) William Heinemann published the play in the spring of 1895, but a production did not take place until November 1896. In early 1895 Heinemann had granted the rights to Elizabeth Robins, who sought a West End producer, but without success. Then Heinemann shifted the rights to the* Independent Theatre, *which under the new leadership of Charles Charrington tried to put together a production in early 1896, but this effort failed.*

This letter – and the following three – concerned Shaw's efforts to control the IT *production, which never got off the ground. Throughout this period – from December 1894 to November 1896 – Shaw offered advice, often unsolicited, on how to cast, stage, and publicize Ibsen's play. He insisted that Janet Achurch should be in the production. His campaigns can be traced in letters to over a dozen people, including Achurch, Charrington, Heinemann, Archer, and Robins. In March 1896 the play reverted to Robins, who finally mounted a production in November 1896. Thus, controversies and conflicts were a constant feature of the* Little Eyolf *event, from the copyright reading in December 1894 to the production which finally occurred in late 1896.*

No extant letters from Shaw or Archer have survived from the period of the rehearsals and performances in November and December 1896. It is evident, nonetheless, that Shaw continued to stir up controversies. The production of Little Eyolf *finally opened on 23 November 1896 at the Avenue Theatre for a week of matinee performances. The cast included Robins, Achurch, Mrs Patrick Campbell, and Courtenay Thorpe. Against their better judgment, Robins and Archer agreed to cast Achurch as Rita (despite her alcoholism, drug use, and advanced pregnancy). Robins played Asta and Mrs Campbell took the role of the Rat Wife. With the matinee performances drawing full houses, a financial syndicate stepped forward to fund an evening run. But when Achurch secretly attempted to negotiate an increase in her salary with the new producers, Mrs Campbell was encouraged – either by Robins and Archer or by one of the producers – to underbid Achurch, who was then removed from the production. On short notice Mrs Campbell took over Achurch's role. With the script tied to her waist by a ribbon in the third act, she got through the initial evening performance. Florence Farr then took on the role of the Rat Wife. The evening performances extended the run for three more weeks. (See Prophet: 118–28; Whitebrook: 175–89; Gates: 94–7; Peters: 198–206.)*

Archer published an analysis of the play (DC, 23 November; reprinted in World 96: 306–14). He also briefly mentioned, but did not evaluate, the production in three World *articles in November and December 1896. Shaw wrote two reviews (SatRev, 28 November, 12 December; Dukore 2: 705–11, 717–23). In the first he praised Achurch above all other performers; in the second he lamented her removal, and then praised, with extended irony, Mrs Campbell for removing all defining traits of Rita that Achurch had delivered. He finished this review by proclaiming, 'I do not presume to meddle in the affairs of all these actors and authors, patrons and enthusiasts, subscribers and guarantors.' Nothing could have been further from the truth – for two fulsome years.*

Look here: we must go to headquarters and consult Ibsen about the ratwife. I find that Charrington has your notion – a witch out of Macbeth, red handed from the murder of her lover (Sarah Thorne for preference) with a savage bulldog. I am convinced that this would turn the whole thing into a horrible melodrama. I am for a tiny woman with a small far away voice, four hundred years old, with strange eyes; and I find, on anxious inquiry, that I am not alone in my notion. Mopesman is clearly a beautiful little black Spitz. The point is so important, considering the immense difference to the feeling & effect of the play, that I think Ibsen should be consulted. But mind you put the case fairly. I think photographs of Cissy Loftus and Sarah Thorne might help the old man to an unbiassed decision.

GBS

Like her father and seven brothers and sisters, the actress **Sarah Thorne** (1837–99) toured regularly on the provincial circuits. She occasionally appeared in London, but for many years she served as the actress-manager of the stock company at the Theatre Royal, Margate, where she also ran a successful actor-training program. Janet Achurch, Harley Granville Barker, Violet Vanbrugh (1867–1942), Irene Vanbrugh (1872–1949), and Louis Calvert (1859–1923) were among the many performers who began their careers with Thorne. **Mopseman** is the Ratwife's dog in *Little Eyolf.* **Cissy** (Marie Cecilia) **Loftus** (1876–1943) was a versatile and popular performer. During her long career in both England and the United States, she appeared in the music halls, variety shows, musical comedies, and serious drama. There's no evidence that Archer wrote to Ibsen about Loftus and Thorne.

57 / To William Archer

29 Fitzroy Square W
7th February 1896

[APCU: BL 45296 f 62; CL 1]

Archer's reply to the letter of 2 February is missing, but Shaw's comments here revealed part of what Archer had written.

The Charringtons are at 148 Oakley St, Chelsea, provisionally. I have sent on your card.

Charrington's idea of the ratwife is of course unassailable, and by no means inartistic. On the other hand his objection to Cissy is entirely wrong. He has never seen her, but he deduced her from her heredity, with appalling results, and denounces my notion as nothing but a pantomime fairy. However, I ask nothing better if the pantomime is a good one and the fairy an artist. My suggestion is really based on the position that Cissy has beauty, genius, and a quaint personality that *touches* an audience. These are treasures; and to be turned aside from them by mere logic seems to me the height of Philistine folly. Treat the play logically & realistically, and it will be horrible – brutal. This will delight you and Charrington, the fundamental aim of both of you being the shewing up of the villainy of creation. But it will make the New Drama a message of wrath. Why not at least pay Ibsen the compliment of asking has he any instructions to give? Your point about the Norwegian for Ratwife does not convince me in the teeth of the speeches put into her mouth, & her fascination for the child. That's what indicates the fairy.

[no signature]

58 / To William Archer

29 Fitzroy Square W
19th February 1896

[APCS: BL 45296 ff 63–4; CL 1]

On 18 February Shaw wrote a badgering letter to William Heinemann, insisting that Little Eyolf *had to be staged by the* Independent Theatre *(CL 1: 599–602). Even though he acknowledged that he had 'created the first difficulty' by trying to control the casting for the play, he continued to push his agenda. In the role of Asta he argued against Rhoda Halkett and for Elizabeth Robins, and he pushed for Cissy Loftus as the Ratwife, but he noted that he was 'hooted down by Archer and Charrington.' He even urged Heinemann to publish an edition of the plays of Hermann Sudermann (1857–1928), translated from the German by Janet Achurch. There was no limit to his campaigns for Achurch. Heinemann exploded in anger, and announced in a letter to Shaw on 25 February that he was withdrawing the play from the* IT, *which would then be free to stage a play by Shaw, which must be what he desired. But no* Little Eyolf. *(For Heinemann's letter see the endnote to Shaw's letter of 18 February, CL 1: 599–602.)*

Unable to convince Archer or Heinemann or Charrington to agree with him, Shaw unloaded his frustrations in a long condescending and sometimes nasty letter to Charrington, written in two parts on 19 and 20 February (CL 1: 602–6). Even though his sarcasm was ironic when he listed the character faults of everyone – Archer, Charrington, Heinemann, Achurch, Robins, and himself – he became too meanspirited, especially his anti-Semitic complaint that 'Heinemann is a Jew, with all the consequences of Judaism' (CL 1: 604; see also Shaw's letter to Archer on 18 March 1895). Usually in control of his ideas and style, Shaw floundered in this catalogue of human faults. In a forced operatic analogy, he characterized Archer as Tannhäuser. Then shifting his Wagnerian analogy, he dismissed Charrington as the foolish Parsifal during his 'swan shooting stage.' Straining to control his anger, Shaw ridiculed both Archer and Charrington because of their confused sexual judgments over Rhoda Halkett. Only 'Holy Elizabeth' Robins could save them from their Venusberg seductions.

Over the following weeks a weary Shaw admitted that he had become disagreeable. Although he was getting physical therapy from Mrs Archer, 'I am still hardly safe without a chain and muzzle,' as he wrote to Janet Achurch (24 March 1896; CL 1: 615; see also his letter to Bertha Newcombe, 31 March 1896: CL 1: 618–20).

What is this I hear about your selection, for Asta – Asta the pure and flatchested – of the voluptuous Rhoda Halkett? Can you be serious? Or do you want two Ritas in the play? I have submitted to the Meg Merrilies ratwife; but a Venusbergian Asta is too much.

The proposal of a tentative rehearsal is worthy of a parliament of bats. How could you take a part away from a capable woman like that if you once gave it to her? Siete tutti ammiliati: she has bewitched you all with her prettiness.

Can you not induce Elizabeth Robins to play it? Can't you open her eyes to the mistake she is making in letting it slip?

GBS

The actress **Rhonda Halkett** (1855–1918), who appeared in only three minor roles in the West End theatres during the 1890s, was not cast in the projected IT production of *Little Eyolf*, which William Heinemann cancelled. Elizabeth Robins had declined the role of Asta in an IT production, but nine months later she played Asta in her own production. **Meg Merrilies** is a gipsy woman in Sir Walter Scott's novel *Guy Mannering*. In the popular stage version of the novel Charlotte Cushman (1816–76) performed the role with great authority; she delivered the death scene with terrifying agony yet triumphant revenge. According to a medieval German legend, the Lady Venus held her court in the caverns of **Venusberg**, or Horselberg, the mountain of delight and love. The opening act of Wagner's *Tannhäuser* is set there.

59 / To William Archer

29 Fitzroy Square W
6th March 1896

[ALS: BL 45296 ff 65–6; CL 1]

Shaw was responding to a missing letter from Archer. Because of his frustration with the inability of the IT *to put together a production of* Little Eyolf, *William Heinemann returned control of the play to Robins. Having done so, there was no reason for him to meet with Miss Rhonda Halkett about a possible role in an* IT *production. As to bicycling, Archer had sought guidance on the purchase of a bike. Shaw had established his authority, despite his several mishaps on steep hills. (See his letter of 6 August 1895.)*

I have just had a visit from Miss Halkett. She is in some distress because Heinemann won't see her. I expect he is now, after his spluttering flourish of her colors, going to shew us that *he* has no interest in her – not he, and that his acquaintance with her is of the slightest. He has written to Charrington, who is to impart the gist of the communication to me this afternoon.

As to the bike, I must try and find out what is possible. The absolute crack machines of the moment are the Elswick (19 Great Portland St) and the Osmond (3 Holborn Viaduct). Their net price, new, with gear case, saddle &c, complete is £25; and they make no second grade machines. It might be possible to get second hand ones (1895) for £15 or so; but the agents are apt to shake their heads and swear that an Osmond or an Elswick never comes back once it leaves the shop, so rapturously do the riders cling to them.

Humber, however, makes Beeston machines (the best), Wolverhampton machines, and (I think) Coventry machines; and it is generally possible to get an offer from them of something nominally second hand at a reasonable price. J.K. Starley (not Starley Bros.) also caters for the average man; and his machines are good, sensible ones. The Premier people work the payment-by-installment system energetically.

I suggest the following alternatives. 1. A friend in the trade (any hardware trade) who could order a machine 'for export.' Mrs Emery [Florence Farr] has a convenient pal of this description, I think. 2. Approach Norman on the subject of his admiration for the American bicycle, which may move him to buy one if he can trade off his 'Referee' on you. It is a fairly new machine, as he sold its predecessor (a Starley Rover) to Webb last summer. Pennell might know of something, by the way.

Prices are high just now in consequence of the prodigious boom. Except you light on a rosy private contract, you will not get anything new for £12.10.0 that will be worth buying.

Did Buchanan send you his pamphlet as well as the leaflet? It (the pamphlet) contains a private letter of mine. B. is in immense spirits, 'clinging in desolation and despair to a faith in God.'

GBS

Sir Henry **Norman** (1858–1939) was a member of the editorial staff of the *PMG.* Joseph **Pennell** (1857–1926) was an American artist who wrote art criticism under the pseudonym of 'Artist Unknown' for *The Star.* He became a successful illustrator. Robert Buchanan's self-published **pamphlet**, which appeared in March 1896, was entitled *Is Barabbas a Necessity?* The **leaflet** announced his future plans to become a publisher with his own imprint. Psalm 22 describes a sufferer, assumed to be David, '**clinging in desolation and despair**' to his faith. For some Christians this suffering served to forecast Christ's statement on the cross, 'My God, my God, why hast thou forsaken me?' See Shaw's abridged letter to Buchanan in CL 1: 584–5. Also see the informative headnote by Dan Laurence. Buchanan published sections of the letter without Shaw's permission.

60 / To William Archer

29 Fitzroy Square W
15th May 1896

[APCS: BL 45296 f 67; CL 1]

The Théâtre de l'Oeuvre, under the direction of Aurélien-Marie Lugné-Poë (1869–1940), postponed Peer Gynt *until November. Shaw travelled to Paris for the production, and wrote about in the* Saturday Review *(Dukore 2: 698–704). Archer did not go because he was in the middle of the* Little Eyolf *production.*

Have you heard anything about Lugné Poe's project of doing 'Peer Gynt' next Wednesday at the Théâtre d Oeuvre? Bertha Newcombe, who is in Paris, writes to ask whether I am coming over '*supposing*' they do it, &

offers me a ticket. I have a sort of temptation to go, if half a dozen extra inducements were thrown in. Have you heard about it; and have you any idea of going?

GBS

Bertha Newcombe (1870–1939), an artist who did a portrait of Shaw in 1892, was in love with him. Beatrice Webb and others in the Fabian crowd promoted a match, but he resisted.

61 / To William Archer

29 Fitzroy Square W
6th October 1896

[APCS: BL 45296 f 68; CL 1]

The Lyceum production of Cymbeline *opened on 22 September (88 perfs.). While the play was in rehearsals, Shaw wrote to Ellen Terry on a regular basis, making suggestions on how she should play her role. In his review he dismissed the play as 'stagey trash' and complained that Henry Irving 'disembowels' the text with too many cuts. But he celebrated Terry's 'infinite charm and delicacy of appeal,' and even applauded Irving's acting (SatRev, 26 September; Dukore 1: 660–6). Archer felt compelled to deliver two reviews (30 September, 7 October; World 96: 260–8, 268–76). He praised Ellen Terry's charming acting as Imogen, but contended that in one scene she was too cordial in her response to the villainous Iachimo of Henry Irving.*

I see you find fault with Ellen Terry for not making Imogen a Scotchman in the scene with Iachimo. As a matter of fact she had elaborated a remarkable scheme for playing the scene unforgivingly; and I induced her to give it up by pointing out three things. 1. That the sudden transition was a marked part of the character & was repeated over & over again elsewhere. 2. That Imogen could not possibly make the offer to take the chest into her bedroom consistent with the least suspicion or resentment. 3. That with Cloten & the king & everyone else Imogen is the same – in a childish fury the moment anyone disparages Posthumus, and in a childish ecstasy the moment anyone praises him. She is a most unguarded person, quite unsuspicious & terrifyingly courageous. You haven't half studied her.

GBS

62 / To William Archer

[no address]
[c. 1897]

[ALU: FALES]

The exact date for this partial letter, which is missing its heading and signature, cannot be established. This surviving paragraph resides among the papers of Elizabeth Robins at the Fales Library. A handwritten note at the top of the letter, written by Robins, stated that Archer was responsible for the cuttings. No explanation was provided. In the 1890s Grant Richards (1872–1948) served as secretary and assistant editor to W.T. Stead on the Review of Reviews. *In 1897, however, he founded his own publishing firm. In April 1898 he published Shaw's* Plays Pleasant and Unpleasant. *(For publishing details see Biblio 1: 33–6.) Then a year later he published Archer's* Study and Stage: A Yearbook of Criticism, *which compiled a selection of his book and theatre reviews for 1898. Archer had shifted to Richards after learning that* The Theatrical World of 1897, *published by Walter Scott in spring 1898, would be the last volume of the annual series. Given that Archer and Richards did not become professionally acquainted until some time in 1898, Shaw's letter was likely written in late 1897 or early 1898.*

I was talking the other day to Grant Richards, and found him quite on for 'The Theatrical World,' but rather terrified by the result of an attempt to make your acquaintance some time ago. He was with Miss Robins, who undertook to affect an introduction. She waited for her opportunity (you were all three together somewhere) and said sweetly, 'Do you know Mr. Grant Richards?' To which you replied in a pointedly matter-of-fact manner 'No I don't', and walked off, leaving them staring after you in the utmost taken-abackness. He has been afraid to approach you ever since, but ardently desires your acquaintance.

[no signature]

63 / To G. Bernard Shaw

[no address]
31st July 1897

[*St Paul's*, a journal]

In 1895 Shaw wrote The Man of Destiny, *with the role of Napoleon intended for Richard Mansfield. But he refused the play. Then in 1896 Shaw attempted, with Ellen Terry as an advocate, to get Henry Irving to take it on (Terry/Shaw: 27ff.). For several months Irving avoided a decision, but he had little interest in the play and no respect for Shaw. The possibility of a partnership disappeared in late December 1896 when Shaw reviewed the Lyceum production of* Richard III. *He compared Irving's acting to the puppet Punch (SatRev, 26 December; Dukore 2: 728–34). Although Irving delayed an answer for several months in 1897, he had no intention of staging Shaw's play. Instead, he had decided to present a different Napoleon play,* Madame Sans-Gêne *by Sardou and Moreau. (It ran for 85 perfs.) Shaw's review, which dismissed the play as Sardoodledom, appeared on 17 April. On the same day, a letter of rejection, written by Irving's business manager Bram Stoker (1847–1912), was sent to Shaw. One Napoleon play was quite sufficient for Irving (Holroyd 1: 348–69; CL 1: 747). A month later, in a self-crafted interview, Shaw acknowledged that the negotiations were terminated (*Daily Mail, *15 May; Biblio 2: 604).*

A few weeks later Shaw granted production rights to the actor and playwright S. Murray Carson (1865–1917), who appeared regularly in West End companies. He sometimes co-wrote plays with Louis N. Parker (1852–1944). The Man of Destiny *premiered on 1 July 1897 at the Grand, a suburban theatre in the city of Croydon at the southern edge of Greater London (3 perfs.). Carson directed and appeared as Napoleon, Florence West (1862–1912) was the Strange Lady, and E.H. Kelly played the Lieutenant. Shaw had nothing to do with this production. He invited Ellen Terry to see the third and last performance, but she was ill (CL 1: 777–8). When he saw it, he was appalled, as he wrote to her on 4 July: 'Oh, Lord, Ellen, I've been to see* The Man of Destiny. *It's just as well, perhaps; for I should perhaps have thought, if I hadn't seen it, that my noble brothers the critics were cutting it up, whereas I now boil with indignation at their corrupt friendliness. Picture to yourself the worst you ever feared for it; raise that worst to nightmare absurdity and horror; multiply it by ten; and then imagine even that result ruined by an attack of utter panic on the part of the company in which each made the other's speeches when he (or she) could think of anything to say at all, and then you will have some faint guess of what it was like … The applause at the end – half goodnatured to the actors, half a perplexed tribute to my reputation – was like a groan: it was more pathetic by far than a vigorous hooting would have been. There was something insane & ghastly about the business; for since the dialogue does not consist of obvious jokes (which must either come off or be perceptibly muffed) but has, apart from its comedy, as continuous a grammatical sense as any bluebook, it sounded at once serious and inexplicable, like a dream-play. Fortunately the audience was humble in its agony, and mutely respected Napoleon for saying things it could not understand. It would even make a mouselike attempt to shew its appreciation now & then; but each time it shrunk back lest it should be taking seriously something that was perhaps one of my dazzling jokes. An agonizing experience for the author, Ellen; but an intensely interesting one for the critic' (CL 1: 778–81; Terry/Shaw: 164–6). Except for the unplanned arrival of a 'rowdy little kitten' in two scenes, nothing about the production amused Shaw.*

Because the production was at a suburban theatre, Archer did not review it in The World. *But four weeks later he decided to publish this open letter to Shaw in the journal* St Paul's *(31 July 1897). It carried the title of 'A Theatrical Causerie by William Archer.' His harsh judgment on the play is launched in the third paragraph: 'It represents nothing, illustrates nothing, typifies nothing, caricatures nothing.' This negative phrasing, by way of Shakespeare, echoes yet reverses a statement he made two years earlier about Oscar Wilde's* The Importance of Being Earnest. *Wilde's play 'imitates nothing, represents nothing, means nothing, is nothing, except a sort of* rondo capriccioso, *in which the artist's fingers run with crisp irresponsibility up and down the keyboard of life.' Wilde's play 'creates its own canons and conventions, and is nothing but an absolutely willful expression of irrepressibly witty personality' (World 95: 57). Shaw's play, by contrast, lacked life and failed to transform its conventions. It was, as Archer writes in the last paragraph, 'a piece of mechanical and meaningless claptrap.' Fifteen years later Archer saw another production of* The Man of Destiny *when he visited Japan. (See his letter of 8 June 1912.)*

If Shaw responded to Archer, the letter is lost. He did comment to Ellen Terry on 5 August: 'Did you see Archer's column of weary & disgusted vituperation of "Man of Destiny" in St. Paul's*? I intended to send it to you; but I find Ive left it in the pocket of a London coat' (Terry/Shaw: 179).*

'For the performance of an unpleasant duty,' says Mrs. Porcher, in *The Hobby Horse,* 'no time can be inappropriate.' Therefore, my dear G. B. S., I take this somewhat belated opportunity of informing you that I didn't like your *Man of Destiny* a bit, and begging you not to make ducks-and-drakes of your dramatic talent in this wanton fashion. For you *have* dramatic talent, if only you would condescend to use, in place of abusing, it. You have falsified my prophecy of many years ago that you would never write a play. You have written one play, at least, and possible more. The one play I mean is neither *Widowers Houses,* nor *Arms and the Man.* Were these and *The Man of Destiny* all your dramatic works, I should say you had fulfilled my prophecy, not falsified it. But you have written *Candida*

– and the fact that it is known only by rumour to the playgoing public shows that there is something very rotten in the state of the theatre. Well, we are to see it in print in the autumn, along with other *Plays, Pleasant and Unpleasant,* which as yet I do not know. This is well, since no better may be: but you really do not give the managers a chance to discover the error of their ways when you put your name to nondescript eccentricities like this *Man of Destiny.*

It was not very well acted when I saw it at Croydon the other afternoon. The performance was 'the first on any stage'; the part of the Lieutenant had been taken, at short notice apparently, by a gentleman who was very shaky in his words; and his natural nervousness communicated itself to the other actors. I had intended to make this an excuse for saying nothing about it at present, and reserving my remarks until it is produced at a West End theatre. But playwrights of talent are not so plentiful on the English stage that we can afford to let one of them fritter himself away like this without a word of protest. I don't for a moment suppose that you will listen to it, but I shall have done what I can, and, like the aforesaid Mrs. Porcher, shall enjoy the reward of a good conscience.

Pray forget, for the sake of argument, that you wrote *The Man of Destiny.* Forget that you are a playwright; remember that you are a critic. Let me give you an unvarnished account of the play I saw that afternoon at the Croydon Theatre, and see what you think of it. The time is a few days after the battle of Lodi. General Bonaparte has apparently left the Army of Italy to look after itself, and is enjoying a quiet Saturday to Monday at a roadside inn. He has obeyed the Biblical injunction to take neither scrip nor staff. Except the Lieutenant, to be hereinafter mentioned, there is not a soldier on the premises, or (it would seem) in the neighborhood. This at once, you will observe, strikes the keynote of verisimilitude. To him enters a young Lieutenant of Hussars, who has been entrusted with a packet of despatches for the General. He treats Napoleon with the most offhand, slangy insolence, such as no General on earth could tolerate for a moment; and Napoleon does not even check him in any way. Can you divine the reason, or even the humour, in this? I cannot. Of course it is ludicrous for a time, as any gross incongruity raises a smile; but you will readily understand how quickly it palls. It represents nothing, illustrates nothing, typifies nothing, caricatures nothing.

Between ourselves, I think the fact is that the playwright has a constitutional dislike for authority and subordination, and it pleases him to imagine them flouted and ignored. Well, then, let him flout and ignore them in some realm of imagination, some Gerolstein of comic opera or extravaganza. An undergraduate who should treat his tutor as this subaltern treats Napoleon would most certainly be sent down; but Napoleon takes it quite as a matter of course. What point, what entertainment can there be in such purposeless falsehood of fantasy?

This is the method which the Lieutenant chooses for announcing to Napoleon that he has lost the despatches entrusted to him. And how? Because he met another officer who wheedled them out of him by means of the 'confidence trick'! The author, you see, expects the audience to emulate the Lieutenant in credulity. However, this is a mere piece of maladdress on his part. We are willing enough to pass the confidence trick as a bad joke, and assume, since this is evidently the start-point of the action, that somehow or other the despatches have been stolen.

A nameless lady now appears on the scene, and the chuckle-headed Lieutenant dashes at her and accuses her of being a man in disguise – the man who stole his despatches. With the penetration of genius, aided by a scented handkerchief borrowed from the Scribe-Sardou bag of tricks, Napoleon divines that the lady is not a man in disguise, but the man was the lady in disguise. He sends the Lieutenant off without enlightening him, and, in the most genial way in the world sits down to psychologize with the lady. They examine into the nature of bravery and other virtues and vices, and evidently fancy themselves rather subtle analysts. In reality their psychology is quite rudimentary; they pose each other by a series of verbal fallacies. This, however, is natural enough: they are not bound to be logical, if only they were dramatic. Unfortunately, neither of them is a projected, independent character. They are simply two lobes of the same fantastic brain.

Moreover, any possible dramatic effect of the scene is nullified by the fact that the audience does not in the least know what it is all about. They do not know what is at stake, what the despatches contain, why the lady wants to keep them out of Napoleon's hands, or what will happen if she fails. In short, they glide along the meandering stream of dialogue without the faintest notion whither it is taking them. The author is writing a comedy of intrigue (that is his intention, there is no mistake about it), and he has not been at the pains to make the intrigue comprehensible.

He has taken a leaf, nay, a handful of leaves, out of Scribe's book; but he has jumbled them all together in admired confusion, and interleaved them with random pages from *Cashel Byron's Profession.* He has chosen a theme fitted only for a well-made play, and he has made it exceedingly, deplorably, exasperatingly ill.

Presently the lady so far ingratiates herself with Napoleon that she thinks she can slip through his fingers. Unfortunately she mentions the word 'confidence,' and thus recalls to his mind the adventure of the Lieutenant. At once Napoleon turns upon her, and tells her that if she does not give up the despatches, he will take them from her by force. Seeing that he is in earnest, she gives them up, and changes her tactics. It has gradually dribbled out by this time that her object is to keep out of Napoleon's hands a letter compromising Josephine with Barras, which has somehow got among the papers. She now practically admits that this is the case, but hints to Napoleon that he had much better not read the letter, since, if he does, he will be compelled, as a man of honour, to make a scandal and ruin his own career. And Napoleon finally takes that view of the matter.

Now, here is a really dramatic situation, a conjuncture that tests character and raises wide issues. But we have reached it through such a maze of irrelevancies, and it is so obscurely presented, or rather suggested, that it produces no effect. Not one in ten of the audience, I am sure, understood in the least what was going on. And when the interest of the letter – the whole interest of the play – is at an end, the author has not the tact to stop. It now becomes Napoleon's cue to pretend that the despatches have never reached his hand at all, and to that end he determines to sacrifice the Lieutenant, while the lady determines to save him. Here we are launched upon a new intrigue, which, I regret to say I cannot describe to you, for about this point I fell asleep. The last thing I distinctly remember was hearing the Lieutenant say to the Innkeeper, 'Go and find the General and tell him I want to speak to him.' That was the last straw; exhausted nature could bear no more of that Sub-Lieutenant.

When I returned to consciousness he was (thank Heaven!) gone, the lady had resumed her male attire, and Napoleon was delivering a harangue on English greed and hypocrisy, which the audience mistook for a Jubilee tribute from a generous enemy, and loudly applauded. Then, learning that the lady was an Irishwoman (!) Napoleon suddenly grew somber and remarked, 'If ever I have to face an English Army led by an Irish General, that will be the end of Napoleon Bonaparte!' He ought to have added:

'Especially if night or Blücher arrives in time.' I am sure Napoleon was not the man to do his prophesying by halves.

Now, frankly, my dear Shaw, if Mr. G. R. Sims had introduced such a piece of mechanical and meaningless claptrap into an Adelphi melodrama, what would the *Saturday Review* have said? And why should that in G. B. S. be a stroke of genius, which in G. R. S. would be flat idiocy? And, taking it all in all, *is* this a play of which your critical intelligence can approve? Of course there are 'clever things in it' that I have omitted to notice; but, believe me, the general impression one brings away from it is of something very different from cleverness.'

William Archer

Archer praised a revival of A.W. Pinero's ***The Hobby Horse*** (1886), which was staged on 15 May 1897 at the Court Theatre (World 97: 137–9). To '**make ducks and drakes of**' one's talent is to squander it recklessly. The analogy is to the game of 'ducks and drakes' which requires one to throw a flat stone across water so that it skips precariously along the surface and then sinks. The two volumes of *Plays, Pleasant and Unpleasant* did not see publication **in the autumn**, but instead in April 1898. At the **battle of Lodi** in Lombardy the French forces, led by the young Napoleon, defeated the Austrian army in 1796. **Gerolstein of comic opera** is an allusion to Jacques Offenbach's *La Grande-Duchesse de Gérolstein* (1867, Paris), an *opéra bouffe* that presents a satire of militarism. Archer's disdain for the **Scribe-Sardou bag of tricks** matches Shaw's own dismissal of the plays of Eugène Scribe (1791–1861) and Victorian Sardou (1831–1908). Scribe's *Adrienne Lecouvreur* (1849), co-written with E.G. Jean Baptiste Legouvé (1807–1903), became a vehicle for Rachel (1820–58) and Sarah Bernhardt. Sardou co-wrote *Madame Sans-Gêne* (1893) with Émile Moreau. J.W. Comyns Carr then translated the play for Irving. In a review of Sardou's *Fédora*, Shaw first coined the term 'Sardoodledom' to characterize this kind of well-made play (SatRev, 1 June 1895). Shaw's novel ***Cashel Byron's Profession*** was published in 1886. Few readers of this open letter would have known about the novel. In *The Man of Destiny* Shaw imagined a possible affair between Napoleon's wife **Josephine** (1763–1814) and Paul François Jean Nicolas, the vicomte de **Barras** (1755–1829), a nobleman who joined the Jacobins, yet led the coup d'état in 1794 against Maximilien Robespierre (1758–94). In 1795 he suppressed a Royalist uprising by turning the troops over to the young officer Napoleon, and in 1799 he supported Napoleon's coup d'état. **I fell asleep**: a standing joke between Archer and Shaw was the fact that Archer often fell asleep at productions. Many **Jubilee tributes** were held in 1897 during the 50th year of Queen Victoria's reign. Gebhard Leberecht von **Blücher** (1742–1819), a Prussian field marshal who fought Napoleon in 1813–14 during the War of Liberation, led his army into Paris. He also participated successfully in the Waterloo campaign against Napoleon in 1815. During part of his career **G[eorge]. R[obert]. Sims** (1847–1922) served as editor in *The Referee*; he wrote under the pseudonym of 'Dagonet.' He published Shaw's first paid essay, 'Christian Names,' for fifteen shillings in 1879 (CL 1: 20–1). Sims was best known in the 1890s for the **Adelphi melodramas** that he wrote and co-wrote, often with Robert Buchanan. He also co-wrote farces, comedies, burlesques, and musicals with other dramatists. A fact now forgotten, Sims was a quintessential popular playwright in his era.

64 / To William Archer

29 Fitzroy Square W
13th January 1898

[ALS: BL 45296 f 69]

Miss Martha Morton's A Bachelor's Romance, *staged by John Hare, premiered at the Globe Theatre on 8 January (95 perfs.). In his review Archer lamented: 'There are at the present moment, to my certain knowledge, fifty better plays (many of them by people of literary reputation and social influence) seeking in vain for a hearing; yet this unknown American lady secures two productions within six months at leading West End theatres, and is supported in one of them by the prestige of one of our ablest and most popular actor-managers!' (World, 12 January). Miss Morton's other play,* The Sleeping Partner, *had opened at the Criterion Theatre on 17 August 1897 (42 perfs.). In this complaint Archer had in mind Shaw's plays.*

But Shaw rejected Archer's argument, as he made clear when he published Plays Pleasant and Unpleasant *four month later in April 1898. In the 'Preface' to* Plays Pleasant *Shaw praised the diligence of the West End actor-managers, and argued that 'in the beaten path of drama no unacted works of merit, suitable to his purposes, have been discovered; whereas the production, at great expense, of very faulty plays written by novices (not "backers") is by no means an unknown event. Indeed, to anyone who can estimate, even vaguely, the complicated trouble … involved by the production of a play, the ease with which dramatic authors, known and unknown, get their works performed must needs seem a wonder' (CP 1: 377). And in the 'Preface Mainly about Myself' for* Plays Unpleasant, *Shaw insisted that the search by the Independent Theatre 'for unacted native dramatic masterpieces was so complete a failure that in the autumn of 1892 it had not yet produced a single original piece of any magnitude by an English author' (CP 1: 17). But then timely fate – or singular genius – intervened when an unknown Irish dramatist came to the rescue in December 1892 with his first play,* Widowers' Houses.

There is an alarming statement in your World article about the existence of 'over fifty plays' to your particular knowledge better than 'A Bachelor's Romance.' This concerns me just at present; for in my prefaces to the forthcoming volumes of my dramatic works I have committed myself to the statement that there is no case against the managers for want of enterprise in producing plays – quite the reverse, in fact; and that if works of genius like Ibsen's are left out of account (the laws of nature barring their appreciation at first sight) all attempts to discover really eligible plays that the managers have rejected have proved that no such play exist. By really eligible I mean of course commercially eligible. The Independent Theatre signally failed to unearth anything of the sort. I concluded that the New Century had been no luckier, as it has done nothing but Ibsen, Echegaray & Stevenson & Henley, who are not commercially eligible & were not unknown. But your article suggests that you may have drawn some treasures out of the desks. Is this so? Of course I know that lots of plays exist which have more of this, that & the other quality than 'A Bachelor's Romance': for instance, Murray's 'Carlyon Sahib.' But that's not the point. My case is that there is nothing to be made out of a grievance against the managers – that their need for plays makes them credulous & sanguine in their ventures instead of sceptical & grudging, and that nothing can be done unless the commercial limits are widened or evaded, by endowment or otherwise. Do your fiftyodd plays disprove that?

If you wish to avoid the trouble of mugging up the history of Peter the Great, get my last week's Saturday article. There's nothing more to know touching the play except that Peter kept faith with Emphrosyne & treated her very handsomely, it being obvious policy even to such a dunderhead as he was – to keep up her credit; that the play gathers up into one moment events which were widely scattered over several years; that the legend of Catherine's rescuing Peter's army on the Pruth is all nonsense, P. having simply bought the Turks off; and that the battle of Poltava was an infinitely less respectable event than Sayers or Heeman. If you want to read it up, the shortest account is Melchior de la Vogue's 'Fils de Pierre le Grand,' which gives all the Alexis incident; but for Peter you should read Walisyevsky, who, after completely exposing the ideal Peter, found himself in the middle of the FrancoRussian furore, and had to insert 'this great genius,' 'this Northern Colossus' &c &c &c, each time P's name occurred in his MS, without, however, putting in a single wooden leg for the toppled-over colossus to stand on. A great deal of the apparently boyish farcical stuff in L.I.'s play is authentically verbatim.

GBS

In late 1896 Archer, Elizabeth Robins, H.W. Massingham, and Alfred Sutro (1863–1933) founded a subscription society, initially to help fund the *Little Eyolf* production. Then in February, May, and November of 1897 this society, newly named **New Century Theatre** (NCT), announced its aims to support new drama. It produced three plays: *Mariana* by

José Echegaray (1832–1916), *John Gabriel Borkman* by Ibsen, and *Admiral Guinea* by R.L. Stevenson and William Ernest Henley (1849–1903). Each play received five matinee performances. To generate interest about the plays and productions, Archer wrote three articles about Echegaray and *Mariana* (World 97: 39–50, 50–6, 63–5), two about *John Gabriel Borkman* (World 97: 121–3; *Progressive Review*, June), and two about *Admiral Guinea* (World 97: 319–27, 331–8). Robins and Archer considered but did not produce Gilbert Murray's ***Carlyon Sabib*** – set in India and loosely based on *Peer Gynt*. ***Peter the Great***, written by Laurence Irving (1871–1914), premiered at the Lyceum on 1 January 1898 (38 perfs.). Both Henry Irving and Ellen Terry performed in it. It was based upon events in the life of Peter I (1672–1725), czar of Russia from 1682 to 1725. Because Henry Irving had forbade Shaw from receiving a critic's free pass to the Lyceum, Shaw did not attend the performance. In his review he wrote exclusively about the play itself, describing how it deviates from the historical facts. **Emphrosyne**, one of the Charities or Graces, is the Greek goddess of joy. *Le fils de Pierre le Grand* (1889), which focused on the life of Alexis Mikhailovitch, was written by Eugene **Melchior de la Vogüé** (1848–1910). The biography *Peter the Great* by Kazimierz **Walisyevsky** (Waliszewski) appeared in French and English in 1897. Waliszewski (1849–1935), a long-time resident of France, was a Polish scholar of Russian history. Because of his military successes against Charles XII of Sweden (1682–1718) in the Great Northern War, Peter was sometimes referred to as the **Northern Colossus**; this term also suggested his height of 6'8", as reported in some descriptions. **L.I.**, that is, Laurence Irving, raided several biographies of the Russian czar Peter Alexeyevich – Peter the Great (1672–1725) – for his play.

65 / To G. Bernard Shaw

34 Great Ormond St
14th January 1898

[ALS: BL 50528 f 44]

My dear Shaw

Though 50 is a number one uses vaguely for 'a great many,' I believe it was really within the mark – but remember my point was that Miss Morton's play was contemptible, and that many plays might be better without being positively good. I quite agree with you (& have said again & again) that there is no case against the managers as a body, but only against the system which enslaves them as much as anyone. But of the fifty plays, I can think of only one at the present moment which I myself would with any confidence mount for a run – that is to say spend £1000 on and stake my prestige – & that play is *Candida*. Even *Carlyon*, though it interests me, I wouldn't dream of backing for a run. I forget the exact phrase I used & haven't got the paper here; but I didn't mean to convey that I blamed *Hare* for producing the play. That he *can* do so shows that he has no literary intelligence, but no one ever suspected him of that. The play is, as I tried to suggest, just the sort of mild imbecility that goes down with a certain class of the public (especially the provincial public, I fancy) & simply as a manager Hare was probably quite right to pitch upon it. There is no case against the managers as a body, but *there is against the critics,* myself included, though I'm not one of the worst in that respect. We intimidate the managers by becoming ferociously critical the moment a play begins to have merit, while we're all geniality & tolerance so long as it has no merit at all. This doesn't apply to the mere imbeciles of the fraternity who really prefer the slush – it is a general tendency which it's almost impossible to resist.

Dont be too much puffedup if I break to you the intelligence that you have won the approval of Robertson. He has seen the *Devil's Disciple* in Boston & writes of it with what is (for him) enthusiasm – 'the applause of the which one must in your allowance o'erweigh a whole theatre of others.'

Yours ever
W.A.

The actor-manager Sir John **Hare**, knighted in 1907, began and concluded his career performing the plays of Tom Robertson. Gilbert Murray wrote the play ***Carlyon** Sahib.* Both Archer and Shaw admired the freethinker John Mackinnon **Robertson**, an old friend of Archer's from Edinburgh, who was a radical journalist, then later a liberal politician and Shakespearean scholar. As a rationalist, he loved to argue with Shaw. Richard Mansfield's production of Shaw's ***The Devil's Disciple*** previewed in Albany, New York, on 1 October, then opened in New York City on 4 October 1897 (68 perfs.). It also toured to several cities, including Boston. The royalties provided Shaw's first financial breakthrough, thereby contributing to his decision to retire from reviewing. Though written in 1896, it was not included in the 1898 edition of *Plays Pleasant and Unpleasant.* It was published in *Three Plays for Puritans* (Grant Richards, 1901). Archer modified Hamlet's speech to the players (3, 2): 'the censure **of the which one must in your allowance o'erweigh a whole theatre of others**.'

66 / To William Archer

29 Fitzroy Square W
[21st April 1898]

[TLU; last thirteen words handwritten: BL 45296 ff 153–5; CL 2]

In a letter to Charlotte Payne-Townshend on 21 April Shaw explained that he spent 'most of the morning dictating a fatherly letter to Archer about his Chronicle criticisms. Am a fearful wreck' (CL 2: 33). But after dictating the response to Archer's two reviews of Plays Pleasant and Unpleasant, *he decided not to send the letter. Instead, he saved two sections from the long letter: the following paragraph on Eugene Marchbanks in* Candida *and the postscript on models for the characters in the play. Both sections were enclosed within the following letter of 26 April. Shaw published* Plays Pleasant and Unpleasant *in two volumes on 19 April 1898. Archer then published two long reviews in the* Daily Chronicle *on 19 and 21 April. (And a year later he republished these two reviews as a single essay of 22 pages in* Study and Stage: A Yearbook of Criticism *(Grant Richards, 1899). His two-part evaluation provided his first major opportunity to evaluate Shaw's first decade of playwriting: 'I never have approached a more difficult task than that which now confronts me.' Because he had previously published reviews of* Widowers' Houses *and* The Man of Destiny, *he decided to avoid a repetition of those negative assessments. But he did comment upon* Arms and the Man, *even though he had written a review of the 1894 production. He praised it as a 'brilliant and delightful' farce – though he again rejected Shaw's claims for the realism of the play. (See also Shaw's two letters of 23 April 1894 and Archer's letter of 25 April.) He proclaimed that* Mrs Warren's Profession *– 'this powerful, painful play' – is a 'masterpiece.' It 'is not only intellectually but dramatically one of the very ablest plays of our time.' But he complained about the characterization of Vivie.*

The Philanderer *appalled him, and he called* You Never Can Tell *a 'formless and empty farce,' a judgment he completely reversed by 1906 when he deemed it a 'classic.' His greatest admiration was for* Candida, *a 'work of rare genius.' After having observed the hard-edged and aggressive women in the first three plays – Blanche Sartorius in* Widowers' Houses, *Julia Craven in* The Philanderer, *and Vivie Warren in* Mrs Warren's Profession *– Archer was delighted to see Shaw create the ideal character of Candida. He fell in love with her. He read the play 'with bursts of uncontrollable laughter not unmingled with tears.' Shaw approved of the laughter, but not the tears, as he stated in his next letter.*

When Eugene, with his apprehensive faculty raised to the highest sensitiveness by his emotional state, hears that long speech of Candida's about the household, he takes the whole thing in, grasps for the first time what it really means, what the conditions of such love are, and how it is essentially the creature of limitations which are far transcended in his own nature. He sees at once that no such life and no such love are possible for him, and instantly leaves them all far behind him. To put it another way, he jumps to the position from which the Masterbuilder saw that it was all over with the building of happy homes for human beings.

He looks at the comfort and sweetness and happiness that has just been placed before him at its best, and turns away from it, exclaiming with absolute conviction, 'Life is nobler than that.' Thus Candida's sympathy with his supposed sorrow is entirely thrown away. If she were to alter her decision and offer herself to him he would be unspeakably embarrassed and terrified. When he says, 'Out into the night with me,' he does not mean the night of despair and darkness, but the free air and holy starlight which is so much more natural an atmosphere to him than this stuffy fireside warmth of mothers and sisters and wives and so on. It may be that this exposition may seem to you to destroy all the pathos and sanity of the scene; but from no other point of view could it have been written. A perfect dramatic command, either of character or situation, can only be obtained from some point of view that transcends both. The absolute fitness which is the secret of the effectiveness of the ending of 'Candida,' would be a mere sham if it meant nothing more than a success for Morell at the cost of a privation for Eugene. Further, any such privation would take all the point from Candida's subconsciousness of the real state of affairs; for you will observe that Candida knows all along perfectly well that she is no mate for Eugene, and instinctively relies on that solid fact to pull him through when he is going off, as she thinks, brokenhearted. The final touch of comedy is the femininely practical reason that she gives for their incompatibility.

PS It may interest you to know some of the people who have, or might have, served me as models.

Candida – Ellen Terry, Mrs H. M. Stanley, Mrs Ormiston Chant.

Vivie – Mrs Sidney Webb (an absolutely new type in modern fiction).

Bluntschli v. Saranoff – Sidney Webb v. Cunningham Graham in the Socialist movement. Saranoff's 'I never withdraw' is historical. It occurred in the House of Commons when Cunningham Graham said 'Damn.'

The Waiter standing between Crampton and his family – R.B. Haldane standing between [A.J.] Balfour and [H.H.] Asquith.

Raina – Mrs Besant.

Napoleon – Richard Mansfield and the historical Napoleon.

Cuthbertson – Clement Scott.

Crofts, Frank, Praed, Burgess, and Prossy were very definitely suggested to me by the outward aspect of certain individuals who are not necessarily at all like them in character: for instance, the original of Frank is now my colleague on the Vestry, a County Councillor, a devoted husband, a glutton for public work, and an exemplary citizen in all respects. Cokane is a real individual. Julia is a stormy reality from my own past. Of course all the characters are really composites; but some of them are types as well, the more vivid ones types of character, like Mrs Warren, the less vivid ones types of youth, like the twins in 'You never can tell' (or Hilda Wangel), or of servitude, like Nicola. The only 'work of art' is the Strange Lady in 'The Man of Destiny,' who is only a confection. The sublieutenant in that piece, by the way, is a little masterpiece of character; whilst your friend the innkeeper is almost as nearly borrowed from Dickens as Bohun (see Cavaletto in 'Little Dorrit' and Jaggers in 'Great Expectations'). Mrs Clandon is a composite of the advanced woman of the George Eliot period, with certain personal traits of my mother.

[no signature]

The **Masterbuilder** is Solness in Ibsen's play of this name. **Mrs H. M. Stanley**, also known as Dorothy Tennant (1855–1926), was the wife of the African explorer Sir Henry Morton Stanley (1841–1904); she was a neo-classical painter and author (e.g., *London Street Arabs*). She edited her husband's autobiography. See letter of 29 April 1895 on the identity of **Mrs Ormiston Chant**; she was a most surprising and intriguing model for the character of Candida. R.B. **Cunningham Graham** (1852–1936) was a socialist who served in Parliament. Richard Burton **Haldane** (later Viscount) (1856–1928) was a philosopher and liberal politician who served as war secretary before the First World War. Arthur James **Balfour** (1848–1930) held the post of Conservative chief secretary of Ireland; he opposed Home Rule, and later became prime minister in 1902. Herbert Henry **Asquith** (later Earl of Oxford and Asquith) (1852–1928) was home secretary under Gladstone; he supported Home Rule, and became Liberal prime minister in 1908. The character of **Frank** in *Mrs Warren's Profession* was based on Robert Charles Phillimore (1871–1919), a wealthy, well-established man in the Fabian Society who generated funds for the Webbs and their programs. In the late 1890s and early 1900s he served on the London County Council. The character **Julia** Craven from *The Philanderer* was a version of Jenny Patterson (c.1840–1924), with whom Shaw had his first sexual affair, beginning in 1885.

67 / To William Archer

29 Fitzroy Square W
26th April 1898

[ALS: BL 45296 f 70]

By collecting and publishing seven of his plays, Shaw was gambling that people would buy the two volumes, even though productions had been few in number. Grant Richards printed 1240 copies of each volume. Richards sold 756 copies, at 5 shillings each, during the first six months (Holroyd 1: 404). In the United States

Herbert S. Stone & Co. published the two volumes on the same date of 19 April. Only 374 sets, priced at $2.50 for the combined volumes, were sold by Stone during 1898 (Biblio 1: 33–6) – not 734 sets, as Holroyd reported; this may have been a transposed number from 374 (404). Whatever the exact numbers, the initial market for Shaw's plays did not compare to the success of Archer's translations of Ibsen's Prose Dramas *(1890–1); the five volumes, available separately, sold 16,834 copies by the end of 1892 (Prophet: 51). Nonetheless, Shaw was determined to 'mow down the critics' with his plays. He began to write* Caesar and Cleopatra *on 23 April, just four days after publishing* Plays Pleasant and Unpleasant. *He finished the draft in December.*

Shaw had reached a major turning point in his career and life by the spring of 1898. Charlotte Payne-Townshend had travelled to Italy, not returning until May; the Webbs had left for an extended tour in America and Australasia, not returning until the end of the year. In early April Shaw faced some nasty dental work. Moreover, he was suffering from an infection in his left foot, which hindered his mobility. On 23 April he saw a doctor, but the foot failed to heal. On 9 May the foot was operated on – an event that he dramatized in the Saturday Review *on 14 May. A week later, still writing lamentations on the theme of his injured foot, he announced a 'Valedictory' on his career as a theatre reviewer. After fourteen years of writing weekly reviews on theatre, music, art, novels, biographies, current events, and politics for various journals, he was played out. 'Never again will I cross the threshold of a theatre. The subject is exhausted; and so am I' (Dukore 3: 1061). Two weeks later on 1 June he married Charlotte. They then retreated to the countryside for a recuperative honeymoon. Shaw's physical recovery required more than a year. The couple did not return to London until November 1899.*

My dear Archer

I wrote you a long letter about your Chronicle review; but on looking over it I see nothing in it that would interest you except the postscript, which contains simple information, and an explanation of the 'poet's secret' in 'Candida,' which will dry your tears.

I knew that the book would simply mow down the critics. I pick my way daily through their corpses. I have to hop, by the way, because I have hurt my left – oh, I forgot: you saw my condition at the Globe.

You really are the very blamedest dunderhead – explaining all the most exciting social phenomena of your time as mere aberrations of Shaw.

I have just begun a new play – 'Caesar & Cleopatra.' The Queen's bodyguard, discoursing in the first act in the manner of Sardou's butler & housemaid, has already given the most unexpected touches of local color to the scene.

GBS

PS By the way, did I tell you that I have sent in my notice to the Saturday? I shall drop dramatic criticism at the end of this season.

See the previous letter for Shaw's **postscript** and his description of the characters of Marchbanks and Candida. The production at the **Globe** Theatre was *The Master* by Stuart Ogilvie (1858–1932). It opened on 23 April (63 perfs.). Starring John Hare, the production featured Kate Terry (1844–1924) in a return to the stage after decades away. Shaw offered a beautiful tribute to Terry's acting; his empathetic voice celebrated the charm of her acting. In the process he also praised the stage brilliance and 'artistic conscience' of the Terry family (SatRev, 30 April). In his reference to **Sardou's butler & housemaid**, Shaw evoked the typical exposition scene of the French well-made play, such as *Les pattes de mouche* (*A Scrap of Paper*). Shaw's last article for the **Saturday** Review, 'Valedictory,' appeared on 21 May 1898. He announced that he was 'helpless and disabled' because of his injuries, but he was no longer 'the slave of the theatre.' He was released from 'an unworthy institution and a stupid public.' He closed with a celebration of his own genius.

68 / To G. Bernard Shaw

[no address]
30th April 1898

[ALU: 45296 ff 71–2]

My dear Shaw

If you really want to 'mow down' the critics, write a few more *Candidas* – that's the way to do it. Anyone can achieve the triumph of being misunderstood; it is only the bungler (sometimes, no doubt, a bungler of genius) who makes a virtue of his limitations & pretends to aim at & rejoice in 'mowing down' people. I ask for nothing better than to have it proved that my analysis of your limitations is wrong, imperfect, founded on insufficient or misread evidence. It will cost me nothing, less than nothing, to confess it. But the evidence I want is good plays, not expositions of the excellence of your sociology (which I don't doubt) or assertions that such and such a character is taken from such & such a real person. That I don't doubt either; but the merit of a likeness depends not on whom it is meant for, but on whether it is like; and furthermore, a likeness may be very like & yet a shocking work of art, & especially out of place in a given dramatic picture.

[no signature]

69 / To William Archer

29 Fitzroy Square W
2nd May 1898

[C. Archer: 242–3]

The original of this letter has apparently disappeared, but a partial version was published by Charles Archer (1861–1941) in his biography of his brother.

Well I am DAMNED! Your *analysis* of my limitations! Why, you stupendous ass, you draw a line through my plays which represents your own limitations in your most fatuously lazy mood; and you then proceed to explain that everything outside that line is mere Shawism (which doesn't in the least account for it), and everything inside it is heavenborn genius. You are getting a great deal worse than Clement Scott: everything that is not a stagily sentimental *coup de théâtre* makes you simply petulant ...

I have just begun *Caesar and Cleopatra*. The psychological womantamer, at 50, operating on an Egyptian girl of 16, will require at least 30 columns of the Chronicle for adequate denunciation.

G.B.S.

70 / To William Archer

29 Fitzroy Square W
3rd June 1898

[APCS: BL 45296 f 73]

Hobbling on crutches, Shaw married Charlotte Payne-Townshend on 1 June at the Registry Office, Covent Garden. Archer did not witness the brief ceremony, but a day later he published his version of the wedding in an unsigned note that appeared in The Star*:*

As a lady and gentleman were out driving in Henrietta-st., Covent-garden yesterday, a heavy shower drove them to take shelter in the office of the Superintendent Registrar there, and in the confusion of the moment he married them. The lady was an Irish lady named Miss Payne Townshend, and the gentleman was George Bernard Shaw.

Mr. Graham Wallas and Mr. H. S. Salt were also driven by stress of weather into the registrar's and the latter being secretary of the Humanitarian

League would naturally have remonstrated against the proceedings had there been time, but there wasn't. Mr. Bernard Shaw means to go off to the country next week to recuperate, and this is the second operation he had undergone lately, the first being conducted, not by a registrar, but by a surgeon.

Startling as was the liberty undertaken by the Henrietta-st. official, it turns out well. Miss Payne Townshend is an Irish lady with an income many times the volume of that which 'Corno di Bassetto' used to earn, but to the happy man, being a vegetarian, the circumstance is of no moment. The lady is deeply interested in the London School of Economics, and that is the common ground on which the brilliant couple met. Years of married bliss to them.

Dan H. Laurence speculated, quite understandably, that this anonymous 'journalist scoop' was probably written by Shaw because he often published unsigned notices about himself and his activities (CL 2: 46–7; Biblio 2: B397). Following Laurence, Janet Dunbar gave credit to Shaw for the report (New York edition: 151; London edition: 173–4). Likewise, Michael Holroyd credited Shaw (1: 465). But care sometimes is necessary with an argument by analogy. They have ignored Shaw's letter to Archer on 3 June. It reveals that this anonymous wedding announcement was provided by Archer, who knew that Shaw did not want wedding gifts, and in fact was opposed to gifts. So Archer crafted a non-gift in the style of G.B.S. or Corno di Bassetto. Shaw expressed his appreciation here (and then of course a jesting barb). In this manner Shaw delivered an appropriate thank you note, for he recognized that Archer would find some way to honour the event.

That is the wittiest wedding present of the century. Only, confound you, I believe you never read a line of the Saturday Review, and don't know how clever youve been.

I am off to the country next week, if I live until then. I am making very little headway in the London air.

GBS

The **wittiest wedding present** was the work of Archer, written in imitation of an anonymous note by Shaw. But it still has some earmarks of Archer's voice (and even his forced wit). The notice was published in *The Star*, which Archer's close friend H.W. Massingham edited. The remark about the bride's fortune is a topic Shaw himself diligently tried to avoid in public (though privately he occasionally mentioned her fortune to a few people, such as Ellen Terry). Given that the couple so diligently separated their incomes and even refused to file a joint income tax return, it is hardly likely that Shaw would have declared in public that he was marrying a rich heiress. Also, the somewhat laboured joke about Shaw being a vegetarian is not a Shavian witticism, especially not on this occasion, when various people were blaming his illness on his diet. Indeed, in his letter to Beatrice Webb on 21 June 1898 he remained defensive of this topic: 'I backed vegetarianism to the extent of my life without a moment's hesitation' (CL 2: 51). The unsigned notice reflected Archer's sensibility. He repeatedly teased Shaw in the 1890s about his vegetarianism. As for the last line – 'Years of married bliss to them' – this is Archer's message to the Shaws, his half-move back into his own voice as he wraps up the report.

If we seek Shaw's own humour and wit about the wedding, we have his letter to Graham Wallas on 26 May (CL 2: 45–7). In this jesting letter he justified his scoffing at a present from Wallas, and then launched into a farcical story about searching for someone to perform the marriage, the price of the ceremony, and Miss Payne Townshend's 'final humiliation of buying a ring.' In conclusion he explained the need to invite Henry Salt, not his wife Kate, as the second witness because 'she is quite capable of breaking out and forbidding the banns at the supreme moment' (CL 2: 45–6). Also, at a later date Shaw offered his own version of the wedding ceremony that featured Shaw dressed as a street beggar and Graham Wallas almost becoming the groom. Here we have the Shavian spirit of mischief (Hend 3: 418; partially reprinted in CL 2: 46). Unfortunately, Archibald Henderson failed to provide a date and source for this anecdote. Of note, eight years later, on 24 April 1906, Lillah McCarthy and Granville Barker were married at the same registry office in **Henriietta-st.**, Covent Garden.

71 / To William Archer

29 Fitzroy Square W
6th June 1898

[APCS: BL 45296 f 74; CL 2]

A few days after the marriage at Henrietta Street, and before the Shaws left London, Shaw arranged – or had anticipated – a meeting between Archer and Charlotte Payne-Townshend. He had forgotten that Archer's initial introduction to her had occurred at the premiere of Ibsen's Little Eyolf *on 23 November 1896. The more recent – and second – meeting took place at the Comedy Theatre for a performance of H.V. Esmond's* One Summer Day, *which premiered on 15 September 1897. The meeting likely happened on 8 or 9 October 1897, when the Shaws attended a performance. Shaw did not name the occasion for the upcoming third meeting.*

This letter provides a notable clue that Archer had very little contact with the various women that Shaw was involved with in the years before his marriage. Archer knew Florence Farr, for example, because of her involvement in key productions. And he probably knew that The Philanderer *was based in part upon Shaw's relationships with Farr and Jenny Patterson. But Archer had little or no contact with Patterson. Perhaps in his many conversations with Archer Shaw talked about his affairs from the mid-1880s until 1898, but it was quite possible that Archer's knowledge of – and interest in – these matters was quite limited. As far as their surviving letters were concerned, there was no discussion by Shaw or Archer of these private matters. Also, though Archer had met the Webbs, he was not part of their social and political circle. He had very limited contact with Beatrice Webb, Shaw's model for Vivie in* Mrs Warren's Profession. *For Archer, Elizabeth Robins, not Beatrice Webb, was the ideal representation of the new woman.*

I introduced her to you at the Comedy Theatre. Ladylike woman with green eyes. So when you meet her remember that you know her already.

GBS

72 / To William Archer Pitfold, Haslemere, Surrey
24th June 1898

[APCS: BL 45296 f 75]

During their country retreat following the marriage, the Shaws first settled in Pitfold, Haslemere, Surrey. They had planned to return to London by late October, but Shaw's recovery, which had progressed slowly, was hindered by further damage. So in November, while he was still recuperating, they moved into a larger residence at Blen-Cathra, Hindhead, Haslemere, Surrey.

If you are passing this way at any time, give us a look. This day a week I tried to come downstairs on my crutches, and projected myself into space with such volcanic energy that I broke my left arm & partly wrecked the staircase. So just now I am crippled hand & foot & have to be tended like a baby by a nurse. Altogether, a roaring honeymoon. When I am mended, you might run down some day (or sooner if you like). My wife wants to know Mrs. Archer.

GBS

73 / To William Archer Blen-Cathra, Hindhead, Haslemere, Surrey
27th July 1899

[ALS: BL 45296 ff 76–7; CL 2]

There are no surviving letters between July 1898 and July 1899. Although Shaw and Archer had limited contact during this period, Archer continued to read Shaw's new plays in manuscript, including both Caesar and Cleopatra *and* Captain Brassbound's Conversion. *In this letter, which may be a response to comments Archer made about* Caesar and Cleopatra *during his visit to Haslemere,*

Shaw avoided his normal bantering. Instead, he offered a defensive explanation – not a confidential justification – of the play. Is it possible that his illness tempered Shaw momentarily? Whatever the case, he soon abandoned this reflective voice about 'defects' in the play. Six months later in the letter of 24 January 1900 he returned to his feisty persona with a complaint about Archer's 'dunderheadedness.'

After visiting the Shaws at Haslemere on 23 July 1899, Archer returned to London with the draft of Caesar and Cleopatra *in hand. In a letter to Gilbert Murray on 2 August 1899, he provided his assessment: 'I have got Shaw's Caesar and Cleopatra, which he says I am to send to you. But I am minded to keep it and read it to you; it is not a thing that one can appreciate alone. You don't want to read Pickwick to yourself – you lose half the fun of the thing. I expected to be infuriated by the thing, much as one resents a 'Comic History of Rome' or of England. But really there is amazing cleverness in it, though it is outrageously long, and tedious at some points. I think Shaw has invented a new genre in this sort of historical extravaganza, though fortunately no one but he is likely to practice it' (C. Archer: 245–6).*

While recuperating over the following months, Shaw wrote The Perfect Wagnerite, Caesar and Cleopatra, *and* Captain Brassbound's Conversion. *Archer, by contrast, travelled. He visited New York, Philadelphia, Washington, DC, Boston, and Chicago in March and April 1899. During* The *eight-week trip he published several short articles entitled 'American Jottings' for* The Pall Mall Gazette *and* The New York Times. *Back in London, he published six extended essays in the* Pall Mall Magazine *between September 1899 and January 1900: 'America Today I: North and South'; 'America Today II: The Republic and the Empire'; 'The American Language'; 'The American Stage I'; 'The American Stage II'; and 'The American Stage III.' Also during this period he continued to write for* The World, *and began a revision of his translation of* Ibsen's Prose Drama *(5 vols.).*

Will you send 'C & C', when you are quite done with it, to Gilbert Murray, Barford, Churt, near Farnham. He has just moved in.

I think I will call the play 'Captain Brassbound's Conversion.' I can think of nothing else but 'The Angel in the Atlas' (after Coventry Patmore), which is silly.

The bacillus has turned up in Charlotte's throat, which was a little sore & is now perfectly well. I cannot make the doctor see that this is checkmate to his bacteriological theories. He actually wants her to stay in her bedroom for three weeks, lest the insect should decimate Hindhead.

– Oh, by the way, I forgot that you haven't heard the news. Reeves has diphtheria! At least the bacillus turned up in *his* ulcerated throat; and we are all in a major state of siege, with nurses, carbolic sheets, & devil knows what not. Pints of antitoxin have been squirted into the whole household, excepting only my sceptical self. Perhaps its just as well that you didnt come into contact with him.

The defects of 'C & C' seem to me to be inherent in the *genre* Chronicle Play. I tried cutting & compression; but when I came to read the play to people I found myself forced to restore the cuts – even the most apparently harmless ones. (Try this yourself if you doubt it). Finally I concluded that only one cut was possible – the omission of the third act chockablock. The first act could be played by itself almost: it is very effective; but, as in 'Arms & The Man,' one must pay the penalty of a good dramatic first act by a comparatively expository second one. The chronicle ties you to the exposition of Caesar's position at Alexandria; and there is no drama in it because Caesar was so completely superior to his adversaries that there was virtually no *conflict*, only a few *adventures*, chiefly the hairbreadth escape when he jumped into the harbor. I was desperate about the business until, like Columbus with the egg, I solved the problem by making Cleopatra commit a murder. Of course the main feat to be performed was to do what Willy Shakspere didn't (his object being to heroify Brutus): that is, present Caesar as a great man with a genuine differentiation of character, & view in the greater direction, instead of merely sending on a leading man & saying 'Let us assume that this is Caesar, though he talks like a military Mr Barlow, with a touch of the modern wisdom of the Breakfast Table Autocrat.' It is true that I have done this by making rather small beer of the protagonists; but I think he dwarfs them fairly and that his eminence is something more than an illusion produced by the flatness of the surrounding country. That achieved, I give up the rest as hopeless. The first act clearly cant go on through the play: it exhausts its theme. The chronicle must tell its historical story, which, I repeat, could only be made *melodramatic* in construction as a Relief of Lucknow business which would take all attention from the characters. Besides, if I attempted, with such a construction in view, to start with an exposition, as in 'The Devil's Disciple' & 'Brassbound,' I should damn the play, because though an audience will take in a simple story of a family & a police case patiently & even eagerly before they see the people in it, they *won't* take in an exposition of the Eastern Question, whether Egyptian or Bulgarian, unless their curiosity & interest have been very strongly roused by a piquant adventure with some attractive Egyptian or Bulgarian. The fact is, when you come to do these things, you find out that the peculiar characteristics of the Shakespear chronicle play are not due to his neglect or failure to construct them like Othello, but are produced by the technical conditions of the feat. You say in the chronicle play 'I will accept character and story from outside the drama – from History, not from my own dramatic invention & the needs of the dramatic appetite; and I will make the best play I can out of them.' In the Othello–Devil's Disciple genre, you make the whole thing – character, story & everything else – out of the tree in your own garden.

This is the best explanation I can give of the scatteriness of the play. I cling rather to the hope that some of the bits that seem second rate or superfluous have their function. At least, as I said before, I found that I couldnt make the play fully intelligible & effective without them, bar always the third act, which, except as a bit of light, air, scenery & fun, might as well not exist, though the lighthouse & the carpet are 'historical.'

GBS

Coventry Patmore (1823–1896), a poet and critic, published the poem *Angel in the House* in 1854). This once popular poem, which sold well during the Victorian era, celebrates his blissful marriage to Emily Augusta Andrews. He equates their love to the divine love of God. **William Pember Reeves** (1857–1932), a Fabian from New Zealand who later became director of the London School of Economics, visited the Shaws in Surrey, developed diphtheria, and thus caused a three-week quarantine of the house and household. The popular anecdote of **Columbus with the egg** refers to a demonstration he supposedly performed when some Spanish nobles proclaimed that discovering America was easy. In reply, he challenged his critics to stand an egg on its edge; none of them could. Columbus then demonstrated that difficult tasks often seem obvious after the fact by flattening one edge of the egg and balancing it on the table. In Thomas Day's *Sandford and Merton*, a popular children's book (published in 3 volumes: 1783, 1786, 1789), **Mr Barlow** is a tutor to the two boys. The **Breakfast Table Autocrat** was Oliver Wendell Holmes (1809–94), the American essayist, poet, and novelist who, beginning in 1857, published articles in the *Atlantic Monthly* under of the title 'Autocrat of the breakfast table.' The **Relief of Lucknow** was the British defence in India of the Residency within the city of Lucknow in 1857, when the Oudh and Bengal troops rebelled. *Jessie Brown or the Relief of Lucknow* (1858), the melodramatic play by Dion Boucicault (1822–90), offers a popular and patriotic version of the relief, performed by Scottish Highlanders.

74 / To G. Bernard Shaw

[no address]
22nd January 1900

[TT/C; TLS; FALES, Robins Papers; CL 2]

No letters have survived from August 1899 to January 1900. During the autumn of 1899 the Shaws took a six-week cruise in the Greek Archipelago on the S.S. Lusitania. *Archer visited Christiana for the opening of the Norwegian National Theatre in September, which featured Ibsen's* An Enemy of the People *and a special celebration of Ibsen's career. Archer published two articles in the* Daily Chronicle *about the events (6 and 8 September 1899). A few days later he met with Ibsen at his home; this was their last meeting. The New Century Theatre (*NCT*), under the guidance of Archer and Robins, had become inactive after its production in late 1897 of* Admiral Guinea *by R.L. Stevenson and W.E. Henley. In 1898 and 1899 they searched for a role for Robins, hoping for a West End production, but they failed to find any play to produce. Even Ibsen's* When We Dead Awaken, *which Archer translated quickly in November and December 1899, did not tempt them, though they participated in the copyright performance on 16 December at the Haymarket Theatre. The only activity of the* NCT *during this two-year period was its support of a Haymarket production by Cyril Maude (1861–1951) of H.V. Esmond's* Grierson's Way *in late February 1899 (4 matinee perfs.). Running out of options, Archer finally convinced Robins that they should ask Shaw for a play (Whitebrook: 191–9, 202–3, 209–11). Their plan and hope was that the* NCT, *unlike the Stage Society, could present Shaw's* Candida *for an extended run, as they had done successfully with* Little Eyolf *in late 1896.*

In this series of letters between 22 January and 1 February, Archer and Shaw resume their familiar arguments with one another over the traits and qualities of Shaw's plays. The first taunt was Archer's final comment in this letter, but Shaw quickly expanded the exchanges with a cutting dismissal of the NCT. *And by the letter on 27 January he expanded the teasing and taunts to an indictment of Archer's critical judgment and a lament over Archer's failure to write plays.*

My dear Shaw

The New Century Theatre ought to give its fourth production this spring – why shouldn't it do one of your plays? – either 'Candida' or 'Captain Brassbound.' We have plenty of funds to give you a good production, & I have no doubt we should be able to get you a good cast. My one condition is that Miss Robins shall have the leading part in whatever we do. She has had no part at all in the last two productions of the N.C.T., &, this being the last performance of the series, I am determined that she shall not again have all the work & none of the fun. Of course I can't tell whether she would care for the part in 'Captain Brassbound'; but I know she would be delighted to play Candida.

Failing either of these, haven't you another play in hand that we could do? If you would give us 'Candida' or something that would suit us as well, we would do our best to get an evening production for it; or we might perhaps guarantee you 8 or 10 matinees in place of 4 or 5. Why didn't you give us 'Devil's Disciple' rather than Murray Carson? We'd have given it a much better show.

Yours ever W.A.

PS N.B. NO PHILANDERERS NEED APPLY!

Murray Carson had staged Shaw's *The Man of Destiny* in 1897 (see letter of 31 July 1897). He offered the first British production of *The Devil's Disciple* at the Prince of Wales's Theatre in Kennington (September 1899). Both productions were at suburban theatres.

75 / To William Archer

10 Adelphi Terrace WC
24th January 1900

[TLS: HRC; CL 2]

Responding to Archer's letter, especially the postscript, Shaw fired off several rounds of his rhetorical cannon fire against Archer, Robins, and the NCT. *By the time he dismissed the* NCT *as a 'Sixteenth Century Theatre' company, he had fully achieved his aim of discrediting Archer and Robins as business entrepreneurs. Yet Shaw's more expansive aim was to locate the failures of the* NCT *in the philosophical principles that guided Archer and Robins, principles he aligned with the cultural and ethical ideas of Matthew Arnold, George Eliot, John Stuart Mill, and Lesley Stephen. Against this 'party of Secular Morality' (and its utilitarian rationalism), Shaw offered the ideas of a 'Socialist-Nietzsche generation.' This dichotomy between liberalism and socialism became a recurring theme in the debates between Archer and Shaw during the twentieth century.*

After Shaw's rejection of Archer's appeal for a play, the NCT *suspended operations until 1904. In March 1900 Robins left London, travelling to Alaska in search of her brother Raymond, who had disappeared into the Klondike in search of gold (Gates: 117–29). Although she returned to the London stage in 1902, her last two roles had nothing to do with the* NCT *(John: 242). The* NCT *continued to exist until 1904, when it co-sponsored with J.E. Vedrenne (1867–1930) the staging of Gilbert Murray's translation of Euripides'* Hippolytus, *with H. Granville Barker as director. (See headnote to Shaw's letter of 12 May 1904.) Despite its name the* NCT *barely survived into the new century. By contrast, the Stage Society, founded in 1899 with the official title Incorporated Stage Society, lasted for three decades as a subscription organization. Both companies were marginalized, however, by the success of the Vedrenne-Barker management, 1904–8.*

As luck will have it I have just consented to allow the Stage Society to do Candida. By the way, they told me you had joined that body (which has boomed into intense life with 300 odd members in a most unexpected way); but I havent seen you there. I put it down to influenza when You Never Can Tell was done; but you werent there last Sunday either – at least I didnt see you; and Olivier's play turned out a masterpiece, positively as good as Ibsen, with a very fine native style to boot. I should have sent you invitations both times but for their telling me that you and three or four other critics have come in.

I gave The D's D [*The Devil's Disciple*] to Murray Carson for the trite reason that he had the cheek to ask me for it. You might have obtained it by the same subtle ruse. I dont know what to do for you now. Cleopatra would hardly do for Miss Robins; and Captain Brassbound could only be done by arrangement with Ellen Terry, who would certainly not let anyone else play Lady Cicely. Of course I could write another play for you; but I couldnt possibly begin it until the middle of the year or later. And besides, you probably wouldnt play it. Not that that would matter, as I could probably bring you to your senses; but unfortunately Miss Robins's judgment is disabled in precisely the same way as yours; and I cant make an American George Eliot understand the twentieth century. With you she gets on reasonably, because her American scheme of ethics exactly fits your Sir Walter Scottish social consciousness, and your stupendous ignorance of English life and character. But with me she is a perverse devil, because it is quite impossible to her to conceive my anti-gentlemanly, anti-literary, anti-ethical, anti-virtuous view of life as anything else but mere blackguardism. When one is young, one thinks that these things can be got over: later on, that illusion vanishes. She is quite right about me from her point of view. It so happens accidentally that a single play of mine, Candida, presents to her three people who have read all the books she has read, who speak touchingly in her dialect, and conduct a moving drama the relationship of which to, say, The Philanderer, is no more forced upon her than the implications of the Master Builder, which she plays without understanding, by poetic infection. But even if Candida were available, I am not sure that her enthusiasm for it would stand any revelation at rehearsal of the fact that Candida's nice domestic speech at the end suddenly leads the poet to the Master Builder's discovery that it is all over with the happy home ideal, and that he flies out into the night as a bird flies out of a cage or a trap. And there is not the least likelihood of my writing any more plays which will be not only acceptable to you both, but will also be uncommercial enough to be the business of the N.C.T. And what is the use of entering into friction-creating relations when we know quite well that we shall not be happy in them. As I said before, *you* don't matter: your dunderheadedness will only give rise to your national sport of argument; but with a woman such maladjustments create hatred. On the whole, it will be far better for you to arrange an appearance for her in some correctly Ethical play (why not ask Mrs Humphrey Ward to write it?) and reserve me for some later occasion when it can be managed that we shall not meet.

My difficulty is, of course, to convince you that there is anything in all this solid and real enough to obstruct a concrete proposal to perform a play. But there is. You are becoming such a disgraceful old ruffian now that years of wallowing in theatrical love and murder have wiped all the intellectual passion out of you, and even extinguished your sense of humor, that unless I stimulate your jaded appetite with the brutalities of Mrs Warren, or soften you with the blandishments of a nice fat amiable ladylike Candida, who is a mother first, a wife twentyseventh, and nothing else, you outdo Clement Scott in your protests. It is positively indecent, the way you go on about the play. You are worse than Ian Robertson, who has just spent half an hour trying to persuade me to rewrite the third act of the D's D for Forbes in the spirit of a gentleman, with Richard in love with Judith, and a general flavor of the Only Way about it. I refuse to pander to these Renaissance sensualities. I will not create Haymarket heroes whose blood goes into their erotics (do you remember the disgraceful phrase 'bloodless erotics'?) instead of into their metaphysics and politics. I will write no more glorifications of marriage, the only one of our institutions that is rooted in its avowed and utter licentiousness. If marrying Candida is to be accepted as the one noble and complete fulfillment of the human will, then you will get two sorts of drama: one, the Adelphi drama of lies; and two, the realistic drama of Zola and Maupassant (have you read Fecondite? if not, do), or the romance of Casanova glorified by Mozart or Byron into Don Juan. In the Philanderer I have shewn you the real Don Juan, the man whose blood has gone to his head, and left him with nothing but an appetite which entangles him ridiculously with a woman who is still very violently in the 'flesh and blood' stage. You are just like all the managers: you want my talent and even my subjects with the ungentlemanly consequences left out. You will take Mrs Warren on condition that I leave in the prostitution, hot and strong, but leave out the inevitable complication that the prostitute's child never knows its brothers and sisters, and is dramatically certain to find them turning up unexpectedly in the third act. You attribute my insistence on this to the sensual attraction of the subject for me. And all the rest of my work is accounted for by the fact that all the characters are a projection of myself. I put on the stage for the first time a dramatization of those three generations which we have both seen arise: the old fashioned pious people, the generation of Mrs Fawcett, Lydia Becker, Stuart Mill &c, and the new Socialist-Nietzsche generation. I contrive with such labor and skill that not only does this history of the three generations come out as the most striking part of the performance, but that it presents itself in the guise of a perfect comedy, full of fun and character. But the subject is not an erotic one, and consequently does not exist for you, scandalous debauchee that you are. 'A tedious farce' is your verdict, with a rider to the effect that it is a bad acting play – the most completely asinine piece of technical incompetence that has ever disgraced a once promising critic. I ask you, what do you mean by it? Where is your sense of shame? How have you the cheek to come to me for plays for your ridiculous Sixteenth Century Theatre, where I am to be treated as a Philanderer reformed by Candida? Do you suppose, because I am patient with the rest of the world, that I am bound to be patient with you, who have some brains if you were not too lazy a voluptuary to use them. Every day I expect to meet you in an overcoat with an astrachan [i.e., astrakhan] collar, and your hair dyed purple, talking literature, and living in a world of worn out shadows that still has its misty modes set by

Hamlet and Falstaff. I am to devote my few remaining days to writing plays for your amusement and Miss Robins's, am I? Bother Miss Robins! To the dusty shades with the New Century Theatre – even the Euston Road is ashamed any longer to call itself the New Road. Get out.

The right thing for the N.C.T. to do now is to specialize in the George Eliot direction. I am quite serious in this. The Stage Society has altered the situation for you completely. It has caught on to the modern side of things by simply doing two plays which were lying ready to your hand if you had wanted them. The fact that you didn't want them really settles the question of your function in the movement. You must embrace your fate and set to work seriously to provide a theatre for the party of Secular Morality – the party of Matthew Arnold, George Eliot and Mrs Humphrey Ward, of the Ethical Society of America, of South Place, Leslie Stephen, and so on, with what you call a seamy side of Zola-Maupassant realism, all brought up to date. Now nobody can catch up all those threads better than the authoress of An Open Question. And nobody can help her better than Norman Britton. There's your line – an excellent and honorable one. It is not new; but by attacking it resolutely it will lead you somewhere, perhaps to the real new drama which my Irish eighteenth centuriness and rhetoric and obsolete laugh catching may miss. Anyhow there is nothing to be done by ridiculously sitting on your funds and doing nothing but asking me for work which you two may admire, but which you dont respect. When we found long ago that there was no new drama in existence, I turned my hand to the stage and supplied my own demand. You must do the same thing. What I supplied is not what you want: well, follow up Alan's Wife: even if you fail, it will freshen you for other successes. There: that's my advice to you and to Miss Elizabeth.

Can you come to lunch tomorrow (Friday) at half past one? Or on Friday next week if you are engaged tomorrow? If I dont hear from you we shall expect you.

G.B.S.

Both Archer and Elizabeth Robins admired the novels of **George Eliot** (1819–80), especially *Middlemarch* (1871–2). **Mrs Humphrey Ward** (1851–1920) was the niece of the poet and critic Matthew **Arnold** (1822–88) who wrote *Culture and Anarchy* (1869). She wrote popular novels (e.g., *Robert Elsmere*), and was founder of a London settlement house. Shaw's statement about her was prescient: in late 1902 Elizabeth Robins's last stage role was in an adaptation of Ward's novel *Eleanor* (Royal Court, 15 perfs.). **Ian Robertson** (1858–1936), the younger brother of (Sir) Johnston Forbes-Robertson (1853–1937), was a minor actor who often served as a stage manager and producer for his successful brother. The

Stage Society presented Sydney **Oliver's play** *Mrs Maxwell's Marriage* on 21 January 1900. It fell quite short of being a masterpiece. In February 1899 ***The Only Way***, an adaptation by Freeman Wills of Charles Dickens's *A Tale of Two Cities*, was staged at the Lyceum Theatre (168 perfs.); it starred John Martin Harvey (1863–1944). Archer's complaint about the **bloodless erotics** of the love scenes in Shaw's plays began in the 1890s with his critiques of *Widowers' Houses* and *Arms and the Man*. Zola's *La* ***Fécondité*** was published in Paris in 1899. Shaw read it as soon as the English edition appeared in 1900. Millicent Garrett **Fawcett** (1847–1929) and Lydia E. **Becker** (1827–90) were advocates for women's suffrage. **Leslie Stephen** (1832–1904), the father of Virginia Woolf (1882–1941) and Vanessa Bell (1879–1961), was a literary biographer and critic; he co-edited the *Dictionary of National Biography* (63 vols, 1882–1900), providing almost 400 entries himself. By the time of the quite successful productions of *You Never Can Tell* in 1905, 1906, and 1907, Archer would retreat from his description of the play as **a tedious farce**. Writing under the pseudonym of C.E. Raimond, Elizabeth Robins published the novel ***The Open Question*** in 1898; it was influenced by George Eliot's *The Mill on the Floss* (1860). The reviews were positive, and it sold quite well, with William Heinemann publishing three editions. Her identity was revealed just before the second edition appeared in December 1898 (Gates: 106–10). Soon after, Shaw wrote a lengthy letter to her (13 February 1899) in which he chastised her for hiding part of her talent from him. He then wrote a critique of the novel, in part because 'you are, as an authoress, more exactly like George Eliot than any two original novelists have hitherto been like another.' He appealed to her, however, not to share the 'fatalism' of Eliot's novels, to escape the trap of Victorian ethics (CL 2: 76–8). As often happened in the 1890s, Shaw's sardonic persona, along with his critical judgments, angered her (Peters: 267). **Norman Britton** was a pseudonym that Archer used in the 1880s. For the controversies over **Alan's Wife**, see letters 38, 39, 40, and 41.

76 / To G. Bernard Shaw

[no address]
25th January 1900

[TLS: FALES, Robins Papers]

Like the NCT, *the Stage Society was a subscription society for a few hundred supporters of the new drama. Its first production was Shaw's* You Never Can Tell *(26 November 1899). Over the next four years, the* SS *presented* Candida *(1 July 1900),* Captain Brassbound's Conversion *(16 December 1900),* The Man of Destiny *(29 March 1901),* Mrs Warren's Profession *(5 and 6 January 1902), and* The Admirable Bashville *(7 June 1903). These 'private' productions for members only, usually for one or two performances, circumvented the censorship of the Lord Chamberlain's Office. The last four productions featured a brilliant young man named Harley Granville Barker, as performer or co-director. Although these productions did nothing for Shaw's finances, they advanced his London reputation as a playwright. And they brought about the friendship and partnership of Shaw and Barker. These events became the precursors for the creation of the Vedrenne-Barker management, which produced eleven of Shaw's plays between 1904 and 1907.*

Archer was wrong about Ellen Terry and Captain Brassbound's Conversion. *Despite her initial judgment that the play was not right for her (Terry/Shaw: 244–5), she did the copyright reading on 10 October 1899, and then acted in the Court Theatre production that opened on 20 March 1906. She would later tour the play in the United States in 1907.*

My dear Shaw,

If we have really missed CANDIDA only by a chance, I am exceedingly sorry – for your sake as well as the N.C.T.'s, for I don't see what you get out of a Stage Society performance, however good. I can't think why you should allow Ellen Terry to sit on CAPTAIN BRASSBOUND – she will never do it, & couldn't if she would – As for CAESAR, we would gladly do it (at least *I* would) if we had twice as many thousand pounds as we have hundreds. I didn't suggest you should write a play for us – I thought you might have been writing one during the autumn.

As for your diatribe in which an a priori you, an a priori me, & an a priori Miss Robins play a number of fantastic tricks before high heaven, it is so utterly aloof from all reality that it simply leaves me dumb. There is only one thing I want to say, & that is that you are utterly & unaccountably wrong when you say that I attribute your insistence on the Vivie-&-Frank business [in *Mrs Warren's Profession*] to 'the sensual attraction of the subject for you.' I never dreamt of such a thing. I attribute it partly to the wrong-headed logic by which you here defend it, partly to the sheer pleasure it gives you to *épater le bourgeois* – a pleasure which I believe quite genuinely translates itself in your consciousness into a duty. Having logically convinced yourself that this question of uncertain paternity is an essential part of your theme & must be brought out, you wouldn't for untold gold flinch from doing it. Morally I admire your attitude, bating always the fact that, where there is any shocking to be done, duty & pleasure largely coincide; but artistically I protest. I don't think your logic [is] in the least cogent; & if it were, there are ways & ways of doing a thing, & I don't like the Vivie-&-Frank way. But heavens above! I never dreamt of its having any 'sensual attraction' for you. As for the play in general I don't care a brass farthing whether it's about prostitution or what it's about; I call it a masterpiece because many of its scenes are intensely dramatic, & some of its 'repliques' are dramatic 'Trouvailles' – I can't be bothered translating into English.

No, I have not joined the Stage Society because I am too old & too busy to take much interest in that sort of thing. The history of the N.C.T. sufficiently shows that I am a bad hand at coterie-theatre work. I haven't the faculty of persuading myself that a play is a good play merely because it is unconventional. It seems to me that my one gift as a critic is that of distinguishing 'live' work from dead work; anyway, rightly or wrongly, I have strong prejudices on the point, & my recollection of Olivier's play is that, whatever cleverness there may have been in it, it was dead as a doornail – therefore precisely fitted for a Sunday evening performance. I don't mean to say that 'You Never Can Tell' was in the same case – but it never interested me much & was not a type of play that N.C.T. could advantageously tackle. But believe me the N.C.T. is not & never has been guided by any of the superb moral or literary theories you manufacture for it. Give it a play that *is* a play – a play that is not merely commonplace or merely épatan*t* – & that comes within its pecuniary means, & we will do it like a shot.

I can't lunch with you tomorrow, but will try to do so next Friday. Please tell Mrs. Shaw that if she does not hear from me to the contrary she may expect me. But of course if anything should come in the way on your side, just put me off.

Yours W.A.

Archer avoided translating his assertion that some of the **repliques** (replies, retorts)] in *Mrs Warren's Profession* are dramatic **Trouvailles** (creative or fortunate discoveries), but he was suggesting that in those cases the exchanges between characters revealed their values, not just Shaw's own desire to épater le bourgeois. Archer continued to argue for this principle of dialogue and character development when he wrote *Play-making* (1911).

77 / To William Archer

Beacon Hotel, Hindhead
27th January 1900

[ALS: BL 45296 ff 78–6; CL 2]

Apparently some extra time and effort went into the writing of this letter of nine pages. At the top of the letter Shaw wrote '(Saturday to Monday).' He obviously enjoyed the opportunity to offer a sharp critique of Archer's statement about his confidence in his critical judgment. This statement was an open invitation to Shaw to make fun of Archer, for this statement echoed his self-satisfied claim a decade earlier that he was an incorruptible theatre critic. In that case Shaw portrayed him as Archer the Anchorite. (See the letters of 7, 9, and 10 November 1891.) Now he was free to call Archer 'the worst critic now alive' because he failed to recognize that Shaw had become 'the best English-language playwright since Shakespear.' How could Archer have any confidence in himself as a critic when he had made such blunders in his judgment on Shaw's plays? Of course, in this chastisement of Archer's expression of self-confidence, Shaw saw no reason to limit his own statement of supreme confidence.

Beyond the pleasure of scoring rhetorical hits, Shaw felt the need in this letter to express some of his frustration with Archer, who seemed unwilling or unable to break free from his fixed ideas about dramatic form. Why had Archer, who had been so astute in his understanding and advocacy for Ibsen's drama, become so resistant to Shaw's innovations? Perhaps, if Shaw could finally convince Archer to write plays, his friend might discover within himself a more expansive creative, not just critical, conception of modern drama and its possibilities. He criticized Archer for not sitting down and writing a play for the NCT. *But he did not know that Archer and Robins had done just that. They had written a realistic play called* Mirkwater *in 1895 that had traits of* Alan's Wife *and* Little Eyolf. *They had no luck, however, in placing it. Their final gambit was* Benvenuto Cellini, *a historical melodrama that they had secretly written together in 1899–1900, with Robins turning out drafts that Archer revised. H. Beerbohm Tree took an option on it, but then backed away. Both plays remained unperformed and unpublished. (See Whitebrook: 179–81, 211.)*

You really are an utterly impossible chap. However, let us work out the position your way. Let it be granted that we three, Elizabeth, William & George Bernard, are three angelic and infinite cuttle fish; that we are not what you call Apry Ory beings, meaning that we have no temperaments and belong to no categories, biological, psychological, dramatic, literary or political; that we are unconditioned and universal; and that, consequently, the differences and destinies which lead other friends into divergent paths do not exist for us. True Pionians, all three.

Very well.

Now let us waive my previous remarks, based on a mistaken estimate of us as human beings. The parole is to you.

A voice as from an astrakan [astrakhan] collar suddenly claims as its one critical gift, that of distinguishing 'live' work from dead. It doesn't care a rap what theories or principles are behind a play. It has no prejudices: it means business. Give it a good play, 'a play as *is* a play – a play that is not merely commonplace or merely épatant' – and it will do it 'like a shot.' It has 'swallowed all the formulae,' has this voice, and knows only two sorts of play, good ones and bad ones.

Alas, it needs no New Century Theatre to tell me this. For this, in letter and spirit, without word, thought or attitude altered by the shadow of a shade, is the voice of Tree, Alexander et hoc genus omne. Why should I give *you,* New Century Theatre manager, with your few paltry hundreds, a play that Her Majesty's, the St James's, the Haymarket & all the rest, are clamoring for? *That* is what I mean by the astrakan collar. You have in process of time dropped into the practical attitude – the attitude into which experience drives all men who aim at *success,* whether pecuniary or simply artistic – and you say spontaneously and unconsciously exactly what all the other practical men say.

But you do not stick to it. The moment you are taken at your word and confronted with Mrs Warren & You Never Can Tell, you suddenly cease to be infinite and unconditioned and admit there are things in those plays that you 'don't like' and 'never interested you much.' Is this much more infinite or less conditioned than John Hare, who will say if you ask him, 'Give me a *good* play by Ibsen, and I'll do it tomorrow.' You suggest the Wild Duck. Immediately he assures you that the Wild Duck is not a good play. By which he means that he doesn't like it. You didnt like You Never Can Tell, which happens to be an almost diabolically good play technically; and you solemnly assured the public that it is tedious farce, and doubted whether even the most skilful acting could make it tolerable. And very likely if you had seen the performance at the Royalty, you would have felt thoroughly confirmed in your judgment, & slept as soundly as [Frank] Harris did during the Wild Duck. And your care is worse than Harris's. He slept because the thing was above and beyond him. You see things – the same things – differently; and that is fatal. The difference is so biassing that the Shawish quality of my characters produces the same effect on you as the blackness of a negro does on a white man in a white country, to whom all negroes are alike, no distinction of age, complexion, good or bad looks being apparent to him. For example, to me the snubnosed Swiss soldier in Arms & The Man is a simple & unaffected man. Napoleon is exactly the opposite, an incorrigible actor, self conscious to his finger nail. The contrast (to me) is emphasized by the fact that they are both, as professional soldiers, alike in their freedom from vulgar illusions about war, though Bluntschli's experience stops short of Napoleon's generalized observation & reflection. Now to you these two opposites are alike. They are not even real men: they are only projections of a disagreeable affectation of my own. This is not the same thing as your disbelief in Vivie Warren & the Widowers' Houses people. *That* is pure Arcadian innocence: Sir Walter Scott would have said the same thing about them. But Bluntschli & Napoleon are within your scope: they belong to the world which the literary man exposes imaginatively, whereas Miss Blanche Sartorius, Vivie & Co, belong to the vast English antiliterary majority of whose existence & characteristics I myself had not the faintest conception 20 years ago, and whom you have not discovered yet.

This being so, it's not possible for you to like my plays. Napoleon the Subtle duped easily by a woman, Bluntschli the Simple absolutely invulnerable – all these strokes & turns of comedy have no interest – no existence for you. You simply feel 'I wish Shaw wouldnt go on like that.' And you convince yourself that when I do really good work you can appreciate it, because you like Candida. But everybody likes Candida; Wyndham drops a tear over Candida; Alexander wants the poet made blind so that he can play him with a guarantee of 'sympathy'; Mrs Pat wants to play Candida; Ellen Terry knows she *is* Candida; Candida is everybody's play except the utter groundlings'. Candida vindicates every wife & mother and every suburban home to her and itself. To me it does nothing of the kind: it shews how important the woman's part in the arrangement is; but it does not justify the arrangement itself; and indeed the original of Vivie Warren, who is not susceptible to the sexual sentimentality which gives the Candida household its false charm, heads a party which denounces the play as disgusting.

Now you may say that all this is idle, because you like my last three plays. No doubt you do. The first was written for Terriss, and is a melodrama. The second was written for Forbes Robertson & Mrs Pat, and is literary. The third was written for Ellen Terry, round a part which is about as realistic as Rosalind. All three have strong & moving situations which appeal to you and to me exactly as they appeal to every man in the pit. For that reason, they have nothing to do with the New Century Theatre.

And now, to what end all this insistence on the fact that my plays are antipathetic to you? Have I spent all this black lead and excellent valuable time on mere amertumous recritication? Not a bit of it. I am hammering at my old point: you must write the plays you want yourself, or at worst make others write them. You will tell me, with the modesty of ingrained laziness, that you are not a playwright. Unfortunately for your credit on such points, you formed an equally strong opinion that *I* was not a playwright, and did what a sincere wellwisher could to prevent my exposing my obvious incapacity to the whole world. As a matter of fact I am by a very great deal the best Englishlanguage playwright since Shakespear, and considerably *his* superior on a good many points. If you made that colossal blunder about me, how can you feel any confidence in your judgment of yourself? You have immense confidence in yourself as a critic, though you are in many ways the worst critic now alive, declaring Olivier's play a dead thing, and Secret Service a masterpiece and deuce knows what not. How do you know that playwriting, if you could once get on your destined plane, is not your forte after all. At all events, you have failed to get the plays you want from other people. Even Ibsen doesnt convince you: you always want to cut his plays; and you have left the League of Youth to the Stage Society. In me you have hatched a cockatrice. Olivier is equally a failure. 'Alan's Wife' is the only seed that has come up as you wanted it. Well, here you are with a New Century Theatre and funds for a performance or two. It has plenty of talent on hand – yourself, Mrs Clifford & Miss Robins. Why dont you meet and say 'The land is barren: we must make a play.' There is more where 'Alan's Wife' came from, and more where 'Clive' came from. What is more, you three are not amateurs of an effete period: your vein has never been worked dramatically. Its a regular Rand.

This is all I have to say, and I am absolutely and perfectly right about it. And it is time for you to look to it, for we are both over 40, and your astrakan collar is growing rather alarmingly. The sooner you become as a little child again, the better. After all, it does not take so long to write a play; and it will be some expiation for flattering the Americans, and informing a stupended public that the verb 'to scrap' is unknown in England. Cashel Byron could have told you that it is as hackneyed in the London streets as 'copper' for policeman.

If you WONT, then hand over your NCT funds to the Stage Society, and it will do something with them.

We shall expect you on Friday, as arranged.

GBS

With his coinage of **Apry Ory beings** Shaw scoffed at Archer's version of 'a priori' thinking, mentioned in the previous letter. Shaw's reference to **Pionians** repeated an accusation in an earlier letter (21 August 1893) that Archer – detached from reality – lived in Piona, the fantasy world dreamed up by Archer's young son Tom. Likewise, Shaw's accusation that Archer wore **an astrakan collar** repeated a similar charge made in the letter of 24 January 1900. There Shaw imagined Archer 'in an overcoat with an astrachan collar' and with his 'hair dyed purple.' Although the spelling of 'astrakhan' eluded him, Shaw knew exactly how to represent the tight fitting image of Archer's critical rigidity. These two versions of Archer as an aesthetic type with fixed (and false) ideas about art should be distinguished from Shaw's description a decade earlier of Archer wearing 'incorruptible collars.' In that case Shaw insisted that a high, rigid collar was a perfect fit for Archer's high-minded defence of his critical integrity. (See letter of 7 November 1891.) On several occasions Shaw joked that Archer **slept** at performances, including Shelley's *The Cenci* in 1886 and the reading of the unfinished *Rheingold* in Archer's flat in 1887. Shaw continued to repeat versions of this anecdote on several occasions, including his memorial essay in 1927 on Archer (3 Plays: xiii). ***The Wild Duck*** was produced by the IT in May 1894 (3 perfs.) and May 1897 (5 perfs.). Whatever Archer's initial reservations over the play, he came to rank it among Ibsen's greatest achievements (13 June 1894: World 94: 136–43; 29 May 1897; World 97: 146–51). Shaw likewise was amazed by the play (SatRev, 22 May 1897; Dukore 3: 852–8). If Shaw had the 1897 production in mind, he was referring to Frank **Harris**, not Augustus Harris, who died in 1896. As for the three IT performances in 1894, it is most unlikely that Augustus Harris attended. Shaw's **last three plays** (or most recent plays) were *The Devil's Disciple*, *Caesar and Cleopatra*, and *Captain Brassbound's Conversion*. They were published in January 1901 as *Three Plays for Puritans*. William **Terriss** (1847–97) was a popular actor in melodrama. He never acted in *The Devil's Disciple* because he was stabbed to death outside the stage door of the Adelphi Theatre on 16 December 1897 by a fellow actor. Johnston **Forbes-Robertson** played Caesar in *Caesar and Cleopatra* in 1906 and 1913, the year he was knighted. In 1912 Shaw wrote an opening prologue for Forbes-Robertson, who appeared before the audience in a hawk's head in the persona of Ra, the Egyptian god. Shaw's forced coinage of **amertumous recritication** is apparently a bilingual pun on the French word *amertume*, which means bitterness. The obscure phrase has the traits of professional jargon, as if Shaw suffered from a medical ailment. Whatever the case, he resented the need to repeat his criticism of Archer and the NCT. ***Secret Service***, the popular melodrama written by and starring the American William Gillette (1855–1937), opened on 15 May 1897 (Adelphi and Comedy, 79 perfs.) – not on May 1895 at Terry's, as noted in CL 2: 140. In May 1897 Archer wrote an enthusiastic review, calling it 'the best drama of adventure and situation written within my recollection in the English language' (World 97: 130). It was revived at the Adelphi on 24 November by an English company, featuring Terriss; performances continued until 16 December, when he was murdered. Ibsen's ***The League of Youth***, presented by the Stage Society on 25 February 1900, was directed by C. Charrington (Vaudeville, 1 perf.). Shaw mistakenly identified Mrs W. (Lucy) **Clifford**, the novelist and playwright, as a member of the NCT management. **Clive** was an early, unpublished play by

Archer. Because **Rand** is defined as a vein of gold that glitters and is also the monetary unit of South Africa, Shaw may have intended both meanings, gold and money. It is also defined as a strip, edge, or border of land or leather. In his complaint that Archer failed to know that the verb **'to scrap'** exists in British popular idiom, Shaw was responding to Archer's essay on 'The American Language' in the *Pall Mall Magazine.* It was one of six long essays that Archer published between September 1899 and January 1900 on American society, language, and theatre.

78 / To G. Bernard Shaw

[no address]
1st February 1900

[TLS: BL 45296 f 87; also published in C. Archer]

Because Shaw's last letter repeated some of the complaints and challenges from letters of the last decade, Archer found it easy to dismiss or ignore most of the critiques. With the idiomatic phrase Und damit basta *(enough of this), he quickly deflated the tone and terms of their debates. And perhaps intentionally he transformed Shaw's misspelled 'astrakam collar' into an 'Astrakhan coat,' which would fit comfortably around the shoulders instead of tightly around the neck – just the attire for luncheon with the Shaws, especially if Shaw wore his Jagger suit. What a pair for Mrs Shaw to contemplate!*

No doubt some of Shaw's complaints had merit, but Archer was not prone to worrying over such matters. As Shaw recognized, Archer's self-confidence left little room in his mind for self-doubts or self-questioning. Of course, this was true of both of them.

Unfortunately, this is the last extant letter from Archer until 1 September 1903 – almost four years of silence. As is clear from Shaw's statements in some of the following letters, several of Archer's letters are missing. Quite possibly many others disappeared.

My dear Shaw

As the man says in Stevenson, 'Golly, what a letter!'

I write to you suggesting that the N.C.T. might do one of your plays; you haven't a play that we want free for us to do; one would think nothing could be simpler. But somehow a 'position' is set up, which has got to be 'worked out' laboriously, with tons of black lead lavished upon it. There is no 'position' whatever. We have never agreed about plays, & we never will. There is not the least reason why we should. I have never given a red cent for the ideas in plays. You & other people have had to point out to me the ideas in Ibsen's plays. Some of them I see, some of them I don't (nor, I believe, does Ibsen). But the play has always been the first thing to me; it is the last thing to you.

Never was black lead more hopelessly wasted than in this letter. You haven't even persuaded me that I ought to be ashamed of myself for admiring your later plays. As for the other plays, a few minutes after I read your letter I read a manuscript preface by Gilbert Murray to one of his own plays in which he says: 'I see that I am approaching the common pitfall of playwrights who venture upon prefaces, & am beginning to prove how good my play ought to be!' For 'prefaces' read 'letters.' I think I have solved the mystery of your friend Shakespeare's premature end: he no doubt broke a bloodvessel in trying to prove to Ben Jonson that TITUS ANDRONICUS was a good play & HAMLET a bad one.

The amazing appearance of Mrs. Clifford upon the theatre of war leads me to conjecture that you think she wrote ALAN'S WIFE. She didn't, nor did Miss Robins, nor did I. *Und damit basta.*

Expect me at one tomorrow, Astrakhan coat & all.

Yours W.A.

The line **'Golly, what a letter!'** appears in the comic novel *The Wrong Box* (1889) by R.L. **Stevenson** and Lloyd Osbourne (1868–1947). Osbourne was the stepson of Stevenson. Besides *The Wrong Box,* they wrote two other novels together: *The Wrecker* (1892) and *The Ebb-Tide* (1894). He was twelve years old when his mother Fanny married Stevenson in 1880. When Stevenson went to the South Seas in 1888, Osbourne was part of the family group. In 1924 he published *An Intimate Portrait of R. L. S. by His Stepson.*

79 / To William Archer

10 Adelphi Terrace WC
21st February 1900

[APCS: BL 45296 f 88]

Shaw sent the poetry book Maoriland and Other Verses *because he knew that Archer was preparing to publish* Poets of the Younger Generation. *Shaw was not alone in admiring Archer's assessment of America in his new book* America Today: Observations and Reflections *(1900). When the separate articles were first published in the American press in late 1899, the governor of New York, Theodore Roosevelt, wrote to Archer: 'I cannot deny myself the pleasure of writing to compliment you upon your altogether excellent articles on the conditions of affairs in America, both as to the relations between the North and the South and between America and England. What I especially liked about your article was that it was so eminently sane and moderate' (C. Archer: 246–8). There was nothing moderate, however, about Archer's enthusiasm for America and New York, which he visited in 1899. In a letter to his brother Charles he proclaimed: 'I am more than ever charmed with America. The people are simply delightful, and I am convinced that twenty years hence New York will be one of the most beautiful cities in the world' (C. Archer: 245). By contrast, Shaw held negative views of America, and only visited once in 1933, when a cruise ship made stops in San Francisco and Los Angeles.*

The book herewith 'Maoriland and Other Verses' by Arthur H. Adams, has been sent to me with a request that I would put it in the way of being reviewed by the English Press. I can produce an impression of having done so if I report that I have placed it on your desk: hence the unwelcomed offering. However, I always open such books to sample the beginnings of poetry in the colonies. A small sample of this man will suffice for the present.

Some of your American book is very good — I mean supergood enough to leave a mark, especially the North & South article. I begin to have hopes that you will do me credit yet.

By the way, the Ibsen play is powerful, and *frightfully* moral. The best review I have seen is in the last Speaker. It *must* be played.

GBS

Maoriland and Other Verses (1899) was written by Arthur Henry Adams (1872–1936), a journalist who also wrote poems, plays, and novels. Born and educated in New Zealand, he moved to Sydney in 1898. Two years later, living in China, he covered the Boxer Rebellion for the *Sydney Morning Herald*. In 1902 he moved to London, then returned to Australia in 1906, working primarily as a journalist, but continuing his literary output. He published his *Collected Verses* in 1913. The **Ibsen play** was *When We Dead Awaken*. Archer and Shaw remained diametrically opposed on its merits. Despite having translated and published the play (1900), Archer felt that it was a failure because it sacrificed 'surface reality to the underlying meaning' (Ibsen Essays: 287). Not constrained by principles of realism, Shaw admired both the translation and the symbolism of the play. The review in the **Speaker** may have been by Edmund Gosse. But perhaps the **best review** actually appeared in the *Fortnightly Review*. It was written by the eighteen-year-old James Joyce (1882–1941). Over 8000 words, the article celebrated the play as the 'greatest' achievement of Ibsen's work. When Ibsen learned of Joyce's article, he asked Archer to convey to Joyce his appreciation, which Archer did. Joyce replied to Archer: 'The words of Ibsen I shall keep in my heart all my life' (Meyer: 792). He did so, as the many references to Ibsen and his plays in *Finnegans Wake* illustrated. Joyce's review, in contrast to Archer's negative response, might well be seen as an emblematic touchstone and turning point in the history of modernism. And even though Shaw shared Joyce's enthusiasm for Ibsen's last play, he struggled to embrace Joyce's own contributions to modernism (Holroyd 2: 383–4; 3: 198–200).

80 / To William Archer Blackdown Cottage near Haslemere
8th July 1900

[ALS: BL 45296 f 89; CL 2 partial]

This warning about a possible 'homicidal turn' by this 'lunatic,' who remained unnamed, was no joke. Shaw recalled the murder of William Terriss in December 1897 by Richard Arthur Prince (1865–1936), a deranged young actor who blamed Terriss for his unemployment. Of unsound mind, Prince spent the rest of his life in the Broadmoor Criminal Lunatic Asylum. Candida, *which Janet Achurch, Charles Charrington, and Edith Craig (1869–1947) had first performed in Aberdeen (30 July 1897), was given its London performance, a matinee, at the Strand Theatre by the Stage Society on 1 July 1900. The role of Marchbanks featured the young Harley Granville Barker whom Archer already knew. In 1898, when Barker and Berte Thomas (1883–1966) had submitted their play* The Weather-Hen *to the* NCT, *Archer had rejected it as unplayable. A year later, however, when the play premiered at Terry's Theatre on 29 June 1899 and transferred to the Comedy Theatre for a two-week run, Archer called it 'very clever' in his review for* The World *(Whitebrook: 222–3). After regaining his health and resettling in London in 1900, Shaw resumed a busy schedule. Besides the commitments to his Vestry work and the Fabian meetings, he drafted* Fabianism and the Empire, *prepared the Fabian* Election Manifesto, *and corrected proofs for* Three Plays for Puritans *(which was published on 15 January 1901). He was also rehearsing Johnston Forbes-Robertson in* The Devil's Disciple. *After three years of nudging by Shaw, he had agreed to play the role of Richard Dudgeon. Shaw directed the production at the suburban Coronet Theatre; it opened on 7 September 1900.*

Your correspondent is a lunatic. He is a house painter, who, years ago, wrote me a few letters which I answered offhand under the impression that he was one of my socialist acquaintances & a member of the Fabian. He turned up at a meeting in a state of speechless shyness; and I then discovered that he was the usual March Hare. His letters break out at long intervals: just now he is suffering from a rather acute attack. He believes that I am at the head of a vast and subtle conspiracy to defeat, baffle, suppress, disparage, and blight him, both in his literary ambitions and his love affairs (which are quite imaginary). Sometimes he writes when he is sane – at least he used to – and then his accounts of books he had read, and Roman Catholic services he had attended, were quite presentable. But the only safe course with this sort of case is never to let him hear any reverberation of his explosions. His egotism is fantastically extravagant: he only needs a homicidal turn (at least I hope he is not already provided) to be another Prince – I mean the man who killed Terriss. I shall not shew the letter to Charlotte, as this sort of thing makes her a little nervous.

I am very sorry that the Stage Society gave you up just when they had a chance of getting you to a performance. There has been a box always reserved for you hitherto; but I suppose your persistent neglect, the demands for seats for Candida, and the growing grumblings of the members at reservations of seats for everybody (since they have to scramble), broke down their hopes that you would come. I took it for granted that they would ask you, and so took no steps, worse luck.

Yes: the poet – Granville Barker – was the success of the piece. It was an astounding piece of luck to hit on him. He is a very clever fellow – very young, but *very* expert – began with his mother (elocutionizing) at six, and has been on the stage 9 years. Charrington began well as Morell; but he soon became so deeply affected by the part that his powers of speech departed; he wallowed in it internally; and if there had been 5 acts instead of 3, he would have been speechless in 4th and motionless in the 5th. And as emotion takes a bilious form with him, he became uglier as he felt more deeply, and ended as a clerical Caliban, putting Prossy's complaint beyond all credibility. Janet has now lost all power of doing anything but her own particular *io son io*, which is not Candida's by any means; but her ancient flame of genius finally kindled, and she won at the post, so to speak.

The H.R. article meant – but I will write again about it. At present I am prostrate with acute overwork for a week over The Devil's Disciple & the printing of Three Plays for Puritans, not to mention the Vestry &c &c. For the moment I am really done up. I daren't write another word. I have had to *conduct* the rehearsals for Forbes Robertson; and this for my credit's sake I had to do well – a matter involving elaborate study beforehand.

GBS

Lewis Carroll (1832–1898) created the character of the **March Hare** for the tea party scene in *Alice's Adventures in Wonderland* (1865), but the idiom 'mad as a March Hare' has a history that predates Carroll. It refers to various bizarre and unpredictable antics of European hares during their breeding season in March and other spring months. Early examples of the idiom appear in English literature of the sixteenth century. The phrase **io son io** refers to a particular style of bel canto aria, as displayed in G,F. Handel's *Guilio Cesare* and Francesco Cilea's *Adriana Lecouvreur.* For what Shaw **meant** to say about the **H.R.** (*Humane Review*) article, see the following letter.

81 / To William Archer Blackdown Cottage near Haslemere, Surrey
9th July 1900

[ALS: BL 45296 ff 90–3; CL 2]

Shaw published 'A Conflict between Science and Common Sense' in the Humane Review *(April 1900). He warned against the contemporary faith in the pronouncements of science, including the excesses of prophylactic medicine. We are too gullible. He also mounted an attack on vivisection. But besides these warnings against human credulity and mistreatment of animals, he seemed to have concluded that all science is quackery. Surely he was joking, but perhaps not. In the next* HR *issue, Joseph H. Levy, editor of* Personal Rights, *complained about Shaw's 'clowning.' Archer also wrote a response, 'A Humanitarian Hoax' (ML, 23 June 1900). In the past, he explained, he has always prided himself on being able to distinguish between Shaw's serious and humorous statements, but he has now become unsure about the latest statements. Does Shaw really believe that the moon is only 37 miles from the earth? But then the truth revealed itself to Archer: 'My eye falls on the date of the review containing Mr. Shaw's article – it is April 1! All is explained, and if I do not think the joke a good one, that is doubtless only the natural resentment of a victim of a successful hoax.' On many occasions Shaw challenged the certainties of modern science and the authority of scientists, doctors, and engineers. In his questioning of scientific theory and methodology, he would sometimes push his ironic analysis to a reductio ad absurdum. Though often clever, his scepticism and denials were usually dismissed as misguided satire. And of course he could be wrong, as he was in his dismissal of Darwinian theory. Yet for all of his drollery, he was completely serious in his assaults on false authority, dogma, self-delusion, and idols in the scientific world.*

To resume – the object of the Humane Review article was to call attention to the fact that we have slipped into a doctrine of Omniscience & Infallibility as regards Science, of precisely the same kind as the old doctrine as to Religion.

Also to shew that the parallel (or rather the identity) is so complete, that even the people who imagine themselves in a critical attitude towards Science, are shocked when anybody jokes about it, just as Deists used to be shocked at the jokes of Voltaire.

I have succeeded with ludicrous exactness. Even 'Personal Rights,' which has been denouncing 'the medical priesthood' for years, and is edited by a man who poked fun at the Bible every week in the National Reformer, protests with horror against my 'clowning' in the presence of this ineffably serious & sacred subject.

And I observe, with a chuckle, that even you, in the matter of the fireproof floor, are so absolutely convinced of the validity of the strain calculating system that you assume that the engineer made 'a mistake in his calculation,' of which there is not the smallest evidence, the plain fact being that the moment a floor was introduced which was heavier than the old floors, the house came down and proved, as the bicycle and a hundred other things have proved, that in mechanics as in art, theory comes after practice, and is mostly a pure figment. Yet when people are told by a guide that Beauvais cathedral fell because it was top heavy, they ascribe that to the ignorance of the Middle Ages; but when the Forth Bridge collapses, they think there must have been a mistake in the calculation. Mind: I do not propose to be an expert in these matters: I simply point out the conclusions that would be drawn as a matter of common sense, if there were no superstition to be deferred to.

Even my joke about the moon is not altogether a joke, although it is jocular enough for the test abovementioned. The story about Broadstairs pier and old Perigal is perfectly true. He was an FRS; and I had exactly the same warrant for the validity of his geometric chuck calculation as for the Newtonian one: that is, none at all. As to the millions & billions of miles, they are of course as possible as millions & billions of inches or millionths of inches. But that the astronomic talk about them, and the popularity of that talk, is pure miraclegaping megalomania, I have not the smallest doubt. The agreement among the physicists as to the measurements is as imaginary as the agreement about nitrogen, oxygen & carbon dioxide accounting for the atmosphere.

I rejoice to see that Wells, in his last book 'Mr. Lewisham,' blows the gaff on the system of proving theories to students by shewing them faked experiments. He introduces a spirit medium [James Chaffery] (who professes himself a pupil of mine!) who defends his impostures on the ground that they are the easiest way of teaching the truths of spiritualism, exactly as the professors who fake their experiments in the St Januarius manner contend that it is the easiest way of teaching students the truths of science.

I see by your article that you cannot get science on to a purely secular plane; but that will come later on.

Your article on Ibsen & the Pinero-Jones dukes has given unqualified delight to all & sundry.

I have been reading Sutro's Cave of Illusion. *When* will people realize that [of all] undramatic and stupid no-thoroughfares of subjects adultery is quite the worst? Sutro could write a decent play if he could only get away from it.

I pant to redress the moral balance by beginning my Don Juan.

GBS

The **Beauvais cathedral** in northern France was begun in 1225, but the gothic vaulting collapsed in 1284, perhaps because of poor masonry work. The **Forth Bridge**, a cantilever railway bridge of steel over the Firth of Forth near Edinburgh, was begun in 1882 and opened on 4 March 1890. In his anecdote about Henry **Perigal** (1801–98), a fellow of the Royal Astronomical Society (i.e., FRAS, not **FRA** as Shaw typed), Shaw recalled a summer evening on the Broadstairs pier when Perigal outwitted Shaw in calculating the moon's distance from the earth. After praising Shaw's method of reasoning, Perigal explained that the exact distance of thirty-seven miles could be determined by tracking a star by means of a **geometric chuck** of a lathe. Charmed and outfoxed by a man of 'a hundred and two years of age,' Shaw repeated a version of the anecdote two decades later in 'Foundation Oratory' (reprinted in Platform: 149–51). **Broadstairs** is a coastal town in east Kent, on the island of Thanet. Herbert George **Wells** (1866–1946) published his novel ***Love and Mr. Lewisham*** in June 1900. According to legend, the dried blood of **St Januarius** (AD 272–305), the patron saint of Naples, miraculously turns to liquid annually. It is stored in a silver reliquary. Archer took up the debate about **Ibsen & the PineroJones dukes** in three stages. In a review of W.L. Courtney's new book, *The Idea of Tragedy in Ancient & Modern Drama* (1900), he attacked Courtney's claim that tragedy must feature great individuals at the top of society. Courtney dismissed Ibsen's drama as 'mean, commonplace, and parochial' because it features common people (DC, 15 June). In 'The Dukes of the Drama' Archer presented his own witty version of a reductio ad absurdum: the plays of Pinero and Jones must be grand tragedies because they feature dukes and barons, whereas poor Ibsen is parochial because he only writes about middle-class people (ML, 9 July). Then in 'The Dukeries Once Again' – written a few days after this letter from Shaw – Archer described the limitations of English drama that represents upper-class and aristocrat life in Mayfair and Belgravia, to the exclusion of the rest of society (ML, 14 July). In all three reviews, Archer praised the tragic greatness of Ibsen's drama. Alfred Sutro's play ***Cave of Illusion*** was first published in 1900, with a preface by Maurice Maeterlinck (whose *La mort de Tintagiles* and *Aglavaine et Sélysette* Sutro had recently translated). In a review Archer had praised Sutro's play (DC, 8 June 1900). In May, with Mozart's *Don Giovanni* as a catalyst, Shaw began to write the '**Don Juan** in Hell' scene that became the third act of *Man and Superman.*

82 / To William Archer

10 Adelphi Terrace WC
28th November 1900

[APCU: BL 45296 f 94]

On the evening of 29 November, Archer and the Shaws procured gallery seats to see Forbes-Robertson in The Devil's Disciple. *The production, which Shaw directed, had opened on 7 September at the Coronet Theatre in Notting Hill. After a limited run, it toured in the provinces for several weeks before returning to the same suburban theatre for a few more performances. Dismayed by the uneven quality of the acting, Shaw proclaimed to Charrington on 30 November: 'Oh Lord! Underdone opera bouffe!' He quickly decided to 'drop the notion of a West End production' (CL 2: 201). The decision probably pleased Charrington because he and Shaw were still struggling to complete the casting for* Captain Brassbound's Conversion, *which was staged in December by the Stage Society on the 16th (Strand Theatre) and 20th (Criterion Theatre). Directed by Charrington, the production featured Janet Achurch, Laurence Irving, Courtenay Thorpe, and Harley Granville Barker. Ellen Terry attended the Strand performance; this was her first meeting with Shaw, after eight years of their letter writing. In his review of the* SS *production, Archer castigated the West End managers for not producing Shaw's plays (World, 26 December 1900). To protect the American copyright of* Three Plays for Puritans, *one copy was published on 27 November. Six weeks later, on 15 January 1901, Grant Richard published 2000 copies of the book. In 1904 Richards published 1000 corrected copies. (For publishing details see Biblio 1: 47–9.)*

Charlotte tells me that there are only stalls (6/-) left for Saturday afternoon at the Coronet. Prices seem creeping up: suburban stalls used to be four shillings. Perhaps Shaw & Shakespear are two shillings extra.

The P.M.G. contains nothing but some quite superficial particulars which I gave to Golding Bright – merely the chapter headings. But the [Daily] Chronicle quoted a sentence which is going the round of the press, how obtained I dont know, certainly not from a complete copy or the quotation would have been fuller. The book was technically published yesterday – one copy sold formally to secure American copyright. You shall have the earliest advance copy issued.

[no signature]

In the letter to R. **Golding Bright** (1874–1941), an aspiring journalist who worked as a manager for a play-agent, Shaw described the preface headings for the three plays; he also noted that the book would feature photogravure plates of a bust of Caesar, a portrait of

General John Burgoyne, and 'an Italian photograph of the mosaic in St Marks representing the lighthouse of Alexandria' (CL 2: 190–1). Bright publicized the forthcoming book in the **P.M.G.**, *Pall Mall Gazette.*

83 / To William Archer 10 Adelphi Terrace WC
18th February 1901

[ALS: BL 45296 f 95; CL 2]

On 4 March 1886 Archer had sent a copy of Shaw's first published novel, Cashel Byron's Profession, *to R.L. Stevenson, who was recuperating at Bournemouth. Stevenson replied a few days later, praising Shaw's 'genuine and remarkable narrative talent – a talent that few will have the wit to understand, a strength, spirit, capacity, sufficient vision, and sufficient self-sacrifice, which last is the chief point in a narrator.' Stevenson announced that he had 'howled with derision and delight' over the character of Bashville. 'I dote on Bashville – I could read of him forever; there is only one Bashville, and I am his devoted slave ... It is all mad, mad, and deliriously delightful; the author has a taste in chivalry like Walter Scott's or Dumas's, and then he daubs in little bits of socialism; he soars away on the wings of the romantic gryphon ... It is HORRID FUN.' In a parenthetical statement, he wrote: 'I say, Archer, my God, what women!' (BL 45295 ff 90–1; Stevenson 5: 224–5). Archer wrote back on 10 March: 'Your diagnosis of Shaw's case is delicious. I look forward to reading it to him – it will infuriate him and do him all the good in the world. I am always assuring him that he is an* a priori *novelist, which he doesn't like at all; but to be told that he is a sentimentalist & romanticist will drive the shaft three barbs deeper' (BL 45295 ff 94–6). Archer showed Stevenson's letter to Shaw on the same day (Diaries 1: 152).*

In 1901 Shaw printed part of the letter in 'Novels of My Nontage,' the preface to the revised English edition of Cashel Byron's Profession *published by Grant Richards (Biblio 1: 4–10). He took special pleasure in reproducing Stevenson's list of five possible influences on Shaw's novelistic talent: Henry James, Charles Reade (1814–84), Benjamin Disraeli (1804–81), his own 'struggling, overlaid original talent,' and his 'blooming gaseous folly' (Prefaces 1: 103). According to Stevenson Disraeli's influence was 'perhaps unconscious,' but the largest influence was Shaw's own original talent. Archer, in his reply to Stevenson in 1886, doubted that any of these three writers influenced Shaw, but he agreed about Shaw's unique, independent genius. 'In short, he is a remarkable man, one of the most interesting studies in character, I ever came across' (BL 45295 f 96).*

Archer reviewed Three Plays for Puritans *a day after its publication (DC, 16 January 1901). He noted that in the preface Shaw complained that many plays on the London stage are 'obsessed with sex' and 'sensuous ecstasy' (CP 2: 24, 28). By contrast, Shaw's three plays, which require 'intellectual activity' from readers and potential spectators, appeal to people with a puritan sensibility of mind. A month later Archer returned to this topic in 'Why for Puritans?' (ML, 16 February). Rejecting Shaw's critique of West End theatres, Archer asserted that the current 'serious stage' does not minister to sensuality. He challenged Shaw to name any play produced between Pinero's* The Second Mrs Tanqueray *in 1893 and Jones's* Mrs Dane's Defence *in 1900 that owed its 'success to any sort of "voluptuous" appeal, to any titillation of sensuality in any sane spectator.' Then seeking another debate with Shaw, he announced that 'no dramatist is more subject than Mr. Shaw himself to the obsession with sex.'*

Have you got that letter of Stevenson's about Cashel Byron's Profession which was mutilated by Colvin for the second volume of the Letters, p 96? I want to print the omitted uncomplimentary part in the preface to a new edition of the book, which will consist of a Preface (as usual), the novel, an essay on prizefighting, another preface, and a play in blank verse in the style of Marlow, entitled The Admirable Bashville, or Constancy Unrewarded. This latter masterpiece has been forced on me by the necessity for keeping the American adaptations off the English stage. I had to make an adaptation of my own in a hurry; and as I, or any fool, can write blank verse as fast as the pen will travel (this is the real secret of Shakespear's big output) I plunged into that medium, which proved very effective in bringing out the dramatic qualities of the tale.

Unless you dislike the publication of the suppressed passages of the letter, will you lend it to me, or let me have a copy, which would perhaps be safer.

I gather from The Morning Leader that my Three Plays preface has turned your brain. You forgot that the appeal to Puritans is a flat plagiarism from yourself in The Morning Leader as ever was. You raised the same cry, used the same 'profaneness & immorality' quotation, and so moved Massingham that he lifted up his voice beside you. I am only the third Anabaptist in the trio: you are the first. I can't meet your mad challenge to name the plays in which the heroes & heroines do 'all for love,' because Parke would not give me space enough; but I can hardly think offhand of any plays I should exclude (barring Wilde's, Shakespear's & my own) except The Triumph of The Philistines & Trelawney. There is only one instance in my plays of a couple meeting for the first time before lunch & being engaged after dinner; and that is a dread example of the fate of 'the duellist of sex,' who is swept into the *family* which is the real subject of this really great comedic sociological study like a butterfly. Read all the plays again, six times over.

By the way, if you want to understand why Brassbound was written at such a moment, read Stanley's African expeditions & then Miss Kingsley's. You will then begin to see dimly how I get my Brassbounds & Cicelys and why they appear so unnatural & unreal in that blessed old *pays de Cocagne* in which you have sat (in a stall) for 20 years. You really are

LOSING
YOUR
FACULTIES

GBS

In 1900 Sir Sydney **Colvin** (1845–1927) edited Stevenson's letters in two volumes, followed by two more volumes in 1911. He misdated and abridged some letters, including the one to Archer. Colvin removed some of Stevenson's comments on Shaw and *Cashel Byron's Profession*, including Stevenson's suggestions on possible influences on Shaw. A complete, scholarly edition by Bradford A. Booth and Ernest Mehew is now available (9 vols, 1994–8). Stevenson's letter to Archer is no longer abridged or **mutilated,** as Shaw stated. Elizabethan blank verse, including that of Christopher Marlowe (1564–93), not **Marlow**, served as Shaw's poetic model for ***The Admirable Bashville.*** Written quickly in January 1901, the play had its copyright reading on 13 March 1901. It was published in tandem with the third, revised edition of *Cashel Byron's Profession* on 23 October. Ernest **Parke** (1860–1944), the crusading journalist who edited *The Star*, apparently did not publish Shaw's letter. H.A. Jones wrote ***Triumph of the Philistines*** in 1895; A.W. Pinero wrote ***Trelawney of the 'Wells'*** in 1897. Henry Morton **Stanley**, the journalist for the *New York Herald*, explored Africa, most famously in his search in 1871 for Dr David Livingston, the Scottish missionary. He published *In Darkest Africa* (1890), which influenced Joseph Conrad's *Heart of Darkness* (*Blackwood's Magazine* 1899; book, 1902). Mary Henrietta **Kingsley** (1862–1900), an ethnographer, writer, and niece of the writer Charles Kingsley, explored parts of Africa on several trips in the 1890s, often travelling alone. Unlike Stanley, who killed hundreds of Africans, she sought to defend Africans, and was critical of European imperialists and Christian missionaries. She died in South Africa, nursing prisoners of war during the Boer War. Her *Travels in West Africa* (1897) is a classic. In a 1912 leaflet distributed for the revival of *Captain Brassbound's Conversion*, Shaw again mentioned Stanley and Kingsley (CP 2: 428–9). **Pays de Cocagne** (or Cockaigne) was a mythical land of idle living. Tom Archer's dreamland of Piona was located there.

84 / To William Archer

10 Adelphi Terrace WC
22nd February 1901

[ALS: BL 45296 ff 96–100; CL 2 partial]

Archer's reply to Shaw's previous letter is missing; but as the following letter clarified, he showed R.L. Stevenson's 1886 letter to Shaw. Shaw continued his critique of Archer's article 'Why for Puritans?' And he defended the preface to Three Plays for Puritans. *Years later in a 1916 letter to Frank Harris Shaw admited that 'Archer's early complaint that my plays reeked with sex was far more sensible than the virgin-eunuch theory which half-penny journalists delight in' (Harris: 54). By adding* Man and Superman *and* Fanny's First Play *to his explanation for Harris, Shaw made the case that several of his plays had put 'the sex problem on the stage' (CP 2: 496), as he stated in his Epistle to* Man and Superman, *his Don Juan play.*

You had better ask Colvin, as he would have to refer to you in any case: you being the addressee of the letter.

Of course I meant plays in which love is the sole motive. But all that I meant, with its limitations, exceptions, & various modes, is set out most elaborately & completely in the preface.

The typical poetically voluptuous play – love the sole motive, and lovers in gorgeous robes & spectacular setting the sole personages, is Herod. Now the whole history of the Lyceum is the history of Herodifying Shakespear – getting the brains & realism out & the Belsize Park suburban Jewish glamor in. Ellen Terry & Forbes Robertson as Guinevere & Lancelot in Comyns Carr's King Arthur was Lyceum ritual in excelsis. Herod is the same game; only Phillips can write verse & is a bit of a poet much as Leighton was a bit of a painter – and Carr was a duffer.

On the grosser plane you have The Conquerors, with the rape on the stage, and the woman, when she recovers from the faint which saves public decency at the last moment, falling in love with the hero because she believes that the rape was consummated during her swoon. Then you have Carton's Tree of Knowledge, with the strangling match (same two performers) substituted for the rape. Leading up to this you have Mrs. Ebbsmith, with the (to A.W.P.) unreal, imaginary Trafalgar Square life suddenly changed into a glorious reality when the woman puts on a fashionable dress, & the man, at sight of her naked shoulders, knows what life & love are at last, & so does she. Then came [H.A. Jones's] Michael & His

Lost Angel, still under the influence of the overpowering *odor di femmina* from Mrs P[atrick] C[ampbell]. The same moral: the parson's social & religious work an unreal thing: love sweeping it away as the only real thing in the world. Then Pinero again [*The Princess and the Butterfly*] with the old Maupassant tragedy: the horror of passing 40 & being shelved sexually. Next variation: redemption for the roué by a Shunamite woman. Good Lord! & you ask me to name a single play &c.

However, you probably dont notice those things after quarter of a century in the theatre, just as water has no taste for us because it's always in our mouths. And yet from time to time youve howled, called for the Puritans, protested against the odor di femmina, tried to champion the unvoluptuous against Lily Hanbury & Mrs. Fred Terry. But in the main you are a lost man, and, with that other disgraceful old father of a family A.B.W. [Walkley], have complained that my erotics are 'bloodless' and clamored at me for reality, flesh & blood &c, meaning the aforesaid lovely Lily and the *odor*.

I blush for you.

In haste
GBS

As editor of R.L. Stevenson's letters, Sydney **Colvin** maintained publishing rights to the 1886 letter to Archer, even though he had failed to publish the full letter in 1900. **Belsize Park** is located in northwest London. ***Herod*** by Stephen Phillips (1864–1915) was staged by H.B. Tree at Her Majesty's; it opened on 22 October 1900 (78 perfs.). Henry Irving staged Comyns Carr's ***King Arthur*** in 1895. The painter and sculptor Frederic **Leighton** (1830–96) was honoured for his classical and religious works. He was knighted in 1878; he died a day after attaining peerage as Baron Leighton. George Alexander staged ***The Tree of Knowledge*** by R.C. Carton (1856–1928); it opened on 25 October 1897 (114 perfs.). Alexander also staged ***The Conquerors*** by Paul M. Potter (1853–1921), which opened on 14 April 1898 (48 perfs.). Both productions featured Julia Neilson (1868–1957). During the 1890s **Lily Hanbury** (1874–1908) and **Mrs Fred Terry** (i.e., Julia Neilson) were cast in roles of 'sensuous ecstasy.' The **Maupassant tragedy** is *Yvette.* By **Shunamite woman** Shaw meant the Shulamite woman – the maiden in the *Song of Solomon* (6:13).

85 / To William Archer

10 Adelphi Terrace WC
6th June 1901

[ALS: BL 45296 f 101]

In his 1886 letter to Archer about Shaw's Cashel Byron's Profession, *R.L. Stevenson had mentioned Shaw's socialist message and his attempts at realism, but he also identified 'a taste in chivalry' in Shaw's characterization. Then in his postscript Stevenson returned to the topic of Shaw's imaginative chivalry:* 'Vixere Fortes – *O, let him remember that – let him beware of his damned century; his gifts of insane chivalry and animated narration are just those that might be slain and thrown out like an untimely birth by the Daemon of the Epoch. And if he only knew how I had adored the chivalry! Bashville,* O Bashville! J'en chortle *(which is fairly polygot)' (BL 45295 f 96). Perhaps Stevenson's 'polygot' was supposed to be 'polyglot,' for the recent editors of his letters changed the word without comment (Stevenson 5: 225). Yet because he used the word 'chortle,' which is a portmanteau word that Lewis Carroll created in* Through the Looking Glass *(1872) by combining 'chuckle' and 'snort,' Stevenson may have offered his own playful word of polygot, as Dan H. Laurence and Daniel J. Leary suggested (Prefaces 1: 103).*

When Shaw published The Admirable Bashville *in late 1901, Archer reviewed it. He wrote: 'To me, Mr. Shaw's blank verse dramatization of his own novel,* Cashel Byron's Profession, *seems one of the most delicious of jests ... It seems to me the best burlesque of rhetorical drama in the language' (ML, 26 October 1901).*

Thanks for the letter: I return it, having copied the missing postscript. Two words I cannot decipher: the adverb to 'polyglot' in the last line, and the fifth word – Something of the Epoch: I guess Damon, but am very doubtful – in the fifth line from the end. Can you make them out? You were familiar with his fist.

The warning – Vixere fortes &c – is interesting: he went back to the XVIII century to avoid the XIX, instead of going on to the XX. I believe that was why he did not impress me much at the time: I regarded him as a man I had not time to attend to, whereas now I delight in his romances (prefer the Black Arrow to Jekyll & Hyde) and boil with indignation at the Philistinism which complains of Macaire as a billiard marker complains of classical music. As I grow older I become professionalized, and expect presently to find myself outdoing Walkley, Wedmore & Henry James in self-complacent cabotinage.

Bashville is certainly a masterpiece. Henry Arthur [Jones] implores me to pursue this wonderful vein & recognize that my true genius lies in burlesque. Unfortunately, as I have to write the works I burlesque, I should have to spend the latter half of my life caricaturing the former half, which I am likely enough to do without any prompting & with the most serious intentions.

What is the Poet's book?

GBS

PS By the way I have written a preface to Bashville on the subject of blank verse. When I get a proof I will send it along.

I will alter the passage about the published letters & make it inoffensive.

Your query about Thackeray alarms me. Did he not contest a seat with Gully, who began his career by vanquishing Jem Belcher in the ring, & ended in parliament? Or is my memory playing me a trick?

The phrase **Vixere fortes** in R.L. Stevenson's 1886 letter to Archer is an allusion to a famous line in an ode by Horace (65–8 BCE): 'Vixere fortes ante Agamenona Multi' – 'Many brave men lived before Agamemnon' (*Odes*, 4, 9, 25). Stevenson published ***The Black Arrow*** in 1888 and ***The Strange Case of Dr Jekyll and Mr Hyde*** in 1886. Stevenson and W.E. Henley published ***Macaire****, A Melodramatic Farce*, in 1895. The adjective **billiard** is derived from the noun 'billiards.' A billiard marker, for Shaw, was a Philistine whose artistic taste failed to recognize and appreciate not only classical music but the artistic heritage. A.B. **Walkley** was a theatre critic; Sir Frederick **Wedmore** served as an art critic. In the mid-1880s Stevenson and **Henry James** became friends; they corresponded regularly. The word **cabotinage** is Shaw's noun derived from the verb *cabotage*, the act of sailing safely along a coast. In the letter to Archer of 18 February 1901 Shaw had complained that Stevenson's letter to Archer had been 'mutilated by Colvin.' When he drafted his preface for *Bashville*, Shaw had complained about Colvin. But he decided to remove this offensive **passage**, apparently after receiving an appeal from Archer in the missing letter to Shaw. The preface was published in 1901 (see Prefaces 1: 90–103, especially 102–3). Shaw's memory may indeed have been partial, but he correctly recalled that both **Jem Belcher** (1781–1811) and John **Gully** (1819–88) were English bare-knuckle boxers. Belcher died young in poverty; Gully sat in the House of Commons from 1832 to 1837. Shaw's question about **the Poet's book** is unclear because he is responding to a missing letter from Archer. Likewise, we do not know what Archer asked about William Makepeace **Thackeray**.

86 / To William Archer

10 Adelphi Terrace WC
2nd January 1902

[ALS: BL 45296 f 102]

Charlotte Shaw handled some of GBS's correspondence in the days before the planned production of Mrs Warren's Profession *by the Stage Society. It had originally been scheduled for December 1901, but no theatre could be found because 'Mr. Redford wouldnt license' the play, as Shaw wrote to Mrs Patrick Campbell on 22 November (CL 2: 241). After the Royalty Theatre cancelled an agreement, the production shifted to the tiny New Lyric Club for the afternoons of 5 and 6 January 1902.*

Clement Scott refused to review the presentation by the SS, despite Shaw's appeal to him on 4 January (CL 2: 250–1). J.T. Grein found the play 'needlessly unpleasant' and the production 'painful,' especially because the 'majority of women [had] to listen to that which could only be understood by a minority of men' (Morgan: 19).

Dear W. Archer

Thank you a thousand times for your kind New Year's thought of me: the clear little pocketbook will be most useful.

For the last week I have been on the point of writing to you every day to ask you to come and have luncheon with us, & every day I have been obliged to put off as some fresh complication in our affairs turned up! We have had unheard of troubles over Mrs. Warren! After a promise of nearly a fortnight standing, permission to produce it at the Royalty Theatre next Sunday was suddenly withdrawn. The management declared they had only just found out that the play was unlicensed: but that is only an excuse. As they *did* know when they let us the Theatre: they have evidently been 'got at.'

Of course all our tickets and programmes were printed & just going out & we were dearly distracted. After a great deal of negotiations & many unsuccessful attempts in various directions, we have had to fall back upon the Lyric Club, but we can only have it for Sunday *afternoon*, not evening, so we produce there on Sunday & Monday next; unless new complications arise.

G.B.S. is delighted with the cast: I never saw him so satisfied with rehearsals before: he says Miss Fanny Brough as Mrs. Warren is superb! The others are Vivie – Miss Madge Mackintosh [McIntosh]. Frank – Granville Barker. Clergyman – Cosmo Stewart (*very* good). Praed – Julius Knight; & Crofts – Goodhardt [Charles Goodhart].

I cannot ask you to come here tomorrow or nextday, as we live in a whirl: but I am longing to hear all about Rome & to have a good chat; so a little later on you must come. I will write again.

Kindest remembrances to Mrs. Archer & I am yours most sincerely

C.F. Shaw

PS I have got a New Year's gift for you – a most striking one! – but I really don't know if I shall have the courage to give it to you! Try & guess what it is.

In 1893 J.T. Grein declined to stage *Mrs Warren's Profession* because it was an **unlicensed** play; then in 1898 when the play was published, G.A. **Redford**, the Examiner of Plays, refused a licence even for its copyright reading, despite Shaw's appeal (CL 2: 13–14). **Fanny Brough** (1854–1914), a member of a well-known acting family of the nineteenth century, performed regularly in the West End theatres, often in comic roles. Shaw would later cast her *The Admirable Bashville* (1903) and *Getting Married* (1908). She was featured in the 1906 Jubilee for Ellen Terry at Drury Lane. **Madge McIntosh** (1875–1950) and **Julius Knight** (1863–1941) were regulars in the West End theatres. **Cosmo Stewart** and **Charles Goodhart** (d. 1910) usually played secondary or 'lines of business' roles. Archer travelled to **Rome** with his son Tom in December 1901 (Whitebrook: 221). Charlotte Shaw's desire to have a **good chat** with Archer about his visit to Rome was probably enhanced by her memories of her own trip in March and April 1898. Her calculated absence, at the time of Shaw's misery over his infected foot, contributed to his sense of being deserted, as he wrote to her: 'Oh Charlotte, Charlotte: is this a time to be gadding about in Rome' (7 April; CL2: 27–8). She returned in May; one month later they were married. (See also Shaw's letter to Archer on 26 April 1898.)

87 / To William Archer Piccard's Cottage, Guildford
7th January 1902

[ALS: BL 45296 f 103]

As Mrs Shaw noted in this letter, Archer reviewed the private production of Mrs Warren's Profession. *Unlike J.T. Grein, he was not bothered by the topic of prostitution. He praised Shaw's 'extraordinary dramatic talent,' but he criticized Shaw's 'insistent didacticism.' This 'defect,' not evident in later plays, reveals Shaw's 'inability to touch pitch without, so to speak, wallowing in it' (World, 15 January 1902).*

Dear W. Archer

I am so sorry I remember that just before I asked you to luncheon on Friday next – I had accepted an invitation to luncheon for ourselves for that day! It is very bad luck, as we have not another day this week in Town.

I am so sorry; but G.B.S. says that as he is sure you are going to say most severe things about Mrs. Warren, it is just as well you should be left to write your article in peace!

Next week I hope to see you. I will write on Monday & let you know what days we shall be in Town. I never know until the Sunday.

Yours Sincerely,
C.F. Shaw

88 / To William Archer

Piccard's Cottage, Guildford
24th February 1902

[ALS: BL 45296 f 104]

Mrs Shaw also wrote this letter. Archer had resumed his campaign for a National Theatre in 1901, with articles in several journals. He then initiated discussions on building requirements with the architect Edwin O. Sachs (1870–1919), who had designed several London theatres, and had installed electricity at Drury Lane Theatre. They began to compile a 'Blue Book' for a National Theatre. By the summer of 1902 their ideas led to the founding of a Theatrical Reform Committee, consisting of Archer, Sachs, Gilbert Murray, Granville Barker, the journalist Hamilton Fyfe (1869–1951), the scholar Sidney Lee (1859–1926), co-editor of The Dictionary of National Biography, *Spenser Wilkinson (1853–1937), who edited the* Morning Post, *and A.C. Bradley (1851–1935), professor of poetry at Oxford. The members of the National Reform Committee met often in 1902, exchanging ideas on a National Theatre (Whitebrook: 226–30).*

*Two days before Mrs Shaw sent this letter Archer had published an article, 'A Brace of Morals' (*The Morning Leader*), that offered a contrast between England and German/Austria in the production of major dramatists. He compared the number of productions of plays by five canonical dramatists that were presented in the English- and German-language theatres for two seasons, 1899–1900 and 1900–1:*

	Germany	*England*
Schiller	*1,818*	*0*
Goethe	*878*	*0*
Lessing	*374*	*0*
Molière	*276*	*0*
Calderon	*161*	*0*

Archer noted that 600 productions of Shakespeare were staged every season in Germany and Austria. In the case of London, according to the calendar prepared by J.P. Wearing, there were 15 Shakespearean productions in 1900, 12 in 1901. There were some productions outside of London each year, but these additional productions were at most a dozen or two for each year, and probably less. Obviously, the challenge of transforming the cultural taste and mindset of people in England was daunting. Perhaps, though, the creation of a national theatre would begin to change things – at least in a small measure.

Dear W. Archer

We *heartily* approve of the project of the National Theatre 'Bluebook.' It is a splendid idea & we will gladly subscribe to the guarantee fund.

G.B.S. strongly objects to a 'School of Acting.' Cant you come & talk it over – say on Thursday or Friday next at luncheon – 1.30? We should be delighted to see W. Sachs too; do you think he would care to come?

Yours sincerely
C.F. Shaw

89 / To William Archer Piccards Cottage, St Catherine's, Guildford
1st and 2nd March 1902

[ALS: BL 45296 ff 105–18; CL 2]

Archer and Edwin O. Sachs had begun to develop possible plans for the construction of a national theatre. This had led to the formation of the Theatrical Reform Committee (see previous letter). By 1903 Archer and Barker had begun to organize and transcribe these discussions, and then in 1904 they drafted Scheme & Estimates for a National Theatre, *which was privately printed and distributed to the committee members and a few dozen interested people, including the Shaws. Then Archer and Barker continued to modify and refine their recommendations. In 1907 they published* A National Theatre: Scheme & Estimates. *Throughout this period Shaw contributed to the discussions and debates, as he does here (Whitebrook: 226–34).*

Dear W.A.

I write in the train: hence joggling. Hope you can decipher.

I am game to back the SachsArcher book as you may direct. But I implore you to get rid of that superstition – the Dramatic School. In fact, I will contribute that section myself & present you with the copyright, and get Alexander to sign it, or sign it myself or impose the authorship on you, as you please, if you like.

My idea is this. Acting cannot be taught, as Tree, Irving &c are fond of telling us. But men can be physically trained for public life. Politicians, barristers, clergymen, lecturers, naval & military officers all depend greatly for their success on the style in which they can stand before an audience and address them or order them about. Toastmasters, servants, shopmen, auctioneers, bookmakers, and beadles also require deportment and oratory. Now what I want to agitate for is the addition of a Physical School of the Arts of Public Life to the schools of the London University, giving courses of instruction and training in platform accomplishments; so that a man or woman holding a certificate or diploma or degree from such a school could be depended on to deliver a lecture at the Royal Institution, preach a sermon, open a case in court, give an order in the field or from the quarterdeck & so on without making him- or herself ridiculous by the ineptness of the novice & the amateur. A National Theatre could demand such a degree from all its novices, just as a bishop demands a minimum of Greek before ordaining a curate. If the bishop demanded the physical degree too, and the same qualification was imposed for the bar and the services (including certain civil services), the School would become important, and its students would rub shoulders & criticisms with men of all classes, social & intellectual. The would-be actor would go there & have his horizon enlarged. He would not learn to act any more than the would-be barristers would learn to plead & cross examine, or the clergymen to save souls, or the general to win battles; but he would go on the stage, as the others would go into court & pulpit & camp *personally* qualified to begin. This plan would not only avoid the Puritan objection to subsidizing a theatrical school out of the rates, but place the theatrical profession on the level of the learned professions in the only possible way. And the school, supported by all the professions, could be on a scale impossible to any mere dramatic academy. It could get endowments from people & grants from public bodies who would not leave or give a penny to a National Theatre.

I do not mean that the apprenticeship of the future societaire should be wholly haphazard. The National Theatre would want supers. These supers should be for the most part young people 'walking on'; but a teacher of dancing, pantomime &c should be kept for them; and the wardrobe master should be a bit of an artist, like Teddy Craig. They should do all the curtain raising, and the special performances for children at holiday times (and all times) not by performing inane little novelettes, but masques, pantomimes, Planché extravaganzas, harlequinades & so on – things requiring dancing & dressing & tomfooling and high spirits. In this way they could pick up 'plastique,' costume &c, and such acrobatism as may be good for them – enough to jump through a trap, at all events.

(And this reminds me that one of the needs of a National Theatre would be an extra stage to enable two rehearsals to proceed simultaneously, and even a second theatre for the intimate performance of Ibsen plays & the like to small & superior audiences). There should be a strict age limit for this sort of thing; so that the apprentice-super who wished to devote his life to tomfooling & knockabout, or who was not graduated into the stock company of fully fledged actors, should be driven off to the music halls & commercial theatre at 24, say.

And this brings me to the necessity (later on) for a larger collectivism in the theatre than can be achieved by a single central house. The main artistic objection to stock companies is that they finally destroy dramatic illusion. Portia, Juliet, Imogene & Ophelia are different women: to make them all Ellen Terry ends in people going to the theatre to see Ellen Terry & accepting all sorts of conventions & absurdities in their forgetfulness of the play. This difficulty can be overcome only by circulation of companies; and this means that all the great centres of population should have national theatres, and that their artists should have an indefensible right to play all their roles once a year (or two or three years) in London. This development would be useful commercially too. At present London is becoming more & more a place for advertisement, whilst the provinces bring in the money. The provinces should feed London, if necessary, in the same way under a scheme of national theatres; and the profits should be used to finance incursions to small and growing towns to set up a standard of taste there and lay the foundations of additional national theatres.

Provisions should be made for long runs in the constitution of the theatre; not only for the sake of the theatre, but for the sake of attracting authors. For instance, there are plays of mine which I could not recommend any commercial manager to produce for a run, which yet might conceivably hit the public fancy either on their own account or through the fascination of somebody in the cast. Under such circumstances the national theatre should either hire another theatre and run the play for all it was worth or sublet it to one of the regular managers if he was ready & willing. At any rate they should either leave the author free to do this or else guarantee him a minimum number of performances of the play as a box office price for two or three seasons. Mind, I am not suggesting that such proceedings should be obligatory, only that the powers of the

N.T. should extend so far. I regard power to lease supplementary theatres on occasion as very important.

It is worth considering whether a public dramatic library should not be established, with an obligation on dramatic authors to deposit a copy of every published play as a condition of copyright (though a clause ought to attach to *all* public library copies of books to enable the author or publisher to recover the cost price of very expensive books).

However, all these are stray considerations. My main point is that the Dramatic School notion, intended to secure a stock company of the pupils of John Coleman and Henry Neville – even with the voice production by Hermann Vezin, assisted by Mrs. & Miss Behnke – is in every way a disastrous mistake, and that its functions should be undertaken by a University School of, say, Rhetoric (with a touch of Sandow). You have a precedent in the London School of Economics & Political Science, which grew out of the need of technical training for voters, which led to the need of technical trainings for town clerks & other municipal experts, which led again to the discovery that the staffs of railway companies, banks &c &c &c were in need of much the same training, and which is now a school of the London University with students using it as the spring board to jump off into scores of different careers. In this way only will you ever get the actor out of his cabotinage and give him the University stamp as distinguished from the professional stamp. For please remember that the present anarchy has the advantage of destroying the old Crummles professionalism; and that the return to order by way of a National Theatre will revive it if the dramatic student is to be educationally segregated from the other professions.

In haste
GBS

PS Charlotte is in bed with influenza.
PPS In one of my prefaces to Plays Pleasant & Unpleasant I sketch a plan for developing a repertory theatre out of an opera subsidy to an established manager.

Shaw initially opposed the formation of a **Dramatic School** as part of a national theatre, but in later years he became a major supporter of the Royal Academy of Dramatic Art (RADA). He served as a RADA administrator and provided major funds from his royalties (see the letter of 8 June 1922). Edward (**'Teddy'**) Gordon **Craig** (1872–1963) and Edith ('Edy') Craig began their stage careers as performers at the Lyceum Theatre, but by 1902 he had become a stage designer and she served as a costumer and wardrobe mistress. James Robinson **Planché** (1796–1880), a playwright, musical director, and costumer, staged popular burlesques, pantomimes, and extravaganzas in London for several decades; he published *History of British Costume* in 1834. The technique of **plastique** is an action and method for making slow movements in dance or pantomime. The **trap**, such as the 'Star Trap' or the 'Vamp Trap,' was a device in playhouses for projecting a performer onto the stage, either from below the stage or through the scenery. The cauldron in *Macbeth* was raised from a trap. Pantomime shows featured many trap scenes, as did melodramas. Both **John Coleman** (1830–1904), an actor-manager and occasional playwright, and **Henry Neville** (1837–1910), an actor, ran acting studios at the end of their careers. **Hermann Vezin** (1829–1910) was an American-born actor and teacher of elocution; he performed regularly on the London stage from the 1860s through the 1890s. **Mrs** Kate **Behnke and Miss** Kate Emil **Behnke**, the wife and daughter of Emil Behnke (1836–92), used his teaching methods in their voice training courses for public speaking and singing. They published a series of books on voice mechanisms, singing, and stammering. Florenz Ziegfeld (1869–1932), the American entrepreneur of popular entertainment, put Eugen **Sandow** [Friedrich Wilhelm Müller] (1867–1925) on display as a strongman at the Chicago World's Fair (1893). Sandow later developed his Institutes of Physical Culture in London, and in 1901 at Royal Albert Hall he staged the first bodybuilding competition. Old **Crummles** is a travelling actor in Charles Dickens's *Nicholas Nickleby*. Shaw described his plan for a **repertory theatre** in the preface to *Plays Pleasant* (Prefaces 1: 46–7)

90 / To William Archer

Piccards Cottage, Guildford
4th March 1902

[ALS: V&A, GB 71THM/368/4/4/38; CL 2 partial]

*Archer's response to Shaw's letter of 1 and 2 March has not survived. Shaw continued to offer here some of his ideas for a national theatre. Of note, a month later in an article entitled 'The Case for Endowed Theatres' (*Clarion, *11 April 1902), Archer argued that an endowed theatre might be the appropriate place for staging Shaw's* Mrs Warren's Profession. *Although the play had been performed privately by the Stage Society (5, 6 January 1902), it was forbidden from public presentation until 1924. Although the commercial theatre, under the leadership of the West End actor-managers, supported the censorship system of the Lord Chamberlain's Office, Archer envisioned a national theatre that would have open-minded leadership – that is, people of the calibre of those on the Theatrical Reform Committee.*

No: I dont agree about voice production as part of the business of the National Theatre staff. It belongs to the University School; and even there it would probably be a piece of quackery if it were specially taught. All that is needed in the theatre is somebody in the gallery at rehearsal, to say (as Mrs Charles Kean used to say to Ellen Terry) 'I can't hear you,' and somebody in the stalls to say 'Dont bawl like that.' You must be frightfully careful to limit your proposals for a staff of instructors to the differentia of the theatre. Voice production is needed by the whole human race: the theatre might as well teach reading and writing. Stage dancing, pantomime, costume and makeup, are the specialities of the theatre. And there should be a salle d'armes where stage combats & wrestlings could be practiced – a gymnasium, in fact; but this ought not to attempt to supply the place of general physical schools. Above all, do not call these things a 'Dramatic School.' It is allimportant that people should *think* rightly about the subject: at present their ideas are confused. The theatre must not have any taint of the school about it: the stage manager and ballet master should be taken as a matter of course like the carpenter and not promoted to a Chair.

Dont get hold of the idea that a University School of the Arts of Public Life is necessarily a longer way off than a National Theatre. It is probably much closer, as it appeals to a far larger public, and is commercially urgent. And as it is only emerging as a distinct idea, it has the enormous advantage of being new and setting people talking. The fact is, the intelligent, managing, initiative people wont stand the theatre: they will yawn in the face of a Théâtre Anglais; but they will prick up their ears at a big educational scheme. Gladstone did not trouble himself about the theatre; but he studied Charles Kean carefully in training himself as an orator (at least so Miss Glyn told me).

In any case, you must understand that as you will only get a tenth at most of what you ask for, you cannot possibly ask for too much provided your demands are interesting. We got 24/- a week for County Council laborers by strenuously demanding the socialization of land, capital & all the instruments of production & exchange. The only thing your book can do is to make people think & shew precedents to the politician.

Once more, be careful about voiceproduction. The case for putting Mrs. Archer on the staff is really much stronger than the case of putting Mrs. Behnke on it; and the claims of 'Bartitsu' follow irresistibly. As to your damned elocution professors, they might be shunted; but on their ruins comes the phonetician, whose case is the strongest of all. So beware.

GBS

Ellen Terry's career as a child actress began at the Princess's Theatre of **Charles Kean** (1811–68). In 1856 **Mrs Charles Kean** [Ellen Tree] (1806–80) coached nine-year-old Terry in the role of Mamillius, the young price in *The Winter's Tale.* William Ewart **Gladstone** (1809–98), who served as prime minister on four occasions for the Liberals, was famous for his oratory. In 1879 Shaw met the actress Isabella **Glyn** (1823–89) at the home of Lady Jane Wilde (1821–96). **Mrs Archer**, under the influence of Annie Payson Call (1853–1940), developed a physical therapy program that involved exercise techniques to relax the muscles and nerves. She sometimes treated Shaw. **Mrs Behnke** offered sessions in voice training. **Bartitsu,** a martial art of self-defence, was developed and promoted in England between 1899 and 1902 by Edward William Barton-Wright (1861–1951), an engineer. He adapted Jujitsu methods that he had learned when living in Japan. Sir Arthur Conan Doyle (1859–1930), taking up Barton-Wright's ideas, identified, but misnamed, the fighting art of 'baritsu' in a Sherlock Holmes story from 1903, 'The Adventure of the Empty House.'

91 / To William Archer

Piccards Cottage, St Catherine's,
Guildford, Surrey
26th March 1902

[ALS: BL 45296 f 119]

In 1902 Lillie Langtry (1852–1929) and Lewis Waller (1860–1915) appeared together in Mademoiselle Mars. *Written by Paul Kester (1870–1933), this costume drama was staged at the Imperial Theatre (78 perfs.). In his review in* The World *on 29 January 1902, Archer dismisses the play: 'If Scribe had never lived, nor Sardou, nor Mr. Sydney Grundy, Mr. Kester might have been congratulated on the invention of a novel and ingenious method of theatrical story-telling ... As it is, Mr. Kester only gives us the sensation of seeing a thing indifferently done which we have seen well done a hundred times, and which was never very much worth doing. Criticism of detail, in such a case, would be idle.' Of Mrs Langtry he writes that she 'acts with practiced plausibility – the next best thing, no doubt, to real talent.' Shaw had denied* Captain Brassbound *to Archer and the* NCT. *And Ellen Terry was still resisting Shaw's overtures to perform the play (though she would finally play the role of Lady Cicely in 1906). He did not give it to Langtry.*

Mrs Langtry wants to produce Captain Brassbound. Is this at all a possible proposal? I have not seen her act for some years: in fact, except for her old experiment as Rosalind (a part in which it is not possible to fail, nor, in a sense, to succeed) I may say that I have never seen her act at all. Agatha Lylden I forget; and the only other effort of hers I witnessed – it was at the Haymarket, I think – couldnt possibly have been worse. Courtenay Thorpe declares that she is very coachable. The question is whether she can do the things I can coach her in with sufficient charm to carry the play through. I am very loath to throw 'Captain B' away; for I stand just now at a point where a failure would put me quite out of court, and a success would 'cheer me ever.' At the same time it is against my business instincts to refuse the first comer on the chance of doing better with the next.

On the whole, as you have seen Mademoiselle Mars, I should like to know what you think as to her possibilities as Lady Cicely. Let me have a line (to Guildford) by return if you can, as I may have to give a definite answer tomorrow.

GBS

Lillie **Langtry**, daughter of the dean of Jersey, was a great beauty. Her marriage in 1874 to the diplomat Edward Langtry established her as a society woman. In the late 1870s she went on the stage. Throughout the 1880s and 1890s she performed in London and on tour. Then in 1901 she became the manager of the Imperial Theatre, which she renovated. Besides popular melodramas, she produced the medieval *Everyman* and Ben Jonson's *The Alchemist*, both directed by William Poel (1852–1934), who was the leader of the Elizabethan Stage Society. *Agatha Tylden*, not **Agatha Lylden**, was a Haymarket play by Edward Rose (1862–1904), performed in 1892 with Mrs Langtry, Lewis Waller, and Cyril Maude (52 perfs.). The actor **Courteney Thorpe** appeared in several Ibsen productions in the 1890s, including *Little Eyolf* (1896). He also played Marchbanks in the Aberdeen performance of *Candida* (1897). The phrase '**cheer me ever**' is from *Macbeth*, act 5, scene 2. When not in London, the Shaws stayed at Piccards Cottage in **Guildford**, Surrey, from mid-November 1900 to April 1902. In his last sentence Shaw asked for a **definite answer tomorrow** to Guildford. In the days before the arrival of the telephone the mail delivery in England was so dependable that a letter could often be mailed and delivered within a few hours, not only throughout the London metropolitan area but to the surrounding counties, such as Surrey. Despite the war, the Shaws acquired a telephone for Adelphi Terrace in 1915 (see letter of 11 March 1915) and another one for Ayot St Lawrence in 1916 (see letter of 4 February 1916).

92/ To William Archer

Piccards Cottage, Guildford
27th March 1902

[TLS: BL 45296 ff 120–1; CL 2]

Archer apparently responded to the previous letter, but his reply is missing. As Shaw noted, Archer was a steady advocate for the production of Shaw's plays in the West End theatres. For example, in his review of the Stage Society's production of Captain Brassbound's Conversion *in December 1900, Archer had made the case that this play and the three 'pleasant' plays deserved productions by the West End managers (World, 26 December 1900).*

Dear W.A.

For this advice, much thanks. I quite agree with its principles; but in applying them to my case you must bear in mind that I am not suffering from lack of production. Eight of my ten plays have been produced and noticed and so forth; and there is now no question as to my competence and vocation. What remains undecided is the point you have so nobly championed: namely that my 'Pleasant' plays would be commercially and fashionably successful on ordinary West End conditions. Now the decision on this point will turn on what happens the first time such an experiment is tried. If Mrs Langtry made a mess of it, the public might be taken in by a forced run; but the managers would not. They know me well enough now, and are sufficiently tempted by my parts, to be very curious as to how *their* public would take me: in fact, some of them shiver on the brink from time to time until I persuade them to put on their clothes again and wait a bit. That is what I meant by saying that a failure at the Imperial would put me out of court.

I should not countenance the proposal at all without Waller. I gather from what you say that the reputation which I have so carefully cultivated for being an impossibilist at rehearsals has reached and impressed you; but you need not bother about that. I now conduct my own rehearsals; and I never have any trouble. On the contrary, my difficulty is to prevent the performance coming as an anticlimax to the rehearsals. It is possible, of course, that in this matter I may be the dupe of a consummate hypocrisy on the part of my companies: if so, I can only say that I wish they could act as well on stage as off.

As to Thorpe, the quality you mention is by no means lost on my nerves; but he is a clever character actor. As the Judge in Brassbound, which he rehearsed hastily for me when nobody else would touch it, he took me aback by an unrehearsed makeup which was ludicrously wrong, and which shewed me that he had not really got hold of the character at all. But it is he who has made Mrs Langtry read the play. Now suppose she is willing to give him the part. Vezin would be the right man for it; but Vezin was one of those who refused to play it originally. Under these circumstances, as I can correct Thorpe's makeup, and as he is quite clever enough to get hold of the part by the right end when I talk to him about it, I am bound to stand by him. Of course what he would like would be to play Brassbound; and there, if you like, his curious effeminacy would be appalling.

You will see that things are pretty complicated for an author who has to form a party, as it were, to get his plays into action. However, this business may come to nothing; for I have replied to Mrs Langtry not only with strong dissuasion, but with a warning that I cannot promise her exclusive provincial rights, as a provincial actormanager named Harold Nielson has offered to try the play in Manchester for a fortnight with Janet Achurch as Lady Cicely; and this, again, I of course cannot refuse to sanction.

GBS

Lewis **Waller**, a popular and versatile actor, appeared often in costume dramas as the romantic lead. He often acted with the theatre companies of H.B. Tree and Charles Wyndham, and had some success in Shakespeare, including *Henry V* in 1900. But his acting in Wilde's *An Ideal Husband* in 1895 was, according to Archer, 'sufficient without being distinguished' (World 95: 19). Hermann **Vezin** played the role of Fergus Crampton in the Stage Society's 1899 production of Shaw's *You Never Can Tell.* Courtenay **Thorpe** played the role of Sir Howard Hallam in the private Stage Society production of *Captain Brassbound's Conversion* in December 1900 (2 perfs.). **Harold V. Neilson**, not Nielson (1874–1956), was the manager of the Queen's Theatre in Manchester. He staged *Captain Brassbound's Conversion,* with Janet Achurch and Charles Carrington, in May 1902 (6 perfs.). The play was also produced in 1906 by the Vedrenne-Barker management in 1906 (89 perfs.), featuring Ellen Terry as Lady Cecily Waynflete.

93 / To William Archer

10 Adelphi Terrace WC
20th June 1902

[ALS: BL 45296 f 122; CL 2]

Regrettably, Archer's letter in which he commented upon Shaw's draft of the scene entitled 'Don Juan Dream' has not survived. Archer may have also written notes on the pages of the draft. Whatever the case, his remarks apparently convinced Shaw to 'lengthen' the draft. This scene, which Shaw began to create in 1900, would become act 3 in Man and Superman. *But in his reply Shaw was not responding to that lost letter. Instead, he addressed Archer's article 'Mrs Warren, Once Again' (ML, 21 June 1902). Archer had shared the page proofs with Shaw. The publication of a separate edition of* Mrs Warren's Profession *provided yet another opportunity for Archer to voice his reservations yet again about the play, even though he thought it was a masterpiece. In his new preface, 'An Author's Apology,' Shaw quoted Archer's earlier complaint in* 'Mrs Warren's Profession' *(World, 15 January 1902) that Shaw 'cannot touch pitch without wallowing in it.' That January article, in which Archer criticized the scene between Vivie and Frank in act 4, was a review of the private production of the play by the Stage Society on 5 and 6 January.*

Six months later in the Morning Leader *article Archer apologized for the pitch metaphor because it is 'violent and excessive.' He declared, however, that he was not condemning* Mrs Warren's Profession, *but just questioning Shaw's artistic handling of some of the moral issues in the play (and in* The Philanderer*). He explained that he concurred with the play's moral indictment of society. 'I think it cogent, crushing, and at many points admirably dramatic. I do not quarrel with a word in his play that is in any way necessary to the full, frank, and dramatic thrashing-out of the theme.' But Archer felt that the scene between Vivie and Frank was clumsy and that they were forced together because of Shaw's wilfulness. Thus, the issue between them 'cannot possibly be said to present a typical incident in the history of a polyandrous group, and has the air of being dragged in simply for the sake of unpleasantness.' Archer asked: did Shaw realize 'how fatally such a fault of technique, or rather of logic, may mar the general impression produced by a play? Show us that a horror is inevitable, and we admire while we shudder; leave us with the feeling that it is gratuitous, and it is only too probable that weak human nature may "wallow" a little in metaphors of reprobation.'*

Thanks for the Don Juan dream. I am greatly afraid that the process of pulling it straight will lengthen it instead of shortening it; but the rest of the business will be so outrageous that this will be the merest trifle.

I dont approve of your Morning Leader article: you should push your attack home & see what comes of it. The wallowing in pitch phrase was a capital one: I seized on it because it exactly & forcibly expressed the effect produced by the play. What is more, it is justifiable in all the implications from which you shrink out of your reluctance to say anything that sounds personally nasty. A dramatist *must* wallow: the moment he ceases to wallow he ceases to be dramatic. You can see this plainly if you think of him as refusing to wallow in things that are congenial to you. When a conventional author introduces a character supposed to represent one of your own heterodoxies, and makes comic relief of him, or holds him up as a warning, (like the Woman's Rights young lady in Rebellious Susan, for instance) you feel at once that the character is unreal – that the dramatist must take a character from its own point of view, and must actually wallow in that point of view if he is to make that character live. You cannot absolve Shakespear from all complicity with Falstaff: he wallowed in Falstaff, and in Thersites. The elegant remark of Lucio when he meets the lady of the pavement: – 'How now. Which of your hips has the most profound sciaticia?' must have amused Shakespear or he couldnt have written it: he was Lucio when he wrote it. I believe that to people with no sense of humor & strong & refined conscientiousness, there must be something hideous in the derision of 'the comic spirit.' When I wallow in that serious point of view I feel that horror myself. So stick to your guns as to the wallowing: it may be the biggest part of your critical function to challenge the lawfulness of the ecstasy of derisory blackguardism which makes comedy so enormously amusing.

The paragraph about 'inevitable' is all topsyturvy. The customary thing in the polyandrous group is for the Franks & Vivies to be playmates from childhood, or at least acquaintances. My long arm of coincidence, instead of forcing in the dilemma artificially, actually sacrificed its normal inevitability for the sake of the main situation, which made it necessary that by hook or crook Mrs Warren & Vivie should be practically strangers to one another.

But the odd thing to me is that you should so dislike the Frank & Vivie courtship (which does not shock me in the least) and overlook the episode between Mrs Warren & Frank, which is to me the most exquisitely atrocious passage in the play. I know of a real case in which a young man, having very gallantly seduced a lady a good deal his senior, was taken aback by being told contemptuously that he was not half the man his father was. The Dilke case gives you the same thing with the man as the senior of the woman. It is, I believe, quite common in circles of the Mrs Warren type for this twogeneration complication to arise. If you study the housing question & Westermarck & so on, you will see that the way in which Mrs Warren is enveloped in a web of possibilities of incest, Mrs Warren narrowly escaping an affair with the son of her old associate, Crofts wanting to have the daughter as her mother's successor even with a possibility of the daughter being his own, & Frank & Vivie making love to one another, is part of the situation. You really have not sounded the depths of the pitch or appreciated its blackness or you would not dwell on this comparatively rosewatery part of it.

Your final conclusion is right from your comparatively innocent point of view. But if you ever get to mine, you will laugh at many things that now seem very solemn to you; and you will also take some things very seriously that now seem to you to be mere paradoxes. You may observe that though I walk through hell with my bells jingling, I lose my temper a good deal when I walk through heaven. My moral perspective is not wrong from my standpoint. My discords will not annoy you so much when you catch my way of resolving them. Damn it, you cant have my plays *all* your own way.

GBS

Henry Arthur Jones wrote *The Case of* ***Rebellious Susan*** (1894). In *Measure for Measure* it is the First Gentleman, not **Lucio**, who makes the statement about Mistress Overdone, the '**lady of the pavement**' (1, 2). The Victorian novelist and poet George Meredith (1828–1909) wrote the popular essay 'On the Idea of Comedy and the Uses of the **Comic Spirit**' in 1877. The **Dilke case** or scandal of 1886 featured the notorious sexual activities and divorce case of Sir Charles Wentworth Dilke (1843–1911), the Liberal Member of Parliament from Chelsea. He was accused of not only carrying on an affair with a married woman but also seducing the woman's daughter. Two trials followed, the second of which proved devasting for him. The investigative journalism of W.T. Stead led to Dilke's downfall and the loss of his seat in Parliament. Edward **Westermarck** (1862–1939), a Finnish anthropologist, wrote *History of Human Marriage* in 1891.

94 / To William Archer Overstrand Hotel, Cromer, Norfolk
12th January 1903

[ALS: BL 45296 ff 123–4; CL 2]

In November 1901 Siegfried Trebitsch (1869–1956), an Austrian writer, visited Archer, whose criticism he admired. Archer urged him to read Shaw's plays. Upon his trip home Trebitsch began reading Plays Pleasant and Unpleasant *and* Three Plays for Puritans. *In March 1902 he appeared at the door of 10 Adelphi Terrace, with an introduction from Archer. He offered to translate Shaw's plays into German. Shaw agreed. Starting with* Candida, Arms and the Man, *and* The Devil's Disciple, *Trebitsch became Shaw's translator and theatrical agent in Austria and Germany. In December 1902 Trebitsch published* Drei Dramen von Bernard Shaw. *(For the accounts of these meetings see Samuel A. Weiss's introduction in* Bernard Shaw's Letters to Siegfried Trebitsch*: 3–7.) Trebitsch's first name surely charmed the author of* The Perfect Wagnerite *(1898).*

On 29 December 1901, the Danish critic and literary historian Georg Brandes (born Morris Cohen), who was best known for his masterful Main Currents of Nineteenth Century Literature *(1872–90, 6 vols), published 'Bernard Shaw's Teater' in* Politiken, *a Copenhagen newspaper that he and his brother Edvard founded in Copenhagen. Its motto was 'The paper of Greater Enlightenment.' In his review of Trebitsch's translations Brandes identified Shaw as 'the most original dramatist in the British Empire of to-day.' Each of the three plays, he insisted, has its own distinct style. Two weeks later, on 10 January 1903, Archer's 'The Two Georges' appeared in the* Morning Leader. *Archer knew and admired Brandes, and in fact in 1899 had published translations of Brandes's* William Shakespeare: A Critical Study *and* Henrik Ibsen, Björnstjerne Björnson: Critical Studies. *Archer opened his review with a lament over the 'monstrous and almost incredible anomaly' that West End theatre managers had failed to stage Shaw's plays. He described Brandes's positive assessment of Shaw's plays, including his claim that* The Devil's Disciple *was a masterpiece of historical drama. But Archer rejected Brandes's praise for Shaw's ability to create various types of characters: male and female, American, English, and Bulgarian. 'Dr. Brandes seems to be unconscious of the intense personal peculiarity, whimsicality, mannerism, that runs through all Mr. Shaw's work, and sometimes gets between us and the high qualities which the critic quite justly discerns.'*

Nine days later Shaw wrote to Trebitsch: 'Do not be anxious about Archer's astonishment that Brandes does not appreciate my Shawishness. Archer knows me so well personally that he cannot understand how anybody can read my books without seeing that it is "only Shaw talking," and not literature' (Trebitsch: 37).

I think you might draw the moral of your Two Georges article more definitely in favor of an endowed theatre. At present Trebitsch (whose translations, apart from the mere mistakes, which are mighty ones and millions, are so good that I prefer them in many respects to the originals) has a contract with money down for The Devil's Disciple at the Raiemund Theatre in Vienna, and is negotiating with the Hamburg theatre & the Deutsches (Berlin) for 'Helden' (alias Arms & The Man). The Burg Theatre also flatters him with hopes for Candida, with Kainz as the rolypoly poet. That august institution the German Theatre in London (meaning Grein & Miss Halstan's father) is presently to produce Der Schlachtenlenker, ci devant Man of Destiny. All this, thin as it is, intoxicates Trebitsch with dreams of glory, and enables him to survive my unbounded comments on his translations without any worse consequences than six weeks in a Nerven Anstalt. You should see the metaphysics he has elaborated for Burgess in Candida because the poor old man exclaims 'Blame me if it didnt come into my head once or twyst that he must be off his chump.' 'Tadeln Sie mich &c &c &c.'

However, though it may all come to nothing, it is worth pointing out that our London system does cut off masterpieces which are eagerly sought after from Aberdeen to Cracow (my present limits) in the old world. Given theatres of the German type in England and my difficulties would be over at once. The managers are not hostile: they cant afford to be hostile. The interests at stake are too pressing to allow of much indulgence of personal feeling. If I would play their game tomorrow thoroughly they would jump at me, just as they have to put up with the autocracy of Pinero & Sardou & the empfindlichkeit of H.A.J., all of whom treat them in an unspeakable manner.

But the difficulties are very great. The only play I have myself blocked is Candida. I wrote that long ago as a sort of consolation prize for Janet Achurch for the Doll's House; and under the circumstances it would have been rather mean to hand it over to anybody else. But for that it would have been played. Mrs. Pat Campbell & others inquired about it; but I hold out so that Janet should create the part in London. By that time, though she played certain bits of it – for instance, the scene with Morell in the second act – as nobody else could have done, yet she had grown out of the part. She has plenty of strength, and is beyond all the others in lucidity when there is intellectual tissue to be dissected; but Candida wants patience, tenderness & sweetness of a much more mawkish brand than Janet can supply, clever as she is. When she played it I considered the bargain off; and now Candida is free as air.

I have stopped two productions of The Devil's Disciple – or rather three, because it was impossible to cast it successfully. I refused to let Miss Granville produce it with Waring. Waring would have done it on his own account if he had been able to finance it himself; but Miss G. naturally would not pay without playing, and I told her she would not succeed in it & that she must not throw away her money on it. I have stopped Forbes Robertson twice. The first time the conditions (at his short, late season at the Comedy) were positively exclusive of success or of its complete exploitation if, by a miracle, it occurred. The second time was the other day, as a stopgap before Othello. I told him he would have to put Lena Ashwell into the part his wife took in the provinces, because Lena has an unrivalled power of appealing to *pity*, which is exactly what Judith must do ('Mitleid' – patented by Parsifal – being the key to Richard) whereas Gertrude Elliott is absolutely incapable of arousing pity: she is indignant when she should be horrified, and playful when she should be childishly helpless. Her character is too positive. Well, I put it to Forbes whether he had not better follow up Mice & Men with a play which had a good part for her, instead of changing his leading lady in the face of the public. I suggested Much Ado as good business for both of them, as it would come in on tour as a Shakespearian repertory play even if it was not a great success on the spot. You Never Can Tell broke down purely over the cast: I did not withdraw it until I made Frederick Harrison attend a rehearsal & admit that the end of the second act was impossible for Aynesworth. So that as the superficial facts stand, it is the regular theatres that are unable to cast my plays, whereas the Independent Theatres can always make some sort of shift with them.

Of course these difficulties are really created partly by the illiterateness of the managers. The proposals they make are proposals to fool with my plays: there is generally an idea at the back of their minds that if they could get complete control of one of my plays they could adapt it as Daly adapted Shakespear. Frohman actually sounded me as to rewriting You Never Can Tell under his direction; but the ecstatic delight with which I embraced the suggestion struck terror into his soul, and the proposed interviews never came off. Still, the fact remains that when it comes to the point of a concrete proposal, neither you nor I could conscientiously recommend the manager to go on with it. For example, Alexander wanted to play Brassbound. Well, what could I say to him? I told him that it was a woman's play, and that he would have to get somebody like Ada Rehan or Ellen Terry, who would reap all the personal success. I also told him that Brassbound was a part that half a dozen melodramatic young Terrises in the provinces could play as well or better than he could, whereas his own special qualities would not shew at all, or if they did so much the worse. Naturally he did not pursue the project. I also refused to let him have the Man of Destiny unless he played Napoleon himself, unless of course he gave me H.B. Irving, in which case I pointed out that he would be definitely relinquishing the lead at his own theatre. This system of telling our actormanagers the exact truth is not always delightful to them; but it has the advantage that the proposals they make are dealt with on their merits and do not fall through because of irrelevant personal squabbles. They would much rather, perhaps, be promised gold mines by an eager and infatuated poetaster; and it spreads unspeakable terror; but still it is the only possible course for me or for any author who writes at a certain level and is serious about it.

I note that you are still fundamentally amazed at the fact that a man whom you know, and whose voice you can hear in every line of his books, can appear to any sane person as a real author. This is really an enfantillage. That intense peculiarity which you cannot get away from, and which you are amazed to find not affecting Brandes as it affects you, is simply my style. I have to have a style like anybody else: I cant help it. Ben Jonson never could quite get over the absurdity of the Shakespearisms which he knew so well at the Mermaid passing off in cold ink as literature; and – though Lord forbid I should compare you to so dull a dog as Ben! – to the end of your life you will remonstrate with Europe for not distinguishing between mere Shawism & real serious proper impersonal judicial drama.

Brandes is of course quite right about my genius for differentiating nations. You do not appreciate my extraordinarily happy command of classes & grades of civilization. You think Brandes has been taken in by a mirage. You are wrong: no doubt the thing is a mirage in the sense in which every picture, play or statue is a mirage; but if you consider that the one overwhelming characteristic of my plays is the friction between people on different planes of thought, of character, of civilization & of class prejudice (the overwhelming characteristic of the ordinary PineroJonesGrundy play being that all the characters are on exactly the same planes in these respects, and the friction is purely external & artificial) you will see – or you would if you would take the trouble to criticize literature instead of amusing yourself with it – that these contrasts of which Brandes speaks are just the ones that interest me and are handled by me with the greatest care. My Bulgarians are wonderfully well done considering how restricted my sources of information were; and there is an American in my new play who is a masterpiece.

GBS

The Devil's Disciple was the first Shaw production on the German-language stage; it occurred at the Raimund, not **Raiemund**, Theater in Vienna, 25 February 1903 (see playbill in Trebitsch: 45). Josef ***Kainz*** (1858–1910), an esteemed Austrian actor of Hungarian birth, performed in Austria and Germany, and toured in the United States. He was praised as a great Hamlet, and played a wide range of roles in Shakespeare, Molière, Schiller, Hugo, and Grillparzer. He also appeared in the contemporary plays of Ibsen and Rostand. H.A. Hertz, founder and financier of the **German Theatre in London**, planned to stage ***Der***

Schlachtenlenker, the German version of *The Man of Destiny*, in London during January 1903, but the production was cancelled (Trebitsch: 26, 37). Hertz was a member of the executive committee of the Stage Society. His daughter Margaret **Halstan** (1879–1967) acted in the 1899 production of *You Never Can Tell*, and played the Strange Lady in the single matinee of *The Man of Destiny* (29 March 1901); H. Granville Barker played Napoleon and directed. Shaw was of two minds about the German title for *The Man of Destiny*, *Der Schlachtenlenker* [*Ruler of Battles*], that Trebitsch offered (Trebitsch 26, 34–6). A **Nerven Anstalt** is a nerve institution. In his dealings with London theatre managers, the playwright H.A. Jones suffered from **empfindlichkeit**, a case of being overly sensitive, touchy, and thin-skinned. Charlotte **Granville** (1863–?) performed regularly, usually in secondary roles, with George Alexander and other actor-managers. Herbert **Waring** portrayed Helmer in *A Doll's House* (1889) and Solness in *The Master Builder* (1893). For several decades he performed leading roles in West End productions. **Lena Ashwell**, later Lady Simson, gained fame in *Mrs Dane's Defence* (1900). Shaw admired her acting and valued her friendship. Between 1907 and 1915 she managed her own company at the Kingsway Theatre. In 1910 she played the role of Lina Szczepanowska in *Misalliance*. Johnston Forbes-Robertson staged ***Mice and Men*** by Madeleine Lucette Ryley (1865–1934) at the Lyric Theatre (opened 27/1/02; 365 perfs.). He and his wife **Gertrude Elliott** (1874–1950) played the leading roles. An American, Elliott had married Forbes-Robertson in December 1900. In a letter to her in June 1903, Shaw proclaimed that she should not play Judith in *The Devil's Disciple* because she lacked 'the quality that excites pity: to wit, weakness' (CL 2: 330). By contrast Lena Ashwell could deliver this quality, **Mitleid** – that is, the kind of compassion and sympathy that is achieved by the character of Parsifal in Wagner's opera. In *The Devil's Disciple* the character of Richard Dudgeon requires this quality from the character of Judith Anderson. Frederick **Harrison** (1853–1926) was the manager of the Haymarket Theatre, in partnership with the actor-manager Cyril Maude (1862–1951). For more details on Shaw's withdraw of *You Never Can Tell* in 1897, see his letter of 7 September 1903. Allan **Aynesworth** (1865–1959) was a journeyman actor in London. (Shaw expanded on this Haymarket anecdote in the letters of 7 September 1903 and 14 December 1924.) Between 1893 and 1895 Aynesworth he was a member of the company of Augustin **Daly**, the American manager and playwright whose core performers included John Drew (1853–1927) and Ada **Rehan**. Daly's Theatre, built by George Edwardes, opened in London in 1893. Both Shaw and Archer criticized Daly's cuttings of Shakespeare's plays, but they praised Rehan's performances (e.g., in *The Taming of the Shrew* in 1893). There may have been half a dozen young Terrisses, not **Terrises**, who acted in the melodramatic style of William Terriss, who was murdered in 1897, but Shaw does not bother to describe this style of acting. After attending Oxford University and participating in the Oxford University Dramatic Society, **Henry Brodribb Irving** (1870–1919), the eldest son of Sir Henry Irving, performed with George Alexander and other actor-managers. He became a popular actor-manager, appearing in Shakespeare and revivals of several of the history plays that his father had staged. Charles **Frohman** (1860–1915) was an American producer who transferred popular London productions, such as George Edwardes's musicals, to the United States. In 1905 he leased the Duke of York's, where he staged *Peter Pan* by James Barrie (1860–1937). Then in 1910 he established a short-lived repertory company at the Duke of York's, featuring plays by Shaw, Barrie, Barker, and John Galsworthy (1866–1933). He also presented *Chains* by Elizabeth Baker (1876–1962). Frohman drowned in 1915 when the *Lusitania* was torpedoed. Mr Malone is the **American** in *Man and Superman*.

95 / To William Archer

10 Adelphi Terrace WC
23rd February 1903

[APCS: BL 45296 f 126; CL 2]

In a letter on 1 March Shaw apologized to his German translator Siegfried Trebitsch for telling Archer and Golding Bright about the censorship imposed upon Arms and the Man *in Austria. Bright published the news in the* Daily Express, *along with an interview with Shaw, who talked up the 'Shaw boom' in Germany and Austria. To Trebitsch, Shaw wrote: 'I had no idea that there was any secrecy about the action of the censorship. When you first told me of it I mentioned it to Archer and to another journalist. This other man promptly published it (I meant him to), and the enclosed cuttings are the result. I hope no harm will come of my indiscretion' (Trebitsch: 44).*

I have to inform you triumphantly that in view of the political disturbances in the Balkan states, the Austrian Censorship forbids the Burg Theatre to produce Arms & The Man at present.

This tribute to the political actuality and ethnographical verisimilitude of my play will, I hope, be a warning to you not to disparage my historical researches in future.

GBS

96 / To William Archer

Grand Hôtel, Brufani, Perugia (Italy)
15th April 1903

[APCS: BL 56296 f 127]

Edward Gordon Craig designed and staged Ibsen's The Vikings at Helgeland *at the Imperial Theatre (15 April 1903, 30 perfs.). Edith Craig prepared the costumes. Archer provided a revised translation. Mrs Langtry leased the theatre to Ellen Terry, who produced the play for her son. In order to attract an audience she agreed to play the role of Hjördis. Archer, who a decade earlier had encouraged Janet Achurch to play Hjördis (24 November 1893; CUL), felt that Terry was quite inappropriate for the role. But he praised most of the acting and costuming. And though he criticized the 'murky blue haze' and the 'atmosphere of strained & fantastic mysticism,' he stated that Craig 'deserves credit for some novel & really ingenious effects of lighting, shadow, and colour.' Overall Craig 'has done his work well' (World, 21 April 1903).*

Between 10 April and 4 May the Shaws toured in Italy: Parma, Perugia, Assisi, Orvieto, Siena, Genoa, and Milan. They returned in time to see the Ibsen production on 14 May. In his letter to Ellen Terry (15 May 1903: CL 2: 323–6), Shaw criticized the costume that Edy Craig had designed for her mother, but he reserved most of his criticism for the lighting effects by her brother. 'If Master Teddy wants to use plays as stalking horses for his clever effects, let him write them himself ... You cannot run a theatre on moonlight.' Craig should 'become an impressionist painter and paint nocturnes; for there is no career for him on the stage.' Shaw granted that Craig possessed a visual imagination, but that talent was imposed onto Ibsen's play. 'If he did that to a play of mine, I would sacrifice him on the prompter's table before his mother's eyes' (325).

This letter is missing from Ellen Terry and Bernard Shaw: A Correspondence *(1931/2). Shaw withheld some letters that discussed living people, especially Gordon Craig. Christopher St John, the editor, offered no specific explanation for this missing letter, but she noted that Craig defended his production in his book on Henry Irving (1930: 144–51). Besides offering an attack on GBS and* The Man of Destiny, *Craig provided a paragraph on* The Vikings. *Quoting selectively from Shaw's letter to his mother, he demonstrated that it was Shaw, not Craig, who misrepresented Ibsen's stage directions (151). Over the years Craig and Shaw continued to have a long, troubled history of discord that culminated with the fight over the publication of the Terry/Shaw letters (1931). See also Craig's* Ellen Terry and Her Secret Self *(1931) and its attached* Envoy *of twenty-nine pages entitled 'A Plea for G.B.S.' (On these publications and personal battles see Holroyd 3: 182–7.)*

I am curious – partly for business reasons – as to the prospects of The Vikings at the Imperial. Will you drop me a card to this address to say whether, as far as you can guess, it will run. If it does, you ought to translate the Feast at Solhang to follow it.

G. Bernard Shaw

Ibsen wrote ***The Vikings*** *in Helgeland* in 1857. Archer's initial translation appeared in volume 3 of *Ibsen's Prose Drama* in 1890. Ibsen wrote *The Feast at Solhoug,* not **Solhang**, in 1855 and revised it in 1883. Archer's revised translations of all plays appeared in *The Works of Henrik Ibsen,* 12 vols (London, 1906–8).

97 / To William Archer Strachur, Argyllshire (Scotland)
27th August 1903

[ALS: BL 45296 ff 128–9; CL 2]

In an article entitled 'Mr. Shaw and Mr. Pinero' (ML, 22 August 1903), Archer lodged a complaint about the series of negative critiques that Shaw wrote about British drama for the Saturday Review. *Shaw tried to 'discredit, crush, and stamp out the new movement,' especially the plays of Pinero. In a letter to the* ML *editor (28 August), Shaw rejected Archer's complaint. But instead of mounting an argument against Archer, Shaw stated, 'I will remonstrate with him privately,' as he did in this letter. Writing from Scotland, Shaw addressed this letter to Archer, living in 'L'Inghilterra.' In this compressed history of their joint campaign for the new drama, Shaw transforms Archer's 'New Movement' into Shaw's version of a 'Grand School' of modern thought.*

Saul, Saul: why persecutest thou me? What do you mean by this conduct in the Morning Leader? I warned you that I was going to make such a blinding brain display as has not occurred in the British drama since Shakespear's advent – and to make it for your sake, too, to give you a decent asset to put in the window of that shop which you are so heroically trying to save from its manifest intellectual bankruptcy – and yet you go and lose your head – your buffle head – because your poor nurslings cannot live up to me, and thoughtlessly force A.W.P's neat little perambulator right across my motor car when I am going 80 miles an hour. Nobody would have thought of his venerable Paula anymore than of Audrey Lesden (Jones doesnt really deserve this; but I sacrifice him to propitiate you) or the New Magdalene or the Lady of the Camellias or Iris or any other version of the old formula: I tell you that these things cease to exist on the plane to which I lift my readers.

Just think of your dates a little. You started dramatic-critic in 1876, before Pinero & Jones were born (playwrightfully) & when Grundy was complaining of a 'ring.' I began in 1895, when P. J. & G were absolute masters of the commercial situation. Well, we did them handsome: you, having nursed Pinero as a son & Jones as a stepson, continued the treatment; and I backed you, except that I gave J a turn as son & P. as stepson – and even that was due to the outrageous way you were spoiling him by – but see Max's excellent picture of the situation. I was unkind about Mrs Ebbsmith pulling the Holy Bible out of the stove & [George]

Alexander sitting on the drawingroom table with a paper foolscap on his head; but what would you have had me say? did I not damn myself almost by my praises of [Pinero's] Trelawny & the Benefit of the Doubt & the revived Hobbyhorse? Did I not retire in time to save myself from absolutely killing & burying the author of Iris, who would have never done it if you had not lured him to his doom by your flatteries? But the point is that what you call the New Movement – meaning the substitution of Pinero for Robertson, Grundy for Albery, Farnie & Reece, Jones for Boucicault, & Cecil Raleigh for Pettitt, with Charles Reade & Wilkie Collins still awaiting their successor in Barrie – was no more a New Movement in 1895 than the Robertson movement was new in 1889, though Clement Scott still thought it so. It did not need any bottle feeding then; and your refusal to wean it – due probably to a strain of Esquimaux blood in you – was becoming an open scandal.

In any case, what had I to do with 'New Movements'? My business is to fight for the Grand School – the people who are building up the intellectual consciousness of the race. My men are Wagner, Ibsen, Tolstoy, Schopenhauer, Nietzsche, who have, as you know, nobody to fight for them, especially since you have, with pathetic selfabnegation (I am really serious) constituted yourself commercial traveller to our West End Theatre because your overgrown nursling cries for Praise, Praise, Praise. I have also to keep my good words for such neglected things as Barker's Ann Leete, by far the finest bit of literature since Stephenson's Prince Otto, and of a much more original quality of excellence too. To imply, as you do, that the dreadful leadingarticle clichés which serve for 'literary' dialogue in Iris is the work of a master & a leader, whilst Ann Leete is not worth noticing, is to commit a crime for which you ought to be condemned to sit out a Pinero Festival. Can you not let the man sit safely on his little throne with his well filled treasury, and turn the limelight on his good deeds, and not on his follies, instead of forcing him into a position which he knows he cannot hold or defend? He is a sensitive man: you can hear the nerve quiver in his plays at times if you listen; and you are just torturing him by dragging him into *my* arena.

I find this country quite native to me: my descent from Macduff was at once admitted by the cook, who belongs to the elder branch herself.

In haste – yrs ever
G.B.S.

In Acts 9:4 the voice of Jesus addressed Saul (later named Paul), who was on the road to Damascus: '**Saul, Saul, why do you persecute me?**' Saul fell to the road, blinded by the flash of light from heaven. His conversion appears in Acts 9:1–31. The **blinding brain display** was *Man and Superman.* In the Epistle to the play Shaw discussed the 'new movement' in drama. **Audrey** [i.e., Audrie] **Lesden** is a character in Henry Arthur Jones's *Michael and His Lost Angel* (1896). Mrs Patrick Campbell withdrew from the role before the premiere, in part because the character is a temptress who commits adultery with a priest, yet continues to seek him out, even after he confesses his sin before his congregation. Wilkie Collins (1824–89) adapted his novel ***The New Magdalene*** for the stage in 1873, with Ada Cavendish (1839–95) in the role of Mercy Merick. In 1875, while still living in Ireland, Shaw saw the touring show, falling 'wildly, madly, suicidally in love' with her (CL 1: 11). Alexandre Dumas fils wrote ***La dame aux Camélias*** (1852). A.W. Pinero's ***Iris*** was staged in 1901. Both Shaw and Archer wrote sharply negative reviews of Sydney Grundy's *Slaves of the Ring* (1895), which represented couples unfairly imprisoned by the wedding **ring** because of marriage laws. **Max's excellent picture** refers to Max Beerbohm's satiric drawing 'A Touching Coronation Scene – Mr. W. Archer and Mr. A. W. Pinero,' which represented Pinero being crowned with a wreath by Archer. In December 1901 the drawing was featured in Beerbohm's one-man show at the Carfax Gallery. In a letter to Beerbohm on 17 December, Shaw commented on the drawing, which Charlotte Shaw had bought (CL 2: 247–9). In his catalogue of playwrights, Shaw named T.W. **Robertson**, author of *Society* (1865), *Ours* (1866), and *Caste* (1867); James **Albery** (1838–89), author of *The Two Roses* (1870); Henry B. **Farnie** (d. 1889), author and adapter of light operas; Robert **Reece** (1839–91), writer of burlesques and domestic dramas; Dionysus **Boucicault**, a master of melodrama, including *The Octoroon* (1859), *The Colleen Bawn* (1860), and *The Shaughraun* (1875); Cecil **Raleigh** (1856–1914), writer and co-writer of Drury Lane melodramas; Henry **Pettitt** (1848–93), writer and collaborator of popular dramas; and Charles **Reade**, novelist and dramatist, including *Masks and Faces* (1852), *The Lyons Mail* (1854), and *It's Never Too Late to Mend* (1854). The Scottish novelist and playwright Sir James M. **Barrie** established himself with *The Little Minister* (1897), followed by *Quality Street* and *The Admirable Crichton,* both in 1902. His fame grew for two decades, from *Peter Pan* (1904) to *Dear Brutus* (1917) and *Mary Rose* (1920). He would join Archer and Shaw in the campaigns against censorship. The Stage Society's production of H. Granville Barker's *The Marrying of* ***Anne Leete*** had two performances at the Royalty (26 and 27 January 1902). In 1885 Robert Louis Stevenson, not **Stephenson**, published ***Prince Otto****: A Romance.*

98 / To G. Bernard Shaw

National Liberal Club SW
1st September 1903

[ALS: BL 50528 ff 47–54]

The catalyst for this heated, nine-page letter was not only Shaw's letter of 27 August but also the newly published Man and Superman. *In his review, 'Mr. Shaw's Pom-Pom' (DC, 24 August 1903), Archer explained that 'Mr. Shaw's type-writer is the pom-pom of the literary battlefield.' His play and its sections – including the Epistle Dedicatory, the Revolutionist's Handbook, and Maxims for Revolutionist – 'crackle with wit and tingle with cerebral activity.' The book 'swarms with quips' in Shaw's 'best manner.' But Shaw has failed to match and build upon 'the representation of life' that he had begun to develop in the earlier plays, including* Candida *and* Mrs Warren's Profession. *Struggling to define the play's form, Archer called it a 'symbolic extravaganza,' a 'morality in four acts and a dream,' and an 'allegorical farce.' Whatever its genre, the play is 'primitive in invention, second-rate in execution.' Most of the characters are just 'colourable variations of Mr. Shaw's stock types.' Consequently, Shaw is in danger of parodying himself.*

In this assessment of Man and Superman *Archer was likely constrained by his own categorical imperatives for realistic drama. Yet he shared the judgment of Elizabeth Robins and other independent women who rejected Shaw's Life-Force doctrine, which represented Ann Whitefield as 'Nature's blind and ruthless instrument, inexorably bent on fulfilling herself in motherhood.' Archer rejected this idea of a woman 'tracking down her victim' to the ends of the earth. It represented a reductive, insulting allegory about 'the wiles of women.' Likewise, Shaw's idea of a Superman, derived partially from Nietzsche, may offer a 'whimsical' and ironic reversal of the Don Juan legend, but Shaw's 'logic of allegory' also provided a crude and primitive version of masculine and feminine identities. 'Simplification and exaggeration are the law of allegory.'*

In contrast to Archer's judgment, Beatrice Webb expressed great satisfaction when Shaw read the play to the Webbs over three evenings. She was 'genuinely delighted at his choice of subject,' as she wrote in her diary for 16 January 1903. 'To me it seems a great work, quite the biggest thing he has done. He has found his form, *a play which is not a play but only a combination of essay treaties, interlude, lyric – all the different forms illustrating the same central idea, like a sonata manifests a scheme of melody and harmony.' She felt that she and Sidney 'cannot touch the subject of human breeding,' but 'GBS's audacious genius can reach out to it' (Webb 2: 267).*

My dear Shaw

I wish you had read my notice of 'Man & Superman' before you wrote, & had given me all the vials of your wrath at once; but ever since I read that Nietzschean motorcar, I have had vials of remonstrance simmering within me which the possession of your address causes to boil over. Let us put aside Pinero – I know as well as you do that he hasn't enough intelligence, or rather enough education, to do full justice to his quite extraordinary talent. In that respect he is like Shakespeare & Dickens & Thackeray, & a good many other worthy people. Somehow in England creative genius tends to be divorced from speculative intelligence. But in a man whose business *is* to create, I prefer genius to intelligence; and any way, as regards the English stage, beggars mustn't be choosers. Nor is it your treatment of Pinero alone that seemed to me disastrous in your critical campaign. I referred mainly to him, because the type play you had in mind was evidently 'Mrs Tanqueray.'

But I don't care one tenth part about your treatment of Pinero than I do about your treatment of yourself. You are not doing yourself justice or anything like it. I don't mean merely as a dramatist – I mean that in no way are you making the mark either upon literature or upon life, that you have it in you to make. The years are slipping away – I have painful reason to know, to a few months, how old you are – and you have done nothing really big, nothing original, solid, first rate, enduring. If you were to die tomorrow, what would happen? In the history of literature you would find a threeline mention – like that we now give to Peacock or Beddoes as an eccentric writer, hard to classify, whose writings a few people still remember with pleasure. I think it highly probable that for thirtyyears or so Shaw Societies would spring up from time to time, especially in Boston – and I can't imagine a more doleful way of going to oblivion. In political history you would be still more briefly dismissed as perhaps the most brilliant & futile of the brilliant and futile group of Fabians. If you are content with this, good & well; but I am not content for you. You are a great force wasted; & I am Scotchman enough to detest waste. If I had half your talent it would go hard but I would make a mark in the world. If I had even your leisure, I would contrive to do something worth doing. But you, with all your talent & all your leisure, are doing nothing but 'abounding in your own sense' to the mingled entertainment & exasperation of the few hundred or few thousand people in England & America that have a taste for literary oddities. The great world goes on its way unconscious, or at most with a shrug & a smile. You are one of the little notabilities of the time whom the halfpenny paper reporters know that they can rely on for a comic interview. Great heavens, man! is *that* all you were made for!

You say '*your* men are Wagner, Ibsen, Tolstoy, Schopenhauer, Nietzsche' – I should reverse it & say you are *their* man. Why should this be? Why should you always be flying somebody else's banner, and shouting somebody else's warcry, with only the addition of your own Irish accent? I have always said, & I now say it more emphatically than ever, that your great intellectual foible is credulity. The moment someone comes along with a nostrum, you seize upon it as the last word of human wisdom. Here is Nietzsche with his Superman, for instance – a brilliant piece of philosophic mythology, giving definiteness & tangibility, so to speak, to a more or less unformed ideal that has been hovering in the air ever since 'The Origin of Species' was published – but, after all, only a piece of transitory jargon, the catchword of a decade or halfcentury, which will 'have its day & cease to be' very likely in our own time. Well, you seize upon this concept, & you rethink your whole mental system in the light of it, and produce your 'Revolutionist's Handbook' and Aphorisms – a glittering jumble of untested, unweeded, unharmonized thought, devoid of perspective or proportion, the old humanitarianism cropping out every here & there through the new Nietzscheism, a good deal that is really profound in it, a good deal that is hasty & superficial, and not a little that is merely personal, crotchetty, Shawesque – in short, a philosophical treatise composed in a hopelessly unphilosophical spirit – and treating, I repeat, a new nostrum, a new piece of jargon, as though it were the 'Open Sesame' of all light & truth. Nietzsche is all very well, & so are Wagner and Ibsen – and they come out very quaint & entertaining when refracted in the Shaw medium – but what I want to see you do (as the drillsergeants say) is to go beyond Nietzsche, Wagner and Ibsen, and especially beyond Shaw, and carry thought a step further towards clarity, towards permanence, towards dynamic efficiency, in a book or books that shall attract & influence all the great intelligences, instead of making some passing chatter among the amateurs of oddity.

I don't mean to say that I despair of you as a dramatist; but I am bound to confess that 'Man & Superman' rather dashes my hopes. I think, with all your extraordinary talent, you want a measure of mental discipline before you can produce a real work of art, which it is rather late to think of your attaining. I don't despair, but I am not sanguine. On the other hand, I believe that you want only a little additional patience & power of selfsuppression to carry you very far in political & philosophic work. You do not essentially belong (with Meredith, Browning and Whitman) to the race of the mere selfpleasers. When I used to go to your lectures in the old days, I used specially to admire your power of answering objections – not flattering the hecklers as the unskillful do, but really placing yourself at their point of view, & understanding & meeting their difficulties. Now *that*, on a longer scale, is just what you now want. You have, to my thinking, almost unequalled powers of exposition. The way you used to make the technicalities of music fascinating was, & is, a marvel to me. Very likely, if I had been a musician, your musical criticism would have enraged me as your dramatic criticism did; but that doesn't alter the fact that your power of exposition was masterly. It is evident, then, that you *can* adapt yourself to your audience – and that, in expository & persuasive writing, is the indispensable secret of success. Of course it involves a good deal of selfrepression; but I am sure you have the power, if you only had the will. Of late you have become a slave to your own talents – master them again (as you could, at a pinch, fifteen years ago) and, with your additional thought & experience, you will put my carping to shame. Heaven knows I envy you your wit – but I wouldn't have it as a gift if I had to accept along with it your (frequent) inability to refrain from being witty. So, too, with your power of startling people & making them sit up. Startling is useful in its way – it is one element in the power of persuasion – but when you startle all the time you cease to startle. That's a piece of wisdom as old as Aesop; but it's as true as anything in Nietzsche.

I know you will poohpooh all this, & I daresay I am mistaken in many details; but some of what I say is certainly right & may, in spite of yourself, sink in. Just for the fun of the thing, clear your mind of all 'flattering unctions,' humorous or serious, and ask yourself soberly '*Are* you satisfied with your position or your work in the world? *Have* you done, and are you in the way of doing, all your powers entitle you to do?' If you can sincerely answer in the affirmative, then all I can say is your own ambition is much lower than my ambition for you. You once said, with some justice, that I was 'incurably modest on my friends' behalf'; but now the tables are turned & it is you that are modest & I overweening. On the other hand; if you *can't* answer in the affirmative, I am sure you are too sane to take refuge in the delusion of the halfbaked genius, and blame the stupidity of the world, and imagine a conspiracy of inappreciation. If you have been, not a tocsin, but a tinkling cymbal in the world's ear, the fault is in yourself. I don't say you have it in you to be a great leader of men – I think you have too much humor for that – but you certainly have it in you to be more than a vivacious vestryman. If you would only think patiently, do your best to eliminate the personal equation, clear your mind of theories of human nature which, if not absolutely a priori, are founded mainly in a study of your uncles & aunts – an inadequate basis for an instruction – if you would do this, & then express your thought with the consummate artistry you have somewhere in you (overlaid for the moment by the selfpleasing habit) you would take us a long way beyond quintessences of Ibsen, Wagner, or Nietzsche, however brilliant and amusing. What we want is your own thought, your true thought, your inmost thought, sincerely, patiently, persuasively expressed, – not a freakish echoing of thoughts 'made in Germany.'

Remember me kindly to Mrs Shaw, if she *can* remember me at all kindly, & believe me.

Yours ever
W.A.

I never got off such a sermon in my life before.

Thomas Love **Peacock** (1785–1866), a novelist and poet, was best known for his satiric wit. He wrote *Nightmare Abbey* (1818), which features surrogates for Coleridge, Byron, and Shelley. He maintained a close friendship with Shelley. Thomas Lovell **Beddoes** (1803–49), a minor English playwright, spent much of his short life in Germany, supporting revolutionary movements. He committed suicide in 1849. Archer worried that by taking up **Nietzsche with his Superman**, Shaw was just 'shouting somebody else's warcry.' But Shaw never claimed to be a disciple of Nietzsche or Schopenhauer. In a letter of 5 September 1905 to Archibald Henderson (1877–1963), Shaw stated that he had read only a limited number of translations: 'The truth is I am rather an imposter as a pundit in the philosophy of Schopenhauer & Nietzsche … There is a fashion now of referring my philosophy to Schopenhauer and Nietzsche, partly because, to people without philosophy, all philosophies seem the same, and partly because I have often referred to them to remind my readers that what they call my individual eccentricities and paradoxes are part of the common European stock' (BL 50564 ff 63–6).

99 / To William Archer

Strachur, Argyllshire [Scotland]
2nd September 1903

[ALS: BL 45296 ff 130–1; CL 2 partial]

Still on vacation in Scotland, Shaw responded to Archer's long letter. Each of them, in his own way, lamented that the other had not done justice to his talents. And each of them, full of self-confidence, rejected the other's complaints. Shaw's comments here on A.W. Pinero, H.A. Jones, and J. Barrie echoed and expanded upon some points he had made in his letter of 27 August.

The weather here is gradually producing a sense of awe. Two fine days since the 1st August! One half&half day (the rainy half very terrific) we went to the Inverary sports, and saw the two mile race won by Major Charles Archer. I had no idea he was an athlete; but he is evidently a famous one; for he was the most heavily handicapped of all the runners. The extraordinary promptitude with which the competitors stopped the moment it was clear that they were not going to be placed (a place meaning a few shillings) gave a sordid complexion to the races; and I was surprised at Charles making such an effort for one pound ten. Lest he should be carrying on a clandestine business as athletic pot hunter and boldly deny my testimony, I took the precaution to snapshot the field in the last lap but one, and I have got him very microscopiable, but still unmistakable over the shoulder of the first man. He was then running third. He spurted and won on the post at the last moment. Some evening next winter I will enlarge him & send you a print.

Your Chronicle review roused the greatest indignation here. Charlotte declared you a gross imposter – a man absolutely without perception of greatness. I argued feebly for your intellectual competence for the whole afternoon; but the weight of evidence against me in the Chronicle was overwhelming. Fortunately your letter has to some extent rehabilitated you. Charlotte, I regret to say, has no sense of humor: indeed she thought your toleration of the heliograph joke a most unreasonable encouragement to my vulgarest weakness; and she also objects to what you happily call my waving the banner with an Irish accent. To that extent therefore she is willing to concede your possession of a limited critical faculty.

As for me, I find you more modest than ever on my account. I feel as Harmsworth or Pierpont Morgan might feel if you wrote to exhort them to turn over a new leaf and make a little money. All that you ask for is there, not only in Man & Superman, but in my early immature scrawlings. You are asking me to begin, not seeing that I began years ago far ahead of where you expect me to leave off. Your review, apparently colossally stupid, is really blind and careless. Let me give you a single simple example. In the fougue of your theme, which is that the book is a mere rechauffée of stale Shavianized Nietzsche &c, you say that the cycle theory is Nietzschean. Now you knew Thomas Tyler. Nobody could ever have enjoyed that privilege without having it burned into his brain that Shakespear was a cyclist. Laplace and Carlyle between them rubbed the physical theory of cycles as hard as possible into us before Nietzsche was ever heard of. It is news to me that Nietzsche ever alluded to the subject – I must really read some of his stuff. The cycle theory has been one of the staples of Pessimism ever since Pessimism existed. It was inevitable that my Devil should trot it out. But as far as I know, nobody before Don Juan has ever given the simple answer that the perpetual motion may be effected by a pendulum mechanism – that the notion that a clock does not go because the bob of the pendulum does not seem to get any forrader is the notion of a blackbeetle on the wall and not of a man setting his watch by Big Ben. No doubt that answer has been given; but it has been forgotten; and to describe its statement as being a mere repetition of Tyler's despairing difficulty is a most outrageous piece of carelessness. Read the book again. Read it fifty times over. If it leaves you exactly where Nietzsche & Darwin & Ibsen & Wagner & Tolstoy have left you, then I have nothing more to say, except that you have never really troubled yourself about philosophical questions and dont really believe that it matters whether Thackeray's view of life is right or Bunyan's. In that case, my work can never have any reality for you because it must appear to you passionless and therefore fundamentally undramatic. The first act of the Superman, for instance, will be to you, not a tragedy, but simply a sell, and that not in the best taste.

The odd thing about it all is that you, with this apparent amblyopia for every passion except divorce & police passion, should yet be so susceptible to the philosophic poetry that you get quite upset by it. If your review were the placid utterance of a color blind man criticizing Titian – or, to take an actual case, of the famous physicist Young describing Mrs. Siddon's Volumnia – there would be nothing more to say. But it is an outburst of recalcitrance, the splutterings of a protesting, incommoded, deeply stirred victim. It is the same with Ibsen. You translate Ibsen; you cry over Ibsen; you have forced Ibsen on the English stage; but when it comes to criticize or produce him you declare that he is mad, disgraceful, deplorable; and you cut his plays to pieces for representation. Compare your treatment of When We Dead Awaken to Walkley's. You first protest with all your might against such a scandal as the performance must be in any case; and then you half apologize for the play, half denounce it as an infamy. Walkley walks up to it with his boulevardier air, duly chaffs it in his manner, but finally says 'Do not misunderstand me, ladies &

gentlemen,' and takes off his hat to genius as he retires. Whereas you kick the thing, shewing that in some way it has hurt you.

You really are a very curious character. You admit the superiority of my talent and wit. You are quite wrong. Incredible as it sometimes seems, you have just as much talent and wit as I have. You have all the tools of the trade, but you have no conscience. There are a great many men who sin against the light because they cant do without wine & cigars & a thousand a year or ten thousand. They go to hell because the train has first class carriages, whereas the train for heaven has third class ones. There are other men so fond of money that they take the hell train because the ticket costs twopence less than the other. But you are perfectly content with plain living, and care so little about money that any publisher can get the better of you in a bargain; and yet dont think the train to heaven is worth taking. There is an absolute gratuitousness about your perversity that is inexplicable unless one sees you as a sort of child in fairyland who has never learnt to live in the world and who resents the intrusion of moral problems as angrily as it joyfully welcomes the advent of the poetic glamor. Blugginess you dont object to at all – quite the contrary. Fun is quite acceptable. But conscience avaunt! You turn pettish at the first taste of it. If Tom had not a mother as well as a father he would never to the end of his days walk out of Piona.

Now that you have exhausted all that talent & wit can do for you, you are falling back on the excuse of incapacity. But you are capable enough; and your bolt is not shot yet, though mine is. To all your heartsearching questions I answer without a moment's hesitation or affectation. Yes. I am astonished at what I have done with so little means. I am as willing to hang up my *théâtre* beside Shakespear's – leaving everything that has been written for the stage in the interim out of account as completely negligibly – as Turner was to hang his landscapes beside Claude's; and I attach no importance whatever to that or any other comparison. But you have done nothing that bears the same relation to your talent as my output does to mine. In your letter to me, you say the absolute truth about Pinero; but when you write about him for the public, and *for himself* (which is the main thing) you will lie like a Trojan about him & lure him down to further Iris abysses with a horrible childish ignorance of the fact – which can be learned only in public life, not divined by wit & talent – that flattery will ruin a man more surely & swiftly than any extremity of abuse. Walkley has done Jones no harm. I have encouraged Jones; but if you read my notice of Michael, you will see that I dealt faithfully with him. You have almost destroyed A.W.P.: another Iris and, with Barrie already far outrunning him, he is lost. And all this to keep up a pretense, which imposes on nobody, that William Morris was an ignorant & foolish person who was incapable of appreciating the greatness of the British Theatre. If you want to be an advocate, put on your wig & go in the courts; but while you are a critic, be a critic.

The sun is shining. I have not half finished, but must go & bathe before lunch. More anon – on sufficient provocation.

GBS

Charles Archer, five years younger than William, went to Sandhurst Military Academy and became an officer in the army. He was assigned to the British India Staff Corps. As a major, then a lieutenant-colonel, he served as a political agent and commissioner for the Raj Empire during the Edwardian era. He was posted to Baluchistan in northwest India (now part of Pakistan). On leave in August 1903, he visited family in Scotland. Archer's essay on *Man and Superman* appeared in the Daily **Chronicle** on 24 August. The **heliograph joke** derived from the opening stage-direction in which Shaw described the polished head of Roebuck Ramsden: 'on a sunshiny day he could heliograph his orders to distant camps by merely nodding.' In his review Archer quoted and praised this witty quip. Alfred **Harmsworth** (1865–1922), Viscount Northcliffe, was a journalist and owner of newspapers. **Pierpont Morgan** (1867–1943), the son of J.P. Morgan, was a US financier. In his review Archer complained that the **cycle theory is Nietzschean**. In 1890 **Thomas Tyler** (1826–1902) edited Shakespeare's sonnets. When Shaw withdrew in 1884 from editing the index and glossary of the works of Thomas Lodge (1557/8?–1615) for the New Shakespere Society, founded by Dr F.J. Furnivall, Tyler replaced him. Peter Simon, Marquis de **Laplace** (1749–1827), was a French astronomer and mathematician. Thomas **Carlyle** (1795–1881), the Scottish philosopher and essayist who settled in Chelsea, was famous for his historical studies (e.g., *The French Revolution, On Heroes*). **Titian** [Tiziano Vecellio] (c. 1490–1576) was a Venetian painter. The condition of **amblyopia** is the lack of sharp vision. Shaw also accused Archer of suffering from this default in the letter of 24 April 1894. The actor Charles M. Young (1777–1856), not the physicist Dr **Thomas Young** (1773–1829), described Mrs Sarah **Siddons** (1755–1831) in the role of Volumnia in *Coriolanus*. Shaw's statement '**you cry over Ibsen**' was a reference to Archer's reading of *Little Eyolf* to a few friends in December 1894, soon after he had translated the play. Overcome with emotion, Archer could not finish the reading. He had to ask Shaw to finish it. Despite his 'wooden' exterior, Archer was a passionate and sentimental man, as Shaw insisted. (See Shaw's memorial essay on Archer, the foreword to *Three Plays*: x.) On several occasions Shaw claimed that Archer cut Ibsen's **plays to pieces** for productions. On this disagreement see the letter of 8 September 1903; also those of 6 September 1919 and 20 June 1923. For Archer's assessment of ***When We Dead Awaken*** see the letter of 21 February 1900. Shaw's comment that **the train for heaven has third class** carriages contradicts the statement by Higgins to Eliza in act 5 of *Pygmalion* that 'there are no third-class carriages' in heaven (CP 4: 774). On several occasions, when Shaw wished to dismiss Archer's artistic sensibility and critical judgments, he accused him of abiding in **Piona**, a fantasy realm that young Tom Archer dreamed up (e.g., see letters of 21 August 1893 and 12 May 1904). J.M.W. **Turner** (1775–1851), the English painter and watercolourist, was a master of nature painting, especially of the sea. **Claude** Lorrain [born Claude Gellée] (1600–82) was a French landscape painter and draughtsman who lived and worked in Italy. In English he is often referred to as Claude. H.A. Jones's ***Michael** and His Lost Angel* premiered in 1896, A.W. Pinero's ***Iris*** in 1901.

100 / To William Archer Springburn, Strachur, Argyllshire
7th September 1903

[ALS: BL 45296 ff 132–47; CL 2]

The Shaws continued their visit in Scotland. On 2 September Archer published 'Das moderne Drama in England' in Die Zeit. *He argued that the commercial system that controlled the theatre managers in London was mainly responsible for the absence of Shaw's plays from the West End theatres. In these expansive letters from Scotland, from 27 August to 27 September, Shaw was obviously enjoying not only the abiding pleasure of arguing with Archer but also the opportunity to share his reflections upon London playwrights and players. Regrettably, some of Archer's replies have disappeared.*

(Dictated) (From Shaw – handwriting Mrs S's)

William Archer

I have just been reading an article of yours in Die Zeit which proves beyond all question my contention that you are not a nincompoop but a perfectly disinterested liar. I can only hope that neither Pinero nor Jones are familiar with the German language; for the callous brutality with which you tell the truth in German when the mere monotony of telling lies in English becomes unbearable, would lead to a straining of personal relations which would end in Pinero inviting me to dinner and Jones taking Walkley to his breast.

However, what I want you to do is to complete the picture by shewing the effects of the situation on the actors. One of the noteworthy points about my own situation is that though I get performed by the Stage Society only, I have no difficulty in getting casts quite as good as & in some respects better than Jones & Pinero can get at the regular theatres. Even in the early days, up to & including Brassbound, when there were overwhelming extraneous difficulties of one kind & another, I never had to face such hopeless misfits as the casting of Gerald Du Maurier for the old actor in Trelawney, or Ellis Jeffreys for the second woman in Mrs. Ebbsmith, or the various misfortunes which make Jones declare that casting a play has become impossible, even apart from the obligation to give the acting manager the leading part. As to Mrs Warren & Bashville, I could not have got even an approach to my Stage Society casts at any regular theatre. One reason for this you have mentioned in passing: it applies to Farren Soutar as Bashville. I found that he was quite capable of first rate work; & of course the result is that he is mopped up by musical comedy. But the main point that wants bringing out is that the player with a specific acting talent has been driven off the stage by the walking toff. Although what you say in the article about my plays being kept off the stage because they are not toffish is roughly true, yet this does not apply to 'You Never Can Tell,' which was deliberately manufactured to admit of enough Saturday to Monday millinery & champagne to pass muster. What really shipwrecked the Haymarket production of that play was just the state of things you have described in your article. When the question of casting the play came up for settlement, the management was bent on having Allen Aynesworth. I at once said that it was quite impossible; that Aynesworth was an amusing farce actor & had done very well in 'The Prisoner of Zenda' & still better in 'The Importance of being Ernest,' but that the end of the second act of 'You Never Can Tell,' the failure of which must inevitably mean the failure of the whole play, was utterly beyond any power that he had ever shewn. Cyril Maude pleaded that he had never had a chance; that I ought not to refuse to let him shew what he could do; that he had never failed; & finally (& this was of course the whole secret of it) that he was a very nice fellow; that he had rooms in Bond Street; & that he was, in short, a Paffick Genlmn. Of course the onus of naming an alternative was thrown on me. I could only name, as men whom I would accept, Drew, Fred Kerr, Bourchier, or Yorke Stephens. It so happened that the first three were not available; & I was flatly met by the objection that Yorke Stephens was not a gentleman! The end of it was that I had to give Aynesworth his chance; & the result was precisely and exactly what I had predicted. He broke down at the end of the second act; & I got them all out of a very painful difficulty by withdrawing the play and promising to support any version that might be most convenient of its being dropped; for I saw that if the real reason reached the public Aynesworth would be undeservedly damaged, just as Granville Barker was the other day by Jones taking the part in 'The Princess's Nose' away from him. I say undeservedly because Aynesworth rehearsed all the scenes that were in his line extremely well, & it was entirely my fault & Maude's folly that he was wrecked on a scene that was out of his line. Consequently my play was shelved; I got a reputation for impossibility at rehearsals which lasted until the Stage Society enabled me to live it down; & finally the play was performed by the Stage Society with Yorke Stephens in the part.

The next serious proposal from a West End theatre was Alexander's for Brassbound. I had to tell Alexander that if he produced the play he would have to play Brassbound; that it was just the kind of part that any secondrate young leading man in provincial melodrama could play just as well as he, if not better; that it was wholly the woman's play & not Brassbound's; that his leading lady was no use for Lady Cecily; & that, in short, I could not honestly advise him to produce the play.

Next comes Forbes Robertson. I had let him take the Devil's Disciple into the provinces at a time when he was so desperately hard up that there was clearly nothing better for him to do. He wanted to produce it in London on two occasions: first, at the Comedy, & second after 'Mice & Men' & before 'Othello.' I refused on both occasions, solely because we could not cast the play. Of course he was very angry: they are always angry when you save them from obvious and certain ruin; but you will see by what I have put up with & made the best of in the way of scratch performances & appalling scenery in the Independent Theatre & the beginnings of the Stage Society that I am not an Impossibilist in these matters.

Now if you put all these things together; if you reflect on the fact that until 'Mr and Mrs Daventry' & 'Mrs Warren's Profession' were produced Fred Kerr & Fanny Brough had never got a chance of doing anything but comic relief; that Yorke Stephens & Kate Philips & others with a genuine modicum of temperament & skill languished for years without engagements whilst parts that they could have played with perfect dexterity were being amateured through by people who were simply more eligible acquaintances for socially ambitious managers; that Kate Terry could not get the succession to Rose Leclercq though she bid for it at the psychological moment; that Hermann Vezin couldnt get anything at all, then you will see that the case you have made out as to the effect of the fashionable play or dramatic authorship holds good also as to its effect on actorship; & that just as I have had to fall back on the Stage Society along with Barker & Brieux & all the rest of the author geniuses so it has come to be recognized in the Profession that the serious actor's only chance lies on the same distinguished boards.

Thus the expression used by your German translator 'Halb-amateur theater' to describe the Stage Society is just the wrong word; for the half-amateurs are at the West End theatre walking through the smart plays, whilst the skilled temperamental professionals are playing for the Stage Society, ostensibly for honor & glory alone, but in some cases, I am greatly afraid, because the two guineas 'expenses' are not a matter of indifference to them.

I suggest the working out of this to you because there is some truth in the current complaint that the critics care nothing about acting, & that you in particular, whilst you are never tired of watering that hardy annual the fashionable drama (upon which, in Austrian papers, you lavish a gallon of weed killer) the unfortunate actor never gets more notice from you than the few crumbs which a particularly importunate dog might coax from a man who disliked animals.

There is one other aspect of the case to be worked out; & that is the reaction of the actors' incapacity on the dramatist. It is perfectly possible, up to a certain point, to produce an illusion of acting from marionettes, & this is what the modern author has to do. I went a little into this in my notice of 'The Benefit of the Doubt,' where I shewed how Pinero, having ventured to keep a popular leading man & leading lady continuously in evidence on the stage for nearly half an hour, instead of cleverly bustling them about for five minutes & getting them off before the audience had found them out, practically wrecked his piece, & confirmed himself in his scepticism as to the wisdom of allowing the actor any initiative whatever.

It seems to me that if you were to add two articles on these lines to the one in Die Zeit – the three would make an excellent view of the English stage during the toffification period which culminated in the knighting of Irving; & it would only be fair to shew that though dramatic literature & the art of acting were practically left out of account in this period, & although the actor in striving to make himself a gentleman has only succeeded in making himself eligible for stockbroker's dinner parties, yet it is an open question whether the general clearing out of the old

Bohemian dirt & drunkenness & slatternliness may not be worth the temporary artistic sacrifice.

I have now spent the whole morning writing to you, or rather making my wife write to you; & I decline to go on.

GBS

Sir **Gerald du Maurier** (1873–1934), the son of George [Du] Maurier (1834–96), acted in H.B. Tree's company in the 1890s, including a small role in *Trilby*, which was based upon his father's novel. He had roles in James Barrie's *The Admirable Crichton* (1902) and *Peter Pan* (1904), then major success as a charming criminal in *Raffles* (1906) and *Arsène Lupin* (1909). In 1922 he was knighted. **Ellis Jeffreys** (ca. 1868–1943) performed occasionally in Gilbert and Sullivan operettas and Pinero's plays; she was a West End regular with most of the actor-managers. As a young actor J. **Farren Soutar** (1874–1962) played juvenile parts; he also sang in musical comedies. Besides adapting plays, he was a director and producer. In 1903 he played Bashville in the Imperial Theatre production of *The Admirable Bashville*, directed by Shaw. Shaw's phrase **walking toff** refers to the secondary role of the *walking gentleman* which is one of the 'lines of business' in a conventional stock company. During the 1890s Allan, not **Allen**, **Aynesworth** appeared often in West End productions, including those of A.W. Pinero's *The Cabinet Minister* (1890) and *The Second Mrs Tanqueray* (1893), H.A. Jones's *The Crusaders* (1891) and *The Bauble Shop* (1893), Edward Bulwer Lytton's *Money* (1894), Oscar Wilde's *The Importance of Being Earnest* (1895), and Edward Rose's *The Prisoner of Zenda* (1896). The cancelled production of ***You Never Can Tell*** at the **Haymarket** Theatre in 1897 became a recurring topic in Shaw's correspondence. In Laurence's *Collected Letters*, see Shaw's letters to Ellen Terry on 9, 10, 12, 16, and 29 April and 11 May 1897 (CL 1: 740–1, 741–2, 742–3, 744–6, 750–1, 759–60). See also Terry's letter to Shaw on 24 April (Terry/Shaw: 142–3) and the letter to Beatrice Mansfield on 21 October 1899 (Theatrics: 32–4). He wrote an anonymous and sanitized version of the episode for Cyril Maude's *The Haymarket Theatre* (1903). In communication with Archer he raises the topic in a previous letter on 12 January 1903. And the cancelled production is even resurrected in his final letter to Archer on 14 December 1924. The American actor John **Drew** appeared in London with Augustin Daly's company in the 1890s. ***Mice and Men***, written by Madeleine Lucette Ryley, was produced at the Lyric (365 perfs.); besides Johnston Forbes-Robertson and his wife Gertrude Elliott, it featured Ben Webster (1864–1947) and Mrs Theodore Wright. **Frederick Kerr** (1858–1933), a regular player in the West End theatres, acted in plays by T.W. Robertson, Robert Buchanan, Sydney Grundy, Pinero, and Jones. In 1900 he appeared in Frank Harris's play ***Mr and Mrs Daventry***, which Oscar Wilde had sketched out in 1894, then later sold to Harris (and several other people). It opened at the Royalty on 25 October (116 perfs.). The production, which Mrs Patrick Campbell managed, also featured Gerald [Du] Maurier and George Arliss (1868–1946). Two decades later Arliss, a British actor who would make his career in America, became the star of Archer's *The Green Goddess*. Shaw commented on Frank Harris's derivative play in a letter to Harris on 4 November 1900. **Fanny Brough** was best known as a comic actress; she appeared, for example, in Oscar Wilde's *An Ideal Husband* (1895) and Shaw's *Getting Married* (1908). **Yorke Stephens** played Bluntschli in the 1894 production of *Arms and the Man* and the Dentist in the 1899 and 1900 productions of *You Never Can Tell*. The actress **Kate Phillips** (1856–1931), who performed with Irving and many other actor-managers, was quite versatile. For instance, she portrayed Mistress Quickly in H.B. Tree's 1896 production of *Henry IV, Part I* and Gina Ekdal in the Independent Theatre's 1897 production of Ibsen's *The Wild Duck.* She also performed in Christmas pantomimes. As a child actress **Kate Terry** performed in Charles Kean's company. After marrying in 1867, she retired from the stage for several decades. **Rose Leclercq** (1845–99), a comic actress, appeared in *The Importance of Being Earnest* (1895) as Lady Bracknell. One of her last roles was in H.A. Jones's *The Manoeuvres of Jane* at Cyril Maude's Haymarket (29 October 1898; 281 perfs.). **Hermann Vezin**, actor, elocution teacher, and occasional dramatist, portrayed Crampton in *You Never Can Tell* in the 1899 and 1900 productions. He also acted in José Echegaray's *Mariana* in 1897, produced by the New Century Theatre Company. Eugène **Brieux** (1858–1932), the French playwright, wrote naturalistic dramas. His *Blanchette* had a matinee performance at the Court (24 May 1901). *La Robe Rouge,* produced by Mrs Langtry, was staged in French by Réjane (1857–1920) at the Imperial (4 June 1902; 3 perfs.). **Arthur Bourchier** (1863–1927), husband of Violet Vanbrugh, was educated at Oxford; he was a co-founder of the Oxford University Dramatic Society. He played various Shakespearean roles when acting with H.B. Tree's company. In 1896–7 he managed the Royalty Theatre, then in 1900 became actor-manager of the Garrick Theatre.

101 / To William Archer

Springburn, Strachur, Argyllshire
8th September 1903

[ALS: BL 45296 f 148; CL 2]

*Archer's reply to Shaw's letter of 2 September is missing. Because Shaw expanded here upon the topic of cutting Ibsen's plays, it seems quite likely that Archer mentioned the topic in the missing letter, and perhaps denied the charge. Also, Archer probably discussed the topics of pessimism and life's cycles which Shaw took up again in this letter. Besides responding to the missing letter, Shaw returned to Archer's letter of 1 September in which he predicted that Shaw's future fame would be no greater than that of Thomas Love Peacock and Thomas Lovell Beddoes. And Shaw had more to say about the two earlier reviews by Archer: 'Mr. Shaw and Mr. Pinero' (*Morning Leader, *22 August) and 'Mr. Shaw's Pom-Pom' (DC, 24 August).*

Archer's cutting of the texts of The Pillars of Society *and* The Wild Duck *for productions occurred as follows. In December 1880, after failing to find a publisher for his first Ibsen translation, Archer adapted* Pillars *into a play he entitled* Quicksands. *It had a single matinee performance. He soon regretted the liberties he had taken with the text. In January 1881, he travelled to Rome to meet Ibsen for the first time; he was worried that Ibsen would be angry about the adaptation. But the meeting went well. Ibsen accepted 'my rather lame excuses,' and soon Archer was proudly calling Ibsen 'my friend' (C. Archer: 101, 104). As for the matter of cutting* The Wild Duck, *Shaw repeated this assertion in 1919 and 1923. In both cases Archer adamantly denied that he had anything to do with cuts made in either of the productions in 1894 or 1897 that the Independent Theatre Company staged. (See letters of 2 September 1903, 6 September 1919, and 20 June 1923.) In the published translation, though, he had avoided publishing a few obscure Norwegian words and titles.*

All right: I am quite satisfied: Archer still lives. I do not even ruefully ask why I should be pilloried in the Leader as the traitor who bit the hand of my unquestioned leader as he brought me up out of the land of Egypt. But I wish Pinero could see my private protests that I always flattered him and yours that you always exposed him.

The connexion between Pessimism & the cycles is obvious. If the theory is true, we are only squirrels in a revolving cage; and our frantic efforts to keep the thing going are purposeless. That's Shakespear. But perhaps it turns something. That's Shaw. What the deuce does it matter? That's Archer – the unconscionable.

You villain, you cut Ibsen to ribbons for the stage – first, Pillars; and then the first act of The Wild Duck. I didn't mean the books. The old man's brain is about as soft as a Brazil nut: the only effect of age is to make him utterly reckless in his stonethrowing.

As to whether the biographical dictionaries will give me a paragraph with Beddoes or ten pages with Shakespear I care not one single damn. Whatever drives me to sweat Superman & the like for the benefit of the world is certainly not driving at my personal posthumous fame. I have no doubt that a course of serious Bashville would raise me to a pinnacle higher than Lytton, Knowles or even Calmour. But the matter isnt really in my hands. I have to say [the] things that seem to me to want saying; and if you consider that one thing is as well worth saying as another and that the thing is to say it (whichever it is) in such a way as to have my life written in the XXIII century by the S. L. Lee of that age, you dont understand my internal mechanism in the least. I look on at the Superman just as helplessly as you do: I could not have produced anything else. But I have great hopes that my fate may set a very beneficial example to the rising literary generation. I am, as you perfectly well know, by no means such a stupendously clever person as I seem just at present. If I lived as Pinero lives & ate what he eats, I greatly doubt whether I should ever have written a play at all. My twelve years of stump oratory, my six years of lighting & paving & dust collecting, my twenty years of Fabian agitation, on top of a childish grounding in Mozart, Beethoven, Verdi, Meyerbeer, Donizetti, Gounod &c &c &c: all that is within the reach of everybody; and when others, convinced by my example, follow it, do you really suppose I shall be anybody in particular? Not a bit of it: everybody's shop window will blaze as tawdrily as mine by the time I am 80.

G.B.S.

Edward Bulwer **Lytton** (1803–73), a novelist and playwright, had popular successes with *The Lady of Lyons* (1838) and *Richelieu* (1839). Both W.C. Macready and Henry Irving mounted productions of these melodramas. James Sheridan **Knowles** (1784–1862) was an actor and playwright; Macready staged his *Virginius* (1820). With *The Hunchback* (1832), Knowles created a popular vehicle for young actresses. Alfred Cecil **Calmour** (1857–1912) wrote *The Amber Heart,* a sentimental trifle which Ellen Terry performed at the Lyceum in 1887 and revived on many occasions in both England and America. Besides serving as co-editor, then editor, of the *Dictionary of National Biography,* **Sydney L. Lee** wrote scholarship on Elizabethan drama and theatre, and published *The Life of William Shakespeare* in 1898.

102 / To William Archer

Strachur
16th September 1903

[ALS: BL 45296 f 149]

Archer's letter is missing. He may have replied to the preceding letters of 7 and 8 September, or he may have written on separate matters. Whatever the case, he apparently asked Shaw's advice about publishing a collection of his 'Study and Stage' articles from the Morning Leader. *Although he continued to publish weekly theatre reviews for* The World *until January 1906, he also wrote regularly for the* Morning Leader *and the* Daily Chronicle. *The* ML *articles, which had the title 'Study & Stage,' began in April 1900 and covered a range of reflective topics, including commentary on Shaw's published plays. Despite Shaw's encouragement here, Archer decided against publishing a separate collection of* ML *articles.*

Shaw once again returned to Archer's letter of 1 September in which he predicted that Shaw's future fame would be no greater than that of Thomas Love Peacock and Thomas Lovell Beddoes. Despite Shaw's assertion in his letter of 8 september that he cared 'not one single damn' about future fame, he felt compelled a week later in this letter to dismiss any concern for his place in the biographical dictionaries of the future.

Yes: these are most excellent articles: I remember them very well. In fact I take in the Leader solely because of Study & Stage. As far as our present controversy is concerned, the articles are simply proofs of your guilt: in them I appear as the sole asset of the advanced school in England, & Pinero & Jones as the benighted reactionaries. Why, then, am I now to be executed as a traitor to my undoubted leaders Pinero & Jones? However, your reply – that you cant keep on saying the same thing ad nauseum (I can & do, by the way) – somehow appeals to me. At bottom you are right; but through not sorting it out carefully enough you have stated it all wrong.

As to the biographical dictionary, who can tell? For my part, I believe this is a passing craze of yours, due chiefly to your knowing me too well to be able to entertain me as a Panjandrum. But I am very much afraid I am destined to be a Panjandrum & to be the curse of English literature for the next 300 years at least. It is really not my fault: it is that in the country of the blind the one-eyed is king.

GBS

103 / To William Archer

Strachur
27th September 1903

[APCS: BL 45296 f 150]

George Edwardes was the leading producer of popular theatre in London (see Edwardes: 80–102). In 'The Slump in Musical Comedy' (ML, 19 September 1903) Archer had complained that musical comedy is sinking 'in the slough of sheer silliness ... Why not commission Mr. Barrie to write the text of an extravaganza?' Archer had major doubts about George Edwardes's plan to develop a light opera based upon Madame Sans-Gêne, *the Napoleon play by Victorien Sardou and Émile Moreau. Edwardes knew, however, that J. W. Comyns Carr had successfully adapted the French play for Irving and Terry at the Lyceum in 1897 (revived in 1898 and 1901). So he decided to transform that play into* The Duchess of Dantzig. *He hired Henry Hamilton (1853–1918), who wrote melodramas for Drury Lane and other theatres, to write the libretto and Ivan Caryll (1861–1921) to compose the music. It opened on 17 October at the Lyric Theatre (238 perfs.). Evie Greene (1876–1917) played the role of Catherine 'Sans-Gêne' Upscher and Holbrook Blinn (1872–1928) took on the character of Napoleon, a serious, non-singing part. The production lacked the comic traits of a typical Edwardes musical, but the public still 'liked George Edwardes' newest concoction' (Gänzl 1: 833–6, 852–3). Ten days later, on 27 October, Edwardes opened the new Gaiety Theatre with* The Orchid *(559 perfs.), a musical comedy starring the beloved Gertie Millar (1879–1952).*

Besides these two productions, two additional Edwardes vehicles were still drawing audiences: A Country Girl *at Daly's (opened 18 January 1902; 729 perfs.) and* The Girl from Kay's *at the Apollo (14 November 1902, 432 perfs.). And* A Toreador *had just closed out the old Gaiety theatre (17 June 1901; 675 perfs.). For two decades Edwardes was the 'Gov'nor' of musical comedies (see Edwardes: 80–102).*

Edwardes could obviously ignore Archer's sour judgment. By the Edwardian period (which perhaps should have been named after him), he had established himself as the master of London popular theatre, just as Shaw soon established himself at the Court Theatre as the master of modern drama. A London partnership between these two giants of theatre might have been a special achievement: a Napoleon entertainment far superior to either The Duchess of Dantzig *or* The Man of Destiny. *But it was not to be.*

In your last Study & Stage but one (yesterdays has not yet arrived). You are unjust to Edwardes. He asked *me* to write the Duchess of Dantzig years ago: perhaps he asked Barrie too. D'Oyly Carte also offered me a commission to write a libretto for Sullivan or any composer I pleased. Lowenstein offered me a large retaining salary & a third of the profits of my operas. Quite lately Miss Minnie Chappell came to me & said that the dream of her life was to produce a light opera by me, and that she was ready at last. Grundy actually did write one for the Savoy. Probably Pinero has been asked. And surely Barrie did one – Jane Annie or something like that – for the Savoy. The truth is that the moment a writer shews serious talent in London he is implored to write a comic opera, & *wont.*

GBS

PS On the 30th go to Glasgow to the Central Station hotel until the 5th.

J.M. **Barrie** and Arthur Conan Doyle wrote the book for *Jane Annie, Or the Good Conduct Prize,* which Richard **D'Oyly Carte** had commissioned. It premiered on 13 May 1893, but only had 50 performances. It was the first box-office failure at the Savoy Theatre since it opened in 1881. *Jane Annie* had followed *Haddon Hall* by Sydney Grundy and Arthur Sullivan, which ran for 204 performances (Gänzl 1: 460–1, 487). Henry Lowenfeld (not **Lowenstein**) was the 'Kops Ale' tycoon. He staged *La Poupeé* in 1896, revived in 1898. Also in 1898 he produced Maurice Maeterlinck's *Pelléas and Mélisande* for Mrs Patrick Campbell and Johnston Forbes-Robertson. He often featured comic musicals, in competition with George Edwardes, but he even staged a matinee performance of *Nora oder Ein Puppenheim* (*A Doll's House*) by the visiting Deutsches Theater from Berlin (4 April 1901). **Miss Minnie Chappell** failed to fulfill her dream; her stage career did not develop. After spending almost two months in Scotland at Springburn, Strachur, the Shaws went to **Glasgow** for a few days in early October. He delivered a talk to the Fabians, 'Is Free Trade Dead or Alive?,' and another to the Independent Labour Party, 'Socialist Unity' (Gibbs 1: 157).

104 / To William Archer

Maybury Knoll, Woking
7th November 1903

[TLU: BL 50528 ff 55–6]

John Mackinnon Robertson, like Archer, was a Scottish secularist and rationalist who launched his career in England as a liberal journalist. He and Archer met in the Edinburgh Secular Society. *He served as assistant editor, then editor, of Charles Bradlaugh's* National Reformer. *In the* Free Press, *which he founded in 1893, he supported atheism, evolutionary theory, free trade, and neo-Malthusian ideas. In 1899 he published* A History of Freethought in the Nineteenth Century. *In 1901, in opposition to the South African War, he attacked supporters of British imperialism, including Arthur Conan Doyle. Active in many progressive groups and movements, he was an aggressive and caustic debater. As a Shakespeare scholar he published* Did Shakespeare Write Titus Andronicus? *(1905) and* An Introduction to the Shakespeare Canon *(5 vols, 1922–30). He argued that many of the plays credited to Shakespeare were co-written or written by other playwrights. Self-taught, he had knowledge of six languages. He published over 100 books and pamphlets, and over 1000 articles. In 1925, after Archer's death, Robertson edited* William Archer as Rationalist, *a collection of his 'Heterodox Writings.'*

When Robertson stood for Parliament in 1903, he became outraged by statements by Henry Montague Villiers (1837–1908), vicar of St Paul's, Knightsbridge, who slandered him by suggesting he was a sodomist. The attacks were carried forward by the Leeds Mercury *newspaper. Robertson mounted an aggressive counterattack, but lost both the court case on slander and the chance for a seat in Parliament that year. Three years later, however, he was elected the Liberal Member of Parliament for Tyneside, serving from 1906 to 1918.*

Shaw also had a disagreement with Villiers (CL 2: 571–3), who objected in 1905 to profane statements in Man and Superman, *but Shaw avoided a lawsuit.*

My dear Archer

I saw the Robertson case reported in the Times and Daily News. The moment I saw the heading I gave Robertson up as hopeless. I saw straight through to his bankruptcy without troubling about the details. There are some errors of judgment that are made only by doomed men. What can one say except that a man with a temper like that must either keep out of public life, or be careful to hold only the most conventional opinions?

I do not see that we can do much for him. A subscription to pay the costs of the Leeds Mercury and the bill of the solicitor who allowed

Robertson to take this hopeless action is not likely to be much of a success. He had better make up his mind to file a petition. His own lawyers deserve no sympathy; and as the Leeds Mercury calculated its blow so nicely, I presume they also calculated the recoil, and made up their minds to pay Clarke in consideration of the bankruptcy disqualifying J.M.R. from standing at the election. Probably they never dreamt that he would be so mad as to try and fight them in court. They were very wary. If you had been on the jury yourself, I dont see how you could have disagreed with the verdict.

It is very hard to judge from a report how a case has been handled. There was only one chance; and that was to bring out very strongly and sensationally the fact that Villiers was a propagandist of sodomy as a sort of religion. If Robertson had then stuck to the Malthusian guns; said that he had always preached neoM. and always would; that he did not protest against Standring's advertisements because he approved of them; that he did not care whether the jury approved or disapproved of his opinions, but that he left it to them to say whether it was English fair play to take advantage of his outspokenness to imply that he was a preacher of sodomy, he might have won, if he could have convinced them that the libel carried that innuendo. But there is not a sentence in the report which suggests that this was mentioned.

Of course the proper thing to do was to get a testimonial signed by a number of good names to the effect that the L.M. had completely mistaken his literary standing and the character of his work; and a copy should have been sent to every elector on the register. This would have cost something; but it could have helped him at the polls and would have been much cheaper than the present political and financial disaster.

It is amazing how newspaper attacks drive men out of their senses even when they are experienced journalists. If I proposed to take actions against the papers who have taken Redford's view of Mrs Warren's Profession, Robertson would see quite clearly that I was simply going to spend a thousand pounds on a verdict to confirm Redford's view. And yet he expected a jury to say that the National Reformer and the Free Review were organs of polite society!

Can you suggest anything practical? I cant. A testimonial will not be of much use now; and clearly it must have other signatures than those of Havelock Ellis, Edward Carpenter, William Platt, and the author of Mrs Warren. The signature of Conan Doyle would be, for this purpose, worth ten of mine; but you are not likely to get it, because when Robertson wrote his counterblast to Doyle on the war question, he treated him, as usual, as a moral delinquent, denied his good faith, sneered at his novels, and would, I am afraid, have LeedsMercury bled him without remorse if Doyle had left himself open to any such handling. What Robertson has done to Doyle he has probably done to everybody who differs from him politically and about whom he has had occasion to write. When we go signature hunting we will find this tripping us up; so that the final list of supporters may turn out rather more damning than the verdict.

To sum up the case against Robertson, I dont think you will get a really influential testimonial: that is, a nonparty one; and I doubt if Robertson has any right to ask his friends to put their hands in their pockets to pay the lawyers when it is open to him to file a petition. I should be sorry to give him this cold comfort, because it would do him no good, and embitter him (quite superfluously); but I give it to you privately by way of warning, as there is no use in your involving yourself in a hopeless attempt to prove a miscarriage of justice. Grantham's utterance about abortion was quite worthy of him; but its omission would not have saved the verdict. Personally, as you know, I am friendly to J.M.R.; but the above is the frozen truth of the matter as the common sense of the world will see it. Still, we must make the best we can of a bad job; for the damage to him will be very serious: the publishers, who are just beginning to accept him as a fashionable writer, will be frightened off him for two or three years; and no sane liberal causes will accept him as a candidate until the affair is forgotten. And that raises the question whether it is wise to advertise it any further. It is devilishly perplexing. Do you wish me to draft the testimonial & protest?

[no signature]

Clarke may have been William Clarke; see Shaw's detailed description of him in a letter to Archibald Henderson on 3 January 1905 (CL 2: 495). George Alexander **Redford** (1846–1916), as the Lord Chamberlain's Examiner of Plays, had denied a licence in 1898 for *Mrs Warren's Profession*, which was not granted a public performance until 1924, eight years after his death. **Havelock Ellis** (1859–1939), a physician and social reformer, wrote scientific studies of human sexuality, including *Studies in the Psychology of Sex* (7 vols, 1897–1928). He also was an early supporter of Ibsen's drama, and in 1888, two years before Archer published *Ibsen's Prose Drama*, he edited and published *The Pillars of Society and Other Plays*, including *Ghosts* in Archer's revision of Mrs Francis Lord's translation and *An Enemy of Society*, translated by Eleanor Marx-Aveling. **Edward Carpenter** (1844–1929), an English poet, philosopher, and socialist, wrote *Love's Coming of Age* (1896). Influenced by Whitman and Thoreau, he was an activist for sexual rights and for what he called 'homogenic love' and the 'third sex.' With William Morris he produced the Socialist weekly *Justice*. In 1897 he edited *Forecasts of the Coming Century*, for which Shaw wrote 'The Illusions of Socialism.'

105 / To G. Bernard Shaw National Liberal Club, Whitehall Place, SW
17th November 1903

[APCS: BL 50528 f 57]

Although Shaw's letter is missing, he apparently had sought information on Scandinavian publishers. He followed Archer's advice on the publisher, but not the translator. In 1907 Gyldendal published a translation of Plays Pleasant and Unpleasant *in Copenhagen.*

My dear Shaw

I don't know anything about Mergnussen, but will ask Braekstad, who may know him. The Gyldendal firm is absolutely the best in Scandinavia, & you can't do better than let them have your *Théâtre* if they want it.

Dr Adolf Hansen who wrote an article about you in a Danish magazine knows English perfectly & would translate well. Yours, W.A.

106 / To William Archer 32 Via di Porta Pinciana, Rome
12th May 1904

[ALS: BL 45296 ff 151–4; CL 2]

A year after their first trip to Italy in 1903, the Shaws made a second visit, from 1 May until 10 June. They visited Turin, Pisa, and Rome, then returned by way of Geneva. On 27 April A.B. Walkley published a brief report in The Times *on the production of* Candida, *which opened on 26 April at the Court Theatre (6 matinees). Then on the 29th he offered a full review in the* Times Literary Supplement. *He complained that Shaw is a 'fantasist' who presented a travesty of life; Shaw makes a 'joke' of life.* Candida *is a 'mathematical demonstration' of Shaw's intellect. Archer's own review appeared on 3 May in* The World. *After dismissing the limitations of other reviewers, he proclaimed that* 'Candida, Mrs Warren's Profession, *and* The Devil's Disciple *prove that Mr. Shaw possesses in a very high degree the specific gifts of the dramatist.'* Candida *is 'the most human of Mr. Shaw's plays, and the one in which he is most successful in concealing himself behind his puppets – or rather in distributing himself among them.' But Archer repeated his lament that most of Shaw's plays are platforms for Shaw's ideas; if only Shaw would 'keep in check' and subdue 'the multiplicity of his other gifts, might be one of the leading playwrights in Europe.' Both Walkley and Archer complained that Shaw's characters were masks for G.B.S.*

The response of Siegfried Trebitsch, Shaw's German translator, to Walkley's short review amused Shaw, who wrote to Trebitsch on 15 May: 'The Times critic is Walkley, to whom Man & Superman is dedicated. I shrieked with laughter over your comment on the notice, & promptly sent it on to him. I now send you Archer's notice. I wonder will you like it any better' (Trebitsch: 70). In turn, in this letter to Archer Shaw shared Trebitsch's comments on Walkley's review.

The production of Candida, *which featured Harley Granville Barker as Marchbanks, Kate Rorke as Candida, and Norman McKinnel (1870–1932) as Rev. James Morell, was produced by J.E. Vedrenne, with additional support from the* New Century Theatre Company. *A month later* NCT *and Vedrenne co-produced Gilbert Murray's translation of Euripides'* Hippolytus *(4 perfs.), a major undertaking with two dozen actors. Barker was director/producer. This production, which packed the house on the third and fourth afternoons and had a profit of £400, was the final venture by* NCT, *but not for Vedrenne. The production proved to be the penultimate step and final justification for the formation of a new team: the Vedrenne-Barker management at the Royal Court theatre in Sloan Square. In October* Hippolytus *was revived for six performances as the first official production of the new management. Then* Candida *was revived for eight performances in late November and early December. Over three seasons (1904–7), the Court productions would establish Shaw as 'one of the leading playwrights in Europe,' if not 'the greatest dramatist of the XX century,' as Shaw proclaimed in this lettter. The year 1904 was thus the dawn of the Vedrenne-Barker enterprise, but the dusk for* NCT. *(For the early history of* Candida *see letter of 28 December 1894.)*

My dear Archer

Trebitsch's howlers are certainly mighty ones and millions, though I think I got them driven out of the dialogue of the Schlachtenlenker. But how can I reproach him when he sends me the following, which I am sending on to Walkley.

> 'The Observer has sent me the Times-critic about Candida. Who is that desperate impostor, who wrote all this frightful nonsense? Not even his

grand-children will be able to understand this deep and poetic work. I did not finish to read that writing: it would have caused me neuralgics.'

I shall send him your criticism in the hope of extracting some further blossoms from him. By the way, there is one naiveté in your notices which you always produce with ingenious pride; and that is nothing less than the discovery that Caesar, Napoleon &c &c are only masks through which G.B.S. speaks. The implication that Hamlet, Macbeth, Falstaff, Georges Dandin, Don Juan &c are authentic realities with which Shakespear & Molière had no more to do than a reporter has with [Joseph] Chamberlain, is stupendous. Confound you for a romancing idiot, with your imagination always in Piona, what did you expect my people to be? Bluntschli & Napoleon are as violently differentiated as any man whose charm lies in his perfect simplicity can be from an inveterate poseur – Sidney Webb is not more distinct from Mansfield – but of course the two are the work of the same hand, stamped with the same style, getting their effects by the same stage tricks. How can that be helped, except by having every part written by a different author? Burgomaster Six, old Mrs Van Rhyn and Saskia are all Rembrandts; Peter & Paul and Christ are all Raphaels; and Napoleon, Caesar, Dick Dudgeon, Captain Brassbound & Candida are all Shaws. There is nothing in that as you state it: it sounds as if you were announcing with a penetrating air that Sloane Square is not Victoria Park and 5 in the afternoon not 10:30 at night. You must either drop it or else carry it very much further. For my own part, I am amazed at how little a touch of emotion will carry off the most monstrous unrealities. Candida's 'I give myself to the weaker of the two' is the climax of all impossibility; yet it passes. The situation is true; the characters are true; the solution is the right one; but the actual words uttered, and the state of clear intellectual consciousness of the situation which they imply, is outrageously unreal.

Now if you will only sit down and tell yourself that Shakespear & Co have never been real men to you, and that in my plays you have for the first time faced the big drama (for I assure you in all unhumility I am the greatest dramatist of the XX century) with such a personal knowledge of the man behind it that for once, in spite of Piona propensities, the author is more real to you than the play, you will get some hermeneutical advance out of it. You are behind the scenes for the first time in your life; and you are complaining that instead of a scenic illusion, you find nothing there but obvious carpentry and seamy-side-of-the-canvas rigged up by me. Just as Ben Jonson could never for the life of him see that Shakespear was such a dramatist as his idolaters made out; so you, whilst heaping encomiums on my wit &c &c &c, are always wondering that people cannot see that it is all Shaw, Shaw, Shaw, nothing but Shaw. Critically, this leads you to an abuse of your private knowledge of me. I *cannot* illude [see note] a man who knows me, just as Kate Rorke cannot persuade me that she is anybody but Kate Rorke. But she has a right to demand that I shall discount this in criticising her acting; and I claim, too, that you should either allow me the same discount in criticising my plays, or else discount your own criticism by announcing at the start that you are not at the optical point of the ordinary spectator, and can hear the sound of my voice in every line I write.

This ought to furnish you with materials for at least a dozen Study & Stage articles.

Has Borup *finished* The Man of Destiny? If so, I shall get a copy type written by Miss Dickens & try to arrange a performance in Denmark. Mrs Weeks tells me that Gyllendal is *afraid* to touch my books.

Yrs ever
GBS

Trebitsch's **howlers** appeared in *Der Schlachtenlenker* (*The Man of Destiny*). **Piona** is the fantasy realm that Tom Archer imagined. The word **illude** was probably a spelling error, yet it may have been a Shavian coinage that combines illusion and elude. **Kate Rorke**, who began her career with John Hare and Charles Wyndham, acted with most of the leading actor-managers. In 1906 she was appointed professor of dramatic art at the Guildhall School of Music, where she trained a new generation of performers. Jens Martin **Borup** (1880–1960), a Dane who resided in London, had recently begun to translate *Plays Pleasant and Unpleasant.* The Danish publisher **Gyldendal**, after overcoming initial reservations about Shaw's plays, published all seven of them in 1907. Mrs Ethel **Dickens** (1864–1936), a granddaughter of Charles Dickens, provided a typing service on Tavistock Street that Shaw used for many years.

107 / To William Archer 10 Adelphi Terrace WC

13th June 1904

[ALS: BL 45296 f 156; CL 2]

Archer's letter is missing. He apparently resumed the argument he had made in his review of Candida *(World, 3 May 1904). He once again lamented that Shaw's plays are dominated by Shaw's own voice.* 'Candida, Mrs Warren's Profession, *and* The Devil's Disciple *prove that Mr. Shaw possesses in a very high degree the specific gifts of the dramatist. If only he could keep in check, and subdue to artistic uses, the multiplicity of his other gifts, he might be one of the leading playwrights in Europe.' No matter how often Shaw dismissed this complaint, Archer kept repeating it, to Shaw's frustration. When Archer published* The Old Drama and the New *in 1923, he was still making this lament – even though he also argued that Shaw deserved the Nobel Prize in Literature. (See the six letters in June 1923 for the culmination of their duels over Shaw's plays.)*

I have written to Meyerfeldt to come at 1 instead of half past; so come along. I will do the talking; and you can spare yourself for Tree & get a comfortable lunch & have plenty of time to get to the Haymarket.

As to your letter, all I can say is – Yah! go and stereotype your own confounded article. If you keep hitting the same key you naturally get the same note. You are quite wrong about the others saying the same thing. A few who know me set up the same cliché; but they have had the sense to drop it because they cant get any further with it. As to your knowing other dramatists who dont reproduce their own views & ideas, the explanation is obvious: they havnt any to reproduce – at least none peculiar to themselves. They deal in the readymade article, which is as characteristic of the first score of men you meet in the Strand as of themselves. Their heroes are not themselves because their heroes are not heroes at all, but nobodies. My heroes are all Shaws because, like myself, they are somebodies. As to Shakespear, if you cant see the underlying identity of Iago, Richard III, Edmund, and Thersites, of Hamlet, Macbeth, the Duke in Measure for M., Ulysses and Prospero, of Timon & Jacques &c &c &c, then you are no critic, but only a beglamoured joskyn in a booth. But what is the use of arguing as if Shakespear's or my 'creations' *could* be anything but impersonations? Of course one can read the police news in different voices, like Sloppy in Our Mutual Friend: one can do Faust & Mephistopheles, Athos & Aramis, Romeo & Mercutio, Morell & Eugene, Napoleon & Caesar; but after all what is it but Goethe or Dumas or Shakespear character-acting? These men, like me, understand that men fundamentally *are* identical: they seek for their characters in themselves, and know how to say 'But for the grace of God there go I.' It has been said of me repeatedly of late that I do not do this; that I am an observer only & not a sympathizer; and this, though false, is further on the way to the truth than your inane formula, which only shuts the path in your own face. If you write a play with the characters all Archers, it will be a good play; and you will be astonished to find how many different people you are. As to my disappointing you, it bereaves me of breath. You infernal lazy scoundrel, which of us has had to produce works of genius for both – you or I? Who went to sleep over Widowers' Houses & has never woke up since? Disappointed! Million millions!!! You ought to be shot for such a reproach.

GBS

Max Meyerfeld (1875–1952), not **Meyerfeldt**, was a German critic who wanted to replace Trebitsch as Shaw's German translator. Shaw defended Trebitsch against Meyerfeld's attacks, even when Meyerfeld came to Adelphi Terrace 'with a heap of flowers for my wife' (Trebitsch: 82). Meyerfeld continued his public critiques, but in 1908, as Dan Laurence pointed out (CL 2: 412), Trebitsch and Shaw settled scores by criticizing Meyerfeld's translation of Wilde's *De Profundis.* In June 1904 at His Majesty's Theatre H.B. **Tree** staged a revival of *The Merry Wives of Windsor,* with Tree as Falstaff, Ellen Terry as Mistress Page, and Constance Collier as Mistress Ford (9 perfs.). There was no matinee performance on 13 June, but there were matinees on 21 and 24 June (Wearing 1900: 299). So the luncheon may have been held on one of those dates. Two years earlier Terry and Mrs Kendal had joined Tree in *Merry Wives* for 56 performances. When Shaw referred to **others saying the same thing**, he likely had in mind both A.W. Walkley and Max Beerbohm. Both of them regularly complained that Shaw's plays serve as platforms for his political agendas. The phrase **joskyn in a booth** refers to a 'joskin,' British slang for a bumpkin. Shaw likely had in mind this type of character in a puppet booth, a rustic clown or low character of the penny gaff. In Charles Dickens's ***Our Mutual Friend*** Mrs Higden explains to Mr and Mrs Boffin that her ward **Sloppy** is a beautiful reader of the newspaper: 'He do the Police **in different voices**.' T.S. Eliot (1888–1965), when writing *The Waste Land,* used this statement as a working title for his poem. **Athos & Aramis** are characters in *The Three Musketeers* by Alexandre Dumas père (1802–70). Archer supposedly **went to sleep** when Shaw read to him the draft of the unfinished play in 1887, not during the 1892 production of *Widowers' Houses.* Shaw repeated several versions of this anecdote about Archer nodding off, almost as often as Archer complained about the dominance of the GBS persona in the plays.

108 / To William Archer

The Old House, Harmer Green, Welwyn
17th June 1905

[APCS: BL 45296 f 157]

There is a break in the extant correspondence from 14 June 1904 to 17 June 1905, probably because of missing letters. In May and early June 1905 Shaw wrote Passion, Poison and Petrifaction or the Fatal Gazogene (A Brief Tragedy for Barns and Booths). *This burlesque of melodrama was commissioned, as*

Shaw later explained, 'at the request of Mr Cyril Maude, under whose direction it was performed repeatedly, with colossal success, in a booth in Regent's Park, for the benefit of The Actors' Orphanage, on 14 July 1905' (CP 3: 203). It featured Irene Vanbrugh, Cyril Maude, and Eric Lewis. Shaw did not see the performance because he and Charlotte left on 6 July for County Cork, Ireland. This 'tomfoolery,' as Shaw explained to Archibald Henderson, had its origin in 'a story about a cat' that he told to Tom Archer and other children 'in the early days of William Archer's married life.' In this story Shaw narrated 'how at one time my aunt was interested in making little plaster-of-paris figures; and one day the cat came along, and thinking it was milk, lapped up the liquid plaster-of-paris. It then curled up and went to sleep on the hearthrug. Hours elapsed, and it never stirred. At last my aunt, alarmed at its immobility, attempted to lift it, and found it a ponderous mass of cement.' When one of the children asked what happened, Shaw said that his aunt used the cat to prop open the back door of the house. 'There it remained for ever after.' Archer 'shrieked with laughter at the back door touch. Mrs. Archer never believed a word I said afterwards' (Hend 3: 567).

Huneker is not in England as far as I know. At least he has not notified me of his arrival or intention of coming; and there are reasons why he should if he intended the trip. His address is The Carrollton, 981 Madison Avenue, New York.

Have you seen the title of my new play – 'Poison, & Petrifaction, or the Fatal Gayogene'? It may interest Mrs Archer to know that Petrifaction alludes to a great human development of the tragedy of the plaster cat.

G. B. S.

James Gibbons **Huneker** (1860–1921), an American critic of the arts, published *Iconoclasts* in 1905. It featured a section on Shaw. In the New York *Sun* (25 October 1903) he reviewed the publication of *Man and Superman*. Like Archer he loved *Candida*, but dismissed *Man and Superman* as unactable talk. He did come to London later in 1905, but he gave Shaw 'the slip' (CL 2: 526). In 1906 he published in New York a selection of Shaw's theatre criticism from the *Saturday Review* under the title of *Dramatic Opinions and Essays* (2 vols). Shaw provided a short preface, 'The Author's Apology' (v–viii), in which he justified his attacks on Shakespeare and Henry Irving and his battles for Ibsen and himself. Sloppy editing and typesetting marred the texts of the reviews, and many of them were abridged. Also, though Huneker featured 113 of Shaw's articles, he deleted 38. Among those he removed were 'Mr William Archer's Criticisms' (13 April 1895),' The New Century Theatre' (10 April 1897), and 'Archer's Annual' (19 March 1898). (Concerning these 38 articles that were deleted, not merely truncated, see Biblio 1: 190–1; this helpful list of the missing articles corrects a misleading statement in Biblio 1: 70.)

109 / To William Archer Berry, Rosscarbery, Co. Cork
[c. 27th September 1905]

[APCS: BL 45296 f 158]

The Shaws visited Charlotte's family estate in Derby, County Cork from 7 July until 29 September. It was Shaw's first trip to Ireland since leaving in 1876. After returning to England in early October, the Shaws visited Charlotte's sister, Mary Cholmondeley (c. 1855–1929), and her husband, Col. Hugh Cecil Cholmondeley (1852–1941), who lived in Shropshire. This photographic postcard showed a profile of Shaw, wearing glasses. Beneath the portrait Shaw inscribed 'Ole Shaw.' Archer probably replied, but the letter is missing.

Do you by any chance know Ole Bang's address? If so, pop it on a postcard & send it to 10 Adelphi Terrace where I shall be on Saturday morning on my way hence to Shropshire.

G.B.S.

Oluf Lundt Bang (1870-?), known as **Olë Bang**, was a Norwegian playwright. In January 1905, upon the invitation of the American actress Minnie Maddern Fiske (1863–1932), he had given a public reading in Norwegian of scenes from *Peer Gynt* in New York City at the Manhattan Theatre, which Mrs Fiske managed. In May, as Archer noted in *The World* (30 May 1905), he presented this reading in London. This Olë Bang should not be confused with Oluf Lundt Bang (1788–1877), the dramatist, or with Hermann Joachim Bang (1857–1912), the Danish novelist and theatre critic, whom Ibsen asked to advise Lugné-Poë at the *Théâtre de l'Oeuvre* in Paris for rehearsals of *Rosmersholm* (1893) and *The Master Builder* (1894). Nor should Olë Bang be confused with Olë Bull [Bornemann] (1810–80), the famous Norwegian violinist and composer. In July 1886 Shaw wrote a book review of a memoir about him by his wife Sara Chapman Bull (1850–1911), his young second wife (Tyson 1: 156–64). At Archer's house in May 1887 Shaw attended a violin performance by Olë Bull's Son, Alexander (Diaries 1: 269).

110 / To Mrs Frances Archer 10 Adelphi Terrace WC
27th October 1905

[ALS: HRC, folder 32.4]

In September 1904 Mrs Archer had developed a Nerve Training Colony at King's Langley in Hertfordshire. The service provided physical therapy that relaxed muscles and nerves.

Dear Mrs Archer

I have got so screwed up into nervous knots by overwork lately that I have serious thoughts of asking you to unscrew me. I have quite lost the power myself. Have you a vacancy for a patient? You warned me against getting old; but I have been doing it ever since; and unless you can stop me I shall be eighty in a few months.

Have you anything in the nature of a card of terms? My beautiful Superwoman at the Court Theatre (alias Lillah McCarthy) would be very much the better for a course of unstiffening; and I should like to persuade her to go to you. The American superwoman, who is having a prodigious success, is a prior pupil of yours – Fay Davis.

In the afternoons between 3 and 5 is my only free time. I am generally in a black knot by then. I will call tomorrow (Saturday) at 3. If you are engaged then, or have left, leave a line with the housekeeper for me. I called today & learnt that you are expected tomorrow.

Yours sincerely
G. Bernard Shaw

Lillah McCarthy (1876–1960) played the role of Ann Whitefield in the production of *Man and Superman* (minus act 3) at the Court Theatre. H. Granville Barker played Tanner. Produced by the Stage Society and Vedrenne-Barker, it opened on 23 May for 14 matinee performances. The production was revived, again minus act 3, at the Court Theatre by Vedrenne-Barker for 68 evening performances from 23 October to 30 December. **Fay Davis** (1872–1945), an American actress, played Ann in Charles Dillingham's New York production of *Man and Superman* (minus act 3), starring Robert Loraine (1876–1935) as Tanner. It opened on 5 September 1905 and ran for over six months; then it toured for another seven months. Shaw's fame in America was rapidly expanding. Instead of his standard signature of G.B.S., as he signed his letters to Archer, he provided **G. Bernard Shaw** for Mrs Archer.

111 / To William Archer

10 Adelphi Terrace WC
8th November 1905

[ALS: BL 45296 f 159; CL 2]

Following a try-out in New Haven, Connecticut, on 27 October, Mrs Warren's Profession *opened in New York City on 30 October at the Garrick Theatre. Arnold Daly (1875–1927), who played the role of Frank, was the director. After one performance the police closed the production. Anthony Comstock (1844–1915), a postal inspector who prided himself on destroying 'obscene' literature and pictures, was the secretary of the New York Society for the Suppression of Vice. He warned*

Daly that he was opposed to the staging of a play written by an 'Irish Smut Dealer.' But Daly ignored Comstock's threats and also Shaw's warnings of possible problems. The performance sold out. The audience was polled by a handout distributed by the New York World *newspaper. Some 304 people voted that the play was 'Fit' for production; 272 voted 'Unfit.' But close to 400 did not vote. Several newspapers condemned the 'immoral' play for 'glorifying prostitution.' Daly quickly withdrew* Mrs Warren's Profession, *and revived* Candida *for the rest of the week. On 1 November Shaw published a statement in the* New York Sun *entitled 'Shaw Proud of His Play.' This statement also appeared in London in the* Daily News *on 2 November (Biblio 2: C1501).*

The police commissioner, William McAdoo, who attended the performance, issued arrest warrants for Daly, the actress Mary Shaw (1854–1929), and various others involved in the production. They were charged with disorderly conduct, but only the house manager, Samuel W. Gumpertz, was charged with being a public nuisance. A hearing at the Court of Special Sessions imposed guilty verdicts, but seven months later everyone was acquitted. Accordingly, on 7 July 1906 Shaw proclaimed 'America Kinder than Britain' in the New York American *(Biblio 2: 1545).*

Back in London Archer and Shaw continued to take advantage of the dispute. Archer published 'America and Mrs. Warren' in the Morning Leader *on 4 November 1905. He satirized the 'philistine public ... for being shocked,' and he dismissed the closed-minded press: 'The critic who denies the extraordinary ability of the play has evidently been thrown into a condition of moral panic that has paralysed his perceptions and judgment.' He praised 'the play in which Mr. Shaw gave unmistakable evidence of his rare dramatic talent.' Yet despite his campaigns since the 1880s against stage censorship, including his defences of the 'private' performances of Shelley's* The Cenci *and Ibsen's* Ghosts *(plays also about incest), he made a surprising argument that the closing of the New York production expressed the will of the people. 'If one inquires whether the police authorities have done wrong in stopping the performance of* Mrs Warren, *I am inclined to think that the answer must be in the negative. I doubt whether any other course was open to them. It is manifest that the play did not edify, but genuinely scandalized the public. Those who went to see subsequent performances would have been attracted, not by its dramatic merits or by its morality, but by its supposed immorality; and it cannot be public policy to permit an entertainment which, whatever may have been the author's intention, appeals to the baser instincts of the public. The moral qualities of a work of art does not reside in itself, but in the relation to the percipient mind.' He thus concluded, despite the play's artistic virtues, that* Mrs Warren *invited public resistance because of the way Shaw presented the incest theme.*

In a long letter to the editor of the Morning Leader *on 7 November, Shaw rigorously defended his play, and countered Archer's argument. The rebuttal is one of Shaw's powerful statements against censorship and for an open society (Biblio 2: C1502). A day later he sent the following letter to Archer, and enclosed a 'spare proof' of the newspaper copy of his abridged letter to the editor of the* New York Sun *on 1 November.*

I send you a spare proof [of] the part of my reply which was meant for American consumption only.

Apart from the emergency created by the trial in America, I am glad to have the opportunity of making you reconsider your old explanation – that I cannot touch pitch without wallowing in it &c &c. The incestuous part of Mrs Warren is a genuine part of the original plan because it is what you call an anecdote, or rather two anecdotes. I knew of a case of a young man who, on being initiated by a modern Madame de Warens (observe the name), was rather taken aback by her reproaching him for being 'not half the man his father was.' I also watched the case of a man who was a friend of my mother in her young days: when my sister grew up he became infatuated about her and wanted to marry her. And there was, of course, the famous —— case, where a young married woman was seduced (in the street from which Mrs. W's name was taken) by a man who had formerly seduced her mother. A certain inevitability about these cases had struck me as being dramatic long before I wrote Mrs Warren, also a certain squalid comicality consisting partly, I think, in the fact that there was such an utter absence of any tragic consequences when there was no exposure. These and many confirmatory observations made the solid mass of 'Mrs W's P' – there is really no side issue.

Thanks for letter in today's Leader – just the thing.

G.B.S.

The **part of Mrs Warren** was played by Mary Shaw, a supporter of women's rights. She had performed in *Ghosts* and *Hedda Gabler* in 1903 and 1904. In 1909 she staged Elizabeth Robins's *Votes for Women.* **Madame** Françoise-Louise **de Warens** (1699–1762), divorced from her husband in 1726, met Jean-Jacques Rousseau (1712–78) in 1728 and became his his benefactress and mistress. They lived together in 1735–6. Rousseau writes about her in his *Confessions.* The **friend of my mother** was Vandeluer Lee, who had carried on an affair with Shaw's mother in Dublin. Lee later attempted to seduce Shaw's sister Lucy in London, but she rejected him. Shaw provided the long dash in **the famous —— case**. In Archer's **letter in today's Leader** he reaffirmed his opposition to censorship. The letter was a follow-up to his article 'America and Mrs. Warren' (ML, 4 November) and Shaw's letter to the editor of *ML* on 7 November.

112 / To William Archer

10 Adelphi Terrace WC
15th November 1905

[TLS: BL 45296 ff 160–3; CL 2]

In this letter Shaw was responding to a missing letter from Archer (c. 9–14 November). Apparently Archer had made some comments about family affections and the effect of blood relations upon human behaviour. And he again commented upon Mrs Warren's Profession. *Whatever the case, he said more than enough to launch Shaw into a rebuttal on the theme of incest. Ranging widely, he considered the topics of botanical science, consanguinity, sexual attraction, human psychology, societal attitudes toward incest, and even his childhood experiences. He settled into a full debating mode of delivery. But because he offered in this letter a series of arguments by analogy on the general topic of human sexuality, his generalizations masked or evaded the specific nature of Archer's artistic concerns. From Archer's viewpoint, as he explained in the following letter of 18 November, these scientific, cultural, and personal topics were beside the point. They did not address his basic complaint that Shaw had failed to integrate the incest theme into* Mrs Warren's Profession. *His reservations were artistic, not ethical or social. Archer continued to admire the play, but he also continued to disapprove of the incest scene between Vivie and Frank.*

In 1905, not surprisingly, Shaw rejected any and all negative comments on the play. But two decades later, in calmer times, he was quite capable of entertaining his own negative judgments. For example, after the Lord Chamberlain's Office finally allowed public performances of the play in London, he declared to the actress Gertrude Kingston (1866–1937): 'I can't stand anybody as Mrs Warren, because I can't stand the play itself … Ugh' (16 February 1925; Holroyd 1: 295). On occasion he would even criticize several of the early plays. But these doubts were temporary.

My dear Archer

You are the laziest man in London. The way you calmly leave me to do all your thinking for you is beyond words.

Now listen.

Carry your mind back to the case of Linnaeus, who first explained the fertilization of plants. His book was immediately denounced as immoral. So it was. The instructive bee, improving the shining hour to the edification of the infant mind, became an infamous go-between; and every hedgerow became a pornographic exhibition.

Now can you conceive it possible for Linnaeus to have returned to the assumption that every flower came straight from the hand of God? Suppose he had seen the whole of Europe proceed straight from the study of botany to the wildest sexual excesses, could he have withdrawn his discovery on that account? Clearly not.

Well, no more is it possible for me to give a false answer to any question raised by the human relations with which I deal merely because the consequences of the true answer may be this, that, or the other. If the avowal of Vivie and Frank that the suggestion of Crofts made no difference in their feeling towards one another – as under those circumstances it most assuredly would not – resulted in the immediate committal of incest by every brother and sister witnessing the play, I could no more alter the passage on that account than Linnaeus could alter his treatise on botany. It is useless to preach the refusal of knowledge and of the consequences of knowledge.

Now as to the family question. I have never denied the existence of family love in the sense in which you describe it. I should as soon think of denying the existence of the affection of schoolfellows or shipmates or any other of the forms of affection resulting from intimate association. I do not deny, for instance, that you have a strong affection for Charles. But why you should deny him all credit for that, and insist that his being a nice fellow has nothing to do with it – that it is a mere symptom of consanguinity – I cannot understand. If you come to that, *I* like Charles, and should probably have formed a strong affection for him if we had been brought up in the same house at the same ages. Besides, you confess to a preference in the matter, though your other brothers are equally close in blood. Consanguinarily they are all equally near to you. But are they all equally dear to you? Not a bit of it. You paint the degrees with a graphic pen. For Charles, strong affection. For Jim, benevolent affability. For the others, apologetic indifference, with a perceptible vagueness as to their names and numbers. That is to say, exactly the feeling you would have towards schoolfellows of different ages and generations. A more convincing demonstration of the wisdom and scientific soundness of my refusal to accept the popular theory of family affection as a result of consanguinity could hardly be adduced.

One of the objections to that theory is this. It is obviously expedient that sexual intercourse should be ruled out as between brothers and sisters under our family system. It is equally obvious that it must be ruled out in a mixed school, the reason being the same in both cases: that is, the danger of sexual precocity. It should be a point of honor not to make love to your sister, your schoolfellow, your friend's wife, a nun &c.; and the most important case is the housemate in childhood, whether relative or stranger in blood. Young children need not be bothered about it: I find that they like Mrs Warren's Profession because to them the crowning charm of the Babes in the Wood courtship is that the babes turn out to be brother and sister. In the same way, if you ask a little boy whom he would like to marry, he is as likely as not to say his mother. But when childhood is over, and reasons have to be given, it is a hideous error to bring in the consanguinity theory and represent incest as being 'wrapped in a strange cloud of sin and shame.' From that you get The Cenci, Parisina, and the sharpening of Crofts's pursuit of Vivie by the morbidity of his imagination.

Note, in passing, that the incest in Die Walküre has never been felt to be incest at all, because Siegmund and Sieglinde were not brought up together.

What is the general evidence on the subject? Clearly, it is that the tables of affinity are conventional, not natural. The convention varies from country to country. Among Christians marriage between uncle and niece and between first cousins is lawful in one country and incestuous in another. So is marriage with a deceased wife's sister. The refusal of a man to marry his deceased brother's wife is in some societies the climax of unnatural horror. There are actually cases in which a widow is expected to marry her own son to provide a head for the family: and you may remember that Caesar's dream about his mother before he crossed the Rubicon was considered by him a happy omen, and is recorded without the slightest revolt by Plutarch. We are more horrified by incest between parent and child than between brother and sister, though the consanguinity between brother and sister is the closest possible – much closer than between parent and child, the reason being, obviously, that it is more inconvenient socially, and therefore more unbecoming. A union between stepmother and stepson would horrify us equally, though here there is no blood relationship at all.

Why has all this such an interest for me? I think you have sometimes suspected me of a quite unholy fancy for it. But to anybody whose main work is to fight for real morality in its continual struggle for life with the spurious morality of mere custom, it is too valuable and interesting as an illustration not to recur pretty frequently. There is no other case in which a pure convention masquerades so effectually as a human instinct. The next best is an equally unpleasant one: namely, the fact that a man who will commit the horrible wickedness of marrying when he has syphilis, will shrink with genuine repugnance from walking down Bond St in the afternoon in a frock coat and bowler hat. But in spite of the enormous irony of this, it is not so good an illustration of the force of custom and convention as incest, because after all, nobody pretends that the bowler hat is anything worse than an offence against good taste, whereas people have been burnt alive for marriages which under other codes are regarded as quite normal, and even desirable.

Whether consanguinity has a real effect in sexual relations is very doubtful. Let me explain what I mean by a real effect. When I was a small boy I once saw a jar in a chemist's shop labelled Ipecacuanha Lozenges. I thought the name fascinating; and I thought all lozenges were sweetmeats. I went in and asked for some. The chemist asked me would I have an ounce. I said I would have a pennorth, that being the utmost of my means. He gave me about a dozen; and I ate them and rather liked them. Half an hour later I was a retching, belching, spewing, agonized worm. I call that a real effect, because it occurred without suggestion, without expectation, in flat violation of my mental attitude towards the lozenges. Now imagine yourself lunching with a Fijian chief. He gives you some excellent pork; and it agrees with you perfectly, as he is careful not to inform you that it is really the remains of his deceased uncle. But if somebody came in and let the cat out of the bag, you would probably be hideously sick. That is not a real effect of the uncle on your stomach, but of our customs on your imagination.

Suppose now you had committed some crime or had some adventure in your youth that caused you to leave the country and settle in America under an assumed name, concealing your action from your family. Suppose one of your sisters afterwards emigrates also and marries, thus changing her name. Suppose you meet her and, in entire ignorance of your relationship, are led to contemplate sexual intercourse with her. Do you believe you would both avoid such a thing by instinctive repugnance? I see no reason to believe that you would. But if you would, then it seems to me that the repugnance must affect all the sympathetic sentiments more or less, and that, as Tanner says, 'the tables of consanguinity have a natural basis in a natural repugnance.' My own belief is that the case would be the Fijian one over again: that is, that if you discovered your relationship next morning you would both be shocked, or even take a quite morbid view of the situation, according to the strength of your prejudices, but that if you were never the wiser you might marry and bring up a large family without the smallest misgiving or anybody being a penny the worse.

However, this does not mean that I consider that the ordinary laws of attraction and repulsion are altered by consanguinity. It is roughly true that liking goes by contraries; and sisters and brothers are commonly too like one another to attract one another. If you try the experiment of walking from end to end of Oxford Street and counting the women whom you would care to entertain sexually, you will probably be surprised by your own fastidiousness. Two per cent would be a quite Turkish proportion. I should expect you to find that the odds against any particular woman attracting you are about 5000 to 1. Under these circumstances the fact that our sisters do not attract us needs no consanguinity theory to explain it. I am disposed to insist on this view of the matter because I think it is the less morbid one. I think our imaginations are systematically inflamed by surrounding sex with imaginary and imputed horrors, and that a great deal of the fuss we make about such things is as absurd and mischievous as the fuss savages make about touching anything that a menstruating woman has touched. I deliberately make a point of 'callousness' on the subject; and I think I am right.

My more extreme views on the sex question are to be inferred from a remarkable (and consequently unremarked) passage in Man & Superman, where Don Juan asks Dona Ana whether the sex relation is really a personal one. 'Do my sex the justice to admit, Senor, that we have always recognized that the sex relation is not a personal or friendly relation at all.' ANA – Not a personal nor friendly relation! What relation can be more personal! more sacred! more holy! DON JUAN – Sacred and holy if you like, Ana, but not personally friendly. Your relation to God is sacred and holy: dare you call it personally friendly? &c &c &c.' I feel quite sure that in the long run it will be seen that the arch-incest is the sexual intercourse of husband and wife, and that the intercourse from which the race will be bred will be an intercourse between people who do not know one another, and who will make it a most sacred point of honor not to associate their breeding intercourse with any further intrusion whatever. Suppose such a state of things to have taken place, then incest would no longer have anything to do with consanguinity, because there would be no necessity for people to know their parents or their relatives. Incest would then mean intercourse between housemates – an important matter if children were brought up in households of ten or so in consequence of the common observation that the children of large families are the most humanized and successful.

I have not time to work this out further for you; so you must take it with a reasonable construction, and not conclude that I am a lunatic on the strength, not of what I expect, but of the many associations which people without my fine analytic mind persist in attaching to things that do not involve them in the least.

yours ever,
GBS

Carolus **Linnaeus** (Karl von Linné, 1707–78), the Swedish botanist and taxonomist, gained international renown for his binomial nomenclature for plants and animals. During his adult years Archer was close to his brother **Charles**, to whom he wrote often, but had limited contact with his brother **Jim** and other members of the family. Archer's parents, Thomas (1823–1905) and Grace (1833–1911), had nine children. The family moved often, with residencies in dozens of places in Scotland, Norway, England, and Australia. In 1912, when on his world tour, he visited his sister Grace Stedman in China (see letter of 15 June 1912), and spent several months with Charles in India. The legend of the ***Babes in the Woods*** derived from sixteenth-century ballads and folktales, which may be based upon an event in Norfolk. The sad tale described the abandonment and deaths of a young brother and his sister in the woods. The birds covered over their bodies with leaves. A version of the legend was adapted for a Christmas pantomime show at Drury Lane in 1897 and 1907. In his *Saturday Review* assessment of the 1897 production, Shaw was quite dismissive of the spectacle (1 January 1898; Dukore 3: 972–5). The line '**wrapped in a strange cloud of sin and shame**' is from Shelley's *The Cenci* (5,5). The text for Donizetti's opera ***Parisina*** (1833) is based on Byron's poem (1816) of this name. **Siegemund** and **Sieglinde** are brother and sister in Wagner's *Die Walküre,* the second opera of *Der Ring des Nibelungen.* In *The Life of Julius Caesar* Plutarch describes one version of **Caesar's dream about his mother**, reporting that on the night before crossing the Rubicon Caesar dreamed that he committed incest with his mother. Also, Suetonius, in *The Lives of the Twelve Caesars,* relates that Julius Caesar dreamed of sleeping with his mother.

113 / To G. Bernard Shaw [no address]
18th November 1905

[ALS: BL 45296 ff 165–8]

In a reply to Shaw's letter of 15 November, Archer, in turn, launched into his own rebuttal. In the process he expressed his frustration that Shaw seemed determined to exasperate him and to misinterpret his statements in his previous letter, which has not survived.

*On 5 October 1928, four years after Archer's death, Shaw attached a note to this letter, perhaps intended for Blanche Patch (1879–1966), his secretary. The note had the address of Whitehall Court, the London residence for the Shaws in 1927. He wrote: 'This has just turned up. You had better add it to your collection, as his letters should be kept together as much as possible.' Also, in the left margin of the first page of this letter, Shaw wrote: 'I do not see how the possibility and probability of the situation which arises in the play [*Mrs Warren's Profession*] can be fairly excluded from any presentation of promiscuity or group marriage. This does not seem to have occurred to W.A. Its introduction seemed to him to be gratuitous. G.B.S.' This marginal notation, with its verbs in the past tense, was likely written in 1928.*

My dear G.B.S.

I never in my life read a document more utterly beside the mark than your letter. Man alive, I agree with you on every point, and tried to say so. (I don't know, of course, about the speculation at the end as to impersonal breeding, but that too is a quite conceivable development.)

(1) I never for a moment suspect you of any 'unholy fancy' for any topic whatsoever; but I have suspected you – no, that is not the word – of a perverse fancy for saying things to startle & exasperate rather than to enlighten.

(2) I have never conceived incest as 'wrapped in a strange cloud of sin & shame.' I said so emphatically in my letter. I regard the objection to it as a pure convention, but as a most valuable & convenient convention, for which it is worth while to make any legitimate fight. You admit its convenience yourself, but apparently dont see that it is just what you deny (by implication) in 'Mrs Warren.' Psychologically, too, you are wrong about Frank & Vivie. If they were normal young persons, on the revelation of their consanguinity, the convention – mark you, not the consanguinity but the convention – would take them by the throat, just as, in your

illustration, the knowledge that he had been eating 'fake pig' would act as an emetic to a civilized man (I dont think it would to me, but let that pass). The truth is, of course, that in 'Mrs Warren' you raise the complex & delicate issue & dismiss it in half a page, having said nothing that was worth saying, & merely opened the door to all sorts of misunderstanding. Is it worth while, at this time of day, to give people the idea that you cordially approve of the marriage of brother & sister, when as a matter of fact you only intend a jibe at the exploded superstition of the *voix du sang*?

(3) I seem to have confused you by passing from the subject of incest to that of family affection. They were entirely distinct in my mind, the two points of my letter having no more connection than if the one had been on astronomy & the other on the tariff question. In all you say I entirely agree. I never dreamt of founding family affection upon consanguinity. I think, indeed, that similar heredity has a certain influence in predisposing to concord; but it cuts both ways – there are many cases (I admit) in which it predisposes to friction. In short, my analysis of family affection is exactly your own. It arises from habits of companionship, common memories, common vanities, common tastes (the result of companionship at impressionable ages – partly perhaps, too, of similar heredity) and from a score of other perfectly natural and tangible causes. I no more believe in the *voix du sang* imposing family affection than I believe in it prohibiting incest. But whatever its source, family affection is a great & potent *fact* in human relations: and it is your persistent denial of the *fact* that seems to me sociologically unscientific and artistically tedious.

Now make a great effort, and try to conceive that I am not an idiot: whence it will follow that when you are controverting something idiotic, the chances are you are controverting something I didn't say. On political questions I may often be practically an idiot, simply because I have never had time to give them any study. But on such elementary questions of morals & psychology, it is really no good assuming that I am a superstitious ass. The assumption is all the less reasonable as, point for point, I agree with you on the moral & psychological plane. The trouble is that when you come to translate theory into art, you are so jolly apt (in my judgment) to do it at once inartistically & illogically & thus to repel your audience while falsifying your own real conviction. So there!

Yours ever
W.A.

114 / To William Archer

10 Adelphi Terrace WC
1st January 1906

[ALS: BL 45296 f 169; CL 2 partial]

The autumn season of the Vedrenne-Barker management in 1905 offered two revivals and three premieres. The revivals were Ibsen's The Wild Duck *and Shaw's* Man and Superman. *The premieres were* Major Barbara, The Voysey Inheritance *by H. Granville Barker, and* The Return of the Prodigal *by Edward St John Hankin (1869–1909). Archer was deeply impressed by Barker's play, less so by Hankin's.* Major Barbara *opened on 28 November (52 perfs.). Annie Russell (1864–1936) played Barbara, Barker was Cusins, and Louis Calvert was Undershaft.*

In his review (World, 5 December 1905) Archer stated that 'Mr Shaw is taking his revenge on Messrs. Vedrenne and Barker for having, in their production of Man and Superman, *omitted the dialogue in hell between Don Juan, Donna Ana, the Commander, and the Devil. He has determined to prove, to them and to all of us, that he can make a mere discussion "as good as a play." And he has unquestionably succeeded:* Major Barbara *is a fascinating entertainment.' Archer interpreted the play as an allegory of Shaw's life and ideas. The character of Barbara represents 'the optimistic socialism of Mr. Shaw's younger years, when he used to deliver a dozen lectures a week.' Undershaft, 'an admirable figure,' represents Shaw today. 'There is a passionate and even poetical conviction in many of his sayings that is intensely dramatic and thrilling.' As for Shaw of the future, Archer becomes philosophical. 'But over the Shaw of the past and Shaw of the present there hovers a third Shaw, the Shaw of the fourth dimension, typified in the Euripidean ironist, Adolphus Cusins ... His is the philosophic intellect which can get outside Time and Space, shake off the tyranny of the categories, and criticize the frame of things from the standpoint of pure reason.' This was a clever but fanciful reading. Ironically, though Archer repeatedly complained that Shaw's plays represented the G.B.S. persona, he proceeded to praise the play for being a biographical reproduction of the stages of Shaw's identity. Of course, Shaw rejected this imposed biography.*

In January Archer shifted jobs from The World, *a weekly journal, to* The Tribune, *a new liberal daily. He published his last column for* The World *on 16 January. He had spent twenty-one years there, but would spend just two at* The Tribune. *Each week at* The Tribune *he wrote not only a column called 'About the Theatre' but also short reviews on select productions.*

My dear Archer

I have only just heard of your transfer from The World to The Tribune. Have you any influence in the choice of your successor? If so, and it is not already bespoken, the absolute-best man in London for it is Cecil Chesterton, 11 Warwick Gardens, Kensington W. I induced Hodge of the Saturday to put him on when Max was unwilling to criticise Fagin at His Majesty's; and he wrote a most brilliant & sound article. He is a brother of Gilbert. It is very important that I should nominate all the dramatic critics for the next ten years or so; and Chesterton will hear out all you can say in his favor, besides being a good Shavian who understands my religious views.

Your article on 'Major Barbara,' the worst you ever wrote, delighted me. The complete success with which I wrecked your mind and left you footling – simply footling – was really the greatest proof of your fundamental sensibility to my magic. The third act is so novel and revolutionary that it will never get across the footlights – at least on top of the second – at one hearing; but the second has been completely grasped by Stead, who has written an admirable notice of it, and by Lodge (Sir Olivier of that ilk – see The Clarion). You, wretched atheist that you are, must see it again tonight. It is a MAGNIFICENT play, a summit in dramatic literature.

Yrs
G.B.S.

Cecil Chesterton (1879–1918), the younger brother of G.K. Chesterton (1874–1936), supported the Fabian Society until 1907, but by 1912 had abandoned socialist politics and became a conservative Roman Catholic like his brother. In 1912, as editor of the journal *New Witness*, he carried out sustained attacks on two Jewish members of the Liberal government, Sir Rufus Isaacs (1860–1935) and Herbert L. Samuel (1870–1963). (Stella Issacs, the sister of Issacs, was married to the playwright Alfred Sutro.) Chesterton accused Issacs and Samuel of purchasing shares in the American Marconi company when the government was secretly negotiating a major contract for radio transmission. The 'Marconi Scandal' generated charges and countercharges about the misuse of political information, but a select committee of the Liberal government cleared Isaacs and Samuel. In 1918, having received major wounds in the war, Chesterton died in a French hospital. H. Beerbohm **Tree** opened his production of *Oliver Twist*, adapted by J. Comyns Carr, at His Majesty's in September 1905 (112 perfs.). Tree presented a nasty but popular caricature of Fagin as 'a dirty old Jew' (Pearson Tree: 153). W.T. **Stead** reviewed *Major Barbara* in the *Review of Reviews*. **Sir Olivier Lodge** (1851–1940), a scientist and principal of the University of Birmingham, reviewed the Court Theatre production in *The Clarion*. He praised Shaw's treatment of the Christian religion in act 2 of *Major Barbara*. This act was 'one of the finest pieces of dramatic art that has been seen for a long time.' But Lodge felt that the final act at Undershaft's factory was 'diabolically cynical' (Evans 160–2).

115 / To G. Bernard Shaw [no address]
3rd January 1906

[ALS: BL 73484 f 30]

My dear G.B.S.

I had promised Phil Carr if I resigned the *World,* to recommend him as my successor & I did so in sending in my resignation. So I'm afraid I can't put forward another man, unless I were to hear that Carr has no chance. I am fairly sure that neither Carr nor Chesterton is in the running but that some one of the Harmsworth gang will get the place.

I wanted to see you on Monday night, but 'Major Barbara' had a disastrous effect on Tom, who came to the theatre with a headache & had to leave towards the end of the second act, feeling very sick. I even hastened our departure a little, for fear it might seem like a protest against 'My God why hast thou forsaken me.' By the bye, in this monstrous farrago at the Shaftesbury, a crucifix is introduced in a way that *I* would consider shocking, if I were in the way of being shocked.

Yours ever,
W.A.

Philip Carr (1874–1958) served as the London critic for the *Manchester Guardian.* As Archer predicted, neither Carr nor Chesterton received the appointment. W. Hamilton Fyfe (1878–1965) replaced Archer at *The World* (Whitebrook 257). Fyfe, a classicist, would later become headmaster of Christ's Hospital. Alfred **Harmsworth** (latter Viscount Northcliffe) controlled several newspapers and journals. The shocking melodrama at the **Shaftesbury** Theatre was *The Jury of Fate* by 'Hugh Morton' (C.M.S. McLennan, 1865–1916), staring H.B. Irving and Lillah McCarthy.

116 / To William Archer The Old House, Harmer Green, Welwyn
7th June 1906

[ALS: BL 45296 ff 171–2; CL 2 partial]

Along with this letter, which was dictated to Mrs Shaw, Shaw enclosed two items: a draft of 'First Aid to Critics,' which became a section of the 'Preface' to Major Barbara, *and a copy of his obituary article on Ibsen. Shaw still used Archer as an editor for drafts of some of his essays (but not the plays). On 9 June Archer published in* The Tribune *an article entitled 'The English Drama in Germany – A Talk with Dr Meyerfeld – Oscar Wilde, Bernard Shaw, Gordon Craig – German Managers and Authors – The Kaiser and the Theatre.' Archer had introduced Dr*

Leon Kellner (1859–1928) to Shaw in 1898. A literary scholar and philologist from Vienna, Kellner published the first German article on Shaw's drama. In 1903 he criticized Trebitsch's translation of Candida, *and as the subsequent translations of Shaw's play appeared, Kellner continued his public assault on Trebitsch. Dr Max Meyerfeld also wrote a negative review of Trebitsch's* Drei Dramen von Bernard Shaw. *Although Trebitsch revised* Drei Dramen *in 1904, Kellner waited until 1911 to acknowledge this (Trebitsch: 38–40, 47–52, 58–9, 141).*

Ibsen died on 23 May; Shaw's obituary essay appeared in The Clarion *on 1 June. Praising Ibsen as the 'greatest dramatic genius of the XIX century,' he provided a perspective on the Ibsen campaign in London, Ibsen's dramatic techniques, and Ibsen's influence on British drama (Dukore 3: 1126–32; Wisenthal: 239–45). He also praised Archer's translations. Archer's obituary notice appeared in the* Morning Leader *on 26 May. He also published 'Ibsen as I Knew Him' (*Monthly Review, *June 1906) and 'Ibsen's Craftsmanship' (FR, July 1906; reprint in Ibsen Essays: 107–24, 125–38).*

(Dictated)

My dear Archer

Charlotte terrifies me by the news that you are going to let loose on the Continent a selection from the staggering hallucinations which you firmly believe to be a sound critical biography of my unfortunate self. Will you therefore read through & return to me the enclosed first draft – rather a scrawly one I am afraid – of part of the Preface to my next volume of plays. The Schopenhauer-Nietzsche stereo may not matter much in England, as it seems impossible to knock any national self-respect into English literary journalism; but when you are addressing a foreign audience you really must not talk as if England were an intellectual vacuum into which the ideas of half a dozen foreign writers rush like the east wind into the receiver of an air pump.

As to Kellner, he came to see me in 1898 on Hindhead, – played billiards with John Burns & Massingham whilst I was taken out for a walk on crutches by my nurse. Thenceforth I regarded him as having Eaten my Salt; so that I was not free to make a personal attack on him of any kind even if I'd wanted to, which I didnt; for Kellner struck me as being a very worthy chump. However, he wanted to translate some of my works; & I would not let him do it because it was absolutely necessary for me to find some young man who would devote himself to reproducing my entire oeuvre in German, exactly as you have reproduced Ibsen in English, whereas all that Kellner wanted was to translate Candida, for which he had a snivelling affection, & perhaps to make a further selection of what he might happen to think worthy of me. I found my man in Trebitsch. Trebitsch began with Candida. He was foolish enough to rush a first-edition of his translation into print before I had been through it. In his utter ignorance of London local government, & of the construction of front gardens in the Hackney road, & also of English Socialist literature, he came quite indescribably to grief in Burgess's references to the Vestry, in the preliminary description of the neighborhood of Victoria Park, & in the list of books in Morell's library. Kellner, eine feste Burg of sound information on these & all other concrete points, took advantage of them to publish a slashing attack on poor Trebitsch, who was held up without mercy as an ignoramus & impostor, le dernier des derniers. Trebitsch has no power of defending himself against attacks of this kind; but he has fought 3 duels. He declared that Kellner was an infamy, & that he must give him an ear-box; & Kellner would probably have fallen beneath his avenging sabre if I had not pacified him by declaring my satisfaction with the translations.

In the meantime exactly the same thing had begun in Germany & Vienna as has been going on about your translations of Ibsen. Journalists who didnt know English tried to imply that they spoke it like natives by pooh poohing Trebitsch as impossible. Journalists who did know English & wanted to supplant him as translator did the same thing; & some of them actually wrote me private letters on the subject which might have made me very uncomfortable if I had not been warned by your experience, & known enough of German to be able to ascertain for myself that the case against Trebitsch rested on mistakes that did not matter & not on real incompetence. In short, there was Meyerfeld in Germany just as there was Gosse in England; & though I have no more reason to complain of Meyerfeld personally than you have of Gosse, everything was done that could be done to discredit Trebitsch with me. Naturally I was not going to let them play the Hedda Gabler trick on me. When they all jumped at Kellner's attack & rejoiced in it, I made it clear that I attributed a good deal of the hostility to him to the feeling of would-be rival translators. No doubt Kellner put the cap on – I shall not pretend to think it was altogether a misfit – but I of course did not attack him personally. As far as he was hit on the *ricochet*, he brought it on himself. His attack on Trebitsch was bitter and contemptuous; and the intention to damage Trebitsch to the utmost of his opportunity was unmistakeable. I went no further in my defence than loyalty to Trebitsch required: in fact Trebitsch was very rueful over the good humor with which I took his ill usage.

Unless you saw my correspondence you could form no idea of what arrant blacklegs & impudent pirates there are in translation business in Germany. I have at last had to let loose the law at them.

Have you seen the enclosed Clarion article on Ibsen? As usual I have had to use up my space in contradiction of current fallacies rather than in affirmation of the old man's qualities: however, he can look after himself in that respect. Until I read the Monthly Review I had no idea that you had seen so much of him. It throws a light on the gross secretiveness of your disposition. Apparently the only person you ever tell anything to is Charles [Archer].

G.B.S.

By the late nineteenth century the word **stereo** was beginning to be used in physics, chemistry, and other scientific fields to identify a method of transmission in multiple channels and procedures. So Shaw apparently adapted the word to suggest a process for combining and delivering the philosophical ideas of the two German philosophers. The phrase **Eaten my Salt** means that a person has accepted one's hospitality; this act establishes a social bond between host and guest. It would thus be inappropriate to speak ill of the person. **John Burns** (1858–1943), a socialist colleague of Shaw's since the 1880s, was active in the Social Democratic Federation, and head of the Progressive Party of the trade unionists. He participated in the 'Black Monday' demonstration in 1886 and 'Bloody Sunday' in 1887, and led the famous London Dock Strike in 1889. Burns served as an M.P. for Battersea from 1892 to 1914. He was the model for Boanerges in *The Apple Cart.* In his discussion on **Trebitsch**, Shaw apparently forgot that in 1901 Archer urged Trebitsch to read Shaw's plays, and provided the introductory letter to Shaw that Trebitsch presented in March1902 when he requested permission to translate the plays. The reference to Kellner's **snivelling affection** for *Candida* was also a backhanded tease of Archer, whose sentimental admiration of the play amused Shaw. The phrase **eine feste Burg** derives from Martin Luther's famous hymn *Ein feste Burg ist unser Gott* (A mighty fortress is our God), which J.S. Bach used for a cantata (BWV 80). In 1891 Edmund **Gosse** obtained permission, by way of William Heinemann, to translate *Hedda Gabler.* Archer published an angry critique of the inadequate translation. He then gained permission to publish his version of the play, which appeared in late 1891.

117 / To G. Bernard Shaw

King's Langley
8th June 1906

[TLS: BL 45296 f 173]

Archer selectively responded to Shaw's letter of 7 June and its two enclosed items. His comments here on Trebitsch's translation mistakes in Der Schlachtenlenker *(*The Man of Destiny*) repeated concerns he had raised in May 1904. See Shaw's letter of 12 May 1904 for additional controversies over Trebitsch as a translator.*

*Archer postponed a reading of Shaw's draft of 'First Aid to Critics,' which was clearly aimed at Archer and his complaints about Shaw's dependence upon Schopenhauer and Nietzsche. And though he read Shaw's obituary notice on Ibsen (*The Clarion, *1 June; see Dukore 3: 1126–32) when Shaw sent a copy to him, Archer delayed his written response to it until he had published his two Ibsen essays in the* Monthly Review *and the* Fortnightly Review *(see note to previous letter). Then, in 'Death and Mr. Bermard Shaw' (Tribune, 14 July), he took the measure of Shaw's complaint that 'Ibsen seems to have succumbed without a struggle to the old notion that a play is not really a play unless it contains a murder, a suicide, or something else out of the* Police Gazette.*' Archer felt compelled to counter this assessment. 'If, in Mr. Shaw's own phrase, 'the illumination of life' is the main purpose of drama, what illuminant, we may ask, can be more powerful than death? To compare a tragic dramatist's preoccupation with death to a morbid tourist's haunting of the Morgue is ... to talk very idly.'*

My dear G&B&S&

(Observe the results of my purchase of a Blickensderfer Type-Writer, largely determined by your reported approval of them.) Make your mind easy – I am neither addressing a foreign audience, nor am I talking about Schopenhauer & Nietzsche. Were it my cue to do so, I should not go to Meyerfeld for prompting. I am only giving, in the course of an interview on the German stage in general, some purely external data as to the performances of your plays. Of course nothing whatever is said as to rival translators or anything of that sort. I don't know how I came to mention Kellner's complaint to MRS. Shaw, but anyway it had nothing to do with the interview. I respect your loyalty to Trebitsch, & I have no doubt he is useful; but since I read carefully about half of his version of the MAN OF DESTINY, I feel that you ought to insist on having his translations revised by some thoroughly competent German – your own German;

unless it has vastly improved, [it] is quite inadequate to cope with master T's enormities, which *must* present you in a distorted light to the German public. As he admits the fact of numerous errors, I don't see that he could reasonably object to a revision, so long as the right of ultimate decision rested with him.

As there is no immediate danger of my saying anything I didn't oughter, I have not read the ms – I mean MS. One always gets a wrong impression of a thing one has to spell out; & your handwriting has not improved any more than my own. On the other hand, I must keep the CLARION article in the meantime – I will try to get a copy for myself in Fleet Street, & then return yours. I am writing about the Old Man's technique for the FORTNIGHTLY, but of course there is nothing new to be said about that. What interests me is the question of violence, bloodshed, avalanches, &c. & their place in the machinery of drama. Your Maeterlinckian [views] are rendered interesting by the fact that you more or less act up to them, while Maeterlinck does the very reverse.

I hope Mrs. Shaw gave Eustace Miles a good wigging.

Yours (and hers)
W.A.

In his article on 'Death and Mr. Bernard Shaw' (Tribune, 14 July 1906), Archer commented upon the **Maeterlinckian** features of Shaw's drama. 'Practically, though not explicitly, Mr. Shaw adopts M. Maeterlinck's famous contention that tragedy is a relic of barbarism – that what art should now aim at is the reproduction of 'life itself,' as distinct from 'a violent, exceptional moment of life.' In his criticism of Ibsen tragic action, Shaw has adopted this idea of drama that Maeterlinck articulated in his essay 'The Tragic in Daily Life' (1896). In May 1906 **Eustace Miles** (1868–1948) opened the Eustace Miles Restaurant in London. Shaw was one of the shareholders. Miles, who was educated at King's College, Cambridge, was a tennis player who won a silver medal in the 1908 Olympics. He supported the suffrage movement, whose leaders often met at the restaurant. Miles published books on health, diet, Roman history, and Latin grammar. It is unclear, however, why he needed a 'good wigging' from Mrs Shaw. Perhaps she scolded or censured him for the food in his new restaurant.

118 / To William Archer

10 Adelphi Terrace WC
7th July 1906

[ALS: BL 45296 f 174; CL 2]

Archer's Tribune *article entitled 'Gilbert and Sullivan Opera' (7 July) called for the revival of the Savoy operettas. He noted the popularity of French comic operas in London, but criticized the 'hack adaptors' who failed to capture the poetic quality of the French librettos and lyrics. These hacks 'substituted for the graceful French lyrics abhorrent jingles equally devoid of metre and meaning.' In his historical overview of comic opera and operetta, he wrote: 'The opera-bouffe of Meilhac and Halévy, Offenbach, and Lecocq was a cynical but witty and graceful product of the feverish period which preceded and followed the war of 1870.'*

In this article Archer was somewhat vague about which of these opéra-bouffe works appeared before and which after the Franco-Prussian war. Henri Meilhac (1831–97), who is best known for his libretto for Georges Bizet's Carmen *(1875), wrote comic librettos for Ludovic Halévy (1834–1908), Jacques Offenbach (1819–1880), and Jean-Robert Planquette (1848–1903). Meilhac and Halévy provided librettos for Offenbach, whose great Parisian successes included* Orphée aux Enfers *(1858),* La Belle Hélène *(1864), and* The Grande Duchesse de Gérolstein *(1867). Adapted for the London stage during the 1860s and 1870s, Offenbach's works – both opéra bouffe and opéra comique – remained quite popular, as Archer pointed out.*

My dear Archer

There is an error in your Tribune article today which is of profound historical importance. Offenbach was a characteristic product of the Hohenstiehl-Schwangau empire. La Belle Helene could not possibly have been written after 1871. The genre gave a last kick in La Fille de Madame Angot, and was succeeded by Les Cloches de Corneville &c &c.

Also, you have smitten W.S.G. inadvertently in your contemptuous dismissal of the English adaptations of the opera bouffe. One of the most popular of them was The Brigands; and the author of that adaptation was Gilbert.

I dont think it can be honestly said that any Gilbert-Sullivan opera touched La Grande Duchesse or Fra Diavolo; and in my opinion a revival of Savoy opera would be resurrection pie with a good deal of ptomaine in it. It is of considerable importance to have Strauss's Salome done here; but nobody will be the worse if The Pirates of Penzance &c are left on the shelf. Trial by Jury is the only really vital product of the collaboration: the rest were market pieces, with an entirely spurious air of what the Daily Telegraph calls 'wholesomeness.' Dont get sentimental about old times: you are much too young to play the veteran. Sullivan's operas are no more worth reviving that Robertson's plays. Call for a revival of Mrs Warren if you like.

This week I have seen The Man from Blankley's and been up in a balloon. I never saw a meaner play or felt more acutely what it would be like to stand on the tip top of the Eiffel Tower on one toe. Today I saw seven balloons from my window; and I thought I was mad until I called the parlormaid & found that she saw them too.

G.B.S

In the reference to the **Hohenstiehl-Schwangau** empire, Shaw made a spelling mistake. In English it is common to identify it as Hohenstiel-Schwangau, without the third 'h' in Hohenstiehl. In this statement Shaw may have had in mind not only the collapse of the decadent Second Empire of Napoleon III, which was overthrown during the Franco-Prussian War of 1870–1, but also Robert Browning's poem, which takes up the topic of Louis Napoleon's government. Browning published his poem *Prince Hohenstiel-Schwangau, Saviour of Society* in 1871. Schwangau is in Bavaria. Charles Lecocq wrote ***La Fille de Madame Angot*** (1872); it appeared in a London adaptation in 1873, and by September 1874 'six different Angots were playing on the touring circuits' (Gänzl 1: 66). Jean-Robert Planquette composed ***Les Cloches de Corneville*** (1877), which was a major London hit during 1878–9. Daniel-François-Espirit Auber (1782–1871) composed **Fra Diavolo** (1830). W.S. Gilbert adapted Offenbach's Les **Brigands** (1869) in 1871. Gilbert and Sullivan's **Trial by Jury** (their second work together) premiered in 1875; it was often revived (e.g., four times in the 1890s, three times in the 1900s). Of special note, from Archer's perspective, it was revived as part of Ellen Terry's Jubilee on 12 June 1906. The matinee performance featured over 100 performers. *The Tribune*, with Archer providing the leadership, organized the campaign for the Jubilee. ***Salome*** (1905), the opera by Richard Strauss (1864–1949), had its London premiere in December 1910 (Covent Garden, 10 perfs.). It was based upon Oscar Wilde's *Salome*, written in French in 1881 and published in French and English in 1893. The play, not the opera, was banned from any London public performance in English until 1930. It was performed in London, however, in a French production on 27 February 1911 by the visiting Théâtre de l'Oeuvre company (2 perfs.). Thomas William **Robertson's plays**, including *Caste*, were popular in the 1860s. ***The Man from Blankley***, a comedy by F. Anstey (Thomas Anstey Guthrie, 1856–1934), was originally staged in 1901 (119 perfs.), and revived at the Haymarket Theatre on 24 March 1906 (281 perfs.). Shaw's trip in a gas **balloon**, the 'Norfolk,' occurred on 3 July 1906. The other passengers were Harley Granville Barker, the actor Robert Loraine, and Mary Cholmondeley, the younger sister of Charlotte Shaw. They rose to a dizzy-inducing height of 9000 feet (I&R: 210), hence Shaw's analogy of standing **on the tip top of the Eiffel Tower on one toe**. Their descent landed them in the field of an unhappy farmer. Perhaps this event served as a catalyst for the crashing aeroplane in *Misalliance*.

119 / To William Archer

10 Adelphi Terrace WC
10th July 1906

[ALS: BL 45296 f 175]

Archer's reply to the previous letter is missing. Throughout the 1860s and 1870s Offenbach's works were quite popular in England. A version of Barbe-Bleue *(1866) transferred to London in June 1866. Likewise,* La voyage dans la lune *(1875) made a quick shift from Paris to London. At least in London the Franco-Prussian War of 1870 did not diminish Offenbach's appeal. During the early 1870s John Hollingshead – who staged* Thespis *(1871), the first Gilbert and Sullivan operetta – presented over a dozen versions of Offenbach's works at the Gaiety Theatre. For example, in 1870 he staged* La Princesse de Trébizone *(1869), starring J.L. Toole (1830–1906) and the charming Nellie Farren (1848–1904). In 1879 Offenbach's* Madame Favart *(1878) opened at the Strand Theatre; it 'enjoyed a West End run of 502 performances and established itself as a genuine favourite in the following years with regular tours and revivals' (Gänzl 1: 144). In 1880 two of the most popular London musicals were Offenbach's* La fille du Tambour Major *(1879) and Gilbert and Sullivan's* Pirates of Penzance. *In great measure Offenbach prepared the London stage and audiences for Gilbert and Sullivan.*

In 1898, when You Never Can Tell *was published, Archer rejected the play as a 'formless farce.' But two years later in an article entitled 'The Drama: An Optimistic Survey,' he wrote that 'Mr. Bernard Shaw's* You Never Can Tell *[is] a brilliant farce with a brilliant intellect behind it.' He praised the play's 'intellectual vigour and originality' (*Pall Mall Magazine, *January 1901). Then by July 1906 when he saw the Vedrenne-Barker production, he went even further in his praise: 'What is a classic? It may be defined, perhaps, as a piece of work to whose faults we have grown blind, and if this definition be accepted,* You Never Can Tell *is in a fair way of fulfilling it ... The farce has never before been so well acted as it was last night' (Tribune, 10 July). In the Court Theatre production Henry Ainley (1879–1945) played the role of Valentine; Lillah McCarthy was Gloria, and Louis Calvert was the waiter. A year later, in September 1907, when the play was revived yet again by Vedrenne-Barker at the Savoy Theatre, Archer compared this 'irresistibly whimsical comedy' to* The School for Scandal *and* Hamlet. *Like these classic plays, he proclaimed, it has retained its appeal for audiences, production after production: 'Its humour has a quality that does not pall' (Tribune, 17 September 1907). This critical reversal is striking, but it is matched by Shaw's own about-face. In 1896, soon after writing the play, he decided that it is 'an* *appalling failure. The play's no use: I looked for my gold and found withered leaves. I must try again & again' (Diaries 2: 1142). But a decade later, as he declared in this letter, the play is not just a 'masterpiece'; it is 'a poem and a document, a sermon and a festival, all in one.'*

Madame Favart doesnt count, nor La Fille du Tambour Major, nor Le Voyage dans la Lune. The real Offenbach was the Empire-Schwandau Offenbach of La Grande Duchesse [de Gérolstein], La Belle Hélène, Princesse de Trébizone, Barbe Bleu, & Orphée [aux Enfers]. It was during their vogue that opera bouffe overran & swamped the English theatre. Favart was simply a Strand piece. 1871 made a complete break.

Your remark in the Tribune that a masterpiece is a play whose faults you learn to endure is a perfect breath-bereaver. You discover that my faults were only your blunders; and that is how you put it! And you still talk about 'a farce.' The thing is a poem and a document, a sermon and a festival, all in one. As to Valentine bamboozling the girl, was there ever such a confusion of thought as your conclusion that he was unpoetic & insincere? He won her by perfectly legitimate strategy, she having defied him and pitted her heartlessness with contemptuous confidence against him. Surely Ainley & Lillah got all this out at last for you, imperious Scotch rationalist as you are. Oh Jerusalem, thou that killest the prophets!!! —

You came up against it last night for the first time; and you only smile & scratch your nose as if I had poked it with an umbrella.

G.B.S.

Shaw's lament **Oh Jerusalem, thou that killest the prophets** is derived from the talk of Jesus Christ to the multitudes and his disciples: 'O, Jerusalem, Jerusalem, thou that killest the prophets, and stone them which are sent unto thee, how often would I have gathered thy children together, even as a hen gathereth her chickens under her wings, and ye would not!' (Matthew 23:37, King James version). Shaw's familiarity with the Bible was probably not as extensive as that of Ibsen, who kept a Bible in his study, as Archer discovered upon a visit to Christiania, but Shaw did read the Bible. His study of Jesus Christ was central to the writing of *Androcles and the Lion* and its lengthy *Preface on the Prospects of Christianity*. (See also the letters of 4 January, 18 July, and 30 December 1916.) Yet this engagement with Christianity was that of a 'Pagan,' as Gilbert Chesterton insisted (Holroyd 2: 217; and see Chesterton: 24–37 on the 'Puritan' Shaw), and should be placed in the context of his beliefs in Creative Evolution. See also Shaw's essay 'The Religion of the Future' in Religion: 29–37.

120 / To William Archer

Pentillie, Mevagissey
R.S.O. Cornwall (until 5th Sept.)
[Late August 1906]

ALU: BL 45296 ff 179–80)

This statement served as both a public and private response to Archer's article 'Death and Mr. Bernard Shaw' (Tribune, 14 July 1906). After sending the handwritten copy to Archer, with the two added comments at the bottom, Shaw published this statement, without the comments, in The Tribune. *It can thus serve as an open letter that Shaw aimed primarily but not exclusively at Archer. Just as Archer had published open letters in response to* The Quintessence of Ibsenism *(letter of 25 October 1891), the production of* The Man of Destiny *(letter of 31 July 1897), and the wedding announcement for the Shaws (see headnote to letter of 3 June 1898), so Shaw decided on a special private and public response to Archer's article, which in turn was a response to Shaw's obituary article on Ibsen (*The Clarion, *1 June).*

Shaw had criticized Ibsen and other modern playwrights for clinging to violence and death in their plots. (See letter of 7 July 1906.) He argued that drama should offer 'an illumination of life,' not a representation of death. But Archer rejected Shaw's statement as a false dichotomy. He declared that the genre of tragedy, as the pinnacle of dramatic literature, provided the fullest illumination of both life and death. For the greatest playwrights death is 'the ultimate adventure of humanity' and 'the most penetrating search-light in the armoury of his craft.' In opposition to Shaw's reductive version of Ibsen's drama, Archer insisted that 'death is still the touchstone of character, the supreme test of fortitude, the refuge of despair, the consecrator of greatness, the desecrator of loveliness, the crass intruder and the deliverer yearned for in vain, the matchless stimulant, the infallible anodyne, [and] the signature to the stave of life.' Accordingly, it is 'not the glory, but the limitation of Mr. Shaw's theatre that it is peopled by immortals.' Those immortals include the four characters in the Don Juan in Hell act of Man and Superman.

Taking up the implied challenge of Archer's article, Shaw began to write The Doctor's Dilemma *on 11 August, as he explained in a letter to Archibald Henderson: 'The fortunes of the Court theatre depend on my writing a new play this year; and not until this morning had I a notion of what it is to be about. I know now, and will probably be unable to resist working at it to the neglect of everything else.' Two days later, in the same letter to Henderson, Shaw added this comment: 'I have begun the new play, and am already through the best part of the first act. This means a devouring and importunate job; but I think I see my way through it quickly. The subject is modern serumpathy, if you know what that is. My hero will be a doctor' (CL2: 640–1). By mixing serum with empathy, Shaw conceived his own version of tragic catharsis; but if the 'hero' was to be a doctor, was Louis Dubedat the villain? He wrote rapidly, finishing the play on 12 September.*

In late August he sent the following statement to both Archer and The Tribune. *This handwritten version contained two final remarks – 'What price tragedy now? Yah!' – that are not in the version published in* The Tribune. *(Someone, at a later date, wrote '1907' at the top of the page for this undated statement by Shaw. The date, however, had to be August 1906.)*

Exclusive to The Tribune

Mr Bernard Shaw has been taking advantage of his seaside holiday in Cornwall to write a new play. It will be of special interest to readers of The Tribune, as it is the outcome of the article in which Mr William Archer penned a remarkable dithyramb to Death, and denied that Mr Shaw could claim the highest rank as a dramatist until he had faced the King of Terrors on the stage. Stung by this reproach from his old friend, Mr Shaw is writing a play all about death, which he declares will be the most amusing play he has ever written. However, he has not evaded the challenge by a quip: the play is in five acts, with the fatal situation in the correct position – at the end of the fourth. The death scene will be unlike any ever before represented; and the consultations of the doctors will give full scope for the author's knowledge of modern therapeutics and for his views on the medical profession. The play which is to be called 'The Doctor's Dilemma' will be one of the features of the forthcoming season under the Vedrenne-Barker management. The heroine will be played by Miss Lillah McCarthy.

What price tragedy now?
Yah!

121 / To William Archer 10 Adelphi Terrace WC
14th November 1906

[ALS: BL 45296 f 176; CL 2]

Both Shaw and Granville Barker wrote to Archer on this date, asking him not to attend the rehearsal of The Doctor's Dilemma *because his presence would disturb the actors (BL 45290 f 48). In addition, on this same day, the drama critic Archibald Haddon (1872–1942) published in the* Daily Express *a detailed synopsis of the play and some dialogue from the Epilogue. Despite Shaw's letter to the editor, which demanded the identity of the informant, Haddon refused to reveal his source. During the last week of rehearsals only those directly involved with the production were admitted into the Court Theatre. Even Lillah McCarthy's mother was forbidden entry.*

The play opened a week later on 20 November at the Court Theatre, produced by the Vedrenne-Barker management. After a week of matinees, performances shifted to the evenings, continuing through December and into early January, for a total of 50 performances. The production featured Barker as Dubedat, Lillah McCarthy as Jennifer Dubedat, William Farren, Jr (1853–1937) as Sir Patrick Cullen, and Ben Webster as Sir Colenso Ridgeon. Archer published his initial review for The Tribune *on 21 November, and then followed with three more assessments on 29 December, 1 January, and 19 January. For the most part he praised the play: 'Up to the end of the fourth act, it is daring, original, and, to my mind, admirable … Mr. Shaw has never been more witty, more penetrating, or (in a sense) more human.' But Archer criticized the death scene, which was his primary concern in his follow-up reviews. Barker, who struggled with the fourth-act scene, informed Archer that 'Louis Dubedat was a bad performance,' but he disagreed with Archer on the reasons (BL 45290 f 49). In a letter to Trebitsch Shaw would subsequently admit that 'Barker made it ghastly; … he missed the peculiar softness & prettiness that gives pathos to the death, and made it hard & frightful. Of course the critics did not know what was wrong; they never do' (Trebitsch: 137).*

My dear W.A.

If Barker asks you to a rehearsal of The Doctor's Dilemma, please put him off with an apology. It is utterly impossible that a rehearsal can be a rehearsal with you present. Some of them would act frantically: others would walk through with no other thought than to make it clear that they were walking through. I should very much like to have you concealed in a box & consult with you afterwards; but that is not possible, & wouldnt be fair to the company. You cannot imagine – or rather you *can* imagine – how impossible your position as a critic makes you on such an occasion. When Barker suggested it I said 'Yes, of course,' as I wish you to be considered a privileged person in all my enterprises & affairs; but unless Barker will undertake to conceal you even from me (so that I shall not have to be disloyal to my company by cheating them) I depend on you to get me out of the scrape by excusing yourself.

Some wretch in the theatre has just given away the whole plot & some of the dialogue to the Express. I am hunting down the traitor.

G.B.S.

Shaw participated in the **rehearsal**, of course, because he regularly directed his plays. (See Dukore's *Bernard Shaw, Director* on this aspect of his talents.)

122 / To William Archer

10 Adelphi Terrace WC
Monday morning [19th November 1906]

[ALS: BL 45296 f 178]

Charlotte Shaw wrote this note to Archer on the day before the opening of The Doctor's Dilemma, *which occurred on Tuesday afternoon, 20 November. Two weeks previously the Shaws had moved to Ayot St Lawrence in Hertfordshire. Barker and McCarthy had been their weekend guests (CL 2: 660).*

Dear W. Archer

We have only come up from the country this morning & G. B. S. has had to go straight off to the theatre without answering his letters.

It appears that Mr. Vedrenne is quite obdurate about admitting you to the dress rehearsal – I understand G. B. S. can do nothing with him – & *Barker* undertook to let you have a script of the play. No doubt you have it by this time.

We have not seen you for ages. Will you lunch 1:30 on Wednesday?

Yours sincerely,
C.F. Shaw

123 / To William Archer

10 Adelphi Terrace WC
19th November 1906

[ALS: BL 45296 f 177]

Shaw wrote this letter after the dress rehearsal of The Doctor's Dilemma, *which opened the following afternoon.*

My dear Archer

I have only just left the theatre; and the last thing I got there was a message from Barker asking me to send you *my* copy of the D's D. script, as the one which he was to have sent you was not available. But he did this not knowing that I had made an appointment to coach one of the scenes before the performance, as it was all wrong today. So I cannot let my script go.

However, the play will not puzzle you: it is a Child's Guide compared to Major Barbara, which I now hardly understand myself. It is quite simple and clear. If you follow the scientific lectures in the first act carefully, you will be all right. Remember also that phagocytosis means the theory that the white corpuscles (phagocytes) eat the disease germs; and that the modern theory of Sir Almroth Wright of St Mary's Hospital is that the effect of injecting a vaccine is that Nature immediately fries the germs in a toothsome sort of dripping, called by Wright opsonin, to encourage the phagocytes to eat them. BUT the production of this dripping rises and falls in a series of actions & reactions called the positive & negative phases; & to inject a vaccine during the negative phase is deadly. Consequently the vaccine in the hands of a man who does not know Wright's discovery of the phases is a most dangerous weapon. Grasp this & you will follow the scientific side of the play with ease. The dramatic side is as easy as Box & Cox.

In haste, ever yrs
G.B.S.

The chemical sauce or 'toothsome dripping' of **opsonin** is a substance that invites phagocytes to attack and destroy foreign blood cells. The treatment and the term were invented by Sir Almroth **Wright** (1861–1947), a bacteriologist and immunologist who specialized in vaccine therapy for microbe infections. He was associated with **St Mary's Hospital**, Paddington, and was principal of the Institute of Pathology. Shaw visited Wright's laboratory in 1905, and took the famous doctor as a model for Colenso Ridgeon ('Preface on Doctors' in CP 3: 225–320; Holroyd 2: 157–64). The one-act farce ***Box and Cox***, first performed in 1847, was written by John Maddison Morton (1811–91).

124 / To William Archer [no address]
[26th and 27th May 1907]

[ADU; BL 50682; CL 2]

In 1906 James G. Huneker published in New York a selection of 113 of Shaw's theatre reviews from the Saturday Review *under the title* Dramatic Opinions and Essays of G. Bernard Shaw. *When the revised British edition appeared in 1907, Archer used the occasion to offer another defence of Pinero's* The Second Mrs Tanqueray. *The review, entitled 'A Talk on Technique' (18 May, Tribune), offered a rebuttal to Shaw's complaint about Pinero's 'naïve machinery of exposition,' especially the use of letters, confidants, 'sham' characters, and several stage doors. Archer pointed out that similar plot devices appear in the plays of Ibsen and Shaw.*

The following week Archer published 'Youth in the Judgement Seat' (25 May, Tribune), a response to a young, angry reader who had accused him of being a doddering old critic who stood in the way of the new generation of playwrights. The young reader concluded that Archer's criticism of Shaw revealed that he 'dislikes Mr. Shaw's drama ... and is delighted with any opportunity to cross swords with him.' Defending himself, Archer replied: 'I do not dislike Mr. Shaw's drama ... Out of Mr. Shaw's fourteen or fifteen plays, I dislike three and a half; the remainder I hold in different degrees of esteem, but all of them I relish more or less, and some of them intensely. The merits of Mr. Shaw, the playwright, are not for a moment in question ... Mr. Shaw is a law unto himself. It is a mistake to apply to him the criticism of a pedestrian realism. He is so original a dramatist as to be above the trammels of technique. His sins against it are trifling in comparison with his abounding merits.' In the latter part of the article Archer returned to his defence of Pinero. He insisted upon the realism of Pinero's stage architecture of French windows and several doors by noting that his own home has the same 'ordinary' features.

Shaw, who had read both of Archer's articles, wrote the draft of this letter on the back pages of one of his Fabian notebooks, where Dan Laurence discovered and photographed it. Although Laurence set the date at '20th–24th May 1907,' this draft was written on 26 May. In a letter to Barker on 24 May he explained, 'I am in two minds about going down to Fernherst on Sunday.' Then in his P.S. he announced: 'I had just settled the Destiny rehearsal for the afternoon and decided to come down to Haslemere' (Barker: 84; CL2: 689). On Sunday, 26 May, Shaw took 'a S.W. express' train at 5 pm to the cottage of Barker and Lillah McCarthy in Fernhurst, Surrey, just south of the Halsemere station. He returned Monday morning, 27 May, in time for the afternoon rehearsal of Man of Destiny *(Barker: 87–8). Shaw apparently forgot to remove the letter from the Fabian notebook and mail it to Archer. This draft thus has an uncertain status in their correspondence (yet to Laurence's credit, we have this important statement).*

At the top of the first page, Shaw wrote the following two lines.

for publication if you like.
Excuse joggly writing. I am in a S.W. express

My dear W.A.

I cannot agree with the proposition laid down in your article of last Saturday: to wit, that the number of doors and windows in a man's drawingroom is proportionate to his income. I have not observed it. The fact – amazing as it is – that your own house has four doors and a French window or two per room is not evidence. As a dramatic critic you would naturally build a house that way. Or, if you did not build it, you would choose one of that sort. For all you know, your house may have been built by Mr Pinero. Just as stage morals and manners, as our police & divorce reports shew, get copied in real life; so does stage domestic architecture.

As you very rightly said in conclusion, all this does not matter *now*. But in my time it did matter very much. The stage was in process of evolution from the scenery of our boyhood, when the side walls of stage rooms were represented by open wings. In those days there were three entrances on each side even when a practicable door had to be introduced for the sake of some special bit of business; and people walked calmly off and on through the wainscotting, like ghosts. Long after the stage was really walled in as it is today, the traditions of the old plan lingered as pure superstitions. I never objected to the Criterion farces in which there were more doors than even in that wonderful house of yours, because these doors were a necessary part of the machinery of the play. But when authors, managers & actors of serious plays kept on assuming, as they persistently did, that the 1st 2nd & 3rd entrances, and the practicable entrance in the centre of the flat were indispensable to the stage presentation of every proper West End play, it became necessary to laugh them out of that delusion, all the more as it interfered very seriously indeed with the naturalness of the acting. When my Arms & the Man was produced in 1894, all its alleged novelties were as old as Richardson's Show: the real novelty, which nobody off the stage noticed, was that Major Petkoff's library had only one door. The Reverend James Morell's room in 'Candida' was in the same predicament; but to this day American and (I believe) German stage management has not dared to face the innovation; and St Dominic's semidetached parsonage is provided with a door into the next house. For the matter of that I have often seen a stage room with a door into the open air on the third floor, close beside the window.

I found, in my own practice, that by accepting the ordinary conditions of life on the stage as far as possible, I greatly improved my plays. Later on Mr Granville Barker, in The Voysey Inheritance, not only presented a room with one door, but filled it up with a huge dining table, which left only a narrow strip of floor round it for the actors to squeeze themselves about in. I defy you to deny that the staging of The Voysey Inheritance produced much more illusion than the staging of The Second Mrs Tanqueray. Take another illustration. I am a rather old fashioned stage manager. I presented the second act of Man & Superman with an empty stage, save for the inevitable garden seat (for two) right centre. Mr Robert Loraine, a contemporary of Mr Granville Barker, persuaded me to pitch the garden seat into the property room & fill up the stage with a huge motor car. I was naturally furious at being taught my business by a younger man – I, the highly superior critic of Mr Pinero – but the improvement was so prodigious that I had to capitulate. Please observe that I do not offer the blocking up of the stage with dining tables & motor cars as indispensable to good stage management: I am only mentioning two convincing examples of the advantage of discarding traditions which arose from mechanical conditions long since superseded.

As to the activity of the stage postman & the stage telegraph boy, I may remind you that in Sardou's 'Delia Harding,' written for Mr Comyns Carr in the Tanqueray period, the postal and telegraphic system was so completely substituted for the nervous & emotional system that on the first night the gallery broke into open derision during the performance. No doubt you will now ask me why letters & telegrams should be excluded from the stage. You will assure me that you get stacks of letters every day, and that the telegraph messenger is a frequent knocker at your door. You will remind me that the Swiss captain gets a letter in the last act of Arms & The Man, and that Candida's husband actually gets a reply paid telegram. The objection to that style of argument is not that it is illogical, but that, if you get into a confirmed habit of it, your room with the four doors & the two French windows will be replaced by a room with one window (barred), one door (locked on the outside), no razors or clothes pegs, and padded walls. If you cannot see the difference between Monmouth & Macedon because there is a river in both or between Delia Harding & A Doll's House because there is a letter box in both, or between the stage craft of The Second [Mrs] Tanqueray & The Voysey Inheritance because there is a dining table in both, or between 'Charles his friend' and Iago or Foldal because they are both confidants, or between the coincidence of Hamlet's arrival in Denmark just when Ophelia is being buried & the coincidence of Box & Cox taking the same lodging, then, Father William, you are no longer fit to be at large.

What is the explanation of all this affectation of an impossible addle-headedness – this burlesque argument in favor of superfluous doors and tooopportune telegrams? Is it to combat my 'violent prejudice against Mr Pinero'? Bosh! I am much too deeply interested in the theatre to be prejudiced against any dramatist: I always start with violent prejudice in favor. It is you who are openly & shamelessly prejudiced: the thing is a positive scandal. In the eighties & nineties, you said, 'We must make English dramatic literature serious. We must banish the adaptation from the French. We must praise and encourage the men who are doing the best work. If we can not have what we admire, let us at least admire what we have.' Mr Pinero was your first and chief victim. When, having followed his own bent, and made the Court Theatre the leading theatre of London by writing original comedies, he suddenly relapsed into producing old fashioned trade articles like The Profligate & The Second Mrs Tanqueray, you, instead of heading him off as I tried to do, lured him on the downward path by declaring that there was a new English drama, a new literary departure, a native master arisen in London. And because we all crowded to see Miss Kate Rorke's wonderful teetotum faint and to hear Mrs Patrick Campbell play the piano, nor to mention the inevitable failure of Mr Pinero's strenuous attempt to write thoroughly bad plays, circumstances seemed to favor your attempt. Fortunately I came upon the scene as a critic when matters got as serious as The Notorious Mrs Ebbsmith. All the king's horses and all the king's men will not set that shocking misconception of the public women of England up again on the pinnacle where you sought to place it. Mr Pinero meant no harm: he erred in pure ignorance of public life; but you should have known better. I had no prejudice against Mr Pinero: I simply loathed and abominated The Notorious Mrs Ebbsmith, and do so still and always shall.

What would you say if I accused you of a violent prejudice against Wilson Barrett because you loathed & abominated The Sign of The Cross, and were angry with me because I could not, for the life of me, take the play seriously, and saw importance & hope in the move it made towards getting the chapel & churchgoing public into the theatre.

Your policy – borrowed unconsciously from the grand duchess of Gerolstein – was in the long run an impossible one. Its generosity made it seductive and easy; and there is always an air of common sense and good humor about making the best of a bad job. And it is well established in England, where the worse our generals are the more we pretend that they are Caesars & Hannibals, and the more helpless our diplomatists are, the more gravely do we hold them up as Cavours & Bismarcks. But political emergencies expose political humbugs, whereas in the drama there are no emergencies, and if you lower the standard you debauch the theatre. There were certain quite hideous deficiencies in the drama we criticized. Chief among them was the absence of any conception of the higher passions, moral passion, intellectual passion, philosophic passion, religious passion, poetic passion. Not a single character had any real motives except appetites: the other motives were all undisguised conventions. Contemplating these plays, one asked oneself amazedly whether the authors had ever met a decent dog, much less a decent human being. The one sign of grace about Mr Pinero in this period was that he at least knew that since his heroines saw no interest in life but love, and no tragedy in it but the tragedy of growing old and unattractive, they were harlots, dramatically tolerable only because they were so pitiable. The other authors mostly presented such women without the faintest sense that they were not everything that a woman could possibly be or desire to be. The special horror of Mrs Ebbsmith was that Pinero here deliberately took a woman of the type of George Eliot, Mrs Josephine Butler, Mrs Besant, Mrs Wolstenholme Elmy, Miss Eva Maclaren, Mrs Creighton, Miss Tuckwell, Mrs Sidney Webb (I could give you fifty convincing names) and explained to the public that these were all Mrs Tanquerays & Irises to whom the one supreme moment of their lives was that in which they threw a man into a state of erotic excitement by putting on a low necked evening dress for him. When you let that pass without reproach you practically announced that you were going to manufacture your modern school of London dramatic literature without the slightest regard to the elementary decencies of criticism. Yet Mrs Ebbsmith was not worse than the dramatisation, in the case of Quex, of the countryside superstition that a man can cure himself of venereal disease by ravishing a virgin.

[The draft ends here; no signature]

Richardson's Show was a small, portable booth that John Richardson (c. 1763–1837) developed for travelling pantomimes and other entertainments. A **huge motor car** appeared in act 2 of *Man and Superman* for the 1907 production that opened on 27 May. Robert Loraine took the role of Tanner, and was responsible for adding the car to the production. The car was not used, however, in the premiere production in 1905, with Barker in the role. In Shakespeare's *Henry V* Fluellen makes the comparison between **Monmouth & Macedon.** His yoking of Macedonia and Monmouthshire was part of an attempt to compare Alexander the Great to 'King Henry' of Wales: 'There is a river in Macedon; and there is also moreover a river in Monmouth ... and there is salmons in both' (4, 4). Shaw's early use of this Shakespearean trope appeared in his 1885 review of Franz Liszt's Dante symphony (Music 1: 215). Victorien Sardou's ***Delia Harding*** was adapted and staged by J.W. Comyns Carr. Featuring Cyril Maude, Fred Terry, and Rose Leclercq, it opened at the Comedy Theatre on 17 April 1895, but ran for only 28 performances. In his criticism Archer was quite capable of mounting assaults similar to those that Shaw offered in this letter. He attacked the 'ready-made and bran-stuffed characters' in Carr's adaptation. The plot, he complained, offered 'an abuse of coincidence' that required 'incessant juggling with letters and telegrams' (World 95: 128–9). Lewis Carroll's poem 'You Are Old, **Father William,**' which was delivered as a parody of Robert Southey's 'The Old Man's Comforts,' appeared in *Alice's Adventures in Wonderland* (1865). Comte Camillo Benso di **Cavour** (1810–61) was a leader in the Italian national movement for unification. Prince Otto von **Bismarck** (1815–98), the 'Iron Chancellor,' was the Prussian leader who unified the German empire in 1871–90. In playscripts and theatre programs the list of characters had identifications such as **Charles his friend**. This listing was a typical way to identify a secondary character whose name appeared just below that of the primary character. Vilhelm **Foldal**, a clerk in Ibsen's *John Gabriel Borkman*, is the confidant of Borkman. *La Grande* ***Duchesse de Gérolstein***, an *opéra bouffe*, was written by J. Offenbach. **Josephine Butler** (1828–1906), Elizabeth C. **Wolstenhome-Elmy** (1834–1918), Mrs Eva McLaren (1852–1921), not **Miss Eva Maclaren**, Louise **Creighton** (1850–1936), and **Gertrude M. Tuckwell** (1861–1951) were all participants in the British women's suffrage movement. Pinero's *The Gay Lord* ***Quex*** premiered in 1902.

125 / To William Archer

10 Adelphi Terrace WC
3rd June 1907

[APCS: BL 45296 f 185]

Archer's letter to Shaw is missing. He had recently returned from a trip in April and early May to the United States, where he served as a member of the Simplified Spelling Board, a campaign supported by President Theodore Roosevelt, Dr F.J.

Furnivall, Andrew Carnegie, Brander Matthews, and others. Enclosed with the missing letter, probably written on 1 or 2 June, was a copy of 'The Revival of Billingsgate,' published on 1 June in The Tribune. *This was Archer's response to two nasty articles on Shaw's* Dramatic Opinions and Essays. *(See also letter of 17 June 1905.) The first assault appeared in the May issue of* The Bookman, *signed by Alfred Noyes, and the second in the June issue of* Blackwood's Magazine, *signed by 'Z.' The anonymous 'Z,' who dismissed Shaw as a 'Charlatan' and an 'ignorant jackanapes,' proclaimed that 'the tide has turned for the decadents as a body, and that Mr. Shaw is being found out with the rest of the morbid and mediocre crew.' Angered by the tirades of 'two intemperate Shaw-haters,' Archer declared that the rant by 'Z' 'is no clever attack, no reasonable criticism; it is a torrent of hysterical abuse, and I cannot but express the disgust with which I read it.' Archer also speculated that 'Z' was Noyes.*

My dear W.A.

I havnt read Z: I *have* read Noyes. It amused me, and didnt strike me as beyond the bounds.

'I like to see young heroes
Ambitioning like this.'

I should say, let him alone; but of course do as you please.

Why shouldnt I be blasphemed against?

Thanks for the impulse to defend me; but I should be magnanimous if I were you.

G.B.S.

Yet again, because Archer's letter is missing, Shaw's letter must serve as the source for our speculations about what Archer wrote. But by expanding our investigation to Archer's publications at this time, it is still possible to recover vital aspects of Archer's thoughts and emotions when someone attacked Shaw. Indeed, because we have several of his articles in June, including 'The Revival of Billinsgate,' we can discover Archer's commitment to defending Shaw, despite their many arguments with one another. The public domain serves as a register of the private self.

Billingsgate was the London fish market. Alfred **Noyes** (1880–1958) was a prolific English poet. In the 1920s he attained praise for his verse trilogy *The Torch-Bearers* (1922–30), but perhaps has remained best known for his famous poem 'The Highwayman,' published in 1906. Shaw's quoted lines about **young heroes** is from *Hans Breitmann's Ballads* (1871), written by the American journalist, folklorist, and humorist Charles Godfrey Leland (1824–1903). Archer resisted **the impulse to defend** Shaw in a public debate with Noyes. Instead, he found various ways to feature Shaw by publishing four articles in June, starting with two in *The Tribune.* On 5 June he reviewed the productions at the Court Theatre of *Don*

Juan in Hell, which he admired, and *Man of Destiny*, which he did not. On 6 June he hailed the reception of both Ibsen and Shaw in America. He described productions he saw in April, including *Mrs Warren's Profession* with Mary Shaw. He also saw Robert Loraine in *Man and Superman* in Pittsburgh and Ibsen's *The Pretenders* at Yale University). And he noted the recent Anerican tours of *Caesar and Cleopatra* (Forbes Roberson and Gertrude Elliott) and *Captain Brassbound's Conversion* (Ellen Terry). (On Archer's American trip see C. Archer: 287–90; Whitebrook: 264–5.) Archer also published a separate article on the month-long run in New York City of *Mrs Warren's Profession* with Mary Shaw (June, *The Independent*). Just two years earlier the police had closed down the production of this play. (See letters of 8, 15, and 18 November 1905.) Then at the end of June he published 'G. B. S.' (29 June, *Morning Leader*), which compared Shaw to Mark Twain. He argued that each of them was 'a victim to his own humor.' As 'jesting wise-men' they had often been misapprehended and undervalued. Making the case for Shaw's intellectual significance, Archer praised the 'brilliant' preface to *Major Barbara*: 'What a splendid piece of work it is! How strong as literature! How vital as thought!' His plays had established Shaw as 'one of the great figures of our time, who will probably bulk at least as large in the history of the early twentieth century as either Carlyle or Ruskin in that of the middle-nineteenth century.'

126 / To William Archer

10 Adelphi Terrace WC
13th November 1907

[TLS: BL 45296 f 190]

Archer's letter is missing. The third year of the Vedrenne-Barker management at the Court Theatre concluded in June 1907. In 'From the Court to the Savoy' (29 June 1907, Tribune), Archer presented an assessment of the Court Theatre achievements and a forecast of the new venture at the Savoy Theatre. He pointed out that the three seasons at the Court had featured 32 plays by 17 dramatists. Eight of the plays were one-acts. Three were Greek tragedies by Euripides, translated by Gilbert Murray. Eleven of the plays were written by Shaw. Out of a total of 988 performances, 701 were of Shaw's plays.

In support of the Savoy initiative Archer published 'The New Spirit in Drama' (14 September, Tribune). He praised the Court productions, and urged readers to support the Savoy season, which opened with You Never Can Tell, *a proven success at the Court. The plan was to follow this popular play with H. Granville Barker's* Waste, *Gilbert Murray's translation of Euripides'* Medea, *and a new play by Shaw. But the Examiner of Plays refused to license* Waste; Medea *had only eight matinee performances, and Shaw failed to get* Getting Married *written in time. Its staging was delayed until May 1908 for performances at the Haymarket Theatre.* Waste *was replaced by* The Devil's Disciple *(79 perfs., counting a transfer to Queen's Theatre), with Barker playing Burgoyne, though he disliked the role and play (CL 2: 714–15). The Savoy season then offered two more of Shaw's plays that opened in November and December:* Caesar and

Cleopatra, *with J. Forbes-Robertson and Gertrude Elliott, followed by* Arms and the Man, *with Barker and Lillah McCarthy.* C&C, *which Archer reviewed on 26 November (Tribune), had either 28 or 40 performances (Wearing 1900: 610 vs. CL 2: 735);* Arms, *which Archer reviewed on 31 December (Tribune), had 77 or 56 performances (Wearing 1910: 622 vs. CL 2: 739).*

My dear W.A.,

Your letter conveys to me an appalling sense of something forgotten – something that I should have answered at once and did not. Anyhow, whatever it is, I cannot go to Oxford. I have just been to Cambridge; and the Fabian Society has filled me up for the rest of the winter to the utmost limit of my energy, and indeed beyond it, as they have no sooner filled up the cup than other people begin to drop marbles into it.

I have been fearfully rushed of late. The affairs of Vedrenne and Barker and of the Stage Society would quite fill up two men's time, without counting the boom in Socialism, which has fallen very heavily on me, and my own literary work. My new play, which ought to have been finished before this, is virtually not begun.

Business at the Savoy is perfectly devilish: the stalls are either out of town or broken by the bank rate; and we think ourselves lucky if we take £650 a week.

Yours ever,
G.B.S.

In October Shaw travelled to **Cambridge** to lecture to the Fabians. Because of censorship on *Waste*, the **Stage Society** presented two private performances. **Business at the Savoy** caused financial difficulties for the Vedrenne-Barker management. To help bankroll a season at the Savoy Theatre, which was a much larger and more expensive theatre than the Court, Shaw loaned £2000 to Vedrenne and Barker (CL 2: 702–4; 706; Barker: 126–7, 129). By December he had advanced an additional £500 (CL 2: 742). His loans over the years to Vedrenne and Barker exceeded £5000 (see, for instance, CL 2: 807–9). In 1911, accepting financial facts, he cancelled the loans to the management (Holroyd 2: 178).

127 / To William Archer 10 Adelphi Terrace WC
17th June 1908

[APCS: BL 45296 f 191]

No letters are extant from 14 November 1907 to 17 June 1908. On 19 March 1908 Archer and Barker sailed to New York City, where American millionaires were building the New Theatre on Central Park West. They sought the advice of the men who had written A National Theatre: Scheme & Estimates. *The founders of the New Theatre were also considering Barker as a possible director when the building opened in late 1909. Both men were quite willing to offer advice, and Archer would later become a consultant on European drama, but Barker was unimpressed by the enterprise. He turned down the position of director and returned to England in April. He got back in time to see the opening of Shaw's* Getting Married *at the Haymarket on 12 May (54 perfs.).*

Archer, however, extended his visit in order to carry out research for a study of 'the race problem' in America. The day after he returned to London on 15 June, he quickly read Getting Married *and attended a performance at the Haymarket Theatre. But he delayed his review for two months because he was in the process of shifting from* The Tribune *to the* Morning Leader *as a theatre critic. On 15 August in 'What of the Drama?' he evaluated Shaw's play, along with three other new plays of the 1907–8 season that the Vedrenne-Barker management had produced: the verse drama* Nan *by John Masefield (1878–1967),* Joy *by John Galsworthy, and the censored* Waste *by Barker – 'the biggest play of the year.' Shaw's play was a disappointment, even though the first act was 'exceedingly brilliant and entertaining.' But by the end of the second act the 'characters began to talk round and round their subjects.' Archer then announced in his review that an 'accident [actually a disabling performance by a drunk actor] prevented me from seeing the third act; and, truth to tell, I found no difficulty in tearing myself away, and leaving the actors to continue in my absence their game of intellectual ping-pong across that deanery table. No –* Getting Married *is really not quite good enough. It might almost be a piece of self-parody, exaggerating the G.B.S. mannerism, and giving us very little else.' Archer concluded that Shaw 'must – and will – do better than this next time.'*

The ways of genius are unaccountable, especially when it puts an enemy into its mouth. I have just been to the theatre to see the understudy play; and lo! no understudy but the delinquent in her very finest form, voice clear, face radiant, not a word or a point missed, not an instant's hesitation, audience alert & delighted! Amazing!

G.B.S.

The **genius** in this case was the actress Fanny Brough, who played Mrs George Collins. She became sick during the matinee that Archer had attended, apparently from a drinking problem. This was the **enemy** that hindered her performance. In a letter to Barker on this same day of 17 June Shaw declared that the matinee was a 'tragedy.' He noted that 'Archer left after a few minutes of Act III.' J.E. Vedrenne doctored Brough with 'soda water and strict diet' for five hours, and she recovered in time to perform her role in the evening performance. Shaw went to the theatre that evening, expecting to see the **understudy** Auriol Lee (1880–1941) in Brough's role. But as he reported to Barker, 'F.B. absolutely at her best: a splendid performance' (Barker: 124) This was not, however, a singular event, as Shaw reported to Barker on 21 June: 'Next day, hopeless intoxication until evening.' The 'drink question' remained 'troublesome' throughout the week (Barker: 123–5). And even more troublesome were the financial problems that dominated Shaw's letters to Barker in June and July. Disagreements between Vedrenne and Barker multiplied. In consequence, except for packaging some touring shows, the Vedrenne-Barker management came to an end that summer.

128 / To William Archer

10 Adelphi Terrace WC
3rd July 1908

[TLS: BL 45296 ff 192–6; CL 2 partial]

Two letters are missing, one by Shaw and one by Archer. Shaw had sent a draft to Archer of the report for the Society of Authors as an enclosue in his missing letter. Then, with this most recent letter he sent a document, perhaps a letter by Dr Leon Kellner that expressed his displeasures over the translation of Shaw's plays into German. Both Kellner and Max Meyerfeld continued to criticize the translations by Trebitsch. (See letters of 7 June 1906, 29 June 1908.) They also complained to Archer during their visits to London (Trebitsch: 138–43). Yet Shaw maintained his support of Trebitsch's translations, including Arzt am Scheideweg *(*The Doctor's Dilemma*), which was published serially in* Nord und Süd *(October–December 1908) and as a book on 21 November 1908 in Berlin (Biblio 1: 85). The German premiere in Berlin, directed by Max Reinhardt (1873–1943), opened on the same day at the Kammerspiele des Deutschen Theaters for a run of 82 performances (32 more than occurred two years earlier at the Court Theatre premiere in London).*

In March 1908 40 dramatists who were dissatisfied with the leadership of the Society of Authors announced plans to establish a new, independent organization, with A.W. Pinero as the acting chairman. Their discontent was aimed at the leadership of George Herbert Thring (1859–1941), the society's secretary (1892–1930). The rebels were also frustrated with the management committee, on which Shaw had served since February 1905, and the dramatic sub-committee, on which he had served since March 1906. He, in turn, was unhappy because the authors failed to defend themselves financially against the publishers. In an attempt to forestall the rebellion, the society reconstituted the membership of the dramatic sub-committee. Archer, whom Pinero actively supported, was one of the new appointees.

As a vocal critic of the sub-committee, Pinero expressed his frustration to Archer in a letter on 30 June 1908 (BL). But after weeks of negotiation, he agreed to continue his service in 1908, and when the revolt was settled in 1909 Pinero became the chairman. Both Shaw and Pinero appealed to Archer to support their agendas.

The campaign for a national theatre had fitfully gained momentum in 1902 when Archer had organized a Theatrical Reform Committee. Two years later Barker and Archer drafted Scheme & Estimates for a National Theatre, *which was subsequently revised and published in 1907 as* A National Theatre: Scheme & Estimates. *Many but not all of the members of the theatre community supported this 'Blue Book' proposal, but no funding was forthcoming from the government (Whitebrook: 226–34). In the summer of 1908 a Shakespeare Memorial National Theatre Committee of 21 members was formed, consisting of theatre people, Shakespearean scholars, and a select group of lords, earls, and viscounts. Among the theatre people were Archer, Barker, Pinero, and H.B. Tree. Shaw also participated, primarily after a summer trip to Sweden and Germany, and a month in Ireland. An appeal for £500,000 was announced, but five years later only £100,000 was raised for a possible building. Its possible location remained undecided.*

My dear W.A.,

You are of course quite right about 'only too glad.' But I really had at the back of my mind certain very troublesome experiences with the French Société des Auteurs, and some observation of the Society of Authors here. The Société is 'only too glad' with a vengeance. It not only takes the author's affairs into its hands by violence, but proceeds to mismanage them and to defeat all the attempts of the unfortunate author to set them right. The Society of Authors will have exactly the same tendency unless looked after. It is much more troublesome to educate an author and make him understand his own business than it is to take it out of his hands and to treat him like a child, which is what all Societies rather tend to do except when they tend to do nothing. However, all this would not be present to the readers of our report; so by all means let 'only too glad' be expunged. I only explain to justify my own use of the phrase. I used it quite unconsciously; and I should be greatly alarmed for my literary integrity if I found myself culling literary weeds for my buttonhole without any justification.

I send you a copy of a letter, which you may destroy, as a sample of the documents in the Meyerfeld-Trebitsch campaign. Kellner would be inexpressibly delighted at one of Trebitsch's achievements in his translation of The Doctor' Dilemma. I described the manners of one of the characters as 'propitiatory.' Trebitsch's version of this is 'eigentümlich'!

In steering this Authors' Society business, you must bear steadily in mind that the thing we have got to do is to educate our men, and that all these reports and draft agreements and so forth have that as their first function – possibly also their last. They have to be educated, not only in the economic and practical business they have to face, and in public procedure, of which, as you can see for yourself, they are all childishly ignorant, but above all in the impersonal habit of mind – the committee habit – without which every attempt to face and deal with the simplest hard fact leads to wounded feelings, squabbling, resignations, and, generally, the sort of baby stunt that Sutro treated us to the other day. Also, we must keep a perfectly open mind as to which body finally captures the position. I am at present applying all my driving force (which, you will observe, consists simply in sitting down and doing the work that nobody else will do) to make the Authors' Society Committee out-do, out-think, and out-goodmanner the other Committee. The effect has already been to straighten up the new Committee tremendously, and to set them at work at the agency scheme of which Marshall spoke yesterday, and of which, a month ago, they were as incapable as a litter of kittens. I shall continue at every opportunity to goad them with insults to further exertions. I have already done my best, by kindly and patronizing insolence, to make them feel that they will be simply like infants in my hands and those of the Authors' Society unless they really put their backs into the affair. The effect of this will be altogether good, because neither side can conceal its operations from the other. In a rash moment the new body invited me to attend one of their meetings; and five minutes after I had entered the room I had in an innocent manner raised the question of preliminary expenses and sent the hat round with a sovereign of my own in it. With the sovereign I purchased their souls: they can no more keep me out of their councils now than the Society of Authors can keep them out. Each side will benefit by all the work the other does; and whether the result is a new Society or a complete regeneration of the dramatic committee of the old Society, all the intermediate work will be to the good. On the whole I lean towards the side of literary solidarity, not only for financial and general human reasons, but also because I rather mistrust the tendency of the old gang of dramatic authors towards the traditions of the Savage Club. Do what you can while I am away to keep things wholesome; and remember that nothing whatever can be done as long as the authors are inactive. In the Authors Society in the old days (meaning in fact yesterday) we really did all we could to galvanize the dramatic committee into life; but the authors simply would not take any interest in it. When Pinero found that nothing was being done, instead of saying that something must be done and doing it, he acquiesced in the situation with a relief which was human and natural enough in the circumstance. Edward Rose and Grundy, like Jones, were driven to the same fatalistic acceptance of the uselessness of getting the dramatic authors to assemble and put in any work. At last, Hawkins and myself made the Executive Committee add us to the Dramatic Sub-Committee; and we did what we could until the censorship agitation gave us our chance. But we should collapse again tomorrow if the old apathy set in again.

Now for a bit of diplomacy in which you might help me. I have made up my mind to make Pinero a knight. In this National Theatre scheme we have a lot of knight-actors; but we have no knight-dramatists except Gilbert, who is too old and not really representative. Pinero is the man. The other day, when Pinero, Hare, Lytton, and myself met at Lord Plymouth's, I sounded Pinero as to whether he would accept a knighthood if it came his way. His position, like Irving's, is strong enough to save him from any suspicion of wanting a knighthood on personal grounds; and the accolade would undoubtedly strengthen the theatre movement. He said that it had never occurred to him, and that he would rather have something in the way of a little red ribbon; but he is prepared to suffer knighthood on public grounds. So yesterday I made the heroic sacrifice of going into Society. I went to Mrs Asquith's garden party, and told her flatly that A.W.P. must be made a knight. She said she could not do it until next November. I said next November would do. Finally the whole assembly of duchesses and other social daisies began discussing it; and though of course the whole thing was wildly irresponsible, I think it quite possible that something may come of it, because Mrs Asquith quite understood that I was in earnest about it, and quite agreed that it would be a very proper birthday honour. Will you take any opportunity you may have of propagating the idea, in print or in private. But take due care not to let anybody compromise A.W.P. or make him ridiculous. It is rather desirable that he should know what is going on; but I cannot tell him because I cannot make him an accomplice in my wire-pulling. All the more reason why you should tell him if you get the chance.

I am now going off into the wilds, leaving no address; but any letters addressed here will be forwarded at such moments as I am discoverable. This also, by the way, is rather queer English; but 'twill serve.

Yrs ever
G.B.S.

In the missing letter to Shaw, Archer had warned him that he was overusing the phrase **'only too glad'** in his writing; the phrase appeared in his draft report for the Society for Authors. The German adjective **'eigentümlich'** means 'proprietary,' but Shaw had used 'propitiatory' in his description of Dr Shoemaker in *The Doctor's Dilemma* (CP 3: 325). The playwright Robert **Marshall** (1863–1910) wrote farces, comedies, and romances, including *The Second in Command*, which featured Cyril Maude in 1900. The **Savage Club** was a male preserve – not always sedate – for food, drink, and partying. Anthony Hope **Hawkins** (1863–1933) is best known for his novel *The Prisoner of Zenda* (1894), which **Edward Rose** adapted for George Alexander's St James's Theatre in 1896 (255 perfs.). Robert George Windsor-Clive (1857–1923), 1st Earl of **Plymouth**, held a meeting at his home on 30 June 1908 to discuss the plans for a national theatre. Shaw and the actor Sir John **Hare** were among the participants. Victor **Lytton** (1876–1947), 2nd Earl of Lytton, also attended the meeting. A supporter of the arts, Lytton would later serve as president of the Royal Society of Literature and chairman of the Old Vic Association. The **censorship agitation** was over Harley Granville Barker's play *Waste*. The Stage Society presented two private performances at the Imperial Theatre on 24 and 26 November. Barker played Henry Trebell and directed (Wearing 1900: 610). Archer voiced his disapproval of the Lord Chamberlain's Office in *The Tribune* on 27 November 1907 and 28 December. 'Waste is a great play. It not only stands on the highest level of our modern drama – it stands on that level and in a place apart. It reveals a new combination of technique and intellectual qualities' (27 November). In opposition to this censorship, seventy-one playwrights, including Shaw, published a letter in *The Times* on 29 October to protest against the Lord Chamberlain's Office (CL 2: 714–15). Shaw also published two articles against censorship on 16 November 1907 and 8 February 1908 in *The Nation* (Agits 93–101; 101–4), which was edited by H.W. Massingham. Earlier in the year, before the controversy erupted over *Waste*, he had published 'The Solution to the Censorship Problem' in *The Academy*, 29 June 1907 (Dukore 3: 1139–48). Shaw's talk with Margot **Asquith** (1864–1945), wife of the new Liberal prime minister, proved successful, for a knighthood was arranged for Pinero the following year. (See letter of 3 November 1908.) Shaw and Mrs Shaw disappeared the following day **into the wilds** for their trip to Sweden and Germany. They were on the Continent from 4 July until early September, and then sailed to Ireland, where they spent four weeks, from 7 September until 4 October.

129 / To William Archer

Gothanburg [Göteborg, Sweden]
7th July 1908

[APCS: BL 45296 f 203]

The writer Hugo Vallentin (1888–1963), who translated Shaw's plays into Swedish, joined Shaw and Mrs Shaw on the first stage of their trip. They began their tour of Sweden by steamer, with Stockholm as their designation. Shaw hoped to attain a meeting with August Strindberg (1849–1912). This picture postcard displays a park scene: Trädgårdsföreningen in Göteborg. Shaw wrote above the scene: 'Fountains playing in honor of G.B.S.'s arrival in Sweden.'

I am just starting for Stockholm by the Götha Canal – expect to arrive there on the 9th, in the evening. I shall stay at the Rydberg Hotel. The North Sea performed its long moon silvered roll very unpleasantly on the way over, I regret to say. Was only too glad to land. I now find that I have acquired this locution as an inveterate habit.

G.B.S.

Archer had cautioned Shaw about overusing the phrase **only too glad**. In his letter of 3 July Shaw acknowledged this lapse in 'my literary integrity.'

130 / To William Archer

Hotel Rydberg, Stockholm
10th July 1908

[APCU: BL 45296 f 204]

Shaw, Mrs. Shaw, and their translator Hugo Vallentin arrived in Stockholm on 9 July. The picture postcard shows an image of an owl on a tree branch. At the bottom of the card the words 'SKANSEN Lappuggla' are printed. Next to this inscription and below the owl, Shaw wrote 'anti-Ibsenitica.' In September 1905 Shaw had informed Archibald Henderson that he had read only 'one book and one play by Strindberg' (BL 50564 ff 63–6). Very few of Strindberg's works were available in English during the first three decades of the twentieth century, and these few were usually derived from German or French translations. As for the production of Strindberg's plays, the first in London took place in 1909 for a fifteen-minute matinee of the one-act The Stronger *(written in 1888). In 1912 single performances of* Miss Julia *(1888) and* The Creditors *(1888) occurred. A few other plays were staged in minor productions in the 1920s. Chelsea Arts Theatre staged the first production of* A Dream Play *(1901) in 1930. By contrast,*

Max Reinhardt had staged seventeen of Strindberg's plays in Berlin by 1933 (the year the Nazis took possession of his theatres). When Shaw won the Nobel Prize for Literature in 1925 he used the award money to create an Anglo-Swedish Literary Foundation that would support the translation of Swedish literature, including the plays of Strindberg.

Arrived here yesterday. Strindberg has *not* called. If he does, I think I shall suggest a new set of translations by you.

[no signature]

131 / To William Archer [Stockholm]
[16th July 1908]

[APCS: BL 45296 f 205; CL 2]

This picture postcard, postmarked 17 July, reproduced a half-figure portrait of August Strindberg that was painted in 1905 by his friend Richard Bergh (1858–1919). On the wall behind Strindberg, partially visible, are three landscape paintings – perhaps painted by him. At this point in his career Strindberg was staging his plays at his new Intima Teatern, which he had established in 1907. His plays had not yet been performed in London, and translations were almost non-existent.

In a postcard to Harley Granville Barker, Shaw provided a rather flippant version of the meeting, but it shared some details with this message to Archer: 'This great man reached the summit of his career when he met the immortal G.B.S. at the Theatre Interne at Stockholm on the 16th July 1908 at one o/clock in the afternoon. At 1:25, he said in German, 'At two o/clock I am going to be sick.' On this strong hint the party broke up' (Barker: 130).

In yet other versions of this event, recounted in 1927 and 1928, Shaw provided more details. In 1928, for example, he stated: 'I thought it my duty to pay respects to a great man whom I considered one of the great dramatists of Europe.' In these memories from twenty years later Shaw reported that he had sent a note to Strindberg, asking for a meeting. Strindberg had replied in a long letter written 'in several languages – French, German, and English – any language but Swedish.' The meeting took place at the Intima Teatern. Both Shaw and Mrs Shaw met with Strindberg, and apparently Hugo Vallentin also met with him. (See Shaw's letter to Strindberg on 16 March 1910: CL2: 906–9.)

After Shaw's failed attempt to hold a conversation in French, Mrs Shaw communicated with Strindberg primarily in German. In the 1927 report, as told to Judge

Henry Neil at a luncheon, Shaw recalled that they 'found Strindberg in a mood of extreme and difficult shyness; but his sapphire-blue eyes were irresistible; the man of genius was unmistakable.' Strindberg told the Shaws that he lived in complete seclusion and was 'dying of a mortal disease.' In all versions of the interview, Shaw stated that at a certain point in the meeting Strindberg pulled out a watch and announced that he was going to be sick at two o/clock. (For the 1927 version, see I&R: 416–17; for the 1928 versions in three newspapers – Manchester Guardian, Baltimore Sun, New York Times *– see Holroyd 2: 195–6 and 4: 263; there is yet another derivative version of this event from 1981 that Holroyd also drew upon.)*

At this interview Strindberg invited them to attend a hastily arranged performance of Forken Julie *(*Miss Julie*) on the next day. Strindberg apparently attended the performance with them. Following the performance, the Shaws sailed for Germany on the same day.*

I achieved the impossible – a meeting with Strindberg – today. He said 'Archer is not in sympathy with me.' I said 'Archer wasnt in sympathy with Ibsen either; but he couldnt help translating him all the same, being accessible to poetry, though otherwise totally impenetrable.' After some further conversation, consisting mainly of embarrassed silence & a pale smile or two by A.S. & floods of energetic eloquence in a fearful lingo, half French, half German, by G.B.S., A.S. took out his watch & said, in German, 'At two o'clock I am going to be sick.' The visitors accepted this delicate intimation & withdrew.

GBS

132 / To William Archer

Bayreuth
27th July 1908

[APCS: BL 45296 f 206]

This picture postcard offered an exterior view of one side of the Richard Wagner Festspielhaus in Bayreuth. Archer's letter is missing, but he reported on a meeting of the SMNTC. *As noted in the letter of 3 July 1908, Robert George Windsor-Clive, the 1st Earl of Plymouth, Victor Lytton, the 2nd Earl of Lytton, Sir John Hare, A.W. Pinero, and H.B. Tree served on the committee, which had a total of 21 members.*

Your letter arrived this morning. Plymouth is a hopeless muddler: what does he suppose we (Hare, Pinero, Lytton, Esher, & myself) went to his house for? I think I shall appeal to Tree not to attend, as we really do want to get the theatre built.

GBS

Shaw clearly wrote **muddler**, not meddler; his coinage derives from *muddle.* Reginald Baliol Brett (1852–1930), the 2nd Viscount of **Esher**, had served as a Liberal Member of Parliament.

133 / To William Archer

[Bayreuth]
[c. 27th July 1908]

[APCU: BL 45296 f 208]

This picture postcard provides a view of the interior of the Margravial Opera House, built in the 1740s on designs by French architect Joseph Saint-Pierre (c. 1709–54). The baroque interior was designed by Giuseppe Galli Bibiena (1696–1757). Taken from the stage, the photograph displayed the main floor, three levels of ornate boxes, and the ceiling. Below the image Shaw wrote his brief message.

Talk of the Court Theatre! Can anything be more courtly than this?

[no signature]

134 / To William Archer

[Bayreuth]
28th July 1908

[APCS: BL 45296 f 207]

This picture postcard shows the exterior entrance to the Richard Wagner Festspielhaus. Shaw, Archer, and Edward Rimbault Vere Dibdin (1853–1941) had visited Bayreuth in July 1889 for performances of Parsifal, Tristan und Isolde, *and* Die Meistersinger. *Dibdin, who continued to be one of Archer's closest friends since their days together in Edinburgh, lived in Liverpool, where he served as an art critic (1887–1904), then as curator of the Walker Art Gallery (1904–20). Hans Richter, about whom Shaw wrote his first music article for the* Dramatic Review *in 1885 (see letter #1), was a renowned Wagnerian conductor. At Bayreuth in 1908 he conducted Wagner's* Der Ring des Nibelungen. *As Shaw explains in a detailed letter to J.E. Vedrenne (CL 2: 803–5), he and Mrs Shaw saw the* Ring *performances between 25 July and 1 August. They also saw* Lohengrin *and* Parsifal, *which Shaw described as 'the most perfectly managed performance I ever saw (and I had seen 6 before at Bayreuth).'*

This place, as far as the theatre is concerned, is incredibly unchanged: it is exactly as if you & I & Dibdin (Dibdin's dead, by the way, isn't he?) were there yesterday. The industrial end of the town has developed: there are more factories. The lunatic asylum has the same air of being deserted for the theatre. Richter looks older: so do I: otherwise it only needs you to be here (since you dont change) to make the illusion of yesterday complete. You will collapse some day like the one-horse shay if you dont age naturally. G.B.S.

With the arrival of the automobile, which Shaw loved, the **one-horse shay** and other carriages were displaced as standard modes of transportation. (And with Shaw driving they were in danger of being chased off the roads – a forced method for collapsing them.)

135 / To William Archer Hotel Vier Jahreszeiten, München
6th August 1908

[ALS: BL 45296 ff 209–10]

In a missing letter Archer reassured Shaw that Eward Rimbault Vere Dibdin was alive, and serving as the Curator of the Walker Art Gallery in Liverpool (C. Archer: 304). Besides seeing performances of Candida *and* How He Lied to Her Husband *in Munich, the Shaws saw a performance of Mozart's* The Marriage of Figaro. *In a letter to H. Granville Barker Shaw provided a drawing of the two German actors, arrayed in their mismatched costumes, who played Marchbanks and Morrell in* Candida *(CL 2: 806).*

I am not at all satisfied about this Dibdin business. I saw the man's obituary notice; I said, 'Alas, poor Yorick!' over him; I reflected on the shortness of the period during which I could hope to survive him; I thought of the many worse men I would have better spared; and at last I became resigned to the loss, and invested his memory with a certain poetry. And now he upsets me and falsifies history by not being dead at all. I am not disposed to accept your rather offhand and unfeeling statement without some investigation. I am going to Liverpool to lecture in October; and I shall make a point of visiting the Walker gallery (the name is suspicious) and satisfying myself that the alleged curator is really Dibdin. If not, I shall tell the impostor what I think of him. If so, I shall do my best to resume our old relations with as little sense of anti-climax as possible.

Somehow, strange things are happening. You will not attempt to deny that Davenport Adams has been dead many a long day; yet I saw him tonight at the Residenz Theater listening to Mozart's Figaro's Hochzeit – in which, by the way, the part of Figaro was taken by T.P. O'Connor. Perhaps he is dead too: I havent seen an English paper for a month past. There was a time that when the brains were out, the man was dead; and if there was a man in the world at whom Macbeth might have pointed this remark, it was Davenport Adams; and yet there he was pushing the Residenz opera goers from their stalls as large as life. I have not met Joe Knight yet, but shall probably do so in the course of the week.

The hand of Providence was shown plainly on my arrival here yesterday by the sudden revival at the Residenz, for one night only, of Candida & How He Lied. I asked the hotel porter to get me tickets. He told me that I was mistaken about the play – that it was in German & that I would not understand it. I said I would go all the same. He then told me to pay at the door, as the house would be empty. I thanked him & took his advice, which I found to be based on fact. Eugene was a thick necked young motor agent out for a bank holiday, in a striped suit & collar of the flashest fancy. Morell was an Archimandrite who would have put Moses out of countenance on Mount Pisgah. His hair came down to his shoulders, and his coat came down to his ankles. Candida was not at all bad for a Gertrude Kingston sort of woman. Burgess made me laugh & even gave me some tips in the way of stage business. They played it straight through in 90 minutes, dropping the curtain for a moment only, and hurrying on as if the police were at their heels. In How He Lied (same cast) Morell lifted Eugene on to the keyboard of the piano and bumped the bass with him. The woman was again good; but the thick necked Bursch made the piece simply disgusting. On the whole, it was a devastating experience, and confirmed my opinion that Germany has everything to learn from Vedrenne & Barker.

GBS

By evoking Hamlet's **'Alas, poor Yorick!'** Shaw set up the 'fellow of infinite jests' as the emblematic herald for this letter of laments and jests about dead people. Perhaps the name of the **Walker gallery** was supicious to Shaw because it reminded him of A.B. Walker, one of several critics named in this letter of suspicions. Unlike E.R.V. Dibdin, William

Davenport Adams (1851–1904) was dead. He had been theatre critic for several London papers including the *Globe*. **Joseph Knight**, who had served as the theatre critic for the *Athenaeum* and editor of *Notes & Queries*, died in 1907. ***Hochzeit*** means wedding. **Thomas Power O'Connor**, an Irish journalist and Liberal MP, founded *The Star* in 1888. For a short period in 1888 Shaw wrote some political articles for O'Connor, but soon shifted to musical criticism as Corno di Bassetto. O'Connor was a quite versatile man and still alive, but he had not expanded his activities to being a performer in the German theatre. Shaw paraphrased Macbeth's statement, upon seeing the ghost of Banquo: 'the time has been, That, when the **brains were out**, the man would die' (3, 4). An **Archimandrite** was the head of a monastery in the Eastern Orthodox Church. **Gertrude Kingston**, an actress-manager, began her career, as did H. Granville Barker, with Sarah Thorne's company in Margate. She played the role of Aurora Bompas in the Court production of *How He Lied to Her Husband* in 1905. She staged and acted in several revivals of Shaw's plays in the 1910s and 1920s. Shaw wrote *Great Catherine* (1913) for her.

136 / To William Archer

10 Adelphi Terrace WC
3rd November 1908

[TLS: BL 45296 f 211]

Back in London, Shaw resumed his attendance at the meeting of the SMNTC. *He also continued his campaign for a knighthood for Pinero by discussing the matter with Reginald Baliol Brett, the Viscount of Esher. Several months earlier he had initiated the proposal with Mrs Asquith, wife of the prime minister. (See letter of 3 July 1908.) The knighthood was awarded in 1909 at the June Birthday Honours. W.S. Gilbert and John Hare had been knighted in 1907; Herbert Beerbohm Tree was also knighted in 1909.*

My dear W.A.,

After the Committee this morning I sounded Esher on the question of the dramatic Knighthood that I mentioned to you. He jumped at the idea very cordially and said he had no doubt that it could be managed next June; but he fears it is too late for the 9th of November. He is on the honours list himself for the 9th, and has probably seen the entire list of names. A few days ago I wrote to Mrs Asquith about it; but I have not yet had any reply. However, I had no serious hope of getting anything done within the three months (mostly holidays) which have elapsed since I mooted the suggestion; but since Esher has taken to it so kindly I feel sanguine about its coming off next June. All the same, I wish we could get it done at once. It would be of great assistance to the theatre scheme.

Yours ever
G.B.S.

137 / To William Archer

10 Adelphi Terrace. WC
4th March 1909

[TLS: BL 45296 ff 212-213]

In late February Shaw drafted a 'Letter to Millionaires' (BL 45296 ff 214–21; reprinted in Dukore 3: 1157–61). It was addressed to 'the very small number of rich and influential public men in England who realize the enormous national importance of the theatre and the hopelessness of trusting to commercial competition to make the best of it.' The aim of this appeal was to gather £500,000 that would provide the initial commitment to build a Shakespeare Memorial National Theatre. It would be developed according to the plan that Archer and Barker had presented in A National Theatre: Scheme and Estimates *(1907). In his draft letter Shaw described the operation of the Vedrenne-Barker management at the Court, Savoy, and Haymarket theatres between 1904 and 1908. He noted that a final deficit of £6000 faced the Court and Savoy ventures (a deficit primarily covered by loans from Shaw who later forgave the debt). The Vedrenne-Barker management, despite its accomplishments, proved that a commercial model of repertory theatre could not sustain itself in London. (See letters of 13 November 1907 and 17 June 1908.) Although the committee members rejected Shaw's 'Letter to Millionaires,' he published a long letter to the editors of* The Times *on 10 May that expressed many of the same points (Dukore 3: 1161–3).*

The Archers continued to maintain two residencies: a home in King's Langley, which was a Hertfordshire village, and a flat in London. During March 1909 Archer moved into a temporary flat in London at 44 Great Russell Street, WC. Then in November the Archers took a flat at 27 Fitzroy Square, W1, which became their permanent London residence during the rest of his life. Typically, he would be in London during the week, usually alone. Mrs Archer used the back room of the Fitzroy flat on Wednesdays and Saturdays for her nerve treatment business, but otherwise she usually stayed in King's Langley, which had become the location for her Nerve Training Colony (Whitebrook: 234–5).

My dear Archer,

I ordered a copy of my draft letter to be sent to you as well as to Barker and to Mrs Lyttelton; but the only address I know was King's Langley. I shall have to ascertain your new address through the telephone.

As neither you nor Mrs. Lyttelton approve of my draft, we must let it drop; and you must go to work in your own way. In drafting it, I proceeded on two lines. First, as the newspapers from time to time describe me as the Socialist millionaire, with the result that I immediately get applications for money from all sorts of people, I have formed a strong opinion as to the sort of letter that is likely to survive in the postal struggle for life. Second, I regard the Vedrenne-Barker business as the strongest card we have to play; and it was my deliberate intention to suggest that the National Theatre would be Vedrenne-Barker rescued from its pernicious dependence on Shaw – a dependence, which, I may observe, was often very bad for Shaw, as it compelled him to consent to productions which, artistically speaking, ought never to have been made. The Philanderer was a glaring instance.

If you proceed with millionaires on the general assumption that people are stupid, you will come to grief with them. A millionaire may be ignorant or philistine or puritanical; but the necessity for handling and investing his capital, and of defending his income from the attacks of every conceivable kind of projector, prompter, beggar and swindler, knocks out of him scores of illusions that have to be tenderly dealt with in the case of poor men, and, in particular, makes him very impatient of general plausibilities, and anxious to get to the points of actual practice and any previous experience available in the matter. However, it is clear that you don't see the millionaire that way, and probably none of the rest will either, the notion of my making a dash personally to try to save a desperate situation perishes; and nothing remedies but to set Gollancz on the scheme of Sir Walter Lawrence, which will suit him down to the ground. It still involves getting round your millionaires to guarantee the site and so on; so we had better try your letter on them. Probably they will object to Matthew Arnold as an atheist; but one has to chance these things.

Yours ever,
G. Bernard Shaw

Edith S. **Lyttelton** (1865–1948), second wife of Alfred Lyttelton (the famous athlete, 1857–1913), served on the executive committee of the Shakespeare Memorial National Theatre. For her friend Mrs Patrick Campbell, she wrote plays (CL 3: 139–41), including *Warp and Woof,* which represents the working conditions of sweat labour. The play was staged at the Vaudeville Theatre (27 June 1904; 21 perfs.). In 1917 she was made a Dame Commander of the Order of the British Empire for her support of war refugees, and was inducted into the order in 1929. The first public production of ***The Philanderer*** was staged at the Royal Court Theatre for eight matinee performances in February 1907. Shaw claims here that he was **compelled ... to consent** to the production. But on 28 December 1906, weeks before the production opened, Shaw had made a pitch to Barker for staging *The Philanderer*. 'It is the best of my plays, and when I work it up with a little extra horse play it will go like mad' (Barker: 73). Barker disliked the play, but consented. Ben Webster portrayed Charteris; Mary Barton (d. 1970) played Julia Craven after Lillah McCarthy, who rehearsed the role, withdrew because of an emergency operation. Shaw and Barker directed. The production, **artistically speaking**, was a glaring flop. Most reviewers blamed the playwright. Archer, who also disliked the play, did not write a review. Israel **Gollancz** (1864–1930), who was knighted in 1919, was the honorary secretary of the Shakespeare Memorial National Theatre and director of the Early English Text Society. He taught English literature at King's College, London, from 1903 to 1930, and edited the popular Temple Edition of Shakespeare's plays (1894–6). Both Lyttelton and Gollancz remained dedicated members of the Shakespeare committee for two decades. **Sir Walter Roper Lawrence**, 1st Baronet (1857–1940), served in the Indian Civil Service, and wrote a study of the geography and customs of the people of Kashmir, *The Valley of Kashmir* (1895).

138 / To William Archer

Ayot St Lawrence, Welwyn, Herts.
10th August 1909

[ALS: BL 45296 f 222]

Shaw was responding to a missing letter from Archer, who had commented upon the lengthy Statement of the Evidence *that Shaw had prepared for the Joint Select Committee of both Houses of Parliament. The committee carried out an investigation of stage censorship and the status of the Lord Chamberlain's Office. In his letter Archer may also have commented on the letter of 28 July that Shaw had produced in multiple copies and mailed to the members of the new Dramatists' Club (CL 2: 848, 851–3). In his* Statement, *which he printed in 1911 as the Preface to* The Shewing-up of Blanco Posnet *(CP 3: 673–762), Shaw spelled out his case against censorship and offered an alternative system to that of the Lord Chamberlain's Office. He recognized that the West End theatre managers were quite comfortable with the present system, but he felt that his plan, which would place all entertainment under the control of the London County Council, should appeal to the managers of Variety entertainment. If any legal issues or problems emerged, the Department of Public Prosecution or the attorney general could regulate such matters (CP 3: 747–9).*

Between 29 July and 24 September the Joint Select Committee conducted public hearings. Forty-nine witnesses testified. In preparation for his testimony, Shaw delivered to the committee's members not only his printed Statement *but also copies of his three censored plays. He was interviewed on 30 July (Dukore 3: 1173–88), but the members refused to accept or discuss the* Statement, *which was excluded from the committee's published records of the hearings. And when he returned on*

5 August to continue his testimony, the chairman announced that the committee had no further questions for him. Adding to Shaw's frustrations, the Dramatists' Club's members failed to offer a united front in opposition to censorship. Also, Archer, H.G. Barker, Gilbert Murray, and James Barrie resisted his guidance when he tried to direct and control their testimony before the committee. They did not feel a need to follow a script he had prepared, and instead made their own separate statements. (For Dan Laurence's description of these events see CL2: 747–50; also see letters in CL2: 850–1, 853–5.)

Shaw's battles in 1909 against stage censorship stretched across much of the year (Holroyd 2: 224–38). The campaign was engaged when The Shewing-up of Blanco Posnet, *written in March and April for H. Beerbohm Tree, was denied a licence in May by G.A. Redford, the Examiner of Plays. Shaw issued a public protest on 22 May (CP 3: 800–2). Redford then compounded his opposition to Shaw's drama in June by refusing a licence for* Press Cuttings *(CL 2: 843). This banned play, which offers a satire of militarism and the mishandling of the suffrage movement by the Asquith government, was announced by the Women's Suffrage Society. The first line of the play is 'Votes for Women!,' the title of Elizabeth Robins's 1907 play that was staged at the Court. In late June Shaw again registered his protest against censorship with five statements in* The Times *and* The Observer *between 26 June and 16 July (CP 3: 884–95). When the Stage Society presented a private staging on 9 and 12 July, Archer joined the protest against Redford with 'The Censor's Heroism' (17 July 1909,* The Nation*).*

Blanco Posnet *was subsequently performed in Dublin in late August by the Abbey Theatre, but not before another legal dispute took place when the under secretary of the Lord Lieutenant at Dublin Castle threatened to disallow a production. Even though the British crown had no authority over Dublin productions, the under secretary aligned himself politically with the judgment of the Lord Chamberlain Office. But Lady Augusta Gregory (1852–1932) and William Butler Yeats did not give in to threats from the Irish government. The production opened on 25 August, and was a notable success for the Abbey. (See letters in CL 2: 855–68.) The Shaws were in Ireland by this time. Charlotte attended a performance with her sister Mary Cholmondeley, but Shaw stayed in western Ireland at the Great Southern Hotel in Parknasilla. He was writing* Misalliance. *Later in 1909 he arrange for the Abbey to stage* Blanco Posnet *in London on 5 and 6 December, under the 'private' auspices of the Stage Society.*

Yet despite the efforts of Shaw, Archer, and others to campaign against stage censorship, the government, in accord with the West End theatre managers, was quite satisfied with the current system. The select committee's report, published in November, suggested only a few minor modifications in the procedures, and when Parliament met in its next session, the members were quite satisfied to do nothing. For an earlier and more concise critique of stage censorship by Shaw, see 'The Censorship of the Stage in England' in the North American Review, *August 1899.*

Dear W.A.
I am down here until Thursday, when I shall come up to see what the Select Committee will do, and to pack for a holiday flight to the west of Ireland.

I thought the D. of Pub. Pros. *was* the Attorney General. Sidney Webb told me that when the Sabbatarians prosecuted the Brighton Aquarium as a disorderly house for giving concerts on Sunday, an Act was hastily passed, restricting the initiative in such cases to the A.G. That was my precedent.

I have drafted a circular for our witnesses & told my secretary, Miss Gillmore, to send you a few copies when they are mimeographed. What's the matter with my plan, except that Barker muddled it & Barrie ignored it? I see no other on the cards. The variety managers ought to support it because it will protect them from abuse of the authority they are already under; and the legitimates ought to support it (failing their beloved status quo) because they will most likely, if there is any change, be delivered over to the local authorities.

What I want to know about the Advisory Council is who the distinguished dramatist was who offered to tell the Lordly whether Pinero's plays & mine & Jones's & Barrie's & Carton's &c &c were fit to produce. Gilbert? Someone suggested him.

In haste for post
G.B.S.

Georgina 'Judy' **Gillmore** (1885–1974) was the daughter of Arabella Gillmore (1856–1941), who was the half-sister of Shaw's mother. Miss Gillmore was Shaw's full-time secretary (1907–12). The **legitimates** was a reference to the West End theatre managers. The **Advisory Council** was the Joint Select Committee on censorship. The **Lordly** – that is, the Lords on the Select Committee – were unimpressed by Shaw and his arguments. R. C. **Carton** was a playwright; his farce *Mr Preedy and the Countess* had 236 performances in 1909. In the letter of 22 February 1901 Shaw had expressed disdain for Carton's *The Tree of Knowledge*, which was staged in 1897.

139 / To William Archer Ayot St Lawrence, Welwyn, Herts.
11th August 1909

[APCS: BL 45296 f 223; CL 2 partial]

Shaw was responding to a missing letter or communication from Archer. The American photographer Alvin Langdon Coburn (1882–1966) studied with Edward Steichen (1879–1973) and exhibited in the New York gallery of Alfred Stieglitz (1864–1946). He later settled in England and then Wales. Working primarily in England at this time, he completed a series of photographs in 1909 of London and Edinburgh. Besides cityscapes, he excelled at portrait photography, featuring famous writers and artists. He first photographed Shaw in 1904 (CL 2: 435), and in 1906 joined Shaw in Paris when Auguste Rodin did the sculpture of Shaw. He photographed Rodin, and in the same year he took the nude photograph of Shaw in the pose of Le Penseur. *In 1906 Shaw provided the preface for Coburn's exhibition catalogue at the Royal Photographic Society (Biblio 2: 624, C1518). Coburn instructed Shaw on photography, and may have contributed to Shaw's lecture 'Photography in Its Relation to Modern Art,' delivered on 18 October 1909 at the Photographic Salon. A Coburn headshot of a Satanic Shaw from c. 1910 appeared in Archibald Henderson's* Man of the Century *between pages 320 and 321.*

I did not send you the Coburn group: I saw it at Coburn's house, but did not annex a copy. He must have sent it to you himself.

I liked the Chipperfield Sheeny, & will be specially civil to him; and I like the house; but Charlotte would have none of it. She wants a park; & I daren't tell her we can't afford it. So we are waiting until Blenheim or Haddon Hall is to let.

G.B.S.

The **Coburn group** may have been the recent series of photographs that Coburn had taken of Edinburgh. The series was intended for Robert Louis Stevenson's *Edinburgh: Picturesque Notes,* but the book was not published until decades later. **Sheeny**, a derogatory word for a Jew, was all-too prevalent in the racial discourse of the era, and Shaw felt comfortable using the term. Of course, Shaw felt comfortable making this remark to Archer because they both used such terms. For instance, when Archer was negotiating for a production of *The Green Goddess* in New York, he was pleased that he had not 'fallen into the hands of an 'Ebrew Jew like [David] Belasco,' the producer and playwright (Whitebrook: 363). It is unclear who Shaw was referring to, but Archer knew the person whose home was in the village of **Chipperfield**, which was part of King's Langley, where the Archers lived. Although the Shaws had settled into their home at Ayot St Lawrence in November 1906, they continued to look occasionally at alternative residences in the Hertfordshire region. Of course, the Churchill family was not giving up **Blenheim** Palace and the eleventh-century **Haddon Hall** was unavailable.

140 / To William Archer Ayot St Lawrence, Welwyn, Herts.
15th May 1910

[APCS: BL 45296 f 224]

No correspondence has survived for the period between 11 August 1909 and 15 May 1910. In the spring of 1910, after returning from a freezing trip to Warsaw and Moscow in March, April, and early May, Archer was commissioned by Cameron McKenzie (1882–1921) of McClure's Magazine *to investigate the trial and execution of Francisco Ferrer y Guardia (1850–1909). Ferrer, a free-thinker, dissident educator, and critic of the Spanish government, became known internationally as 'the Spanish Dreyfus' because he had been unjustly accused of being the author and instigator of the 1909 'Revolution of July' in Barcelona. The military trial, defended by the Catholic Church, was a gross injustice.*

Archer already had some knowledge of Spanish, and during the summer he immersed himself in a colloquial language course. He then studied the documents and published literature on the case. Also, with Shaw's guidance, he learned how to operate a camera for taking photographs during the trip. His research carried him to Paris, Barcelona, and Madrid in late summer and early autumn. He met with people who had been involved in the Barcelona riots, and with people connected to Ferrer and the trial. The investigation led to the publication of two long articles in McClure's Magazine *(November and December 1910), and then to Archer's book in the early spring of 1911,* The Life, Trial, and Death of Francisco Ferrer, *which was widely reviewed and praised. Deeply impressed by the book, A.W. Pinero wrote to Archer: 'If there is ever to be a Day of Judgment your book will lie on the Judge's table!' (See C. Archer: 313–15, 323; Whitebrook: 284–6.)*

On reflection I think your best plan as to the photographing will be to borrow a camera from me. I shall have to send it to the makers to adjust the shutter properly, as it has rusted & gone out of order during the winter; so it will probably not be available for a week at least; but it will do all you require. I shall have to instruct you in the use of it, as if you go snapping at random, you may spoil half your films & make bad pictures of the rest. I can put you in the way of succeeding creditably every time. The films will cost three shillings a dozen, and perhaps twice as much for developing and printing; but McClure ought to pay for this. A pound would cover the cost of a dozen illustrations. A new camera of the class of the one I can lend you would cost from ten to fifteen guineas, which would be an absurd expenditure for a single job.

G.B.S.

141 / To G. Bernard Shaw

Tokyo
8th June 1912

[APCS: HRC Texas and DHL]

There are no surviving letters between 15 May 1910 and 8 June 1912. In 1912, under contract to write articles for McClure's Magazine *and the* Daily News and Leader, *Archer commenced a world tour. He left Liverpool on 23 March 1912 and did not return to London until early February 1913. He arrived in New York City on 4 April. After a short stay, he took a train across the country to San Francisco, where he sailed for Japan by way of Honolulu. Arriving in Tokyo Bay on a May morning, he saw Mount Fujiyama 'floating lightly above the interlopping hill-crests like a giant bird with wings outspread' (C. Archer: 330). He spent nearly two months in Japan (early May to late June), visiting various cities, hiking in the mountains, staying at village inns, and writing articles about Japan. In Osaka he saw Bunraku puppet theatre and in Tokyo he attended performances of both Kabuki and Noh theatre (Whitebrook: 290–3). He also saw productions of* A Doll's House *and Shaw's* The Man of Destiny, *the latter staged by a Japanese experimental theatre company of students at Waseda University. The performers were Harnake Doi (Napoleon), Seiichi Kato (Lieutenant), Sumako Matsui (Strange Lady), and Tetteki Togi (Giuseppe).*

Archer's message to Shaw extended across two postcards. The reverse sides of the cards revealed photographs of two scenes from the production. He also sent a third postcard, with the brief message: 'Note the wind being and thunder guy.' The card featured two photographs of the famous carvings at Nikko, Japan of 'The God of Winds' and 'The God of Thunder' in threatening poses. Instead of mailing the cards separately, he inserted all three in a mailing envelope.

My dear G.B.S.

Here are two scenes from 'The Man of Destiny,' as performed at a sort of experimental (private) theatre, belonging to Dr. Tsubouchi, father of Sheko Tsubouchi whom I think you have seen. The performance was far from bad considering – the innkeeper was capital, the lady inoffensive, Napoleon not too Mongolian (rhyme unintentional) and the officer amusing. His attitude in this card is very Japanese, but I don't remember that he did much of that sort of thing. The tragic acting of the Japanese stage is almost barbarous, but they do comedy very well.

In order to see that M. of D. I stayed a day longer than I intended, and was rewarded by seeing a performance of a 'No' play, or 'No' drama which is the queerest thing I ever observed. I suppose it is the oldest form of theatrical art at present extant in the world – it is just as if we had preserved exactly every movement, costume and tradition of the fifteenth-century 'interlude.' The 'No' theatre is curiously like the Elizabethan stage in its design & proportions, but the performance is immobile and hieratic in the last degree – the reverse of Elizabethan.

Hope you are flourishing. Love to Mrs Shaw, H.G.B., Mrs H.G.B. & all.

Yours
W.A.

Sheko Tsubouchi or Tsubouchi Sheko (Shökö) (1859–1935) was a Japanese novelist, playwright, director, and critic who taught at Waseda University. The son of Dr Yuko Tsubouchi, he introduced the plays of Ibsen and Shaw to Japan. He also translated some of Shakespeare's plays into Japanese, and novels by Sir Walter Scott and E.G.E. Bulwer-Lytton (1803–73). He visited London, and his writing appeared in Gordon Craig's *The Mask*, which attempted to introduce aspects of Japanese theatre to Western readers. For instance, his article 'The Drama in Japan' appeared in the April 1912 volume. Perhaps the designation of **Mongolian** for a Japanese person was a joke, but a poor one. Whatever the case, the word was applied broadly in the era by anthropologists to people with 'yellow' skin. In the late nineteenth century the term was even applied to native peoples of Lapland and the Eskimo of North America. The physical **attitude** of the lieutenant in the photograph suggests a tense pose of physical challenge. His crouching body appears ready to spring forward, with the left arm bent in a defensive gesture before him (as if holding a shield), while the right arm is extended straight behind him in preparation to swing his sword towards the actor portraying Napoleon, who stands tall, resolute, and unafraid. The English **interlude** or dramatic sketch derived its name from the Latin *interludium* (between + play); it shared some traits with the Italian *intermezzo* and the Spanish *entremés*. These forms developed in the fifteenth and sixteenth centuries. Archer extended his love to Mrs Shaw and **H.G.B., Mrs H.G.B.** – that is, the recently wedded couple of H. Granville Barker and Lillah McCarthy.

142 / To G. Bernard Shaw

Shidzuoka, Japan
15th June 1912

[APCS: HRC Texas]

The photograph on this postcard showed Archer and two unindentified Japanese men sitting at a table and having tea. Above Shaw's address Archer wrote, 'Via Siberia.' Archer discovered that he was known in Japan, primarily because of the Ibsen plays. He was invited to lecture at Waseda University on 'The Future of the Drama.' During the last two weeks of his visit, he was joined by his sister, Grace Stedman. She and her husband ran a tea plantation in Dairen (i.e., Talien, a port city in northeast China on the Liaoning Peninsula where the Japanese had fought the Russians at Port Arthur during the Russo-Japanese War in 1904–5). On 27 June Archer and his sister sailed to Dairen from Kobe. During July he travelled alone in China, visiting Peking, Tientsin, Shanghai, and Canton. He was disgusted by the poverty, urban squalour, and dire social conditions following the collapse of the Manchu dynasty (C. Archer: 331–2; Whitebrook: 294).

P.S. To former card. As we were going through the library of Waseda University, Tokyo, with an American lady who is somehow on the staff, my sister said, 'I see you have *Man & Superman* there.' 'Oh yes' was the reply. 'We have all Ibsen.'

W.A.

143 / To G. Bernard Shaw Galle Face Hotel, Colombo, Ceylon
7th August 1912

[ALS: BL 50528 f 58]

The 'enclosures' with this letter have not survived. Among them was a theatre program for Candida. *Archer arrived in Ceylon [Sri Lanka] in late July. He stayed for two weeks, mainly in Colombo, but he made a short trip inland to the city of Kandy, not 'Candy.' This name, which is derived from 'Kanda Uda Pas Rada' (the five areas of the mountain), was provided by the English colonial government. Located in the mountainous centre of Ceylon, Kandy served as an administrative capital, with Colombo on the coast being the commercial centre. The Buddhist Temple of the Tooth, a sacred site for a tooth of Siddhartha Gautama Buddha, is a primary attraction in Kandy. During British rule the temple became the residence of the government agent. Since the independence of Sri Lanka, the temple, once a royal residence, serves as a Buddhist shrine, with daily rituals performed in the inner chamber. It experienced a new type of commercial colonialism in 1984 when it served as the location for the film* Indiana Jones and the Temple of Doom.

Upon leaving Ceylon in mid-August, Archer travelled north by rail from Tuticorin and Madura [Madurai] to Poona [Pune], Bombay [Mumbai], and Ahmadabad. He continued northwest to the mountains of Baluchistan, now part of Pakistan, where his brother Charles was the officiating agent for the British Raj. Charles was located at the hill station at Ziarat, 8000 ft. above sea level. Archer stayed with Charles and his wife Alice for a few weeks. He then departed, travelling through the Northwest Frontier to Peshawar [Pakhawar], then south to Lahore and Amritsar, where he toured the Golden Temple, the holy Sikh shrine. Then he went to Simla and Delhi (Whitebrook: 296–7). In Agra, visiting the Taj Mahal, he ran into E.M. Forster; they struck up a friendship. Archer wrote an unfinished poem on the Taj Mahal, which included the lines: 'a fabric of enchantment, hewn / From lucent quarries of the moon' (C. Archer: 341). He was appalled by the living conditions and squalour of Calcutta [Kolkata], the base of the East India Company and British rule over India. He also travelled to Trichinopoly [Trichies], Bangalore, the sacred city of Benares [Varanasi], founded by the god Shiva, Allahabad, and back to Bombay. After five months in India, he departed for England on 7 January 1913, sailing on the SS Circassia.

My dear G.B.S.

I think you owe me a salary as Travelling Inspector of your *théâtre*. After *The Man of Destiny* in Tokyo, I came in for *Candida* here. The theatre was about half full, which was not bad considering the counter attraction of Mr. R. G. Knowles & his wife, (described as 'the Kubelik of the banjo'). The performance, of which I saw 2 acts, was quite respectable, considering they played *Othello* the night before & were to do *The Sign of the Cross* next night. Both Morell & Eugene were quite decent; the people loved Burgess ('Don't be vulgar Candy' was the success of the evening); & the Candida had the good fault of being too young for the part – she looked quite as young as Eugene. In this way she was the most inadequate of the lot – but she was agreeable. You will see from the enclosures what an excellent dodge it is to write your own criticism & print it on the program.

Such is your popularity in Ceylon that the name Candy has been given to the capital. I spent the day there & only returned to Colombo in time for the performance.

My first impression on the threshold of India is that we are a hopelessly insignificant & vulgar lot in comparison with the extremely handsome and distinguished people we rule over. You see sinister & even ugly faces here, but scarcely any that are common, half baked, shapeless. And the number of noble & impressive figures is extraordinary. I daresay they are awful scoundrels but aesthetically they are magnificent.

Love to Mrs Shaw from

Yours ever
W.A.

Richard George **Knowles** (1858–1919), born in Canada, was a music hall comedian whose rapid-fire jokes and songs were popular in London in the 1890s; he had long runs at the Trocadero and the Empire Theatre. He later performed in Australia, and occasionally toured in southeastern Asia. He usually appeared with his **wife**, Winifred Johnson, who played the banjo. Jan **Kubelík** (1880–1940) was a Czech violinist and composer. He toured extensively before the First World War. One of his eight children, Rafael Kubelík, became a successful conductor. ***The Sign of the Cross***, a spectacle of Christian martyrdom set in Nero's Rome by Wilson Barrett, was staged in London in 1896. (See the letter of 29 January 1896.)

144 / To William Archer

10 Adelphi Terrace WC
10th July 1914

[APCS: BL 45296 f 225]

There are no extant letters between Archer and the Shaws from 7 August 1912 to 10 July 1914, another unfortunate gap, for surely some letters were exchanged. Mrs Shaw is responding to a missing letter from Archer, so the identity of the visiting 'poetess' is unclear. H.W. Massingham, who had previously edited The Star *(1890–1),* Daily Chronicle *(1895–9), and* Daily News *(1901–6), became editor of* The Nation *in 1907; he continued in this role until 1923. Archer and Shaw had written for each of these journals and newspapers. For example, Archer served as theatre critic for* The Nation *between August 1908 and December 1910. Both Archer and Shaw admired Massingham and his editorial skills. He remained a friend and ally for both of them until his death in 1924. (See Shaw's memorial essay in Pen Portraits: 203–11.)*

Dear W. Archer

I am *so* sorry, but we are engaged to spend the whole day next Sunday with the Massinghams at Wendover. Mrs. Massingham specially asked us to stay to tea as I think she has some people coming.

It is a great pity as we should both of us like to see *you* – let alone the Poetess!

My kindest remembrance to Mrs. Archer.

Yours sincerely
C.F. Shaw

145 / To G. Bernard Shaw [no address]
10th November 1914

[TLS: BL 45296 f 227]

On 7 November Shaw published in The Nation *and* The New York Times *his quixotic 'Open Letter to the President of the United States,' which appealed to President Woodrow Wilson (1856–1924) to organize the neutral nations as a moral force that could urge both sides in the war to withdraw from Belgium.*

In early July 1914, just before the war began, Archer, Shaw, Gilbert Chesterton, and Lord Howard de Walden participated in the making of a farcical film about cowboys that J.M. Barrie conceived. He wrote the screenplay and operated the camera; Granville Barker directed the action, which was filmed in Hertfordshire. A surviving photograph of the four aging men in cowboy costumes, complete with hats and guns, captured the silliness of their 'Cowboy adventures,' but the light-hearted mood of the escapade would soon vanish when German soldiers marched into Belgium on 3 August. Archer's son Tom returned by steamer from the United States as soon as the war commenced. He enlisted as a lance corporal in the London Scottish regiment, which went into battle on 31 October wearing kilts. In early November he had his first military engagement, a disaster of defective rifles and chaotic leadership in the trenches of Flanders. Over 400 men, half of the regiment, were killed. Tom survived.

My dear G.B.S.

At risk of breach of confidence, I really must pass on to you a compliment of which you ought not to remain in ignorance. It occurs in a letter from my brother Jim to a cousin of ours. He writes: –

Did you see Shaw's appeal to President Wilson in last NATION? It seems to me to do more credit to Shaw's heart than to his head.

I feel sure that this is the testimonial, of all others, that you will most prize, if only on account of its rarity.

Since London Scottish were in action ten days ago, we have been very anxious about Tom; but we heard yesterday that he came through it all right.

How many centuries it seems since our Cowboy adventures! Love to Mrs. Shaw, though, as Johnson said of Mrs. Boswell, I fear she does not love me.

Yours ever W.A.

146 / To William Archer Ayot St Lawrence, Welwyn, Herts.
11th November 1914

[TLS: BL 45296 f 228; CL 3 partial]

Shaw's letter, the first surviving letter to Archer since 15 May 1910, expressed his anger over the war. He was responding to Archer's letter of 10 November. Although he surely wrote several cards and letters during the four and one-half years, they have disappeared.

For both Shaw and Archer the war set the agenda for their publications over the next four years. On 14 November, just a week after his 'Open Letter to the President of the United States' had appeared, Shaw published Common Sense about the War *for the* New Statesman, *the Fabian journal. The pamphlet of 35,000 words, printed as a 'Special War Supplement' in the journal, condemned British as well as German militarism, and attacked the foreign policy of Sir Edward Grey (1862–1933). (For short and long descriptions of Shaw's political activities and publications during the war, see Dan Laurence's summary in CL3: 239–41 and Michael Holroyd's perspective in Holroyd 2: 345–82.)* Common Sense *turned many people against Shaw. He was accused of treason in some quarters for offering an apology and justification for Germany's actions. Although he was not worried about upsetting the leaders of the Liberal Party, he risked offending friends when he refused to join Archer, Barker, Barrie, Chesterton, Murray, and Wells, who had signed a propaganda declaration prepared by the government in support of Western ideals of freedom and against Prussian militarism (Journey: 38; Holroyd 2: 351). He had previously refused to put his name to a open letter that Gilbert Murray had crafted in support of Russian colleagues in the arts and humanities (see CL3: 260–1).*

Unlike Shaw, Archer supported the British government. He was one of several writers who went to work for the new Secret War Propaganda Bureau, located at Wellington House in Buckingham Gate. Except for an assignment in Edinburgh for a few weeks as a censor of mail, Archer spent the war in London as a governmental employee. He wrote and published official critiques of Germany. Even though he had criticized British militarism in some of his weekly articles for the Daily News, *he held German leaders responsible for the invasion of Belgium and the resulting atrocities. In 1915 he published* The Thirteen Days: July 23–August 4 1914: A Chronicle and Interpretation, *which indicted Germany and defended the British leaders. In that same year he wrote* Fighting a Philosophy, *a pamphlet that placed the writings of Schopenhauer and Nietzsche within the context of German war policy and cultural identity. In 1917 he published* 501 Gems of German

Thought, *a compilation of statements that illustrate 'German self-laudation and contempt for the rest of the world' (xv). Archer's aim was to offer a perspective on German ambitions, ruthlessness, and militarism. Then in 1918 he published* The Pirates' Progress: A Short History of the U-Boat.

My dear Archer

I am naturally touched by Jim's tribute; but it is hardly deserved. The truth is, we have been plundering American ships in such a highhanded manner, especially at Gibraltar, where they allege trade with Italy, that matters are becoming extremely strained; and we shall have to pay for our last big haul of copper. Fisher's lunacy in declaring that we should sink burn and destroy every ship in the north sea at sight, no matter what flag it flew, would have put the lid on if it had affected America as much as Scandinavia. There was a real danger of Wilson coming down on the wrong side; and it was absolutely certain that he would not come down on the right one for our sakes. Meanwhile we did nothing to conciliate him but tell him what splendid fellows we are and what swine the Germans are, with Reims and Louvain trimmings *ad lib.*, and a visit from Harold Begbie thrown in. The only thing to do was to point out that if America declared for Germany, it would also be dealing another blow to Belgium; and this would hardly be stood by American public opinion, even where it is antiest-English. Hence my Open Letter. The sentiment was piled on for America. However, it was legitimate enough, though I have information (communicated by Belgian wounded to Englishmen who speak French well enough to be mistaken by Flemings for Frenchmen) as to the savage slaughter of German prisoners at Liège which throws some light on the *furia Tedesca.*

I did not realize that Tom was in the London Scottish. It is a sickening business this sending lambs to slaughter because we are governed by bloody fools wirepulled by damned thieves. However, if Tom has survived that first scrimmage where the six hundred fell, he may be considered immortal, and I wish him a safe deliverance with some confidence. If any of his childish talent for fiction remains in him, what a time he will have of it telling the tale of his campaign!

What about Charles? Is he in command of our Ghoorka cutthroats at the front, or is he still in India drinking the health of the Tsar?

Next Saturday the New Statesman will contain my War Supplement, which will not bring the unbidden tear to the cheek of James.

You must come see us presently. In Charlotte's absence (she has gone up to Adelphi Terrace by the early train) I cannot fix a day now; but I will consult her this evening.

G.B.S.

John Arbuthnot **Fisher** (1841–1920), first Baron Fisher of Kilverstone, held the post of first sea lord of the Admiralty. In *Common Sense* Shaw wrote about the shelling of the **Reims** Cathedral and the destruction of **Louvain**. Edward **Harold Begbie** (1871–1929), an English author known for his children's stories, wrote recruiting poems such as 'Fall In' when the war broke out; he visited the United States to stir up support for the war. The Italian phrase ***furia Tedesca*** means Germanic rage. The Brigade of Gurkhas, not **Ghoorka**, was the term for the Nepalese soldiers in the British Indian Army and the East India Company. The term derived from the town of Gorkha. Besides taking part in the Relief of Lucknow, the Gurkha regiments were part of the British army in both world wars. Of course, Charles Archer did not fight with them; nor did he support the **Tzar**. The joke was ill conceived. (See letter of 14 December 1924 for Archer's concerns about Shaw's occasional 'failures of tact,' both minor and major.)

147 / To William Archer

Ayot St Lawrence, Welwyn, Herts.
23rd November 1914

[APCS: BL 45296 f 229]

The 'nice letter' that Charlotte Shaw mentioned has disappeared. Despite their political differences over the war, Shaw and Archer did not part company. For the most part, it would seem, they avoided both personal contact and public debates with one another. Serving the government in several capacities throughout the war, Archer maintained a quite busy schedule, primarily in London. By contrast, the Shaws were seldom in London during the war. Sometimes they were at Ayot St Lawrence, but they were often in Torquay, where they stayed at the Hydro Hotel. For example, Shaw wrote Common Sense about the War *there. And they also visited Ireland on several long visits during these four years.*

Thank you for your *very* nice letter which gave us both great pleasure.

We *will* meet soon again! The obstacle with us is our being down here so much which makes our two days in London (Thursday & Friday) get completely filled up week after week. But it is an obstacle that can & shall be got over!!

C.F.S.

148 / To Frances E. Archer

10 Adelphi Terrace WC
23rd January 1915

[TLS: BL 45296 ff 230–1]

*The letter from Mrs Archer is missing. Shaw's reply offered only partial information on Dr Lipinska's identity, the nature of her profession and scientific training, and the reason she sought to communicate with the famous pianist and composer Ignace Jan Paderewski. Years earlier, when Shaw wrote the first of his several reviews on the London recitals of Paderewski, he praised his piano performances (*The Star, *16 May 1890; Music 2: 66–7). Shaw's one complaint, which he repeated in several reviews during the 1890s, was that Paderewski's playing was too passionate and violent. Many years later, in 1939, he wrote a letter of praise that was printed, with Shaw's permission, within Mary Lawton's 'Foreword' for the British edition of* The Paderewski Memoirs *(Biblio 1: B280: 454).*

Dear Mrs. Archer

I hardly know what to do about Dr Lipinska. I am very doubtful about writing to Paderewski for two reasons. First, the very utmost resources one can credit him with must be so fearfully overtaxed by the distress in Galicia, where the Russians have been doing just what the Germans have been doing in Belgium, or possibly a good deal worse, that he is not likely to have either money or patience left for a lady in London who has some friends and the possibility of practicing a profession. At all events, I know what happens when such applications are made to me. Second, it is only too possible that my name may be a household word to Paderewski; that it may have been so for the last twenty years or so; and that the words may be entirely unfit for publication. I was at my zenith as 'a musical critic of European reputation' when Paderewski gave his first recital in London to a small audience. I dont remember what I said about him: but perhaps he does; for foreign musicians trying their fortune in London for the first time attach an importance to their press notices which seems ridiculous enough to the world at large. I am pretty sure I did not mistake him for a second rate player; but I do remember that he had some really frightful habits of hammering forte passages which must have slipped a thorn or two into any crown I may have conferred on him. On the whole, since there is never any harm in being on the safe side, and as Paderewski is far too big a lion himself to be in the least impressed by my mane and tail, I think it would be better to get someone else to write the letter. You will see from my first reason that I rather doubt whether the letter will do any good anyhow: still, as it cannot do any harm to Dr Lipinska, and can, at worst, only provoke an impatient imprecation from Paderewski, it had better be sent.

I suppose, as Dr Lipinska has been scraping along for six months, the generosity of her personal friends has run dry. Why not try the Prince of Wales's Relief Fund, or some of the War Emergency Funds which seem to exist all over the place. She has a claim on any scientific fund that may exist as well as on such political ones as may apply to a Galician Pole – if she *is* a Galician Pole. If any private fund can be raised, I daresay I can squeeze out a few guineas, though the war has such a brutalizing effect on me, as it has on everyone else, that I am growing callous to human suffering. It is a villainous business, from beginning to end.

Yours sincerely
G. Bernard Shaw

149 / To William Archer

10 Adelphi Terrace WC
11th March 1915

[APCS: BL 45296 f 232]

Because Archer's letter has disappeared, the identity of this person cannot be established. As this telephone number illustrates, Shaw continued to embrace the new technologies of the modern world – typewriters, bicycles, automobiles, gas balloons, photographic equipment, motion pictures, motorcyles, telephones, and whatever else the engines of innovation put before the public. He was the ideal customer for capitalist enterprise. There were, though, physical as well as economic prices to be paid: bicycle smashups, a dangerous accident in a gas balloon, and a taxing automobile trip in France in 1913, as he informed Trebitsch: 'My journey of 4000 kilometres by car, supposed to be a holiday, has left me a wreck' (Trebitsch: 168).

All right: I'll see him. Am writing to him giving him an appointment. My telephone number is 8131 City.

Make a note of it, as it is not in the book.

GBS

150 / To G. Bernard Shaw

27 Fitzroy Square W.
4th January 1916

[TLS: BL 50528 f 59; copy in BL 45296 ff 233–4]

Shaw's letter to Archer has disappeared, but he apparently expressed some ideas about Jesus Christ ('J.C.') that he had also articulated in the preface to Androcles and the Lion. *The play had its London opening and premiere on 1 September 1913 at the St James's Theatre. It had either 52 performances (CL 3: 202) or 63 performances (Wearing 1910: 379). Whatever the case, the production lost money, despite the large audiences during the early weeks. Staged by H. Granville Barker, it featured Lillah McCarthy as Lavinia and O.P. Heggie (1879–1936) as Androcles. Archer reviewed the London production in* The Star *on 2 September 1913: 'What a delightful, not to say a rollicking, time at the St. James's last night; and to me it was none the less delightful for being not in the least strenuous ... There is philosophy in the farce no doubt, but it is neither very obtrusive nor very baffling; and if you prefer to ignore the philosophy, you may simply yield yourself up to an hour-long revel of wit, humor and comic invention.' Archer complained, however, that the 'Shawpenhauerism' in the dialogue expressed 'Shaw's familiar contempt for rationalism.' (See also letter of 18 July 1916.)*

Max Reinhardt had staged Androcles *in Berlin at the Kleines Theater on 25 November 1913 (not in 1912, as is often reported). Trebitsch's translation,* Androklus und der Löwe, *was also published on 25 November 1913. In January 1915, despite the war and the dangers of being torpedoed, McCarthy and Barker took the production to New York. The play – along with the lengthy preface that Shaw wrote in December 1915 – was published with* Overruled *and* Pygmalion *on 21 April 1916 in New York by Brentano's. The English edition, despite the shortage of paper during the war, followed a month later on 25 May.*

My dear G.B.S.

Very glad to see your typewriting once again, but you take a most unscrupulous advantage in replying to a lot of criticisms of mine which I have totally forgotten. I have no objection in the world to your making out a sort of proportion sum: as was J. B[aptist] to J.C., so was J.C. to G.B.S. – only I think you ought to do it (like George Moore) by way of romance, & not try to prove it by the documents, which are stubborn things & simply won't fit in. It is all very well for you to represent the King walking through a thunderstorm with one of your umbrellas; but if you put under the picture: 'His Majesty walked out today with his inseparable companion, a G.B.S. Impermeable Gossamer Bomb-Proof Four-&-Ninepenny Gingham' – *Court Circular* such-&-such a date – & if people turn to the *Court Circular* & find that His Majesty did nothing of the sort, the effect of the advertisement is discounted.

But anyway, why worry about J.C.? Whatever else he may have been, he was the most colossal Failure on record. If he could have foreseen a millionth part of the devilries & insanities that were to be enacted in his name, he would have said like Peer Gynt:

Beautiful earth & beautiful sun.

You were foolish to bear & give light to my mother —

& would have rushed down a steep place into the sea. You say 'Why not try Christianity?' But I say 'Why go back 2000 years for a religion when any decently intelligent man can make a better religion for himself any day in the week?' And even if there were any particular value in the sincere milk of the Word (which I don't believe) the first essential would be to get an Act of Parliament to free it from the name of 'Christianity,' & purge it of all association with the tear-drenched, blood-dripping maniacal absurdities connoted by the word. I have taken to reading history in my old age, & I have come very near to the conclusion that the birth of Christ, whether real or imaginary, was the greatest calamity that ever befell mankind. There is only one thing to be said for Christianity, namely that it is par excellence the religion of hypocrisy, & that when faith means intellectual & moral degradation, hypocrisy becomes a virtue. I feel a good deal of tolerance for Protestantism when I am in a country – like Russia, or Spain, or India – where people really believe in their religion. Protestantism is nowadays only a cowardly alias for agnosticism. It is a pitiful thing, but better than belief. But all this harking back to Judaea is mere waste of time. Let us make a clear Exodus from Houndsditch instead of trying to clean & press & patch & disinfect the blood-stained & verminous Old Clo.

I don't believe Anno Domini has anything to do with your sticking [Christians] in your play – it is the war that is at fault. You haven't the heart to talk nonsense, & you know that if you talked sense you'd empty the theatre, so you temporarily dry up. I keep on watching myself for signs of dotage, but as yet in vain. I never had any memory, so can't well lose it, & my other faculties are 'in their frail ordinar'.'

By the bye I have discovered from Froude's Henry VIII that you are a lineal descendant from an Earl of Desmond of that period. When he was examined before the Privy Council prior to having his head chopped off, he made exactly the same replies which you (or one of your heroes, which is the same thing) would have made under the circumstances.

Yours
W.A.

The bracketed insert in **J. B[aptist]** was by Archer. In 1916 the Irish novelist **George Moore** published *The Brook Kerith, A Syrian Story*. It offered a fictional account of Christ who, lacking divinity, does not die on the cross, but instead is nursed back to health and then travels to India in search of wisdom. **Houndsditch**, which received its name in the thirteenth century, was originally a defensive channel in the earth that the Romans dug outside of the city wall of Londinium. By medieval times the ditch was seventy-five feet wide. Residents used it as a garbage pit for waste and even dead dogs. Because cleaning it was a major problem in modern times, the city authorities covered it over. It became a London street in the Aldgate area. But in 1989 an archelogical excavation was carried out in selective places. The cry of **Old Clo** was used by peddlers who sold and bought old clothes in the Monmouth Street area. Charles Dickens documented the activities of the street peddlers in *Sketches by Boz*. Rejecting Shaw's efforts **to clean & press & patch & disinfect** Christianity, Archer assigned the vestments of Christianity to a condition of rags and tatters – frocks that clothe the moral poverty and **blood-stained** history of religion. The English historian James Anthony **Froude** (1818–94) published a multi-volumed history of England during the sixteenth century, extending from the reign of Henry VIII to that of Elizabeth I (1856–70, 12 vols). In his various publications he supported British authority and hegemony over the church, Ireland, and the colonies. The **Earldom of Desmond** in southwest Ireland was ruled over by the Fitzgerald clan from the twelfth century to the late sixteenth century. The Fitzgeralds resisted English control over Ireland during the Desmond Rebellion. In 1583 the fifteenth Earl of Desmond was defeated by Queen Elizabeth's forces, and when the sixteenth Earl attempted to regain control of the title and lands he was captured and executed in 1603.

151 / To William Archer

Ayot St Lawrence, Welwyn, Herts.
[4th February 1916]

[APCS: BL 45296 f 235]

Archer's letter to Shaw has disappeared. The phone number is for Ayot St Lawrence. A year earlier the Shaws had a phone installed at Adelphi Terrace. Shaw's note, written on a French carte postale, *has a postmark of 4 February 1916. It was mailed from Welwyn post office, not France. His most recent trip to France had been in 1913. A small French flag with the tag of 'Se vend au profit des orphelins de la guerre' appears on one side of the card. On the other side a cartoon represents an angry, overweight man pounding a table and spilling an inkwell while another man holds a bag of money in one hand and some papers in the other. The caption – in French and English – proclaims: 'Qui ne nous aime pas est vendu' and 'Whoever does not like us is bought by the other side.' Perhaps this image suggested to Shaw the nefarious dealings of governmental politics.*

Gerrard 331 is the telephone number. The Androcles volume with the evangelical preface is passed for press & will be out when the American printing is through. The F.O. would not object to my going to Sweden – or to Jericho: the difficulty would be to get back again.

GBS

Because of the war, publishers faced governmental restrictions on the supply of paper. Shaw was pleased, perhaps even surprised, that the British edition of *Androcles and the Lion, Overruled,* and *Pygmalion* was **passed for press**. It was published on 25 May 1916, 5000 copies bound, 5000 sheets 'on reserve' (Biblio 1: 129–30). A month earlier the American edition was published on 21 April by Brentano's. Shaw sent a copy to Archer as soon as the London edition was published. See Archer's letter of 18 July 1916 for his response to the play and the **evangelical preface**. Shaw suggested that the **F.O.** (Foreign Office) might stop him from returning to England, if he were to travel to Sweden or elsewhere because of how unpopular he was with Asquith's government. He had maintained a public campaign in the newspapers and journals against the government over both its war policy with Germany and the Irish crisis. Nonetheless, on 6 January 1917 Field-Marshall Sir Douglas Haig, commander of the Western Front, invited Shaw to visit France to observe the war effort. Accepting the invitation, Shaw spent a week at the front during February, visiting the Somme and other sites (Holroyd 2: 371–4). He even rode in a tank. Upon his return he published a three-part essay in the *DC* about the tour: 'Joy Riding at the Front' (Biblio 2: 669, C2113).

152 / To William Archer Ayot St Lawrence, Welwyn, Herts.
23rd February 1916

[APCS: BL 45296 f 236]

Archer's letter to Shaw has disappeared. Shaw did not identify the specific topic that engaged him here, but the basic issue was obvious: the leadership of the British government under Asquith and Grey, Tweedledum and Tweedledee. In a general proposal for 'The World after the War,' he had suggested that in any future war the first one to die should be the prime minister or leader of a country. He also voiced opposition to the Conscription Act that the government had put forward (Biblio 2: 662–3). The crafting of pamphlets, articles, and letters to the press about the war had delayed or displaced the writing and publication of plays. Shaw did finish the manuscript of Heartbreak House *in 1917, but it was not published until 1919. The premiere occurred in New York in November 1920, staged by the*

Theatre Guild. Likewise, O'Flaherty, V.C., *written in 1915, was not available in England until 1919, though an amateur production arranged by Robert Loraine was presented by officers of Royal Flying Corps on the Western Front in 1917. After the war, when he completed the preface to* Heartbreak House, *he described 'How War Muzzles the Dramatic Poet.' In his concluding paragraph to the play he proclaimed: 'War cannot bear the terrible castigation of comedy, the ruthless light of laughter that glares on the stage ... Truth telling is not compatible with the defence of the realm' (CP 5: 57–8).*

I shall certainly oppose any serious depredations, though I expect we shall have to take some cheap part in the business.

I am all for pluck and imperturbability: the old women who dig their patches and hang out their washing under shell fire are heroines if you like, though I dont think they would make good ministers or generals. But we really shant win on uncriticized mendacity, jobbery, venality, tyranny, concealment, and claptrap for fools and rascals without even claptrap for decent people. Tweedledum may not be congenitally better than Tweedledee; but Tweedledee impure may be very much worse than Tweedledum after he has seen Tweedledee hanged.

G.B.S.

153 / To William Archer

10 Adelphi Terrace WC
9th March 1916

[TPCS: BL 45296 f 237]

Along with this brief letter, Shaw sent to Archer the page proofs (BL 45296 ff 238–40) for his review of The Author's Craft *(1914), a practical manual written by the novelist Arnold Bennett (1867–1931). Bennett was well known and admired for his novels, including* Anna of the Five Towns *(1902),* The Old Wives' Tale *(1908) and* Clayhanger *(1910), but he was also a successful playwright in 1912 with* Milestones *(Royalty Theatre, 608 perfs.), which he co-authored with Edward Knoblauch (1874–1945), and* The Great Adventure *(1913, Kingsway Theatre, 674 perfs.), which Granville Barker directed.*

In his manual Bennett claimed that it is easier to write a play than a novel. This was sufficient provocation for Shaw, who offered a lighthearted parody of the way that novelists tend to overlay a narrative event with superfluous scenic details. The tone of this review was notably different from that of the arguments about the war that Shaw and Bennett had exchanged a month earlier in the Daily News. *Shaw's review offered a burlesque of how novelists like Bennett, H.G. Wells, and John Galsworthy would describe the sword-fighting scene between Macbeth and Macduff. The action is delayed as the narrator delivers Macbeth's thoughts on insect life in the castle, the blue sky, golden gorse, and the many crows, jays, larks, martens, and hawks in Scotland. Macbeth is quite taken with the songs of wood pigeons – 'Tak two coos, Taffy: tak two coos, Taffy' – but this enjoyment is interrupted by the sight of a walking oak tree from Birnam Wood, 'coming up at a rattling pace.' Macbeth, 'a country gentleman, is infuriated 'that another country gentleman should move his timber without acquiring any rights.' Finally, he takes up his claymore and yells, 'Lay on, Macduff.' Then, after Macbeth is reduced to 'mince,' the narrator informs readers that Macbeth and his wife are buried 'in God's quiet acre in the little churchyard of Dunsinane.' Shaw concluded: 'There! That is what is called novel writing.'*

My dear W.A.

If you are stumped for a subject for your weekly article, the enclosed may start you on a controversy as to whether novels or plays are easier to write. Anyhow, it may amuse you as an expiring flash of the moribund humor of Corno Di Bassetto.

It is much more a parody of Galsworthy than of the other two. I wrote it immediately after reading Freelands. Its publication has been delayed to synchronize with the American issue.

Ever
G.B.S.

John Galsworthy published the novel ***Freelands*** in 1915. Shaw's review, 'Mr. Arnold Bennett on Playwriting,' was published on 11 March in *The Nation* (reprinted in *Pen Portraits*: 46–54). The **American issue** appeared a month later in *Cosmopolitan* (New York) under the title 'On Writing Plays.'

154 / To G. Bernard Shaw

27 Fitzroy Square W.
12th March 1916

[TLS: BL 50528 f 60; copy in BL 45296 f 241]

Archer fully supported Shaw's handling of Arnold Bennett, yet Shaw's spoof opened the door for Archer's own tease of the formal complexities of Getting Married *and*

Misalliance. *At the top left corner of this letter Shaw had added a note, written several months after Archer's death: 'Corno di Bassetti [*sic*] (the name of a now disused musical instrument of the wood wind family) was the signature I used to my weekly article in* The Star *in 1888 or thereabouts. G.B.S. 12/6/25.' Shaw actually began the Corno di Bassetto reviews for* The Star *in February 1889. He continued the column until May 1890, when he became music critic for* The World *until 1894. He identified himself there as 'GBS.'*

My dear C. di B.,

I am delighted to see that the last of the di Bassetti [*sic*] is still going strong, & that that illustrious race is in no danger of extinction. Arnold Bennett richly deserves to have that ridiculous affectation shown up. I enjoyed the exposure all the more as I had just been wading through 'These Twain.' Really there is almost a touch of charlatanism in that book, clever as it undoubtedly is. It is the sort of thing that

Might, 'ods bobs Sir, in judicious hands,
Extend from here to Mesopotamy.

It is a study, not even of two temperaments, but of two tempers, & the psychology is absolutely arbitrary. At every one of the innumerable little revulsions or reactions of feeling that they go through, you think: 'Yes, that is plausible enough – but the exact opposite would be equally plausible.' That is not the method of a great master. He gives you a sort of substratum or backbone of character, and then makes you feel that every emotional process through which the man or woman passes is rightly and inevitably related to it. If his psychology is capricious, he has the art to conceal it. Bennett is a man I admire exceedingly – but not his long novels.

At the same time, I think if C. di B. were to look up the works of G.B.S., he would find in *Getting Married* and in *Misalliance* plays that might just as well have been novels so far as any difficulty of form goes.

Yours,
W.A.

These Twain (1916) is the third of four novels in Arnold Bennett's *The Clayhanger Family* series that includes *Clayhanger* (1910), *Hilda Lessways* (1911), and *The Roll-Call* (1918). Archer derived the lines beginning **Might, 'ods bobs Sir** from 'The Cock and the Bull,' a humorous poem by Charles Stuart Calverley (1831–84). He had also quoted the lines in a review published in *Study and Stage* (1898: 189).

155 / To G. Bernard Shaw

27 Fitzroy Square W.
18th July 1916

[TLU: BL 45296 ff 242–3]

When the edition of Androcles and the Lion, Overruled, Pygmalion *was published in London on 25 May, Shaw mailed a copy to Archer. The quality of Shaw's feisty prose in the long 'Preface on the Prospects of Christianity' (completed in December 1915) impressed Archer: 'There are might good things throughout.' But he rejected Shaw's revisionist arguments about Jesus Christ. Archer thus suggested in this letter some possible revisions that Shaw might consider for a later edition of the preface. (See also the letter of 4 January 1916.) During the summer of 1916 Shaw continued to publish political broadsides. When not arguing about the war, the Irish Rising for independence, and the government's intention to execute Roger Casement as a traitor, Shaw debated with Gilbert and Cecil Chesterton on the topic of Christianity in the* New Statesman *(Biblio 2: 665–6). But Shaw's arguments failed to change minds and events. The Asquith government ignored him, the leaders of the Irish campaign dismissed him, Casement was hanged in August, and the Chestertons rejected Shaw's ideas on Christianity.*

My dear G.B.S.

Many thanks for ANDROCLES. It – the play I mean – reads delightfully. So does the preface for that matter – it is one [of] your best. You have most ingeniously created J.C. in your own image. If I were Bernard Partridge, I would do a new version of Holman Hunt's 'Light of the World' for a frontispiece to the volume with your benign countenance beneath the crown of thorns. And your Christ is extremely plausible until one turns to the Gospels; & then, lo & behold' he doesn't dovetail a little bit. You say that a 'startling change' occurs in Matt. XVI, when Peter says 'Thou art the Christ, the Son of the living God.' But this was no new idea to Jesus. In Matt. X, 32, 33, he distinctly poses as the Son of God. In Matt. XII 40, he prophecies his death & resurrection – already on the John Barleycorn tack – & he calls himself a greater [person] than Solomon, evidently meaning that he is a divine personage. In Matt. XIV, 33, 'They that were in the boat worshipt him, saying, Of a truth thou art the Son of God' – a phrase implying that it was the current idea. You cannot get over these (& I think other) passages except by a criticism which would equally invalidate the passage on which you rely. The truth is, of course, that the whole record is too confused & corrupt to have any evidential value, especially as to a point of chronology.

Then as to miracles, how can you possibly make out that Jesus 'agreed with Rousseau' & disagreed with Matthew? See Matt. XI, where he first appeals to his miracles when John the Baptist asks for his credentials, & then denounces woe upon Chorazin, Bethsaida, &c., because they have taken no stock in the 'mighty works' which have been done in them. Of course Matt. or his authority may have lied; but they are much more likely to have lied when they represented him as trying to keep his miracles secret – this looks very like a means of getting over the fact that in such-&-such a village no one had heard of the mighty works alleged to have been wrought in it.

Now as to 'Judge not' – the point, no doubt, is partly a linguistic one – I should like to hear Gilbert Murray upon it – but the whole context seems to me to show that what he meant was 'Criticize not, that ye be not criticized' – that he was warning against carping censoriousness, which, by the way, does more harm than the King's Bench & the Old Bailey put together. The illustration of the mote & the beam is evidently aimed at self-righteousness, not at the penal code. There are lots of J.C.'s utterances, both in straight talk & in parables, from which it might be very plausibly argued that he not only believed in the punishment of crime, but that he thought it should be vindictive, not merely deterrent. Of course other texts could be cited, to the opposite effect. But that merely shows that there IS no consistent J.C., & that any one, by judicious selection & suppression, can call him as a witness to any doctrine he pleases. For instance Torquemada could cite Matt. XVIII, 34.

Page lxxv, short paragraph: try this – 'When the sea leaks through the Dutchmen's dyke, they generally stop the breach, not considering that if the dyke were effective, the sea would never leak through.'

Page xli, 'The only suggestion of a feat of arms on his part in the gospels.' Is this a joke? His vanishing through the crowd is evidently supposed to be a miracle.

Page lxii, 'My reproach to you for having the poor always with you.' It was no reproach. J.C. was a true Oriental in considering the poor a providential opportunity for acquiring merit by alms-giving, though he liked it to be done unostentatiously.

Summa summarum – It is impossible to get any consistent economic doctrine out of the gospels, because J.C. was no more a consistent, systematic thinker than Ibsen was – indeed much less. But you have shown what he ought to have thought & said, which, after all, is the main thing. The part about Paul is extremely good, & there are might good things throughout. It makes one feel young again to come upon your fine old wheezes about the distance of the sun & so forth. They are as refreshing in this iron age as a volume of PUNCH of the Du Maurier period.

I am going to read the other pieces in due course. If I had waited until I had done so before writing, I should have forgotten all about ANDROCLES.

Did you see the Barrie film? & was it any fun?

Yours ever
W.A.

Sir John **Bernard Partridge** (1861–1945), painter and illustrator, served as the chief cartoonist for the satiric journal *Punch.* In the 1880s and 1890s he acted under the name of Bernard Gould. William **Holman Hunt** (1827–1910), one of the founders of the Pre-Raphaelite Brotherhood, painted 'The Light of the World' in 1853–4. The image, which is based upon a passage in Revelation 3:20, represents Jesus knocking on a door. The painting is located in a chapel at Keble College, Oxford. **John Barleycorn**, a British folk song that emerged in the sixteenth century, has many versions, including one by Robert Burns (1756–96). The personified character of John Barleycorn is usually thrashed, beaten, and killed (and sometimes resurrected), a process of rough treatment that parallels the stages of preparing barley for beer and whisky. The name is now a synonym and metaphor for alcohol. Christ pronounced woes upon the villages of **Chorazin** and **Bethsaida** in Matthew 11:20–3 and Luke 9:10 because the villagers resisted his mission. **Gilbert Murray** was a linguist who knew Greek and Latin. **King's Bench** was the supreme court for English common law. In the past the king or queen sat on a raised bench. **Old Bailey** was the common term for identifying the English criminal court located in London on Old Bailey Street. Tomas de **Torquemada** (1420–98), a Spanish Dominican monk, served as the Grand Inquisitor of the Spanish Inquisition. With the support of King Ferdinand and Queen Isabella, he was zealous in his mission of removing Jews from Spain. Matthew 18:34, which **Torquemada could cite**, states: 'And his lord was wroth, and delivered him to the tormentors, till he should pay all that was due unto him' (King James version). Archer's statement about '**fine old wheezes about the distance of the sun**' was a reference to Shaw's 'A Conflict between Science and Common Sense,' which the two of them discussed in the letter of 9 July 1900. George **Du Maurier,** the father of the actor Gerald Du Maurier, was a French-born British cartoonist. He provided work for *Punch* and other periodicals from the 1850s to the 1890s. He also wrote the popular novel *Trilby* (1894), which Herbert Beerbohm Tree, playing the role of Svengali, staged in 1895 (Haymarket, 240 perfs.). The **Barrie film,** organized by J.M. Barrie, was shot 4–7 July 1914. H. Granville Barker operated the camera. The series of farcical scenes featured Shaw, Archer, Gilbert Chesterton, and Lord Howard de Walden, dressed as cowboys and doing silly things in the Hertfordshire countryside. (See also the letters of 10 November 1914 and 30 December 1916.)

156 / To William Archer

10 Adelphi Terrace WC
30th December 1916

[TLS: BL 45296 ff 244–8; CL 3]

Archer sent a copy of Play-making, A Manual of Craftsmanship *to Shaw. It was a belated gift, having been published in 1912. The book was the catalyst for Shaw's initial comments in this letter, but he also replied to Archer's letter of 18 July about the preface to* Androcles and the Lion. *Moreover, a missing letter or perhaps a recent conversation contributed to his response.*

Shaw's comments on W.S. Gilbert and Widowers' Houses *were not triggered by the two short references to Gilbert in* Play-making. *In the right-hand margins to the second and fourth paragraphs of this typed letter, Shaw added two handwritten notes about his secretary's misreading of two words in his shorthand draft. I have placed these marginal notes within parentheses in the text, directly after the misidentified words.*

My dear W.A.

Thanks for the book. It is an invaluable document; for it describes precisely how plays were, and still are, written by people whose conception of drama is wholly theatrical. Art for art's sake can go no further. Observe that Gilbert, who did really hold the mirror up to nature, was led to believe that his mirror was a distorting one because it did not reflect theatrical characters, and so missed his chance of importance as a serious dramatist. Last year I happened to see the Yeomen of the Guard in the provinces, for the first time. In it Gilbert attempted to escape into serious opera; and the extremely depressing result was that he purposely and laboriously forced himself back into a flat mixture of Harrison Ainsworth romance and Italian opera – The Tower of London and Rigoletto.

The visit to the seaside or run to Paris to freshen the author up when he is exhausted by cobbling at his play is quite of a piece with the three names Brown, Jones and Robinson. I wonder they did not die of it. The proper modern term for such productions is synthetic plays. The natural play writes itself. One of my plays has a plot: Captain Brassbound's Conversion. Another, Caesar and Cleopatra, being a chronical play, (This is my secretary's spelling. As it is quite defensible I do not correct it.) is nailed down to history. They are more helplessly dependent on the acting than any other of my plays, the plot and the chronical being absolutely dead wood.

By the way, it *is* odd, as you say, that Gilbert should have hit on the idea of Widowers' Houses, and not used it. I distinguish between an idea for a play, and a plot. You made a plot for Widowers' Houses; and you can claim the Rhine scenery of the first act, and the idea of the tainted treasure. I had no difficulty with the Rhine, and no difficulty with the idea; but the plot was no use: the play somehow wouldnt write itself round it.

I wish, by the way, the play I have in hand at present would write itself. I have written enough for a first act, filling the stage with the most delightful characters under the pleasantest circumstances; but whether it is preoccupation with the war, and with business, and with all sorts of interest more urgent than the theatre, I have left them there for months and months, hopelessly stuck. This has never happened before. Neither has my sixtieth birthday. I fear the two facts are connected. My faculties are decaying horribly; but I have no doubt I shall be able to finish the play someday, and perhaps not badly. Age always imagines that though it can no longer win prizes by sprint running, later and more mystical faculties are only boding at eighty. (Secretary again. God knows what I wrote in the original shorthand! Probably 'budding.')

I never answered your letter of the 18th July about Androcles. You have forgotten it by this time; but I want to warn you against too precipitate a reliance, for the confutation of my assumption that Jesus lost his head and believed he was really John Barleycorn, on earlier texts in which he spoke of himself as the Son of God and was worshipped as such. I did not overlook this; and I disregarded one of them on the ground that the whole passage was repeated later on, thereby destroying its chronological value (if it can be said to have any). But the other passages were reconcilable. You must bear in mind that the Barleycorn tradition was not a sudden mad fancy which came into Jesus's disordered mind when Peter hailed him as the Christ. It was strongly rooted in the popular imagination; and the people's heads, including Peter's, were full of it; so that any miracle set them at once hailing Jesus as God. He himself had his characteristic theory that the kingdom of heaven is within us, and that we are incarnations of God, and therefore the sons of God. There is therefore nothing inconsistent with my hypothesis in his speaking of himself as a divine person when he was quite sane, or in the people hailing him as a supernatural personage. My suggestion is that when his mind gave way under the strain of his campaign *gegen die Dummheit* (his depression and discouragement are expressly mentioned), he gave way to the popular illusion, and began to talk about himself as the Son of God, not for the first time, but for the first time in the literal popular sense, and he took to himself all the Barleycorn superstitions as a form of sticking straws in his hair.

But of course the whole position is desperate as far as the evidence goes. The only thing that is to be said for my hypothesis (Renan's also, I am told) is that it explains what is otherwise quite unaccountable: his determination to be crucified and his suicidal demeanour at the trial. All that is possible is to construct a perfectly natural and credible historical character who might have given rise to the gospels as attempts at biography, or rather hagiography.

For the rest, if I were an umbrella maker I should exhibit posters representing the king carrying one of my umbrellas. Not being an umbrella maker but a patentee of certain doctrines, I represent Jesus as preaching those doctrines. If the umbrella is not unworthy of the king and the doctrine of the prophet I do not think anyone can complain of the arrangement, especially as it is so obvious.

There is nothing in the Rousseau view of miracles that is inconsistent with the miracle worker damning the stupidity of witnesses who refuse to be impressed by them. I may desire to be known as a prophet rather than as a playwright, much as Mahomet fought all his life against the taunt that he was only that disreputable thing, a poet; but when Walkley says that my plays are not plays, I may remonstrate as Jesus remonstrated with Chorazin and Bethsaida.

As to your point that Jesus, when he said 'Judge not' could not have been thinking of the criminal law because he sometimes expressed a hearty vindictiveness, I refer you to a passage in Caesar and Cleopatra, where Caesar says he feels no horror of Rufio, who has just cut a woman's throat, but that if he had sat in judgment on her and condemned her to death in the name of justice he could never have taken his hand again. Nobody thinks the worse of Romeo for killing Tybalt in a fit of red hot vengeance; but if he had had Tybalt arrested and tortured, and especially if he acted as judge in the case himself, he would have become too odious to be a sympathetic hero.

As to the 'feat of arms' implied in Jesus making his way through the crowd who wanted to lynch him because he said in the synagogue that there were just as good Gentiles as Jews, you say that 'his vanishing through the crowd is evidently supposed to be a miracle.' Why? There is not the smallest suggestion in the narrative that anyone marvelled at it, or that it converted or surprised the crowd. If I saw it stated that you had made your way to Kings Cross, I shouldnt assume that you had levitated yourself through the air. I think this is one of the numerous cases in which we read into narratives superstitions which would never occur to a Chinaman reading it without preconceptions.

And I dont see why you should attribute to Jesus conventional oriental (also Catholic) views as to the poor, and the acquirement of merit by almsgiving, any more than you should attribute to me the views of the Charity Organization Society. There are plenty of incidents and sayings which shew that he was not a Pharisee, and did not conceive himself as a merit hunter. If you are dealing with a genius, you must not reduce him to the common denominator.

I saw the Barrie film: why did not you ask him to shew it to you? There were several reelingsoff of it. It wasnt in the least funny. Chesterton has possibilities as a comic film actor – or had before his illness spoilt his figure – but the rest of us were dismal failures as amateur Charlie Chaplins. The Savoy supper was the most interesting.

Ever
G.B.S.

William **Harrison Ainsworth** (1805–82), an English novelist, became famous by the 1840s for his historical novels, such as *Jack Sheppard, Guy Fawkes,* and *The* ***Tower of London.*** He also edited *Ainsworth Magazine* and other journals. Verdi's ***Rigoletto*** has its own literary origin, for it was derived from Hugo's drama *Le roi s'amuse.* Shaw's **secretary** was Ann M. Elder (b. 1892). She had replaced Georgina ('Judy') Gillmore in 1912, and remained in the position until 1920, though she took two leaves in 1919 and 1920 (Holroyd 3: 25). Blanche Patch became the secretary and business manager in 1920. She stayed with Shaw until his death. The **play I have in hand** was *Heartbreak House,* which Shaw was writing in 1916. Although he claimed in the play's preface that he began to write it before the war broke out in August 1914, most of the evidence has placed the writing between March 1916 and May 1917 (CP 5: 10). The phrase ***gegen die Dummheit*** means 'against stupidity.' Joseph Ernest **Renan** (1823–92), a French scholar of Middle Eastern languages and cultures, wrote *La vie de Jésus* (1863), which represented Jesus as a human rather than divine person who purified Christianity by ridding himself of his Jewish traits. This interpretation supported the idea of Jesus as a racial Aryan. Jean Jacques **Rousseau** wrote about miracles in *Lettres de la montagne* (*Letters Written from the Mountain*) in 1764. In the preface to *Androcles and the Lion* Shaw call's Rousseau's work 'the classic work on miracles as credentials of divine mission.' **Mahomet,** in this context, is Mohammed, the prophet and founder of Islam. In Matthew 11:21 and Luke 10:13, Jesus pronounced woe upon the cities of **Chorazin and Bethsaida** because of the unbelief of the inhabitants. **King's Cross** is the busy rail station that opened in 1852, not the inner city neighborhood. On 3 July 1914 J.M. Barrie presented a **Savoy supper** for over 100 invited guests from the theatrical world and society, including Shaw and Prime Minister Asquith. For this 'Cinema Supper,' held at the Savoy Theatre, Barrie presented a revue entertainment by various performers. He filmed the guests and the sketches. His plan was to incorporate some of these scenes into the cowboy film farce that he and Granville Barker co-directed a few days later. (See the letters of 10 November 1914 and 18 July 1916.) The overall film project was never completed, and Barrie subsequently destroyed the prints (Journey: 16–18). Only a photograph survived, showing Shaw, Archer, G. Chesterton, and Lord Howard de Walden in their cowboy costumes, hats, and holstered guns (Whitebrook: 276–7). See illustration on page ci.

157 / To William Archer

10 Adelphi Terrace WC
[c. March 1919]

[APCS: BL 45296 f 278]

There are no surviving letters between Shaw and Archer for 1917 and 1918. Charlotte Shaw's note to Archer apparently referred to books on dreams, as the following letter revealed. Ever since 1913 Archer had been keeping a daily record of his dreams, and he knew the writings on dreams by Sigmund Freud (1856–1939), Henri Bergson (1859–1941), Havelock Ellis, and others. In 1924 he was preparing a book on the topic, but his death prevented publication. An edition of his study was published in 1935 under the title of On Dreams, *edited by Theodore Besterman (1904–76) who was a psychical researcher, bibliographer, and scholar on Voltaire. Most notably, he edited the 107 volumes of Voltaire's letters.*

Mr Williams sent me these yesterday evening.

Read them. Keep them as long as you like & return them at your leisure. I shall be curious to know what you think of them.

Charlotte F. Shaw

Mr Williams was possibly Harcourt Williams (1880–1957), the actor whom Shaw referred to in the letter of 19 April 1919.

158 / To William Archer

Ayot St Lawrence, Welmyn, Herts.
7th April 1919

[APCS: BL 45296 f 249]

Along with the book he returned to Adelphi Terrace, Archer left a note, no longer extant. Although he was quite familiar with Freud's Die Traumdeutung *(*The Interpretation of Dreams*), which he read in German, he questioned some aspects* *of Freudian symbolism, including Freud's general statement that the fulfilment (*Erfüllung*) of a wish is the meaning of every dream. Archer granted the 'theoretical validity and the practical usefulness of Professor Freud's method,' but he insisted that the method does 'not in the least depend upon its being applicable to all dreams whatsoever' (Dreams: 107).*

You were most welcome to the book, & might have kept it longer as I am not using it now. I went to some classes at which we took it as a text book, but I agree with you, it is not much good. A clever friend of mine said the other day that this whole Freudian business was like getting into a palace by means of the drains. I rather agree.

I was so sorry to miss you when you came to Adelphi Terrace the other day.

Best Remembrances,
C.F.S.

159 / To William Archer Ayot St Lawrence, Welwyn, Herts.
19th April 1919

[TLS: BL 45296 ff 250–3; CL 3]

In 1918, during the last year of the war, Archer wrote a play entitled War Is War, or the Germans in Belgium. *The process of writing the play allowed him to address the suffering and horrors of war. The three-act play draws upon the evidence that Archer had gathered when he published* The Thirteen Days: July 23–August 4, 1914: A Chronicle and Interpretation *(1915), which indicted Germany. But* War Is War, *unlike* The Thirteen Days, *humanized the indictment by representing the moral struggles and compromises of a German soldier who attempts to resist the militarism that led to the massacres of innocent people, including women and children, at Aerschot in Belgium during the outbreak of the war in 1914. Archer attempted to seek funding for a production, but the dark topic was probably not what the West End theatres sought for their audiences. In March 1919 he settled for publication (Whitebook: 324–8). The published play contains a long epilogue in which Archer explained that his presentation of the massacre of Belgian villagers is based upon documentary evidence.*

Ever since April 1918 the primary concern for Archer was the report that his son Tom was 'wounded and missing in action.' Archer did not know that Tom had died in a German hospital a few days after he had been wounded. The Archers and Tom's young wife, Alys, did not receive confirmation and details of his death and burial in Flanders until July 1921 (Whitebrook: 322–3, 334–8). Contending with his grief, Archer consulted spiritualist mediums in 1919 and 1920. Despite his rationalism and scepticism, he hoped to make contact with his son. He discussed these efforts with Robins, who tried to discourage him, and with Gilbert Murray, who had served as president of the Society for Psychical Research, but not with Frances, Alys, or Shaw.

As the war finally concluded, both Archer and Shaw joined the debates about the treaty negotiations and peace conferences. In October 1918 Archer published 'Obstacles to a League of Nations' in the Fortnightly Review. *He outlined the problems that an international forum would face. A few months later, on 12 March 1919, Shaw published* Peace Conference Hints. *Archer reviewed the book in the* Daily News *on 12 April. He supported Shaw's call for the founding of a 'supernational tribunal' and 'legislature' that President Wilson had outlined in his campaign for a League of Nations. But he objected to Shaw's argument that 'incompatible nations' beyond America and Europe should be excluded from the international organization. Responding to Archer's review, Shaw wrote a letter to the editor of the* Daily News *on 15 April (Agits: 236–7). He reiterated his opposition to an 'unstable League of All Mankind' that would include all nations, stretching 'from China to Peru.' This allusion to the opening lines of Dr Johnson's 'The Vanity of Human Wishes' failed to impress Archer. The two friends also disagreed on how to deal with Germany. Archer, who was facing the uncertainty over the fate of his son, believed that Germany should be held responsible for the war. Shaw argued, however, that if the winning nations punish Germany, 'we may as well drop the whole project and prepare for the next war' (Agits 236–7). Most sadly, he was correct on this warning.*

Although political issues had been paramount for Shaw and Archer during and after the war, they still found time for theatrical matters. In April 1919 they commenced a debate over the cutting of Shakespeare's plays. Archer's review of a revival of Romeo and Juliet *(Lyric Theatre, 12 April, 72 perfs.) provided the catalyst. The production featured the return of Ellen Terry to the stage in the role of the Nurse. The scenery was designed by Edith Craig. Archer found the painted scenes 'original and beautiful,' but because of the lengthy pauses needed for scene changes, he suggested that additional 'cutting of the text' might be required for a performance that ran for over three hours (14 April,* The Star*). That suggestion* *was all Shaw needed. Starting with this letter on 19 April, this debate carried over to several of their letters and publications during 1919. For Shaw, the foremost issue was a matter of artistic integrity. Shakespeare's plays, like Wagner's operas at Bayreuth, should be performed without cuts. In support of this argument, Shaw praised William Poel for presenting uncut texts of Shakespeare's plays in his Elizabethan Stage Society productions. This praise must have made Archer see red because he was a relentless critic of Poel's productions. Shaw's claim was completely false. The prompt-books for Poel's productions reveal his substantial 'abridgement and rearrangement' of playtexts (Speaight: 12). Archer reported, for example, that 250 lines of* Twelfth Night *were cut in Poel's production in 1895 (World 95: 223). Likewise, in the 1899 production of* Richard II, *with the young H. Granville Barker in the lead role, Poel removed many of the introspective lines from the king's speeches (Speaight: 151). He was still slashing Shakespeare's plays three decades later when he offered a 'drastically abridged' production of* Coriolanus *(260). Throughout his career, Poel removed lines and speeches from the plays (Speaight: 104, 150, 197, 259–61).*

*This debate over cutting Shakespeare was also vented in meetings of the Shakespeare Memorial National Theatre Committee. For Shaw the issue came to a head when the committee, after attempting for over a decade to found and build a Shakespearean theatre in London, decided to support a plan for a Shakespeare Memorial Theatre (*SMT*) in Stratford-upon-Avon. Although the* SMNTC *did not abandon plans for a London theatre, the members, in a divided vote in May 1919, selected William Bridges-Adams (1889–1965) to be the director of the new company. After he attended Oxford University and participated in the Oxford University Dramatic Society, he had begun his career with Laurence Irving, William Poel, and Harley Granville Barker. Although skilled as an actor and scene designer, he was primarily a director. Between 1915 and 1921 he staged nine productions of Gilbert and Sullivan for D'Oyly Carte's Savoy Theatre. When appointed director for the* SMT, *he requested a subsidy of £10,000 for the first summer season, but this was trimmed to £3000. Also, though a tentative proposal for a touring company was discussed, the plan was dropped. Despite these compromises, Archer and Bridges-Adams, who had been secretly developing this Stratford-upon-Avon project since 1918, had succeeded in their overall strategy (Whitebrook: 348–50). Although Shaw had been out-manoeuvred and out-voted, he maintained his opposition to the new theatre company. When members of the* SMNTC *stopped listening to him, he shifted his bullying tactics to Bridges-Adams in a threatening letter on 26 May (CL 3: 611–14).*

My dear W.A.

When I sent that letter to the Daily News, I rashly asked them why they didnt send ME your play to review, and give me a chance to get a bit of my own back. Lynd promptly took me at my word; and I finished the review yesterday. It is a philippic about the war, naturally; but it will help to boom the play. It is quite a good play and suggests that you may, like Lady Gregory, begin a career as dramatist at an age when most dramatists are retiring. What has inhibited you so far has not been your utterly wrong theory of dramatic biology, but simply that you have had no conscience. The war has at last made you feel strongly enough to compel you to genuine dramatic utterance; and lo! the whole thing comes easily. I always told you, on the strength of your youthful Clive, that you had the faculty. But you never really wanted to use it. You wanted to write a play just as a tramp wants to get a million of money. That's no use – wanting a thing if you can get it for nothing and being quite prepared to do without it if you cant. Why didnt you write Widowers' Houses? It is now evident that you could have done it as easily as I did if you had cared to set about it. Just because you didnt want to say anything. Why did I write it? Not because I wanted to write a play particularly, but because I wanted to shew up the slums and the cash nexus between them and the squares. And by simply finding out the best way to effect the exposure I achieved a masterpiece of the very sort of construction you repudiated me for neglecting. It makes me laugh now when I read it (not that I ever do). It is so Scribesquely constructed that you can see its ribs sticking out all over it.

Another thing has lamed you more than you realize. You are quite right in saying that Germany went wrong in the middle of the XIX century. So did we all. She got it from us. In our reaction against Evangelicalism we threw the baby out with the bath and became blind to life, trying to account for it as a matter of mechanics, chemistry and accident (called Natural Selection). Butler cried in vain in the wilderness to warn us. Darwin led to Weismann; and Weismann led straight to the devil. George Eliot was sterilized by the movement; and your attempts to get anything dramatic on George Eliot's lines were attempts to get blood out of a stone. I wrote my last rationalist novel in 1880, and then turned bang round and wrote my next with Beethoven as its hero. Just think of what you and I have seen since then. Parliament so completely reduced to a Maskelyne trick cabinet that its Acts are used to drive bargains between placemen, and carried out or put on the shelf according to the upshot of the deal. A man who had had to apologize to the House for prevaricating about a speculation in which he had used his political knowledge to guide his investments made Lord Chief Justice. Smith made Lord Chancellor. Asquith selling his party secretly to Bonar Law for votes enough to keep him in power. In India men sentenced to penal servitude after the jury had acquitted them; and now the Rowlatt laws, which would make the Kaiser sick and stagger even Torquemada. Grey wallowing in savage atrocities and being universally accepted as a perfect gentleman until he perished politically in the ocean of blood he had led us to. And nobody minding particularly because there was no longer any standard, any principle, to measure conduct by: nothing but the laziest opportunism. The king of Brobdingnag had reason enough for his remarks on Gulliver's sketch of XVII & XVIII century history; but what would he say now, except that we had achieved the apparently impossible feat of going from bad to worse.

All this will seem to you exaggerated instead of, as it is, far short of the whole frightful truth. I have kept up a running fight with it for forty years, and am naturally more acutely conscious of it than people who were interested in other things. But at last you got a job which involved your tracing it in its operation in Germany. It has made you very indignant. But you will find that as far as there was any lead in the matter, we gave Germany the lead. The mere blackguardisms of the war in Belgium can be capped anywhere where soldiers are in an enemy's country. The significant and radical evils which led two great centres of civilization to try to starve one another to death belong to the whole body of European thought; and the only movement in which there is any real interest is the reaction to religion and philosophy. Out of the chaos left by the demolition of Glassism and its cognates a creed of Creative Evolution has been gathering into consciousness, and will soon inevitably proceed to organization. Man & Superman is the first attempt to dramatize it in English. My Life Force is Bergson's *élan vitale.* My biology is J. S. Haldane's new biology. The old vitalism, the old will of God and grace of God, are coming back with a rush in a scientific form, immensely enriched with postevolutionary discoveries and concepts. Man, having for half a century been so much sodium, so much potash, so much phosphorus, again becomes a miracle: the commonest people will soon be saying 'Damn your sodium and phosphorus: will you tell us what holds these salts and minerals together in this magical form instead of leaving them to lie about or be shovelled into bottles and salt cellars? What is Life?' If it were not for the emergence of this, who would waste another thought on Shakespear's angry ape and Swift's Yahoo?

It seems to me that you would have written plays by the dozen, like me, if you had not shrunk away from Glassism into George Eliotism, and then virtually dropped the subject because there was nothing doing in that quarter. The world, instead of being your oyster, became rather your Peer Gynt's onion. My rule of thumb that a logic which leads to an impasse is really a reductioadabsurdum of the argument did not occur to you, apparently. Now, however, you are awakening to a political conscience. In the book on India there are traces of the old Malthusian antivitalism; but there are always such traces in human work. There is the right Ibsen impulse to get away from idolatry and get to the truth regardless of shattered ideals and ripped-up Rabindranaths. And this impulse to get at realities and away from figments (apply it to Neutrality, by the way) is an infallible signpost to the right path through all subjects.

Here endeth the thousand and somethingth lesson. I must now get on to Shakespear and Scissors.

Your plaidoyer is perfectly sound. Shakespear *is* long, dull, tedious, wearisome, nonsensical, and everybody's enemy except his own. Hence Lyceum Shakespear, Daly Shakespear, Tree Shakespear, and now Archer Shakespear. You dont want to hear Romeo warbling verbal jazzes like 'O single soled jest, solely singular for the singleness' because you dont care for Lewis Carrollism and word music. I dont want to hear the Seven Ages of Man because it is twaddle; and all the actors except Jaques will agree with me because it does not advance the action of the piece. The scientific members of the committee will cut out Beatrice's ridiculous statement that a star danced at her birth, because it [is] unsound obstetrically and astronomically. As to Romeo & Juliet, whenever I read it my fingers itch to cut out all the puns and the attorney's clerk's 'conceits' and leave nothing but the bare and beautiful poetry. Not a man on the cutting committee but will have his knife in somewhere.

And how much will be left at the end of the process? Just about half as much as can be got from any actormanager, who has only his own dislikes to consult, and who can at least be depended on not to cut his own part very drastically, or from any commercial entrepreneur who is only one cutter instead of six. Once let us loose on the cutting job, and we shall not only do nothing that the commercial stage will not do, but do much worse. We shall gut the plays that commerce will only chop. Commerce will give you Cibber's Richard, which is a first rate job of its kind: we will give dull selections from Shakespear consisting of what is left after you and I and Gollancz and half a dozen other knifers have all mutilated the poor old Bard to our heart's content. And, as we shall have no stars to make the mess go down, the public will rightly prefer Wilkie Bard.

The alternative is then clear. Either we do what nobody else will do for Shakespear: that is, what Bayreuth does for Wagner, or else we do something worse for him than Commerce and Martin Harvey do already.

Performances at full length are perfectly practicable. If Barker could play Twelfth Night and the Winter's Tale within fashionable hours, we can do Hamlet by beginning at six and all the others by beginning at seven. That such beginning is practicable is proved by the fact that Man & Superman was repeatedly played in Glasgow at that length and at that hour. No doubt the people suffered agonies: no matter: they paid their money; came; saw; and I conquered. They did so because the play was presented as a masterpiece of dramatic art by a great author, demanding sacrifice and endurance. Glasgow sacrificed and endured. That is exactly what we must do in the case of Shakespear. It is the only thing we can do that Martin Harvey cannot do better. The tour should be a pilgrimage: its visits a festival. That is how Bayreuth has succeeded, and led the Munich Prinz Regenten Theater to follow its example.

Now as to side questions. You must place Poel and Barker more carefully. Poel played more outrageous tricks with Shakespear than ever Tree did, even to the point of making Polonius the chief figure in the closet scene in Hamlet (Poel played Pol. himself); and if I recollect aright, after his early production of The Comedy of Errors he never gave an uncut performance or anything near it. Having to do the whole thing single-handed with very little money, he could compass, not a motion of the Prodigal Son, but a few experiments in the course of what purported to be a complete performance of a play. Some of these experiments; for instance, Thersites played by a woman in a fantastic jester's dress, demonstrated nothing but a method of preventing the audience from understanding a word of the part, as the lady spoke it in dialect, and quite inaudibly at that. Others, like making Romeo and Juliet a boy and girl according to the ages indicated by Shakespear, were amazingly and convincingly successful. Harcourt Williams and Dorothy Minto will always be for me the only credible R. & J. I have ever seen. In Hamlet, Poel had time to coach the king in his first speech, which was extraordinarily good; but all the rest of the king's part was the vulgarest stage commonplace: an instructive contrast. Thus, in bits like the curate's egg, Poel shewed what might be done, especially as to delivery and acting on the lines instead of between them.

Barker, who began by playing Richard II for Poel, learnt his lessons; and it was Barker who restored Shakespear to the stage. Why anyone should propose to go back from Barker to Ben Greet except for the sake of the box office and the bars, God knows. And Barker could not have done it if he had not inexorably made Shakespear the supreme authority and not himself. If he had not made that his dogma he would have started on an inclined plane on which there was no stoppage possible until the level of His Majesty's was reached.

Asking why Shakespear did not issue a collected edition of his works is very like asking why he did not get his photograph taken. It was not done until the value of his works forced Heminge[s] & Condell to invent the Family Shakespear. None of the Elizabethans dreamt of such a thing as possible; and if anyone had proposed it they would probably have objected violently for the same reason as Barrie, who for years refused to follow my example, or even the quieter ones of Pinero and Jones[,] because the publication of his plays made a present of them to the pirates in America and elsewhere.

The notion that Shakespear wrote more than he intended to have acted will not hold water. He may have known that it was not possible to have it acted under the existing conditions, just as I knew that Man & Superman could not be acted under them, and therefore designed it in such a fashion that it could be played without the third act. But I fully intended every word of it to be given when my Bayreuth is founded. Ibsen was compelled to acquiesce in a happy ending for A Doll's House in Berlin, because he could not help himself, just as I have never been able to stop the silly and vulgar gag with which Eliza in Pygmalion, both here and abroad, gets the last word and implies that she is going to marry Pygmalion. But would you therefore play A Doll's House in Jones's

Breaking a Butterfly version, or allow Eliza to gag in a production of Pygmalion for which you were responsible? Peer Gynt is exactly in the predicament of Man & Superman, except that it suffers infinitely more by the attempts to cut it to the measure of the two hours traffic. I have never read a single line of Shakespears (in a play) which had the least air of being written 'for the closet.'

There is only one 'standard authoritative acting edition of Shakespear'; and that is the first folio. Granted that Shakespear is as great a bore as Wotan in The Ring, and that his utterances are interminable rigmaroles. That is a reason for restricting his share in the National Theatre to his bust in the vestibule, but not for performing his plays at the expense of the theatre funds. Wagner said 'If you will send your singer to me and let me coach him, Wotan will not bore *my* audiences.' Barker accepted the implied responsibility with sufficient success to shew that complete success is not impossible. If [Bridge-]Adams is not prepared to take on that responsibility he shant have our £6000 if I can help it. He comes from Barker's theatre as Barker came from Poel's; and he must carry on the tradition.

I am totally exhausted. I am too old for these long letters.

G.B.S.

Robert **Lynd** (1879–1949) was the literary editor of the *Daily News.* **Clive** was an unpublished one-act play by Archer, written when he was young, on the topic of suicide. Whereas the rich people, in control of the **cash nexus,** lived in the urban **squares** of trees, flowers, and fine homes, the poor lived in ugly slums.] Shaw embraced the evolutionary ideas of Samuel **Butler** in 1887, when he reviewed *Luck, or Cunning?* (Tyson 1: 277–81). In 1919 he still agreed with Butler's rejection of Darwinism, though he acknowledged that Butler's narrow-minded views and mean-spirited rhetoric did not help in the dissemination of his ideas on evolution (Tyson 2: 383–98). Dr August **Weismann** (1834–1914), a German biologist who investigated heredity, performed experiments to disprove the concept of acquired habits in evolution. Shaw, who was writing *Back to Methuselah* in 1919, discussed the ideas of both Butler and Weismann in the preface to the play. The novels of **George Eliot** greatly impressed Archer, who admired her secular perspective as well as her realism and liberalism. Shaw, however, rejected the materialism and determinism in her novels and essays. His '**last rationalist novel**' was *The Irrational Knot* (1880). It still showed some influence of Eliot's writings on scientific materialism (Gibbs 2: 92), but by 1881, when he wrote *Love among the Artists,* he had rejected materialist philosophy. The novel featured '**Beethoven as its hero**,' a creative genius of self-willed independence. John N. **Maskelyne** (1839–1917) was a popular magician and illusionist who performed regularly at London's Egyptian Hall. Sir Rufus Isaacs, a Liberal MP and cabinet member, **'had to apologize to the House'** because of his involvement in the Marconi Company scandal of 1913. He was later acquitted. He served as Lord Chief Justice of England (1913–21), and later Viceroy of India (1921–5).

He was the first Jew to hold these positions. He became Viscount of Reading in 1916, Earl in 1917, and Marquess in 1926. Frederick **Smith** (1872–1930), first Earl of Birkenhead, was appointed Lord Chancellor in 1919. Andrew **Bonar Law** (1852–1923) served as a Unionist MP. In 1914 he supported the war policy of the Asquith government. When David Lloyd George (1863–1945) became prime minister in 1916, Law became the leader of the House of Commons. The **Rowlatt laws** of 1919, which defined criminal activities in India, were developed by Sir Sidney Rowlatt (1862–1945). He served as the judge of the King's Bench and was chairman of the Indian Sedition Committee that imposed punishments in India. The **king of Brobdingnag** appears in part 2 of *Gulliver's Travels* (1726) by Jonathan Swift (1667–1745). The king is disturbed by Gulliver's accounts of European politics and war. Despite Shaw's disgust over European politics and the war, he did not share the pessimistic mindset of Swift. He was not drawn to satire, either Horatian or Juvenalian. And even though human beings may have some of the base traits of **Shakespear's angry ape** – that is, Caliban in *The Tempest* – and **Swift's Yahoo** in part 4 of *Gulliver's Travels*, Shaw had not abandoned his basic ideas of human progress and wilful evolution. Shaw was greatly influenced by the ideas of Henri **Bergson**, especially his book *Creative Evolution* (1907). **John Scott Haldane** (1860–1936) was a Scottish physiologist who carried out research on human respiration. He investigated gases in coal mines, and identified toxic gases that the coal miners faced. During the First World War he invented the gas mask because of gases being used along the trenches. In 1917 he founded the *Journal of Hygiene*. He was the father of the even more famous J.B.S. Haldane (1892–1964), who carried out research in the field of population genetics. Counter to Shaw's rejection of Darwinian theory, he unified the theory of natural selection with Mendelian genetics. **Glassism** was Shaw's term for a separatist religious movement developed by John Glas (1695–1773). This Christian sect was cast out of the general assembly of the Kirk in Scotland. The Glasites opposed the authority of any established church. Archer's **book on India**, *India and the Future* (1917), was based upon his five months of travel in India in 1912. Sir **Rabindranath** Tagore (1861–1941), a Bengali poet and philosopher, used colloquial language instead of the traditional verse based on Sanskrit models. He also denounced the British Raj. In 1913 he won the Nobel Prize of Literature.

Under the topic of **Shakespear and Scissors**, Shaw launched into Archer's plea for cutting the plays in production. The French word **plaidoyer** means a plea or petition, a defensive argument. Colley **Cibber** (1671–1757) cut *Richard III* in half, then inserted additional scenes taken from Shakespeare's other history plays. The Shakesperean scholar Isaac **Gollancz** was a member of the SMNTC, as were Shaw and Archer. Willie Shakespeare the bard gives way to **Wilkie Bard** (1874–1944), a performer in the music halls and pantomimes. In the pre-war years the actor-manager **Martin Harvey**, who began his career as a romantic actor in melodrama, staged *Hamlet*, *Richard III*, and *Henry V*. In 1912 he starred in Max Reinhardt's production of *Oedipus Rex*. In August 1919, at the conference of the new Drama League, held at Stratford-upon-Avon, he praised the new Shakespeare Memorial Theatre under Bridges-Adams, but he also urged the establishment of a national theatre in London. The **Munich Prinz Regenten Theater**, which opened in 1901, was built on principles similar to those of Bayreuth. It was a festival hall for Wagner's operas. **William Poel**, founder of the Elizabethan Stage Society in 1894, led the campaign for presenting Renaissance drama on a platform stage. He staged several Shakespearean plays between 1895 and 1905. Unlike the **Prodigal Son**, who wasted his fortune, Poel never possessed the funds for grand productions. Several years after his apprenticeship with the Elizabethan Stage Society, Harley Granville **Barker** staged nearly full-text versions of *Twelfth Night* (1912),

The Winter's Tale (1912), and *A Midsummer Night's Dream* (1914). **Thersites**, the vituperative commentator in *Troilus and Cressida*, was played by Mrs Robertson Scott, who affected 'a querulous male voice' (Speaight: 196). The actor and director **Harcourt Williams** began his career with Frank Benson (1858–1939) at Stratford-upon-Avon. He acted for several West End companies before the war, and also appeared in revivals of *You Never Can Tell* in 1907 and 1908. He later served as director of the Old Vic Theatre between 1929 and 1933. **Dorothy Minto** (1886–1957) began her acting career with Benson and Poel. In the Edwardian era she appeared in plays by Shaw, Galsworthy, Barker, J.M. Barrie, and Elizabeth Robins. In 1905 she listed her birth date as 1891 in order to suggest that she was 14 years old when she portrayed Juliet in Poel's production of *Romeo and Juliet.* The Romeo, however, was not Harcourt Williams, but Esmé Percy (1887–1957), who was 19 years old in 1905. Percy performed regularly in Tree's Shakespeare productions and played Pentheus in Gilbert Murray's translation of *The Bachae* at the Court Theatre in 1908. In the 1920s and 1930s he directed and acted in several revivals of Shaw's plays. Sir Philip **Ben Greet** (1857–1936), a Shakespearean actor and director, performed with the Elizabethan Stage Society, and later staged many of Shakespeare's plays for Lillian Baylis (1874–1937) at the Old Vic. John **Heminge** or Heminges (1566–1630)] and Henry **Condell** (1572/6–1627) edited the First Folio and wrote the Preface (1623). Shaw was wrong that **none of the Elizabethan** dramatists dreamt of publishing a collection of plays. Ben Jonson published his collected *Works* in 1616, seven years before the publication of Shakespeare's First Folio. In 1884 Henry Arthur **Jones** and Henry Hermann staged ***Breaking a Butterfly***, their adaptation of Ibsen's *A Doll's House.* (See letter of 3 May 1885.)

160 / To G. Bernard Shaw

[no address]
22nd April 1919

[TLU: BL 45296 f 254]

Robert Lynd, the literary editor of the Daily News, *sent Shaw a copy Archer's play* War Is War, or The Germans in Belgium. *In his review, published on 9 May, Shaw judged it 'a good play, achieved not by any of the methods which Mr. Archer has recommended to playwrights, but by the only method that has ever produced a good play: that is, having a story to tell; feeling strongly that it ought to be told; and using the device of theatrical representation to tell it effectively.'*

The appointment of William Bridges-Adams as the director of the Shakespeare Memorial Theatre inaugurated a professional change in the performance practices in Stratford-upon-Avon. Year by year, from 1886 to 1916, Frank Benson had gamely put together and managed a make-shift company for Shakespearean productions during the summer. Over these years he presented all the plays except for Titus Andronicus *and* Troilus and Cressida, *and he trained a generation of young actors, many of whom began their careers with him. In 1919, Bridges-Adams organized a repertory program for Shakespeare, supported by the* SMNTC. *Despite Shaw's efforts to prescribe the production policy, Bridges-Adams was not impeded by Shaw or the committee. Between 1919 and 1934, he produced 29 of Shakespeare's plays. He preferred an uncluttered stage so that the action could flow quickly from scene to scene. Like Harley Granville Barker, his mentor, Bridges-Adams was committed to largely uncut texts of the plays. Because he was opposed to the traditional kinds of abridgements that had been prevalent for two hundred years of Shakespearean production, he became known as 'Unabridges-Adams,' though he did make limited cuts (along the basic lines that Archer advocated).*

My dear G.B.S.

I'm delighted to hear that Lynd has sent you WAR IS WAR. I have no doubt that you will 'deal faithfully' with it; but it's far better to be murdered than to be still born.

Your remarks on me as a potential playwright are a fine example of your *a priori* method. You have built an ingenious & impressive theory in airy disregard of the simple fact – on which my evidence must be taken as conclusive – that I have no power either of character-drawing or of writing dialogue. If a man is born without hands, it is quite unnecessary to provide a psychologico-philosophical explanation of his not playing the piano. When I try to write drama, I produce an essay cut into lengths & delivered by penny-in-the-slot puppets. That description applies to WAR IS WAR – I make you a present of the right criticism – but I thought that, while the war fever was on, people would be interested in a dramatic essay – an object-lesson with comments – on German methods in Belgium. And so they would have been if I had been in the field a year earlier. The armistice queered my pitch.

As I gather you are in a fighting mood over the Shakespeare question, I will reserve my fire. Let me only say that when you talk of a 'cutting committee' slashing at Shakespeare, you are talking of something which nobody contemplates, & with which I, for one, would have nothing to do. Bridges-Adams, in a weak moment, agreed to submit his texts to the Joint Committee, & that agreement must of course hold. If I had been he I would have told them to go to blazes. I would be personally responsible for my texts, & if the committee didn't like them they could dispense with my services at the date stipulated in the agreement. However, I can't be more Bridges-Adamite than Bridges-Adams, & the texts must be submitted. But that cannot be understood as giving the committee the right to CUT a single line. They can, if they are much misguided, veto Bridges-Adams's cuts, but that is all. It is instructive that (thanks to you) we should encounter on the threshold such a glaring instance of the impossibility of committee-management in theatrical matters.

Yours
W.A.

In a letter of 26 May 1919 to Bridges-Adams (CL 3: 611–14), Shaw raised the topic and problem of **committee-management**, including ideas about a grand tour of Shakespeare in England. But Shaw threatened to resign from the SMNTC unless the plays were 'absolutely uncut ... like the Bayreuth Wagner performances' (612). Bridges-Adams insisted, however, that production decisions belonged to him, not the committee members, including Shaw. And he rejected the plan for a 'Grand Pilgrimage' of Shakespeare as Shaw envisioned matters.

161 / To William Archer 10 Adelphi Terrace WC
17th May 1919

[TLS, except for last two lines, which are ALS: BL 45296 ff 255–6; CL 3]

This letter was Shaw's reply not only to Archer's letter of 22 April but also – and more substantially – to a draft of Archer's essay 'On "Cutting" Shakespeare,' which Archer shared with him before it was published in June in the Fortnightly Review. *In his attempt to establish criteria for making judicious cuts, Archer insisted that all words, lines, and scenes that pertained to the characters and plot action should not be cut. But he argued that obscure vocabulary and references as well as some of the bawdy language could be removed. In August Shaw responded in the* Fortnightly Review. *His short article was entitled 'On Cutting Shakespeare.' He rejected Archer's justifications for cutting the plays.*

Archer continued the debate, but shifted it to The Nation. *On 9 August, as drama critic for the journal, he reviewed the productions of* The Merry Wives of Windsor, Julius Caesar, *and* The Winter's Tale *– three of the six plays that Bridges-Adams had put in repertory that month at the new Shakespeare Memorial Theatre. Archer offered full praise for the stagings, but he expressed concern that Shaw's argument in the* Fortnightly Review *had induced Bridges-Adams to present mostly uncut texts of the plays. Archer insisted, for example, that some statements by Leontes in* The Winter's Tale *(1, 2) should have been cut because they are 'incomprehensible' and 'meaningless to modern ears.' This review set in motion in* The Nation *a series of weekly debates from 9 August to 13 September on cutting Shakespeare. Joining the debate between Archer and Shaw, the playwright John Drinkwater (1882–1937) argued against Archer and William Poel offered limited support.*

My dear W.A.

As you saw, I was kidnapped last night just as I was manoeuvering to go back with you. I did not see Poel's indiscretion; but I did see – I think it was in the Daily News – an announcement of the endowment of Bridges Adams as a *fait accompli.*

Like Nelson putting the telescope to his blind eye, you have put the stethoscope to your deaf ear over Romeo's nonsense verses. The passages you cite are not jeux d'esprit; and they have not ceased to be comprehensible because they never were comprehensible in that sense: they are what they always were, pure jingling nonsense – what Lombroso called echolalia. Shakespear was always doing it. He delighted in nonsense rhymes. I have a horrible suspicion that you are going to play the stage Scotchman in the Fortnightly, and gravely prove that as there is no species of bird known in Warwickshire whose note resembles 'hey ding a ding ding,' the line must conceal some topical allusion the point of which is now lost, and that it should be cut, along with a great deal of doggerel, not now resolvable into intelligible reflections on human nature, uttered by Grumio, the Dromios, and by practically the whole cast of Loves Labor Lost. Did you ever read the description of Mrs Siddons by Young, the inventor of the undulatory theory of light, and compare it with Hazlitt's? It is odd that a man capable of an undulatory theory of light should have refused to form an undulatory theory of Mrs Siddons, and seen in the famous rolling gait of Volumnia nothing but locomotor ataxy. Beware, or you will pillory yourself with Young.

Unless you can make your actors and actresses, in lovely dresses and in lovely lights, go off suddenly into dances of words and rhymes like children at play you cannot put Shakespear on the stage. If you cut them out, there is no Shakespear: nothing but Mr Wopsle and the Melancholy Dane. Cut out the Seven Ages of Man if you like: the play will be none the worse and much the livelier; but a Romeo who is not boyish enough to cap nonsense verses – here I have to rush off to the Local Government Conference, of which I have the honor to be Perpetual Grand.

See you on Monday afternoon, probably

ever
G.B.S

If the shorthand version of this letter was written on 15 May, as Dan Laurence posited (CL 3: 610), the meeting at which Shaw was '**kidnapped last night**' was his lecture in Hampstead, 'The Present Predicament of the Theatre.' **Poel's indiscretion** was either a comment he might have made at the lecture (if he attended) or something he wrote in his monthly newsletter about the decisions of the SMNTC, on which he served. An **endowment of Bridges Adams** was provided by the committee in support of his plans for a theatre at Stratford-upon-Avon. He opened his first season in the summer of 1919. Horatio Nelson (1758–1805) supposedly put **the telescope to his blind eye** during the Battle of Copenhagen in 1801 when the signal flags called for the retreat of the British forces. Nelson claimed that he he did not see the signal, and proceeded with the attack. His bravery led to his assignment as commander-in-chief of the fleet. In *As You Like It* two pages sing 'When birds do sing, **hey ding a ding ding** / Sweet lovers love the spring.' They also sing 'With a hey, and a ho, and a hey nonino' (5,3). In *Hamlet* Ophelia laments 'hey non nonny, nonny, hey nonny' (4, 5), and in *King Lear* the Fool sings 'With hey, ho, the wind and the rain' (3, 2 or 9). Shaw was obviously right about the playfulness of the verse, even in times of despair and madness. Cesar **Lombroso** (1836–1909), a physician, was an Italian criminologist who claimed that criminal behaviour was inherited, and that the physiognomic traits and physical anomalies of criminals, such as large ears or slopping foreheads, could be identified. Their physical traits reveal recurring, atavistic features of primates. According to these discredited theories, anatomy reveals criminality. The concept of **echolalia** – to talk, to prattle – means repetition by someone of the vocalizations or gestures of some other person or sound. It can be onomatopoetic; it can even be an uncontrolled mental disorder. As he had previously done, Shaw confused the physicist Dr Thomas **Young** with the actor Charles M. Young. (See endnote for Shaw's letter of 2 September 1903.) Mrs Sarah Siddons played **Volumnia** in *Coriolanus.* William Hazlitt's review of her is collected in *A View of the English Stage* (1818). See also *The Characters of Shakespeare's Plays* (1817). The condition of **ataxy** (i.e., ataxia) is the inability to coordinate voluntary body movements. Mr **Wopsle**, a clerk in Dickens's *Great Expectations,* becomes an actor, but is unsuccessful in his performance of the role of Hamlet.

162 / To G. Bernard Shaw

27 Fitzroy Square W.
6th September 1919

[TLS: BL 50528 f 61]

Besides offering a critique of Archer's argument for cutting Shakespeare's plays, Shaw had also used his article in the Fortnightly Review *to accuse Archer of cutting the first act of Ibsen's* The Wild Duck *'to the bone.' Archer refuted this charge in* The Nation *on 23 August, and accused Shaw of distorting the evidence. In his response Archer had assumed that Shaw was referring to 'a few phrases' that had been removed from the translated text of the play. Archer defended himself by insisting that he had only removed a few words of the Norwegian dialogue because they lacked 'an effective English equivalent.' But Shaw's complaint was not directed at the published translation. Instead, he had in mind the major cuts in the first act when the play was staged in 1894. Yet these cuts were not by Archer, who did not participate in the production. So they were arguing at cross purposes about Ibsen, if not Shakespeare. Shaw made this charge in 1903 and repeated it 1923; see letters of 8 September 1903 and 20 June 1923.*

In 'Lord Grey, Shakespeare, Mr. Archer, and Others' (6 September, The Nation*), Shaw attempted to clear up the misunderstanding over the Ibsen cuts by a clever apology that in fact strengthened his argument against cuts. At the same time, he continued the debate over cutting Shakespeare. He accused Archer of telling a stupendous 'whopper' in his article of 23 August when he proclaimed that Leontes's speech in* The Winter's Tale *is incomprehensible. 'I take the privilege of old friendship, and tell Mr. Archer that he knows as well as I do' what the lines mean. (A week later John Drinkwater made a similar argument in* The Nation.*)*

In this letter, written on the same day as Shaw's article – Archer ignored the ironic thrust of Shaw's apology. Although Archer made a grand gesture of sheathing his rhetorical sword, he ignored the fact that Shaw had not conceded anything to him about cutting Shakespeare. But Archer's tactic of implying that Shaw had apologized for both Ibsen and Shakespeare served his desire to get Shaw 'to collaborate with me in a play!' Despite this ploy of declaring a truce, Archer returned to the debate on 13 September in The Nation *when he attempted yet again to counter Drinkwater by insisting that several passages in* The Winter's Tale *are incomprehensible. Summing up, he insisted that he was only arguing for 'the paring away of dead tissue.' This position was 'surely a simple act of common-sense.'*

At a later, unspecified date Shaw added a handwritten note at the top of this typed letter: 'ans? [i.e., answer] 10/9/19. No condition. No veto. Play to be his as Widowers' Houses *is mine.' He also wrote on this letter: 'File A.' But as the following letters reveal, Shaw did not veto his involvement until 18 October 1919.*

My dear G.B.S.

'I blush, & hide my sword' – the more readily as you give your case away with both hands, which, as the Nurse says, 'is a courteous, & a kind, & a handsome, & I warrant a virtuous thing to do.'

But now to be serious – I want you to collaborate with me in a play!

An idea came to me the other night in a dream, & has now grown into a tolerably complete scheme for a romantic melodrama, which only needs your co-operation to be infallibly

THE PLAY OF THE CENTURY.

There are two characters which are simply cut out for you – the Raja of a wholly imaginary & impossible independent state in the depths of the Himalayas, & his English valet.

Don't turn this down without further enquiry. I am perfectly serious in thinking there might be no end of money in this thing if you could tame your haughty genius to working within a commonplace but by no means hackneyed framework; & I believe you would love the part of the Raja. Moreover, you owe me a collaboration ever since you took the bit between your teeth & bolted with my (or rather Augiers') plot for 'Widowers' Houses.' This time the plot doesn't come from any Frenchman but direct from God Almighty.

But as collaborators invariably quarrel more or less, I suggest that we lay down certain conditions in advance:

(1) The object of the partnership is TO MAKE MONEY, not to épater le bourgeois or put the utmost possible strain on the patience of the audience.

(2) Each partner to have an absolute veto on anything proposed by the other.

(3) If an irreconcilable difference of opinion results in a deadlock, the plot & appurtenances to revert to me (as the concessionaire of God Almighty) together with the liberty of annex[ing] any inspirations of genius that you may in the meantime have given forth. The last may seem a large order; but fragmentary inventions would clearly be of no use to you apart from the general scheme which would (by hypothesis) revert to me.

When are you to be in town? I could at a pinch send you a rough scenario, but would much rather bring it to you & talk it over. I have the first two acts, out of four, pretty clear in my mind, & the fourth act as well, except in so far as it depends on Act III. That I can't get on without help from an expert in wireless telegraphy – I am trying to find one.

If you let me down, I shall have to fall back upon H.G. Wells – a sad anticlimax.

Yours
W.A.

The opening quotations are from *As You Like It* (2, 7) and *Romeo and Juliet* (2, 5). The plot for *Rhinegold* that Shaw transformed into *Widowers' Houses* was derived by Archer from *La Ceinture Dorée* by Émile **Augiers.**

163 / To William Archer

Presteign (leaving on Saturday)
17th September 1919

[APCS: BL 45296 f 257]

Shaw wrote to Archer on 10 September, but that letter is not extant. Archer then responded to Shaw's missing letter, but his letter is also missing. So, this letter of 17 September was a response to a letter that Archer wrote between 10 and 17 September. Although we lack the details on how Shaw initially responded to Archer's propostion, it is possible to determine from this letter and the one on 9 October that for a few weeks Shaw was helping Archer to develop the narrative details of the plot, even though he probably rejected Archer's conditions for a business partnership, as spelled out in the letter of 6 September. Finally, on 18 October Shaw separated himself completely, and urged Archer to go forward on his own.

During this same period, Archer also asked A.W. Pinero and Harley Granville Barker – but not H.G. Wells – to be co-authors, but they too urged him to complete the play himself. In 1920, however, when The Green Goddess *was in rehearsal in New York City, Barker offered some revisions to the dialogue of the last act. Otherwise, the play, with its melodramatic and romantic conflicts, was conceived and written by Archer.*

The plot of *The Green Goddess* requires wireless communication.

Note that wireless *telephony*, being transmitted by Hertzian rays & not by atmospheric air, goes through to Mars (or Sirius for that matter) if the ether goes so far.

Your difficulty about play flash is your common sense. Use your artistic sense; and it will come all right. The process of writing fiction is the process of making an ass of yourself.

G.B.S.

Hertzian radio **waves** or electromagnetic radiation, discovered by the physicist Heinrich Rudolf Hertz (1857–94), resulted from electrical oscillations. The meaning of **play flash** is unclear because it apparently depended upon something Archer had described in his missing letter. The play, as staged, began with a plane that has just crashed and concluded with bombs exploding offstage. Perhaps Archer considered visual effects in conjunction with either the crashed plane, from which three survivors crawled out, or the exploding bombs.

164 / To G. Bernard Shaw

[no address]
9th October 1919

[TLS: BL 50528 f 62]

My dear G.B.S.

Here is the sketch-plan of the great melodrama. I had intended to have made it much more sketchy, & brought it down & expounded it to you; but I found that the only way to make the process of events clear was to fill in a good deal of the dialogue; so now it can tell its own story. I have not troubled about the last act, which presents no structural difficulties, though it will no doubt be the most difficult of all to write.

All the wireless business would have to be thoroughly studied with an expert. I had one talk of a couple of hours with a very good man, & I think what I have planned is, roughly speaking, possible; but it wants all sorts of touching up.

I will come & talk it over with you whenever you please.

Yours
W.A.

165 / To William Archer

10 Adelphi Terrace WC
18th October 1919

[ASU: BL 50528 f 62; CL 3]

Shaw wrote the draft of this letter in shorthand at the base of Archer's letter of 9 October 1919. He dated the reply 18 October. Dan Laurence had the shorthand draft transcribed and then printed in Collected Letters, *vol. 3: 639–40. The letter itself, if indeed it was sent, has not survived. Shaw withdrew as an adviser for Archer's developing play at this point, not earlier when Archer first proposed a partnership on 6 September.*

Archer had provided the sketch-plan, in some detail, for three of the four acts. He was still trying to convince Shaw to become a collaborator. History had repeated itself, for Archer was recreating a version of what happened in 1884 when he gave Shaw the plot outline for The Way to a Woman's Heart. *In 1887 he rejected Shaw's version of* Rheingold, *which became* Widowers' Houses*; now in 1919 Shaw returned the favour by rejecting* The Raja of Rukh, *which became* The Green Goddess. *In both cases, all was well that ended well.*

My dear W.A.

I somehow overlooked your letter, and was consequently much taken aback when the play stopped so abruptly that it set me hunting in vain for the fourth act.

Of course I could write your scenes in for you; but why should I? Your threat to go and ask someone else is quite dastardly in its incorrigible laziness. Have you no conscience, no shame? There is in your plot either no money at all, or enough to be taken very seriously. Yet you [are] willing to throw away half of it, and hamper yourself for life in dealing with your play, sooner than sit down for a week and write some dialogue that you are quite as capable of writing as any collaborator who shares your laziness sufficiently to accept a collaboration instead of doing his own work for himself. What work of any value can come from so worthless a pair?

Now, I am not going to abet you in a disgraceful evasion. You have clearly no right to ask me for a stroke of work until you have exhausted your own powers. You havent even tried. You excuse yourself by saying that you cannot do it. Then, when I refuse to do it, you excuse me by saying that *I* cannot do it. Whom will you ask next? Calmour is dead; but, alas! he has successors. Dont be that most hopeless sort of sluggard, the sort that overwhelms himself with small jobs to stave off big ones. I tell you you can write plays well enough if only you get your mind really free from the ghastly determinism that strangles the children of your imagination as they are born. Let them rip instead of proving that they dont exist, and see what happens. You might have been writing plays all your life if you had not prevented yourself so strenuously.

You will not find that fourth act so easy as you think, if it is to have any life in it. But if you let your characters go their own way they will write it for you.

Now sit down and write me a long letter explaining that I know nothing about plays, and that this is why my plays are not plays, and why I shall never be able to write plays, and why Broadbent in John Bull is a brilliant Shaw soliloquy in dialogue. Then ask yourself how you can be such a godforsaken fool as to write such nonsense, and tear it up, and write your play. If you make an honorable failure, and I can help you out, I will; but there is not the slightest risk of this: the completion of the play is well within your powers, and may lead you to fuller discovery of them. You are not so young that you can spend any more time trifling with yourself.

ever
[unsigned]

Alfred Cecil **Calmour**, who died in 1912, was author of *The Amber Heart*, a 'Poetical Fancy in Three Acts,' which Henry Irving acquired exclusively for Ellen Terry. Audiences loved her in this sentimental play.

166 / To William Archer

10 Adelphi Terrace WC
8th November 1920

[APCS: BL 45296 f 258]

There are no extant letters between 18 October 1919 and 8 November 1920. During this period, after having completed a draft of The Green Goddess, *Archer became involved in production decisions. He had initially conceived of H.B. Irving in the role of the Raja, but Irving died in 1919. None of the other London actors seemed appropriate to Archer, and he also rejected Henry Ainley and Norman McKinnel. So, instead of pushing for a London production, he accepted Granville Barker's suggestion that he should negotiate with the American director Winthrop Ames (1872–1937) for a New York production and consider George Arliss for the role of the Raja. This turned out to be a brilliant plan. Ames, who came from a wealthy New England family, and spent much of his fortune on theatre during his lifetime, had managed the New Theatre project. Barker and Archer met him at that time (see letter of 17 June 1908). Dissatisfied with the large New Theatre, Ames built the Little Theatre (1912) and the Booth (1913). A supporter of new American drama, he was an accomplished director.*

With a copy of the play in hand, Barker went to Ames in January 1920 and read the play to him. Ames accepted it with enthusiasm, and he agreed with Barker that Arliss was an excellent choice to play the lead role. Production plans went forward in New York with Ames fully in charge. During the spring and summer Ames and Barker nudged Archer into revisions of the fourth act (but he refused to eliminate the triangular relationship between the heroine, her husband, and the hero who loves her because of its private parallels to his own marriage and secret relationship with Elizabeth Robins). By November 1920 the cast was mostly in place, though Archer continued to worry about the role of the Raja.

In this letter Shaw replied to a missing letter from Archer. From Shaw's response it is clear that Archer, the epitome of the nervous and pessimistic playwright, still had second doubts about Arliss in the role of the sophisticated yet devious Raja, and was again considering a London actor as an alternative choice. But no one else, including Shaw, saw any need to change the casting. Finally, by mid-November Archer concurred. He sailed to New York City and settled into the Pennsylvania Hotel as rehearsals went forward in December. Although he could not control his anxieties, he at least had an advance of £2000 from Ames, who was convinced that The Green Goddess *was going to be a hit (see Whitebrook: 360–7).*

The chap is a very capable actor; but as there must be dozens of men of his age and caliber to be had in America, I can see no point in exporting him. Ames would expect something special, and be prepared to pay a special salary; and he would not feel that he was getting it, or getting value for the extra money: he would say (or think) that he could have picked up just as good a man on Broadway for an ordinary salary. So, on the whole, I shouldnt bother about him.

G.B.S.

Because Archer's letter has not survived, the **chap** remains nameless. Whoever he was, he could not have topped Arliss in the role.

167 / To William Archer Ayot St Lawrence, Welwyn, Herts.
16th March 1921

[TLS: BL 45296 f 259; CL 3]

The Green Goddess *was a grand success. It had premiered on 27 December 1920 in Philadelphia at the revamped Walnut Street Theatre. The spectators and critics loved the play (C. Archer: 373–5). After the two successful tryout weeks, it opened at the Booth Theatre in New York City on 18 January 1921. Winthrop Ames had crafted a winner, as Archer knew; when he published the play in New York he dedicated it to Ames. Besides George Arliss, who was marvellous as the Raja, the production featured a combination of British, American, and Australian actors, including Herbert Waring, who years earlier had played Helmer in the 1889 London production of* A Doll's House. The Green Goddess *ran for 440 performances until February 1922, and then toured the northeastern states for over a year. By the end of the touring, it totalled over 800 performances. (On the play and production see Whitebrook: 359–69.) The London production opened on 6 September 1923 at the St James's Theatre and ran until December 1924, closing only a few days before Archer died (416 perfs.). Arliss again played the Raja, but the rest of the cast was new. An Australian production, which ran for half a year, was presented in 1925. The silent film version appeared in 1923, followed by a sound film in 1930. Both film versions starred Arliss, who was nominated for an Academy Award in 1930. A radio version was broadcast on 6 January 1935, starring Claude Rains (1889–1967), and the* Theatre Guild on the Air *delivered yet another radio version on 20 October 1946. The play was even turned into a popular novel in 1922 by Louise Jordan Miln (1864–1933), and a film,* Adventure in Iraq, *was loosely derived from Archer's text in 1943. (For a study of the play, films, novel, and Australian staging, see Kelly: 2–124. Kelly also provided her edited version of the play.)*

After a lifetime of living on a limited income, Archer hit the financial jackpot during the last four years of his life. The royalty payments from The Green Goddess *provided a small fortune. After four decades of reviewing for newspapers and journals, he was able to retire as a theatre critic. With this steady flow of income the Archers purchased additional property and buildings that adjoined their King's Langley property. This allowed Mrs Archer to expand her physical therapy business. The flow of funds also allowed Archer to travel extensively during these last years. With his wife and daughter-in-law he made a solemn visit to Tom's gravesite in Belgium in 1921. In the same year he travelled to Majorca with his brother James and to Norway with his brother Charles. Then during the last three years of his life he made trips to Spain, Italy, New York City, Cuba, Jamaica, Panama, Bermuda, Florida, North Carolina, Boston, Providence, Copenhagen, and Christiana. For most of these trips he travelled alone. Travel was inscribed in his bones, beginning with the childhood trips to Norway each summer to visit relatives. His trip to Australia in 1876, and return by way of America, was the first of many ocean voyages. Not even the shipwreck of the* Merida, *sailing in the fog from the Caribbean to New York City in 1911, deterred Archer's travels, though he and 350 other frightened people had to abandon the sinking ship for lifeboats during a foggy night (C. Archer: 317–20; Whitebrook: 287–9). Archer wrote about the harrowing adventure a month later ('A Shipwreck,' ML, 10 and 16 June 1911). A year later, as his letters from 1912 testify, he travelled around the world, spending several months in India, which contributed directly to key motifs and themes in* The Green Goddess.

My dear W.A.

I hear that your play has been a big success in America. I do not know whether you have come back yet; but I take my chance of this reaching you in London.

Your fees and your film rights will bring you in a lot of money; but, unless you are careful, the United States Government, the State of New York, and the British Exchequer will strip you of half of it or more. You cannot escape both Income Taxes; but if you pay the American tax and immediately invest the balance there (not necessarily in American securities) so that it reaches this country in the form of capital, you need not pay British income tax on it, nor on the proceeds of your subsequent sale of it if you sell it.

You need have no compunction in taking advantage of this privilege which the capitalists have reserved for themselves, because the taxation of author's royalties is taxation of capital in a very thin disguise; and by tearing the disguise off you obtain no advantage that is not already enjoyed by every financier.

Perhaps you know all this; but then again perhaps you dont. I did not know it myself until very recently. Hence this letter.

I am greatly pleased by your success. It proves that I was quite right all along, and that you might have achieved it long ago if you had not been the laziest man (Socratically lazy) on earth.

You can now go ahead with the original Widowers' Houses, and dream a few more plots to go on with when it is finished.

Do not let your film rights go too cheap; and do not, as the silly American authors do, give the manager half. I have been offered 20,000 pounds sterling (not dollars) per year for five years for two films of my old plays each year. That sort of insanity has gone bang now; but still it indicates how much money there is in the business.

ever
G.B.S.

On the whole problem of **taxation** Archer struggled to understand the complications that attended his new financial situation. Some of the tax controversies were not settled until two years after his death (C. Archer: 382; Whitebrook: 378). Shaw's advice on **film rights** was helpful. Shaw took great pride in his business knowledge and negotiating skills – even though Blanche Patch, his secretary of 30 years, thought that he was a poor 'Man of Business' (Patch: 241–61). In his negotiations with the film industry, however, Shaw proved to be a financial wizard. (See Dukore 4: 1380–1 for a brief statement of Shaw's views on contract negotiations with the publishing and film industries. Also see the informative introduction in Dukore's edition of *The Collected Screenplays of Bernard Shaw*.)

168 / To G. Bernard Shaw

27 Fitzroy Square W.
22nd June 1921

[TLU, with handwritten marginal additions and two signatures; BL 50528 ff 63–4]

On 20 July 1919 Shaw had informed Siegried Trebitsch that he was 'working on a huge tetralogy (like Wagner's Ring).' Over two decades earlier in 1898 Shaw had written The Perfect Wagnerite. *There he had spelled out Wagner's historical ideas on 'the three main orders of men' (Wagner: 29). Now Shaw planned to top Wagner with an even more ambitious work that presented the history of mankind since the fall of the gods. At that point in 1919 three plays were written and he was working on the fourth, which was supposed to be set 'a thousand years hence.' But by the time he finished writing the play in 1920,* Back to Methuselah *had become five plays. The undertaking was 'a colossal affair, with, alas! No money in it' (Trebitsch: 202–3 CL 3: 624–5).*

Back to Methuselah, *which was composed between March 1918 and May 1920, was published in New York on 1 June 1921; the London edition appeared on 23 June. The first production was staged nine months later in New York City by the Theatre Guild. Parts 1 and 2 opened on 27 February 1922; parts 3 and 4 on 6 March; and part 5 on 13 March. Each ran for a week. Shaw had conceived the play as his grand work.*

My dear G.B.S.

All the time I have been reading 'Back to Methuselah,' I have been mentally writing you a series of letters that would fill a small volume. Now that I have come to the end, I have providentially forgotten most of them; but Providence (or Satan) having arranged that I should have a little time on my hands, I can't resist the temptation to give you a few extracts from the fragments that remain.

And first of all I want to protest against your affectation (p. lxxxvii) of being a He-Ancient. It won't do. Your mind was never more infernally agile, your intellectual muscle was never better. To put it another way, you never were further from years of discretion. Throughout the play (I'm not speaking of the preface) you are almost indecently young & irresponsible. When a man can walk on a tight-rope over the Falls of Niagara, turning three summersaults to a minute, it's no use his appealing to the census-paper to prove himself decrepit.

There is, then, no just cause or impediment in your age to prevent you from accepting the following challenge: Why not prove once for all the reality of Creative Evolution by creatively evolving from the privileged lunatic all the world knows (I remember when Tom used to call it 'privileged loonatit') into a Leader of Men and a Saviour of Society? If this last Bible of yours is ever going to have any effect, it will be 100 or 1000 years hence; & it's tomorrow that needs salvation. If there are today a few intellectual smelters who can separate the gold from the slag, they are about as many as can understand Einstein. The mass of people will simply laugh, shrug their shoulders & pass on. What's the use of a wisdom concealed in indecipherable hieroglyphics, however amusing?

There are two really tragic passages in the preface: 'I have spent forty years writing in this fashion without, as far as I can see, producing any visible effect on public opinion' and, with regard to MAN & SUPERMAN, 'The effect was so vertiginous, apparently, that nobody noticed the new religion in the center of the intellectual whirlpool.'

I doubt if there is any case of a man so widely read, heard, seen & known as yourself, who has produced so little practical effect on his generation. I am strongly under the impression (I may be wrong) that you have less of a following today than you had twenty years ago. Don't tell me that that's merely the natural effect of the lapse of time, a new generation having supplanted the generation that hailed you as a delightful novelty. Neither Carlyle nor Ruskin (great writers, but men of very limited intelligence) had, at your age, lost any part of his influence. It isn't as if any newer prophet had arisen to oust you. You have no serious competitors (Wells might be one if his voice, physical and literary, were less squeaky), but your public (small blame to them) declines to take you seriously. Can't you fix your will upon the high-growing frondage of Practical Influence & elongate your neck so as to reach it?

You will say it's no use badgering you to 'hatch yourself over again & hatch yourself different.' But that's just what, on your own showing, Creative Evolution should be able to do. Besides, it wouldn't really be a matter of Creation, but rather of Suppression. The wisdom is *in* you, right enough; it has only to be liberated from the tyrannous, irrepressible idiosyncrasy. Do your own smelting: let us for once, or twice, or thrice, have the gold without slag; working it into whatever artistic form you please. Say, for instance, a great play, realistic or symbolic, that should go to every city in the world, & shake the souls of people instead of their midriffs. Or a sober analysis of the situation, exact in statement, moderate in invective, silent upon your pet aversions where they are not indispensable to the argument. Vivacious but not undignified, brilliant but not freakish. A book to be translated into every civilized language & read from Tangier to Tokyo.

To put the same idea in another way, why not set the dramatist in you to work, & project a new avatar of your godhead, persuasive & convincing, instead of merely startling & titillating. The G.B.S. we know is partly a deliberate creation; & it has done its work. Why not shift the mask, & adapt the voice & manner (not the essential matter) to a new & more ingratiating prosopopoeia?

You may think it rather unfair of me (not to say d—d cheek) to seize upon two casual sentences & make them the text of a sermon. But it isn't a sermon – it's an appeal. I believe firmly in the wisdom of the essence of your thought: there are hundreds of pages in your prefaces that I read with a passion of assent & admiration. I believe there is no one living who has more light & leading in him, if you would only purify your light & condescend to give a little study to the psychology of leadership, or rather of followership.

What we really want is a great orator – a 'spell-binder' – who should be at the same time a thinker & a right thinker. I don't suppose even Creative Evolution could make you a Bright or a Bradlaugh, effective debater though you be. But all that the pen can do you could [achieve] if you would. I think you have quoted with approval Ibsen's 'To be yourself you must slay yourself'; I hold that a grossly overstated doctrine; but anyway no one was ever further from acting up to it than you – I mean, of course, in a literary sense.

Do you know that reviews of 'Back to Methuselah' are pouring in from America?

I am starting on Saturday for a fortnight's trip to Norway, with my wife & my daughter-in-law.

Yours ever
W.A.

The **He-Ancient** is a character in part 5 of *Back to Methuselah,* which is set in the distant future of the year of 31,920 when select people, bred in test tubes, have willed themselves to live eternally. Archer's ironic challenge to **elongate your neck** was a tease of Shaw's misguided ideas on evolution, derived from the theories of Jean-Baptiste Lamarck (1744–1829). If indeed 'living organisms change because they want to,' as Shaw proclaimed in the preface to *Back to Methuselah* (CP 5: 271), then Shaw should be able to apply his Neo-Lamarckian will power to expand his 'Practical Influence' on world events – just as giraffes wilfully elongated their necks to reach foliage high in trees. Both Brian Tyson (Tyson Story: 3–4) and Michael Holroyd (3: 80) made the case that this letter, especially Archer's appeal for a **great play, realistic or symbolic**, triggered Shaw to write *Saint Joan.* Holroyd, who quoted much of this paragraph, also identified several people, including Charlotte Shaw, who urged Shaw to write a play on the Maid. John **Bright** (1811–89) and Charles **Bradlaugh** (1833–91) were successful public speakers and political reformers. Shaw commented on Bradlaugh in the preface to *Back to Methuselah.* Shaw probably responded to Archer's heartfelt **appeal** to evolve into a world leader, but regrettably the letter has not survived. The statement '**To be yourself you must slay yourself**' appears in act 5 of *Peer Gynt,* when the Button-Molder confronts Peer. Archer's reference to reviews **pouring in from America** was to the newly published book, not to the production, which occurred a year later. Just before Archer, Mrs Archer, and Alys Archer, Tom Archer's wife, made their **trip to Norway** in 1921, they had received word from the Ministry of Defence – after three years of uncertainty – that a likely gravesite for Tom had been identified. He was no longer missing in action. Soon after they returned from Norway, the Ministry of Defence provided definite information that Tom had died in a German hospital on 28 April 1918, and was buried in grave number 29 of row C at the communal cemetery in the city of Coutrai (Kortrijk), located in Belgium in West Flanders. The three of them then made a pilgrimage later that summer to the gravesite (Whitebrook: 337–8).

169 / To William Archer

Ayot St Lawrence, Welwyn, Herts.
10th January 1922

[APCS: BL 45296 f 260; CL 3 partial]

Archer sent Shaw the proofs for a forthcoming article he had written on Shakespeare's All's Well That Ends Well.

Proofs to hand: thanks.

All's Well is S's only really interesting comedy. Leave out of the question its extraordinary literary beauty – miles ahead of Love's Labor Lost. What have you left? A middle class heroine, with the middle class outlook and ambition, determination and courage, deliberately indifferent to her Junker's feelings because she knows that if she can get him safely married to her she can wear him down by sheer superiority. A Junker hero with no quality but his class quality, just as Thackeray might have drawn him. There are miracles of unstaginess even to this Ibsenite day. Lafan, Parolles, and the lovely old Countess, as good as Polonius and less conventional; far better than Pistol or Bob Acres, being a genuine human type like Lever's Potts or Dickens's Lammle; and the noblest and finest of all S's old women. It is all so fresh and serious and interesting compared to As You Like It or Much Ado that I am tempted to believe, like J.F.R., that it is a combination of Chapman's best with S's best. So *there*!

G.B.S.

In *All's Well That Ends Well* the **Junker hero**, as Shaw imagines him, is Bertram, whom Helena tricks and marries. As the son of the countess, he becomes the Count of Rousillon upon his father's death. There is no character named **Lafan** in the play. Shaw was likely referring to Lafeu, the old lord who opens the play with the **Countess** of Roussillon. It is unlikely he meant Lavatch, the clown figure who serves as the countess's servant. **Pistol** is Falstaff's ensign in Shakespeare's *Henry IV, Part 2*; he marries Nell Quickly in *Henry V*. In *The Merry Wives of Windsor* he participates in the baiting of Falstaff. **Bob Acres** is a foolish and pompous character in Sheridan's *The Rivals*. **Potts** is a quixotic hero in *A Day's Ride: A Life's Romance* (1863), a novel by the Irish writer Charles **Lever** (1806–72) who wrote popular novels, often full of humor and sentiment. Thackeray admired his conversational and witty writing style. Alfred **Lammle** is a fortune hunter in Dickens's *Our Mutual Friend*. The playwright George **Chapman** (c. 1560–1634) wrote for several London companies between 1595 and 1610. He collaborated with Ben Jonson and John Marston (1576–1634), and possibly with Shakespeare. In *An Introduction to the Study of the Shakespeare Canon* (5 vols, 1922–32, John Mackinnin Robertson provided further support for Shaw's argument that Chapman was the co-author of *All's Well*. **J.F.R.** was the actor Johnston Forbes-Robertson.

170 / To William Archer

10 Adelphi Terrace WC
8th June 1922

[TLS, with handwritten postscript: V&A: GB71 THM/368/4/4/38]

The letter from Archer is missing, but Shaw's 'disgruntled' response suggested the tenor of Archer's 'memorandum.' Shaw had become frustrated with the SMNTC *and sceptical about finding major donors. Only £100,000 had been collected by 1914, and very little had been added to the small nest egg since then. Also, between 1909 and 1919 Shaw had often been outmanoeuvred and out-voted on key decisions by members of the committee. In 1909 he had written the 'Letter to Millionaires,' but the committee members had rejected it (see letter of 4 March 1909). Then in 1919 he had opposed the plan to set up a Shakespeare Memorial Theatre in Stratford-upon-Avon under the leadership of William Bridges-Adams (see letters of 19 and 22 April 1919). His judgment on Bridges-Adams and his productions had improved by 1922, but his attitude toward the* SMNTC *continued to be dismissive. Hence this 'cold and weary' reply to Archer.*

By contrast, Archer remained committed to the campaigns for a national theatre. He and Barker had decided that the time was right for updating and transferring the key features of A National Theatre: Scheme and Estimates *(1907) into Barker's new book,* The Exemplary Theatre. *In January 1922 they edited the proofs; then the book was published in 1923. Also, from 1919 forward, they became advocates for a new organization called The Drama League. Its mission was to support playwrights and the development of new drama throughout the country. Shaw, however, kept his distance from the Drama League. He preferred to support the Royal Academy of Dramatic Arts.*

My dear W.A.

Your able memorandum leaves me cold and weary: you may be right; but I cannot begin all that over again. The Drama League and the repertory theatres just manage to keep going: there is no sign of their overflowing to the tune of a million. We did not get anything out of the Mayors and Millionaires; but to whom else can we go now? The thing may catch on this time as a monstrous job, with knighthoods and baronetcies and peerages in it for people who will plank down the money, and lucrative contracts and soft jobs in it for the people on whom the money will be spent. You can try, if you feel fresh enough and apt enough at that particular kind of stunt. I am more interested in developing the Bridges Adams enterprize now that Providence has rescued us from the Old Vic wreckers.

I shall be in London from the 13th to the 17th, and shall be engaged at the Royal Academy of Dramatic Art from 3 to 5 on the 13th, and all the morning on the 15th and 16th. Barring these hours I could work in a meeting.

Ever,
G.B.S.

PS I am afraid the above is disgruntled; but I am keener on the desperate little half amateur or only would-be professional follies which really keep the theatre alive than in the monumental part of the business. When we get our Anglais it will open, under Bancroft's direction, with a repertory of Money, London Assurance, Still Waters Run Deep, and (to satisfy the advanced spirits) Its Never Too Late to Mend.

Upon the founding of **The Drama League** in 1919, an advisory committee was established. Lord Howard de Walden, who had been one of the four cowboys along with Shaw, Archer, and Chesterton (see letter of 10 November 1914). A financial supporter of the arts, he served as the Drama League's designated president. The practical leadership was provided by Geoffrey Whitworth (1883–1951) as honorary secretary, and Barker as chairman of the council. Several viscounts and Members of Parliament served as vice-presidents, and the council was composed of two dozen theatre people, including Lewis Casson (1875–1969), Edith Craig, Ben Greet, and the designer Norman Wilkerson (1882–1934). Ironically, though in 1919 Shaw had opposed the **Bridges Adams enterprise** of the Shakespeare Memorial Theatre in Stratford-upon-Avon, by 1922 he had become a supporter. **Old Vic Wreckers** is a reference to Lilian Baylis (1874–1937), Ben Greet, Russell Thorndike (1885–1972), and others at the Old Vic Theatre, where all of Shakespeare's plays were performed between 1914 and 1923. Although Shaw and Archer dismissed Baylis's efforts, many people supported and praised her, including Ellen Terry, Sybil Thorndike (1882–1976), Edith Craig, and Cicely Hamilton (1872–1952). Shaw's views on Baylis improved in the 1930s when the Old Vic staged some of his plays (I&R: 372–4). No doubt the efforts of Archer, Barker, Shaw, and the SMNTC had established the initial ideas and campaigns of a national theatre, but Baylis, in her idiosyncratic ways, became the decisive person in the birth and development of not only a national theatre company but also the national dance and opera companies. The **Royal Academy of Dramatic Art**, which received its royal charter in 1920, was founded in 1904 by Herbert Beerbohm Tree for the training of actors. A stage was added to one of the building on Gower Street in 1921. Besides serving on the council of RADA from 1911 to 1941, Shaw sometimes gave lectures to the students and contributed funds for new buildings on Gower Street. In 1912 he donated the royalties from *Pygmalion* (and eventually *My Fair Lady*) to RADA, and upon his death he left one-third of his royalties to RADA (Holroyd 4: 112, item #40). One of the **desperate little half amateur** companies that Shaw supported was Edy Craig's Pioneer Players. Shaw was dismissive of the SMNTC because the members would settle for a Théâtre **Anglais** that would be managed by an old-timer such Sir Squire **Bancroft**. The national theatre would then stage popular plays from the pre-Ibsen days such as Edward Bulwer Lytton's ***Money***, Dion Boucicault's ***London Assurance***, Tom Taylor's ***Still Waters Run Deep***, and Charles Reade's ***Never Too Late to Mend***. For similar complaints about the Shakespeare Memorial National Theatre, see Shaw's letter to William Poel in 1916 (CL 3: 382–4) and his open letter to J.T. Grein in 1921 (Dukore 4: 1362–4). In both letters he trots out *London Assurance* and *Still Waters Run Deep* as the plays that will be revived.

171 / To G. Bernard Shaw

27 Fitzroy Square W
10th June 1922

[TLS: V&A; GB 71 THM/368/2/13]

In this response to Shaw's 'disgruntled' letter and postscript of 8 June, Archer made the case for continuing the campaign for a national theatre, as he and Barker were doing.

My dear G.B.S.

Mrs Lyttelton suggests Thursday afternoon for the subcommittee meeting – at her house & at your time – let me know as soon as you can whether this is all right.

I see in the papers that you have been apologizing to posterity for something or other. I think you'd better set about preparing your apology to posterity for this amazing note. For the benefit of posterity I may say that I refer to a type-written document with a MS postscript, dated June 8 1922 – it will doubtless appear in your Collected Correspondence, somewhere in Vol. XXV. Good heavens, man, why turn & rend a project for which you've been working, and working well, for twenty years past! Why get cold feet just at this point? The sudden refrigeration would be comprehensible, though not heroic, if it arose from the conviction that the thing is impossible. Perhaps it is – if your panic were to spread, it certainly would be. But your plea is not that of impossibility – you turn around & say that the thing is not worth doing, & that you look for the aesthetic nourishment of your old age to the savory messes out of the Phoenix Society. The MS postscript is especially amazing. That argument has been laughed out of court five-and-twenty years ago. Of course the S.N.T. will not be the home of Futurist & Expressionist & Psycho-Analyst experiments. These things have their uses: they are the screen of skirmishes before the main body of theatrical progress. I hope & trust that there will always be Vedrenne-Barker movements along side of the S.N.T., if only to train the managers & producers of the S.N.T. & other repertory theatres. But there is not the slightest reason to suppose that the S.N.T. itself will produce anything more old-fashioned than YOU NEVER CAN TELL. And anyway, what sense is there in arguing that we ought not to construct a fine machine because there is a possibility of it being misused? There always is such a possibility – you can't construct a fool-proof theatre any more than a fool-proof motor car; but that consideration has not prevented the invention & development of the automobile. There was some serious danger of misuse if the thing had come into being 20 years ago. There it was possible that one of the Old Guard of actor-managers might have intrigued himself into the management, by way of finding his Invalides at the public expense. But the actor-manager is now extinct, & all the Lodges & Doyles in the world can't call back

Beerbohm Tree from the Shades. (Bouchier is not a serious danger – no one takes him seriously.) Come, come – take a brisk walk & warm your feet – this letter shows alarming symptoms of cerebral anemia.

You say 'I am more interested in developing the Bridges Adams enterprize' – but that is precisely what I am interested in too. We cannot develop it to any purpose with our present resources. We *must* have more money – at least £100,000 – & I believe if we can get £100,000, we can get £1,000,000.

Yours W.A.

PS Of course the first Director ought to be H. G.-B. but if he shirks, then Bridges Adams or some one of his kidney.

The **Phoenix Society** came into being after the war. A spin-off of the Stage Society, its aim was to stage Renaissance and Restoration drama. Between 1919 and 1925 it presented 26 plays, including works of Marlowe, Jonson, Farquhar, Congreve, Dryden, and Wycherley. Norman Wilkerson was the regularly designer; Edith Craig and Allan Wade (1881–1954) were directors. The first production on 23 and 24 November 1919 was Webster's *The Duchess of Malfi* (Lyric Hammersmith, 2 matinee perfs.). Among the performers were Cathleen Nesbitt (1888–1982), Robert Atkins (1886–1972), and Edith Evans (1888–1976). In a minor role was C. Scott Moncrieff (1889–1930) who most famously translated Proust's À *la recherche du temps perdu* as *Remembrance of Things Past.* Most of these people were a generation younger than Shaw and Archer (though some of the Phoenix regulars, like Wilkerson and Wade, first worked with Barker). The efforts of the Phoenix Society failed to satisfy Archer, who sought a national theatre not another version of the Stage Society on a shoestring budget. On 11 June, a day after this letter, Siegfried Sassoon (1886–1967) reported a conversation with Archer, who 'expressed extreme abhorrence for the Phoenix Society' (*Diaries 1920–2*, Faber, 1981: 171; Whitebrook: 379). The **S.N.T.** or Shakespeare National Theatre that Archer envisioned would be distinct from Bridges-Adams's Shakespeare Memorial Theatre. It would be a professional repertory company, located in London in its own building.

Lodges and Doyles: both Sir Oliver Lodge, who lost a son in the war, and Sir Arthur Conan Doyle were involved in the spiritualist movement, including the meetings of the Society for Psychical Research. They entertained ideas about the mind surviving death, and believed that it was possible to contact spirits from the netherworld. Archer himself investigated séances and clairvoyants in 1919 and 1920, in hope of making contact with his son Tom. But nothing came of these endeavours, so he dismissed the efforts (Whitebrook: 334–7). But it is noteworthy that in *The Green Goddess,* written during this same period, Archer introduced the topic of spiritual ties between the living and dead. In the last act Lucilla and Traherne are facing death. She wonders if she will still have contact with her children as a 'purified spirit.' Traherne replies: 'You may be with them this very night – with them, unseen, but perhaps not unfelt' (Goddess: 117). When Herbert **Beerbohm Tree** died in 1917, Archer wrote an obituary notice in *The Nation,* 4 October 1917. **H. G.-B.** was Harley Granville-Barker.

172 / To William Archer 10 Adelphi Terrace WC
13th June 1922

[ALS: V&A; GB 71THM/368/4/4/38]

This card is written in the hand of Blanche Patch, Shaw's secretary, but it is signed by him. His scepticism over the activities of the SMNTC *was apparently warranted, for six months later the* SMNTC *faced major difficulties in its operations. In response, Shaw sounded his public judgment in 'The Sad Case of Shakespeare: Memorial Muddle,' published in* The Observer *on 17 December (Biblio 2: 695). Then in 1925 its financial contributions to the Stratford-upon-Avon theatre company were declared illegal.*

Keep your hair on: you are perfectly welcome to your N.T. if you can get it: it will have a certain value for the drama as St Paul's has for religion; and far be it from me to kick a single brick from its ponderous walls. But I have done far more than my share for it; and now younger men may take up the running. They can have my blessing if they desire it.

I have arranged with Mrs Lyttelton for 3.30 on Thursday next, the 15th, and told her I would tell you.

G.B.S.

The wait for a **N.T.**, a National Theatre, would extend two generations beyond the SMNTC. Finally, with the births of the Royal Shakespeare Company in 1961 (Stratford-upon-Avon and the Alywych Theatre in London) and the National Theatre in 1963 (Old Vic Theatre, then the new National Theatre in 1977, both in London), the promise of a national theatre was fulfilled, with governmental funding for both operations. **Mrs Lyttelton** was a member of SMNTC's executive committee.

173 / To William Archer 10 Adelphi Terrace WC
8th June 1923

[TLS: BL 45296 ff 261–4]

There are no extant letters between 13 June 1922 and 8 June 1923. This letter is the first of six fully engaged exchanges between Shaw and Archer in the month of June 1923 on the topic of playwriting. The publication of Archer's new book, The Old Drama and the New: An Essay in Revaluation, *provided the catalyst for their debate. Archer had read (or reread) hundreds of plays for this study, which was based on 14 lectures he delivered to teachers at King's College in 1920 and 1921. The primary topic of the book is the history of English drama, which he placed within the history of theatre architecture, staging practices, and acting methods. Archer argued that the development of English drama since the Renaissance was a 'process of perfecting the element of Imitation, and gradually extruding the element of lyrical and exaggerative Passion' (142). Shaw admired several aspects of Archer's historical analysis, especially the chapters on Renaissance and Restoration drama, but he felt compelled to challenge Archer's ideas on realistic illusionism and plot construction. And he rejected Archer's assessment of his own plays. He therefore offered in this and the following letters a dramatic and a psychological critique of Archer's 'gaffes.' In turn, Archer defended his ideas on plot construction, and succeeded in getting Shaw to justify his method of writing that gave primacy to characterization and dialogue.*

In the sections of Old Drama *on Shaw's drama, Archer praised* Candida *as 'a pure work of art' (348), and had many positive things to say about* Mrs Warren's Profession, Arms and the Man, You Never Can Tell, The Devil's Disciple, Captain Brassbound's Conversion, John Bull's Other Island, *and* Major Barbara. *He quibbled, however, about the love-making scenes in several plays, and he repeated his long-standing complaint that the truculent behaviour of Blanche in* Widowers' Houses *was unnecessary. As for the discussion plays –* Getting Married, Misallance, *and* Heartbreak House *– he complained that they were 'without any structure.' Although Archer admired Shaw's talent for creating witty dialogue and fascinating characters, he felt that the late plays, in comparison to the earlier ones, lacked well-developed plots. Also, because Archer believed that playwriting, acting, and scenic design were supposed to culminate in modern times in the perfecting of realistic 'Imitation,' he was frustrated whenever Shaw deviated from this historical mandate. He remained adamant about this belief in the progressive development of drama.*

Despite these reservations, Archer insisted that Shaw had 'the most powerful intellect at present expressing itself in dramatic form, not only in England, but in the world' (355). 'Taking his prefaces with his plays, I think we are bound to acknowledge that he is one of the great voices of our time' (356). Yet here too Archer had a reservation. He lamented that Shaw lacked the ability to 'discipline his idiosyncrasies' (355). Unlike Shakespeare, Molière, and Ibsen, he had failed to suppress his personality in his playwriting (342). He took too much pleasure in 'guying his own genius' (350). The 'clowning' had limited his ability to influence human behaviour and political conditions in the modern era.

My dear W.A.

I have not had time to read The Old Drama and the New; nevertheless I *have* read it in three gulps, to the great delay and detriment of less postponeable matters.

On the whole I approve of it strongly for the same reason that led me to approve of the book on India. It is a challenge from a champion of civilization to the beachcombers, with their Beggar's Opera and their Phoenix bugaboo. The Englishman's civilization is always reluctant: he goes Fantee at every opportunity; and it is necessary for his own salvation that he should be soundly persecuted occasionally. I am delighted to see you play Grand Inquisitor, wiping the floor with the flabby souls whose battle squeak is *Tout comprendre: c'est tout pardoner.* Naturally, as I was one of the first to cock a snook at Lamb and Swinburne, I rejoice to see them receive the *coup de grâce* from you.

I think, however, that you will have to cultivate your main thesis both intensively and extensively in a lecture or series of lectures on the new drama alone. Hastily, here are a few points on which you might expatiate.

The Robertsonian stage is not the consummation of scenic illusion, but the repudiation of it, and the substitution of material reality. The modern stage drawingroom is a real drawingroom, with real furniture, carpet rugs, fireplace, windows and so forth. The fact that the walls are canvas instead of brick does not affect the situation. The missing fourth wall is only the invisible wall which every drawingroom has for us when we are in it. One of the effects of this new departure was to make the spectator conscious of the unrealities and absurdities of illusory scenery, and thus began the movement back to the Shakesperean stage.

The real drawingrooms crippled the drama very badly for a long time. It shrank to drawingroom topics and drawingroom treatment of them. Long speeches were dropped; and with them went all the large subjects which call for rhetorical treatment: religion, politics, philosophic comedy and everything interesting except adultery and fornication, and a little general theft and forgery. The mind of the theatre contracted to such an extent that Robertson and Pinero, whose culture was confined to that of theatrical society, were badly hampered in their constant attempts to follow Dickens and Thackeray and Trollope in getting away from the old notion of holding the mirror up to human nature, and holding it up to human society in its specific forms: the castes, the classes, the parties, the sects, and the professions. The titles of Robertson's plays shew this ambition; and his limits are set by his ignorance long before the natural limits of his intellectual capacity are reached. The same thing is true of Pinero, who is, like Robertson, an incorrigible preacher: every play since Letty has been a sermon, which is greatly to his credit. But (as you point out) it is the men who have come into the theatre from the big world outside it, and have wakened up its frightful ignorance, that have stretched the real stage drawingrooms to their utmost capacity. Take as the climax (so far) The Cherry Orchard and Heartbreak House. Here the stretch is partly due to the fact that drawingroom culture in real life has greatly developed since the days of Robertson. But still, the old set of drawingroom caricatures of social types are developed into psychological studies of social tendencies which gain intense dramatic interest from the fact that they are like the water near the brink of Niagara, hastening to the abyss.

But though nobody could have supposed 40 years ago that so much could be got into a villa and its garden, the drama can no more be kept within the limits of realistic staging than the fisherman's djinn could be kept within the sardine tin. In When We Dead Awaken Ibsen burst the realistic form hopelessly: his second act is a mechanical impossibility; and his third possible only on condition of being ridiculous. If I attempted to keep my Joan of Arc within the limits of realistic staging I could not possibly make it complete, as I should have to sacrifice to the stage carpenters at least 50 minutes of the three hours grudgingly granted to me for the entire performance; and I should also shatter the attention of the audience by making the representation like a motor ride interrupted by four bad punctures. I therefore go back to the Elizabethan stage, or at least the Granville Barker adaptation of it. Thus, though the convergence of drama towards a realism in illusion that ended in complete reality reached a focus in the XIX century, the rays were bound to cross and expand again into the old tribune stage from which gods and heroes pontificated on human destiny. Unless you seriously regard the development from Robertson to Tchekov and Shaw as a degeneration, making Sardou a summit in dramatic civilization, I do not think you can sustain your thesis that the Scribean cat's cradle represents play construction at its highest evolution.

Some of the charm of your book is a chintz and lavender charm of the age of literary innocence. There are passages that might have been written by Dr Watts. Your stage still allows no heroine more earthly than Walter Scott's plus George Eliot's: their little hands were never made to tear each other's eyes. You are still scandalized – after fortyfive years in England – at a world in which people are so quarrelsome that temper plays a very large part in their affairs; and the vulgar and violent daughter, only one remove from the washtub, of a *parvenu* father, still seems to you a monster that never was on sea or land. But the young people, and by this time even the middle-aged, will tell you that they find Blanche Sartorius a bit stilted and Victorian, though of course, a familiar type; and they tell me, not without some truth, that people in real life are never so good-humored as they are in my plays. And if you tell them face to face, as you do in the book, that I am a sophist and a mountebank (like John Wesley) heaven help you!

What leads you into these *gaffes*, which discount the impression made by your best pages, is that you are still in reaction against the Glasism of your grandfather. You are a bigoted rationalist materialist agnostic of the days of John Morley and Leslie Stephen and the old Westminster and Fortnightly Reviews. Well, more power to your elbow; but as a King's College professor you must face the fact that the drama has become metaphysical, and that Herbert Spencer, whose definition of evolution you have almost burlesqued in your formula of the evolution of the drama, has now been replaced by Bergson. The factors of creative energy and continuous inspiration, which had dropped completely out of the drama, and thereby reduced it to a barrenness in which plays had to be 'constructed' like artificial flowers, have been reintroduced, with the result that the drama has become vital again. It used to have only one vital subject (like Crofts in Mrs Warren's Profession): to wit, sex; and yet, as I pointed out in the preface to Man and Superman, its plays, with all their eternal triangles, and visits by innocent ladies to gentlemen's rooms at midnight, and duels and so forth, were really so sexless that even the gross profligacy of Restoration comedy was a relief from their wooden unreality. When I, instead of making plays out of dolls' divorce cases, put sex on the stage in a natural manner, I was held up between the old school who were unspeakably shocked, and the new school of young monkeys who complained that I was a Puritan. But if you compare the sex scene which is the climax of the last act of Man and Superman with anything written between Romeo and Juliet and the scenes the Kendals used to act, you will see that what occurred was a revolution. And if you compare the conversion scene in the second act of Major Barbara, and look for anything in the whole range of previous drama since medieval times to compare it with, you will find no case of a playwright who could for the moment have dreamt of such a thing as possible in the theatre, much less thrilling. It is perhaps because the ghost of your grandfather makes the Salvation Shelter repugnant to you that you neither feel the thrill nor the importance of the scene in dramatic history; but you cannot really handle the history of the theatre during your own time if you are insensible or recalcitrant to such changes. To leave out Wagner's Ring, Hardy's Dynasts, the third act of Man and Superman, and Back to Methuselah, or to imply that they are merely regrettable aberrations from the Scribe formula, is to commit a sort of retrospective suicide on the first night of The Silver King. You may approve or disapprove, like or dislike, agree or disagree; but to stand with the thing towering over your head and just pick up a pin like Arms and the Man and say you think this will last longer than anything else in the vicinity (on which point you may be right) is to put yourself in a situation which is ridiculous unless you shew that you are fully conscious of it.

I have no time for more. I am very glad you have stuck up for Barker, about whose future I am anxious, as the last play [*The Secret Life*] he sent me (after an interval which should have produced half a dozen masterpieces) seemed to me the fruit of a sybaritic and uxorious Henryjamesism from which I hope your tribute to his former greatness will rouse him. Also I think you have done Pinero a needed justice. As you know, I have always considered the Profligate-Tanqueray-Ellsmith outburst as a Parisian aberration for which there should now be an amnesty; but the subsequent phase that culminated in The Thunderbolt has never been sufficiently appreciated.

By the way, you should have said a word as to the effect of Ibsen on criticism. At his first onset he put up the standard to such a pitch that Shakespear was knocked silly – see my own criticisms of that date. What could the others expect?

Ever
G.B.S.

PS By the way, you have forgotten the details of our collaboration in Widowers' Houses. When I had finished the shorthand draft of the first act I went to you and said that I had not yet come to your plot and had forgotten it; so would you tell it to me all over again. This, after vehement protest, you at last consented to do, with the result that a few days after I said that I had used up all your story in the first two pages of the second act and wanted some more to go on with. On that you retired with dignity. I retired myself when, on my insisting on reading you what I had written, you fell fast asleep (I did not then know your inveterate Glasite habit). Of course I did not really want your scenario; but I found that when you told me the story it set my imagination working in its own way, which was a very genuine method of collaboration. But from the beginning I was utterly refractory to the Scribe formula, which I knew could produce only an artificial entertainment and not a natural dramatic growth. My plays are miracles of dramatic organization because I have never constructed them: there is not an ounce of dead wood in them: every bit of them is alive for somebody. To me constructed plays are all dead wood, bearable only for the sake of such scraps of sentiment or fun or observation as the artificer has been able to stick on them.

Archer's **book on India**, *India and the Future* (1917), criticized aspects of British rule, yet he was still convinced that the Raj empire could help India gain its freedom from the inhibiting rituals and religious beliefs which he opposed. The book displeased those who supported and those who opposed British colonialism. John Gay's *The **Beggar's Opera***, a burlesque of popular Italian opera, premiered in 1728. The **Phoenix** Society presented Thomas Otway's *Venice Preserved* in 1920. This production followed the company's initial 1919 production of John Webster's *The Duchess of Malfi*. In *Old Drama* Archer found fault with the two plays and the Phoenix productions (52–61, 110–15, 160–5). To go **Fantee** meant to go native, to adopt the habits of natives, as does the policeman Strickland in Rudyard Kipling's short story 'Miss Youghai's Sais' in *Plain Tales from the Hills* (1888). Archer criticized Charles **Lamb** (1775–1834) and Algernon Charles **Swinburne** (1837–1909) for their excessive praise of Renaissance and Restoration dramatists. 'Swinburne ... gave us the Lamb doctrine through a megaphone' (*Old Drama*: 29; also 52, 59–60, 65, 70). Years earlier in his theatre criticism Shaw had complained on three different occasions about the indiscriminate support for Renaissance and Restoration dramatists by Lamb and Swinburne (SatRev, 25 May 1895, 11 July 1896, 19 February 1898). In *Old Drama* Archer claimed that English drama produced only a few worthy plays between 1660 and 1860. He gave credit to **Tom Robertson** for revitalizing London theatre. His plays – *Society* (1865), *Ours* (1866), and *Caste* (1867) – had moved the stage forward 'in its progress towards verisimilitude – the genius of the common place' (260).

Ibsen's ***When We Dead Awaken*** (1899) displeased Archer, primarily because of its unrealistic features. He translated and published the play, but opposed a production by the New

Century Theatre Company. (See letter of 21 February 1900.) A.W. Pinero's ***Letty***, featuring Irene Vanbrugh, premiered on 8 October 1903 at the Duke of York's (122 perfs.). In one of his last theatre reviews Archer criticized the 1920 production of Chekhov's ***The Cherry Orchard.*** The acting was poor, but the larger problem was the dramatic method: 'Nothing whatever happens' (*Illustrated Sporting and Dramatic News*, 24 July 1920). He returned a week later to give the play a second chance, but he remained unimpressed (*The Star*, 31 July 1920; Whitebrook: 341–2). Shaw's **Joan of Arc** play, which he was still composing in June, was completed as *Saint Joan* in August when he was in Ireland (his last visit to his homeland). **Dr Isaac Watts** (1674–1748) was the nonconformist theologian and hymn writer. **John Wesley** (1703–91), an Anglican cleric, founded the evangelical movement of Methodism.

The religious doctrine of **Glasism** was propounded by John Glas, the founder of a religious sect that separated from the Kirk of Scotland in 1730. Archer's maternal grandfather James Morison and his mother Grace Morison were Glasites. Archer's paternal grandfather William Archer (1786–?) and his father Thomas Archer were Walkerites, part of a similar separatist sect founded in Dublin in 1804 by John Walker (1758–1833). Although Charles Archer informed Shaw in a letter of 18 August 1926 that 'no Archer ever was a Glasite' (HRC), the Archer family was exposed to both sects. At home in the 1860s young William Archer had to participate in the Sunday readings of the Bible, led by his father or grandfather. And during the early 1870s he was 'moderately regular' in his attendance at Glasite meetings (C. Archer: 35). In 'How William Archer Impressed Bernard Shaw' (Three Plays: vii–xxxvii; reprinted in Pen Portraits 1–32), Shaw presented a fairly accurate summary of these religious practices in the Morison and Archer families, and of Archer's break from all religious beliefs. But Shaw focused too exclusively on the Glasite heritage. (See Whitebrook: 3–9.) **John Morley**, a political radical and agnostic, was editor of the *Fortnightly Review* between 1866 and 1882. A supporter of Home Rule, he served as chief secretary for Ireland (1886, 1892–5) in the Liberal government of William Gladstone. In 1908, he became Viscount Morley. As a pacifist he opposed entry into the war. When the government declared war against Germany in 1914, he resigned from the Asquith cabinet. Sir **Leslie Stephen**, the father of Virginia Woolf, was an agnostic; he wrote regularly for the *Fortnightly Review* and other journals. In 1886 he published *History of English Thought in the Eighteenth Century*. Archer was not a **King's College professor**, but Shaw was referring to the series of fourteen lectures that Archer delivered there in 1920–1 on the history of British drama. He spent much of the spring and summer of 1922 revising the lectures into the book. For this letter Shaw made several handwritten corrections to mistyped words. At one point, upon correcting 'bareness' to **'barrenness,'** he added a marginal note: 'Forgive my typist: she knows not what she does.' **Herbert Spencer** applied – and often misapplied – Darwinian ideas on evolution to human history. Raised as a nonconformist, he developed systematic ideas about society, the individual, and progress. **Thomas Hardy** was one of the people Archer interviewed in *Real Conversations* (1904). Archer admired Hardy and wrote several reviews of his poems in the 1890s and 1900s. When Hardy's grand historical drama ***The Dynasts*** was published in 1904, Archer reviewed it. This epic drama on 'the war with Napoleon' was an ambitious attempt to enlarge upon the moral agendas of Leo Tolstoy's *War and Peace.* Ten years later, when H. Granville Barker staged an abridged version of the ambitious play at Lena Ashwell's Kingsway Theatre (71 perfs.), Archer provided a supportive review (*The Star*, 26 November 1914). Presented during the early months of the war in 1914–15, the production drew upon the patriotic spirit of the country (see Whitebrook: 313). ***The Silver King*** (1882, 289 perfs.) was a melodrama written by Henry Arthur Jones and Henry Herman. Shaw's complaint about the **sybaritic and uxorious Henryjamesism** in Barker's *The Secret Life* (1923) was repeated in his last letter to Archer on 14 December 1924. Besides praising Pinero's popular plays – *The Profligate, The Second Mrs Tanqueray,* and *The Notorious Mrs Ebbsmith* – in *Old Drama,* Archer made a case for ***The Thunderbolt,*** which 'has never been adequately appreciated' (320). Staged at the St James's Theatre in 1908, with Louis Calvert, George Alexander, and Stella Campbell, it had only 58 performances. Over the years Shaw and Archer offered contending versions of their failed **collaboration in Widowers' Houses**. The project began in 1884 as *The Way to a Woman's Heart*; it then became *Rhinegold,* then *Rheingold,* and finally *Widower's Houses* in 1892.

174 / To G. Bernard Shaw

27 Fitzroy Square W.
12th June 1923

[TLS: BL 50528 ff 75–7; copy in BL 45296 ff 365–6]

The day before he wrote this letter to Shaw, Archer had written to H. Granville Barker, offering a critique of Barker's new play The Secret Life. *Archer also commented upon Shaw's response to* The Old Drama and the New*: 'The same post that brought me your proofs brought a long epistle from G.B.S. He agrees with the* Times *reviewer in thinking me an old dodderer talking in my sleep about some obsolete fetish called 'construction.' But it's nonsense to say, like the* Times, *that construction is as exploded as the unities. The unities never had any common sense behind them, whereas construction is as common-sensical as the human skeleton – mankind, without it, would have only the intelligence of the oyster, or at best the bee ... Of course, I don't mean to say that* The Secret Life *is an unconstructed play, like* Heartbreak House, *which lives moment to moment by the mere shillelagh-whirling of its dialogue. The trouble is, I fancy that its construction is too subtle, too carefully dissembled. The mind gropes for it, and, not finding it, is disoriented.'*

In his analysis of The Secret Life, *Archer asked if the play was written for the stage or the study. He admitted that he did not understand it: 'I am at least three generations removed from it.' In an attempt to soften his criticism, he wrote: 'It is true I thought comparatively little of Ibsen's greatest play –* The Wild Duck *– the first time I read it. That ought to make one humble' (11 June 1923; BL 45290 ff 121–4).*

My dear G.B.S.

I spent all yesterday writing to Barker about his play. Today, fortunately, circumstances put a time-limit to my answer to your very welcomed epistle; for I must give the afternoon to Duse & GHOSTS. But what can be said in 2 ½ hours shall not be left unsaid.

In most of what you say about Robertson & Pinero I the more heartily agree as I have said it at greater length in my book. But I don't agree that the realism of externals consummated & symbolized in the 'box room' is exploded, or is ever likely to be. Not that I want to shut up all drama in the 'box room.' To every style its appropriate setting. But the power of reducing to a negligible minimum the element of convention in a stage setting is a real gain, which is not going to be renounced or suffered to fall into disuse. Of course it is being applied every day to the most trivial & vulgar ends; but it is none the less capable of being applied to the very highest ends. ROSMERSHOLM, perhaps the very summit of modern drama, not only lives & moves within a couple of box rooms, but is I am convinced (& I am sure Ibsen would agree with me) *dénaturé* & ruined by being treated symbolically or expressionistically or Craigishly in any form. The tragedy gains enormously by its commonplace surroundings. Place Ulric Brendel in a fantastic setting & you reduce *him* to commonplace. All Ibsen's prose plays are a demonstration of what can be done with the box room. Of course he did not confine himself to it – who would? – but he did not always gain by deserting it. The great acts of JOHN GABRIEL BORKMAN are the box-room acts. But Why drag in Ibsen? HEARTBREAK HOUSE, that Matterhorn among the lesser Alps of your theatre, is a box room play. Even the garden scene, as excellently staged in New York, was absolutely realistic. The box-room stage, in short, is an admirable tool for the attainment of a very high order of effect, & I see no reason to suppose that it will ever be abandoned till all mankind lives in palaces – or in caves.

The attempt to apply box-room principles to Shakespeare was, as every one admits, foolish & futile. Barker & Bridges Adams – Bridges Adams in particular – have arrived at an excellent compromise between the pictorial & the platform stage, & you do well to adopt it for Joan of Arc. But if you apply it to securing a nonstop performance, you go utterly wrong. The Act was a great invention of the Greeks, & no great dramatist has ever ignored it. Only ignorance maintains that Shakespeare did. The mechanical objection to the waste of time in changing scenes is wholly irrelevant. In the first place you may have as many acts as you like in a single scene; in the second place there are a hundred devices for reducing to next to nothing the time required for changing even a heavy scene. Why should we base our dramaturgic theories on the inadequate equipment of the modern London theatre? Your simile of a motor ride broken by four bad punctures is psychologically unsound. The attention of the average man or woman to even the most absorbing action or fascinating dialogue absolutely demands relaxation at intervals of from 30 to 45 minutes. The Greeks filled up the intervals with choral odes; the Elizabethans filled them, as we do, with irrelevant music, a practice I don't hold with, but the point is inessential. I don't think any interact should exceed five minutes; but the point is that there must be *some* breathing-space. And the need for a breathing-space providentially coincides with the need which the born dramatist (like me) feels to develop his action & his psychology by certain stages, which often demand a considerable lapse of imaginary time between stage & stage. We see therefore, dear brethren, that the Act was ordained by Jehovah before the world began, & that it is impious & damnable to rebel against it. Besides, what would become of the bars?

You don't seem able to grasp my objection to Blanche. It is not that she has a fiendish temper, but that her fiendish temper has nothing to do with the play. You seem now to justify it as a probable characteristic of a daughter of Sartorius. I admit Blanche is a more probable daughter of Sartorius than Candida of Burgess; but the case cannot be argued on the basis of abstract probability. The point is that, probable or improbable, this mental malformation is irrelevant. It is exactly what I have called it in my book – a red-herring across the trail. For you will scarcely pretend that Providence habitually afflicts slum-landlords with termagant daughters.

As to constructed plays: your arguments are valid only against *ill*-constructed plays, which of course abound. You speak as if I were a devotee of Scribe. I have insisted again & again that Scribe existed only to be outgrown & superseded. Scribe's function was so manifestly indispensable to the development of modern drama that I wouldn't mind betting that he has his analogues in other arts. For instance, I know nothing about the history of piano-playing: but was there not at some time a virtuoso who carried mere agility of manipulation, *Fingerfertigkeit*, to a previously unexampled pitch, which influenced all subsequent playing, though the greater men who came after learned it only to unlearn & renounce it? You think, it appears, that the future is to the unconstructed, amorphous play; I think it isn't; we are prophets between whom the future must decide. But I can call the whole past in witness. I said to Barker yesterday, & I say to you today: ALL THE PLAYS THAT HAVE HAD MORE THAN AN EPHEMERAL LIFE IN THIS WORLD ARE MORE OR LESS WELL-CONSTRUCTED PLAYS. I rack my brains to think of an exception to this rule.

As luck would have it, I have been twice in the last ten days to see MAJOR BARBARA. I went first of my own accord (& paid in); the second time I took Winthrop Ames to see some of the actors. I enjoyed it immensely both times; but I had a rather remarkable experience. After the second act, I took Ames to see Macdermott, & Macdermott said something about the fourth act of the play. I thought 'That's a slip of the tongue: of course he means the third act' – & I was positively amazed when the curtain rose on Lady Britomart's drawing-room, & not, as I had expected, on Undershaft's works. After an interval of one week I HAD FORGOTTEN THE EXISTENCE OF THE THIRD ACT, & thought we went straight from the Salvation Shelter to Undershaft's. My memory, I admit, is dreadful; but if anything essential had been done or said in the third act, do you think even I could have totally forgotten it? It amused me very much on the second hearing; likewise on the first; but now, four days later, I remember practically nothing about it. I am quite sure that if Act III had been casually omitted, not a soul in that theatre would have been conscious of any gap. *Is* it quite reasonable to cons [construct] – I mean to emit plays in which an act can be dropped out without leaving a perceptible hiatus?

I have only a few minutes left to deal with your old superstition about my hard-shell rationalism. Why, even Dean Inge sees that I am not a rationalist in any offensive sense of the word; & only last night I had a letter from Galsworthy accusing me of having abandoned the whole rationalist position in the enclosed pamphlet. The trouble with me is that I am too old a metaphysician to be taken in by metaphysics. I know too well that each new philosophy is only a new terminology – in fact a new dialect – &, fundamentally, a new failure to express the inexpressible. I don't despise the inexpressible – in a sense, there is nothing else that matters. But in expressible things I think reason, however imperfect, is the best & only guide we have. The trouble with you, on the other hand, is that you are incurably credulous. Someone comes along & tells you that wool is the only wear; & instantly you go in for woolen boots, which lead, in due time, to a course of crutches. Then Wagner comes along, & you are a

Wagnerite. Ibsen, & you are an Ibsenite (I never was); Nietzsche, & you are a Nietzschean; Bergson, & you are a Bergsonian. And all the time you are no whit nearer the real secret of things. All these men, I admit, had something to say, though Nietzsche to my mind was only a crackbrained poseur who was vastly overrated in his little day. But the best of them has only advanced the border of light a little way, & has shed no penetrating beam into the surrounding darkness. What has Wagner's Ring to do with the English acted drama, which happens to be my subject? You might as well blame me for leaving out the Book of Job. Of course if I were writing a series of twelve lectures upon *you*, I should have to try to estimate the influence of Wagner upon you, in spite of my ignorance of music & my insensibility to much the greater part of it. But at King's College I could only give about a quarter of one lecture – that is to say a quarter of an hour – to you. As for the 'Dynasts,' I think it a magnificent thing, & have said so; but it does not belong, & is not intended to belong, to the English acted drama. You think my criticism of you narrow, peddling, rationalistic, almost mid-Victorian; & of course it does not begin to deal with your philosophy. But, believe me, your philosophy would last longer & would carry further – your *influence* both present & to come would be far, far greater – if your works were not open to my narrow & niggling criticism. I admit it does not touch the essence of your *Wesen*; but so far as it goes it is right & important. I would give a great deal to think that it wasn't.

Who but must laugh if such a man there be?
Who would not weep if G.B.S. were he?
I am much more inclined to weep than to laugh.

Yours always
W.A.

The **shillelagh**, named after a village in County Wicklow, Ireland, was a club or cudgel, often made from the local oak trees. Eleonora **Duse**, who had not appeared in England since Ellen Terry's Jubilee in 1906, performed in May and June 1923 at the New Oxford Theatre, the converted music hall. Sixty-three years old, she presented matinee productions of Ibsen's *Ghosts* and *The Lady from the Sea*. After London, she went to America for her last tour. She died in Pittsburgh in 1924. Archer was opposed to **Craigishly** scene design in the 1920s, but he had praised aspects of Gordon Craig's scenic, lighting, and costume designs for Ibsen's *The Vikings at Helgeland* in 1903 (see letter of 15 April 1903). In *Rosmersholm* **Ulric Brendel** is the revolutionary figure who had once been the tutor of Johannes Rosmer. He returns to the village to give a lecture, but discovers that he has nothing to say. In November 1920 **HEARTBREAK HOUSE** had been staged in New York by the Theatre Guild. Archer saw the production when he was in New York for the rehearsals and opening of his play *The Green Goddess*. ***Fingerfertigkeit*** is the German noun for a nimble-fingered skill or talent in musical performance. **Winthrop Ames**, who had produced *The Green Goddess* in New York City, was in London to oversee the London production, which opened on 6 September at the St James's Theatre (416 perfs.). Norman **Macdermott** (1889–1977) was the producer, manager, and designer who founded the Everyman Theatre in Hampstead. He staged several 'Shaw Seasons' in the early 1920s. Archer was not alone in finding **Act III** of *Major Barbara* forgettable; when Max Beerbohm reviewed the production in 1905, he made a similar complaint (SatRev, 9 December). In his capacity as dean of St Paul's Cathedral from 1911 to 1934, William Ralph **Inge** (1860–1954) often commented upon philosophical topics and social issues in his publications, including *Outspoken Essays* in 1919 and *Outspoken Essays, Second Series* in 1922. The **enclosed pamphlet** was Archer's *The Dean's Apologia … (Dean Inge Answered)* (London: Watts & Co., 1923). The pamphlet, which presented a secular critique of the Dean's ideas, was an expanded version of Archer's review in 1922 of the *Second Series*. Shaw was on **crutches** in 1898 and 1899 when he had two operations on his foot because of a bone infection. It was a stretch, of course, to blame Shaw's woollen boots for the disability, but at the time some people blamed his vegetarian diet. **Wesen** is the German noun for the concepts of being, essence, nature, substance, and character. For the couplet that concluded this letter, Archer modified Alexander Pope's *Epistle to Dr Arbuthnot* (1734), which served as a prologue to Pope's *Imitations of Horace*: '**Who but must laugh**, if such a man there be? / Who would not weep, if Atticus were he?' Atticus was Pope's representation of the writer Joseph Addison.

175 / To William Archer

Ayot St Lawrence, Welwyn, Herts.
19th June 1923

[TLS, with APCU postscript; BL 45296 ff 267–70; CL 3 partial]

The recurring debate about 'plot construction,' which served as the primary topic of these six spirited letters in June 1923, had its distant origin in the attempt of the two friends to write a play together in 1884 and 1887. Their anecdotal accounts of the unsuccessful partnership can be traced in several of their letters, including those of 4 October 1887, 14 December 1892, and 24 and 27 March 1893. Archer had articulated his version of those events in his review of Widowers' Houses *in 1892, explaining that he had provided a 'rounded and perfect organic plot' for* Rheingold, *but Shaw had misused it. Then in May 1893, when Shaw's first play was published, he delivered his rebuttal: 'I had then, have now, and have always had, an utter contempt for "constructed" works of art' (CP 1: 40). Over the following years, they occasionally renewed this debate about dramatic plotting, especially when Shaw published a new play. Then, with the publication of* Old Drama, *Archer revived the topic of the writing of* Rheingold. *Not surprisingly, Shaw felt compelled to counter with his own memory, as he did in the letter of 8 June 1923. Each of them insisted that his memory provided not only the accurate history but also the correct interpretation of what happened and why.*

It should be clear that their basic disagreement over playwriting was not really about organic versus mechanical plots, for both of them were advocates for organic plots. In this sense, as Michael Holroyd concluded, Archer and Shaw, 'by their own accounts, ... were each saying roughly the same thing' ever since their dispute in 1987 (Holroyd 1: 276). As theatre critics they had been comrades in the battles against the French well-made play, which Shaw had dismissed as 'Sardoodledom' (SatRev, 1 June 1895). And even years before Shaw fired his guns at the French playwrights and their British imitators, Archer had dismissed the well-made play of France in several essays and reviews (e.g., 'The Dying Drama,' New Review, *September 1889). But if they were in the same camp, why did they argue so intensely and repeatedly over plot construction? Were they just having sport with one another? Or were they in fact saying the same thing, yet unable to recognize and acknowledge their shared perspective? It seems most unlikely that this was a case of mutual blindness, yet they continued to argue.*

At least one thing is obvious. In 1923 Shaw gained the rhetorical advantage by portraying Archer as the defender of artificial and mechanical plays, such as those written by Scribe. From his opening statement in this letter of 19 June – with the witty dismissal of Archer's 'impervious knowledge box' – Shaw took control of the debate, even though the yoking of Archer to Scribe and Sardou was, as he must have known, a false ploy. Yet Shaw was not merely scoring rhetorical points. He gained control of the debate in this letter because his vision of modern drama was far more expansive than the one that Archer presented in Old Drama. *Shaw understood and appreciated how modern drama in the twentieth century was developing.*

But Archer, despite his progressive and sometimes revolutionary campaigns in the theatre for over four decades, was becoming conventional and prescriptive in his artistic judgments. He ignored – or failed to recognize – that Shaw's discussion plays, though unconventional, could still be well constructed. Ibsen's plays were important to Shaw when he wrote Candida, Mrs Warren's Profession, *and even* Pygmalion, *but they no longer provided the guiding light for* Misalliance, Getting Married, *and* Heartbreak House. *Shaw had opened up new possibilities for dramatic form that Archer could not accept. Just as he was unable to appreciate the brilliance of Chekhov's plays, he could not perceive the creative order of* Heartbreak House.

My dear W.A.

Oblige me with a hammer, a saw, a beetle and a couple of wedges that I may operate on your all but impervious knowledge box.

There is no such thing as an amorphous play. That Boyg of the theatre need not make you anxious, because he is impossible; and your Peerlike slashes at him will only wear your heart out. There are, as you say, bad plays; but as most of them are 'constructed' plays, and the great plays of the world, including the most perfect in form, are not constructed, the bad plays do not help you.

The plain fact is that there are two sorts of plays: natural growths and constructions, just as there are two sorts of flowers, natural ones and artificial ones (made mostly in France). Just as the doctors of the second half of the XIX century were able to do some very clever things, and even occasionally benefit their patients, by treating the human body as if it represented a purely mechanicalcumchemical problem; so the playwrights of that godless period did some very clever things, and occasionally pleased their audiences, by treating the plays as if they presented a mechanistic problem only. But the success was never due to the construction, but always to the attraction of the performers and of such scraps of wit and humanity as the artificers were able to stick on to their frame of 'dead wood.' When dramatic invention revived, and the constructive method was contemptuously scrapped, it was found that bushels of these constructed plays could be cut down to half hour sketches with great advantage, because the only vital bit was the 'situation' at the end of the last act but one. The audience were spared the tedium of watching the scaffolding brought in (the exposition) and then removed (the last act, which was so seldom even a denouement). Now it is not impossible for a genuine dramatic poet to go through the ceremony of constructing his play. Ibsen constructed his Doll's House in the French manner: I remember being startled by its artificiality the *second* time I saw it. Considering that he had begun by writing plays in asides and so forth (Lady Inger is an appalling example) it was just as well that he did. It was a progress from a greater artificiality to a less: besides, he clothed the cucumber frame with such a wealth of living flower and fruit, all quite stout stemmed enough to dispense with it, that it did not matter, just as it did not *always* matter (it often did) when Mozart tied his operatic numbers down to sonata frames. But it did matter with the lesser practitioners: their scenarios and sonata forms killed them.

When you are writing a play it is of the first importance that you should not for a moment allow your attention and interest to be diverted from the interest proper to drama: that is, an interest common to yourself and your audience. Now the interest of carrying out a scenario is like the interest of piecing together a jigsaw puzzle: it has nothing whatever to do with dramatic interest, and though it is absorbing to the operator, it is unbearably dull to the lookeron. You must always go where the dramatic interest takes you; and if you do this you will find that the dramatic interest, a live thing, will organize itself so marvellously (like the natural flower) that the final result will be held up by critics as a triumph of construction. But the moment you let yourself be seduced into the jigsaw business, your audience will begin to cough unless the actor or actress can keep it enthralled by personal fascination. When the fascinating London casts refused to tour; and the constructed plays went on tour with ordinary actors, the provincial theatre died of them. And when the natural drama revived in London it turned out that the fascinators could not act. They had complained bitterly that the authors expected them to make bricks without straw; but when the straw was provided they did not know what to do with it.

The colossal absentmindedness of your discovery that Blanche Sartorius's temper 'has nothing to do with the play,' is a choice Archerism, by which I mean a prodigy of stupidity by a conspicuously clever man. Yet it is a necessary consequence of your assumption that the incidental peg on which a play hangs is the play itself. In Widowers' Houses your peg was the mistake of a young man who wooed the poor heroine and then found out that she was the rich one. My peg was the unsuspected social and economic reaction of a mortgage. If, as you contend, the peg's the thing, then undoubtedly a perfectly placid Blanche could have had her income mistaken and married a man with a mortgage on her father's property just as well as an irritable one. Blanche's savage temper, like Mrs Tanqueray's malicious temper and Hotspur's apoplectic temper, are as gratuitous as the frescoes in the Sistine Chapel are irrelevant to the construction of that building. Mrs Tanqueray might have been Sweet Lavender and yet met an old lover inopportunely. Hotspur might have been Hamlet and Falstaff Malvolio without affecting the battle of Shrewsbury. Indeed any character at all on their part is an irrelevance, which explains why it was that the constructed drama did not produce any Hotspurs and Falstaffs, Hamlets and Malvolios. When you start arguing like the unimpeachably logical Regan in King Lear you soon get rid of every element of real drama as effectually as she got rid of Lear's knights, and on exactly the same ground, that of superfluity. You cut Shakespear on the same principle, and get rid at once of the last act of The Merchant of Venice, written through Shakespear's oversight of the fact that 'the play' (meaning the pound of flesh) was over. You clear out the third act of Major Barbara; and you shoot off St John Ervine's leg, as he writes just as well without it. And when you have cleared all the clothes off the peg, you will find that the peg is no use without any clothes to hang on it; and you will clear that away too.

My plays and their acts and their characters happily exist for their own sake, and not for that of any peg or plot or scenario; and if you don't like them you can lump them.

There *is* a limit to the endurance of an audience; but it is the limit to the endurance of a railway passenger in a carriage without a corridor or of a diver under the sea. That limit has long been fixed at two hours, which is the length of the first act of Die Götterdämmerung and the last act of Die Meistersinger. Bridges Adams does Hamlet with one interval of 10 minutes; and it is quite enough. Your 30 to 45 minutes is the limit of the acts of a constructed play in three acts when the carpenters have to strike and set between them: it has no relation on earth to human endurance, as any orchestral concert at Queen's Hall will shew you.

I agree that the plays written for the box room stage should be played in box rooms on the general principle that every play ought to be performed under the conditions for which the author planned it when he was not under duress and making the best of a bad job. But you may have noticed that at the Everyman, where there is a conventional stage adapted by a few mere hints to the three scenes of Major Barbara, the effect is just as good, and in the last act distinctly better, than it was at the Court Theatre, where there were three scenes, solemnly painted with views of East Ham, Perivale, and Wilton Crescent. The four scenes of The Doctor's Dilemma are played in that same conventional scene, and are equally and sufficiently effective.

It is no use defending such horrors of boredom as Hackett's production of Macbeth, with its mutilations and interminable entr'actes, by saying that with a revolving stage the most elaborately built up sets could have been made to succeed one another as quickly as the turns at the Coliseum. The drama has to live in the theatre as it is, and not as it might be if every play licensed for theatrical entertainments had a Utopian equipment. If plays cannot endure a good deal of managerial poverty the drama will perish. I say nothing of the first act of Pygmalion in the Ring Theatre in Vienna, where they shewed not only the porch of St Paul's (the wrong church, of course), but the Tower of London, the British Museum, Westminster Abbey with the Houses of Parliament and the Thames flowing down the middle of the stage, and the whole British fleet, submarines and all, manoeuvring on it. It was magnificent, and would have delighted you; but not a line of my act secured the attention of the ravished audience. What I do say is that your photographic and finally cinematographic would-be illusive scenery is as deadly to drama as your confounded scenarios, because, like all merely mechanical photography, it is utterly unselective, whereas the imagination, skilfully prompted, selects just what is necessary and no more. Crummles with his pump and two tubs could produce Arcadia, whilst the Ring Theatre, insisting on the whole of Kew Gardens, with a thousand varieties of real flowers, could produce nothing but a curiosity like the chariot race in Ben Hur, guaranteed to distract the attention of any audience from the play. Nothing requires more judgment than a realistic stage, because the first condition of dramatic success is that it should not be real.

I must stop. I have read the Inge pamphlet. I reviewed that book of his for The Nation, and made quotations from The Dean and The Philosopher alternately and so forth. But I do not see the use now of calling your grandfather's Bible worship Christianity. You have to count nowadays with the preface to Androcles and the Lion.

By the way, I have never met Winthrop Ames. If he would care to meet me, and you would care to fetch him along, I daresay we could arrange lunch for Thursday* or Friday the 28th or 29th. All my London days are jam full until then; but if he is going away before then I might manage to see him in the country, as we are within an hour of King's Cross via Hatfield and thence by car.

Ever,

G. Bernard Shaw

*PS Since writing the above I have had to make a lunch engagement for the 28th which bars Ames as far as that meal is concerned.

The **Boyg** is a character in *Peer Gynt.* Ibsen's ***Lady Inger*** *of Östråt,* a history play, was written in 1853 and revised in 1874. It was staged in London on 28 January 1906 at the Scala Theatre (2 perfs.), with Edyth Olive (c. 1872–1956) in the lead role. The translation by Charles Archer was revised by William Archer for his edition of *The Works of Henrik Ibsen* (1906–8, 12 vols). Archer remained troubled by **Blanche Sartorius's temper** in *Widowers' Houses.* Ever since his review of the 1892 production, Archer had expressed his distaste for Shaw's portraits of certain kinds of hard-edged women, especially if they lacked social propriety and displayed an aggressive sexuality. Archer expressed this judgment in his review of *Plays Pleasant and Unpleasant.* (See letter of 21 April 1898.) ***Sweet Lavender*** (1888), a sentimental drama, was written by A.W. Pinero. Shaw had previously teased Archer that he was a sentimentalist who 'gushes over *Sweet Lavender*' (SatRev, 13 April 1895). Shaw's comment that Archer would **shoot off St John Ervine's leg** was a reference to Ervine's wound in the trenches during the war that resulted in the amputation of his leg in 1918. The **Everyman** Theatre revived *Major Barbara* on 27 August 1923. *The Doctor's Dilemma* was staged by the Everyman in both 1921 (Edy Craig as director) and 1923 (Norman Macdermott as director, with Claude Rains and Cathleen Nesbitt). Between 1921 and 1924 Macdermott produced 17 of Shaw's plays, all with limited scenic effects. Edy Craig directed seven productions in 1921. For most of the other productions between 1922 and 1924 Macdermott served as the director and designer. In November 1920 at the Aldwych James K. **Hackett** (1869–1926), a Canadian actor who had established himself in the United States, portrayed Macbeth, with Mrs Patrick Campbell as Lady Macbeth. Shaw commented on her acting in a letter to her on 22 December 1920 (Dent: 245–7). The production had numerous cuts in what is Shakespeare's shortest play. The London **Coliseum**, built in 1904 by Oswald Stoll (1866–1942), was a venue for music hall and vaudeville performers who presented their brief **turns** or routines, one after another. The **Ring Theatre in Vienna** was devastated by a fire in 1881, and was not rebuilt. *Pygmalion* premiered at the Burg Theatre in October 1913. It also had productions in Prague and Budapest before its London opening in April 1914. In Dickens's *Nicholas Nickleby* **Crummles** is a touring actor. Both the novel of **Ben-Hur** (1880) by Lew Wallace (1827–1905) and the London stage production by William Young (1847–1920) concluded with a grand chariot race (3 April 1902, Drury Lane, 122 perfs.). The stage version had horses running on treadmills. The musical called *Arcadians* (not ***Arcadia***) was a fantastic spectacle with elaborate scenic effects; it opened on 28 April 1909 at the Shaftesbury Theatre (810 perfs.). It was one of the major musical successes of the Edwardian era (Gänzl 1: 1029–34, 1041–3). In the **preface** to ***Androcles and the Lion*** Shaw offered his updated version of Christianity that reinterpreted the books of the New Testament and reimagined Jesus in terms of modern theories of economics and biology. On the **Inge pamphlet** see endnote for 12 June letter. Shaw reviewed Dean Inge's *Outspoken Essays, Second Series* in *The Nation* on 9 December 1922 (Pen Portraits: 161–8). He had previously reviewed the first series of *Outspoken Essays* on 22 November 1919 (Tyson 2: 406–12; Pen Portraits: 154–61). The **Bible worship** of Archer's maternal grandfather was Glasism. The religious practice of the paternal grandfather was Walkerism. Shaw ignored – or was unaware of – these distinctive branches of Scottish Protestantism. (See letter of 8 June 1923.)

176 / To G. Bernard Shaw

27 Fitzroy Square W.
20th June 1923

[TLS; BL 50528 ff 78–9; copy in BL 45296 f 271]

My dear G.B.S.

It won't do. In your determination to defend your later manner of play-writing against all the rest of the world, your earlier self included, you have undertaken to re-make the English language. I say a cat is a quadruped, with a brain, a backbone, and (unless of the Manx variety) a tail. You say, 'Oh no – a cat is a round, mushy, iridescent object with long streamers, usually observed on the shingle at low tide.' 'Why' I reply, 'that is not a cat but a jelly-fish.' 'Nonsense!' you say, 'Your natural history is mid-Victorian. It may have been called a jelly-fish about 1870; but Tchekhov has changed all that, & we now call it a cat – & furthermore the only admissible form of cat. It is true that Shakespeare, Ibsen, Sophocles & other pre-Tchekhovians had not *quite* mastered the art of dispensing with vertebrae. But by carefully neglecting the articulations of their works, we can reduce them to very plausible imitations of the Tcheko-Shavian cat.'

The substantial points on which we differ are really few, though not quite unimportant. Your wild & whirling methods of dialectic make them seem greater than they really are. We differ as to HEARTBREAK HOUSE; we don't really differ as to THE WILD DUCK, ROSMERSHOLM, HEDDA GABLER, and THE MASTER BUILDER, though it suits you to call them unconstructed plays, whereas in fact they are the most complex jig-saw puzzles ever invented in this world. Ibsen was as convinced a constructor as Sardou; but he was also a poet, & he had elaborated the art (in which he had been anticipated by Sophocles) of constructing his plays backwards instead of forwards, whereby he gave them a new depth & richness of texture.

As to the question of the act, you confound *attention* with *retention.* It is possible for human beings to sit still in one place for 2 hours & even considerably longer without suffering unbearable physical discomfort; but it does not follow that they won't suffer severe mental discomfort if they have to sit for two hours, unsoothed or unstimulated by music, listening to your characters scoring off each other. I know too little of music to judge how far it affects the question of attention; but I am inclined to think you are wrong if you imagine that any considerable proportion of a Wagner audience do not feel their attention overstrained by his stupendous non-stop efforts.

It would save a great deal of time & type-ribbon if you could get it out of your head that I want to cut either Shakespeare or Ibsen in order to fit them to a narrowly realistic stage. As to Shakespeare, I entirely approve the common-sense principles laid down by Granville Barker in the preface to his new edition, & the practice of Bridges Adams. I don't approve the ignoring of the act division, but I don't want it marked by any lapse of time worth mentioning. As for Ibsen, you once accused me of cutting him 'to the bone.' I said that, coming from any one else, that would be a very serious accusation; upon which you said that I called you a liar. Of course that was nonsense – I meant that everyone made allowance for your habit of wild exaggeration where it suited your argument. The truth is that (apart from my 'adaptation' of PILLARS OF SOCIETY away back in 1880) I never cut a line in Ibsen that was translateable into comprehensible English. That means, perhaps, on an average, three lines in each play. The only passage I can think of that calls for any cutting worth mentioning is the dialogue between the Chamberlains at the beginning of THE WILD DUCK – & even that (to the best of my recollection) I never cut, because I was never actively concerned in a production of the play. When I talk of cutting incomprehensible lines, I of course don't mean incomprehensible on account of any obscurity or subtlety of thought, but on account of the sheer linguistic difficulty in finding an English equivalent. There are Norwegian customs &c. quite unknown in England, which it is impossible to make comprehensible without a footnote. Surely even you would admit that the dialogue of a play should not need footnotes. And the passages in Ibsen (I speak of his modern plays) to which this applies are infinitesimal in number & extent.

To return to yourself, let me put your history in a nutshell. I remember perfectly your saying to me that you were a whale on dialogue, but could not invent a plot, or words to that effect. I believe you actually used the word 'plot' – nowadays an obscenity, but in those days as current in polite speech as 'whore' in Elizabethan. Therefore I undertook to provide you with a plot – & hence WIDOWERS' HOUSES. Then in THE PHILANDERER you tried to do without plot, but it didn't work. Then, being diabolically clever, you saw that you must tackle this uncongenial art, & from MRS WARREN onwards you invented some quite good plots. But you never had the patience to finish them off respectably – except in the case of CANDIDA. You either lost interest in your last acts, or you were content with glaringly artificial devices, like the idiotic conduct of Anderson in THE DEVIL'S DISCIPLE in rushing off without telling his wife what he was going to do. Then, when you found yourself independent of the ordinary manager & the ordinary public, you promptly threw plot overboard – no, I am wrong, you did it gradually – & at last convinced yourself that the ideal drama was a non-stop logomachy. Well, that was all right for you – no one wants to prevent you from abounding in your own sense. But I, for one, call a halt when you want me to believe that this was the ideal of Shakespeare, Ibsen, & the great men of the past.

Unfortunately Ames returns to America on Saturday. His wife is expecting a baby, & it is uncertain whether he will even be able to be here for the last rehearsals of THE GREEN GODDESS. He goes to the Barkers' tomorrow but will be in town again on Friday. I am sure if he thought he could meet you, he would come back by the earliest possible train. Couldn't you manage to be in town on Friday afternoon? Ames is at the Berkeley Hotel, Piccadilly.

Yours, with head nor bloody nor bowed,

W.A.

In 1923 **Granville Barker** began to publish his *Prefaces to Shakespeare.* On 21 June 1923 Archer sent detailed notes to him on the proofs for the prefaces to *Cymbeline* and *Macbeth.* In 1880, before he met Ibsen in Rome, Archer made an **adaptation** of *The Pillars of Society.* It was entitled *Quicksands,* and had a single performance. Despite Shaw's accusations in 1903, 1919, and now in 1923, Archer was not responsible for the cuts in the first act of *The Wild Duck,* as staged by the Independent Stage Society in 1894. (On this recurring disagreement about the cutting of plays see the letters of 2 and 8 September 1903 and 6 September 1919.) Shaw portrayed himself as the absolute defender of playwrights, whose plays should never be cut in performance. But in fact he sometimes sanctioned cuts in his own plays, and he also called for cuts in plays by other playwrights. For example, when the Stage Society was considering James Joyce's *Exiles* for production, Shaw insisted that the text should be 'blue penciled' because of obscene words. He vetoed a production (Holroyd 3: 199). Archer's idea of **the act division** in Shakespeare's plays and Greek tragedies does not accord with scholarship today on how the plays were written and staged – in scenes, not acts. These plays have often been published, however, with act divisions. Yet again, in the argument over **plot** and **dialogue**, Archer responded to the writing of *Rheingold,* which became **WIDOWERS' HOUSES** in 1892. See headnote for the letter of 19 June 1923 for a summary on this disagreement.

In *Old Drama* Archer did not comment upon the **idiotic conduct of Anderson** in *The Devil's Disciple,* but a decade earlier in *Play-Making* (309–10) he had complained that in the second act when Reverend Anthony Anderson rushes out of the house without any explanation of his intentions, Shaw unnecessarily kept Anderson's wife and the audience in the dark. The phrase **with head nor bloody nor bowed** is a modification of the second stanza of the poem 'Invictus' by William Ernest Henley (1849–1903):

In the fell clutch of circumstances
I have not winced nor cried aloud
Under the bludgeonings of chance
My head is bloody, but unbowed.

The poem, written in 1875 when Henley was struggling to save his second leg from amputation, concludes 'I am the master of my fate. / I am captain of my soul.' A century later this poem became important to Nelson Mandela (1918–2013) during his 27 years of imprisonment in South Africa.

177 / To William Archer

10 Adelphi Terrace WC
22nd June 1923

[TLS, with handwritten postscript: BL 45296 ff 272–4; CL 3 partial]

This is the fifth and perhaps the most important of the June letters. Except for the removal of one sentence and the postscript, Dan Laurence included this letter in the Collected Letters. *And in his headnote he provided three paragraphs from Archer's letter of 20 June.*

Archer's unbending defence of the principle of plot construction led Shaw to pause temporarily in his debate with Archer in order to explain his own creative methods as a playwright. Although Shaw began this letter with a typically aggressive reply and closed with a renewed attack, he felt compelled to offer an explanation of how his plays were written (if not constructed). By distinguishing between his and Ibsen's creative techniques, he identified the 'vital process' by which 'the first crystallizations of the magic fluid' generated a new play for him. Creativity occurred first, craftsmanship came second. But instead of dismissing the concept of plot construction, as he had done in the previous letters, Shaw granted that a partnership existed between creativity and craftsmanship. Imagination was paramount but it was not exclusive.

To Archer's credit, he got this explanation from Shaw by doggedly proclaiming his own theory of plot construction – by way of Aristotle, Ibsen, and his own progressive ideas on evolution. In this case, Archer was the apriorist, *and Shaw, if we take him at face value, was the artist of vital organic processes. He did not explain, however, how these creative moments occurred in relation to theoretical ideas derived from Nietzsche, Bergson, or anyone else.*

My dear W.A.

You haven't got it yet. The alternatives are not a cat and a jellyfish, but a clockwork cat and a live cat. The clockwork cat is very ingenious and very amusing (for five minutes); but the organisation of the live cat beats the construction of the mechanical one all to nothing; and it amuses you not for an age but for all time.

Ibsen's method was the vital method, not the mechanical one. Instead of writing a play straight away, as I do, he wrote stories about his characters until he knew them and their histories quite intimately. Then he arranged the result for the stage. My way is not essentially different. I write my dialogue (which involves creating the characters and doing all the vital work), as it comes. I then go over it and arrange it for the stage. This, though it often takes longer than the creative operation, is a mere matter of cleverness and craftsmanship; though nothing seems more amazing than the apparently miraculous way in which the vital process provides for the mechanical one. Developments of character created purely as such turn out to be indispensable cogs in the stage engrenage.

I have never used any other procedure than this. Once, in the case of Captain Brassbound's Conversion, when I used an actual case brought forward by Cornwall Lewis in the House of Commons, and described to me by the late Frederick Jackson of Hindhead, I did work to a rough plan of the exposition of the case which makes the first act smell a little of the workshop; but in no other case did I depart from the path of pure inspiration. But sometimes the thing begins with a situation or even a quite trivial repartee. Thus The Devil's Disciple began with the situation of the arrest of Dudgeon, John Bull's Other Island with the Irishmen laughing at the accident to the pig and the motor car and the Englishman taking it seriously, and Man and Superman with 'I am a brigand: I live by robbing the rich' 'I am a gentleman: I live by robbing the poor' – a complete irrelevance. But these are only the first crystallizations of the magic fluid: I do not work constructively to them: they simply suggest people to whom they might have happened; and these people behave as God pleases.

Mrs Warren's Profession is a crude melodrama; and The Philanderer is a tragicomedy (exquisitely put together, as I perceived when I saw it at the Everyman lately) on the very subtle subject of the operation of the

Ibsenist changes in feeling about marriage and sexual relations in a society mainly quite impervious to Ibsen, even when it tried to be fashionably advanced in his name. But they were both created in the same way. The only differences are purely circumstantial: for instance, the first scene of The Philanderer is an artistic version of a scene that actually occurred; and Mrs Warren's Profession was written to please Beatrice Webb by introducing to the stage the Vivie Warren type of modern girl and dramatizing a strong social and economic subject. But neither play is a ravelling and unravelling of a plot: both are straightforward stories depending for their interest on their present action, and for their significance on their roots in the past and suggestions of the future. My play grows until it stops, just as an animal does. If, as in the case of Methuselah, it grows until it takes two afternoons and three evenings to perform, well, that is its natural size. If, like Androcles, it is not long enough to fill an evening, well, something else must fill up the bill. After all, when you come to think of it, there is no other way in which the size of any work of art can come to be determined.

I give you these as the facts of my case. Your notion that I found that The Philanderer 'did not work' is an illusion. It was an unlucky play. Barker's extreme dislike of it, and my own shrinking from production (a sort of neurosis with me that I shall never get over), to say nothing of the unfamiliarity of its subject and the demands it makes on at least two of the actors, kept it from the stage at the Court Theatre for a long time; and when at last it was rehearsed and Lillah was ready with a very fine performance of Julia, she collapsed and had to undergo an operation. The public result was deplorable; but I had seen enough of the play at rehearsal to know that it was a first rate acting play. If you ever see an adequate performance of it, it will convert you to my method. Put out of your head for ever the notion that it put me out of conceit with it.

I saw Duse yesterday in The Lady From The Sea, with scenery that would have converted Augustus Harris to the Elizabethan stage. It was a display, wonderful to the rising generation, of her old gestures, inflections and moods, totally unrelated to the play except to the extent to which all competent stage work is related to every play, until Wangel set her free, when she suddenly gave us three minutes real acting, after which we no longer grudged the 24/ we had paid for our stalls.

To change the subject, what Rationalism means in practice is the belief that the discovery of knowledge is a ratiocinative process, the discovery coming at the end of the reasoning as a result of it. This is believed only by people who have never discovered anything, or by people who, having discovered something, have not observed how they have discovered it. In practice, what happens is that you find yourself in possession of some fresh instalment of knowledge in the form of a fiction, or a hypothesis, or a paradox, or even a vulgar hoax or joke, in which latter cases you may (like Gilbert) be content with the fun of them and not take them seriously yourself. But if you appreciate your new discovery, you set to work to find the reasons for it, and always find that they have been staring you in the face all your life, just as all the reasons you advance against Inge were staring your grandfather in the face, and were even applied by him very cannily in other directions. Thus the discovery comes first, and the reasons after, precisely as in a play the play comes first and the staging after. Inge is a very acute and powerful reasoner; but when he wants to believe anything, he is satisfied with reasons which would not take in a pew opener. We are all the same: you are a perfect idiot as a professor of dramatic Constructionism. I do not know what I am an idiot about or I should not be an idiot about it; but no doubt I share the common lot. Only, as I always ask myself whether a rational demonstration of anything is a proof or a *reductio ad absurdum* (knowing that it may be either), and never lose sight of the fact that experiments are all put-up jobs, I am not a Rationalist.

Ever
G.B.S.

PS I shall see you presently; but as we shall have to entertain Ames, the above may as well remain in writing & not be paid off over his head.

In 1623 Ben Jonson made the famous statement that Shakespeare is **not for an age but for all time**. Shaw was surely the first and perhaps the only person to transfer this statement to a cat. Shaw knew that Ibsen **wrote stories about his characters until he knew them and their histories quite intimately** because Archer had documented Ibsen's methods in great detail in *From Ibsen's Workshop: Notes, Scenarios, and Drafts of the Modern Plays,* the twelfth and final volume in his publication of *The Works of Henrik Ibsen.* Sir George **Cornwall Lewis** (1806–63) was a man of letters who wrote on linguistic and classical topics. As a Liberal MP, he held several governmental offices including chancellor of the exchequer and secretary of war. As secretary he opposed British involvement in the American Civil War. A legal case in the West Indies that he administered was adapted by Shaw in *Captain Brassbound's Conversion.* Shaw met and became friends with **Frederick Jackson** (1832–1915) when living at Hindhead after his marriage in 1898. A retired solicitor who moved from London to Hindhead in 1890, Jackson urged Shaw to attend to his playwriting instead of becoming bogged down in public affairs in London. As Shaw described the five plays of *Back to Methuselah,* their **natural size** called for five separate performances on two afternoons and three evenings. Part 1 should be presented at a matinee, part 2 in the evening of same day, part 3 at a matinee, part 4 in the evening, and part 5 on a third evening. When the Theatre Guild in 1922 played parts 1 and 2 together during one evening, Shaw was angry. He later complained that 'they had to send round buckets of coffee to keep the exhausted audience awake' (CP 5: 714). So, despite his apparent disagreement with Archer over the time length for acts and performances, he was quite conscientious about the time requirements for audiences. **The Philanderer** was staged on 29 January 1923 and revived on 26 December 1924 at the Everyman Theatre, directed by Milton Rosmer (1881–1971). He played Charteris in 1923; Claude Rains did so in 1924. Shaw saw Duse's production of ***The Lady from the Sea*** on 21 June 1923. She died a year later on tour in Pittsburgh. His statement here should be compared to his high praise of her performances in the 1890s (see for example Dukore 2: 361-73). Shaw did meet with Winthrop **Ames** before he returned to New York City. **Augustus Harris**, who staged grand spectacles of melodrama and pantomime at Drury Lane Theatre in the 1890s, required elaborate sets. A **pew opener** is an usher in a church who leads people to their appointed seat.

178 / To G. Bernard Shaw

27 Fitzroy Square W
23rd June 1923

[TLS; BL 50528 ff 80–1; copy in BL 45296 f 275]

In a backhanded way, Archer acknowledged the significance of Shaw's previous letter, but he then quickly returns to the debate in the rhetorical mode of an impatient teacher or mentor. One can imagine the wagging finger. He apparently recognized that a discussion of 'character and action' is more productive than one limited to his idea of 'construction.' In the process, though the two of them had expanded their argument to the key concepts of action, character, and plot in Aristotle's Poetics, *they had reached yet another stalemate. Nonetheless, as sometimes happened with previous debates, Shaw made use of Archer's comments and challenges. We can see, for example, that in his* Preface to Saint Joan, *written in May 1924, he drew upon their dispute over how long a play should last, as described in the letters of 12 and 19 June. Repeating points he made in these letters, he proudly announced in the preface that* Saint Joan *was designed for 'continuous playing' for over 'three and a half hours.' And he teased Archer by placing him among the 'pseudo-critics' who wish to limit plays to a couple of hours (78). Just as Shaw had used part of Archer's review of* Widowers' Houses *when he wrote the 'Author's Preface' in 1893 (CP 1: 37–46), so he drew upon their letters of 1923 for the preface to* Saint Joan *(see CP 6: 74–9; Biblio 1: 155–6).*

My dear G.B.S.

Your account of your methods is most interesting, & shall be religiously preserved for the benefit of your biographer – poor soul! – who, however, will doubtless read it in a critical spirit. A man always views his own mental processes from the same distorting angle from which he views his personal appearance.

The long & short of the matter is this: All drama is, by the necessity of the case, a product of two factors: character & action: the person doing & the thing done. The great dramatists use these two elements in their just proportions. Character is by far the higher element, but action (as Aristotle saw) is the one thing absolutely indispensable – without it there is no *drama*, which means a thing done. You & I are at opposite ends of the scale: I have little eye for character & little power of drawing it: consequently I write carefully-constructed melodramas, much nearer to Scribe than to Ibsen. You, I fully admit, are at the higher end of the scale: you have a keen eye for character, though you see it through the distorting medium of apriorism which is interposed between you & the whole world. Nevertheless, so long as you keep *on* the scale, you produce very interesting plays. But you tend to run *off* the scale – to leave action behind altogether, & let character display itself in pure talk, without any bony framework whatever. Well, possibly that is the drama of the future: but if so it ought to change its name, & call itself logomachy. Or (since there is nothing new under the sun) let us go back to the medieval term 'flyting'; for there were several G.B.S.s in the fourteenth century or thereabouts, before playwrights & public went a-whoring after the meretricious charms of plot.

I have been re-reading the preface to ANDROCLES – I haven't finished it – & my comment is, 'This is all werry capital, but why worry so much about Jesus?' It is manifest in the very terms of the case that the true Jesus is enormously hard to get at. The earliest documents that tell of him falsify him outrageously, & he is buried under mountainous accretions of human folly. You go at the mountain with your pickaxe & flatter yourself that you have disengaged the true Jesus – like a frog in a rock. You are all the more convinced of his authenticity as you find him very like yourself. But other men with pickaxes discover quite different frogs. And meanwhile the one thing clear & certain is that the world-religion of the future is not going to build itself on the back of any excavated frog, but on the firm foundations of that knowledge of the universe of which Jesus had no glimmer.

You have got my grandfather on the brain – he is your Old Man of the Sea. I believe the old gentleman would find a certain malign satisfaction in haunting you if he could only know it. His theology was very simple, & to my mind much more respectable than Dean Inge's. It started from the simple premise: ALL THAT THE BIBLE SAYS IS TRUE. He was by education & environment incapable of conceiving anything else, or of *perceiving* that the Bible contradicted itself at every turn. When the reason with which, in daily life, he was by no means ill-furnished, ventured the smallest criticism of the Bible, he recognized in it the voice of the Devil, & promptly silenced it. Given an infallible Bible & an inimical Devil, this is entirely logical & satisfactory. Dean Inge believes neither in the Bible nor in the Devil, but stifles the voice of reason wherever he finds it convenient, by a pure act of (doubtless subconscious) will. Therefore it amuses me to argue with him.

Yours
W.A.

Given the context here, **The Old Man of the Sea** is not Proteus in *The Odyssey*, but more likely the monstrous character in the fifth tale of Sinbad in *One Thousand and One Nights*, which Sir Richard Burton translated in 1885. When Sinbad's vessel is shipwrecked, the old man enslaves Sinbad by climbing upon his shoulders and twisting his legs around the sailor's neck. He then refused to remove himself, persistently maintaining this position as Sinbad continues his travels.

179 / To G. Bernard Shaw

27 Fitzroy Square W
28th June 1923

[ALS: HRC Texas]

In December 1922 Archer had his portrait drawn by Walter Tittle, an American painter and illustrator. Six months later, after receiving two drawings, he suggested to Shaw that he should sit for Tittle, which Shaw did in January 1924. Tittle's drawing of Shaw is reproduced in Archibald Henderson's Man of the Century *between pages 768 and 769. But then Tittle, after making the drawing, attempted to sell one or more articles to the journals about Shaw's private conversation during the sitting. Shaw blocked an article in* The Bookman, *and then when Tittle asked for another sitting, Shaw chastised him in a letter of 2 April 1925 for his disregard of 'the obligation of English privacy ... You can hardly expect me to give you another chance, can you? Anyhow, I wont' (CL 3: 906–7).*

My dear G.B.S.

Mr. Walter Tittle is anxious to take your head off and include it in a series of crayon portraits of the wise & virtuous which he is doing. I hereby certify that he has 'done' me, that the process was pleasant, and the result illuminating, inasmuch as it brought out my latent likeness to a Prussian General. Seriously, I regard Mr. Tittle as a remarkable artist.

Yours
W.A.

Walter Ernest Tittle (1883–1966), born in Ohio, studied at the New York School of Art. He created drawings, etchings, lithographs, and paintings. He also wrote biographical articles about his subjects for popular magazines. Working in the United States and Britain, he specialized in portraits, though he also painted landscapes. In London in the 1920s his subjects, besides Archer and Shaw, included Henry Arthur Jones, Joseph Conrad, Arnold Bennett, and G.K. Chesterton. He was a member of the Royal Society of Arts. He spent the later years of his life in California.

180 / To William Archer Ayot St Lawrence, Welwyn, Herts.
14th December 1924

[TLS; BL 45296 ff 276–7; CL 3]

Archer published 'The Psychology of G.B.S.' in the December issue of The Bookman *(reprinted in Evans: 300–4). This was Archer's last publication on Shaw. Joining the speculations in the English journals about possible candidates for the Nobel Prize of Literature, Archer identified Shaw and Thomas Hardy as viable contenders. Although Archer greatly admired Hardy and his works, he argued that Shaw was the stronger candidate because 'his renown had reached round the world.' Archer compared his talents and fame to those of Voltaire. Yet unlike Voltaire, Shaw's fame far exceeded his influence. His 'unique temperament' was guided by 'a certain impishness' that greatly hindered his attempts to be taken seriously. Archer also lamented that Shaw's repeated 'failures of tact' had 'retarded' the development of his career. As an illustration, Archer claimed that Shaw, not the public, had been responsible for the long delays in getting his plays produced in the commercial theatres. In 1897, for example,* You Never Can Tell *was 'actually accepted and put in rehearsal at the Haymarket Theatre – and then dropped again.' Why? Shaw failed to accommodate himself to the practices of a West End theatre.*

Shaw dismissed Archer's version of the Haymarket affair. And it was easy for him to ignore Archer's oft-repeated and tired charge that Shaw was an apriorist *who 'does not live in the real world.' But there was some merit in another matter.*

Archer was troubled that his dear friend, despite his many virtues as an artist and intellectual, was often misguided in his 'bravura method of handling a situation.' Repeatedly over the years this psychological trait had caused him to commit 'flagrant errors in [his] method of attack.' As an illustration, Archer mentioned Shaw's misdirected testimony before the Joint Select Committee of Parliament on stage censorship (see letter of 10 August 1909). And Archer probably had in mind additional cases of Shaw's blunders, including his tactless manner of communicating with Elizabeth Robins in the 1890s during the period of the Ibsen productions and his sometimes harsh, disgruntled judgments on William Bridges-Adams and the Shakespeare Memorial Theatre at Stratford-upon-Avon (see letter of 8 June 1922).

Perhaps more consequential was Shaw's mishandling of his relationship with Harley Granville Barker. The loss of the friendship continued to disturb Shaw. What were the causes? One factor, which he raised in this letter, was their difference in age. Sooner or later, he reasoned, this was bound to separate them. But this rationale ignored the fact that Archer, the same age as Shaw, remained in a very close friendship with Barker. The far more convincing explanation was Barker's divorce and remarriage. At the beginning of 1916 he had informed Lillah McCarthy by letter that he wanted a divorce. During the separation, which was difficult for her, Shaw had tried to mediate. He did his best to support and advise McCarthy (see, for example, CL 3: 351–4). In April 1917 the divorce was finalized, and then in July 1918 Barker married the rich American Helen Huntington (1867–1950). In March 1920 McCarthy had married Frederick Keeble, a scientist at Magdalen College, Oxford. By then, Barker and Huntington had already settled at Netherton Hall, their Jacobean manor house in Devon which had 15 servants and a footman in livery. As part of this transformation in social status, Barker had hyphenated his name as Granville-Barker.

After he remarried Barker soon cut his ties to Shaw, in part because his wife could not stand Shaw. Yet Shaw still hoped to re-establish professional ties with Barker. In a letter of early June 1924, which has not survived, he wrote to Barker, announcing an imaginary Barker Relief Expedition that would extract him from Netherton Hall and forcefully return him to the London theatre. Unwilling to accept Barker's decision to turn his back on London production work, Shaw informed Barker that the rescue party included Thomas Hardy, J.M. Barrie, and many other prominent people. Shaw even announced that the raiding party would be led by Col. T.E. Lawrence (1888–1935), best known as Lawrence of Arabia. On 15 June Shaw wrote to Florence Emily Hardy (1881–1937), the wife of Thomas Hardy, about his 'most frightful letter' to Barker. Shaw explained that he had threatened

Barker with the raiding party that would include her husband because 'Harley must be rescued at all costs' (CL 3: 879–81).

Of course, this fanciful ploy of a raiding party was perfect nonsense, and Shaw must have recognized that his attempt to reach out to Barker was a misguided joke. It was unwise and insulting. Unfortunately, all that Shaw accomplished was to anger Barker and his wife and to make other people question his judgment. From Archer's perspective, as he stated in The Bookman *article, the whole matter illustrated Shaw's 'blunders in the art of manipulating human nature.'*

After publishing his article on Shaw's psychology, Archer had worried that he might have displeased his friend. But he need not have been concerned, and was relieved by this letter from Shaw, as he wrote to Barker on 17 December: 'G.B.S. has taken like an angel my article on him in the Bookman' (Add MS 45290 f 169). With the success of Saint Joan, *recently staged in London with Sybil Thorndike as Joan, Shaw could put aside Archer's complaints. Indeed, the Nobel Prize would soon be his.*

My dear W.A.

I have been reading your article about me in the huge Xmas number of The Bookman. What on earth moved you to rake up that old business at the Haymarket? Dont follow it up: it would be extremely illnatured; for I have never said a word in public about it that could give anyone a clue to what really happened, the proof being that you are apparently in the dark about it. In the chapter I contributed to Cyril Maude's history of the theatre (and even that I did not write for publication) I implicated nobody but myself; but of course my subsequent history and that of the play puts that literary lark out of court. Maude's subsequent history also shews how sound my advice to him was to stop fooling with madeup old men, and plunge into juvenile comedy. The truth is, he begged me to give the lead to an actor – you know whom I mean – who had done some farcical young men rather well with Alexander, and who was just ripe for a demonstration of his powers as a comedian. They were great friends; and Cyril was quite sure that he would succeed brilliantly if I would only let him try. I was equally sure that a certain scene in the play, the failure of which would mean the failure of the whole, was beyond him; but I did not feel justified in denying him his chance, and did not like making myself disagreeable to Cyril, who was an amiable baby.

It turned out just as I feared. The scene floored him absolutely and totally. He was so completely at a loss that he was driven to the unpardonable (ordinarily) step of saying to the author 'Let us see you play it yourself' – not offensively, but because he really could not see how it was possible to make any sense of it. The author accordingly gave him a sample. He exclaimed naively 'But that is comedy'! As it was still impossible to convince Cyril that there was anything particularly wrong, or at least anything that Winifred could not pull right, I went to Harrison and told him he must come down to the next rehearsal and see for himself. This settled the matter. After the rehearsal Harrison joined us with such a long face that Maude saw it was all up. It was a miserable moment: they had been a thoroughly happy family; and my confounded play was going to break it up. They had signed the agreement to produce, and could not in any case have thrown me over for the shortcoming of an actor whom I accepted, against my own expressed judgment, to oblige them. I rescued them by saying that 'we' had better withdraw the play and wait for another opportunity. They were enormously relieved, and, I believe, really grateful to me at the moment, though I doubt if Cyril has ever forgiven me for going on as if Harrison was the only adult in the theatre, and for not behaving at least a little badly in common humanity. And that was the end of the affair.

Now this actor who wrecked the production is still to the fore. If he were young enough he could play the part on his head, and wonder what on earth had ever puzzled him in it. In fact he played it very well at the Haymarket except for that one scene. It would, as I began by saying, be wantonly illnatured to rake up this old incident of his nonage against him when it is entirely unknown to the public. And at least he stuck to his part. Fanny Coleman threw up hers because, as she put it, there were no laughs and no exits in it. The McComas shook the dust of the theatre off his feet after the reading, though at the Court later on he was the best McComas we had. Winifred insisted on playing Dolly until she heard me read the play, when she promptly changed over to Gloria. She was the only one who had a glimmering that she had got hold of something, except Brandon Thomas, who was heartbroken at the collapse (a Scot, ye ken). To me it was a respite, as it always was and is to this day. My apparent magnanimity in such matters is a fraud: it costs me nothing except money.

The disappearance of such difficulties at the Court is very simply accounted for. At one of the earliest rehearsals there a question of birthdays arose; and Granville Barker blighted me by remarking 'Oh! youre exactly the same age as my father' (I had up to that moment regarded him as a contemporary). When we became fashionable, Edith Nesbit (Mrs Bland) said to me one day, 'Shaw: IS Granville Barker your natural son?' To my contemporaries my plays were what Wagner's music was to Hanslick. To the next generation they came quite naturally. To the present rising generation they are classics, a bit old fashioned and ponderous in places. When Hanslick-Archer innocently assures it that they never can be popular because of my perverse and cacophonous discords and total absence of melody, though I am a monstrously clever man, it wonders what the sage can possibly mean. The simplicity of George Alexander served him better than your critical experience and acumen. 'We were all wrong about you' said George. Your article says 'Shaw was all wrong about us, and about the Haymarket Theatre, and about the House of Commons. What a pity that so gigantic a talent should be condemned to eternal failure because its possessor is and always has been wrong about everybody and everything!' Complimentary in a way, but perfect nonsense, I assure you.

Do you ever see anything of Harley now; or has he dropped you as he has dropped me? His extinction is an amazing and disconcerting phenomenon. I have tried to stir him up by comparing him to Swinburne at Putney, and inventing an imaginary Barker Relief Expedition consisting of Hardy, Colonel Lawrence, Barrie, and half a dozen others who are pledged to rescue him; but the only effect is to cut off communications completely. Maggie Ponsonby, to whom Helen clings, perhaps because she trails clouds of glory from the court, but certainly also because she is a very good sort, assures me that they are perfectly happy; and if this is so there is nothing more to be said, as Harley is in no wise bound to sacrifice his life to the glory of English literature; but if I had produced nothing in the last twelve years except The Exemplary Theatre and The Secret Life I should regard myself as a damned soul. I take it that under Helen's influence he has relapsed into his natural Henry Jamesism, and found that Henry Jamesism, which was always nine tenths naive American worship of English high life, is a hopeless nothoroughfare. Trotskyism is the open road nowadays; and poor Helen has hardly got over the ungentlemanliness of Washington yet.

I cannot do anything useful, because Helen must hate me for the part I had to take in the divorce, which, thanks to our marriage laws and to the economic predicament of the parties, was the most detestable business you can imagine: just reciprocal blackmail in which I had to do the blackmailing. Lillah, who had the worst of it, has forgiven me; but Helen, whose roseleaves were inevitably crumpled to some extent, and with whose sensitiveness I, face to face with Lillah's suffering, had very little patience, will probably always loathe me; and I shall not blame her, poor dear. Under these circumstances Harley, who can hardly keep up much acquaintance with me without imposing me on her, is forced to drop me. This would not matter, as the difference in our ages would have been bound to tell on our relations soon anyhow, if it were not that he has dropped writing too. Therefore if you are still *persona grata* at Cumberland Place or the place which fashionable ladies call Nethermost Hell (the latest smart joke about the much begossiped situation) do your best to supply the lost Shavian stimulus and get him to work again. Tell him to do something thoroughly vulgar: he needs contact with earth.

On the 26th we sail for Madeira, where we expect to spend a month or so. I dont know whether you are in England or not, and should be glad of a hail if you are.

G.B.S.

Shaw had previously related the **old business at the Haymarket** to Archer in a letter on 7 September 1903 (see that letter's endnote). Two decades later he had forgotten about not only that letter but also the review that Archer had written on Cyril Maude's *The Haymarket Theatre* ('A Playhouse Mixture,' DC, 17 October 1903). Maude's book contained Shaw's anonymously written chapter about the fate of *You Never Can Tell* at the Haymarket. The actor who was **floored** by the part of Valentine was Allan Aynesworth. The actress **Winifred** Emery was married to Maude, and played leading roles at the Haymarket Theatre, which Maude had taken over in 1896. Frederick **Harrison** was the co-manager of the Haymarket with Maude. The actress **Fanny Coleman** (1834–1919) performed regularly in the West End theatres, usually in secondary roles. J.H. Barnes (1850–1925) rehearsed the role of **McComas** in 1897 at the Haymarket. Then in 1905 he performed the role for the Court Theatre production. **Brandon Thomas** (1856–1914) performed regularly at the Haymarket, including the long-running production of J.M. Barrie's *The Little Minister* (330 perfs.), which Maude staged in 1897, soon after the production of Shaw's play was cancelled. **Edith Nesbit** (1858–1924), who had been active in the Socialist movement, was the wife of Hubert Bland (1856–1914), one of the founders of the Fabian Society.

He was a journalist; she wrote novels, poems, and children's books. Shaw met both of them in the mid-1880s. Eduard **Hanslick** (1825–1904), a Viennese musical critic, disliked Wagner's operas, and repeatedly attacked them. In his *Bookman* article Archer had criticized Shaw's method of testifying in 1909 before the **House of Commons** (actually the Joint Select Committee of both Houses of Parliament on Stage Censorship). In Shaw's letter to Barker in June 1924 he apparently had informed Barker that his retreat to Netherton Hall was similar to the withdrawal of A.C. **Swinburne** to The Pines at Putney Hill. But Shaw did not mention that Swinburne's withdraw at the age of 42 was because of poor health. Magdalen **('Maggie') Ponsonby**, who was a friend of both McCarthy and Barker, had reported to Shaw about the new marriage (which occurred on 31 July 1918). Shaw knew her and her husband Arthur Ponsonby (later 1st Baron Ponsonby of Shulbrede), who was a Liberal MP until 1922, when he shifted to Labour and served in the government. In his embrace of **Trotskyism**, Shaw showed that he was familiar with the Marxist ideas of Leon Trotsky (1879–1940), a leader in the Bolshevik government in Soviet Russia. For three perspectives on Shaw's shifting and contradictory ideas on (and alliances with) Leninism, Trotskyism, and Stalinism, see Holroyd 3: 221–54, Davis 2: 120–48, and Yde: 15–16, 37, 62, 105, 145, 201.

181 / To G. Bernard Shaw

[no address]
17th December 1924

[TLS: HRC Texas]

After receiving a series of medical tests on the morning of 17 December, Archer was told that an operation was required, as soon as possible, because of a large tumour on his kidney. Despite this troubling news, he attended a luncheon engagement with the king of Norway and Prince Olaf at the Norwegian Legation. Then in the afternoon he returned to Fitzroy Square to write letters to Shaw, his brother Charles, Barker, and Elizabeth Robins. In the letter to Charles, who was an executor for Archer's estate, he promised to 'leave things in order' and to put together 'all sorts of notes for you as to where things are to be found' (C. Archer: 402). In the letter to Barker, who was in Paris with his wife Helen, he appealed for administrative help, in case of death. Because Charles and the other brother James 'don't know very much about the theatre' (BL 45290, f 169), Archer sought professional oversight by Barker on his dramatic works. Then in a letter to Robins, he confessed to 'a horror of surgery.' He warned her: 'Don't write – my letters would be opened. You may of course take no news for good news, & as soon as I am able I shall let you know how I am getting on. Goodbye for the present, & in any case "tak for alt." Ever yours W.A.' (TLS: HRC Texas). The Norwegian phrase, thanking her for everything, evoked the 1891 production of Hedda Gabler *and the beginning of their close relationship.*

On 18 December Archer went into a nursing home. Two days later the operation was performed, following which, though in great pain, he seemed to stabilize and even rally. But in the early morning of 27 December he died. On the previous day, Shaw and Mrs Shaw had sailed for Maderia. They had assumed that Archer would recover. Shaw later reported that upon arriving at Reid's Hotel in Maderia, he saw the news bulletin that announced the 'Death of Mr. William Archer.' The words 'threw me into a transport of fury. The operation had killed him … My rage may have been unjust to the surgeons; but it carried me over my first sense of bereavement. When I returned to an Archerless London it seemed to me that the place had entered into a new age in which I was lagging superfluous. I still feel that when he went he took a piece of me with him' (Three Plays: xxxvii). Like Shaw, Robins was equally distraught: 'William Archer's death haunts me with a sense of a large part of my own life being swept away' (John: 85). For Shaw, Barker, and Robins the death of William Archer was a sad and painful closure to an era. For decades he had been at the centre of their professional lives. And personally he had been a dear person, greatly admired, greatly loved.

My dear G.B.S.,

Since I wrote you, I have learnt that I shall have to undergo an operation one of these days – I go into a nursing home tomorrow. I don't know that the operation is a very serious one, & as a matter of fact I feel as fit as a fiddle, so I suppose my chances are pretty good. Still, accidents will happen, & this episode gives me an excuse for saying, what I hope you don't doubt – namely, that though I may sometimes have played the part of the all-too candid mentor, I have never wavered in my admiration & affection for you, or ceased to feel that the Fates had treated me kindly in making me your contemporary & friend. I thank you from my heart for forty years of good comradeship.

Whatever happens, let it never be said that I did not move in good society – I lunched today with the King of Norway & Prince Olaf.

Very kind regards to Mrs Shaw, & all good wishes for 1925.

Ever yours
W.A.

At a later date Shaw wrote a single statement at the bottom of this letter: 'He died – killed by the operation – on the 27th December.' Shaw wrote his obituary essay, 'How William Archer Influenced Bernard Shaw,' for an edition of three of Archer's plays. Barker also wrote an obituary essay, 'William Archer,' for *Drama* 4, no. 13 (July 1926): 176–8, 182. But Robins, unable to provide a public statement that could be true to their private as well as public relationship, remained silent. Charles, who knew of the love affair, wrote a three-paged letter to her about the death. In the following years, though she and Archer had agreed to destroy their intimate letters (as he had done with her letters to him), she could not burn all of them. She kept a few, but cut off his signature at the bottom of the handwritten pages. They have remained among Robins's collected papers in the Fales Library, New York University.

Table of Correspondents

Unless otherwise noted, the letters in this edition were written by Bernard Shaw or William Archer. Eight of the letters were written by Charlotte Shaw to Archer. In addition, Shaw wrote three letters to Frances E. Archer. Some of the letters lack a date. In these cases I have provided the likely or certain dates, which I have placed within brackets. Two of Archer's letters to Shaw (#25, #63) and one of Shaw's letters to Archer (#120) were published at the time as 'open letters' in a periodical or newspaper. In each case a copy was also provided to Shaw or Archer.

1 To Bernard Shaw 6 January 1885
2 To Bernard Shaw 7 February 1885
3 To William Archer 16 March 1885
4 To Frances E. Archer from Bernard Shaw 18 March 1885
5 To Bernard Shaw Tuesday [c. late March 1885]
6 To Bernard Shaw Sunday [3 May 1885]
7 To Bernard Shaw Friday night 12 November 1885
8 To William Archer 12 December 1885
9 To Bernard Shaw Sunday evy [13 December 1885]
10 To William Archer 14 December 1885
11 To Bernard Shaw Tuesday mg [12 February 1886]
12 To Bernard Shaw 26 March 1886
13 To William Archer 16 April 1886
14 To Frances E. Archer from Bernard Shaw 12 January 1887
15 To William Archer 4 October 1887
16 To William Archer 4 September 1888

54 To William Archer 6 August 1895
55 To William Archer 29 January 1896
56 To William Archer 2 February 1896
57 To William Archer 7 February 1896
58 To William Archer 19 February 1896
59 To William Archer 6 March 1896
60 To William Archer 15 May 1896
61 To William Archer 6 October 1896
62 To William Archer Undated [c. 1897]
63 To Bernard Shaw 31 July 1897 [open letter]
64 To William Archer 13 January 1898
65 To Bernard Shaw 14 January 1898
66 To William Archer [21 April 1898]
67 To William Archer 26 April 1898
68 To Bernard Shaw 30 April 1898
69 To William Archer 2 May 1898
70 To William Archer 3 June 1898
71 To William Archer 6 June 1898
72 To William Archer 24 June 1898
73 To William Archer 27 July 1899
74 To Bernard Shaw 22 January 1900
75 To William Archer 24 January 1900
76 To Bernard Shaw 25 January 1900
77 To William Archer 27 January 1900
78 To Bernard Shaw 1 February 1900
79 To William Archer 21 February 1900
80 To William Archer 8 July 1900
81 To William Archer 9 July 1900
82 To William Archer 28 November 1900
83 To William Archer 18 February 1901
84 To William Archer 22 February 1901
85 To William Archer 6 June 1901
86 To William Archer from Charlotte Shaw 2 January 1902
87 To William Archer from Charlotte Shaw 7 January 1902
88 To William Archer from Charlotte Shaw 24 February 1902
89 To William Archer 1 and 2 March 1902
90 To William Archer 4 March 1902

91 To William Archer 26 March 1902
92 To William Archer 27 March 1902
93 To William Archer 20 June 1902
94 To William Archer 12 January 1903
95 To William Archer 23 February 1903
96 To William Archer 15 April 1903
97 To William Archer 27 August 1903
98 To Bernard Shaw 1 September 1903
99 To William Archer 2 September 1903
100 To William Archer 7 September 1903
101 To William Archer 8 September 1903
102 To William Archer 16 September 1903
103 To William Archer 27 September 1903
104 To William Archer 7 November 1903
105 To Bernard Shaw 17 November 1903
106 To William Archer 12 May 1904
107 To William Archer 13 June 1904
108 To William Archer 17 June 1905
109 To William Archer [c. 27 September 1905]
110 To Mrs Frances Archer from Bernard Shaw 27 October 1905
111 To William Archer 8 November 1905
112 To William Archer 15 November 1905
113 To Bernard Shaw 18 November 1905
114 To William Archer 1 January 1906
115 To Bernard Shaw 3 January 1906
116 To William Archer 7 June 1906
117 To Bernard Shaw 8 June 1906
118 To William Archer 7 July 1906
119 To William Archer 10 July 1906
120 To William Archer [c. late August 1906] [open letter]
121 To William Archer 14 November 1906
122 To William Archer from Charlotte Shaw Monday morning [19 November 1906]
123 To William Archer 19 November 1906
124 To William Archer [26 and 27 May 1907]
125 To William Archer 3 June 1907
126 To William Archer 13 November 1907

Index

Published works are listed under the names of the authors. Periodicals and newspapers are listed chronologically. Unless otherwise indicated, theatres are located in London.

www.ingramcontent.com/pod-product-compliance
Lightning Source LLC
LaVergne TN
LVHW040154080826
844660LV00014B/958/J

* 9 7 8 0 8 0 2 0 4 1 2 2 7 *